PATHS TO KINGSHIP IN MEDIEVAL LATIN EUROPE, *c.* 950–1200

Medieval Europe was a world of kings, but what did this mean to those who did not themselves wear a crown? How could they prevent corrupt and evil men from seizing the throne? How could they ensure that rulers would not turn into tyrants? Drawing on a rich array of remarkable sources, this engaging study explores how the fears and hopes of a ruler's subjects shaped both the idea and the practice of power. It traces the inherent uncertainty of royal rule from the creation of kingship and the recurring crises of royal successions, through the education of heirs and the intrigue of medieval elections, to the splendour of a king's coronation, and the pivotal early years of his reign. Monks, crusaders, knights, kings (and those who wanted to be kings) are among a rich cast of characters who sought to make sense of and benefit from an institution that was an object of both desire and fear.

BJÖRN WEILER is Professor in History at Aberystwyth University in the UK, with visiting stints at Cambridge, Bergen (Norway), Freiburg (Germany), Harvard and Chapel Hill. He has received grants, among others, from the AHRC, the British Academy, the Huntingdon Library and the Leverhulme Trust. Publications include *Political Culture in the Medieval West, Byzantium and the Islamic World* (2021) (with Catherine Holmes and others); *Representations of Power in Medieval Germany* (2006) (with Simon MacLean); and *Kingship, Rebellion and Political Culture* (2007; rev. edition 2012).

PATHS TO KINGSHIP IN MEDIEVAL LATIN EUROPE, c. 950–1200

BJÖRN WEILER
Aberystwyth University

CAMBRIDGE
UNIVERSITY PRESS

University Printing House, Cambridge CB2 8BS, United Kingdom

One Liberty Plaza, 20th Floor, New York, NY 10006, USA

477 Williamstown Road, Port Melbourne, VIC 3207, Australia

314–321, 3rd Floor, Plot 3, Splendor Forum, Jasola District Centre,
New Delhi – 110025, India

103 Penang Road, #05–06/07, Visioncrest Commercial, Singapore 238467

Cambridge University Press is part of the University of Cambridge.

It furthers the University's mission by disseminating knowledge in the pursuit of
education, learning, and research at the highest international levels of excellence.

www.cambridge.org
Information on this title: www.cambridge.org/9781316518427
DOI: 10.1017/9781009008853

© Björn Weiler 2021

This publication is in copyright. Subject to statutory exception
and to the provisions of relevant collective licensing agreements,
no reproduction of any part may take place without the written
permission of Cambridge University Press.

First published 2021

Printed in the United Kingdom by TJ Books Limited, Padstow Cornwall

A catalogue record for this publication is available from the British Library.

Library of Congress Cataloging-in-Publication Data
Names: Weiler, Björn K. U., author.
Title: Paths to kingship in medieval Latin Europe, c. 950–1200 / Björn Weiler, University of
Wales, Aberystwyth.
Description: First edition. | New York : Cambridge University Press, 2021. | Includes
bibliographical references and index.
Identifiers: LCCN 2020058383 (print) | LCCN 2020058384 (ebook) | ISBN 9781316518427
(hardback) | ISBN 9781009009218 (paperback) | ISBN 9781009008853 (ebook)
Subjects: LCSH: Kings and rulers, Medieval. | Monarchy – Europe – History – To 1500. |
Legitimacy of governments – Europe – History – To 1500. | Europe – Politics and
government – 476–1492.
Classification: LCC D131 .W45 2021 (print) | LCC D131 (ebook) | DDC 321/.609409021–dc23
LC record available at https://lccn.loc.gov/2020058383
LC ebook record available at https://lccn.loc.gov/2020058384

ISBN 978-1-316-51842-7 Hardback

Cambridge University Press has no responsibility for the persistence or accuracy of
URLs for external or third-party internet websites referred to in this publication
and does not guarantee that any content on such websites is, or will remain,
accurate or appropriate.

CONTENTS

List of Maps   *page* vii
Acknowledgements   viii
List of Abbreviations   x
Timeline   xi

Introduction   1

PART I   **Foundations**

1   Politics and Power in High Medieval Europe, *c.* 1000–1200   25

2   Foundational Texts   39

PART II   **Creating Kingship**

3   Becoming King   67

4   Conferring Kingship   95

PART III   **Succession**

5   Duties, Norms and Process   121

6   Designating an Heir   165

PART IV   **Election**

7   Unanimity and Probity   233

8   Choosing a King   259

vi CONTENTS

PART V **Inauguration**

9 Enthroning the King 309

10 Beyond Enthronement 351

Conclusion 399

Select Reading 412
Index 464

MAPS

1 High medieval Europe, *c.* 1100   *page* xiv

ACKNOWLEDGEMENTS

Many more years ago than I now dare to admit, this book began as a footnote to a footnote in my PhD. Other projects intervened, and I returned to kings only during a fellowship at the Radcliffe Institute for Advanced Studies at Harvard (2008–9), and a Senior Fellowship at the Freiburg Institute for Advanced Studies (2010–11). Generous funding from the AHRC and research leave from Aberystwyth allowed for the completion of a first draft.

Too many friends and colleagues now know more about medieval kingship than they may have thought possible, let alone desirable. I offer my sincere apologies, and my deepest gratitude, at Harvard, to David Fischer, Eric Goldberg, Mario Gonzalez, Ilana Gershon, Jim Haber, Hap, Mona Krook, Sarah, Pip and Soci Messer, Joanne Rappaport, Steve Zipperstein and the much missed David Warner for their questions, companionship and counsel; to Zac Smith, Dan Smail and the 'Gang' for their welcome and hospitality; and to Matias Vera for all of the above and the communal exorcising. At Freiburg, Patrick Bernhard, Mark Greengrass, Leonhard Horowsky, Heinz Krieg, Lucy Riall and Till Van Rahden made for another wonderful year and equally inspiring company. Haki Antonsson first set me thinking about concepts and representations of royal authority; Stephen Church gave me the idea to use overlapping stages as a means of structuring the book; Johanna Dale and Thomas Foerster generously shared manuscripts of their then still forthcoming books; and Peter Lambert kept asking about how ideas could drive actions. He and Richard Rathbone also kindly read the manuscript in full, while Nora Berend, Piotr Górecki, Lars Kjaer and Mia Münster-Swendsen offered welcome feedback on individual chapters and sections. The book is a much better one because of their help, advice and criticism.

Gerd Althoff, Jack Bernhardt, Thomas Foerster, Helmut Hughes, Ryan Kemp, Konstantin Klein, Stephan Patscher, Martyn Powell, Tim Reuter, Stephan Schmuck, Simon Taylor, David Trotter, Alex Woolf and Thomas Zotz are only some of the colleagues and friends whose questions, suggestions and criticisms fed into the book. I have learned much from them. Peter Lambert and Patricia Duncker put me even further in their debt by coming up with a title for this book that did not rival a seventeenth-century treatise on alchemy in length. Friends and colleagues at Harvard, in Freiburg, Berlin and

Aberystwyth also provided much needed routes of escape. Writing would have been much less enjoyable without the Kaiser Schnitzel, the Casablanca Burger or the culinary delights of Sissi, April, Jayz and the Ship & Kennel.

Sections, drafts and offshoots were presented at Aberystwyth, Bergen, Bonn, Bristol, Cambridge (both UK and MA), Cardiff, Coburg, Düsseldorf, Freiburg, Glasgow, Heidelberg, Kraków, Kyoto, Leeds, London, Madrid, Minneapolis, Münster, Nicosia, Osaka, Oxford, Palo Alto, Pasadena, Riverside, San Jose, Sofia and Warsaw. I have learned much on these occasions, and am immensely grateful for the opportunity to test several of the ideas underpinning this book.

For permission to reprint previously published materials I am grateful to Caroline Palmer and Boydell & Brewer for 'Kingship, usurpation and propaganda in twelfth-century Europe: the case of Stephen', *Anglo-Norman Studies* 31 (2000), 299–326; and to Allison McCann and the UCLA Center for Medieval and Renaissance Studies for 'The *rex renitens* and medieval ideals of kingship, c. 950–1250', *Viator* 31 (2000), 1–42; 'Crown-giving and king-making in the west, c. 1000–c. 1250', *Viator* 41 (2010), 57–88; and 'Tales of first kings and the culture of kingship in the west, c. 1050–1200', *Viator* 46/2 (2015), 101–28.

Liz Friend-Smith at Cambridge University Press deserves manifold thanks for her trust and patience: I am sorry that the manuscript nearly became a mythical promise, always just beyond the horizon, seemingly forever out of reach. But, as a popular beat combo put it: *nun das Warten hat ein Ende*. I would also like to thank Atifa Jiwa for her help, and, above all, Kathleen Fearn, who has been a wonderfully eagle-eyed and patient copy-editor. At Freiburg, Jan Wacker was the perfect *Mitarbeiter*. He also compiled a list of royal successions that made writing the book so much easier. I would furthermore like to thank the librarians at Harvard's Widener Library, their colleagues at Cambridge, Freiburg, the Staatsbibliothek Preußischer Kulturbesitz Berlin, the Friedrich-Meinecke-Institut at the Freie Universität Berlin, and in the Inter Library Loans department at Aberystwyth, without whose assistance this book would have taken even longer to complete. Despite its best efforts, Microsoft Word could only *delay* the manuscript's completion. And special mention must, of course, be made of Juggles, Coco, Dilys, Lola, Sergej, Suki, Ted, Wolfie and their fellow shipmates. Needless to say, any remaining mistakes are their responsibility, not mine.

ABBREVIATIONS

AfD	*Archiv für Diplomatik und Urkundenforschung*
AKG	*Archiv für Kulturgeschichte*
ANS	*Anglo-Norman Studies*
CCCM	Corpus Christianorum, Continuatio Mediaevalis
CCSL	Corpus Christianorum, Series Latina
CSEL	Corpus Scriptorum Ecclesiasticorum Latinorum
DA	*Deutsches Archiv für Erforschung des Mittelalters*
EHR	*English Historical Review*
EME	*Early Medieval Europe*
f.	folio
FmSt	*Frühmittelalterliche Studien*
HSJ	*Haskins Society Journal*
HZ	*Historische Zeitschrift*
JEGP	*Journal of English and Germanic Philology*
JMedH	*Journal of Medieval History*
MGH	Monumenta Germaniae Historica
MGH	Diplomata Monumenta Germaniae Historica:Die Urkunden der deutschen Könige und Kaiser
MGH SS	Monumenta Germaniae Historica: Scriptores rerum Germanicarum
MGH SS sep. ed.	Monumenta Germaniae Historica: Scriptores rerum Germanicarum in usum scholarum separatim editi
MIÖG	*Mitteilungen des Instituts für Österreichische Geschichtsforschung*
PL	Patrologia Latina
RI	Regesta Imperii
TRHS	*Transactions of the Royal Historical Society*
ZSRG	*Zeitschrift der Savigny-Stiftung für Rechtsgeschichte*

TIMELINE

918	Death of King Conrad I of east Francia; succession of Henry I (919)
983	Death of Emperor Otto II; regency of Theophanu
	Failed plot of Henry of Bavaria
987	Succession of Hugh Capet as king of west Francia
c. 999/1000	Meeting at Gniezno between Boleslaw I of Poland and Emperor Otto III
c. 1000	Conversion of Hungary, kingship of St Stephen
1002	Death of Emperor Otto III; succession of Henry II
1024	Death of Emperor Henry II; succession of Emperor Conrad II
1024–5	Abortive bid for the Lombard (and the imperial) throne by William of Aquitaine
1031	Succession of King Henry I of France
1037	Death of Duke Oldrich of Bohemia
1042 Melfi:	the Normans choose a leader to coordinate their campaigns in Sicily
	Succession of Magnus as king of Denmark
1055	Succession of Spitihnev as duke of Bohemia
1059	Philipp I crowned king of France during his father's lifetime
1063	King Fernando I of León settles his succession
1066	Kingship of Harold II in England (January–October)
	Norman Conquest and coronation of William I
1072	Succession struggle in Castile
1076	Election of Harald as king of Denmark
1077	Election of Rudolf of Rheinfelden as challenger to Emperor Henry IV (r. 1056–1105)
1079	Murder of Stanislas of Kraków
1087	Death of King William I of England; succession of William II
1092	Brestislav II becomes duke of Bohemia
1099	Godfrey becomes first ruler of the crusader kingdom of Jerusalem
	Wladyslaw Herman tries to settle the Polish ducal succession
1100	Death of King William II of England; succession of Henry I
	Death of Godfrey of Jerusalem; succession of Baldwin I, who assumes the title of king
1102	Succession crisis in Poland
1103	Death of King Erik the Good of Denmark

xii   TIMELINE

1106	Death of Emperor Henry IV
1107–10	Crusade of King Sigurd of Norway
1108	Coronation of Louis VI of France
1111	Alfonso VI crowned king of Galicia
1118	Death of King Baldwin I of Jerusalem; succession of Baldwin II
1125	Death of Emperor Henry V; succession of Lothar III
	Self-coronation of Alfonso I of Portugal
1130	Roger II becomes king of Sicily
1131	Murder of Knud Lavard
	Fulk of Anjou chosen as king of Jerusalem
1134	Death of King Niels I of Denmark; succession of Erik the Memorable
1135	Death of King Henry I of England; succession of Stephen
1136	Siege of Exeter
1137	Death of King Erik the Memorable of Denmark
1141	King Stephen of England captured at the Battle of Lincoln
1152	Death of King Conrad III of Germany; succession of Frederick Barbarossa
	King Stephen of England attempts to have his son Eustace installed as king
1153	Treaty of Winchester
	Frederick Barbarossa appoints Wichmann as archbishop of Magdeburg
1154	Death of King Stephen of England; succession of Henry II
	Valdemar I becomes co-ruler of Denmark
1157	Valdemar I becomes sole ruler of Denmark; riots in Roskilde
1158	Frederick Barbarossa grants a royal title to Vladislav of Bohemia
1161	Magnus Erlingsson crowned king of Norway
	First recorded coronation in Norway
1165	King Valdemar I of Denmark ensures the election of his son Knud VI as king during his lifetime
1166	Death of William I of Sicily
1170	King Knud VI crowned king of Denmark during his father's lifetime
	First recorded coronation in Denmark
	Henry the Young King crowned king of England during his father's lifetime
c. 1177	Birkibeinar choose Sverrir as their leader and claimant to the Norwegian throne
1182	Death of King Valdemar I of Denmark; succession of Knud VI
1184	Mainz diet; knighting of Henry VI, king of the Romans
	Death of Magnus Erlingsson
1189	Coronation of Richard I as king of England
	Death of King William II of Sicily
1194	Imperial coronation of Henry VI
1195	King of Cyprus requests a crown from Emperor Henry VI

1195–6	Emperor Henry VI seeks to ensure the succession of his son Frederick
c. 1196	King Lewon II of Armenia receives a crown from emissaries of Emperor Henry VI
1198	Imperial Double Election in Germany
1199	Death of King Richard I of England; succession of John
1202	Death of King Sverrir of Norway
1204	Ioannitsa of Bulgaria requests a crown from the army of the Fourth Crusade
1208	Ioannitsa receives a crown from Pope Innocent III
1214	Death of William the Lion of Scotland; succession of Alexander II
1215	Emperor Frederick II crowned at Aachen
	Magna Carta in England
1222	Golden Bull of Hungary
1249/51	Inauguration of Alexander III as king of Scotland

Map 1 High medieval Europe, *c.* 1100

Map 1 (cont.)

Introduction

This book is about power.[1] How could it legitimately be acquired? To what ends should it be used? What was the relationship between expediency and principle? It pursues these questions with reference to a particular place and time: Latin Europe between the later tenth and the early thirteenth centuries. And it does so with regard to a particular *type* of power: that held by kings.[2] The question of what rights and privileges a ruler can legitimately claim in relation to the people resonates partly because it is one that every political community has to ask itself, and that each generation has to ask itself anew. Men and women in the central Middle Ages were no exception. The ensuing debates over what abstract norms meant in practice, and over how conflicting ideals could – even whether they should – be reconciled, formed part of a political culture that transcended modern political geographies and medieval polities alike. They built on shared cultural legacies and unfolded within shared structural frameworks. Arguments were by no means always conducted peacefully, but a variety of different routes existed along which norms – what should be – could be aligned to practices – what actually was.

---

[1] The concept of power is here approached in the sense outlined by R. Stephen Humphreys, 'Reflections on political culture in three spheres', in Catherine Holmes, Jonathan Shepard, Jo Van Steenbergen and Björn Weiler, eds., *Political Culture in the Latin West, Byzantium and the Islamic World, c. 700–c. 1500: A Framework for Comparing Three Spheres* (forthcoming). That is, it is the ability to get others to do one's bidding. That can be accomplished through material superiority, the employment of symbolic power, the invocation of shared norms, etc. For the concept of 'political culture', see the definition proposed by the 'Political Culture in Three Spheres' project, out of which that volume emerged: http://users.aber.ac.uk/bkw/rulership2008/polcult%20definition.htm (accessed 18 February 2020). The short summary is: '"Political culture" encompasses both the ideology and the practice of "hegemonial" groups. It involves the self-definition (expressed verbally, visually or symbolically), and the actual practices, customs and working assumptions of groups of individuals aspiring to large-scale, long-term hegemony, be it internally (within a given community) or externally (against its neighbours or rivals).'

[2] Here understood as the de facto or nominal secular figureheads of communities that viewed themselves as united by shared legal customs, a common past and a continuous line of rulers. See also Chapter 3 in particular for the role of quasi-regnal polities like Bohemia and, after 1079, Poland, and, of course, for the emergence of new polities.

The period *c.* 950–1200 was pivotal in the development of that political culture. Chapter 1 will offer a fuller discussion of why this was the case. A short outline may nonetheless prove helpful. First, these two centuries and a half witnessed a proliferation of polities whose rulers claimed or were awarded a royal title.[3] This increase in regnal polities derived partly from political fragmentation, partly from the expansion of Latin Christendom by both conquest and conversion and partly from a growing economy that allowed and that sometimes forced princes to seek parity with neighbours or erstwhile overlords. Second, the emergence of new kingships frequently resulted in both external and internal challenges. Neighbours might dispute a royal title. Subjects would try to define their own status in relation to erstwhile peers who now had become their lords. Some even competed with each other to translate their role in the creation of kingship into greater power for themselves. Consequently, disputes over the meaning of common norms, and who would have a say in interpreting them, became common. Third, a growing economy coincided with the wider use of and with wider uses for literacy.[4] The utility of writing manifested itself in a dramatically increased production of administrative documents, including the emergence of entirely new genres, which facilitated new ways of thinking about accountability and power.[5]

---

[3] Nora Berend, ed., *Christianization and the Rise of Christian Monarchy. Scandinavia, Central Europe and Rus', c.900–1200* (Cambridge, 2007); Björn Weiler, 'Crown-giving and king-making in the west, c. 1000 – c. 1250', *Viator* 41 (2010), 57–88; Benedict G. E. Wiedemann, 'The kingdom of Portugal, homage and papal "fiefdom"' in the second half of the twelfth century', *JMedH* 41 (2015), 432–45; Simon John, 'The papacy and the establishment of the kingdoms of Jerusalem, Sicily and Portugal: twelfth-century papal political thought on incipient kingship', *Journal of Ecclesiastical History* 68 (2017), 223–59.

[4] Eltjo Buringh, *Medieval Manuscript Production in the Latin West: Explorations with a Global Database* (Leiden, 2011); M. T. Clanchy, *From Memory to Written Record: England, 1066–1307*, 3rd edition (Oxford, 2012).

[5] Thomas N. Bisson, *The Crisis of the Twelfth Century. Power, Lordship and the Origins of European Government* (Princeton, NJ, 2009). The book is too rich to be easily summarised. One of Bisson's central tenets is that, towards the end of the twelfth century, the spread of rules of accountancy and of bookkeeping replaced a system of accountability of virtue with one of accountability of office. A further key premise is that ethical norms held little sway before then, with violence the chief or even sole means of conducting politics. While Bisson's book remains a learned, sustained and thoughtful attempt to explore the emergence of administrative governance, and one that merits equally thoughtful engagement, some of these underlying premises nonetheless do not hold up in light of the evidence that will be presented here. For a thoughtful consideration of Bisson's book see Theo Riches' review of *The Crisis of the Twelfth Century: Power, Lordship, and the Origins of European Government* (review no. 754), www.history.ac.uk/reviews/review/754 (accessed 31 August 2018). For a critique of the royalist perspective more generally, Timothy Reuter, 'Modern mentalities and medieval polities', in his *Medieval Polities and Modern Mentalities*, ed. Janet L. Nelson (Cambridge, 2006), 3–18. For an important case study: Ulla Kypta, *Die Autonomie der Routine. Wie im 12. Jahrhundert das englische Schatzamt entstand* (Göttingen, 2014).

INTRODUCTION 3

Increasing literacy furthermore encouraged the rediscovery, the revising and copying afresh of foundational texts. Especially in the twelfth century, principles of power were assessed with renewed rigour in relation to the biblical, classical and patristic legacy discussed in Chapter 2. These engagements both created and reinforced a common cultural framework for thinking and writing about kingship and power.[6] Fourth, new actors appeared on the scene, even though they were still part of a numerically small elite. Both among the aristocracy and within the ecclesiastical hierarchy, new movements and institutions laid claim to participation in the political process, such as mendicants, military orders and an increasingly assertive papal centre. The same applies to urban communities, who burst onto the political scene during the eleventh and twelfth centuries.[7] As a result, disputes increased both in frequency and in the range and number of their participants. Finally, towards the end of the period, more formalised mechanisms were developed to channel and resolve the ensuing conflicts and debates. Most immediately, a greater emphasis was placed on written guarantees of established rights, and on formalising previously unwritten rules.[8] We can observe an ever stronger emphasis on defining practices that previously had been determined rather more situationally and in a process that favoured consensus over adherence to clearly set out rules. This book covers the period roughly between the emergence of new polities in the generation either side of the year 1000, and the emergence of new actors and mechanisms around the year 1200.

Kingship provides an especially illuminating angle from which to approach these developments. As a concept, it was universal, even if, as a practice, it was by no means uniform. In the secular sphere, a community would ideally be presided over by a king, or at least by a ruler who performed king-like functions. Even the peasants of Iceland continued to be fascinated by and existed in a very complex relationship with the kings of Norway.[9] In religious thinking, a hierarchical ordering of society, with God as a king-like figure, served to conceptualise the right order of the world.[10] Kingship was representative of how things should be. Moreover, the actions of kings continuously touched upon the lives and

---

[6] Brian Stock, *The Implications of Literacy: Written Language and Models of Interpretation in the Eleventh and Twelfth Centuries* (Princeton, NJ, 1983).

[7] Chris Wickham, *Sleepwalking into a New World: the Emergence of Italian City Communes in the Twelfth Century* (Princeton, NJ, 2015); Knut Schulz, 'Denn sie lieben die Freiheit so sehr ... ' *Kommunale Aufstände und Entstehung des europäischen Bürgertums im Hochmittelalter* (Darmstadt, 1992).

[8] See the case studies discussed in François Foronda and Jean-Philippe Genet, eds., *Des chartes aux constitutions. Autour de l'idée constitutionnelle en Europe (XIIe–XVIIe siècles)* (Paris, 2019).

[9] Theodore M. Andersson, 'The king of Iceland', *Speculum* 74 (1999), 923–34.

[10] John R. Fortin, 'Saint Anselm on the Kingdom of Heaven: a model of right order', *St Anselm Journal* 6 (2008), 1–10; Robert Deshman, '"Christus rex et magi reges". Kingship and christology in Ottonian and Anglo-Saxon art', *FmSt* 10 (1976), 367–405.

4 INTRODUCTION

experiences of elite actors. Monarchs convened assemblies, conducted campaigns, appointed bishops, settled disputes, issued and confirmed grants or visited monasteries, castles and churches. Each activity involved nobles and prelates as recipients, participants, witnesses, petitioners or intercessors. Kings operated in a continuous dialogue with their leading subjects. They practised what the German medievalist Bernd Schneidmüller termed 'rule by consensus'.[11] Secular and ecclesiastical elites functioned as representatives of their regional, dynastic and religious communities, but also as trustees of the people at large.

The standing of elites in relation to each other was established through their relationship with the monarch. Proximity signalled the ability to solicit gifts and influence actions. Rulers and ruled were tied to each other in a relationship of mutual, though by no means equal dependency. But there also was a moral dimension to the role of elites. Both the power and the authority of the king reflected upon his leading subjects, the men close to court, and the ones who had elevated him to the royal dignity. As representatives of the community of the realm, prelates and princes bore a responsibility to ensure that the ruler upheld common principles of royal lordship – that he be a good king, not a tyrant. Kingship symbolised the right order of the world, but it fell to a realm's elites to ensure that someone was chosen as ruler who had the mindset and the means to maintain that order. As the political scientist Rodney Barker has argued, elites desired to be perceived and wanted to view themselves as legitimate. Nobody wished to be the bad guy. Demonstrating adherence to shared values therefore was not just a way of cloaking material concerns. It was essential for the conduct of power relations.[12] Moreover, the pragmatic and the normative were mutually reinforcing. Royal favours were of limited value if they came from a king perceived as weak or illegitimate. Such grants could easily be challenged or might simply be ignored by rivals and competitors. They might even be revoked once a new ruler took the throne. Making sure that kings were kings, not tyrants, was in everyone's interest.

A king's legitimacy was rooted in how he had come to the throne. Indeed, the manner of his elevation was so important that a first step towards formally dethroning a tyrant was to invalidate his accession. He was not deposed, but declared a usurper who had seized a dignity that was not his to hold.[13]

---

[11] Bernd Schneidmüller, 'Konsensuale Herrschaft. Ein Essay über Formen und Konzepte politischer Ordnung im Mittelalter', in *Reich, Regionen und Europa in Mittelalter und Neuzeit. Festschrift für Peter Moraw*, ed. Paul Joachim Heinig, Sigrid Jahns, Hans-Joachim Schmidt, Rainer Christoph Schwinges and Sabine Wefers (Berlin, 2000), 53–97 (shortened English version: 'Rule by consensus. Forms and concepts of political order in the European Middle Ages', *The Medieval History Journal* 16 (2013), 449–71).

[12] Rodney Barker, *Legitimating Identities: the Self-Presentation of Rulers and Subjects* (Cambridge, 2001).

[13] See above, Chapter 5 and, paradigmatically, Michaela Muylkens, *Reges geminati. Die Gegenkönige in der Zeit Heinrichs IV.* (Husum, 2011). See also Björn Weiler, 'Kingship,

INTRODUCTION 5

Moreover, his illegitimacy was rooted both in his actions and character, and in those of the men who had elected, supported or inaugurated him. Only bad people would knowingly choose bad kings. Succession was therefore a key moment for contemporaries. It determined the legitimacy not only of the monarch, but also of the leading men of the realm. To borrow a term from literary studies, it became a textual site. Narrating the process of king-making enabled contemporary and later observers to pass judgement on the events reported, and on those participating in them.

There was a shared framework of ideas and concepts about what kings should do, and what qualified someone to be a king. Chapter 2 will sketch the foundations on which it rested. But these ideals were inherently abstract: rulers were supposed to be pious, just, equitable and warlike. Norms had to be filled with meaning by those participating in the king-making process, and by those writing about it. Different views came to the fore, divergent readings and hierarchies of shared principles, and the inevitable clash between what was desirable and what was feasible. Yet it was precisely in such moments of uncertainty that practices were forged and ideals were defined, that efforts were made to align what was with what ought to be. Defining values extended to the practices of king-making and of being king. They involved not only the ruler, but also the nobles and bishops who chose, advised, and otherwise interacted with him. They touched on the role of the public, the conduct of war, the exercise of justice and patronage, on marriage and education, in short, on every aspect of royal behaviour and of the interaction between ruler and ruled. Attempts to give concrete meaning to abstract norms allow us to see how people in high medieval Europe tried to make ideals work in practice, how they envisaged the interplay between norm and necessity, between pragmatic needs and moral expectations.

I approach these efforts by tracing the several stages in which a king was made.[14] First, kingship had to be established. A polity had to be recognised as sufficiently distinctive, and its rulers as of sufficient status to warrant so elevated a title. Chapters 3 and 4 explore how this could be accomplished. What distinguished a king from a mere duke or count? What did this mean for the relationship between the new monarch, his erstwhile peers, and those who made him king? Ideally, a royal title ought to be passed on to the next generation. Chapters 5 and 6 consider the moral framework within which a succession unfolded, and the practical steps in which it was organised. For reasons beyond the control of any of the actors involved, reconciling moral

usurpation and propaganda in twelfth-century Europe: the case of Stephen', *ANS* 31 (2000), 299–326.

[14] I am grateful to Stephen Church, who first gave me the idea to structure the book in this fashion, but a similar approach had already been taken by Heinrich Mitteis, *Die deutsche Königswahl. Ihre Rechtsgrundlagen bis zur Goldenen Bulle* (Brünn, Munich and Vienna, 1944).

6   INTRODUCTION

norms with practical needs could prove difficult. How could the resulting uncertainty be prevented from endangering not only the stability of the realm, but its very existence? Every succession involved an election, the subject of Chapters 7 and 8. How were kings chosen? Who did the choosing? The process of election was also when, in order to turn one set of norms into reality, another sometimes had to be violated. However, if adherence to norms was central to the legitimacy of the process, and that was integral to the legitimacy of the king, what measures could be taken to ensure that such contradictions did not invalidate the entire process? Once a king had been chosen, he still had to be inaugurated, a process explored in Chapters 9 and 10. In some respects, this was the moment of no return. At the same time, enthronement was not limited to just one event, such as a coronation. It involved a sequence of acts in which the new ruler asserted his right to the throne, during which a kingdom's elites could seek to steer the exercise of power into directions they deemed appropriate and necessary, and in response to which they could, if need be, revisit their earlier choice. How could king demonstrate adherence to norms, but also seize control of the reins of power? And how could the ruled respond?

By answering these questions, several gaps in our understanding of high medieval cultures of power can be filled, and several new perspectives emerge. This book is, for example, the first monograph to explore high medieval kingship as a transeuropean phenomenon.[15] Most modern studies, by contrast, have focussed on the early Middle Ages, and in particular on the example of the empire of Charlemagne and its successors;[16] they have offered case

---

[15] The partial exceptions to the rule are edited collections that set studies of several kingdoms alongside each other, but which also do so across the whole of the Middle Ages. See, for particularly important examples, Anne Duggan, ed., *Kings and Kingship in Medieval Europe* (London, 1993); and Bernhard Jussen, ed., *Die Macht des Königs: Herrschaft in Europa vom Frühmittelalter bis in die Neuzeit* (Munich, 2005). Henry A. Myers, *Medieval Kingship* (Chicago, 1982) seeks to compress modes of royal lordship into a somewhat simplistic pattern that posits supposed Germanic notions of kingship as continuously battling with supposedly Roman (that is to say Christian) ones. See also, below, Chapter 10. Francis Oakley, *The Mortgage of the Past: Reshaping the Ancient Political Inheritance (1050–1300)* (New Haven, CT, 2012) is a wonderfully learned exercise in intellectual history, which is primarily concerned with tracing biblical and classical echoes in theoretical writings about power. Robert Bartlett's *Blood Royal: Dynastic Politics in Medieval Europe* (Cambridge, 2020) was published when this book was already in peer review. His is the rare exception that nonetheless proves the rule. Bartlett is also concerned with rather different questions: the emergence of the concept and the practice of dynastic royal lordship.

[16] Inevitably, any survey will fall short of being comprehensive. Key works include: Walter Ullmann, *The Carolingian Renaissance and the Idea of Kingship* (London, 1969); Simon MacLean, *Kingship and Politics in the Late Ninth Century. Charles the Fat and the End of the Carolingian Empire* (Cambridge, 2003); Franz-Reiner Erkens, ed., *Das frühmittelalterliche Königtum. Ideelle und religiöse Grundlagen* (Berlin and New York, 2005); Roman Deutinger, *Königsherrschaft im ostfränkischen Reich* (Ostfildern, 2006);

INTRODUCTION 7

studies of monarchical rule in particular kingdoms;[17] or of learned discourses from the period after *c.* 1220.[18] However, the Carolingians had a limited impact on tenth-century, let alone eleventh- or twelfth-century modes of governance.[19] Ninth-century discourses cannot explain high medieval practices. And apparent borrowings are often nothing of the kind. Carolingian writers excelled at compiling materials drawn from the Bible, texts from classical antiquity and the works of early Christian theologians. High medieval authors drew on the same materials. But they did so independently.[20] In fact, with the exception of Einhard's *Life* of Charlemagne, few Carolingian texts were copied afresh before the second half of the twelfth century.[21] The ninth mattered because of the importance attached to Charlemagne and his descendants. Legendary forebears, they lent legitimacy to dynastic and institutional claims, to practices and conventions, by offering a link with reputable founders

Ildar H. Garipzanov, *The Symbolic Language of Authority in the Carolingian World* (Leiden, 2008); Paul Kershaw, *Peaceful Kings: Peace, Power and the Early Medieval Political Imagination* (Oxford, 2011); David R. Pratt, *The Political Thought of Alfred the Great* (Cambridge, 2007); Jennifer R. Davis, *Charlemagne's Practice of Empire* (Cambridge, 2015).

[17] John W. Baldwin, *The Government of Philip Augustus: Foundations of French Royal Power in the Middle Ages* (Berkeley, CA, 1986); Sverre Bagge, *From Gang Leader to the Lord's Anointed: Kingship in Sverris Saga and Hákonar Saga Hákonarsonar* (Odense, 1996); Philip Line, *Kingship and State Formation in Sweden, 1130–1290* (Leiden and Boston, 2006); Hans Jacob Orning, *Unpredictability and Presence. Norwegian Kingship in the High Middle Ages*, transl. Alan Crozier (Leiden and Boston, 2008); Judith A. Green, *Forging the Kingdom. Power in English Society, 973–1189* (Cambridge, 2017).

[18] M. S. Kempshall, *The Common Good in Late Medieval Political Thought: Moral Goodness and Material Benefit* (Oxford, 1999). See also the classic study by Wolfgang Berges, *Die Fürstenspiegel des hohen und späten Mittelalters* (Leipzig, 1938).

[19] See in particular Simon MacLean, 'The Carolingian past in post-Carolingian Europe', in *'The Making of Europe': Essays in Honour of Robert Bartlett*, ed. Sally Crumplin and John G. H. Hudson (Leiden, 2016), 11–31; MacLean, 'Shadow kingdom: Lotharingia and the Frankish world, c.850–c.1050', *History Compass* 11 (2013), 443–57.

[20] At best, they might have consulted Bede, who proved to be considerably more popular than almost any Carolingian text bar Einhard:Benjamin Pohl, '(Re-)Framing Bede's *Historia ecclesiastica* in twelfth-century Germany: John Rylands Library, MS Latin 182', *Bulletin of the John Rylands Library* 93 (2017), 67–119.

[21] Rudolf Schieffer, 'Mediator cleri et plebis. Zum geistlichen Einfluß auf Verständnis und Darstellung des ottonischen Königtums', in *Herrschaftsrepräsentation im ottonischen Sachsen*, ed. Gerd Althoff and Ernst Schubert (Sigmaringen, 1998), 345–61, at 347–9; Matthias M. Tischler, *Einharts 'Vita Karoli'. Studien zur Entstehung, Überlieferung und Rezeption*, 2 vols. (Hanover, 2001); Weiler, 'Crown-giving and king-making in the west', 85–7. See, for instance, Hincmar of Rheims, *De cavendis vitiis et virtutibus exercendis*, ed. Doris Nachtmann, MGH Quellen zur Geistesgeschichte (Munich, 1998), 42–7; Hincmar of Rheims, *De Ordine Palatii*, ed. and transl. Thomas Gross and Rudolf Schieffer, MGH Fontes Iuris sep. ed. (Hanover, 1980), 12; Hincmar of Rheims, *Collectio de ecclesiis et capellis*, ed. Martina Stratmann, MGH Fontes Iuris sep. ed. (Hanover, 1990), 31–5.

8 INTRODUCTION

and an equally reputable past.[22] But the claims and conventions themselves were almost entirely the making of later generations.

A focus on distinct polities, meanwhile, is misleading. Indeed, the preference for studying medieval kingship in relation to a distinct geographical area that happens to coincide with a modern nation state owes more to the concerns of nationalism from the nineteenth century to the present day than to any high medieval precedent. Almost any national historiographical tradition claims some kind of exceptionalism or *Sonderweg*, of its past being in profound ways different from something elusively referred to as 'the norm'. However, if everything is exceptional, then nothing truly is. The problem is compounded by defining national or regional exceptionalism against an amorphous European norm. Yet that norm is rarely if ever defined. It exists as a kind of numinous entity that, like Bigfoot and the Loch Ness Monster, is believed to exist without anyone having ever set eyes on it. Unsurprisingly, therefore, when comparative studies are undertaken, they quickly dissolve or invert what was supposed to have been distinctive.[23]

In fact, there was no single realm that somehow distilled the essence of high medieval royal lordship and that could therefore be studied in lieu of all the others. What one finds instead is a common framework, a set of values and practices that were universal without being uniform. It is this framework that this book sets out to sketch. To put this more pointedly, I am not interested in comparing individual trees, but in asking what they reveal about the larger forest of which they formed part.[24] This does not mean that all the trees were identical, but they did share a common environment, and responded to it in similar ways. In the same vein, the framework within which high medieval people thought and wrote about kingship was not a rigid template. It could be

---

[22] Marianne Ailes, 'Charlemagne "Father of Europe": a European icon in the making', *Reading Medieval Studies* 38 (2012), 59–76; William J. Purkis and Matthew Gabriele, eds., *The Charlemagne Legend in Medieval Latin Texts* (Woodbridge, 2016); Thomas R. Kraus and Klaus Pabst, eds., *Karl der Große und sein Nachleben in Geschichte, Kunst und Literatur* (Aachen, 2003); Matthew Gabriele and Jayce Stuckey, eds., *The Legend of Charlemagne in the Middle Ages: Power, Faith, and Crusade* (New York, 2008); Amy G. Remensnyder, *Remembering Kings Past. Monastic Foundation Legends in Medieval Southern France* (Ithaca, NY, 1995).

[23] See, above all, the work of Timothy Reuter, with his most important articles collected in his *Medieval Polities*. Nicholas Vincent, 'Conclusion', in *Noblesses de l'espace Plantagenet (1154–1224). Table ronde tenue à Poitiers le 13 mai 2000*, ed. Martin Aurell (Poitiers, 2001), 207–14; Vincent, 'Sources and methods: some Anglo-German comparisons', in *Princely Rank in Late Medieval Europe: Trodden Paths and Promising Avenues*, ed. T. Huthwelker, J. Peltzer and M. Wernhöner (Ostfildern, 2011), 119–38.

[24] It is worth stressing that a book like this could not have been written without the hard work of those who – to stick with the arboreal imagery – explored individual trees, or even just their branches. The extent of my debt will become apparent in subsequent discussions and references. I do, however, hope that the broader sketch offered here will offer ways of placing the specific within a broader context.

INTRODUCTION 9

amended, adapted and revised to accommodate specific needs – a moment of political crisis, for instance, external challenges and so on. It could also be interpreted differently. Communities might at different times postulate different hierarchies of norms. The attitude of the thirteenth-century Danish chronicler Saxo Grammaticus towards succession practices will prove a case in point (Chapters 5 and 6). In some kingdoms, elites might attach greater importance to some features than others – with the role of elections in Germany an especially striking example (Chapters 7 and 8). But they would still refer back to a shared corpus of foundational principles, and they would employ a shared set of tools. A useful parallel would be the concept of musical variation. There, a theme is subjected to changes in timbre, rhythm, harmony, pitch, counterpoint and so on. While each version is distinctive, highlighting some features, adding or omitting others, responding to the needs of different instruments, etc., the underlying structure remains nonetheless recognisable as the original theme.[25] The same principle applies to high medieval kingship.

Furthermore, I am interested in the interplay between norm and practice. The problem is that, on the surface, most high medieval writers engaged with questions of power solely in the abstract. The genre of king's mirrors – abstract treatises on the principles that ought to guide royal governance – petered out in the ninth century. It was not to be revived again until the decades around *c.* 1200. This does not mean that people did not discuss these issues.[26] They just did so in texts that are unfamiliar vehicles for discussing political ideas, such as

[25] Those of a hardened disposition are invited to seek out the Klezmer, disco, Mongolian throat singing, Bluegrass, and Konzertlied versions of Rammstein's 'Du hast'. For more genteel minds, listening to any available recording of BMV 988 or Beethoven's Op. 120 will prove just as illuminating, and perhaps a bit closer to what I had in mind when referring to variations on a theme: what at first listening may seem wholly different will reveal itself to employ the basic structure of the initial theme.

[26] This is contrary to most modern studies on medieval political thought, which largely skip these centuries, or reduce them to the writings of just one man (John of Salisbury): Walter Ullmann, *Medieval Political Thought* (Harmondsworth, 1975); Anthony J. Black, *Political Thought in Europe, 1250–1450* (Cambridge, 1992); Michel Senellart, *Les arts de Gouverneur. Du regimen médéval au concept de gouvernement* (Paris, 1996); *Fürstenspiegel des frühen und hohen Mittelalters*, ed. and transl. Hans Hubert Anton (Darmstadt, 2006) includes only two late twelfth-century texts, that is, excerpts from John of Salisbury and Godfrey of Viterbo; Frédérique Lachaud and Lydwine Scordia, eds., *Le Prince au miroir de la littérature politique de l'Antiquité aux Lumières* (Rouen 2007), an otherwise splendid collection, also deals with only one high medieval example (John of Salisbury). See, likewise, Cary J. Nederman, *Lineages of European Political Thought: Explorations Along the Medieval/Modern Divide from John of Salisbury to Hegel* (Washington, DC, 2009). For important exceptions, see Jehangir Malegam, *The Sleep of Behemoth. Disputing Peace and Violence in Medieval Europe, 1000–1200* (Ithaca, NY, 2013); Philippe Buc, *Holy War, Martyrdom, and Terror: Christianity, Violence, and the West* (Philadelphia, PA, 2015).

commentaries on the Bible,[27] letters of advice[28] and works of history.[29] Those, in turn, centre on basic principles – what rulers ought to do – rather than on concrete guidance about particular issues and problems. In this sense, thinking about kingship appears as largely divorced from its practice. That can make it difficult to trace how ideas influenced actions. We will be disappointed by the lack of definition of many of the concepts espoused, and by the contradictions between the readings on offer. In the case of historical writing, for example, we might be able to explore the views of a particular author or group of authors, but cannot be certain about how widely these were held, or whether they even circulated beyond a relatively narrow group of literate elites.[30] To avoid these issues, many studies of kingship tend to focus on practices, on *how* rulers ruled. Values and norms are treated only summarily, if at all.[31] Even Gerd Althoff,

[27] Philippe Buc, *L'Ambiguïté du livre. Prince, pouvoir, et peuple dans les commentaires de la Bible au Moyen Âge* (Paris, 1994); Renate Pletl, *Irdisches Regnum in der mittelalterlichen Exegese. Ein Beitrag zur exegetischen Lexikographie und ihren Herrschaftsvorstellungen, 7.-13. Jahrhundert* (Frankfurt/Main, 2000); Julie Barrau, *Bible, lettres et politique: l'écriture au service des hommes à l'époque de Thomas Becket* (Paris, 2013); Werner Affeldt, *Die weltliche Gewalt in der Paulus-Exegese. Röm. 13,1-7 in den Römerbriefkommentaren der lateinischen Kirche bis zum Ende des 13. Jahrhunderts* (Göttingen, 1969).

[28] John Van Engen, 'Letters, schools and written culture in the eleventh and twelfth centuries', in *Dialektik und Rhetorik im früheren und hohen Mittelalter. Rezeption, Überlieferung und gesellschaftliche Wirkung antiker Gelehrsamkeit vornehmlich im 9. und 12. Jahrhundert*, ed. Johannes Fried (Munich, 1997), 97–132; *Briefsteller und Formelbücher des elften bis vierzehnten Jahrhunderts*, ed. Ludwig Rockinger, 2 vols. (Munich, 1863-4).

[29] Foundational: Helmut Beumann, 'Die Historiographie des Mittelalters als Quelle für die Ideengeschichte des Königtums', *HZ* 180 (1955), 449–88; František Graus, 'Die Herrschersagen des Mittelalters als Geschichtsquelle', in *Ausgewählte Aufsätze von František Graus (1959-1989)*, ed. Hans-Jörg Gilomen, Peter Moraw and Rainer C. Schwinges (Stuttgart, 2002), 3–28.

[30] See, though, Martin Aurell, 'Political culture and medieval historiography: the revolt against King Henry II, 1173–1174', *History* 102 (2017), 752–71; Jacek Banaszkiewicz, 'Slavonic *origines regni*: hero the law-giver and founder of monarchy (introductory survey of problems)', *Acta Poloniae Historica* 69 (1989), 97–131; Giovanni Maniscalco Basile, 'The Christian prince through the mirror of the Rus' chronicles', *Harvard Ukrainian Studies* 12:13 (1988–9), 672–88; Anette Güntzel, 'Godfrey of Bouillon: the stylization of an ideal ruler in universal chronicles of the 12th and 13th centuries', *Amsterdamer Beiträge zur älteren Germanistik* 70 (2013), 209–22; Ármann Jakobsson, 'The individual and the ideal: the representation of royalty in *Morkinskinna*', *Journal of English and Germanic Philology* 99 (2000), 71–86; Gábor Klaniczay, 'Representations of the evil ruler in the Middle Ages', in *European Monarchy. Its Evolution and Practice from Roman Antiquity to Modern Times*, ed. Heinz Duchhardt, Richard A. Jackson and David J. Sturdy (Stuttgart, 1992), 69–79; Michael Staunton, *The Historians of Angevin England* (Oxford, 2017), 153–84; Kevin J. Wanner, '*At Smyrja Konung Til veldis*: royal legitimation in Snorri Sturluson's *Magnús Saga Erlingsonar*', *Saga-Book* 30 (2006), 5–38.

[31] See, for instance, Line, *Kingship*; Green, *Forging the Kingdom*.

INTRODUCTION

whose work on ritual and symbolic communication has fundamentally transformed our understanding of high medieval politics, initially viewed the unwritten rules of the game, so central to his approach, simply as a tool with which power relations could be negotiated. Rituals and symbolism communicated not abstract ideals, but hierarchies of material power.[32] How, then, can we get at what contemporaries thought about kingship, and how can we get a sense of the interplay between norm and practice?

These are the major questions underpinning this book. They also pose a number of challenges. How, for instance, can one offer a transeuropean approach that avoids conflating ubiquity with uniformity? The approach chosen here is to combine detailed case studies with examples drawn from across the Latin west.[33] This, as an advance warning, will mean that I will move freely between kingdoms and regions. That is a feature, not a bug. To help with the range and number of examples, readers will find at the beginning of this book a chronological list of the major events to which I will refer. We are, in fact, fortunate in the sheer number of examples on which to draw, even though a precise figure of royal successions between c. 950 and 1200 is difficult to reach. A reliable estimate would be that roughly 160 occurred in this period.[34] Of these, about forty will feature as case studies.

Particular attention will be paid to the monarchies of Scandinavia and central Europe, and those around the Mediterranean, which are rarely treated as part of a common European experience. It is exactly because their regnal status was often challenged and had to be justified that they tell us much about kingship.[35] Still, a degree of flexibility will be required. We are dependent on the survival of sources, and on the willingness and ability of their compilers to describe the processes that form the focus of this book. Chapters 7 and 8, for instance, on elections, will draw heavily on examples from Germany, as German chroniclers (and modern historians of Germany) paid more attention

---

[32] Gerd Althoff, *Spielregeln der Politik im Mittelalter. Kommunikation in Frieden und Fehde* (Darmstadt, 1997); Althoff, *Die Macht der Rituale. Symbolik und Herrschaft im Mittelalter* (Darmstadt, 2003). See, though, more recently, Althoff, 'Christian values and noble ideas of rank and their consequences on symbolic acts', *e-Spania* 4 (2007), 2–13; Althoff, *Kontrolle der Macht. Formen und Regeln politischer Beratung im Mittelalter* (Darmstadt, 2016).

[33] The approach reflects that in Arno Borst, *Lebensformen im Mittelalter* (Frankfurt/Main, 1973).

[34] This number is based on a list of rulers in relevant articles in the *Lexikon des Mittelalters*. Any references to numbers should be understood as approximations, not as precise statistical data. There were, for instance national traditions where, in some realms, competing claimants were considered as co-kings, whereas in others, rivals were labelled rebels and usurpers, and hence not counted. See also Chapter 5 for the extent to which simple figures often cloak more complex realities.

[35] Björn Weiler, 'Tales of first kings and the culture of kingship in the west, c. 1050–1200', *Viator* 46:2 (2015), 101–28.

12   INTRODUCTION

to the issue than their peers elsewhere. Yet once their accounts are placed alongside less detailed ones from across Europe, it will become apparent that we are dealing with differences of degree, not substance. This approach allows us to draw attention to the specific, while simultaneously sketching a framework of high medieval kingship that highlights themes in evidence across Latin Europe.[36] It also enables us to get a sense of what abstract norms and values might have meant in practice. How did high medieval observers expect them to be implemented? How did they seek to reconcile conflicting expectations? And how did observers handle the often considerable chasm between what should be, what could be and what actually was?

Throughout, my focus will be on the interplay between ruler and ruled. The decision is made easier by the fact that, with very few exceptions, the views of kings are difficult to ascertain. This holds true especially of royal self-representation in seals, architecture, manuscript illuminations and other artefacts.[37] Modern scholarship generally assumes that images of kingship, as sponsored by the court, had been designed to secure legitimacy. They often celebrated royal majesty, for instance by representing a ruler as being crowned by God, or copying the style of classical Roman and contemporary Byzantine emperors. There are, however, problems with this premise. Almost twenty years ago, Ludger Körntgen has asked how far images designed for private contemplation, as in Gospels and prayer books, circulated beyond a ruler's immediate entourage. The question is surprisingly difficult to answer. Much depends on context, and on the extent to which wider debates about kingship are taken into account. A defining theme in high medieval thinking about royal power was that royal authority was granted by God. Yet that constituted a duty and obligation on part of the ruler, not an invitation to unfettered rule over others. He would be held answerable both for his failings and those of his

---

[36] See also the studies collected in Reuter, *Medieval Polities*, which similarly combine case studies with broader overviews in order to trace recurring patterns in evidence across the Latin west.

[37] The key figure in this regard is Percy Ernst Schramm: *Herrschaftszeichen und Staatssymbolik. Beiträge zu ihrer Geschichte vom dritten bis zum sechzehnten Jahrhundert*, 3 vols. (Stuttgart, 1954–6); Schramm, *Kaiser, Könige und Päpste. Gesammelte Aufsätze zur Geschichte des Mittelalters*, 4 vols. in 5 (Stuttgart, 1969). In addition to Ildar H. Garipzanov, *Graphic Signs of Authority in Late Antiquity and the Early Middle Ages, 300–900* (Oxford, 2018); Rosa Bacile, 'Stimulating perceptions of kingship: royal imagery in the cathedral of Monreale and in the church of Santa Maria dell'Ammiraglio in Palermo', *Al-Masāq* 16 (2004), 17–52; Thomas Dittelbach, 'The image of the private and the public king in Norman Sicily', *Römisches Jahrbuch der Bibliotheca Hertziana* 35 (2005), 149–72; Jan Svanberg, 'The legend of Saint Stanislaus and King Boleslaus on the 12th-century font in Tryde, Sweden', *Folia Historiae Artium* NS 5–6 (1999–2000), 25–42; Hagen Keller, 'Die Herrschaftsurkunden: Botschaften des Privilegierungsaktes – Botschaften des Privilegientextes', *Settimane di Studio del centro Italiano di Studi sull'Alto Medioevo* 52 (2005), 231–83; Terézia Kerny, 'Das Engelkrönungsmotiv in der Ikonographie König Stephans des Heiligen', *Acta Ethnographica Hungarica* 49 (2004), 313–42.

INTRODUCTION   13

people. He was supposed to be the caretaker of the realm, not its proprietor. Chapter 2 will show just how common this reading was, and how deeply engrained in writing about royal power. Similar points can be made concerning secular models, like Roman emperors: antecedents set standards by which contemporaries could be judged. They were an exhortation – or perhaps even a promise – to do as well as one's fabled and legendary forebears. Consequently, if an image of the king as *imago Christi* appeared in a manuscript designed for private contemplation, should that not be read in light of the king's personal obligation towards his Creator, rather than as propagating an especially exalted view of royal power, aimed at the totality of his subjects? At best, Körntgen argued, these images therefore tell us something about royal piety, but we cannot even be entirely sure how far they reflect the understanding of a particular king.[38] What, for instance, was the role of artists and donors? How far did they reflect royal self-perceptions, and how far did they seek to mould them?

Similar questions arise in relation to charters. The *arenga* – where the issuer explained his motivations and the context of a grant – frequently contains programmatic statements. In 1222, King Andrew II responded to grievances from his nobles by issuing a grant confirming earlier privileges. In the *arenga*, Andrew recounted how the liberties of St Stephen had been 'diminished in many respects by the authority of certain kings, some of whom in personal anger took vengeance, others of whom paid heed to the counsel of wicked and false men'. He therefore vowed to guarantee ancient rights, so as to preserve peace and the royal dignity.[39] The king presented himself as restoring the right order of the world by preserving the legacy of his most illustrious predecessor. The 1222 charter was unusual. Known as the Golden Bull, it continued to be reissued by Andrew's successors until 1916. But comparable statements frequently preface simple property exchanges, confirmations of tax exemptions and so on. They reveal much about concepts and expectations of royal authority – like the relationship with the divine, the obligation to uphold justice and to redress the grievances of one's people.[40] Still, uncertainties remain. Did

---

[38] Ludger Körntgen, *Königsherrschaft und Gottes Gnade: zu Kontext und Funktion sakraler Vorstellungen in Historiographie und Bildzeugnissen der ottonisch-frühsalischen Zeit* (Berlin, 2001).

[39] *The Laws of the Medieval Kingdom of Hungary*, transl. and ed. J. Bak, G. Bónis and J. R. Sweeney, 2 vols. (Bakersfield, CA, 1989), vol. 1, 33–4. The practice survives in the names given to some modern laws, like the American Recovery and Reinvestment Act of 2009 (officially Public Law 111-5).

[40] Agnes Kucz, 'Arenga und Narratio ungarischer Urkunden des 13. Jahrhundert', *MIÖG* 70 (1962), 323–54; Heinrich Fichtenau, *Arenga. Spätantike und Mittelalter im Spiegel von Urkundenformeln* (Graz, 1957); Ralph V. Turner, 'King John's concept of royal authority', *History of Political Thought* 17 (1996), 158–78; John W. Bernhardt, 'Der Herrscher im Spiegel der Urkunden: Otto III. und Heinrich II. im Vergleich', in *Otto III. – Heinrich II. Eine Wende?*, ed. Bernd Schneidmüller (Stuttgart, 2000), 327–48; Heinz Krieg, *Herrscherdarstellung in der*

14   INTRODUCTION

rulers actually dictate the charters issued on their behalf? Or did clerks fashion
in their own words what they knew or assumed to be the king's views? How far
did precedent shape the language of grants? To what extent were form and
content conditioned by established precedent? And how far did recipients
influence the phrasing of a charter? Similar issues arise in relation to coins,
seals and letters.[41]

These questions certainly apply to narrative sources. Before the thirteenth
century, examples of histories being directly composed or directed by kings are
rare. Sverrir of Norway (d. 1202; see Chapters 4 and 6) may have overseen or
even participated in the writing of *Sverrisaga*, but he remained the exception,
not the rule. Similarly, in the 1150s Emperor Frederick Barbarossa commissioned an account of his deeds from Otto of Freising, and even wrote a letter
outlining his chief accomplishments. Yet, given that Frederick could neither
read nor write Latin, we face the same questions as with charters. In any case,
Otto and his continuator Rahewin interpreted the emperor's remit rather
loosely.[42] More commonly, records of the regnal past were produced for
female relatives, or for the benefit of a clerical community, its patrons and
benefactors. Alexander of Telese (Chapter 4) composed his account of the
reign of Roger II of Sicily at the behest of the king's sister. In England, William
of Malmesbury had written the *Gesta Regum Anglorum* (*c.* 1125) at the request
of the queen. 'Gallus Anonymus' (*c.* 1110) and Cosmas of Prague (*c.* 1123)
dedicated their histories of Poland and Bohemia respectively not to the duke,
but to ducal chaplains and senior clerics. And so on. Even authors ostensibly
writing for royal patrons usually tailored a narrative to what they *suspected*
(rather than what they *knew*) the king's self-image to be. Regnal histories –
accounts of a kingdom as a whole – were composed for courtiers and princely
advisors, to guide those who were supposed to counsel the king.[43] They tell us

---

   *Stauferzeit. Friedrich Barbarossa im Spiegel seiner Urkunden und der staufischen
   Geschichtsschreibung* (Stuttgart, 2003). Jochen Johrendt, 'Der Empfängereinfluß auf die
   Gestaltung der Arenga und Sanctio in den päpstlichen Privilegien (896–1046)', *AfD* 50
   (2004), 1–12; Hartmut Hoffmann, 'Eigendiktat in den Urkunden Ottos III. und Heinrichs
   II.', *DA* 33 (1988), 390–423.
[41] Garipzanov, *Symbolic Language of Authority*; John F. Cherry, 'Heads, arms and badges:
   royal representation on seals', in *Good Impressions: Image and Authority in Medieval
   Seals*, ed. Noël Adams, John F. Cherry and James *Kaiser, Könige und Päpste* (London,
   2008), 12–16; Irmgard Fees, 'Die Siegel und Bullen Kaiser Friedrichs I. Barbarossa', *AfD*
   61 (2015), 95–137; Jean-Marie Martin, 'Quelques remarques sur les sceaux des princes
   lombards et normands de Capoue', in *Ut sementem feceris, ita metes. Studi in onore di
   Biagio Saitta*, ed. Carmelina Urso (Acireale, 2016), 437–46; Van Engen, 'Letters, schools
   and written culture'.
[42] Heinz Krieg, 'Im Spannungsfeld zwischen christlichen und adligen Normvorstellungen.
   Zur Beurteilung Friedrich Barbarossas in stauferzeitlicher Historiographie', *FmSt* 41
   (2007), 447–66. See also Chapter 10.
[43] Generally: Karl Ferdinand Werner, 'Gott, Herrscher und Historiograph: der
   Geschichtsschreiber als Interpret des Wirkens Gottes in der Welt und Ratgeber der

INTRODUCTION 15

what the ruled thought about the ruler, but not necessarily what kings thought about kingship.

Far from being a shortcoming, these features present manifold opportunities. Narrative accounts allow us to trace how contemporaries conceptualised kingship, and how they expected abstract norms to be translated into political practice. Commentators and observers included those who had not themselves been privy to the events recorded. Yet they still constructed a narrative that set what they knew against what they thought should be, or what had occurred in a past that they deemed to be normative. To some extent, a fanciful re-imagining, a misunderstood or misconstrued account will be of as much value as one penned by an eyewitness intimately involved in the proceedings reported.[44] Authors may have shaped accounts to tally with what they expected to have occurred, or to pass judgement on a ruler's subsequent actions. But they may also simply have sought to forge from fragmentary accounts, from dim recollections and passing references, a credible rendition of what they thought had likely happened, or what, as a rule, would have happened. The writing of history was always also an act of interpretation. Whatever the motivation of authors, how they came to terms with the process of king-making tells us much about the ideas circulating among a wider elite, and about the tools and mechanisms that observers expected to have been employed – however limited their familiarity with regnal politics may in practice have been.[45]

In addition, narrative sources survive in a wide variety of forms and in astonishing numbers. Geschichtsquellen.de, an online repertory of historical sources for the medieval western empire, divides materials into fifty-five genres, including catalogues of abbots; chronicles of monasteries, bishoprics, regions, kingdoms, people and the world; hagiographical writings; accounts of recent events; travel literature; visions; ruler lists; and much else besides.[46]

Könige (4. bis 12. Jahrhundert)', in his *Einheit der Geschichte. Studien zur Historiographie*, ed. Werner Paravicini (Sigmaringen, 1998), 89–119; Björn Weiler, 'Thinking about power before Magna Carta: the role of history', in *Des chartes aux constitutions. Autour de l'idée constitutionnelle en Europe (XIIe–XVIIe siècles)*, ed. François Foronda and Jean-Philippe Genet (Paris, 2019), 3–26.

[44] Thomas Foerster's concept of political myth, while not quite capturing the phenomenon described here, will nonetheless prove useful: 'Political myths and political culture in twelfth-century Europe', in *Erfahren, erzählen, erinnern: narrative Konstruktionen von Gedächtnis und Generation in Antike und Mittelalter*, ed. Herwig Brandt, Benjamin Pohl, William Maurice Sprague and Lina Hörl (Bamberg, 2012), 83–116.

[45] This follows Graus, 'Die Herrschersagen', and Beumann, 'Die Historiographie'. See also Joachim Ehlers, 'Machtfragen. Aspekte der historiographischen Literatur im lateinischen Europa des Hochmittelalters', in *Macht und Spiegel der Macht: Herrschaft in Europa im 12. und 13. Jahrhundert vor dem Hintergrund der Chronistik*, ed. Grischa Vercamer and Norbert Kersken (Wiesbaden, 2013), 23–40.

[46] See under 'Gattungen' at www.geschichtsquellen.de/filter (accessed 22 February 2021).

16 INTRODUCTION

Auguste Molinier's list of sources for French history from 987 to 1194 resorts to somewhat broader but nonetheless indicative categories: genealogies; local histories; Norman, English, universal and crusading chronicles; ruler biographies; as well as Cluniac, Cistercian and other monastic writings.[47] The range also denotes different audiences, narrative archetypes, models of composition, etc. Just because texts were written in Latin, it does not follow that they unerringly voiced identical views. Audiences, domestic traditions, the expectations of brethren, patrons, informants, the conventions of genre and the availability of sources and resources ensured that a variety of perspectives was preserved.

What one does, however, find are shared expectations about what kings should do. Writers primarily concerned with the affairs of a particular abbey or cathedral would often ignore the deeds and actions of rulers. But when royal actions impinged upon the community, a common catalogue of virtues was nonetheless invoked. Good kings gave grants and gifts, honoured abbots and bishops and appointed pious and capable men to lead an abbey or cathedral. Bad ones incited rebellion. They favoured corrupt and evil clerics. They exploited and impoverished the communities given into their care. In a like vein, dynastic chronicles – accounts of the history of a noble family – could take a deeply hostile view of royal power. The *Historia Welforum*, an account of the Swabian Welfs from *c.* 1190, painted a stark contrast between the family and the rulers unfathomably placed over them. It rested on the Welfs' ability and willingness to perform the functions of kingship, and to do so more consistently and with far greater success than almost any king. Where emperors oppressed the Church, the Welfs were its guardians and protectors. Where rulers acted like tyrants, the Welfs earned the devotion and love of their subjects by upholding justice and securing the peace. They may have lacked the title, but they certainly displayed the qualities of kings. In the house chronicle of the counts of Anjou, kings were largely ignored, beyond an occasional act of patronage. But the *Chronique* still ended with the accession of Count Fulk to the kingship of Jerusalem. Despite being merely a count, he had already performed the functions and duties of kingship. The *Gesta* of the counts of Barcelona followed a similar trajectory.[48] Individual kings could be ignored, or be found wanting when set alongside their noble subjects. But ideas of *kingship* still formed the moral archetype that dukes and counts should seek to emulate,

---

[47] Auguste Molinier, *Les sources de l'histoire de France depuis les origines jusqu'en 1789. I:2* (Paris, 1902), 319–22. My own approach is closer to Molinier's, simply because too fine-grained a level of categorisation obfuscates the ease with which medieval writers could transcend conventions of genre.

[48] Björn Weiler, 'Kingship and lordship: kingship in "dynastic" chronicles', in *The Gallus Anonymus and His Chronicle in the Light of Recent Research*, ed. Krzysztof Stopka (Kraków, 2011), 103–23.

INTRODUCTION 17

and the standard against which their actions would be measured. Universality does not equal uniformity.

Narrative sources also survive in vast numbers. Molinier listed almost 1,250 items,[49] and Geschichtsquellen.de 1,220 for the period 950–1200.[50] Still, considerable imbalances existed over time and between regions. Of the imperial materials, 190 were written in the second half of the tenth century, 520 in the eleventh century and 755 in the twelfth.[51] The spread reflects the increasing textual production in evidence across Europe: a phenomenon replicated in almost every genre of writing, and one reason why so much more can be said about the twelfth century than the tenth. Moreover, narratives were not produced evenly across Europe. In Denmark, all surviving narratives for the entire Middle Ages fit into eight volumes (two of them Saxo Grammaticus). Two suffice for Hungary. By contrast, the *Scriptores* series of the *Monumenta Germaniae Historica* runs to 190 volumes, its English equivalent to 99, and its Italian to 159. Even with such uneven survival, historians of high medieval Europe are presented with a veritable embarrassment of riches.

To put this into perspective: only about 3,500–4,000 charters issued by western emperors remain extant for the period 936–1190, roughly 150 survive from the kingdom of Sicily 1130–1198 and 800 from the kingdom of Jerusalem (1099–1292). These numbers do not include documents issued by lay princes or ecclesiastical institutions, but adding them would do little to change the general pattern. Only about 300 charters of Henry the Lion (*c.* 1129/31–1195) remain, and 140 of Matilda of Tuscany (1046–1115), both leading secular princes in the western empire.[52] The wealth of Latin materials furthermore contrasts starkly with what is available in the vernacular. Of the 1,220 high medieval items on the Geschichtsquellen database, only twenty-one contained extensive passages written in languages other than Latin (fourteen if we also exclude Hebrew).[53] Both Molinier and Geschichtsquellen omit what one might

---

[49] Molinier, *Les sources*, numbers items continuously from volume I.1 in the same series. It starts with no. 950 and ends with no. 2209. Some of these numbers however refer not to texts, but to short summaries of the entries that follow.

[50] Search carried out 12 August 2020.

[51] That the number is greater than 1,220 reflects the fact that some texts were counted at least twice, for instance, because their precise date is uncertain (e.g. *c.* 950–1050), or because it may have been written across the artificial dividing line of a century, as in 990–1010 or 1080–1110.

[52] The imperial figures need to be approached with some caution, as we lack editions of the charters of Henry V (1105/6–1125) and Henry VI (1184/90–1197). For Sicily and the crusader kingdom, I drew on the relevant editions, listed in the bibliography. For Henry and Matilda, see the volumes in the *Dynasten- und Laienurkunden der Kaiserzeit* sub-series of the MGH Diplomata, accessible via www.dmgh.de.

[53] And even that number is misleading: it includes *Keiser und Keiserin*, an ode to Emperor Henry II and St Kunigunde, written at some point between 1200 and 1240; a legendary account of the order of St John, produced at some point in the thirteenth century; the

18   INTRODUCTION

term 'literary sources'. Yet adding these would not significantly change the overall picture. By far the largest corpus of extant vernacular 'literary' manuscripts from the twelfth century was composed in Middle High German, with roughly 200 items. A mere sixty-six survive in Northern French (mostly in Anglo-Norman, and hence likely to be of English provenance).[54] With very few exceptions (pre-Conquest England being one), Latin remained the dominant language of literary production, and narratives of the past one of its most popular outlets.

Most texts were composed by clerics. That vernacular writings were, too, would only constitute a problem if one assumed that clerics and laymen inhabited fundamentally different moral universes. There is no evidence to that effect.[55] Abbeys with royal patrons might hold different views from those with primarily noble or patrician benefactors. Benedictines and Cistercians rarely agreed, and both clashed with secular clerics (the ones not subject to a monastic rule). Bishops and canons were often in dispute. Everyone despised archdeacons. Some favoured firebrand reformers. Others viewed them as endearingly uncouth, or as noisy hypocrites. Canons and monks at monastic and cathedral schools looked down on parish priests, court clerics despised the ethical imperative of their peers

> Cambridge songs, which include only two texts in Middle High German; a *Life of St Ulrich*, also produced in the thirteenth century; a genealogy of the dukes of Austria, translated from the Latin in the thirteenth century; and a fifteenth-century continuation of a set of eleventh- and twelfth-century notes on the history of the monastery of Adelsberg. Without these, eight items remain for the period 950–1200. Of these only two deal in detail with aspects of kingship. Both will be used.

[54] Rodney Thomson, 'The place of Germany in the twelfth-century Renaissance', in *Manuscripts and Monastic Culture: Reform and Renewal in Twelfth-Century Germany*, ed. Alison I. Beach (Turnhout, 2007), 19–42, at 27–8.

[55] Joshua B. Smith, *Walter Map and the Matter of Britain* (Philadelphia, PA, 2017) has pointed out how seemingly folkloric elements in Latin literature formed part of a transeuropean clerical elite culture. On that same transeuropean clerical culture: Elizabeth M. Tyler, 'Writing universal history in eleventh-century England: Cotton Tiberius B. i, German imperial history-writing and vernacular lay literacy', in *Universal Chronicles in the High Middle Ages*, ed. Henry Bainton and Michele Campopiano (Woodbridge, 2017), 65–93; Elizabeth Boyle, 'Lay morality, clerical immorality, and pilgrimage in tenth-century Ireland: Cethrur Macclérech and Epscop do Gáedelaib', *Studia Hibernica* 39 (2013), 9–43; Maximilian Benz and Sylvia Reuekamp, 'Mittelhochdeutsche Erzählverfahren und theologisches Wissen. Bausteine einer historisch spezifischen Narratologie', *Poetica* 50 (2020), 53–82. The phenomenon becomes even more pronounced in the thirteenth century: Haki Antonsson, 'The present and the past in the sagas of Icelanders', in *How the Past Was Used: Historical Cultures, c.700–2000*, ed. Peter Lambert and Björn Weiler (Oxford, 2017), 69–90; Haki Antonsson, 'Salvation and early saga writing in Iceland: aspects of the works of the Þingeyrar Monks and their associates', *Viking and Medieval Scandinavia* 8 (2012), 71–140; Torfi H. Tulinus, 'Honour, sagas and trauma: reflections on literature and violence in 13th century Iceland', in *Literature and Honour*, ed. Aasta Marie Bjorvand Bjørkøy and Thorstein Norheim (Oslo, 2017), 81–94 (www.idunn.no/literature-and-honour (accessed 6 March 2018)); Paul Beekman Taylor, 'Njáll grómr: Christian morality and Norse myth in Njál's Saga', *Mediaeval Scandinavia* 13 (2000), 167–80.

INTRODUCTION

trained in the liberal arts. Most liked the idea of the pope, but far fewer were enamoured by its reality. And so on. The medieval *ecclesia* was not the Borg collective. That there was some uniform world view shared by all clergy may be a frustratingly persistent misconception. That makes it no less erroneous. The same multiplicity of views existed among laypeople, where those can be traced. Moreover, ecclesiastical and secular elites frequently overlapped. The former were the sons, brothers, uncles, nephews and cousins of the latter. Family and dynastic networks existed alongside institutional affiliations. The higher echelons of the aristocracy also shared an educational framework with their clerical neighbours and relatives (see Chapter 6). In practical terms, churches remained dependent on the continuing patronage and support of their lay benefactors. There would be no monasteries if someone didn't think it was a good idea to endow a few, or to give lands and gifts to others. Many ecclesiastical institutions acted as centres of family *memoria* and instruction, as depositories of a dynasty's history, as providers of instruction, solace and legitimation.[56] This does not mean that differences of opinion did not exist. We will encounter numerous examples to that effect, especially in Chapters 8 and 10. But those were not substantially different from the ones that existed, for example, between clerics supporting rival claimants to the throne (Chapter 5).

In practice, lay aristocrats frequently called upon members of the clergy to formulate and communicate shared values. They translated demands about the governance of the realm and their fulfilment into the language of record, and preserved that record on behalf of the community at large. That is certainly what they were expected to do in England when Magna Carta was issued, or in Hungary with the Golden Bull. In both instances, copies were sealed and deposited in the kingdom's cathedrals to ensure their continuing survival and validity. Acting in this manner formed part of the duties for which churches were endowed, supported and protected by their benefactors. This did not prevent clerical authors from imposing an interpretation of their own, or from highlighting aspects that would have been of particular relevance to their peers. Neither, though, does this mean that they spoke only for themselves. Clerics practised literacy not solely for their own benefit, but also on behalf of, and in interaction with the community of the realm at large.

Furthermore, their efforts reflected and sought to shape social reality. They provided a record of useful precedent, and of moral lessons to be drawn from the events of the past.[57] Both were especially important when it came to

---

[56] See, paradigmatically, Nicholas L. Paul, *To Follow in Their Footsteps. The Crusades and Family Memory in the High Middle Ages* (Ithaca, NY, 2012).

[57] Johanna Dale, 'Imperial self-representation and the manipulation of history in twelfth-century Germany: Cambridge, Corpus Christi College MS 373', *German History* 29 (2011), 557–83; Simon MacLean, 'Recycling the Franks in twelfth-century England: Regino of Prüm, the monks of Durham, and the Alexandrine Schism', *Speculum* 87 (2012), 649–81; Steffen Patzold, 'Wie bereitet man sich auf einen Thronwechsel vor?

20

INTRODUCTION

making a king. That process was, after all, an extended exercise in rehearsing, defining and seeking to enshrine normative behaviour on the part of king and king-makers alike.[58] Narratives of the past shared the impetus to direct the exercise of power with the coronation liturgy, charters and letters.[59] A new ruler's charters demonstrated continuity and promised a revival of good governance.[60] Letters confirming a ruler in or congratulating him on his succession also exhorted him to discharge the duties of his office.[61] Historical writing reflected that wider cultural consensus. This does not mean that chroniclers and historians provided a disinterested record of what actually happened. That was only part of what they were supposed to, and it was not always what they could offer. An account still had to echo what was considered to be plausible, and what would fit with a shared understanding of the events described and of the participants in them.

In a way, therefore, upholding norms and values, demonstrating their importance and impact on the past, provided practical guidance. It showed how one should behave in certain situations, outlined the most common points of crisis and the most frequent challenges, recorded how people had responded to them in the past and the dangers that occurred when norms were disregarded, tools of power were abused or rules of conduct were broken. This still leaves us with the dilemma that it will be almost impossible to outline what happened during any particular act. The more detailed an account, the more likely it was written so as to shape future action. It highlighted what should happen, and did so very likely at the expense of what had actually happened. But if writers from across Europe highlighted similar steps as necessary for a succession to be legitimate, we can assume that they reflected shared concepts. As our focus is not on any particular king-making, but on recurring *patterns* of king-making as well as on the debates and practices that these reflected and triggered, we can live with that degree of hermeneutic uncertainty.

Some of the norms espoused in the central Middle Ages will seem familiar. Power should be used for the common good, not private gain; the ruler ought to act as keeper of the realm, not its proprietor; and holding great power required

---

Überlegungen zu einem wenig beachteten Text des 11. Jahrhunderts', in *Die mittelalterliche Thronfolge im europäischen Vergleich*, ed. Matthias Becher (Ostfildern, 2017), 127–57. See, in lieu of a very rich literature, the rather useful collection in *Prologues to Ancient and Medieval History: A Reader*, ed. Justin Lake (Toronto, 2013). Generally: Lars Boje Mortensen, 'The glorious past: entertainment, example or history? Levels of twelfth-century historical culture', *Culture and History* 13 (1994), 57–71.

[58] See, especially, Chapters 3, 5 and 7.

[59] Johanna Dale, *Inauguration and Liturgical Kingship in the Long Twelfth Century: Male and Female Accession Rituals in England, France and the Empire* (Woodbridge, 2019), and below, Chapter 9.

[60] See Chapters 6 and 10.

[61] See Chapters 2 and 9 below, and Weiler, 'Clerical *admonitio*, letters of advice to kings and episcopal self-fashioning, c.1000–1200', *History* 102 (2017), 557–75.

INTRODUCTION

that those wielding it adhere to certain norms of ethics and morals. The habitually mendacious and the inveterately corrupt should not hold public office; grifters and liars should not be kings. High medieval Europeans were not the first – nor will their twenty-first-century heirs be the last – to advocate these ideals, and to struggle to enforce them. Some of the mechanisms developed in the eleventh and twelfth centuries still survive as ideals or hallowed antecedents, such as formalised assemblies that had to consent to a ruler's demands,[62] and the written guarantee of fundamental rights, or of the limits of governmental power.[63] That, at the time of writing, six of the twenty-seven member states of the European Union are monarchies,[64] while four had become republics only in the 1960s,[65] may enhance this sense of familiarity. So may the fact that even presidential government can maintain the vestiges of monarchical rule, as it does in France and the United States. Modern and medieval writers also shared common reference points. Cicero, for example, was as important to high medieval thinking about power as he was to the founding fathers of the American Republic.[66]

But similarities and parallels should not blind us to profound differences. The publics addressed in the political process were fundamentally different.[67] Most modern politicians are not elected for life. And contemporary political leaders invoking divine favour are at best subject to mockery. At worst, they open themselves up to accusations of tyranny.[68] Approaching the high medieval simply as foreshadowing or laying the foundations for the contemporary, as a mere prelude to the present, devalues the experiences of the people who wrote about, who lived through and who suffered the consequences of the events at the heart of this book. They are not mere playthings to wanton moderns. This is not to deny the fact that echoes can be heard across the centuries. If nothing else, the high medieval example suggests that diverging opinions about and disputes over the meaning and ranking of norms have a long pedigree. They form an integral part of the political cultures out of which modern European polities emerged. But we can distinguish echoes and relics of the past from the contemporary only if we approach the former on its own terms.

---

[62] www.parliament.uk/about/living-heritage/evolutionofparliament/originsofparliament/birthofparliament/ (accessed 18 February 2020).

[63] Michael Forsythe, 'Magna Carta exhibition in China is abruptly moved from university', *New York Times*, 15 October 2015.

[64] Belgium, Denmark, Luxembourg, the Netherlands, Spain and Sweden.

[65] Cyprus, Greece, Malta and Portugal. Monarchies also rule in Andorra, Monaco and Norway, which are not in the EU.

[66] Charles Francis Adams, *Memoirs of John Quincy Adams: Comprising Portions of His Diary from 1795 to 1848* (New York, 1875), vol. 4, 361; Jeremy Bailey, *Thomas Jefferson and Executive Power* (Cambridge, 2007), 106.

[67] See Chapters 1, 4, 5, 8–10.

[68] David Roark, 'Is President Trump chosen by God?', *Dallas News*, 20 January 2020.

PART I

Foundations

That the polities making up the high medieval Latin west are best approached not in isolation from, but alongside each other, may seem an obvious point to make. Almost thirty years ago, Timothy Reuter lamented the tendency to superimpose upon the medieval past the political borders and sensibilities of the nineteenth-century nation state.[1] Reuter voiced his disappointment not long after Robert Bartlett's *Making of Europe* outlined the extent to which the economic, social, religious and political culture of medieval Europe was shaped by ideas, movements and institutions that travelled freely across the boundaries of both medieval realms and modern states.[2] That Reuter's and Bartlett's exhortations have largely gone unheeded only serves to highlight how deeply entrenched a national approach to the past still is,[3] and how urgently we need to move beyond it.

The modern preoccupation with the nation state is not entirely without its medieval antecedents. Especially in the twelfth century, a proliferation of regnal histories sought to identify what was distinctive about a community.[4] Because many of these accounts were the first of their kind, they formed the foundations on which modern constructions of nationhood were built. But medieval writers also asserted that regnal communities distinguished themselves by being better at living up to shared ideals. Danes, for instance, were better Romans than the Romans, and, once converted, better Christians than their German or Norwegian neighbours. Similar sentiments surface in England, Germany, Hungary, Poland and Bohemia.[5] These cultural horizons make possible the broad transeuropean

---

[1] Timothy Reuter, 'Modern mentalities and medieval polities', in his *Medieval Polities*, ed. Janet L. Nelson (Cambridge, 2006), 3–18, at 14–16.

[2] Robert Bartlett, *The Making Of Europe: Conquest, Colonisation and Cultural Change* (London, 1993).

[3] For the broader development: Stefan Berger and Christoph Conrad, *The Past as History: National Identity and Historical Consciousness in Modern Europe* (Houndmills, 2015); *The Making of Medieval History*, ed. G. A. Loud and Martial Staub (Woodbridge, 2017).

[4] Alheydis Plassmann, *Origo gentis. Identitäts- und Legitimitätsstiftung in früh- und hochmittelalterlichen Herkunftserzählungen* (Berlin, 2006).

[5] Lars Boje Mortensen, 'Saxo Grammaticus' view of the origin of the Danes and his historiographical models', *Cahiers de l'Institut du Moyen-Âge grec et latin (Université de Copenhague)* 55 (1987), 169–83; Norbert Kersken, *Geschichtsschreibung im Europa der*

approach adopted in this book. Most literate high medieval Europeans shared an understanding of what kingship was, what it was supposed to accomplish and how it should be awarded. Their understanding of what the royal office entailed reflected social realities. What, though, were these? That is the question at the heart of Chapter 1. In the process, some of the conceptual underpinnings of this book will be sketched more fully. What, for instance, is meant by referring to 'the Latin west' or the 'central Middle Ages'? To what extent are these terms rooted in medieval modes of thinking about and practices of ruling? Furthermore, practical and social realities interacted with, and were written about, in relation to a set of foundational texts. These will be at the heart of Chapter 2. What norms and concepts did they uphold? What do they tell us about the foundations on which high medieval engagements with royal power were built?

'nationes'. Nationalgeschichtliche Gesamtdarstellungen im Mittelalter (Cologne, Weimar and Vienna, 1995).

1

Politics and Power in High Medieval Europe, *c.* 1000–1200

Latin Europe provides a convenient, though not wholly accurate, shorthand. It refers to those parts of Europe where Latin remained the primary language of religious practice and written communication. These constituted a mixture of regions that had been part of the western Roman empire, and of those like Scandinavia, as well as much of Germany and central Europe, that only became part of a Latin cultural orbit during the early and high Middle Ages. Latin Europe is sometimes set in opposition to a Byzantine political and cultural sphere, encompassing the successor polities of the eastern Roman empire, such as the Byzantine empire itself (which at the beginning of this period stretched from Antioch into eastern Anatolia, across Greece into the Balkans and southern Italy, and to the Black Sea region), in addition to those where Greek or Old Church Slavonic remained the primary languages of religion and communication, with Serbia and the Kievan Rus chief among them.

Inevitably, reality was more complicated. Latin and Byzantine cultural spheres *did* overlap. Language was no barrier to cultural and economic exchange, political borders were fluid and both eastern and western Europe drew on a shared classical Roman and early Christian legacy. That my focus nonetheless remains firmly on the west should not be misread as implying that Byzantium did not matter. It did, and a detailed comparison, perhaps combined with a history of exchanges between the two spheres, remains a desideratum.[1] It is not, however, what this book sets out to offer. We can only compare western practices of monarchical rule with others once we have a working understanding of what they may actually have been. Furthermore, western Europe was by no means monolithically Latinate. Vernacular cultures

---

[1] Christian Raffensperger, *Reimagining Europe: Kievan Rus' in the Medieval World* (Cambridge, MA, 2012); Jonathan Shepard, 'Byzantium's overlapping circles', *Proceedings of the 21st International Congress of Byzantine Studies* (Aldershot, 2006), 15–55; Roland Scheel, *Skandinavien und Byzanz: Bedingungen und Konsequenzen mittelalterlicher Kulturbeziehungen*, 2 vols. (Göttingen, 2015). Vedran Sulovsky, 'Sacrum imperium: Lombard influence and the "sacralization of the state" in the mid-twelfth-century Holy Roman Empire', *German History* (https://doi.org/10.1093/gerhis/ghaa085) (2020); Nicola Carpentieri and Carol Symes, eds., *Medieval Sicily, al-Andalus, and the Maghrib: Writing in Times of Turmoil* (Amsterdam, 2019), however, appeared too late to be fully used for this book.

26   1. POLITICS AND POWER IN HIGH MEDIEVAL EUROPE

thrived in the British Isles, Ireland and Scandinavia, and from the late twelfth century became more prominent in France, Iberia and Germany. In addition, there was a sizeable Arabic-speaking population in Iberia and Sicily, and Jewish communities existed across western Europe.[2] Latin culture both drew upon these cultures and shaped them.[3] Yet until the period discussed here drew to a close, little of that exchange filtered through into depictions of kingship. The discovery of Aristotle, which revolutionised thinking about power, had its greatest impact in the thirteenth century. Even in Sicily – where rulers drew on a rich medley of Byzantine, Arabic, Lombard and northern European practices – the narrative portrayal of kingship unfolded in Latin, and among a literate elite that viewed the syncretism of Sicilian royal rule with suspicion, or even ignored it entirely.[4] In Iberia, several centuries of close proximity to and, by the twelfth century, a lively interest in Islamic culture were barely reflected in an admittedly sparse and intermittent tradition of narratives about politics, power and kingship.[5] The high medieval Latin west

[2] Brian A. Catlos, *The Victors and the Vanquished: Christians and Muslims of Aragon and Castile, 950–1300* (Princeton, NJ, 2004); Mark D. Myerson and Edward English, eds., *Christians, Muslims, and Jews in Medieval and Early Modern Spain. Interaction and Cultural Change* (New York, 2000); Alex Metcalfe, *The Muslims of Medieval Italy* (Edinburgh, 2009) and 'The Muslims of Sicily under Christian rule', in *The Society of Norman Italy*, ed. Graham A. Loud and Alex Metcalfe (Leiden, 2002), 289–318; Anna Sapir Abulafia, *Christian Jewish Relations, 1000–1300: Jews in the Service of Medieval Christendom* (Cambridge, 2011); Ram Ben-Shalom, *Medieval Jews and the Christian Past: Jewish Historical Writing from Spain and Southern France* (New York, 2012); Jonathan M. Elukin, *Living Together, Living Apart: Rethinking Jewish-Christian Relations in the Middle Ages* (Princeton, NJ, 2007).

[3] Max Lejbovicz, ed., *Les relations culturelles entre chrétiens et musulmans au Moyen Âge: quelles leçons en tirer de nos jours?* (Turnhout, 2005); Stamatios Gerogiorgakis, Roland Scheel and Dittmar Schorkowitz, 'Kulturverkehr vergleichend betrachtet', in *Integration und Desintegration der Kulturen im europäischen Mittelalter*, ed. Michael Borgolte, Julia Dücker, Marcel Müllerberg and Bernd Schneidmüller (Berlin, 2011), 385–466; Michael Borgolte and Bernd Schneidmüller, eds., *Hybride Kulturen im mittelalterlichen Europa* (Berlin, 2009).

[4] Anneliese Nef, 'Muslims and Islam in Sicily from the mid-eleventh to the end of the twelfth century: contemporary perceptions and today's interpretations', in *Routledge Handbook of Islam in Europe*, ed. Roberto Tottoli (London, 2015), 55–69; Charles Dalli, 'Contriving coexistence: Muslims and Christians in the unmaking of Norman Sicily', in *Routines of Existence: Time, Life and After Life in Society and Religion*, ed. Elena Brambilla (Pisa, 2009), 29–41.

[5] Stephen Lay, *The Reconquest Kings of Portugal: Political and Cultural Reorientation on the Medieval Frontier* (Basingstoke, 2009); Peter Linehan, *History and Historians of Medieval Spain* (Oxford, 1993); Stefano Maria Cingolani, 'The myth of the origins and the royal power in the late medieval Crown of Aragon', in *Catalonia and Portugal. The Iberian Peninsula from the Periphery*, ed. Flocel Sabaté and Luís Adão da Fonseca (Bern, 2015), 243–67. See also the important case of the crusader states: Andrew D. Buck, 'Settlement, identity, and memory in the Latin East: an examination of the term "Crusader States"', *EHR* 135 (2020), 271–302.

I. FOUNDATIONS

represented itself as a distinct cultural sphere. That this did not reflect reality is precisely the kind of tension that this book explores. Yet it is also this self-representation that facilitates and enables the approach taken here.

Latin mattered as a language of communication not least because it was the language of western Catholic Christianity. By the eleventh century, it had, with only patchy exceptions, become normative as the language of the liturgy, and also as the medium through which the component parts of Latin Christendom communicated with each other and with an increasingly assertive papal centre.[6] A religion based on written revelation required professional interpreters of sacred scripture, of the exegetical body that had grown up around it and of the legal corpus that emerged just as conversion reached many of the regions treated here. Christianisation necessitated building an educational infrastructure.[7] That, in turn, reinforced the paradigmatic character of classical literature. It was the basis on which Latin was taught, and on which both the Latin Vulgate and early interpretations of the Bible built. The result was that a body of foundational and quasi-canonical texts emerged, and alongside it a shared outlook on how to compose and fashion writing. Vergil, Cicero, Suetonius, Sallust, Ovid, Lucan, Solinus, Orosius, Ambrose, Augustine and Gregory the Great were known and read across Europe. They constituted the framework within which Latinity was practised. Equally, once it came to fashioning accounts of a community's secular or religious past, models and narratives from across western Europe were consulted. Together with the Bible, handbooks of rhetoric and classical historians, chroniclers like Regino of Prüm, Marianus Scotus, Adam of Bremen or Sigebert of Gembloux provided a framework for recording the past.[8] Latinity helped create a transeuropean textual community,[9] where writers and readers used common models and shared foundations to record, evaluate and help shape the realities around them. An approach to high medieval Europe that fails to consider this international and cosmopolitan framework will not be able to grasp the complexity and variety of the world it seeks to analyse.

---

[6] See, though, for important exceptions, Elaine M. Treharne, *Living through Conquest: the Politics of Early English, 1020–1220* (Oxford, 2012); Ramón Gonzálvez Ruiz, 'The persistence of the Mozarabic liturgy in Toledo after A.D. 1080', in *Santiago, Saint-Denis, and Saint Peter. The Reception of the Roman Liturgy in León-Castile in 1080*, ed. Bernard F. Reilly (New York, 1985), 157–85; Jochen Johrendt and Harald Müller, eds., *Rom und die Regionen. Studien zur Homogenisierung der lateinischen Kirche im Hochmittelalter* (Berlin, 2012).

[7] Nora Berend, 'Introduction', in *Christianization and the Rise of Christian Monarchy. Scandinavia, Central Europe and Rus', c. 900–1200*, ed. Nora Berend (Cambridge, 2007), 1–46; Robert Bartlett, 'From paganism to Christianity in medieval Europe', ibid., 47–72.

[8] Matthew Kempshall, *Rhetoric and the Writing of History, 400–1500* (Manchester, 2011); Björn Weiler, 'Historical writing in Europe, c. 1100–1300', in *Medieval Welsh Chronicles*, ed. Ben Guy and Owain Bryn Jones (forthcoming).

[9] A term borrowed from Brian Stock, *The Implications of Literacy: Written Language and Models of Interpretation in the Eleventh and Twelfth Centuries* (Princeton, NJ, 1983).

The period between the end of the first millennium and the early thirteenth century also witnessed the gestation of some of Latin Europe's most important political structures.[10] Many of the actors familiar from the early Middle Ages disappeared, sometimes slowly, sometimes cataclysmically. Around the year 1000, the Anglo-Saxon kingdoms of England had only recently been united by Edgar I, and the realm was about to be subsumed into a Scandinavian empire that also encompassed Norway and Denmark. Just over a decade earlier, in 987, the count of Paris had seized the west Frankish throne from the last ruling descendants of Charlemagne. Nobody could foresee that his heirs would rule until the fourteenth century. In east Francia, the rulers of Saxony, once firmly outside that realm entirely, had occupied the throne for almost a century, and in 962 had revived the Carolingian claim to act as successors to the Roman empire of Augustus. Much of Iberia was still ruled by the caliphs of Cordoba, with Christian polities relegated to the north of the peninsula. In Italy, Lombards and Franks fought for pre-eminence in the north, while the south was a patchwork of territories maintaining nominal adherence to Byzantium, and those ruled by Muslim and Lombard warlords. Few would have imagined that, over the next century, they would be conquered by the Norman mercenaries that had recently begun to arrive. In central Europe, the rulers of Bohemia and Hungary had adopted Christianity only a short while ago, while the process of conversion was still ongoing in Scandinavia.

Two centuries later, England was ruled by the descendants of Norse warlords who had conquered the island kingdom in 1066, and who intermittently sought to extend their authority across the British Isles. In addition, its kings held large swathes of the kingdom of France. Yet most of their mainland possessions would, in just a few years, be seized by those very kings of France. In Iberia, the rulers of Portugal, León, Castile and Aragon had taken control of much of the peninsula, while the caliphate of Cordoba had collapsed. Still, the Almohads from North Africa engaged in a spirited pushback that was not to grind to a halt until 1212. In Italy, the kingdom of Sicily, established by Roger II in 1130 and encompassing the islands of Sardinia and Sicily as well as much of southern Italy, had in 1198 been inherited by the infant son of Emperor Henry VI, while the Holy Roman Empire, as it began to be known, was torn by a succession dispute. Together, over the next half century, Sicily and the Empire would experience both the apex and the nadir of imperial might in western Europe. In Norway, Sverrir was the first king in almost a century not to die at the hands of his successor, and in Denmark Valdemar I had similarly ended

---

[10] The best overviews remain Michael Borgolte, *Europa entdeckt seine Vielfalt* (Stuttgart, 2002); Thomas F. X. Noble and John Van Engen, eds., *European Transformations. The Long Twelfth Century* (Notre Dame, IN, 2012).

a civil war that had lasted nearly a generation. He was the first king in over a century to be succeeded by his son. In central Europe, the rulers of Poland had gained and lost their royal title, those of Hungary had kept theirs and those of Bohemia were about to become kings by hereditary right. Some of the most dramatic changes occurred in the eastern Mediterranean. In 1204, a crusading army was to conquer most of Greece and establish a Latin empire in Constantinople, and in Cyprus a new Francophone ruling dynasty had wrested the island from Byzantine control. In the Middle East, in 1187 Saladin had driven the kings of Jerusalem out of their capital city, barely a century after the kingdom of Jerusalem had first been established, while the rulers of Cilician Armenia engaged in desperate diplomacy between western and eastern emperors, the pope and Saladin.

These developments required elites to refashion and rethink principles and structures of governance. England might serve as example. The pre-eminence of Wessex in the tenth century had a profound impact on the gradual development of a sense of England as but one polity.[11] The kingdom was also twice conquered by foreign rulers. Both brought with them new customs and actors, and both challenged established conventions. Indeed, the Norman Conquest resulted in the widescale replacement of the realm's secular and ecclesiastical elites, and was at least in part legitimised by the promise to reform and remodel the kingdom's religious and ecclesiastical institutions, and to bring them into alignment with the higher standards practised in mainland Europe. Important questions were therefore asked by contemporary and later observers.[12] What was the importance of regnal unity? How was a realm forged out of several erstwhile distinct polities meant to be ruled? What was the importance and what were the rules of succession? How could foreign invaders be fitted within a concept of regnal unity? How could alien elites be made aware of and how could they be incorporated into an established repertoire of ideas and practices of ruler-ship? Similar questions were posed across Latin Europe, and they were addressed with increasing frequency and detail. They were asked in reference to a shared framework of practices and ideals of kingship. In the English case, foreign rulers had to be assured that the customs of the English were not alien to, but rather deeply rooted in a shared European heritage. Similarly, new or newly Christianised polities in Scandinavia and central Europe sought to present their distinctiveness and their membership of a community of Christian nations in a manner recognisable by and acceptable to their

---

[11] George Molyneaux, *The Formation of the English Kingdom in the Tenth Century* (Oxford, 2015).

[12] For some of the answers given, see Emily Winkler, *Royal Responsibility in Anglo-Norman Historical Writing* (Oxford, 2017).

30   1. POLITICS AND POWER IN HIGH MEDIEVAL EUROPE

peers, whose agreement, in turn, served to reinforce the legitimacy of their community's past and current standing.[13] Rapid change led to a deepening engagement with principles of governance and government.

Moreover, polities never existed in isolation. Political borders remained fluid. Most medieval polities did not foreshadow modern ones.[14] Some emerged and then disappeared again. Their ruling families merged with those of distant regions, territories were acquired and lost and so on. While writers imagined a *populus* (people) that constituted the community of the realm,[15] in practice there was no link between ethnicity and polity, not least because, just as ruling elites could move across regnal boundaries, so could their subjects.[16] Newly developed institutions and networks facilitated and necessitated a transeuropean exchange of individuals and ideas. The papal court emerged as arbiter both of political legitimacy and of ecclesiastical disputes, while new religious orders like the Cistercians developed finely tuned transregnal networks of dependency and oversight. In addition, cathedral schools, like those in Bamberg and Cologne, emerging universities in Bologna and Paris and communities like that of the Victorines in Paris (a major centre of theological activity) helped reinforce a transeuropean framework of literary production. Cumulatively, these and other factors established an often vaguely defined but nonetheless widely shared expectation of how a political community should be organised, and how it should be governed. In this regard, the self-representation of high medieval Europeans as part of a transregnal community of norms and cultural practices did reflect social and material realities.

A defining feature of this ideal political organisation was rule by kings. High medieval observers established a direct link between kingship and conversion to Christianity. In Poland, Hungary and Norway conversion was perceived explicitly as a precondition for kingship.[17] Royal status furthermore established rulers as more powerful than their peers, and their subjects as a group distinct from its neighbours. Importantly, however, kingship marked but one stage in the history of a territorially defined community, which often pre-dated the emergence of a ruling dynasty or its royal rank. The resulting tension between realm and dynasty is central to how contemporaries thought and

---

[13] Lars Boje Mortensen, 'Sanctified beginnings and mythopoetic moments. The first wave of writing on the past in Norway, Denmark, and Hungary, c. 1000–1230', in *The Making of Christian Myths in the Periphery of Latin Christendom (c. 1000–1300)*, ed. Lars Boje Mortensen (Copenhagen, 2006), 247–73.

[14] Patrick J. Geary, *Myths of Nations: the Medieval Origins of Europe* (Princeton, NJ, 2003); Carlrichard Brühl, *Deutschland-Frankreich. Die Geburt zweier Völker* (Cologne and Vienna, 1995).

[15] See below, Conclusion.

[16] Michael Borgolte, ed., *Migrationen im Mittelalter. Ein Handbuch* (Berlin, 2014).

[17] See Chapter 3.

I. FOUNDATIONS 31

wrote about royal lordship. Moreover, regnal status coincided with establishing or taking control of a kingdom's ecclesiastical organisation. An even greater prize was for one of these new bishoprics to be raised to metropolitan status – that is, as an archbishopric overseeing a distinct church province that was no longer subject to oversight from foreign prelates.[18] Nidaros (modern Trondheim) in Norway, Lund in Sweden and Braga in Portugal provide some of the best known examples for this development, which was driven by ecclesiastical elites and rulers alike.[19] As a result, new tensions could arise. On the one hand, kingship was assumed to be a gift from God. It signalled divine recognition of an individual's suitability. On the other, it carried with it obligations and duties. Who was to determine what these duties were? Who provided oversight of the king, who ensured that he and his successors did indeed uphold divine law? Where was the line to be drawn between establishing the Church and meddling in its affairs?

Answering these questions was all the more important, as the period witnessed a proliferation of royal titles. Between 1000 and 1200, new kingships emerged in Portugal, Denmark, Norway, Sweden, Poland, Hungary, Bohemia, Armenia, Sicily, Cyprus and Jerusalem. Evidence for plans to claim a title also survives for Estonia, Livonia, Bulgaria and Serbia.[20] By the end of the period, almost every European was ruled by a king. Even Lombard towns and Frisian peasant communities, which in practice existed very much beyond the grasp of royal power, at least nominally recognised the authority of kings. The sole

---

[18] That was one of the reasons why the kings of England sought to thwart efforts at St Davids in Wales and St Andrews in Scotland to become archiepiscopal sees. John Reuben Davies, 'The archbishopric of St Davids and the bishops of Clas Cynidr', in *St David of Wales: Cult, Church and Nation*, ed. J. Wyn Evans and Jonathan M. Wooding (Woodbridge, 2007), 296–304; Ian Campbell, 'The idea of St Andrews as the second Rome made manifest', in *Medieval St Andrews: Church, Cult, City*, ed. Michael Brown and Katie Stevenson (Woodbridge, 2017), 35–50. See also below, Chapter 3.

[19] Horst Fuhrmann, 'Studien zur Geschichte mittelalterlicher Patriarchate, 1–3', *ZSRG (Kanonistische Abteilung)* 39 (1953), 112–76; 40 (1954), 1–84; 41 (1955), 95–183; Luis Carlos Correia Ferreira do Amaral, 'As sedes de Braga e Compostela e a restauração da métropole galaica', in *O século de Xelmírez*, ed. Fernando López Alsina, Henrique Monteagudo, Ramón Villares and Ramón José Yzquierdo Perrín (Santiago, 2013), 17–44.

[20] I use 'kingships' rather than 'kingdoms', given the difficulty of distinguishing between already established conventions of monarchical rule and the establishment of Christianised kingship in the Scandinavian realms and central Europe. The best overview is available in the essays in Nora Berend, ed. *Christianization and the Rise of Christian Monarchy. Scandinavia, Central Europe and Rus', c. 900–1200* (Cambridge, 2007). See also: Bernd Ulrich Hucker, 'Liv- und estländische Königspläne', in *Studien über die Anfänge der Mission in Livland*, ed. Manfred Hellmann (Sigmaringen, 1989), 65–106; James Ross Sweeney, 'Innocent III, Hungary and the Bulgarian coronation: a study in medieval papal diplomacy', *Church History* 42 (1973), 320–34; Marie Luise Burian, 'Die Krönung des Stephan Prvovencani und die Beziehungen Serbiens zum Heiligen Stuhl', *AKG* 23 (1933), 141–51.

exception was Iceland, which explicitly rejected rule by crowned heads. Yet its inhabitants were deeply fascinated by, regularly engaged with and provided the first historians of the Norwegian monarchy whose grasp their forebears had purportedly sought to escape.[21]

The proliferation of regnal communities gave rise to tensions and conflicts. On the one hand, there was a desire to claim legitimacy by emulating established conventions: patronising churchmen, establishing archbishoprics, even adopting ceremonies like crowning and unction. On the other hand, distinctiveness and antiquity had to be asserted. This extended to how contemporary observers imagined and represented the past of these communities. In Sicily, Roger II claimed to resurrect a kingship that had existed in the mists of time. Simultaneously, he availed himself of such relatively modern tools as gaining papal recognition for his title and commissioning a coronation liturgy drawn from Franco-German antecedents. Divergence and conformity existed side by side. In practice, most polities drew upon but modified shared models. Regnal traditions came into play, but also geography and environment. The relatively small territory ruled directly by the kings of France required different modes of governance than those needed in a realm as vast as the empire of King Knud of Denmark, Norway and England. The machinery of government of Anglo-Saxon England, geared towards defence against maritime raiders and towards the extraction of surplus to pay them off, necessitated a more elaborate administrative apparatus of government than the patchwork of lands and territories ruled by the Holy Roman emperors in cooperation with and reliance upon prelates and princes. Yet, important as these differences were, they should not blind us to the overwhelming similarities between the component parts of the Latin west. We are dealing with variations on a common theme, not altogether different tunes. These structures constitute the framework within which contemporaries wrote about kingship, and they provided the tools and mechanisms with which literate subjects sought to shape practices of royal lordship. They merit sketching out.[22]

---

[21] Theodore M. Andersson, 'The king of Iceland', *Speculum* 74 (1999), 923–34; Andersson, *The Sagas of Norwegian Kings (1130–1265). An Introduction* (Ithaca, NY, 2016); Ármann Jakobsson, 'Our Norwegian friend: the role of kings in the family sagas', *Arkiv för nordisk filologi* 117 (2002), 145–60.

[22] For more detailed treatments of what follows see Althoff, *Kontrolle der Macht.*; Althoff, *Spielregeln der Politik*; Althoff, *Verwandte, Freunde und Getreue. Zum politischen Stellenwert der Gruppenbildungen im frühen Mittelalter* (Darmstadt, 1990); English translation: *Family, Friends and Followers. Political and Social Bonds in Early Medieval Europe* (Cambridge, 2004); *European Transformations*, ed. Noble and Van Engen; Karl J. Leyser, *Rule and Conflict in an Early Medieval Society: Ottonian Saxony* (Oxford, 1979); Reuter, *Medieval Polities*; Sverre Bagge, 'Early state formation in Scandinavia', in *Der frühmittelalterliche Staat – europäische Perspektiven*, ed. Walter Pohl and Veronika Wieser (Vienna, 2009), 145–54; Bagge, *Cross and Scepter: the Rise of the Scandinavian Kingdoms from the Vikings to the Reformation* (Princeton, NJ, 2014); Sverrir Bagge, Michael L. Gelting and Thomas Lindkvist,

I. FOUNDATIONS 33

Across Europe, elite power centred on the extraction of surplus from a largely agricultural economy, even though burgeoning trade and urban communities provided additional sources of wealth.[23] The pursuit and the possession of the skills requisite for warfare defined secular elites.[24] They existed alongside and overlapped with a clerical elite that viewed itself as the provider of moral guidance, as well as commemorative and literary expertise. It was both legally and socially distinctive. Its members were exempt from certain types of taxation, but were also supposed to abstain from participating in bloodshed. Furthermore, most were expected to remain celibate, that is, to remain outside established family networks. Nominally, their goods and properties were not theirs, but had been acquired on behalf of and therefore belonged to the religious community of which they formed part. In practice, clerical and lay elites were mutually dependent. Churches relied on protection

---

eds., *Feudalism. New Landscapes of Debate* (Turnhout, 2011); Jürgen Dendorfer and Roman Deutinger, eds., *Das Lehnswesen im Hochmittelalter: Forschungskonstrukte – Quellenbefunde – Deutungsrelevanz* (Ostfildern, 2010).

[23] Henry Fairbairn, 'Was there a money economy in Late Anglo-Saxon and Norman England?', *EHR* 134 (2019), 1081–135; David S. Bacharach, 'Toward an appraisal of the wealth of the Ottonian kings of Germany, 919–1024', *Viator* 44/2 (2013), 1–27; Bernard S. Bachrach, 'Feeding the host: the Ottonian royal fisc in military perspective', *Studies in Medieval and Renaissance History*, 3rd series 9 (2012), 1–43; Caroline Gödel, *Servitium regis und Tafelgüterverzeichnis. Untersuchung zur Wirtschafts- und Verfassungsgeschichte des deutschen Königtums im 12. Jahrhundert* (Sigmaringen, 1997); James Hill, 'The "Catalogus Baronum" and the recruitment and administration of the armies of the Norman kingdom of Sicily: a re-examination', *Historical Research* 86 (2013), 1–14; David Brégaint, *Vox regis. Royal Communication in High Medieval Norway* (Leiden, 2016); Geneviève Bühler-Thierry, Régine Le Jan and Loré Vito, eds., *Acquérir, prélever, contrôler: les ressources en compétition (400–1100)* (Turnhout, 2017); Geneviève Bühler-Thierry, Steffen Patzold and Jens Schneider, eds., *Genèse des espaces politiques IXe–XIIe siècle: autour de la question spatiale dans les royaumes francs et post-carolingiens* (Turnhout, 2018); Benjamin Arnold, *Power and Property in Medieval Germany: Economic and Social Change c.900–1300* (Oxford, 2004); Carlrichard Brühl, *Fodrum, Gistum, Servitium regis. Studien zu den wirtschaftlichen Grundlagen des Königtums im Frankenreich und in den fränkischen Nachfolgestaaten Deutschland, Frankreich und Italien vom 6. bis zur Mitte des 14. Jahrhunderts*, 2 vols. (Cologne, 1968).

[24] François Bougard, Hans-Werner Goetz and Régine Le Jan, eds., *Théorie et pratiques des élites au Haut Moyen Âge: conception, perception et réalisation sociale* (Turnhout, 2001); Timothy Reuter, 'Nobles and others: the social and cultural expression of power relations in the Middle Ages', in his *Medieval Polities*, 113–26; Martin Aurell, *La noblesse en Occident (Ve–XVe siècle)* (Paris, 1997 hxm); Reuter, 'Chivalric culture in the twelfth and thirteenth centuries', in *Riddarasögur: the Translation of European Court Culture in Medieval Scandinavia*, ed. Else Mundal and Karl G. Johansson (Oslo, 2014), 33–56; Jean Flori, *Chevaliers et chevalerie au Moyen Âge* (Paris, 2004); Flori, 'Knightly society', in *The New Cambridge Medieval History IV:1 – c. 1024–1198*, ed. David Luscombe and Jonathan Riley-Smith (Cambridge, 2004), 148–84; Werner Hechberger, *Adel im fränkisch-deutschen Mittelalter. Zur Anatomie eines Forschungsproblems* (Ostfildern, 2005).

34   1. POLITICS AND POWER IN HIGH MEDIEVAL EUROPE

and patronage, and they exercised lordly functions over their lands and estates, and the people working them. Equally, family networks ensured that distinctions were rarely drawn as rigorously as normative expectations would prescribe. Aristocratic kin groups often provided the patrons and protectors of an ecclesiastical institution, as well as many of its members.

Disputes over resources remained a defining feature of politics. They were conducted by resorting to violence, and through a developing apparatus with which judicial decisions could be enforced. The ability to do, receive and enforce justice mirrored the material resources at a claimant's disposal. That meant not just land and material wealth, but above all connections and networks. Violence and judicial process were more successfully employed if one could draw on powerful protectors, friends and relatives. Establishing, defending, and expanding such networks was therefore a necessity. In order to function, they depended on the ability of actors to demonstrate their willingness and capacity to provide protection, secure the peace and ward off enemies. Indeed, the public performance of standing was a recurring feature in the process of king-making, and was expected of rulers and ruled alike. Ties of friendship, family and dependency were all the more important because there was no monopoly on violence. Even the king's peace only extended to some of his subjects, and in practice only to those parts of the realm that he had the resources to reach. There was no public body that would see to it that court judgements were enforced. Claimants had to draw on their own resources to implement decisions.[25] Yet individuals could belong to different networks. These could cooperate as well as clash. Negotiating networks was therefore an essential skill for any political actor.[26]

That many of the functions associated with modern states had to be shouldered by individuals has led some observers to class high medieval polities as stateless societies.[27] This oversimplifies matters considerably. As early as the

---

[25] Gerd Althoff, 'The rules of conflict among the warrior aristocracy of the high Middle Ages', in *Disputing Strategies in Medieval Scandinavia*, ed. Kim Esmark, Hans Jacob Orning and Helle Vogt (Leiden and Bosten, 2013), 313–32; Hermann Kamp, *Friedensstifter und Vermittler im Mittelalter* (Darmstadt, 2001); Paul Hyams, *Rancor and Reconciliation in Medieval England* (Ithaca, NY, 2003); Adam J. Kosto, *Making Agreements in Medieval Catalonia: Power, Order, and the Written Word, 1000–1200* (Cambridge, 2004); William Ian Miller, *Bloodtaking and Peacemaking: Feud, Law, and Society in Saga Iceland* (Chicago, 1990); Wendy Davies, *Windows on Justice in Northern Iberia: 800–1000* (London, 2016).

[26] Althoff, *Verwandte, Freunde*; Jonathan R. Lyon, *Princely Brothers and Sisters: the Sibling Bond in German politics, 1100–1250* (Ithaca, NY, 2013); Stephanie L. Moers, 'Networks of power in Anglo-Norman England', *Medieval Prosopography* 7 (1986), 25–54.

[27] Gerd Althoff, *Die Ottonen: Königsherrschaft ohne Staat*, 2nd edition (Stuttgart, 2005); Althoff, 'Funktionsweisen der Königsherrschaft im Hochmittelalter', *Geschichte in Wissenschaft und Unterricht* 63 (2012), 536–50; Otto Brunner, *Land und Herrschaft*.

I. FOUNDATIONS

eleventh century a clear sense of a transpersonal community of the realm had emerged.[28] The norms and customs of that community were preserved through practice, but also by ecclesiastical institutions acting on its behalf. By definition, monasteries and cathedral churches possessed a degree of institutional longevity that transcended individual lifespans. Even if particular churches could be destroyed or abandoned, collectively they nonetheless possessed the expertise and institutional durability that allowed them to act as keepers and guardians of communal custom. If we are looking for state-like mechanisms, we can do much worse than turn to the institutional practices of the medieval *ecclesia*.[29] Moreover, beginning in the eleventh century, the medieval European economy revived. This period of expansion coincided with a growing range of uses to which literacy could be put, and an equally growing number of men who could provide them.[30] As so often, ecclesiastical institutions took the lead, though they were quickly imitated by their secular peers. One consequence was the increasing codification of customs, procedures and conventions. Most commonly, this occurred by means of what has been termed pragmatic literacy: charters, letters, writs and other documents

---

Grundfragen einer territorialen Verfassungsgeschichte Österreichs im Mittelalter (Vienna, 1973). On the latter: Benjamin Arnold, 'Structures of medieval governance and the thought-world of Otto Brunner (1898–1982)', *Reading Medieval Studies* 20 (1994), 3–12. See also: Jonathan R. Lyon, 'The medieval German state in recent historiography', *German History* 28 (2010), 85–94; Stuart Airlie, Walther Pohl and Helmut Reimitz, eds., *Staat im frühen Mittelalter* (Vienna, 2005); and the poignant remarks by Steffen Patzold, 'Human security, fragile Staatlichkeit und Governance im Frühmittelalter. Zur Fragwürdigkeit der Scheidung von Vormoderne und Moderne', *Geschichte und Gesellschaft* 38 (2012), 406–22. Generally: Susan Reynolds, 'The historiography of the medieval state', in *Companion to Historiography*, ed. Michael Bentley (London, 1997), 117–38. See, for (partial) exceptions, Fanny Madeline, *Les Plantagenêts et leur empire: construire un territoire politique* (Rennes, 2014); Monika Suchan, 'Fürstliche Opposition gegen das Königtum im 11. und 12. Jahrhundert als Gestalterin mittelalterlicher Staatlichkeit', *FmSt* 37 (2003), 141–65; James Campbell, 'The late Anglo-Saxon state: a maximum view', *Proceedings of the British Academy* 87 (1994), 39–65; Alice Taylor, *Shape of the State in Medieval Scotland, 1124–1290* (Oxford, 2016); Marien Ferrer, 'State formation and courtly culture in the Scandinavian kingdoms in the High Middle Ages', *Scandinavian Journal of History* 37 (2012), 1–22; Sverre Bagge, *From Viking Stronghold to Christian Kingdom: State Formation in Norway, c. 900–1350* (Copenhagen, 2010).

[28] Helmut Beumann, 'Zur Entwicklung transpersonaler Staatsvorstellungen', in *Das Königtum. Seine geistigen und rechtlichen Grundlagen*, ed. Theodor Mayer (Sigmaringen, 1956), 185–224. See also Chapters 3–10 below.

[29] Timothy Reuter, 'A Europe of bishops. The age of Wulfstan of York and Burchard of Worms', in *Patterns of Episcopal Power: Bishops in Tenth and Eleventh Century Western Europe*, ed. Ludger Körntgen and Dominik Waßenhoven (Berlin, 2011), 17–38.

[30] Buringh, *Medieval Manuscript Production*; Clanchy, *From Memory to Written Record*. I am grateful to Jonathan Shepard for pushing the importance of the economic transformation of high medieval Europe.

36   1. POLITICS AND POWER IN HIGH MEDIEVAL EUROPE

that recorded fiscal, procedural and legal matters.[31] They established precedent and rooted claims, practices and customs in time. Such writings also reinforced a sense that there was more to a community of the realm than the sequence of monarchs ruling it.[32] This self-perception was at the heart of a new wave of regnal histories that became popular from the early twelfth century. They frequently located a community's origins and principles of political organisation in a remote and distant past. Sometimes, this involved discussing the emergence of monarchical power,[33] but even when a community was assumed always to have been ruled by kings, it still pre-dated the arrival or emergence of any particular family or clan of rulers. Consequently, even if medieval polities do not resemble a Weberian image of statehood, their literate elites nonetheless viewed themselves as part of a transpersonal entity that transcended individual lifespans, and that was unified by customs and practices according to which rulers and leading subjects were supposed to operate. That framework was subject to negotiation The precise meaning of its components remained dependent on context, and the specific crisis or challenge that had to be tackled. But it provided a set of rules according to which abstract precepts could be turned into concrete political realities.

This background casts into relief several recurring themes in high medieval representations of kingship. Kings were meant to be keepers and guardians, not proprietors, of the realm. They had been entrusted by God and their people with upholding the law and keeping the peace, with defending and correcting the community given into their care. They represented and protected the right order of the world. They were expected to use their power not for their own advancement, but on behalf of the people, to protect those who could not protect themselves, and to humble the unjust among the mighty. Therefore, they had to be more powerful than any of their subjects. Ecclesiastical and secular elites should aid the king, and exhort him if he deviated from what was right. This established a set of mutual obligations. Claimants to the throne had to demonstrate that they had the means and moral disposition to act like a king, while those raising them to the royal dignity also had to demonstrate that they had indeed chosen the most suitable candidate for the throne. In practice, even kings were only as powerful as the resources at their disposal. What was desirable was not always feasible. Sometimes, the unjust yet mighty were simply too mighty. Last but not least, normative expectations remained

---

[31] Franz-Josef Arlinghaus, Marcus Ostermann, Oliver Plessow and Gudrun Tscherpel, eds., *Transforming the Medieval World: Uses of Pragmatic Literacy in the Middle Ages* (Turnhout, 2006); Richard H. Britnell, ed., *Pragmatic Literacy East and West* (Woodbridge, 1997); Hagen Keller, Klaus Grubmüller and Nikolaus Staubach, eds., *Pragmatische Schriftlichkeit im Mittelalter. Erscheinungsformen und Entwicklungstendenzen* (Munich, 1992).

[32] Susan Reynolds, *Kingdoms and Communities in Western Europe, 900–1300*, 2nd edition (Oxford, 1997).

[33] See below, Chapters 3 and 4.

I. FOUNDATIONS

fluid and were at times in conflict with each other. One man's justice was another's tyrannical challenge to ancestral right. The expectation that followers should be rewarded could clash with the need to preserve equity and justice. Hence the importance of advice and counsel, the need to deliberate, cajole, persuade, convince and indeed to terrorise elites into supporting the king. The resulting tensions could be violent.[34] But they also led to attempts to reconcile conflicting expectations, to forge reality so that it reflected what should be, and to fashion values so that they coincided with what was feasible and necessary. It is with these efforts that this book is concerned.

Other factors also merit noting. The emergence of new polities was among the most immediately visible changes in this period, as was that of new political actors, urban communities chief among them. The tradition of Carolingian treatises on abstract principles of governance petered out with the demise of Charlemagne's descendants in east Francia. Comparable texts were not composed again with any frequency until the early thirteenth century.[35] By then, however, new genres and conventions of writing had emerged. Biblical exegesis often occupied a place that, during the intervening centuries, had been occupied by letters, charters and chronicles. In the decades either side of the year 1200 we also encounter increasing efforts to turn abstract principles of virtuous rule into concrete legal form. These often ran alongside the institutionalisation of consultative assemblies with an incipient and partial remit to practise oversight of the ruler, or at least of his agents, by the ruled.[36]

---

[34] Jean-Marie Moeglin, '"Rex crudelis": über die Natur und die Formen der Gewalt der Könige vom 11. zum 14. Jahrhundert (Frankreich, Reich, England)', in *Gewalt und Widerstand in der politischen Kultur des späten Mittelalters*, ed. Martin Kintzinger, Frank Rexroth and Jörg Rogge (Ostfildern, 2015), 19–52. A useful reminder of the violence of power relations is provided by: Thomas N. Bisson, *Tormented Voices. Power, Crisis and Humanity in Medieval Catalonia, 1140–1200* (Cambridge, MA, 1998); Robert Berkhofer, Alan Cooper and Adam J. Kosto, eds., *The Experience of Power in Medieval Europe 950–1350: Essays in Honor of Thomas N. Bisson* (Aldershot, 2005).

[35] Wolfgang Berges, *Die Fürstenspiegel des hohen und späten Mittelalters* (Leipzig, 1938); Hans Hubert Anton, *Fürstenspiegel und Herrscherethos in der Karolingerzeit* (Bonn, 1968); M. S. Kempshall, *The Common Good in Late Medieval Political Thought: Moral Goodness and Material Benefit* (Oxford, 1999).

[36] Jörg Peltzer, Gerald Schwedler and Paul Töbelmann, eds., *Politische Versammlungen und ihre Rituale: Repräsentationsformen und Entscheidungsprozesse des Reichs und der Kirche im späten Mittelalter* (Ostfildern, 2009); Thomas N. Bisson, *Assemblies and Representation in Languedoc in the Thirteenth Century* (Princeton, NJ, 1964); J. R. Maddicott, *The Origins of the English Parliament, 924–1327* (Oxford, 2010); Jose M. Cerda, 'Cum consilio et deliberatione episcoporum, comitum, et baronum nostrorum: consultation, deliberation and the crafting of parliamentary assemblies in England and the Spanish kingdoms', in *Podział władzy i parlamentaryzm w przeszłości i współcześnie – prawo, doktryna, praktyka*, ed. Wacław Uruszczak (Warsaw, 2007), 264–76; Joseph F. O'Callaghan, *The Cortes of Castile-León 1188–1350* (Philadelphia, PA, 1989). See for early medieval antecedents: Levi Roach, *Kingship and Consent in Anglo-Saxon England,*

38   1. POLITICS AND POWER IN HIGH MEDIEVAL EUROPE

The early thirteenth century therefore marks a convenient if approximate endpoint for this book. Ideas and values did not change, but the manner did in which their interpretation and enforcement occurred. Precedent became more than merely an ideal to which to adhere. It was – fitfully – transformed into a set of rules by which kings and their people would be equally bound. The process continued to be driven by debates and challenges, and was inevitably violent. In England, for example, rulers faced rebellions in 1213–17, 1233–4, 1258–65 and 1297. Each time, the interpretation of shared norms provided the means by which resistance could be justified. Violence was legitimised with reference to principles that had – or that were believed to have been – enshrined in charters and grants. Similar developments occurred in Germany, Hungary, Castile and Norway.[37] They were a transeuropean phenomenon, which overlapped with developing mechanisms for deposing and replacing rulers because they had proven unsuitable for the office they occupied.[38] Yet these later developments built on, and were rooted in, the ones that this book explores. They drew upon the accumulated experience of previous generations, now enshrined and recorded with far greater frequency, and available to a far wider range of audiences. Documents like Magna Carta or the Golden Bull, institutions like the *cortes*, *Reichstag* and parliament would not have emerged, or at least would not have taken the shape they did, without the principles and practices rehearsed and honed since the beginning of the second millennium.

871–978: Assemblies and the State in the Early Middle Ages (Cambridge, 2013); Paul S. Barnwell and Marco Mostert, eds., *Political Assemblies in the Early Middle Ages* (Turnhout, 2003).

[37] Björn Weiler, 'Rebellious sons: revolt, succession, and the culture of kingship in Western Europe, c.1170 – c.1280', *Historical Research* 82 (2009), 17–40; Weiler, *Kingship, Rebellions and Political Cultures: England and Germany, c. 1215-1250* (Basingstoke, 2007).

[38] Frank Rexroth, 'Tyrannen und Taugenichtse. Beobachtungen zur Ritualität europäischer Königsabsetzungen im späten Mittelalter', *HZ* 278 (2004), 27–54; *Album Elemér Mályusz*, no editor (Brussels, 1976); Edward M. Peters, *The Shadow King: Rex Inutilis in Medieval Law and Literature, 751-1327* (New Haven, CT, 1970).

2

Foundational Texts

Structural frameworks of power make a transeuropean approach both necessary and possible. So do shared cultural foundations. Latinity and Christianisation ensured that a corpus of canonical texts circulated across the west that could then be used for the interpretation of the Bible, for training in literacy and for the religious instruction of both clergy and lay elites.[1] At the same time, many of these texts have long since ceased to be foundational. Most modern readers, myself included, lack any deep familiarity with the likes of Cicero, Seneca, Ambrose, Augustine, Gregory the Great or Isidore of Seville. That puts us at a disadvantage when faced with medieval authors who did. Indeed, echoes and allusions that might have been obvious to medieval readers have escaped even modern editors of high medieval texts.[2] Part of the problem was that these borrowings often reflected ideas that circulated so widely that it can prove difficult to assign them to just one particular source.[3] Still, if we want to understand the normative framework within which high medieval observers thought about kingship, we first need to familiarise ourselves with key concepts on which that thinking was based.

---

[1] The library assembled for the bishopric of Bamberg, an eleventh-century imperial foundation, has been reconstructed, and gives a good impression of the kind of texts deemed necessary for what was intended to be both a religious and an educational centre: www.staatsbibliothek-bamberg.de/digitale-sammlungen/kaiser-heinrich-bibliothek/ (accessed 23 February 2020). Bamberg was, of course, a prestige project on which considerable resources had been lavished. It was by no means representative of *all* medieval religious communities. But it tells us something about the ideal type of a clerical community and its reading matter. For the literary instruction of lay elites see below, Chapter 6.

[2] Paul Hayward, 'The importance of being ambiguous: innuendo and legerdemain in William of Malmesbury's Gesta Regum and Gesta Pontificum Anglorum', *ANS* 33 (2011), 75–102.

[3] See, for instance, the echoes of Isidore of Seville in the Roskilde Chronicle and Walter Map: *Chronicon Roskildense*, in *Scriptores Minores Historiae Danicae Medii Aevii*, ed. M. C. Gertz, 2 vols. (Copenhagen, 1917–18, repr. 1970) vol. 1, 1–33, at 25; Walter Map, *De Nugis Curialium: Courtiers Trifles*, ed. and transl. M. R. James, rev. C. N. L. Brooke and R. A. B. Mynors (Oxford, 1983), v.7, pp. 510–11. On the latter: Björn Weiler, 'Royal virtue and royal justice in Walter Map's *De Nugis Curialium* and William of Malmesbury's *Historia Novella*', in *Virtue and Ethics in the Twelfth Century*, ed. Istvan Bejczy and Richard Newhauser (Leiden, 2005), 317–39, at 328.

40   2. FOUNDATIONAL TEXTS

Providing a comprehensive overview of these foundations would, however, exceed the confines of this book. Instead, the first part of this chapter will focus on the kind of materials with which we can assume most high medieval authors to have been familiar.[4] Discussion will resemble a medley of the greatest hits of biblical, classical and patristic writings. The comparison is apt. Many of the post-biblical materials circulated not only in complete copies, but also in compilations and excerpts, in digests and florilegia.[5] This manner of transmission contextualises the ease with which key phrases and concepts were borrowed and adapted. The second part sketches that pervasiveness. It will draw on works of exegesis, letters of advice and a range of religious treatises. Not every writer of history, charters or liturgical texts was familiar with all of these. But then direct lines of transmissions are less important in the present context than the broader cultural framework within which sources were situated. That, in turn, is appreciated more easily once we are able to recognise at least some of the allusions and echoes in which these materials abounded.

1.1   The Bible, the Classics and the Fathers

The Old Testament provided a storehouse of useful precedent.[6] The first three kings of Israel (Saul, David and Solomon) were especially important. Indeed,

---

[4] See, for instance, Birger Munk Olsen, 'Comment peut-on déterminer la popularité d'un texte au Moyen Âge? L'exemple des oeuvres classiques latines', *Interfaces* 3 (2016), 13–27.

[5] See, for a very useful case study, which, however, appeared too late to be fully incorporated, the discussion of digests of Seneca in Lars Kjaer, *The Medieval Gift and the Classical Tradition: Ideals and the Performance of Generosity in Medieval England, 1100–1300* (Cambridge, 2019). The Bible was no exception: Julie Barrau, 'Sibyls, tanners and leper kings: taking notes from and about the Bible in twelfth-century England', in *Reading the Bible in the Middle Ages*, ed. Janet L. Nelson and Damien Kempf (London, 2015), 119–46.

[6] On the issue in general: Philippe Buc, *L'Ambiguïté du Livre*; Percy Ernst Schramm, 'Das Alte und das Neue Testament in der Staatslehre und Staatssymbolik des Mittelalters', *Settimania di studio del Centro italiano di studi sull'alto medioevo* 10 (1963), 229–56, at 128–30, 134–5; Walter Ullmann, 'The bible and principles of government in the Middle Ages', *Settimane di studio del centro Italiano di studi sull'alto medioevo* 10 (Spoleto, 1963), 181–227, at 190–207; with special emphasis on northern France: Philippe Buc, 'Principes gentium dominantur eorum: princely power between legitimacy and illegitimacy in twelfth-century exegesis', in *Cultures of Power. Lordship, Status, and Process in Twelfth-Century Europe*, ed. T. N. Bisson (Philadelphia, PA, 1995), 310–28; Hugo Steger, *David rex et propheta. König David als vorbindliche Verkörperung des Herrschers und Dichters im Mittelalter* (Nuremberg, 1961); Yves Sassier, 'Deutéronome, royauté et rois bibliques dans le Policraticus de Jean de Salisbury: première et succincte approche', in *Rerum gestarum scriptor. Histoire et historiographie au Moyen Âge. Hommage à Michel Sot*, ed. Magali Coumert, Isaïa Marie-Céline, Klaus Krönert and Sumi Shimahara (Paris, 2012), 387–96; Jan Schumacher, 'Breaking the bread of scripture. On the medieval interpretation of the Bible', *Collegium Medievale* 6 (1993), 107–32; Elizabeth Boyle, 'Biblical kings and kingship theory in medieval Ireland and Norway', in *Speculum septentrionale. Konungs skuggsjá and the European Encyclopedia of the Middle Ages*, ed. Karl G. Johansson and

I. FOUNDATIONS 41

with the exception of Joshua and the Maccabees, no other rulers feature as prominently in high medieval accounts.[7] A short synopsis will thus prove useful. As the prophet Samuel approached old age, the people, hitherto ruled by judges, demanded to have a king, just like their neighbours. Samuel laid their request before God, who did not take kindly to it. In demanding a king, Yahweh declared, the Israelites had rejected him as their lord. Samuel should warn them about a king's prerogatives: he would rule over them unhindered, enslave and exploit them, take their daughters as his wives and force their young men into his armies. Still, the Israelites persisted (1 Samuel 8). God therefore commanded Samuel to grant them their wish, and picked as their first king Saul, a young man who had been lost while searching for escaped donkeys, and whose sole distinguishing feature was that he was taller than all the other Israelites. Samuel anointed Saul, and convened an assembly of all the Israelite tribes, who obediently chose him as their king (1 Samuel 9–10).

In the end, Saul refused to follow God's commands. For that he was rejected by the Lord, who instead ordered Samuel to choose a new king: David, a young shepherd who had been chosen not for his outward appearance, but because of his inner disposition (1 Samuel 15–16). A pivotal episode of David's reign occurred when, having brought the Ark of the Covenant to Jerusalem, and having promised to build the first Temple, he was filled with doubt. The prophet Nathan reassured the king that God would continue to protect him and increase his glory, as long as he obeyed God's will (2 Samuel 7). Just like Saul, David erred from the path of righteousness: he lusted after Bathsheba and arranged for her husband Uriah to be killed in battle before taking her as his wife. Unlike Saul, however, David, on having been reprimanded by Nathan, recognised the error of his ways. He begged for and was granted forgiveness (2 Samuel 11–12). Even so, henceforward rebellions ensued: first by David's son Absalom, then by Sheba (2 Samuel 14–20) and Adonijah, another of David's sons (1 Kings 1). On his deathbed, David chose as his successor Solomon (the second son sired with Bathsheba), exhorting him to remain obedient to God and His laws, as the Lord had promised that David's descendants would rule as long as they showed obedience to the divine will.

After Solomon got married, and undertook to complete the building of the Temple that his father had begun, the Lord invited him to ask whatever he desired. The king requested the wisdom to do what was right, and to be able to obey the divine law. God replied that, as Solomon had asked for discernment in doing justice, and not for a long life or wealth or the death of his enemies, he

---

Elise Kleivane (Oslo, 2018), 173–200; Evan F. Kuehn, 'Melchizedek as exemplar for kingship in twelfth-century political thought', *History of Political Thought* 31 (2010), 557–75.

[7] This will be discussed in greater detail in Björn Weiler, 'Whatever happened to Rehoboam and Jeroboam? The Bible in narratives of kingship, c.1000–1200' (forthcoming). See also Barrau, 'Sibyls, tanners'.

would receive all four (1 Kings 3). Once the Temple had been completed, God appeared once more, and warned Solomon that he would only protect him and his descendants as long as they obeyed his will (1 Kings 9). Inevitably, Solomon, too, began to err. Led astray partly by his 700 wives, he dedicated temples to pagan gods, and thus enraged his Lord. However, in memory of David, Solomon was spared: God would forsake the Israelites only after Solomon's death (1 Kings 11). And that duly came to pass (1 Kings 12).

What are the major themes emerging from this summary? First, the attitude towards kingship remained ambivalent. The Israelites might have defied their Creator by wishing for a king, but once they insisted, the institution received divine sanction. Indeed, it was God who decided who would be king of Israel: he chose Saul, David and Solomon, and he decreed that Solomon's heirs would forfeit their royal status. The Israelites were still invited to consent (Saul, David and Solomon were all formally elected by the constituent tribes), but it was God who decided. Divine backing resulted in a transformation of the monarch, most notably in Saul's case, who received the gift of prophecy after having been anointed (1 Samuel 10). Second, virtue and inner disposition trumped a hereditary claim. It was not Saul's son Jonathan who succeeded him, but David; David was followed not by his eldest son, but by Solomon; and Solomon's sons were deprived of the kingship of a united Israel because of their father's sins. Yet the decision as to who would succeed still rested with God. Indeed, with the important exceptions of David and the disinheritance of Solomon's progeny, no revolt succeeded. But then, strictly speaking Saul had ceased to be king the moment God chose David, while the end of David's line had been sanctioned by the Lord. Third, obedience to the divine will and a desire to do justice made a truly good king. Saul had forfeited his throne when he defied God, while David and Solomon succeeded as long as they tried to abide by the laws of God. That David exhorted his son to show obedience, and that Solomon chose the wisdom to know what was right, ensured a long and prosperous reign. Unrest erupted only when a king violated the law: when Saul defied God, when David not only committed adultery, but also plotted the violent death of Bathsheba's husband or when Solomon built cult sites for pagan idols. Even then forgiveness could be obtained, as long as the errant ruler showed contrition. Equally, though, royal failings translated into disasters for the people at large. Rebellion and unrest beset not only a king who had veered from the path of virtue, but also his people. They had, after all, insisted on being ruled by kings.

Similar themes surface in other parts of the Old Testament. Perhaps the most comprehensive statement on royal power can be found in Deuteronomy 17:14–18. The Israelites should only elect a king chosen by God, and who was not a foreigner. He was not to acquire great treasures or many wives, as those would distract him. Nor was he to lead the Israelites back to Egypt, even to raid it, and, on assuming power, he was to copy out the laws of the Levites – the rules laid down in Leviticus and Deuteronomy – which it was the king's duty to

I. FOUNDATIONS

enforce and uphold. The reference to riches and wives echoes the trajectory of Solomon, who, once he had gained both, abandoned his obedience to God and his embrace of wisdom. Other passages reflect these prescriptions, even if they do not always expound on them in comparable detail. Kings received their power from God,[8] and were owed obedience.[9] In return, they should seek out wisdom, weed out evildoers and obey the law.[10] They should choose prudent counsellors and be moderate in their lifestyle.[11] And they should protect the poor and powerless, with widows, orphans and exiles frequently singled out as especially deserving of protection.[12] Kings depended on their people: 'Love and faithfulness keep a king safe; through love his throne is made secure.'[13]

The Bible provided the essential foundations on which high medieval concepts of kingship were built. These were fleshed out further with references to classical authors. Cicero's *De Officiis* and Seneca's *De Clementia* may serve as examples. They do not exhaust the reception of classical writings read in the central Middle Ages,[14] but Cicero (d. 43 BCE) and Seneca (d. 65 CE) were among the most widely cited Roman authors in the high medieval west, and these were their most popular works.[15] *De Officiis* outlined the qualities

---

[8] Proverbs 8:14–18; Jeremiah 1:3, 1:10, 18:7, 18:9; Ezekiel 28:12, 28:17, 37:24; Daniel 2:21.

[9] Ecclesiastes 8:2, 10:20.

[10] Proverbs 14:31, 16:12, 20:8, 20:26, 29:4, 29:14, 31:9, 11:4; Isaiah 9:7; Ecclesiastes 2:12.

[11] Proverbs 14:35, 16:13, 22:11, 25:5; Ecclesiastes 5:9, 10:16–17.

[12] Leviticus 19:15, 23:22; Deuteronomy 14:29, 15:7, 15:11, 16:11; 1 Samuel 2:8; Job 22:9; Psalms 12:5, 14:6, 68:5, 74:21, 82:3, 113:7; Isaiah 10:2; Malachi 3:5; Ezekiel 16:49.

[13] Proverbs 20:28.

[14] Other popular texts, offering moral instruction with reference to history, rather than as distinctive treatises, were those of Sallust, Suetonius and Valerius Maximus: Beryl Smalley, 'Sallust in the Middle Ages', in *Classical Influences on European Culture A.D. 500–1500*, ed. R. R. Bolgar (Cambridge, 1971), 165–75; Robert A. Kaster, 'The transmission of Suetonius' *Caesars* in the Middle Ages', *Transactions of the American Philological Association* 144 (2014), 133–86; Matthew J. Innes, 'The classical tradition in the Carolingian Renaissance: ninth-century encounters with Suetonius', *International Journal of the Classical Tradition* 3 (1997), 265–82; Hans-Jörg Uther, 'Zur Rezeption der Memorabilia des Valerius Maximus vom Mittelalter bis in die Neuzeit', in *Bilder – Sachen – Mentalitäten. Arbeitsfelder historischer Kulturwissenschaften. Wolfgang Brückner zum 80. Geburtstag*, ed. Heidrun Alzheimer, Fred G. Rausch, Klaus Reder and Claudia Selheim (Innsbruck, 2010), 207–16; Max Manitius, *Handschriften antiker Autoren in mittelalterlichen Bibliothekskatalogen*, ed. Karl Manitius (Leipzig, 1935).

[15] Marcia L. Colish, *The Stoic Tradition from Antiquity to the Early Middle Ages*, 2 vols. (Leiden and Boston, 1985), vol. 1, 14–19; Stephen C. Jaeger, *The Origins of Courtliness* (Philadelphia, PA, 1985), 117; Nicholas Vincent, 'The court of Henry II', in *Henry II: New Interpretations*, ed. Christopher Harper-Bill and Nicholas Vincent (Woodbridge, 2007), 278–334, at 325; Leighton D. Reynolds, 'The Younger Seneca: *De Beneficiis* and *De Clementia*', in *Texts and Transmission: A Survey of the Latin Classics*, ed. L. D. Reynolds (Oxford, 1984), 363–5, at 364; Maddalena Spallone, '"Edizioni" tardoantiche e tradizione medievale dei testi: il caso delle Epistulae ad Lucilium di Seneca', in *Formative Stages of Classical Traditions: Latin Texts from Antiquity to the Renaissance*, ed. Oronzo Pecere (Spoleto, 1995), 149–96; Michael Winterbottom, 'The transmission of

required to engage in public life, the role of expediency and how to resolve conflicts between expediency and right. Public life was meant to be based on the pursuit of wisdom, justice (with its twin charity), fortitude and temperance.[16] The major danger faced in the pursuit of justice was that private ambition and public good could potentially be conflated. Men in pursuit of public office also sought to acquire wealth, partly so as to be able to do good. It was a precondition for being able to lead a public life, for instance, when it came to equipping and funding an army. Yet pursuing wealth and ambition for their own sakes or without restraint turned them into distractions from justice.[17] Generosity was carefully circumscribed. It should not be hurtful to anyone, must be practised within one's means and offered according to merit.[18] One could not be charitable if the resources for one's largesse had been acquired unjustly, if they were spent unwisely or directed at the undeserving. Similar restraints guided the exercise of fortitude and valour. They became vices if devoid of justice, or practised solely for personal aggrandisement.[19] When explaining the role of fortitude, Cicero made a statement that resonated frequently in patristic and medieval sources. Those pursuing public office should 'keep the good of the people so clearly in view that regardless of their own interests they will make their every action conform to that'. They should also abstain from favouritism: 'For the administration of the government, like the office of a trustee, must be conducted for the benefit of those entrusted to one's care, not of those to whom it is entrusted.'[20] Public office was a duty, not an opportunity for self-enrichment. Men seeking to lead others should do so in order to serve, not out of a desire to rule. Self-advancement, the desire to practise revenge or to satisfy one's anger could not be honourable reasons to act, nor should they be allowed to guide one's conduct in politics.[21]

Instead, equipoise of mind was required: 'It is a fine thing to keep an unruffled temper, an unchanging mien, and the same cast of countenance in

---

Cicero's De Officiis', *Classical Quarterly* 43 (1993), 215–42; Winterbottom, 'Cicero: De Officiis', in *Texts and Transmission: A Survey of the Latin Classics*, ed. Reynolds, 130–1; Winkler, *Royal Responsibility*, 31–3; John O. Ward, 'What the Middle Ages missed of Cicero, and why', in *Brill's Companion to the Reception of Cicero*, ed. William H. F. Altman (Leiden, 2015), 307–26. Generally, see Rita Copeland, ed., *The Oxford History of Classical Reception in English Literature. Volume II, 800–1558* (Oxford, 2016), 728, 752, which, despite the number of surviving manuscripts of Seneca and Cicero in England, dedicates chapters to neither; Bolgar, ed., *Classical Influences*.

[16] Cicero, *De Officiis*, transl. Walter Miller (Cambridge, MA, 1913), i.6, pp. 18–21.

[17] Cicero, *De Officiis*, i.8, pp. 24–9.

[18] Cicero, *De Officiis*, i.14, pp. 46–9.

[19] Cicero, *De Officiis*, i.19, pp. 64–5. See also his warning about the dangers of ambition: iii.20–1, pp. 350–9.

[20] Cicero, *De Officiis*, i.24, pp. 86–7.

[21] Cicero, *De Officiis*, i.25, pp. 88–91.

I. FOUNDATIONS

45

every condition of life.'[22] Anger, pride or joy must never cloud the judgement of public officials. Instead, they should remain humble, and invite the counsel of trustworthy friends and advisors who would remind them of the transience of worldly goods, and exhort them to abide by their duties.[23] Temperance acted as further check. Like biblical kings, public servants in the Roman republic were supposed to be moderate in their pleasures, restrain their emotions and serve the common good.[24] However, justice still took precedence. It was to be considered a higher goal than wisdom, fortitude or temperance. The guiding principles of any public servant were to be obedience to the law, and working for the benefit and comfort of human society.[25] Indeed, Cicero explained, the need for justice had underpinned the creation of kingship: 'Men of high moral character were made kings in order that the people might enjoy justice.'[26] For the ability to recognise what was just rested on a good character.[27]

Cicero's concept of public office as duty, as an act of service for the common good, and his emphasis on justice as the root and pinnacle of successful governance, were central to high medieval understandings of the royal office. His writings, and *De Officiis* in particular, lent themselves to appropriation by Christian writers not least because they had so much in common with biblical precepts. Cicero may have viewed the commonwealth as rooted in natural law, not divine authority, but the moral lessons he propagated were nonetheless comparable to the ones contained in the Old Testament. Just as in the case of David, inner disposition was the key to good governance. As with Solomon, wisdom was the key to righteous action. Just as Deuteronomy stipulated that kings remember the Levite laws, so Cicero postulated that law was to be the guiding principle of public life; just like Isaiah, he demanded that wealth and power be used for the benefit of those weaker and poorer. Like Deuteronomy, Proverbs and Ecclesiastes, Cicero insisted that men in public office practise restraint and moderation. The hierarchy of virtues and norms was not, of course, solely Cicero's: he referred to Plato, (unnamed) Stoics and his own teachers. He reflected ideals that surface elsewhere in Latin literature, and was thus by no means the single conduit through which they reached the medieval

---

[22] Cicero, *De Officiis*, i.26, pp. 92–3.

[23] Cicero, *De Officiis*, i.26, pp. 92–5.

[24] Cicero, *De Officiis*, i.28, pp. 98–103; i.35–8, pp. 128–41.

[25] Cicero, *De Officiis*, i.44–5, pp. 158–63. See also ii.9, pp. 202–3 (on the precedence to be accorded to justice); ii.11, pp. 206–7 (justice as the best route to popularity); ii.12, pp. 210–13 (justice as a way of gaining glory); ii.17, pp. 232–3 (generosity best practised when funds are spent on public works, rather than games or lavish feasts); ii.23, pp. 258–9 (justice as the cornerstone of public life).

[26] Cicero, *De Officiis*, ii.12, pp. 209–11.

[27] Cicero, *De Officiis*, iii.5, pp. 290–1. See also Cicero's further exposition of the 'good man': *De Officiis*, iii.19, pp. 346–51.

46   2. FOUNDATIONAL TEXTS

west. But, especially in this period, Cicero, alongside Seneca, proved to be among their most widely read proponents.

Despite having been recognised as turgid even by medieval readers, Seneca enjoyed a surprising degree of popularity – enabled, perhaps, by a preference for digests, with much of the rhetorical ballast removed.[28] *De Clementia* was among the most widely circulating of his works, with a veritable explosion of copies being produced in the twelfth century.[29] Of particular interest is Seneca's account of royal power:

> great strength is admirable only if its power is beneficent. The ability to do damage is, after all, a noxious kind of strength. In short, the only person who has a firm and well-grounded greatness is the one that everyone knows is both their leader and their supporter (*tam supra se esse quam pro se*), the one that they find every day has unsleeping concern for their safety of one and all, the one they do not run away from when he approaches as if some monster or dangerous creature had jumped from its lair.[30]

People, Seneca continued, were willing to defend the king if he acted as their protector, not their oppressor. Like the mind, the ruler was both directing the body, and was protected by it. The king 'quite simply is the link that holds the state together. He is the breath of life to all those many thousands who on their own would only be a heavy weight and easy prey if that mind of the empire (*imperium*) were withdrawn.'[31] His power was absolute. That fact made displays of clemency all the worthier.[32] There was even a moral expectation for the ruler to show clemency: 'Greatness of spirit adorns greatness of standing. If the spirit does not exalt itself to match its station, it drags that station, too, downwards to the ground.'[33] Wrath and anger diminished the serenity of the ruler and hence the loftiness of his office.[34] Indeed, 'an emperor

---

[28] I owe this point to Lars Kjaer.

[29] Seneca, *De Clementia*, ed. and transl. Susanna Braund (Oxford, 2009), 77. For the circulation of other works of his see: Spallone, '"Edizioni" tardoantiche'; Giancarlo Mazzoni, 'Ricerche sulla tradizione medievale del "De Beneficiis" e del "De Clementia" di Seneca', *Bolletino dei classici greci et latini* 26 (1978), 85–110; Mazzoni, 'Ricerche sulla tradizione medievale del "De beneficiis" e dei "De Clementia" di Seneca. III. Storia della tradizione manoscritta', *Bolletino del classici*, 3rd ser. 3 (1982), 165–223; Chiara Torre, 'Seneca and the Christian tradition', in *The Cambridge Companion to Seneca*, ed. Shadi Bartsch and Alessandro Schiesaro (Cambridge, 2015), 266–76; Roland Mayer, 'Seneca Redivivus: Seneca in the medieval and Renaissance world', in *Cambridge Companion to Seneca*, 277–88; Leighton D. Reynolds, *The Medieval Tradition of Seneca's Letters* (Oxford, 1965); Peter Stacey, 'Senecan political thought from the Middle Ages to early modernity', in *Cambridge Companion to Seneca*, 289–302.

[30] Seneca, *De Clementia*, i.3.3, pp. 100–1.

[31] Seneca, *De Clementia*, i.3.4–i.4.1, pp. 100–1.

[32] Seneca, *De Clementia*, i.5.4, pp. 102–3.

[33] Seneca, *De Clementia*, i.5.5, pp. 104–5.

[34] Seneca, *De Clementia*, i.7, pp. 106–7.

I. FOUNDATIONS   47

should adopt for himself the spirit of the gods'.[35] If deities were wrathful, then even the king would not be secure from punishment. If they were reasonable, however, why would the king not emulate them? Precisely because his power over the people resembled that of the gods over mortals, his wrath would terrify his people, not fill them with love and loyalty. For kings, 'their security is more assured by their mildness, because frequent punishment, though it crushes the hatred of a few, rouses the hatred of everyone'.[36] Only tyrants would allow their wrath to go unchecked.[37] True kings, by contrast, acted like fathers. While other titles bestowed upon the emperor – like 'Fortunate' or 'Augustus' – were merely honorific, 'Father of the fatherland' signified that 'he has been granted a father's power, which is the most restrained in the way that it cares for his children and subordinates his own interests to theirs'.[38]

Seneca was concerned not with a systematic outline of the moral underpinnings of public life, but with one particular virtue: clemency. While Cicero had fashioned *De Officiis* as a letter to his son, Seneca addressed the recently enthroned Emperor Nero. The political context within which they wrote was thus fundamentally different: Nero exercised a degree of power far greater than any of Cicero's contemporaries. Still, important parallels emerge, both between them and with the Bible, eagerly seized upon by high medieval writers. Kings had been chosen so as to keep the commonwealth together. They exercised far greater power than any of their subjects, but they were nonetheless dependent upon them. Undue harshness undermined the king's ability to keep the peace and secure the stability of the realm. His power was wielded most justly when it served not to increase his own standing, but the common good. Like a father, the king should put the interests of the people above his own. Only then could he be assured of their loyalty.

Cicero and Seneca reached the Latin Middle Ages by a variety of routes. In addition to copies of their writings being preserved and copied, their continuing reception was ensured by patristic writers, that is, early Christian theologians, who used them as models, or who drew on them because of the cultural prestige that had accrued to them. *De Officiis*, for example, provided the basis for *De Officiis Ministrorum* by Ambrose of Milan (*c.* 340–397), an account of the mindset and duties required of bishops, of which most high medieval cathedral libraries possessed a copy, or at least a digest. While in some ways moving beyond Cicero, most importantly by assigning to the divine will the

---

[35] Seneca, *De Clementia*, i.5.7, pp. 104–5.
[36] Seneca, *De Clementia*, 1.8.6, pp. 108–9. See, similarly, i.11.4, pp. 114–15.
[37] Seneca, *De Clementia*, i.12–13, pp. 114–19.
[38] Seneca, *De Clementia*, i.14.1, pp. 120–1. On the significance of the term: Andreas Alföldi, *Der Vater des Vaterlandes im römischen Denken* (Darmstadt, 1971). For an especially striking example of its medieval reception, see below, Chapter 10: Otto of Freising, *Gesta Frederici, seu rectius Cronica*, ed. Franz-Josef Schmale, transl. Adolf Schmidt (Darmstadt, 1965), ii.58, pp. 390–1.

48   2. FOUNDATIONAL TEXTS

role that natural law had played for the Roman orator, Ambrose nonetheless closely followed the structure and general thematic set-up of *De Officiis*.[39] Cicero and Seneca also formed part of the cultural repertoire on which St Augustine of Hippo (354–430) drew when defining basic tenets of the Christian faith in a manner both accessible and acceptable to late imperial Roman elites.[40] Other Church Fathers adopted similar approaches. Collectively, they amplified avenues of reception for classical Roman ideas about the legitimate exercise of power, even if sometimes they did so indirectly.

The popularity of texts like *De Officiis* and *De Clementia* was enhanced by the ease with which their understanding of the ethics of power could be translated into a Christian universe. That Cicero and Seneca operated in a political environment wholly different from that of most late antique and early medieval writers made it even easier to adapt their thinking to needs and challenges otherwise quite alien to the world of Rome. Cicero's republican thought and Seneca's concern with imperial power could be cast aside precisely because the ethical norms underpinning their writing so closely resembled those in the Old Testament. They could be made to illustrate the dangers of worldly power more generally.[41] To do that, we will need to look beyond specific statements about kings, and explore instead how patristic and early medieval writers engaged with questions of secular might in general. And that means turning to the treatment of bishops. By the fifth and sixth centuries, when many of these foundational texts were written, imperial, let alone royal, power was an absent ideal. It frequently fell to prelates to fill the vacuum created by the absence of governmental authority. Many acted both as secular lords and spiritual leaders. In most of Europe, this dual role continued well into the central Middle Ages.[42] Consequently, ideas about episcopal leadership

---

[39] Marcia L. Colish, 'Cicero, Ambrose, and Stoic Ethics: transmission or transformation?', in *The Classics in the Middle Ages*, ed. Aldo S. Bernardo and Saul Levin (Binghamton, NY, 1990), 95–112; Ivor J. Davidson, 'A tale of two approaches: Ambrose, "De officiis" 1.1–22 and Cicero "De officiis" 1.1-6', *Journal of Theological Studies* NS 52 (2001), 61–84; Giacomo Raspanti, 'Clementissimus imperator: power, religion, and philosophy in Ambrose's "De obitu Theodisii" and Seneca's "De Clementia"', in *The Power of Religion in Late Antiquity*, ed. Andrew Cain and Noel Lenski (Farnham, 2009), 45–55.

[40] Charles Brittain, 'St Augustine as a reader of Cicero', in *Tolle lege: Essays on Augustine and on Medieval Philosophy in Honor of Roland J. Teske, SJ*, ed. Richard C. Taylor (Milwaukee, WI, 2011), 81–114; John L. Treloar, 'Cicero and Augustine: the ideal society', *Augustinianum* 28 (1988), 565–90; Danuta R. Shanzer, 'Augustine and the Latin Classics', in *A Companion to St Augustine*, ed. Shelly Reid and Mark Vessey (New York, 2012), 159–74; Thomas Baier, 'Cicero und Augustinus. Die Begründung ihres Staatsdenkens im jeweiligen Gottesbild', *Gymnasium* 109 (2002), 123–40.

[41] The most extensive coverage of the subject remains: Marc Reydellet, *La royauté dans la littérature Latine de Sidoine Apollinaire à Isidore de Séville* (Paris, 1981).

[42] See, for a convenient overview, Timothy Reuter, 'A Europe of bishops. The age of Wulfstan of York and Burchard of Worms', in *Patterns of Episcopal Power. Bishops in Tenth- and Eleventh-Century Europe*, ed. Ludger Körntgen and Dominik Waßenhoven

I. FOUNDATIONS 49

in the affairs of the world were also applied to secular leaders. What, though, were these ideas?

One of the foundational texts for high medieval understandings of the episcopal office was the *Regula Pastoralis* by Pope Gregory the Great (540–604), of which nearly 500 manuscripts survive from the central Middle Ages.[43] Gregory offered a finely tuned guide on how to provide pastoral care, how to tailor the message to the intended recipient and how to deal with the most common challenges one would encounter in the process. But he also tackled the dilemma posed by wielding power over others. Christ himself, Gregory pointed out, had avoided taking up secular office, not out of fear, but to set an example. Therefore, mere mortals should not desire to wield a power that Christ had refused. For the exercise of worldly authority indubitably brought with it moral corruption. Just as royal *potestas* (power/might) had turned Saul and David from good to evil, so every Christian, placed in charge of others, would find himself exposed to the lures of ambition and greed.[44] At the same time, one must not refuse responsibility when it was thrust upon one. Some faked humility to escape these obligations and dangers, but thereby committed the deadly sins of pride and disobedience.[45] The office of *rector*, of corrector, shepherd and guide of the people, should therefore be assumed reluctantly, with due humility, only at the behest of others and only to work for the common good. Gregory's *Moralia in Iob*, another medieval bestseller,[46] expressed similar ideas. Humility was an essential virtue. For although those were called kings who could control their urges, if carried away by their desires, they succumbed to arrogance, and God would bring about

(Berlin, 2011), 17–38; *The Role of the Bishop in Late Antiquity: Conflict and Compromise*, ed. Andrew Fear, José Fernández Ubiña and María del Mar Marcos Sánchez (London, 2013); Steffen Patzold, *Episcopus: Wissen über Bischöfe im Frankreich des späten 8. bis frühen 10. Jahrhunderts* (Ostfildern, 2008).

[43] Richard W. Clement, 'A handlist of manuscripts containing Gregory's Regula Pastoralis', *Manuscripta* 28 (1984), 33–44. A useful case study of Gregory's medieval significance is Rolf Hendrik Bremmer, Cornelis Dekker and David F. Johnson, eds., *Rome and the North: the Early Reception of Gregory the Great in Germanic Europe* (Paris, 2001).

[44] Gregory the Great, *Regula Pastoralis*, ed. Floribert Rommel, transl. Charles Morel, introduction, notes and index Bruno Judic, Sources chrétiennes 381–2, 2 vols. (Paris, 1992), vol. 1, 136–40. R. A. Markus, 'Gregory the Great's rector and his genesis', in *Gregoire le Grand*, ed. Jacques Fontaine, Robert Gillet and Stan Pollistrandi (Paris, 1986), 137–46; Heinz Hanspeter, 'Der Bischofsspiegel des Mittelalters. Zur Regula Pastoralis Gregors des Großen', in *Sendung und Dienst im bischöflichen Amt: Festschrift der Katholisch-Theologischen Fakultät der Universität Augsburg für Bischof Josef Stimpfle zum 75. Geburtstag*, ed. Anton Ziegenaus (St Ottilien, 1991), 113–36; Reydellet, *La royauté*, 441–502.

[45] Gregory the Great, *Regula Pastoralis*, vol. 1, 148–50.

[46] René Wasselynck, 'Les compilations des "Moralia in Job" du VIIe au XIIe siècle', *Recherches de théologie ancienne et médiévale* 29 (1962), 5–32.

50   2. FOUNDATIONAL TEXTS

their fall.[47] Worse still, if those who had the power to correct failed to lead by moral example, they would drag their subjects with them into the abyss of arrogance.[48] Therefore, it was necessary that whoever was put above others ensure that humility reign supreme in his mind.[49] Worldly authority entailed the obligation to work for the welfare of others, but it also exposed those who exercised it to the dangers of pride and arrogance. Therefore, they had to arm themselves with humility and modesty.

Comparable concerns were voiced by other Fathers. Channelling Cicero, Ambrose of Milan warned of the temptations of worldly power. They were why Christ had ordered his disciples not to possess gold or silver.[50] Ambrose also warned of ambition as the root of all evils: once the pleasures of secular power had been savoured, the desire would arise for more, and the search for glory would dominate the lives of those who had succumbed.[51] St Augustine, likewise echoing Cicero, explained that one should not love honour in this life. The trappings of worldly success were fleeting and vain. Rather, office was to be held by those who were qualified and capable of working for the salvation of their inferiors. Besides, the title bishop denoted not honour, but good works. Therefore, those who enjoyed leading others (*praeesse*), instead of being useful to them (*prodesse*) should not be called bishops.[52] The so-called Ambrosiaster explained that all power rested with and emanated from God.[53] Consequently, if someone assumed office out of ambition and greed, he committed an act of injustice not only against the people entrusted to their care, but also against God. The point was repeated by Isidore of Seville in the seventh century, applying the principle to all clergy.[54] In short, being chosen as bishop or abbot was above all an obligation, not to be embarked upon lightly. Not only did the office entail a responsibility for the spiritual welfare of one's inferiors, it also exposed those who held it to the lures of ambition and greed. Rulers had a divinely ordained duty to mete out justice, to protect and safeguard their subjects, but even good lords could all too easily fall victim to ambition and greed.

---

[47] Gregory the Great, *Moralia in Job*, ed. Marc Adriaen, CCSL, 3 vols. (Turnhout, 1979–85), xi.13.21; vol. 2, pp. 597–8.

[48] Gregory, *Moralia*, xxiv.25.53; vol. 3, p. 1227.

[49] Gregory, *Moralia*, xxiv.25.55; vol. 3, pp. 1228–9.

[50] St Ambrose of Milan, *De Officiis Ministrorum*, PL 16, ii.25, cols. 144–5, no. 128.

[51] Ambrose, *De Officiis*, ii.26, cols. 145–7, no. 131; Ambrose, *Expositio Evangelii secundum Lucam*, in *Sancti Ambrosii Mediolanensis Opera* IV, ed. M. Adriaen, CCSL (Turnhout, 1957), iv.31, p. 117.

[52] St Augustine, *De Civitate Dei*, xix.19, vol. 2, pp. 686–7. The phrase may contain an echo of Seneca, *De Clementia*, 1.3.3, pp. 100–1: *tam supra se esse quam pro se.*

[53] *Ambrosiastri qui dicitur commentarius in epistolas Paulinas*, ed. Heinrich Joseph Vogel, CSEL, 3 vols. (Vienna, 1966–9), xiii.1, vol. 1, pp. 416–19.

[54] *Isidori Etymologiarum*, vii.12.

I. FOUNDATIONS

Similar ideas were expressed when it came to secular power, with Ambrosiaster (*c.* 380), St Augustine and Isidore of Seville (560–636) as the most influential writers. In his commentary on Paul's epistle to the Romans, Ambrosiaster defined kings as princes who had been created in the image of God to correct and to prevent disasters. They had been deputised to exercise divine authority and to spread justice.[55] St Augustine, in turn, juxtaposed David, who reigned justly and piously amidst his worldly possessions, with Solomon who, after a good start, came to a bad end.[56] He also listed the qualities that a Christian emperor should possess. He should rule with justice, maintain humility among excessive praise, employ his power on God's behalf and be moderate in punishment. He was to cultivate self-restraint, amidst power that would make it all too easy for him to gratify his desires, and should act in the service of God, not out of desire for vain glory.[57] These concepts were condensed by Isidore of Seville, whose *Etymologies* remained a standard of work of reference well into the twelfth century: *rex a regere*, king derives from governing, and, *non autem regit, qui non corrigit*, he does not reign who does not correct. This was connected to the two main virtues any king ought to possess: piety and justice.[58]

De xii Saeculi Abusivis by Pseudo-Cyprianus, probably originating in seventh-century Ireland, should be added to these examples, not least because medieval readers variously attributed it to Cicero, Augustine, Gregory I and Cyprian of Carthage. *De Abusivis* was enormously popular, surviving in at least 400 manuscripts.[59] Pseudo-Cyprianus listed such violators of the right order of the world as 'the woman without chastity' or 'the haughty pauper'.[60] Among

---

[55] *Ambrosiastri commentarius*, i, pp. 416–19. For a more detailed coverage of Ambrosiaster's commentary: Affeldt, *Weltliche Gewalt*, 53–84; Sophie Lunn-Rockcliffe, *Ambrosiaster's Political Theology* (Oxford, 2007), 130–8.

[56] Augustine, *De Civitate Dei*, xvii.20; vol. 2, pp. 586–9.

[57] Augustine, *De Civitate Dei*, v.24; vol. 1, p. 160.

[58] *Isidori Etymologiarum*, ix.3. Also: Reydellet, *La royauté*, 505–97.

[59] Aidan Breen, 'Towards a Critical Edition of De XII Abusivis: Introductory essays with a provisional edition of the text and accompanied by an English translation', unpublished PhD, Trinity College Dublin 1988, available at www.tara.tcd.ie/handle/2262/77107 (accessed 9 October 2018), 233–5, 241–61. On the text's medieval reception: Berges, *Fürstenspiegel*, 4; Hans Hubert Anton, 'Pseudo-Cyprian. *De duodecim abusivis saeculi* und sein Einfluß auf dem Kontinent, insbesondere auf die karolingischen Fürstenspiegel', in *Die Iren und Europa im frühen Mittelalter*, ed. Heinz Löwe, 2 vols. (Stuttgart, 1982), vol. 2, 568–617, at 604; Anton, 'Zu neueren Wertung Pseudo-Cyprians ("De duodecim abusivis saeculi") und zu seinem Vorkommen in Bibliothekskatalogen des Mittelalters', *Würzburger Diözesangeschichtsblätter* 51 (1989), 463–74; Mary Clayton, 'De Duodecim Abusiuis, lordship and kingship in Anglo-Saxon England', in *Saints and Scholars: New Perspectives on Anglo-Saxon Literature and Culture in Honour of Hugh Magennis*, ed. Stuart McWilliams (Cambridge, 2012), 141–63.

[60] Pseudo-Cyprianus, *De xii Abusivis Saeculi*, ed. Siegmund Hellmann, *Texte und Untersuchungen zur Geschichte der altchristlichen Literatur*, 3rd ser. 4 (1910) 1–62. For

52   2. FOUNDATIONAL TEXTS

this rogues' gallery, two are of particular interest: the *dominus sine virtute* (the lord without virtue) and the *rex iniquus* (the useless king). Nobody, Pseudo-Cyprianus explained, who lacked virtuous rigour could have *potestas* – the power to rule. Virtue was, however, not a matter of exterior display alone. It had to coincide with an inner readiness to reform and to adhere to strict standards. A ruler who failed to be virtuous deceived not only those he lorded over, but God himself. After good beginnings, Saul had turned God against himself with the arrogance of his disobedience. Solomon was rewarded with lordship over many people and realms due to the wisdom of his rule, but then succumbed to sin and forfeited the throne for his progeny. These examples, the author argued, showed how men who had been elevated to a superior status for the correction of others were often brought low by the moral dangers inherent in lordship. However, there was no virtue without divine help. Without it a ruler could have no strength, nor could he withstand infestations and adversities. There was no power if not ordained by God, who installed the rulers of his people, cast down the mighty and elevated the humble.[61] The same ideas resurface in Pseudo-Cyprianus' comments on the depraved or sinful king.[62] How could he, whose duty it was to correct others, fulfil his obligations if he remained incapable of ruling himself? A monarch's most important duty was to uphold justice: not to exalt the proud, but the humble, to combat evil men, harlots and sorcerers, dispose prudently of the affairs of the realm and listen to sage counsel. Should a king fail to abide by these rules, disaster would strike. Peace would break down and political turmoil ensue, enemies invade the kingdom, harvests fail and natural disasters befall the *rex iniquus* and his subjects, while the dynasty would be discontinued, as had happened to Solomon's sons, who would not be elevated to the kingship because of their father's sins.[63] The duty to mete out justice, to correct and oversee one's subjects coincided with the danger of succumbing to ambition and greed, the hallmarks of a tyrant.

Secular power had been created by God to ensure that justice was done. To this end, rulers had to cast aside ambition, and, like Cicero's Roman patricians, they had to resist succumbing to the temptations of secular wealth. They were

---

a debate on the provenance of the text: Aidan Breen, 'Pseudo-Cyprian *De Duodecim Abusivis Saeculi* and the Bible', in *Irland und die Christenheit: Ireland and Christendom. Bibelstudien und Mission: the Bible and the Missions*, Próinséas Ní Chatháin and Michael Richter (Stuttgart, 1987), 230–45; Rob Meens, 'Politics, mirrors of princes and the Bible: sins, kings and the well-being of the realm', *EME* 7 (1998), 345–57.

[61] Pseudo-Cyprianus, *De xii Abusivis*, 43–5.
[62] Pseudo-Cyprianus, *De xii Abusivis*, 51-3.
[63] For the phenomenon see also: Marita Blattmann, '"Ein Unglück für sein Volk". Der Zusammenhang zwischen Fehlverhalten des Königs und Volkswohl in Quellen des 7. – 12. Jahrhunderts', *Frühmittelalterliche Studien* 30 (1996), 80–102; Meens, 'Politics', *passim*.

I. FOUNDATIONS 53

supposed to be concerned first and foremost with doing what was right, with protecting the law and enforcing it. The debts to the Old Testament are evident, as are those to Cicero and Seneca. Moreover, because prelates and princes held power over others, they faced similar temptations. Arrogance and greed posed a grave danger to them. If they succumbed, they would betray both their Creator and their flock. They would endanger their own eternal soul as well as the material and spiritual well-being of the people given into their care. Power was a privilege, a sign of divine favour and a recognition of virtue. It was also an arduous burden, a grave responsibility that ought not to be shouldered lightly. These ideas were eagerly seized upon by high medieval writers.

1.2 Medieval Readers

Among chroniclers and hagiographers, the parallel between the episcopal and the royal office proved especially popular. In the later ninth century, King Alfred of Wessex oversaw the translation of Gregory's *Pastoral Care* into Old English, and drew particular attention to ruler's responsibility, echoing that of Gregory's *rector*, for the spiritual as well as for the material well-being of his charges.[64] Other writers explicitly linked the norms of episcopal lordship to good kingship. Fulcher of Chartres, when praising the many virtues of Godfrey of Bouillon, the first ruler of crusader Jerusalem, compared him to a monk.[65] The late twelfth-century *Vita* of St Ladislaus of Hungary even cited St Augustine's *De Civitate Dei*: Ladislaus was a good ruler, reluctant to be seen wearing the trappings of royal office, so that he may do good, not lead (*non ut presit, sed ut prosit*).[66] Another parallel is presented by the case of Baldwin I of Jerusalem, who succeeded Godfrey in 1101. He was told, that, as in the case of bishops (*sicut et epsicopo de episcopatu*), wanting to be king meant wanting to do good.[67] This paraphrased Paul's first epistle to Timothy: *qui episcopum desiderat, bonum opus desiderat*, he who wants to become bishop desires to do good.[68] Kings and bishops shared a phenomenology of office. They were

---

[64] Richard W. Clement, 'The production of the Pastoral Care: King Alfred and his helpers', in *Studies in Earlier Old English Prose*, ed. Paul E. Szarmach (Albany, NY, 1996), 129–52; Carolin Schreiber, *King Alfred's Old English Translation of Pope Gregory the Great's Regula pastoralis and its Cultural Context: a Study and Partial Edition according to All Surviving Manuscripts based on Cambridge, Corpus Christi College 12* (Munich, 2003).

[65] Fulcher of Chartres, *Historia Hierosolymitana (1095–1127)*, ed. Heinrich Hagenmeyer (Heidelberg, 1913), 306–10. The discussion of parallels between bishops and kings, of patristic authors and of biblical commentaries summarises, revises and expands upon Björn Weiler, 'The *rex renitens* and the medieval ideal of kingship, c. 950–1250', *Viator* 31 (2000), 1–42, at 18–38.

[66] *Legenda S. Ladislai regis*, ed. Emma Bartoniek, in *Scriptores Rerum Hungaricarum*, ed. Emré Szentpétery, 2 vols. (Budapest, 1937–8), vol. 2, 507–28, at 517–18.

[67] Fulcher of Chartres, *Historia*, 384–90.

[68] 1 Timothy 3:1.

54   2. FOUNDATIONAL TEXTS

subject to similar moral principles and their duties were described in similar
terms. Both rulers and prelates exercised considerable power over their people,
both in this life and the next.

Like bishops, kings looked to God as the source of their power. In 1101, after
the election of Baldwin I to the throne of Jerusalem, the assembled prelates
explained how a king had come to be chosen, and why. In Fulcher of Chartres'
rendering, their main points were as follows: Baldwin had been elected according to law and in accordance with God's will, he had been sanctified (*sancti-
ficatur*) and consecrated with true benediction. As he obtained the *regimen*, the
power to rule, with a golden crown, so he also received the true duty (*onus
honestus*) of maintaining and awarding justice. The prelates then drew
a parallel with the episcopal office: he who desires to be king must desire to
do good works, for there could be no king without justice.[69] Being king was not
so much an honour as a duty. It was a gift from God, neither to be spurned nor
to be accepted lightly. It was not to be taken up for personal gain, but solely for
the rectification of the realm and the guardianship of justice.

Fulcher echoed contemporary thought on kingship, as it survives, for
instance in a series of commentaries on Paul's epistle to the Romans 13:1–7:
Non est enim potestas nisi a deo – 'there is no power, unless it derives from
God'.[70] An anonymous work from the school of Lanfranc, written in the last
third of the eleventh century, used the divine origin of secular and princely
authority to delineate the resulting obligations: to praise the good and admonish the bad, to keep them in beneficial circumstances and to free them from
evil.[71] Other works reiterated that point. In the eyes of Anselm of Laon (d.
1117), the prince wielded the sword of justice.[72] Robert Pullen (*c.* 1080–1146)
explained that all power was ordained by God, and the king held supreme
secular power. Therefore, he should not assume office out of greed or a lust for
wealth and luxury. Ambition would only beget even greater desire for riches
and honours, and would mean that a king failed to meet his obligations
towards God and his subjects.[73] Rupert of Deutz (*c.* 1075/80–*c.* 1129) also
had few doubts about the divine origins of earthly power, and awarded to kings
the rod of discipline, as opposed to the disciples of Christ, who wielded the rod
of pastoral care. However, he too found it necessary to warn against succumbing to a desire for riches.[74] Kings derived their power from God, and therefore

---

[69] Fulcher, *Historia*, 390.

[70] Romans 13. Affeldt, *Weltliche Gewalt*, also presents an edition of previously unpublished
    texts.

[71] Affeldt, *Weltliche Gewalt*, 289–90. Commentary: pp. 146–9.

[72] Affeldt, *Weltliche Gewalt*, 151.

[73] Robertus Pullus, *Sententiae*, PL 186, cols. 919, 921.

[74] Rupert of Deutz, *De Gloria et Honore Filii Hominis Super Mattheum*, ed.
    Hrabanus Haacke, CCCM (Turnhout, 1979), 181, 244, 246. Rupert of Deutz, *De Sancta
    Trinitate*, ed. Hrabanus Haacke, 4 vols., CCCM (Turnhout, 1971–2), vol. 2, 920. For

I. FOUNDATIONS

had a solemn obligation to correct and protect their subjects. This was closely intertwined with warnings not to fall prey to the dangers of secular office. Ambition and greed were a constant threat to the spiritual welfare of the ruler and, by implication, to the general well-being of those whom rulers ought to guard and protect.[75]

The connection appears even stronger when we consult abstract treatises on power. While the Carolingian tradition of *Mirrors of Princes* had petered out,[76] a number of important texts were nonetheless produced. They merit consideration not least because modern studies of medieval political thought have largely ignored them. Both patristic and Pseudo-Dionysian influences surface, for example, in two important eleventh-century texts: the *Institutes of Polity* by Wulfstan of York (*c.* 1023), and the *Libellus de institutione morum*, attributed to St Stephen (d. 1035), the first Christian king of Hungary, but probably composed shortly after his death. The *Institutes* consisted of a rather loose series of short treatises, surviving in several redactions, with no definitive *Urform*. One of the most widely disseminated versions contained three chapters of particular relevance: on the earthly king, kingship and the throne. In Wulfstan's treatise, the primary duty of kings was to promote the Christian faith and to lead a Christian life. They were to offer justice to those seeking it, and to punish evil-doers, yet they must combine rigour with mercy. A good ruler would also study books to acquire the wisdom with which to discern both

---

a more detailed coverage: John H. Van Engen, 'Sacred sanctions for lordship', in *Cultures of Power: Lordship, Status and Process in Twelfth-Century Europe*, ed. Thomas N. Bisson (Philadelphia, PA, 1995), 203–30, at 206–7.

[75] Similar points were made in a collection of proverbs by Wipo, dedicated to Emperor Henry III and probably written in the 1040s: *Wiponis Opera*, ed. Harry Bresslau, MGH SSrG, 3rd edition (Hanover and Leipzig, 1915), 66, ll. 1–3. Among the first duties of a king was to study the laws, for *legem servare est regnare*, to serve the law is to reign. See also Berengar of Tours explaining to King Philip of France *c.* 1072 that, if someone was called to an office, it was a divinely ordained duty to take it up: *Briefe Berengars von Tours*, in *Briefsammlungen der Zeit Heinrichs IV.*, ed. Carl Erdmann and Norbert Fickermann (Hanover, 1977), no. 82. See also Gilbert de Porrée (Affeldt, *Weltliche Gewalt*, 292–3) and William of St Thierry, *Expositio super epistolam ad Romanos*, ed. Paul Verdeyen, CCCM 86 (Turnhout, 1989), 171–2. Radulfus Niger (*c.* 1140–1217) emphasised the importance attached to defending the Church, and religious orthodoxy, an inalienable element of exercising and granting justice: Philippe Buc, 'Exégése et pensée politique: Radulphus Niger (vers 1190) et Nicolas de Lyre (vers 1330)', in *Représentation, pouvoir et royauté á la fin du Moyen Âge*, ed. Joël Blanchard (Paris, 1995), 145–64, at 154–8.

[76] Jonas d'Orléans, *De Institutione Regia*, ed. and transl. Alain Dubreucq, SC 407 (Paris, 1995); Hincmar of Rheims, *De Regis Persona et Regio Ministerio*, PL 125; on Smaragdus: Franz Brunhölzl, *Geschichte der lateinischen Literatur des Mittelalters. Erster Band: Von Cassiodor bis zum Ausklang der karolingischen Erneuerung* (Munich, 1975), 444–9; Otto Eberhardt, *Via Regia. Der Fürstenspiegel Smaragds von St Michel und seine literarische Gattung* (Munich, 1977); on Hincmar: Janet Nelson, 'Kingship, law and liturgy in the political thought of Hincmar of Rheims', *EHR* 92 (1977), 241–79; Rachel Stone and Charles West, eds., *Hincmar of Rheims: Life and Work* (Manchester, 2015).

56   2. FOUNDATIONAL TEXTS

God's will and human law. The foolish king, by contrast, would bring disasters upon his people.[77] Kingship, in turn, rested on the king's virtues (such as steadfastness, honesty, generosity and restraint), and on a mindset that ensured he was righteous, humble before the good and obedient to God.[78] The throne stood in for the kingdom as a whole, built on the pillars of those who work, those who pray and those who fight. Yet, if wisdom, religion and righteousness were abandoned, each of these would collapse, and with it the realm.[79] There was no direct reference to kingship having been instituted by God, but the duty of obedience that the king owed to his Creator was central to Wulfstan's concept of royal authority, as was the need for constancy and justice – an echo of the Bible, patristic writings and Cicero.

Ideas similar to Wulfstan's were voiced by the anonymous author of the *Libellus*.[80] It included sections on preserving the faith and the honour of the Church; treating prelates, princes and knights with respect; practising justice and patience; feeding and protecting strangers; taking prudent counsel; praying; and other virtues, such as piety and mercy. Stephen, the preamble of the *Libellus* explained, owed his kingship to God, who judged and put in place all those who held power. Thus, his son would be well-advised to heed his father's counsel. If he rejected it, he would prove to be no friend to either God or men. Indeed, serious consequences would befall him. When Adam disobeyed God, he was driven from paradise; when humankind rejected God, it was wiped out through water; and the sons of Solomon had forfeited their throne through arrogance.[81] Given the realm's recent conversion to Christianity, it was vitally important that Stephen's son should neither nourish nor protect heretics and apostates.[82] He should treat bishops and clerics as second in standing after himself, like the apostles were in relation to Christ.[83] He should treat princes and counts with respect. They were his warriors, not his servants. He should lead them through

[77] *The Political Writings of Archbishop Wulfstan of York*, transl. Andrew Rabin (Manchester, 2015), 103–5. On Wulfstan: Renée Trilling, 'Sovereignty and social order: Archbishop Wulfstan and the Institutes of Polity', in *The Bishop Reformed: Studies in Episcopal Power and Culture in the Central Middle Ages*, ed. Anna T. Jones and John S. Ott (Aldershot, 2007), 58–85; Patrick Wormald, 'Archbishop Wulfstan: eleventh-century state-builder', in *Wulfstan, Archbishop of York. The Proceedings of the Second Alcuin Conference*, ed. Matthew Townend (Turnhout, 2004), 9–27. Wulfstan's example was not discussed in Weiler, 'The *rex renitens*'.

[78] *Political Writings of Archbishop Wulfstan*, 105.

[79] *Political Writings of Archbishop Wulfstan*, 105–6.

[80] *Libellus de institutione morum*, ed. Joseph Balogh, in *Scriptores Rerum Hungaricarum*, ed. Emeric Szenpétery, 2 vols. (Budapest, 1937–8), vol. 2, 619–27. On the text: Előd Nemerkényi, 'The religious ruler in the *Institutions* of St Stephen of Hungary', in *Monotheistic Kingship. The Medieval Variants*, ed. Aziz al-Azmeh and János Bak (Budapest, 2004), 231–48; Nemerkényi, *Latin Classics in Medieval Hungary: Eleventh Century* (Budapest and New York, 2004), 31–72.

[81] *Libellus*, 619–20.

[82] *Libellus*, 621.

[83] *Libellus*, 621–2. See also 622–3 on the honours due to bishops.

I. FOUNDATIONS   57

humility, mildness and peace, without envy or anger. If he alienated them with avarice or haughty manners, they would forsake him and hand the realm to someone else.[84] Justice should be administered fairly and evenly. Kings judged with patience. Impatient judges ruled like tyrants.[85] Wise judgement required wise counsel,[86] and could be practised only with mercy and constancy.[87] Kingship was almost like a contract, both with God, and the people. The king could maintain his throne only if he served the needs of his people, and of those who required his protection (and who would enhance his power in return), and only if he remained a faithful and obedient servant of the Lord.

Wulfstan and the *Libellus* shared an emphasis on the demeanour and mindset of kings, the importance of justice and the conditional nature of their office. Rulers would remain kings only as long as they performed their duties, remained obedient to God, did not alienate their people and did justice equitably, fairly and to all. In this, they differed little from later writers. The chief innovation of John of Salisbury's *Policraticus* (*c.* 1160), for example, was to cloak some of these concepts in classicising garb.[88] A few decades later, Ralph (Radulfus) Niger, echoing Cicero and Seneca, outlined the duties of kingship in the context of a crusading treatise. All authority was united in the hands of the king, who ought to use his power to rule, protect and defend, but whose actions ought to be accompanied by humility and good manners. Whenever a king was in danger of feeling elated by his good fortune, he should display humility, discipline and modesty. Whenever he was tempted to succumb to vanity, justice, truth and temperance should be invoked.[89] Gerald of

---

[84] *Libellus*, 623–4.
[85] *Libellus*, 624.
[86] *Libellus*, 625–6.
[87] *Libellus*, 627.
[88] Max Kerner, 'Randbemerkungen zur Institutio Traiani', in *The World of John of Salisbury*, ed. Michael Wilks (Oxford, 1984), 203–6; Maximilian Kerner and Hans Kloeft, *Die Institutio Traiani. Ein pseudo-plutarchischer Text im Mittelalter. Text – Kommentar – zeitgenössischer Hintergrund* (Stuttgart, 1992); Thomas Elsmann, *Untersuchung zur Rezeption der Institutio Traiani. Ein Beitrag zur Nachwirkung antiker und pseudoantiker Topoi im Mittelalter und der frühen Neuzeit* (Stuttgart and Leipzig, 1994). For the *Policraticus*: Wilhelm Kleineke, *Englische Fürstenspiegel vom Policraticus Johanns von Salisbury bis zum Basilikon Doron König Jakobs I.* (Halle/Saale, 1937), 21–47. Ernst Robert Curtius, *Europäische Literatur und Lateinisches Mittelalter* (Tübingen, 1948, repr. 1993), 407–10; Ernst Froedrich Ohly, *Sage und Legende in der Kaiserchronik: Untersuchungen über Quellen und Aufbau der Dichtung* (Münster, 1940), 119–28; Gordon Whatley, 'The uses of hagiography: the legend of Pope Gregory and the Emperor Trajan in the Middle Ages', *Viator* 15 (1984), 25–63; John of Salisbury, *Policraticus sive de nugis curialium et vestigiis philosophorum libri viii*, ed. Clemens C. I. Webb, 2 vols. (Oxford, 1909), v.1, v.6, vii.16–17, vol. 1, pp. 281–2, 298–307, vol. 2, pp. 157–66.
[89] Radulfus Niger, *De Re Militari et Triplici Via Peregrinationis Ierosolimitane (1187/88)*, ed. Ludwig Schmugge (Berlin and New York, 1977), ii.1, pp. 131–2; ii.2, p. 132; ii.12, pp. 138–9. On the text see also John Cotts, 'Earthly kings, heavenly Jerusalem: Ralph Niger's political exegesis and the Third Crusade', *HSJ* 30 (2018), 159–75.

58   2. FOUNDATIONAL TEXTS

Wales, whose *De Principis Instructione* was written and revised at various stages between 1180 and 1217,[90] explained that royal authority was divinely ordained. It could be found on all levels of God's creation, among men as well as beasts.[91] He also presented a succinct definition of the differences between kings and tyrants.[92] Kings received their name and power from ruling first themselves and then others, while a tyrant, lacking self-restraint, violently oppressed the people. A king governed the people through personal example, through arms in war and through laws in peace. A tyrant never provided for the safety of his subjects. Not aiming to be of use to others but to lord over them, he corrupted rather than instructed. Furthermore, while kings aimed to be fathers to their people (an echo of Seneca), tyrants destroyed, exploited and oppressed those under their dominion.[93] Most of the theoretical section of *De Principis* was taken up with listing the virtues required of a king: ease of manners,[94] coyness and sexual abstinence,[95] piety,[96] temperance, clemency and prudence[97] – to name but a few. Of even greater importance were a love of justice and modesty. According to Gerald, there was no greater virtue in a prince than justice. It held human society together, impeded the ambition of the great and guarded the tranquillity and safety of the weak.[98] Kings derived their authority from God. Yet, for all its glory, and because of the power it entailed, their position also posed risks, notably succumbing to ambition and greed. Kings therefore had to ensure, in the eyes of God and of their people, that they displayed the virtues and the mindset of a just ruler.[99] Gerald's *De*

---

[90] Gerald of Wales, *Instruction for a Ruler: De Principis Instructione*, ed. and transl. Robert Bartlett (Oxford, 2018). On the text: Robert Bartlett, *Gerald of Wales, 1146-1223* (Oxford, 1982), 69–71; Berges, *Fürstenspiegel*, 143–50; Istvan Bejczy, 'Gerald of Wales on the cardinal virtues: a reappraisal of "De principis instructione"', *Medium Aevum* 75 (2006), 191–201.

[91] Gerald of Wales, *De Principis Instructione*, 35–7.

[92] Gerald of Wales, *De Principis Instructione*, 188–97, 320–3.

[93] See also John of Salisbury, *Policraticus*, viii.17–9; vol. 2, pp. 345–79: a tyrant lorded over the people with violent domination, while a prince reigned through the laws; the former went to war for the oppression and exploitation of the people, while the latter fought to defend their safety and welfare.

[94] Gerald of Wales, *De Principis Instructione*, 44–53.

[95] Gerald of Wales, *De Principis Instructione*, 60–5.

[96] Gerald of Wales, *De Principis Instructione*, 340–95.

[97] Gerald of Wales, *De Principis Instructione*, 74–99, 136–45.

[98] Gerald of Wales, *De Principis Instructione*, 118–35.

[99] The same set of ideas surfaced well into the thirteenth century: Robert Grosseteste, *Templum Dei, Edited from MS. 27 of Emmanuel College, Cambridge*, ed. Joseph Goering and F. A. C. Mantello (Toronto, 1984), chapter ix, p. 8. Particularly useful in the English context: Morton W. Bloomfield, *The Seven Deadly Sins. An Introduction to the History of a Religious Concept, with Special Reference to Medieval English History* (Ann Arbor, MI, 1952), 105–22. See also: Ferdinand Holthausen, ed., *Vices and Virtues, Being a Soul's Confession of Its Sins and Reason's Description of the Virtues. A Middle-English Dialogue of*

I. FOUNDATIONS 59

Principis offered a warning about what would happen to kings who did stray from the path of righteousness. While the first part set out the principles of kingship, the second and third used the examples of Henry II of England (r. 1152–1189) and his sons to show how the Angevins (the English royal family 1154–1399) had forfeited their right to rule through tyranny, greed, lasciviousness and impiety.[100] Failing to abide by the norms of power meant that kings would lose the throne.

Similar concepts were pervasive in letters. The eleventh and twelfth centuries witnessed a flourishing epistolary culture. Not every letter was directed at its nominal recipient. They could be stylistic exercises or could simply serve as a rhetorical device with which to communicate ideas to an audience of friends, peers and immediate dependants. Moreover, what we can surmise about their reception suggests that these were not private communications, but the subject of discussion and deliberation among the entourage of recipients and senders alike.[101] They also provided a tool with which to communicate complex

---

about 1200 A.D., Early English Text Society 89 and 159, 2 vols. (London, 1888–1921), in particular, vol. 1, 4–8, 48–58. Vincent of Beauvais' *De morali principis institutione* elaborated that a desire to rule caused pain and suffering to a king and his subjects (Vincent of Beauvais, *De Morali Principis Institutione*, ed. Robert J. Schneider, CCCM (Turnhout, 1995), ii.12, xxiii.115–20). The Norwegian *Konnungs Skuggsjá* similarly declared that the royal office was ordained by God, but humility was an essential virtue, and justice a prime duty (Berges, *Fürstenspiegel*, 159–84; Sverre Bagge, *The Political Thought of the King's Mirror* (Odense, 1987), 20–3, 92–4. See also *Speculum septentrionale*). Note too Gilbert of Tournai, *Eruditio regum et principum* (Louvain, 1914), 32–6; Egidio Colonna (Aegidius Romanus), *De Regimine Principum Libri III*, ed. F. Hieronymus Samaritanus (Rome, 1607; repr. Aalen, 1967), 125–8. These ideas also surfaced in legal treatises: *De legibus et consuetudinibus Angliae*, commonly ascribed to the English judge Henry Bracton, explained that royal power was supreme, and that it was a king's main duty to ensure the establishment and proper exercise of justice in his realm. Moreover, his plenitude of power had to coincide with modesty and temperance: a king was the vicar and servant of God. (Henricus de Bracton, *De legibus et consuetudinibus Angliae*, 2 vols., ed. George F. Woodbine (New Haven, CT, 1915–22), vol. 2, 305. Note also the *Sachsenspiegel*: Eike von Repgow, *Sachsenspiegel*, ed. K. A. Eckhardt, MGH Fontes iuris Germanici antiqui Nova Series 1–2, 2 vols. (Hanover, 1964–73) iii.52.2 (*Landrecht*). I am grateful to Susan Reynolds for this reference.)

[100] It comes as no surprise that, in its final redaction, *De Principis* was dedicated to Louis, the eldest son of the king of France, who in 1215 had been called upon to seize the throne from John, the last of Henry's sons.

[101] John Van Engen, 'Letters, schools and written culture in the eleventh and twelfth centuries', in *Dialektik und Rhetorik im früheren und hohen Mittelalter. Rezeption, Überlieferung und gesellschaftliche Wirkung antiker Gelehrsamkeit vornehmlich im 9. und 12. Jahrhundert*, ed. Johannes Fried (Munich, 1997), 97–132; Wim Verbaal, 'Epistolary voices and the fiction of history', in *Medieval Letters: Between Fiction and Document*, ed. Christian Høgel and Elisabetta Bartoli (Turnhout, 2015), 9–32; Giles Constable, 'Letter collections in the Middle Ages', in *Kuriale Briefkultur im späteren Mittelalter: Gestaltung – Überlieferung – Rezeption*, ed. Tanja Broser, Andreas Fischer and Matthias Thumser (Cologne, 2015), 35–54; Joel T. Rosenthal,

60   2. FOUNDATIONAL TEXTS

matters widely and succinctly. The letter sent in May 1128 by Pope Honorius II to congratulate Fulk of Anjou on his election as king of Jerusalem was representative of the genre. Fulk's emissaries had assured the pope that the king, who had reached his high office through divine providence, was a lover of justice and religion. Honorius confirmed Fulk's kingship, expressing his hope that Fulk would continue the strenuous defence of the faith practised by his predecessors, and that he would have the strength and humility to bear the vicissitudes of his office.[102] Other popes went a little further in defining what a love of justice and religion entailed, without, however, offering very detailed expositions. In 1071 Pope Alexander II had urged William the Conqueror to 'adorn the churches of Christ in your realm with true religion and just government ... [and] to defend members of the clergy from injustice and to protect widows, orphans, and the oppressed, mercifully coming to their succour'.[103] In 1117, Paschal II exhorted the king of Denmark to be a lover of churches and churchmen, a protector of widows and orphans, to exercise justice efficiently and to oppress those who rejected justice;[104] and in 1136 Innocent II exhorted King Stephen of England to be a lover of men of religion, a cultivator of peace and justice, an anxious consoler of widows and orphans and a devout defender of those who, through their own impotence could not defend themselves.[105]

Kings were supposed to maintain peace and justice by protecting those who could not protect themselves. Good rulers and good princes used their power wisely and reluctantly, and employed it against those who abused theirs. That was possible only if they also possessed the inner mindset and moral disposition necessary to do so.[106] Outward action merely reflected inner virtue. Perhaps the most explicit statement to this effect was a letter sent by Innocent III to Richard I of England in May 1198, in which the pope explained the symbolic significance

'Letters and letter collections', in *Understanding Medieval Primary Sources: Using Sources to Dscover Medieval Europe*, ed. Joel T. Rosenthal (London, 2012), 72–85; Walter Ysebaert, 'Medieval letters and letter collections as historical sources: methodological questions, reflections, and research perspectives (sixth to fifteenth centuries)', in *Medieval Letters*, ed. Høgel and Bartoli, 33–62.

[102] *Honorii II Epistolae*, PL 166, no. 68.

[103] *The Letters of Lanfranc Archbishop of Canterbury*, ed. and transl. Helen Clover and Margaret Gibson (Oxford, 1979), no. 7.

[104] *Paschalis II Epistolae*, PL 163, no. 497.

[105] *Innocentii II Epistolae*, PL 179, no. 250.

[106] *Register Gregors VII.*, ed. Erich Caspar, 2 vols. MGH Epistolae Selectae (Berlin, 1920–3), ii.73, v.10, vi.13, vii.5–6, vii.25. An English translation is available in *The Register of Pope Gregory VII*, transl. H. E. J. Cowdrey (Oxford, 2002), with identical sub-divisions; *Calixti II Epistolae*, PL 163, nos. 146, 156; *Paschali II Epistolae*, PL 163, no. 497; *Honorii II Epistolae*, PL 166, no. 68; *Innocentii II Epistolae*, PL 179, nos. 250, 416, 432; *Eugenii III Epistolae*, PL 180, no. 254; *Alexandri III Epistolae*, PL 196, nos. 29, 204, 1424, 1447; *Epistolae Pontificum Romanorum Ineditae*, ed. Samuel Loewenfeld (Leipzig, 1885), no. 421; *Letters of Lanfranc*, no. 7.

I. FOUNDATIONS   61

of four golden rings with which he presented the king. Roundness, Innocent stated, spoke of eternity, and was to remind the king of his duty to 'advance from the temporal to the eternal'; the number four suggested the equipoise of mind that a ruler was to maintain, 'which should neither be depressed by adversity nor elated by success', but it also stood for the virtues a king should exercise: justice (which Richard ought to maintain in his courts of law), courage (to be shown in times of adversity), prudence (to be exercised in difficult situations), temperance (never to be abandoned in success). Gold signified wisdom, without which other virtues could not be practised (and which, as the example of Solomon had shown, was the fount of just governance). Of the stones, which adorned these rings, the emerald symbolised faith; the sapphire hope; the garnet charity; and the topaz the practice of good works.[107] Justice, piety and charity flowed from a serene mind, courage and an unwillingness to surrender to fleeting emotions.[108] To be a king one had to think and feel like one.

Kingship was an office conferred by God, administered through the people and in recognition of the moral stature of the individual. Kings who violated their duties harmed not merely their people, but their Creator.[109] Their failure therefore provided a means with which to challenge them. In 1023/4, Count Odo II of Chartres wrote to King Robert II of France. He complained that the king had allowed Duke Richard II of Normandy to open proceedings against him without offering the count a fair hearing. Not only did Odo reject the king's right to judge him regarding his benefices (which he held by inheritance) or his services (which he had always provided loyally), but he also challenged Robert. By lending support to Richard, Robert betrayed the foundations of his office. While the discord caused by the king was thus troubling to Odo, it also took away 'root and fruit of your office, that is to say justice and peace'. The count therefore begged to be reconciled with the king.[110] In 1151, Knud, a claimant to the Danish throne, requested that Conrad III of Germany aid him against his rival Sven. The king of kings had selected Conrad to be a father to justice and a son of peace. Therefore, Conrad had to ensure that justice was done and that those who suffered unjust afflictions were consoled. The duty extended to exiles who had fled to the Roman empire for succour. Conrad should recover with his sword the kingship of which Knud had unjustly been deprived, not least because doing so would strengthen his own honour.[111] Both

---

[107] *Selected Letters of Pope Innocent III Concerning England (1198–1216)*, ed. and transl. C. R. Cheney and W. H. Semple (London, 1953), no. 1.

[108] See also *Innocentii II epistolae*, no. 432.

[109] *Register Gregors VII.*, v.10. See also *Innocentii II Epistolae*, nos. 250, 416.

[110] *The Letters and Poems of Fulbert of Chartres*, ed. and transl. Frederick Behrends (Oxford, 1976), no. 86.

[111] *Das Briefbuch des Abts Wibald von Stablo und Corvey*, ed. Martina Hartmann after preparatory work by Heinz Zatschek and Timothy Reuter, 3 vols., MGH Epistolae (Hanover, 2012), no. 315.

62   2. FOUNDATIONAL TEXTS

Robert and Conrad risked betraying the very purpose of their office if they did not protect the weak and powerless.[112]

Whether composing letters, works of exegesis or formal treatises on power, high medieval writers drew on a well-established biblical, classical and patristic legacy. It constituted the framework within which observers and actors Europe engaged with the norms and principles of secular lordship in general, and of good kingship in particular. Yet when it came to translating abstract precept into concrete action, these models offered little practical guidance. At best, they highlighted the need for prudent counsellors. Kings, St Stephen instructed his son, should respect their nobles and treasure their bishops. They should also listen to their clergy, a point repeatedly made in papal letters, too.[113] Abstract principles still had to be imbued with concrete meaning. Patristic writers had sought to mould biblical precepts and classical precedents to fit societies without or with only limited imperial or royal authority. Their later readers had to apply ideas developed in relation to urbanised communities and their ecclesiastical leaders to rather different polities, operating on a considerably larger geographical scale, and within a very different social and political setting. What might have been deemed feasible in fourth- and fifth-century Hippo and Milan might be less suited to eleventh- and twelfth-century Castile and Germany.

In applying this legacy, high medieval observers confronted several challenges. For instance, beyond the actual choosing of a king, biblical, classical and patristic writings envisaged little in terms of formalised mechanisms to ensure good governance. A ruler's character had to suffice as guarantee of future good conduct. Yet bad kings inevitably brought harm and suffering upon their people. They provoked God to unleash famine, pestilence, rebellions and foreign invaders. There was every reason to ensure that the right person was chosen. Indeed, because they had chosen a king, the people were held responsible for his conduct. In Ezekiel 3:18, God had warned: 'If I warn the wicked, saying, "You are under the penalty of death", but you fail to deliver the warning, they will die in their sins. And I will hold you responsible for their deaths.'[114] By failing to upbraid and admonish, the

---

[112] See also the letters sent by the citizens of Rome to Conrad III in 1149/50: *Briefbuch des Abts Wibald*, nos. 197, 199, 340. For the context: Jürgen Petersohn, *Kaisertum und Rom in spätsalischer und staufischer Zeit* (Hanover, 2010), 80–130, and, for events of 1149–51, 113–20; Matthias Thumser, 'Die frühe römische Kommune und die staufischen Herrscher in der Briefsammlung Wibalds von Stablo', *DA* 57 (2001), 111–47.

[113] *Register Gregors VII.*, ii.73; vi.13; vii. 5-6, 25; viii.20, 25; *Calixti II Epistolae*, PL 163, no. 146; *Alexandri III Epistolae*, PL 196, nos. 29, 204, 1424, 1447; *Eugenii III Epistolae*, PL 180, nos. 254, 296; *Innocentii II Epistolae*, no. 426; *Briefbuch des Abts Wibald*, no. 382.

[114] See also Leviticus 19:17; 1 Samuel 8:9; Ezekiel 33:6, 8, 12; 2 Thessalonians 3:15; Matthew 18:15.

people – or at least their leaders – endangered both their eternal souls and that of the king. Similar ideas were expressed by Gregory the Great. Men who held power over others were responsible for the moral conduct of their subordinates: 'For leaders ought to know that if they ever do anything wrong, they will deserve as many deaths as they engender among their subordinates.'[115] It was the duty of the spiritual rector, in turn, to guide, advise and, if required, reprimand the mighty.[116] What, though, did this mean in practice? It was all well and good to know that Samuel and Nathan had admonished Saul and David. But what did their example mean when the Danes were confronted with the likes of King Olaf Hunger – thus named because of the famine he unleashed – or the Saxons with Emperor Henry IV, who, they feared, was about to destroy their liberties and rape their mothers, wives and daughters?[117]

Moreover, because the people chose to have a king, he would have absolute power over them. He could not be challenged, unless he defied the will of God. Even then it fell to God – not the people – to sanction him. That, at least, was the message of the Old Testament. David's transgression might have resulted in rebellions as divine punishment, but the rebels still defied the will of God. Solomon's children may have been deprived of the right to rule, but those who replaced them were nonetheless tyrants. How, then, could the seeming contradiction be resolved between owing absolute obedience to a ruler and restraining him if he transgressed? And what did this mean in situations that neither the authors of the Bible nor Seneca or Cicero could have foreseen? What, for instance, was to be done when new kingships were created? What if there was uncertainty about who was the legitimate heir? What was the role of princes and magnates, of margraves, counts and dukes? The writings of the ancients certainly helped shape the parameters within which such questions were asked. They also provided the conceptual toolkit with which to pose them. But they did not necessarily provide the answers. That task fell to others: to princes and prelates, to their advisors and counsellors and to those who remembered, who wrote about and who sought to evaluate the actions taken and the choices made. It is to their efforts that we now must turn.

---

[115] Gregory, *Regula*, iii.4, vol. 2, pp. 282–90.

[116] See, similarly, Ciceronian concepts of friendship: Cicero, *De Amicitia*, transl. William Armistead Falconer (Cambridge, MA, 1946), xiii.44, pp. 156–7; xxiv.89, pp. 196–7; xxv.91, pp. 198–9.

[117] Steffen Patzold, 'Die Lust des Herrschers. Zur Bedeutung und Verbreitung eines politischen Vorwurfs zur Zeit Heinrichs IV', in *Heinrich IV.*, ed. Gerd Althoff (Ostfildern, 2009), 219–59.

PART II

Creating Kingship

They are most successful at the political game, who sully their hands just enough that the stains of their ambition can be washed off. The central Middle Ages were no exception. What was, however, different was the particular cultural framework, the horizon of expectations within which the game unfolded, the prize awaiting those excelling at it and the cast of players. It is with these three – framework, prize and players – that the following chapters are concerned. In taking this approach, attention is drawn to aspects that rarely feature in modern studies of the origins of regnal status, where the focus has been mostly on disentangling kernels of historical truth from later narratives.[1] With few exceptions, medieval accounts tell us not how royal status had *actually*, but how it had *essentially* been created. What mattered was what the moment of inception revealed about the ideal ordering of the realm. Recovering that story was about constructing lessons for the present, and about finding ways of coming to terms with the tensions inherent in the king-making process – between divine favour and the need for recognition, for instance, or between the premise of overwhelming royal power and the threat of tyranny.

For us, such accounts provide an opportunity. They highlight the range of answers available to contemporary and later observers, and they illuminate how tensions and contradictions could be exploited. They also show that we are dealing not with simple binaries of good vs. evil, but with a complex web of expectations and interpretations. Sometimes these reinforced each other, and sometimes they existed in competition. But navigating them, ensuring that a particular reading was accepted, was essential. Norms bound the parties voicing

---

[1] This is not to deny the value of these efforts. For a magisterial set of case studies, see *Christianization*, ed. Berend. My own approach follows that proposed by Beumann, 'Die Historiographie des Mittelalters' and Graus, 'Die Herrschersagen des Mittelalters'. See also Jacek Banaszkiewicz, 'Königliche Karrieren von Hirten, Gärtner und Pflügern', *Saeculum* 33 (1982), 265–86; Banaszkiewicz, 'Slavonic *origines regni*: hero the law-giver and founder of monarchy (introductory survey of problems)', *Acta Poloniae Historica* 69 (1989), 97–131. I also learned much from Patrick Vinton Kirch, *How Chiefs Became Kings: Divine Kingship and the Rise of Archaic States in Ancient Hawai'i* (Berkeley, CA, 2010) and J. H. Walker, *Power and Prowess: the Origins of Brooke Kingship in Sarawak* (Honolulu, 2002).

them as much as the putative kings who had been exhorted to abide by them. Much therefore hinged on the ability to control and shape that process of interpretation. It could make the difference between success and failure, between being a legitimate participant in the affairs of the realm and a violent disturber of the right order of the world.

3

Becoming King

For there to be kingship, there had to be kings. But how were kings made? If kingship was solely God's to give, did laying claim to regal status not defy the divine will? How then could kings be distinguished from usurpers? Most high medieval observers also accepted that royal status required considerable power, and a willingness to use it. People who abhorred violence and bloodshed were better off joining a monastery. Yet too much force, an inability or unwillingness to view violence as a tool to be used with restraint, was frowned upon. Assessing a potential ruler's suitability required that both the extent of his secular might and his virtue be examined. Recounting the origins of royal status provided an opportunity to outline principles of righteous rule. Because a royal title reflected both virtue and might, their relationship was discussed and conceptualised. And because kingship had to be recognised, such accounts were always about more than just one individual's path to the throne. They provided an opportunity to imagine an ideal order of the world, while also highlighting the snares and pitfalls, the dangers and challenges to be faced in turning abstract norms into political practice.

3.1   The Emergence of Kingship

The history of kings was inextricably linked to that of the communities over which they presided. Yet, when did that history begin? Sometimes its starting point was conditioned by a kingdom's origins: William of Tyre opened his account of the kingdom of Jerusalem with the Islamic conquests of the seventh century, the subsequent history of the Middle East and the First Crusade. More common were points of particular significance in a community's past. William of Malmesbury's *Gesta Regum Anglorum* opened with the arrival of the Saxons in England in 459 CE,[1] the *Chronicon Roskildense* with the baptism at Mainz of

---

[1] William of Malmesbury, *Gesta Regum Anglorum*, ed. and transl. R. A. B. Mynors, R. M. Thomson and M. Winterbottom, 2 vols. (Oxford, 1998–9), vol. 1, 16–17. This section builds on and revises Björn Weiler, 'Tales of first kings and the culture of kingship in the west, c. 1050–1200', *Viator* 46:2 (2015), 101–28, at 105–11, and Weiler, 'Crown-giving and king-making in the west, c. 1000 – c. 1250', *Viator* 41 (2010), 57–88, at 70–1.

King Harald of Denmark[2] and Theodoric the Monk's *Historia de Antiquitate Regum Norwagiensium* with the reign of Harald Fairhair and the discovery of Iceland (*c.* 890).[3] William followed the model of Bede, whose ecclesiastical history of the English had opened with the so-called Anglo-Saxon invasions. King Harald's baptism marked the entry of Denmark into a community of Christian nations. Harald Fairhair had united most of Norway under his control, with the majority of his rivals slain or exiled. The history of the realm long pre-dated a particular ruler's reign. But the latter still marked a new and significant stage in the development of the kingdom and its people.

Even more popular was a short survey of the geography of a realm, perhaps even of its connection with the Bible or classical antiquity. Openings of this type can be found in Thietmar of Merseburg, Richer of St Remi or Henry of Huntingdon,[4] writing respectively in France around 1000, Germany around 1020 and England *c.* 1135–54. The approach seems to have been even more popular in newer realms. It was adopted by the Gallus Anonymus in his *Gesta Principum Polonorum* from *c.* 1110–13;[5] the *Historia Norwegie*, probably written *c.* 1150–75;[6] and the *Gesta Hungarorum* by the 'Anonymous

---

[2] *Chronicon Roskildense*, in *Scriptores Minores*, ed. Gertz, vol. 1, 14. On the text see: Michael H. Gelting, 'Two early twelfth-century views of Denmark's Christian past', in *Historical Narratives and Christian Identity on a European Periphery. Early Historical Writing in Northern, East-Central, and Eastern Europe*, ed. Ildar Garipzanov (Turnhout, 2011), 33–55, at 49–53. See also the *Historia Francorum Senonensis*, MGH SSrG 9, 364, which started with the appointment of Pippin as majordomus in 688, and Rodulfus Glaber, *Historiarum libri quinqui*, in *Rodulphus Glaber: Opera*, ed. and transl. John France (Oxford, 1989), 1–11, starting in the year 900 CE.

[3] Theodorus Monachus, Historia De Antiquitate Regum Norwagiensium, in *Monumenta Historica Norwegiae. Latinske Kildeskrifter til Norges Historie i Middelalderen*, ed. Gustav Storm (Kristiana, 1880), 7–9. On the text: Sverre Bagge, 'Theodericus Monachus: the kingdom of Norway and the history of salvation', in *Historical Narratives*, ed. Garipzanov, 71–90.

[4] Thietmar of Merseburg, *Chronicon*, transl. Werner Trillmich (Darmstadt, 1974) (reprinting the Latin text of *Thietmari Merseburgensis episcopi Chronicon*, ed. Friedrich Kurze, MGH SSrG (Hanover, 1889)), i.2–4, pp. 9–13; Richer of St Remi, *Histories*, transl. Justin Lake, 2 vols. (Cambridge, MA, 2011), vol. 1, 8–11; Henry, Archdeacon of Huntingdon, *Historia Anglorum*, ed. and transl. Diana Greenway (Oxford, 1996), 10–17. On geographical prefaces see also: Lars Boje Mortensen, 'The language of geographical description in twelfth-century Scandinavian Latin', *Filologia Latina* 12 (2005), 102–21; Matthew Kempshall, *Rhetoric and the Writing of History, 400–1500* (Manchester, 2011), 35–52. For a specific case study: Jacek Banaszkiewicz, 'Slawische Sagen "De origine Gentis" (al-Masudi, Nestor, Kadlubek, Kosmas). Dioskurische Matrizen der Überlieferung', *Mediaevalia Historia Bohemica* 3 (1993), 29–58.

[5] *Gesta Principum Polonorum. The Deeds of the Princes of the Poles*, ed. and transl. Paul W. Knoll and Frank Schaer (Budapest, 2003), 10–15.

[6] *Historia Norwegie*, ed. Inger Ekrem and Lars Boje Mortensen, transl. Peter Fisher (Copenhagen, 2003), 23 (for the dating), 52–75. On the text: Lars Boje Mortensen, 'Historia Norwegie and Sven Aggesen: two pioneers in comparison', in *Historical Writing*, ed. Garipzanov, 57–70.

II. CREATING KINGSHIP 69

Hungarian Notary', most likely composed *c.* 1200–30.[7] Furthermore, it was important to demonstrate just how ancient a community was by linking it to Troy, Rome, the Bible or the legendary heroes of antiquity. Perhaps the most famous example for this approach was Geoffrey of Monmouth's imaginary pedigree of the Welsh as descendants of Brutus the Trojan.[8] Just as popular was that chosen *c.* 1235 by Rodrigo Jiménez de Rada. His history of Spain started with the sons of Noah, whose grandson Tubal (the fifth son of Japheth) received Spain,[9] before turning to the deeds of Hercules in the peninsula[10] and ultimately to the origins and history of the Goths and their conquest of Iberia.[11] The vernacular *Kaiserchronik*, or chronicle of emperors (*c.* 1150), embarked on its narrative with a short account of Roman history and the election of Julius (Caesar), but also insisted on the prominent role that the Germans had from the outset played in the affairs of imperial Rome.[12] Antiquity was not always invoked so as to enlist a Roman pedigree. Saxo Grammaticus (*c.* 1200) wrote a history of Danish kings in which events in the north pre-dated or surpassed the most glorious feats of the Romans.[13] Others sought to place the origins of a realm and its dynasty in the mists of time. Cosmas of Prague began with the wanderings of Noah's descendants, some of whom eventually settled in what became Bohemia.[14] Several approaches could be combined, as in Vincent Kadlubek's *Chronica Polonorum*: he asserted that a mythical Roman patrician, Gracchus, was the

---

[7] *Anonimi Bele regis notarii Gesta Hungarorum et Magistri Rogerii Epistolae in miserabile Carmen super destruction Regni Hungariae per tartaros facta*, ed. and transl. Martin Rady, János M. Bak and László Veszprémy (Budapest and New York, 2010), 4–11. On the text: László Veszprémy, '"More paganismo": reflections on the pagan and Christian past in the Gesta Hungarorum of the Hungarian Anonymous Notary', in *Historical Writing*, ed. Garipzanov, 183–201.

[8] Geoffrey of Monmouth, *The History of the Kings of Britain*, ed. Michael D. Reeve, transl. Neil Wright (Woodbridge, 2007), 5–31. See, generally, Kordula Wolf, *Troja – Metamorphosen eines Mythos: Französische, englische und italienische Überlieferungen des 12. Jahrhunderts im Vergleich* (Berlin, 2008).

[9] *Roderici Jimenii de Rada Historia de Rebus Hispaniae sive Historia Gothorum*, ed. Juan Fernández Valorde, in *Jimenii de Rada Opera Omnia I*, CCCM (Turnhout, 1987), 10–14. On the text: Peter Linehan, *History and Historians of Medieval Spain* (Oxford, 1993), 350–411.

[10] *Roderici Jimenii Historia*, 14–19.

[11] *Roderici Jimenii Historia*, 20–38.

[12] *Kaiserchronik eines Regensburger Geistlichen*, ed. Eduard Schröder, MGH Deutsche Chroniken (Hanover, 1895), 81–5.

[13] Martin Groh, 'Das Deutschlandbild in den historischen Büchern der Gesta Danorum', in *Saxo and the Baltic Region. A Symposium*, ed. Tore Nyberg (Odense, 2004), 143–60.

[14] Cosmas of Prague, *Cosmae Pragensis Chronica Boemorum*, ed. Bertold Bretholz, MGH SSrG NS (Berlin, 1923), 4–7; English translation: Cosmas of Prague, *The Chronicle of the Czechs*, transl. Lisa Wolverton (Washington, DC, 2009), 33–6. On Cosmas: Plassmann, *Origo Gentis*, 321–55; Kersken, *Geschichtsschreibung*, 573–82; Lisa Wolverton, *Cosmas of Prague: Narrative, Classicism, Politics* (Washington, DC, 2014).

70   3. BECOMING KING

first ruler of the Poles.[15] All approaches have in common that they asserted and documented just how ancient (and hence legitimate) a community was.

How did authors describe the origins of kingship? In most cases, kingship was assumed to be a constant. The *Historia Norwegie* traced the rulers of Norway back to the Swedish line of god-kings,[16] and in William of Malmesbury's *Gesta Regum* Hengist and Horsa found the British to be ruled by kings already.[17] Only a handful of texts sought to explain the establishment of indigenous rulership, with Cosmas of Prague's *Chronica* the most elaborate. Cosmas drew on the Old Testament account of the origins of Israelite kingship, as well as on influences from classical literature, notably Ovid's concept of the three ages, that is, the gradual decline from a blissful golden age to ones of silver and bronze.[18] The early Bohemians, Cosmas informs us, had lived in innocent bliss. However, as their wealth grew, so did divisions among them. The trend was exacerbated by the fact that they had no prince or lord to do justice for them. In their absence, the Bohemians turned to rich men. One of these, Krok, had three daughters. Among them was Libuše, a prophetess. One day, when Libuše decided a case, one of the claimants felt insulted at being judged by a woman. Libuše responded by declaring that, just as the doves had chosen as their king the kite, who invented new crimes and killed his people, so the Bohemians would acquire a new ruler in the husband she was now going to take. The prophetess and her sisters convened an assembly, where she explained just what it meant to have a duke. He would be easy to appoint, but difficult to depose. Everything the Bohemians owned would be his. They would live in perpetual fear. He would make some of them peasants, some millers, some tax collectors. He would enslave their children and raid their possessions. Still, the people persisted, and so Libuše directed them to find their duke in a man ploughing his fields close to a nearby town. The citizens went to find the duke, Přemysl, who only understood what they desired after they repeated it several times. Before setting out to meet Libuše, the new duke nonetheless insisted that his cheap shoes, made from tree cork, should be taken with him and preserved in perpetuity as a reminder to his progeny whence they had come. Once married to the prophetess, Přemysl 'restrained his savage people with laws, tamed the untamed populace by his

---

[15] Vincent Kadlubek, *Die Chronik der Polen des Magister Vincentius*, transl. Eduard Mühle (Darmstadt, 2014) (reprinting the Latin text of *Magistri Vincentii dicti Kadubek Chronica Polonorum*, ed. Marian Plezia, Monumenta Poloniae Historica Nova Series (Kraków, 1994)), 92–9. On Vincent: Thomas N. Bisson, 'Witness to crisis? Power and resonance in the *Chronicle of the Poles* by Wincenty Kadłubek', in *Gallus Anonymus*, ed. Stopka, 205–13; Darius von Güttner-Sporzynski, ed., *Writing History in Medieval Poland: Bishop Vincentius of Cracow and the 'Chronica Polonorum'* (Turnhout, 2017).
[16] *Historia Norwegie*, 74–5.
[17] William of Malmesbury, *Gesta Regum*, vol. 1, 20–1.
[18] Wolverton, *Cosmas of Prague*, 119–39.

II. CREATING KINGSHIP

command, and subjected them to the servitude by which they are now oppressed'.[19]

Other writers stressed practical needs in the establishment of rulership. The anonymous Hungarian notary recalled that seven leaders of the Scythians had decided to leave their crowded ancestral lands to conquer a new home, the future Hungary. However, they believed that a military expedition was unlikely to succeed unless they appointed a lord and commander. Hence they chose as their leader Álmos, to whom and to whose descendants they and their progeny would forever remain loyal.[20] The office of duke sprang from the demands of war. In Sicily, according to Amatus of Montecassino, the twelve leaders of the early Normans likewise chose one of their number to lead their conquests.[21] Other accounts described as the chief duty of rulers providing their people with laws. St Stephen of Hungary not only introduced Christianity and organised the Church, but also codified its laws.[22] In fact, much of the saint's cult centred on Stephen's codification of legal customs.[23] Finally, when, at the beginning of the twelfth century, Gallus Anonymus looked back to the creation of the Polish kingship a century earlier, he remarked at length on the first Polish king's love of justice:

> if some poor peasant or some ordinary woman came with a complaint against a duke or count, no matter how important the matters [Boleslaw I] was engaged in, amid the throng and press of his lords and officers, he would not stir from the spot before he had heard the full account of the complaint and sent a chamberlain to fetch the lord against whom the complaint had been made.[24]

The beginning of rulership equalled the codification and enforcement of law.[25]

---

[19] Cosmas, *Chronik*, 6–18. English translation: *Chronicle of the Czechs*, transl. Wolverton, 37–49. On the scene and theme: Banaszkiewicz, 'Königliche Karrieren'; Paul Freedman, *Images of the Medieval Peasant* (New Haven, CT, 1999), 209–11; Patrick J. Geary, *Women at the Beginning. Origin Myths from the Amazons to the Virgin Mary* (Princeton, NJ, 2006), 35–41.

[20] *Anonimi Gesta Hungarorum*, 18–19.

[21] Amatus of Montecassino, *Storia de'Normanni volgarizzata in antico francese*, ed. Vincenzo de Bartholomaeis (Rome, 1935), ii.18, p. 76; ii.29, pp. 93–4; Amatus of Montecassino, *The History of the Normans*, transl. Prescott N. Dunbar, rev. and introduced by Graham A. Loud (Woodbridge, 2004), 70, 76. William of Apulia, *La Geste de Robert Guiscard*, ed. and transl. Marguerite Mathieu (Palermo, 1965), ll. 218–40; *Chronicon Monasterii Casinensis*, ed. Hartmut Hoffmann, MGH SS 34 (Hanover, 1980), 299. Theo Broekmann, *Rigor Iustitiae. Herrschaft, Recht und Terror im normannisch-staufischen Süden (1050-1250)* (Darmstadt, 2005), 29–32.

[22] *Legenda maior*, in *Legenda S. Stephani regis maior et minor, atque legenda ab Hartwico episcopo conscripta*, ed. Emma Bartoniek, in *Scriptores Rerum Hungaricarum*, ed. Emerich Szentpétery, 2 vols. (Budapest, 1937–8), vol. 2, 363–440, at 384.

[23] Gábor Klaniczay, *Holy Rulers and Blessed Princesses. Dynastic Cults in Medieval Central Europe*, transl. Éva Pálmai (Cambridge, 2002), 123–34.

[24] *Gesta Principum Polonorum*, i.9, pp. 48–9.

[25] Banaszkiewicz, 'Slavonic origines regni'.

72   3. BECOMING KING

Several of these examples relate to rulership below the level of king. But then the moral obligation to do justice and to lead the defence of one's lands applied to everyone wielding secular power. Between 1059 and 1063, Peter Damian (c. 1007–1072/3), a leading figure at the papal court, expanded on the subject in two letters to Duke Godfrey of Tuscany. Peter berated the magnate for enjoying the fruits of power and shunning its duties. He suggested that Godfrey should either surrender lands if he felt unable to rule them, or appoint suitable men to act in his stead. While he held the power of absolute judgement in his lands, Godfrey would have to account before God for the use he had made of it. Few things would be more pleasing to God than to deter those who were about to commit unlawful acts, to prevent them from incurring divine wrath for their evil deeds, to force them to be content with what they had already and, equally, to ensure that the innocent (in particular widows, orphans and those who had unjustly been robbed of their possessions) would not suffer from crime, that they need not fear for their possessions and that they could freely praise the bounty of the Lord.[26] Lords and kings alike were supposed to act on behalf those given into their care.

Where precisely, though, was the dividing line between noble and royal power to be drawn? As far as high medieval observers were concerned, the key difference was rooted in the material resources that an individual could muster, and in the extent to which his office was dependent on divine backing. Kings were assumed to be more powerful than any of their subjects. Peter Damian praised Godfrey's predecessor, Hugh of Tuscany, who, on realising that he would not be able to perform his duties, had surrendered Spoleto to Emperor Otto III. Unlike Godfrey, he gave his lands to someone more powerful – and hence capable of being a good judge. Peter furthermore hinted at the rewards reaped by Hugh: though not strictly a saint, he nonetheless appeared in a posthumous vision to a Florentine abbot.[27] Ideas comparable to Peter's were expressed when the advisors of Roger II suggested that he resurrect the ancient kingship of Sicily: someone as powerful as he deserved to be more than a mere duke.[28] The *Gesta Principum Polonorum* made the same point.

---

[26] *Die Briefe des Peter Damian*, ed. Kurt Reindel, MGH Epistolae, 4 vols. (Hanover, 1983–93), vol. 2, nos. 67–8. See also Christopher D. Fletcher, 'Rhetoric, reform and Christian eloquence: the letter form and religious thought of Peter Damian', *Viator* 46 (2015), 61–91.

[27] *Briefe des Peter Damian*, vol. 2, no. 68. The spectre requested that the corpse be turned so that it lay on its back, not its chest.

[28] *Alexandri Telesini Abbatis Ystoria Rogerii Regis Sicilie Calabriae atque Apulie*, ed. Ludovica de Nava, with a historical commentary by Dione Clementi (Rome, 1991), 23. For secondary accounts see G. A. Loud, *The Latin Church in Norman Sicily* (Cambridge, 2007), 150–8; Philippe Buc, '1701 in medieval perspective. Monarchical rituals between the Middle Ages and modernity', *Majestas* 10 (2002), 91–124; Hubert Houben, *Roger II. von Sizilien. Herrscher zwischen Orient und Okzident* (Darmstadt, 1997), 53–4, and Josef Deér, *Papsttum und Normannen. Untersuchungen zu ihren lehnsrechtlichen und*

II. CREATING KINGSHIP 73

Recounting how Emperor Otto III had given a crown to Boleslaw I, it had the emperor exclaim that someone as mighty as Boleslaw deserved to be more than just a duke.[29] Yet secular might, and kingship in particular, was also a token of divine benevolence. The connection was made, for instance, in 1077, when Gregory VII outlined to the king of Denmark that it was the monarch's duty to maintain the honour of and defend the kingdom with which he had been entrusted by God.[30] Comparable statements can be found in the coronation liturgy, and they abound in narrative sources.[31] Suggestively, the *Chronicon Roskildense* opened with the baptism of the Danish King Harald in the ninth century. In the *Historia Norwegie*, Olaf Tryggvason, not the first Christian ruler, but the one most energetic in promoting the conversion of his people, stands out for receiving far more detailed coverage than his predecessors.[32] The *Historia*'s comment on Olaf's foster father, Håkon the Wicked, an obstinate pagan who had brought all of Norway under his control, establishes a helpful contrast. He still preferred – 'in the same way as his predecessors' – the title of jarl to that of king.[33] Pagans could – and would – not be kings.

Kings often had their future status foretold in dreams and visions. William of Tyre recorded a vision, in which the mother of Godfrey, the first ruler of crusader Jerusalem, foresaw that the first of her sons (Godfrey) would be a duke, the second (Baldwin, Godfrey's successor) a king and the third (Eustace) a count.[34] The mother of Álmos dreamt that she had been impregnated by a falcon. The bird announced that glorious kings would spring from the fruit of her loins.[35] Gunnhild, while pregnant with the future King Sverrir

---

kirchenpolitischen Beziehungen (Cologne and Vienna, 1972), 214–15; Rudolf Hiestand, 'Zur Geschichte des Königreichs Sizilien im 12. Jahrhundert', *Quellen und Forschungen aus italienischen Archiven und Bibliotheken* 73 (1993), 52–69, at 52–7.

[29] *Gesta Principum Polonorum*, i.6, pp. 34–9. See, for similar examples, *Einhardi Vita Karoli Magni*, ed. and transl. Reinhold Rau, *Quellen zur Karolingischen Reichsgeschichte*, 3 vols. (Darmstadt 1955–60), vol. 1, 168–9; *Narratio de electione Lotharii*, MGH SSrG 12 (Hanover, 1856), 510.

[30] *Register Gregors VII.*, v.10. See also above, Chapter 2.

[31] Reinhard Elze, 'The ordo for the coronation of Roger II of Sicily: an example of dating by internal evidence', in *Coronations. Medieval and Early Modern Monarchic Ritual*, ed. Janos M. Bak (Berkeley, Los Angeles and Oxford, 1990), 165–78, at 170–2; Elze, 'Königskrönung und Ritterweihe. Der Burgundische Ordo für die Weihe und Krönung des Königs und der Königin', in *Institutionen, Kultur und Gesellschaft im Mittelalter. Festschrift für Josef Fleckenstein zu seinem 65. Geburtstag*, ed. Lutz Fenske, Werner Rösener and Thomas Zotz (Sigmaringen, 1984), 327–42, no. 1; Reinhard Elze, ed., *Die Ordines für die Weihe und Krönung des Kaisers und der Kaiserin* (Hanover, 1960), nos. ix.2, 8; xi.6–8. See also below, Chapter 9.

[32] *Historiae Norwegie*, 90–101.

[33] *Historia Norwegie*, 89–91.

[34] *Willelmi Tyrensis Archiepiscopi Chronicon*, ed. R. B. C. Huygens in cooperation with H. E. Mayer and G. Rösch, CCCM, 2 vols. (Turnhout, 1986), vol. 2, 427.

[35] *Anonimi Gesta Hungarorum*, 13–15.

74   3. BECOMING KING

of Norway, had a dream in which she gave birth to an enormous white and
radiant stone from which sparks emanated, resembling those of a furnace.
When she sought to hide the stone, covering it with blankets, it still shone
through its coverings.[36] The meaning of the dream was never stated explicitly,
but later events revealed that Sverrir was not in fact the son of Gunnhild's
husband, but of King Sigurd, and it was on the authority of this revelation that
Sverrir set out to claim the throne.[37] Supernatural endorsements were not
limited to the early years of kings. While on a raid in Britain, Olaf Tryggvason
encountered a hermit who revealed that Olaf would become king of Norway
and a great promoter of Christianity.[38] According to the *Gesta Principum
Polonorum*, in the mists of time two strangers visited the town of Gniezno,
just as the duke celebrated the cutting of his son's hair. When asking for food,
they were turned away. Meanwhile, a ploughman, Piast, was celebrating the
cutting of *his* son's hair. He welcomed the mysterious visitors. The strangers
accepted his hospitality, and expressed the hope that their presence would
bring riches and honour to the peasant and his progeny. In due course, it was
Piast's son who, through divine backing, rose to the rulership of Poland.[39] Nor
was it necessarily the king or his family who experienced such visions.
Alexander of Telese recounted two dreams announcing as imminent the
kingship of Roger II of Sicily to an old woman and a priest,[40] and Albert of
Aachen reported similar visions concerning Godfrey's leadership of crusader
Jerusalem, experienced by a knight and a priest respectively.[41] Godfrey or
Roger did not claim the throne: God assigned it to them.

Divine blessing did not come *ex nihilo*. First kings had been destined for
great things because of their innate suitability. How did that manifest itself?
They were reluctant to assume the royal dignity. Hesitation was sometimes
implied, sometimes publicly demonstrated. Those who were the first to claim
a royal title were never the first leaders of their people. Håkon, not Olaf, had
united Norway; Stephen was not the first duke of the Hungarians, but the first
born a Christian, and the same was true of Boleslaw I in Poland. They did not
usurp power. It was bequeathed to them. Sometimes, rulers even had to be
forced to assume it. Sverrir only claimed the throne once his father's erstwhile

---

[36] *The Saga of King Sverri of Norway (Sverrisaga)*, transl. J. Sephton (London, 1899, repr.
Llanerch, 1994), 2.

[37] Perhaps less spectacularly, the parents of Boleslaw I conceived their first-born son only
after having made a donation to the shrine of St Fides at Conques: *Gesta Principum
Polonorum*, 6–9. See also: *Legenda S. Stephani*, in Scriptores Rerum Hungaricarum, ed.
Szentpétery, vol. 2, 379.

[38] *Historia Norwegie*, 92–5.

[39] *Gesta Principum Polonorum*, i.1–2, pp. 16–23.

[40] *Alexandri Telesini Ystoria*, 84–7.

[41] Albert of Aachen, *Historia Ierosolimitana. History of the Journey to Jerusalem*, ed. and
transl. Susan B. Edgington (Oxford, 2007), 446–51. See also *Legenda minor*, in Legenda
S. Stephani, in *Scriptores Rerum Hungaricarum*, ed. Szentpétery, vol. 2, 412–14.

II. CREATING KINGSHIP

followers had threatened to kill him if he did not.[42] In Hungary Stephen assumed the title of king at the behest of his people, and Álmos led the Hungarians exclusively at their request. Even Roger II had to be persuaded. Only after he had been told on three separate occasions that he *should* be king did he relent.[43] They did not seek the throne, but had it thrust upon them.

Hesitation confirmed that putative rulers possessed the right frame of mind to act like kings. In line with Cicero and St Augustine, they assume the throne out of obedience to wishes of their people and of God, not because they took delight in dominion over others. Nevertheless, moral suitability had to be demonstrated through action. The older legend of St Stephen reports that, immediately following his coronation, the Hungarian king convened an assembly of prelates to codify the laws of his kingdom.[44] According to Sven Aggesen, the first king of the Danes was called Skjold 'because he used to protect most nobly all the boundaries of the realm with the shielding power of his kingship'. It was a pun on his name, which meant 'shield'.[45] Often, kingship was the reward for fulfilling a ruler's duties while the recipient of the honour was still merely a duke or count.[46] In the case of St Stephen, defending his realm against pagan foes and organising the Church prefigured his installation as king.[47] Boleslaw I merited royal title by his extraordinary love of justice, his generosity and his martial prowess.[48] Successful kingship meant seeing that

---

[42] *Saga of King Sverri*, 12–13. See also below, Chapters 7 and 8.

[43] First kings also demonstrated their reluctance in visible ways: in 919, Henry I, the first Saxon ruler of east Francia, refused to receive unction, and Godfrey of Bouillon rejected the title of king of Jerusalem (which, he claimed, belonged to Christ alone): Ernst Karpf, 'Königserhebung ohne Salbung. Zur politischen Bedeutung von Heinrichs I. ungewöhnlichem Verzicht in Fritzlar (919)', *Hessisches Jahrbuch für Landesgeschichte* 34 (1984), 1–24; Jonathan Riley-Smith, 'The title of Godfrey de Bouillon', *Bulletin of the Institute of Historical Research* 52 (1979), 83–6; John France, 'The election and title of Godfrey de Bouillon', *Canadian Journal of History* 18 (1983), 321–9. Björn Weiler, 'The *rex renitens* and the medieval ideal of kingship, c. 950–1250', *Viator* 31 (2000), 1–42', at 1–9, collates further examples.

[44] *Legenda maior*, in *Legenda S. Stephani*, in *Scriptores Rerum Hungaricarum*, ed. Szentpétery, vol. 2, 384.

[45] Sven Aggesen, *Brevis Historia*, in *Scriptores Minores*, ed. Gertz, vol. 1, 96–7. On the text: Mortensen, '*Historia Norwegie*', 59–61.

[46] See also below, Chapters 5–8.

[47] *Scriptores Rerum Hungaricarum*, vol. 2, 383–4.

[48] *Gesta Principum Polonorum*, i.6–7, i.12, pp. 32–7, 40–7, 56–7. See also chapter 2, and the accounts in 'Chronica de Gestis Consulum Andegavorum', in *Chroniques des Comtes d'Anjou et des Seigneurs d'Amboise*, ed. Louis Halphen and René Poupardin (Paris, 1913), 67, 69; *The Gesta Guillelmi of William of Poitiers*, ed. and transl. R. H. C. Davis and Marjorie Chibnall, 2 vols. (Oxford, 1998), vol. 2, 98–101, 104, 142, 150–3; Otto of Freising and Rahewin, *Gesta Fredericus, seu rectius Cronica*, ed. Franz-Josef Schmale, based on the edition by Georg Waitz, transl. Adolf Schmidt (Darmstadt, 1965), 264–5.

76   3. BECOMING KING

justice was done and peace maintained. New monarchs did not merely inherit
power, but used it for the common good.

Moral probity, power and divine backing also translated into concrete duties
and rights, exceeding by far those of a count or duke. They resulted, for
instance, in the right to oversee a kingdom's Church. The authority legitimately to intervene in the appointment of prelates, to draw on their expertise and
skills freely and without dependence on other rulers, separated the king from
a mere duke. The unity, however imperfect, of ecclesiastical and political
organisation marked out a polity's distinctiveness. This line of thinking probably underpinned attempts across eleventh- and twelfth-century Scandinavia
to curtail the authority of the archbishops of Bremen,[49] and those of successive
Portuguese kings to establish Braga as a metropolitan see.[50] In February 1204
Pope Innocent III announced that he was sending Cardinal Leo of St Croce to
present Ioannitsa of Bulgaria with a crown and to bestow upon him the title of
king. He also took the opportunity to confirm that henceforth Ioannitsa's
kingdom would have its own Church province, in the shape of the archdiocese
of Trnovo.[51] Especially among those kingdoms that were newly forged in the
eleventh and twelfth centuries, a process of state formation – the development
of a sense of shared regnal identity and community – coincided not only with
the creation of an indigenous church organisation, but also with the emergence
of communal patron saints, such as St Olaf in Norway, St Knud in Denmark or
St Erik in Sweden.[52] The authority of these saints specifically extended

[49] Eljas Orrmann, 'Church and society', in *The Cambridge History of Scandinavia. Vol. I:
Prehistory to 1520*, ed. Knut Helle (Cambridge, 2003), 421–62, at 428–31.

[50] Ferreira do Amaral, 'As sedes de Braga e Compostela'; Carl Erdmann, 'Das Papsttum und
Portugal im ersten Jahrhundert der portugiesischen Geschichte', *Abhandlungen der
Preußischen Akademie der Wissenschaften: Philosophisch-Historische Klasse* 5(1928),
1–63; Fabrice Delivré, 'The foundations of primatial claims in the western Church
(eighth–thirteenth centuries)', *Journal of Ecclesiastical History* 59 (2008), 383–406.

[51] *Die Register Innocenz' III. Band VII: 7. Pontifikatsjahr, 1204/1205*, ed. Christoph Egger
et al. (Vienna, 1997), nos. 1–12. For an English translation of select items from this
correspondence see *Monumenta Bulgarica. A Bilingual Anthology of Bulgarian Texts from
the Ninth to the Nineteenth Centuries*, ed. Thomas Butler (Ann Arbor, MI, 1996), 217–34.
James Ross Sweeney, 'Innocent III, Hungary and the Bulgarian coronation: a study in
medieval papal diplomacy', *Church History* 42 (1973), 320–34. Royal control did, of
course, also raise the status of those churchmen subject to a king. Writing *c.* 1170,
Helmold of Bosau reported a dispute between the archbishop of Hamburg and the
duke of Saxony over who should appoint bishops. At one stage, the archbishop and his
court argued that investiture belonged to the emperor, the dignity of whose office and
proximity to God raised him above the other sons of man. Bishops invested by princes, by
contrast, would remain mere servants: *Helmoldi Presbyteri Bozoviensis Chronica
Slavorum*, ed. Johannes Lappenberg, revised Bernhard Schmeidler, MGH SS sep. ed.,
3rd edition (Hanover, 1937), 132–3; Joachim Ehlers, *Heinrich der Löwe. Eine Biographie*
(Munich, 2008), 75–9.

[52] Haki Antonsson, *St. Mágnus of Orkney. A Scandinavian Martyr-Cult in Context* (Leiden,
2007), 207–20. See also the Capetian parallel: Gabrielle M. Spiegel, 'The cult of Saint Denis

II. CREATING KINGSHIP

throughout the kingdom, yet rarely stretched beyond it. While there had of course always been patron saints of specific churches or communities, they were unusual on a regional or dynastic level. For all their pretensions to royal status, the Welfs could not claim one patron saint for their various domains, nor could the counts of Barcelona or those of Anjou. Where cults did exist on a non-regnal level, as, for instance, those of St Mágnus on Orkney and St Wenceslas in Bohemia,[53] they existed in polities that were already geographically or politically distinct from those around them.

Much of this framework echoed biblical, patristic and classical models. It sometimes did so explicitly, as when Peter Damian invoked the language of protecting widows and orphans so central to the representation of power and kingship in the Old Testament, or when Cosmas of Prague appropriated imagery from 1 Samuel 8 to describe the origins of ducal power in Bohemia. More commonly, we find allusions to familiar concepts: the ruler as father and protector of his people; the expectation that kings held power so as to serve, not to lead; or the importance of acting righteously, even if this meant surrendering power. Such premises were rarely discussed in the abstract. Instead they were inferred from patterns of action. Divine backing manifested itself in dreams and visions, and in the fact that only Christians could be kings. Rulers did justice by collating and administering the law (in an echo of Deuteronomy), while royal authority was thrust upon rather than sought. The approach reflects the purpose of many of these accounts: to record the past and to draw lessons from it; to show how common norms had been upheld before and how they might be upheld again. It also reflects the audience addressed (to which we will return). It did not need to be told what the Bible said, or Seneca or St Augustine, but it did need to know how moral norms could be implemented and how contradictions could be dissolved in practice. The point has therefore come at which to move from general patterns to specific case studies.

3.2 Gniezno (999/1000)

Probably around 1253, an unknown cleric composed a *Life* of St Stanislas, the bishop of Kraków murdered in 1079 by King Boleslaw II of Poland. After recounting the prelate's martyrdom, the anonymous author lamented the many travails that had subsequently befallen the realm. The royal title, won through humility and piety by Boleslaw I, been lost by dint of the patricidal

---

and Capetian kingship', *JMedH* 1 (1975), 43–70; Jürgen Petersohn, 'Saint-Denis – Westminster – Aachen: die Karls-Translatio von 1165 und ihre Vorbilder', *DA* 31 (1975), 420–54.

[53] For Orkney see Antonsson, *St Mágnus*; for Bohemia: Lisa Wolverton, *Hastening towards Prague. Power and Society in the Medieval Czech Lands* (Philadelphia, PA, 2001), 166–73.

78   3. BECOMING KING

deeds of Boleslaw II. Ever since, the realm had been ravaged by civil war. Just as
the bishop had been decapitated, so Poland, too, had been deprived of its
leader; just as the saint's remains had been dispersed, so Poland, too, had been
subjugated by many lords. However, just as the saint's remains had become
one again through divine benevolence, so Poland, too, could be united once
more.[54] The hagiographer then recounted that he had read in the annals of
Poland and the *Life* of St Stephen of Hungary how Duke Mieszko had once
sought but failed to receive a crown from the pope. Adding to his sources, the
anonymous author explained why God had looked unkindly on these royal
aspirations: the Poles preferred injustice over justice, dogs over humans,
oppressing the poor over obeying divine laws.[55]

The account contains some familiar themes, notably the link between virtue
and kingship. Boleslaw I had gained the crown by his inherent virtue and
humility, while Boleslaw II had lost it by murdering saintly prelates. While
Stephen of Hungary, it was implied, had received his crown through virtue and
justice, Mieszko had failed to carry off a royal diadem because of his and his
people's cruel and violent disposition. The contrast was carefully chosen. The
earliest *Vita* of St Stephen, the *Legenda Maior*, produced *c.* 1083, also emphasised the virtuous origins of Stephen's kingship. In the year 1000, he was,
through divine benevolence, with papal blessing and having been acclaimed by
bishops and clergy and counts and the people, called king.[56] On assuming
power, Stephen issued a series of laws jointly with the prelates, designed to
protect property and to ban his people from attacking each other without due
judgement and from oppressing widows and orphans.[57] In the *Legenda*,
Stephen's success stood in contrast to the sins of his forebears. His father
had been told that he would not be allowed to convert his people, as he had
committed too many heinous sins. Stephen, it was implied, was able to
complete the conversion of his lands precisely *because* he led a good life. He
led it, moreover, in ways that encapsulated key duties of kingship. To the
Church he was a forceful guardian and generous patron. He shone as a keeper
of good law, a fount of justice, a protector of his people and of those who could
not protect themselves. So, already by the later eleventh century Stephen was
remembered primarily as someone who had ensured the right ordering of

---

[54] *Vita Sancti Stanislai Cracoviensis Episcopi (Vita Maior)*, ed. Wojciech Kętrzyński,
Monumenta Poloniae Historica (Lwów, 1864; repr. Warsaw, 1964), vol. 4, 391–2. This
section on Gniezno revises Weiler, 'Crown-giving', 60–5.

[55] *Vita Sancti Stanislai*, 392–3.

[56] *Legenda S. Stephani*, in *Scriptores Rerum Hungaricarum*, ed. Szentpétery, vol. 2, 378–81;
and, concerning Church reform, 383–4; Klaniczay, *Holy Rulers*, 124–7; Klaniczay, 'Rex
iustus: Le saint fondateur de la royauté chrétienne', *Cahiers d'études hongroises* 8 (1996),
34–58.

[57] *Legenda maior*, in *Scriptores Rerum Hungaricarum*, ed. Szentpétery, vol. 2, 384. See also:
Banaszkiewicz, 'Slavonic *origines regni*'.

II. CREATING KINGSHIP 79

society. This status was vigorously maintained well into the thirteenth century and beyond.[58]

This context gave the *Vita* of Stanislas its meaning and its edge. As bishops of Kraków, the successors of St Stanislas were guardians of the Polish royal insignia. Hence it fell to them to judge the legitimacy of anyone desiring to unite the realm under their dominion. The emphasis on the depravity of the Piasts (the Polish ruling family, named after Piast, its legendary ancestor) served to explain the failure of Polish kingship, and to establish a set of norms by which those who sought to resurrect it would have to abide. The *Vita* also reflected an established tradition of painting a stark contrast between saintly Árpads (descendants of Árpad, legendary ruler of the Magyars) and perfidious Piasts. When the anonymous author referred to information he had found in the *Life* of St Stephen, he was probably referring to Bishop Hartwic's reworking of the *Legenda* (c. 1120). According to this version, the duke of the Poles (also called Mieszko), had requested a crown from the pope. The pontiff had commissioned a particularly splendid specimen. It was about to be dispatched to the Polish court, when, on the eve of the crown-giving embassy, the pope had a vision, in which God's messenger announced that, the following morning, emissaries from a so far unknown people would arrive. The crown should be given to them instead – and they, of course, turned out to be Stephen's emissaries. As soon as the pope heard of Stephen's accomplishments, he handed over the crown, and joyfully conceded all the other demands that the king's envoys put before him.[59]

This was neither the first reference to the Piasts' failure to gain a crown, nor was the theme limited to Hungary and Poland. In the middle of the eleventh century, Peter Damian composed a *Life* of St Romuald of Salerno, where he recounted yet another version (this time, involving saints refusing to engage in simoniac practices).[60] The imagery probably reflected the difficulties encountered by both Boleslaw I and his successors in maintaining royal status. In 999/1000, Boleslaw may have received his crown from Emperor Otto III, but already Otto's successor, Henry II (1002–1024) insisted on Boleslaw's vassal

---

[58] *The Laws of the Medieval Kingdom of Hungary*, transl. and ed. J. Bak, G. Bónis and J. R. Sweeney, 2 vols. (Bakersfield, CA, 1989), vol. 1, 34, 42, 48. See also: László Veszprémy, 'The invented eleventh century of Hungary', in *The Neighbours of Poland in the 11th Century*, ed. Przemysław Urbańczyk (Warsaw, 2002), 137–54.

[59] *Legenda S. Stephani*, in *Scriptores Rerum Hungaricarum*, ed. Szentpétery, vol. 2, 412–14. On the text: Klaniczay, *Holy Rulers*, 142–3. Generally: Nora Berend, 'Writing Chistianization in medieval Hungary', in *Historical and Intellectual Culture in the Long Twelfth Century: the Scandinavian Connection*, ed. Thomas Heebøll-Holm, Mia Münster-Swendsen and Sigbjørn Olsen Sønnesyn (Toronto, 2015), 31–50.

[60] *Petri Damiani Vita Beati Romualdi*, ed. Giovanni Tabacco, Fonti per la storia d'Italia (Rome, 1957), 59–60. For the international circulation of the story of Stanislas and Boleslaw, see Jan Svanberg, 'The legend of Saint Stanislaus and King Boleslaus on the 12th-century font in Tryde, Sweden', *Folia Historiae Artium* NS 5–6 (1999–2000), 25–42.

80   3. BECOMING KING

status[61] and in 1032 Conrad II even forced Mieszko II to relinquish his title and
insignia.[62] In combination with the murder of St Stanislas,[63] it was perhaps this
failure to hold on to a royal crown that coloured later representations, in
Poland as elsewhere, of the origins of Piast kingship.

However, precisely because Piast kingship was disputed, other writers went
to quite some lengths to stress the legitimacy of its beginnings and origins.
They may not give a historically accurate depiction of what happened, but they
more than compensate for that by outlining what, from their later vantage
point, were the defining characteristics of kingship. The most important of
these later testimonies is the earliest narrative of Polish history actually written
in Poland. The *Gesta Principum Polonorum* had been composed *c*. 1110–13 by
an unknown cleric, possibly from France (and hence often referred to as
'Gallus Anonymus'), but living in Poland.[64] The *Gesta* is divided into three
parts, treating the achievements of Boleslaw I (r. 992–1025), the decline of
ducal power under his successors and its revival under Boleslaw III (r.
1102–1138). The encounter between the duke and Emperor Otto III at
Gniezno in 999/1000 was a pivotal event in that history.[65] Otto, 'Gallus'

---

[61] Thietmar of Merseburg, *Chronicon*, ed. and transl. Werner Trillmich (Darmstadt, 1957,
      repr. 1974), vi.90–1, pp. 338–41.

[62] Przemysław Urbańczyk and Stanisław Rosik, 'The kingdom of Poland, with an appendix
      on Polabia and Pomerania between paganism and Christianity', in *Christianization*, ed.
      Berend, 263–318, at 289.

[63] The Hungarian kings, too, had faced the hostility of their imperial neighbours, and
      Emperor Henry III (1039–56) had even seized a royal crown and presented it, as
      a token of his triumph, to the papal court: *Register Gregors VII.*, ii.13. See also, for
      a more detailed account, Gábor Varga, *Ungarn und das Reich vom 10. bis zum 13.
      Jahrhundert. Das Herrscherhaus der Árpáden zwischen Anlehnung und Emanzipation*
      (Munich, 2003), 91–141. Imperial hostility can thus not be the sole reason for explaining
      differences between the Hungarian and the Polish experience.

[64] On the text see: Thomas N. Bisson, 'On not eating Polish bread in vain: resonance and
      conjuncture in the *Deeds of the Princes of the Poles* (1109–1113)', *Viator* 29 (1998),
      275–89; Piotr Oliński, 'Am Hofe Bolesław Schiefmunds. Die Chronik des Gallus
      Anonymus', in *Die Hofgeschichtsschreibung im mittelalterlichen Europa*, ed.
      Rudolf Schieffer and Jarosław Wenta (Toruń, 2006), 93–106; Stopka, ed., *Gallus
      Anonymus*; the special issue of *FmSt* 43 (2009); Eduard Mühle, '*Cronicae et gesta
      ducum sive principum Polonorum*: neue Forschungen zum so genannten Gallus
      Anonymus', *DA* 65 (2009), 459–96; Zbigniew Dalewski, 'A new chosen people? Gallus
      Anonymus's narrative about Poland and its rulers', in *Historical Writing*, ed. Garipzanov,
      145–66; Plassmann, *Origo gentis*, 292–320.

[65] The event has triggered a rich literature, of which most recently: Henryk Samsonowicz,
      'Die deutsch-polnischen Beziehungen in der Geschichte des Mittelalters aus polnischer
      Sicht', in *Polen und Deutschland vor 1000 Jahren. Die Berliner Tagung über den 'Akt von
      Gnesen'*, ed. Michael Borgolte (Berlin, 2002), 19–28; and Klaus Zernack, 'Die deutsch-
      polnischen Beziehungen in der Mittelalterhistorie aus deutscher Sicht', ibid., 29–42; Jerzy
      Wyrozumski, 'Der Akt von Gnesen und seine Bedeutung für die polnische Geschichte',
      ibid., 281–92; Roman Michałowski, 'Polen und Europa um das Jahr 1000. Mit einem

II. CREATING KINGSHIP

informs us, driven by a desire to visit the shrine of St Adalbert of Prague, passed through the lands of Boleslaw. The latter greeted Otto with such generosity and splendour that the emperor was at a loss to how he might respond. Eventually, he addressed the duke in the following terms:

> 'So great a man does not deserve to be styled duke or count like any of the princes, but to be raised to a royal throne and adorned with a diadem in glory.' And with these words he took the imperial diadem from his own head and laid it upon the head of Boleslaw in pledge of friendship.... And in such love were they united that day that the emperor declared him his brother and partner in the Empire, and called him a friend and ally of the Roman people. And what is more, he granted him and his successors authority over whatever ecclesiastical honours belonged to the empire in any part of the kingdom of Poland or other territories he had conquered or might conquer among the barbarians ... So Boleslaw was thus gloriously raised to the kingship by the emperor.[66]

The account of Otto's visit was preceded by a list of Boleslaw's conquests and Church patronage,[67] which served chiefly to illustrate the duke's power and wealth. 'In Boleslaw's time', the chronicler informs us, 'every knight and every lady of the court wore robes instead of garments of linen and wool; ... gold in his days was held by all as common as silver, and silver deemed as little worth as straw.'[68] Nor was the crowning the end of the account by 'Gallus'. The emperor spent another three days at the Polish court. Every day, the dishes and plates, the carpets and tapestries exceeded those of the previous day in splendour and value. On the final day, Boleslaw commanded that the 'cups and goblets, the bowls and plates and the drinking horns ... [and] the wall-hangings and the coverlets, the carpets and the coverings' be carted to the emperor's chamber, alongside various vessels, robes and precious stones. All these, the chronicler emphasised, were simply tokens of honour, not a princely tribute.[69]

'Gallus' emphasised just how little Boleslaw was beholden to the emperor. There was, for example, a strong emphasis on parity. The crown placed on Boleslaw's head was merely a token of friendship. It did not signal a superior

---

Anhang: zur Glaubwürdigkeit des Berichts von Gallus Anonymus über das Treffen in Gnesen', in *Der Hoftag von Quedlinburg 973. Von den historischen Wurzeln zum neuen Europa*, ed. Andraes Ranft (Berlin, 2006), 51–72. The maximalist view is represented by Johannes Fried, *Otto III. und Boleslaw Chrobry: das Widmungsbild des Aachener Evangeliars, der 'Akt von Gnesen' und das frühe polnische und ungarische Königtum*, 2nd edition (Stuttgart, 2001). For a convenient overview in English: Nora Berend, Przemysław Urbańczyk and Przemysław Wiszewski, *Central Europe in the High Middle Ages: Bohemia, Hungary and Poland, c. 900 – c. 1300* (Cambridge, 2013), 118–24.

[66] *Gesta Principum Polonorum*, i.6, pp. 34–9.
[67] *Gesta Principum Polonorum*, i.6, pp. 30–5.
[68] *Gesta Principum Polonorum*, i.6, pp. 34–7.
[69] *Gesta Principum Polonorum*, i.6, pp. 38–41.

82   3. BECOMING KING

honouring someone below him in rank.[70] Even the gifts exchanged reflected
this relationship. Otto presented Boleslaw with a copy of the Holy Lance
(among the most prestigious items in the imperial relic collection),[71] and
Boleslaw Otto with the arm of St Adalbert. It is even conceivable that
Boleslaw may have shamed the emperor. When, at the end of the three-day
feast, Boleslaw filled the imperial chamber with gifts, there was no record of
presents being given in return. The inference seems clear: Otto was unable or
unwilling to respond in kind.[72] Furthermore, while the emperor was described
as returning home joyfully, laden with presents, the next chapter reports that
Boleslaw attacked the Ruthenians because of a perceived slight on his
honour.[73] There was a marked contrast between imperial embarrassment
over so splendid a welcome turning into joy over the rich gifts received, and
Polish valour – the true root of Boleslaw's kingship. This is not to say that
Otto's confirmation did not matter. Suggestively, it was only when describing
events *after* the Gniezno conference that 'Gallus' referred to Boleslaw as king.[74]
However, for it to be fully effective, Boleslaw's kingship had to be a token of
respect, acknowledging his might and virtue, and simultaneously also his
parity with Otto. It could not be something that, in any way, placed him in
the emperor's debt.

[70] Which reflected Otto's own view, it seems: Ludger Körntgen, 'The emperor and his
friends: the Ottonian realm in the year 1000', in *Europe around the Year 1000*, ed.
Przemysław Urbańczyk (Warsaw, 2001), 465–88. Matters changed with the succession
of Henry II in 1002: Knut Görich, 'Eine Wende im Osten: Heinrich II. und Boleslaw
Chobry', in *Otto III. – Heinrich II. Eine Wende?*, ed. Bernd Schneidmüller and
Stefan Weinfurter (Sigmaringen, 1997), 95–167.

[71] Peter Worm, 'Die Heilige Lanze. Bedeutungswandel und Verehrung eines
Herrschaftszeichens', *Arbeiten aus dem Marburger Hilfswissenschaftlichen Institut* (2000),
179–216; Percy Ernst Schramm, 'Die "Heilige Lanze", Reliquie und Herrschaftszeichen des
Reiches und ihre Replik in Krakau. Ein Überblick über die Geschichte der Königslanze' in his
*Herrschaftszeichen und Staatssymbolik. Beiträge zu ihrer Geschichte vom 3. bis zum 16.
Jahrhundert*, 3 vols. (Hanover, 1954–6), vol. 2, 492–537. See also below, Chapter 9.

[72] I am grateful to Gerd Althoff for this suggestion. It is worth noting that Thietmar of
Merseburg stressed the honours paid to Otto by Boleslaw, who even escorted him all the
way to Magdeburg: Thietmar of Merseburg, *Chronicon*, iv.45, pp. 160–3; Thietmar of
Merseburg, *Ottonian Germany. The Chronicon of Thietmar of Merseburg*, transl. David
A. Warner (Manchester, 2001), 183–4.

[73] *Gesta Principum Polonorum*, i.7, pp. 40–3. See also below, Chapter 10.

[74] Previously, he had avoided any specific title, though he had referred to Poland as
a *regnum*, a realm, which Boleslaw ruled after the death his father, who, however, was
labelled *dux*: *Gesta Principum Polonorum*, i.6, pp. 30–1. The Gniezno episode could be
read as dismissing precisely the kind of claims later emperors made on the Polish rulers. It
is worth noting that the only other encounter between an emperor and a duke described
in detail was the humiliation inflicted upon Henry V, when, in 1109, he sought to claim
a tribute from Boleslaw III: *Gesta Principum Polonorum*, iii.2–15, pp. 226–47. This
includes a poem, allegedly composed by the German soldiers, in praise of Polish valour:
iii.11, pp. 240–3.

II. CREATING KINGSHIP

This emphasis reflected both the fraught relations with Otto's heirs and the self-inflicted misfortunes of later dukes.[75] While the *Gesta*'s author studiously avoided reporting the murder of St Stanislas in detail,[76] the subsequent loss of kingship became the fate suffered by the dynasty as a whole. Among Boleslaw I's successors, only his namesake, Boleslaw II (who committed the killing), was labelled king.[77] Boleslaw I's reign established the standard against which later rulers could be measured. The section on Boleslaw I concludes with a list of his accomplishments – his magnificence and power,[78] virtuous nobility,[79] arrangements for the Polish Church,[80] that he never harmed the poor and powerless.[81] Only Boleslaw III – whose reign coincided with the writing of the *Gesta* – was not found wanting.[82] The fortunes of Polish kingship were therefore rooted in the virtues and vices of individual rulers, not the gift of a crown by one great lord to another. This line was adopted by later writers. When, around 1201, Master Vincent of Kraków wrote his narrative of Polish history, he clearly drew on but also fundamentally revised the narrative of 'Gallus'. In Vincent's rendering, the display of Polish power was largely omitted, and the emphasis shifted onto Boleslaw's virtue. As in the 'Gallus' version, Otto wanted to visit the shrine of St Adalbert. When meeting Boleslaw, he took the duke aside and declared that all the rumours he had heard about him had proven to be false. Indeed, he was so impressed by Boleslaw's virtue that he felt that the duke should be his equal. Boleslaw's excellence, the emperor declared, exalted the very office of ruler. Hence Otto placed his crown on the duke's head and placed Boleslaw's helmet on his own. While, as Vincent reiterated, Otto admired the duke's splendour and wealth, he was awed above all by his personal qualities.[83] Even more so than in the case of 'Gallus', kingship was rooted in the virtue of the ruler.

---

[75] *Gesta Principum Polonorum*, ii.2, pp. 226–9.

[76] *Gesta Principum Polonorum*, i.27, pp. 96–7.

[77] *Gesta Principum Polonorum*, i.23, i.30, pp. 88–9, pp. 104–5. With Boleslaw III matters changed again, but then only through allusion and rather opaque references. The *Gesta* thus refers to Boleslaw's son as 'of royal stock' (ii.40, pp. 192–3), but record neither a coronation nor the claiming of a royal title.

[78] *Gesta Principum Polonorum*, i.8, pp. 46–9.

[79] *Gesta Principum Polonorum*, i.9, pp. 48–51.

[80] *Gesta Principum Polonorum*, i.11, pp. 54–57.

[81] *Gesta Principum Polonorum*, i.12, pp. 56–9.

[82] Grischa Vercamer, 'Das Bad des Königs – beschreibt Gallus Anonymus ein genuin piastisches/polnisches Ritual? Überlegung zu Ehre und Herrschaftsvorstellung bei den frühen Piasten (Bolesław I. und Bolesław III.) aufgrund des Kapitels 1,13', *FmSt* 43 (2009), 349–72.

[83] Kadlubek, *Chronik der Polen*, 144–7. See also: Grischa Vercamer, 'Vorstellung von Herrschaft bei Magister Vincentius von Krakau (um 1150–1223)', in *Macht und Spiegel der Macht*, ed. Kersken and Vercamer, 309–40.

84 3. BECOMING KING

The *Vita* of St Stanislas, 'Gallus' and Vincent pursued different ends. 'Gallus' wrote a history of Poland that was partly designed to guide those who advised the duke.[84] Vincent revised and reworked 'Gallus' to fashion an extended meditation on the role of virtue in Polish history, and on the imperative of leading a good life.[85] The *Vita*, finally, celebrated the role of the Church of St Stanislas in the affairs of the realm.[86] These differences notwithstanding, for each author the question of kingship provided a means with which to evaluate and guide the affairs of the present. How Polish kingship had been acquired helped explain why it had been lost, and how it might one day be regained. It was rooted in virtue. But it was rooted in the virtue of the ruler, not that of his people. The community of Poland long pre-dated the rise to power of the Piasts. It persisted through the divisions that had plagued the realm ever since the murder of St Stanislas. The meeting at Gniezno set a standard by which putative rulers could be measured. It empowered the ruled, notwithstanding the limited role that they had been assigned in the origin myth of Polish kingship. The meeting at Gniezno had become a pivotal but legendary episode in the history of the realm.

3.3 Palermo (1130)

In their emphasis on virtue and might, and the desire to limit the authority of those who had first recognised a claim to kingship, 'Gallus' and Vincent as well the author of the *Vita* are representative of broader European developments. The extent to which that was the case will become apparent once the events of 999/1000 are set alongside the king-making of Roger of Sicily. At some point during the 1130s, Abbot Alexander of Telese began writing the *Ystoria Rogerii Regis Sicilie Calabriae atque Apulie* (*History of King Roger of Sicily, Calabria and Apulia*). Its first part is taken up with the many campaigns through which, by 1130, Roger II had united under his lordship the Norman principalities of Sicily and southern Italy. Book two opens with several barons approaching the duke to declare that someone as powerful as he should hold the rank of king, not duke. Roger, they further suggested, ought to use Palermo as his capital, because many kings had resided there in ancient times.[87] Roger pondered this

---

[84] See below, Chapter 4.

[85] Przemysław Wiszewski, 'The power of the prince: Vincentius on the dynasty's source of power', in *Writing History in Medieval Poland*, ed. von Güttner-Sporzynski, 199–220.

[86] Jerzy Kłoczowski, 'Saint Stanislas, patron de la Pologne au XIIIe siècle', in *Pascua Mediaevalia. Studies voor Prof. Dr. J.M. De Smet*, ed. R. Lievens, Erik van Mingroot and W. Verbeke (Leuven, 1983), 62–5; Tadeusz Ulewicz, 'St Stanislaus of Szczepanów in old Polish literature and culture', *Aevum: Rassegna di scienze storiche linguistiche e filologiche* 54 (1980), 287–314.

[87] Alexander of Telese, *Ystoria Rogerii*, 23; *Roger II and the Creation of the Kingdom of Sicily*, transl. Graham A. Loud (Manchester, 2012), 77–8. For secondary accounts: Loud, *Latin*

II. CREATING KINGSHIP

85

'friendly and praiseworthy suggestion', and convened an assembly at Salerno. There, he took the advice of 'learned Churchmen and most competent persons, as well as certain princes, counts, barons and others whom he thought trustworthy'. Roger charged them with investigating whether there had indeed been kings of Sicily in the past. Perhaps unsurprisingly, they found this to have indeed been the case, and furthermore declared that Roger ought to be raised to the royal dignity. After all, he held Sicily, Calabria and Apulia as well as other lands, and did so not only by force of conquest, but also by right of inheritance.[88] Roger therefore called yet another assembly, this time at Palermo, and on Christmas Day 1130, 'ordering that all the men of dignity, power and honour from his lands and provinces should gather together'. The audience at Palermo, too, 'approved the promotion to the kingship for him to who[m] had been given such great and virtuous might, so that he might overcome the wicked and preserve justice'.[89] The chronicler then proceeded to give a very general sketch of the coronation itself, writing only that Roger was led to the cathedral, received unction and assumed the royal dignity.[90] Far greater attention was paid to the festivities surrounding the event. Words, Alexander asserted, could not describe its splendour.[91] The royal palace was bedecked with draperies, the pavement strewn with carpets and the horses of Roger's entourage adorned with gold and silver.[92] The finest meals were served, with cups and plates of gold and silver, and the 'glory and wealth of the royal abode was so spectacular that it caused great wonder and deep stupefaction – so great indeed that it instilled not a little fear in all those who had come from so far away'.[93]

Like Boleslaw's, Roger's power surpassed that of a mere prince. That had to be recognised by the award of a title appropriate to the fact. As in Poland, quasi-royal status manifested itself in the lordship over many lands; as at Gniezno, the duke's elevation resulted in a truly festive celebration; as in Poland, the display of wealth was a token of strength. There are equally rich parallels with the Hungarian case, not least in the emphasis placed on the role of the people in establishing Roger's kingship. Roger only claimed the royal title after he had been urged to do so three times: by his close entourage, by

Church in Norman Sicily, 150–8; Houben, Roger II. von Sizilien, 53–4, and Deér, Papsttum und Normannen, 214–15; Reinhard Elze, 'Zum Königtum Rogers II. von Sizilien', in Festschrift für Percy Ernst Schramm zu seinem 70. Geburtstag, 2 vols. (Wiesbaden, 1964), vol. 2, 102–16, at 105; Rudolf Hiestand, 'Geschichte des Königreichs Sizilien', 52–7; Philippe Buc, '1701 in medieval perspective'. The section on Sicily thoroughly revises and departs considerably from Weiler, 'Crown-giving', 65–9.

[88] Alexander of Telese, Ystoria Rogerii, 23–5; Roger II, ed. Loud, 78.
[89] Alexander of Telese, Ystoria Rogerii, 25; Roger II, ed. Loud 79.
[90] Alexander of Telese, Ystoria Rogerii, 25; Roger II, ed. Loud 79.
[91] Alexander of Telese, Ystoria Rogerii 25; Roger II, ed. Loud 79.
[92] Alexander of Telese, Ystoria Rogerii, 26; Roger II, ed. Loud 79–80.
[93] Alexander of Telese, Ystoria Rogerii, 26.

86   3. BECOMING KING

wise and prudent counsellors and by the great men of the realm.[94] We are, moreover, in the fortunate position that a document survives that was likely the *ordo* – the liturgical text – used for Roger's coronation.[95] Like the Hungarian materials, it focusses on the duties of kingship. Before the coronation, it asserts, Roger had to promise that he would maintain the faith, be a protector and defender of the Church and that he would rule and defend with justice the kingdom he had been granted by God.[96] Similarly, after Roger had received unction on his hands, but before he received it on his head, the presiding archbishop offered a prayer. He requested that God grant the king the ability to be a strong protector of the fatherland and a guardian of abbeys and churches, victorious in battle and a terror to his enemies, yet pious, generous and approachable to the great men of his realm.[97]

Roger's elevation needs to be considered in relation to traditions of Norman rulership in southern Italy. Initially, the Normans had delegated authority to twelve equal leaders. However, by 1042 they chose William Ironarm as count, that is, as leader of leaders. When William entered Melfi – which was meant to be shared equally among the twelve leaders – they did homage to him and, Amatus of Montecassino asserts, willingly served as butlers and meat carriers.[98] Parity had given way to hierarchy, though by acting as butlers the original co-leaders of the Normans were still singled out for a role that was both subservient and communicated proximity to their lord.[99] The trajectory continued. In 1059 Robert Guiscard captured Reggio, where he was proclaimed duke by all the Normans.[100] Rank was therefore a direct reflection of power. Each step in the rise of the Guiscard family followed on from the conquest of new territories. They had started out as but one in a group of adventurers and mercenaries who began to make a living from, and became part of, the political communities of southern Italy. As their power expanded, alongside that of their fellow Normans, they assumed ever more exalted titles.

---

[94] This also neatly encapsulates the tripartite division of assembly proposed by Gerd Althoff, 'Colloquium familiare – Colloquium secretum – Colloquium publicum. Beratung im politischen Leben des früheren Mittelalters', *FmSt* 24 (1990), 145–67.

[95] Elze, 'The ordo'. See also below, Chapter 9, for a fuller discussion of the Sicilian ordo.

[96] Elze, 'The ordo', 171. See also below, Chapter 10.

[97] Elze, 'The ordo', 173. See also Thomas Dittelbach, 'The image of the private and the public king', 169–71.

[98] Amatus of Montecassino, *Storia de' Normanni*, 97–8; *History of the Normans*, 76.

[99] See also below, Chapter 9.

[100] Romuald of Salerno, *Chronica*, ed. Giousue Carducci and Vittorio Fiorini (Città di Castello, 1909–35), 182; Geoffroi Malaterra, *Histoire du Grand Comte Roger et de son frère Robert Guiscard; vol. I* (books 1 & 2), ed. Marie-Agnès Lucas-Avenel (Caen, 2016); available electronically at www.unicaen.fr/puc/sources/malaterra/accueil (accessed 28 July 2018), i.35 (no pagination in the electronic edition). The title was then confirmed by Pope Leo IX: G. A. Loud, *The Age of Robert Guiscard. Southern Italy and the Norman Conquest* (Harlow, 2000), 128–30, 186–93.

II. CREATING KINGSHIP

Roger II's elevation completed the journey. He had united all of the Normans' lands under his rule.

The royal title was thrust upon Roger, not sought by him. His reluctance was made manifest in the three meetings convened to deliberate whether he should become king, and in the fact that Roger never desired the crown himself. In Alexander's rendering, Roger merely complied with the advice of prudent men, and the wishes of his people. He showed reluctance. But Roger had also been predestined for so elevated a dignity. Alexander reported two dreams, one experienced by an elderly priest near Telese, one by an elderly woman in the same region. Both preceded Roger's elevation by several years. In the first, Roger was seen as triumphing over and then sparing several of his rivals. Two men in white robes appeared and declared that Roger was victorious by divine will. Roger then placed his spear on top of a hill. A wondrous tree grew out of that spear, and on top of it was a throne, to which the two men in white robes escorted the duke, and where they crowned him. Then the priest woke up.[101] In the second dream, the Virgin Mary appeared to a peasant woman. The latter complained that nobody was willing to free her of the deprivations inflicted by Roger. The Virgin replied that there was little she could do, as Jesus himself had dispatched two guardians to ensure that anyone resisting Roger would be defeated. They were the apostles Peter and Paul, and they would stay with Roger until the last of his foes had been overcome.[102] Both visions, Alexander concluded, clearly showed that resisting Roger was to resist God. No good would therefore come of revolt, and the discontented should bring about peace by surrendering to their rightful lord.

Alexander's was a very Pauline approach. He even quoted directly from the apostle's Epistle to the Romans: 'Let it be recalled what the saying is of the Apostle: "Who resists authority resists the ordinance of God."'[103] Roger's kingship had been divinely ordained. Therefore it must not be challenged. He was protected by Christ. Even the Virgin could not work against him. Nonetheless, when the old peasant woman complained about Roger's deprivations, the response she received framed Roger as upholding peace. The suffering of his people was the work not of the king, but of men who vainly rose up against him. Roger's wars were an instrument of peace. Furthermore, his actions flowed from a virtuous inner disposition, as was to be expected from a first king. While still an adolescent, 'he was so greatly and frequently moved by piety that hardly ever did a poor man or pilgrim leave his presence without rewards'.[104] He wielded power not to enrich himself, but in order to

---

[101] Alexander of Telese, *Ystoria Rogerii*, 84–6; *Roger II*, ed. Loud, 123–4.
[102] Alexander of Telese, *Ystoria Rogerii*, 86; *Roger II*, ed. Loud, 124–5.
[103] Alexander of Telese, *Ystoria Rogerii*, 87; *Roger II*, ed. Loud, 125. Romans 13:2.
[104] Alexander of Telese, *Ystoria Rogerii*, 8; *Roger II*, ed. Loud, 65–6.

88　　3. BECOMING KING

protect the weak, and to enrich the poor. Once Roger succeeded his father as
count of Sicily,

> he showed such activity and demonstrated such admirable firmness,
> ruling the whole province of Sicily so well and strongly, and exercising
> such terrible authority over all that no robber, thief, plunderer or other
> malefactor dared to stir out of his lair.[105]

Like David and Solomon, the young count was blessed with so many riches
that he was feared both in his lands and abroad. Like them, he continued to
work for the common good. Towards the end of the first book, Roger tri-
umphed over and forced into submission most of the Normans. Afterwards, he
convened an assembly at Melfi, where he received the homage and fealty of his
erstwhile rivals. Having united all these domains under his control, Roger
issued a series of decrees. The men of Apulia would henceforth keep the peace
among themselves, and would assist in doing justice. They would not harbour
evil men, but hand over plunderers and robbers to Roger so that we would sit
in judgement over them. And they would extend their protection to all clergy,
pilgrims, travellers, merchants, peasants and villeins.[106] Roger may not have
codified the laws of the realm, but he certainly made sure that they were
obeyed. He was both a servant to and a leader of his people.[107]

How does this compare to the Polish example? Like Boleslaw I, Roger II had
acted in a kingly fashion long before he was elevated to the royal dignity. Like
his Polish counterpart, he was pious, just and stern. Both received a crown
because they were more powerful than a mere duke or count. Their wealth
furthermore revealed their virtue, and demonstrated that they had divine
backing. In this regard, Alexander's portrayal placed Roger firmly within
a broader European paradigm of first or ideal rulers. But it also reflected
aspects particular to twelfth-century Sicily, chief among them the emphasis
on power and martial prowess as the primary qualification for rulership.
According to the chronicler, Roger was predestined to inherit his father's
lands, because, unlike his elder brother, he excelled at fighting even while
still a boy.[108] Once an adult, his conquests and campaigns needed little
justification. Roger had seized Malta, and 'it was his firm intention to occupy
other islands and lands'.[109] Even taking control of Apulia was framed not as an
act of restoring order or of ending the tyranny of an unjust usurper. Either
would have been a common line of justification for a war of conquest.[110]
Instead, Alexander described Roger as *demanding* an inheritance that was

---

[105] Alexander of Telese, *Ystoria Rogerii*, 8; *Roger II*, ed. Loud, 66.
[106] Alexander of Telese, *Ystoria Rogerii*, 18–9; *Roger II*, ed. Loud, 75.
[107] See also the preface: Alexander of Telese, *Ystoria Rogerii*, 1–3; *Roger II*, ed. Loud, 63–4.
[108] Alexander of Telese, *Ystoria Rogerii*, 7; *Roger II*, ed. Loud, 65. See also below, Chapter 6.
[109] Alexander of Telese, *Ystoria Rogerii*, 8; *Roger II*, ed. Loud, 66.
[110] See below, Chapter 10.

II. CREATING KINGSHIP

89

his right, no matter what the people of Apulia, its nobles or even the pope thought of the matter.[111] Roger being pious and just was, of course, important. But what really mattered was that he had been granted power by God, and that he knew how to use it.

That is a rather different image of a first king from that painted by 'Gallus' and Vincent. There, power was certainly important. It was why, in 'Gallus', Boleslaw was made king by Otto. Nonetheless, it remained subsidiary to Boleslaw's virtuous excellence. In Vincent's version, it even became the primary reason for Boleslaw's elevation to the royal dignity. But 'Gallus' also dedicated considerably more space to Boleslaw's piety, doing of justice and religious patronage than to his martial exploits. Alexander, by contrast, praised Roger for his rigorous justice, but never actually *described* him doing justice. But then the Polish case reflected the fraught history of indigenous royal lordship. The past provided a way of coming to terms with the crises and turmoil that had plagued the realm ever since the murder of St Stanislas. Unlike in Poland, Sicilian kingship survived. None of Roger's successors were forced to surrender their title. Roger's neighbours in Byzantium and the west may have viewed him as a parvenu, but unable to dislodge him or his heirs, they eventually sought to embrace them as allies.[112] In fact, outside Sicily later recollections of Roger centred on his power, and sought to garner prestige for foreign rulers by associating them with his elevation.[113] Alexander did, however, share with his Polish counterparts the need to come to terms with the role played by those who had confirmed Roger's kingship. The challenge was to fashion an image that embedded Roger's new title in established conventions of Norman rule in Italy, and that simultaneously justified his attempts to break free of them. Worse still, unlike in Poland, in Sicily there were two groups whose involvement needed to be handled: the great men of the realm and the pope.

Norman rule in Sicily contained a strong electoral element. William Ironarm and Robert Guiscard had not claimed the titles of count and duke. They had been awarded to them by their fellow leaders. The electoral element persisted, with each of their successors chosen by the Norman elites. Consequently, ducal power was inherently fragile.[114] In fact, the more power

---

[111] Alexander of Telese, *Ystoria Rogerii*, 9–18; *Roger II*, ed. Loud, 66–75.

[112] Timothy Reuter, 'Vom Parvenü zum Bündnisparter: das Königreich Sizilien in der abendländischen Politik des 12. Jahrhunderts', in *Die Staufer im Süden. Sizilien und das Reich*, ed. Theo Kölzer (Sigmaringen, 1996), 43–56; Gerhard Baaken, 'Unio regni ad imperium. Die Verhandlungen von Verona 1184 und die Eheabredung zwischen König Heinrich VI. und Konstanze von Sizilien', *Quellen und Forschungen aus italienischen Archiven und Bibliotheken* 52 (1972), 219–97; reprinted in his *Imperium und Papsttum. Zur Geschichte des 12. und 13. Jahrhunderts. Festschrift zum 70. Geburtstag*, ed. Karl-Augustin Frech and Ulrich Schmidt (Cologne, Weimar and Vienna, 1997), 81–142.

[113] See Chapter 4.

[114] Broekmann, *Rigor Iustitiae*, 31–7, 43–56.

90   3. BECOMING KING

the dukes claimed, the more frequent and ferocious were the challenges they faced, and the greater the brutality with which these were put down.[115] Theo Broekmann has suggested that the memory of parity provided those unwilling to submit to ducal might with a means of justifying resistance. The duke's authority had been delegated to him by his peers, but it was not his to do with as he wished. The magnates were within their rights when they restrained a ruler lapsing into tyranny. At the same time, the collective roots of ducal power served to justify the brutality with which resistance was put down. Anyone defying the duke also defied the will of *all* the leaders of the Normans.[116]

This tension defines Alexander's account. Roger is portrayed as rooted in but also as upending traditions of communal rule. After Roger had conquered most of Apulia, he called together its leading men. The assembly took place at Melfi.[117] Few sites were as reminiscent of the premise of shared leadership.[118] Furthermore, once Roger had overcome the last of his Apulian rivals, he returned to Melfi and ordered its fortifications to be rebuilt.[119] He placed himself firmly in a tradition of collective leadership. Yet, where other dukes had been chosen by the magnates, Roger claimed the title by right of inheritance. He acquired it by force and through divine aid (or so Alexander claimed). The will of the great men of the realm was of no concern. They could either accept his claim or, defying both him and their Creator, suffer crushing defeat.

Roger's kingship spelt the end of Melfi's pre-eminence. Its associations with parity became both unwelcome and obsolete.[120] When Roger commissioned learned men to investigate whether there had in the past been kings of Sicily, they not only determined that this had indeed been the case. They also proposed that Roger be made king and reside at Palermo. It was the chief city of the realm, and it was there that the kings of yore had ruled.[121] Roger's kingship flowed from communal action, not individual desire. The people, not Roger, decided that he should be king. But they also enacted a decision that, unbeknownst to them, had already been made. Jesus had singled out Roger for the royal throne long before anyone had pondered the possibility of awarding him a royal title. Moreover, Alexander explained, the ease with which Roger took control of Apulia reflected the fact that 'he was able with the aid of God to

---

[115] Loud, *Age of Robert Guiscard*, 234–46.

[116] This condenses the rather more sophisticated argument of Broekmann, *Rigor Iustitiae*, 30–57, 123–40.

[117] See also Hubert Houben, 'Melfi e Venosa. Due città sotto il dominio normanno-svevo', in *Itinerari e centri urbani nel Mezzogiorno normanno-svevo*, ed. Giosuè Musca (Bari, 1993), 311–32.

[118] William of Apulia, *La Geste*, ll. 316–17.

[119] Alexander of Telese, *Ystoria Rogerii*, 20; *Roger II*, ed. Loud, 77.

[120] *Roger II*, ed. Loud, 19.

[121] Alexander of Telese, *Ystoria Rogerii*, 24; *Roger II*, ed. Loud, 78.

II. CREATING KINGSHIP 91

bring all these lands under his power, since everywhere he ruled he promulgated such mighty and thorough justice that continuous peace was seen to endure'.[122] Roger's royal status was rooted solely in divine will, and the virtuous use he made of the power he wielded because of it. Like the Israelites in 1 Samuel, the people could consent, but they could not choose. They derived no rights from their involvement.

Moreover, unlike in Hungary and Poland, by raising Roger to the throne, they merely *revived* a royal title, but did not *create* one. There had been kings in Palermo long before there ever were counts or dukes. Roger restored an ideal *status quo ante* that preceded and hence nullified Norman conventions of parity. That became possible because of his great power and just rule. Alexander's representation of events not only disqualified the Sicilians further from staking a claim in Roger's governance. He also sidestepped another potential challenger to Roger's power: the pope. After all, just claiming a title was not enough. It also had to be recognised. In the legend of St Stephen, confirmation came from an angel of the Lord, mediated through the pope. In Poland, it came from an emperor, left unable to respond in kind to Boleslaw's lavish generosity. In Sicily, it ultimately came from God, was enacted by the people and was supported by the pope. Though from Alexander of Telese's account one would not have guessed that the pontiff's involvement was at all significant.

Several contemporaries stress that the royal title had been bestowed by Pope Anaclete II.[123] Indeed, in September 1130, several months prior to the coronation at Palermo, Anaclete issued a charter in which he confirmed Roger's kingship. He also specified that the royal dignity would remain Roger's and his heirs', even if a future pontiff failed to renew the privilege.[124] Why would Alexander of Telese fail to mention these details? Roger apart, only a handful of Roman aristocrats recognised Anaclete as leader of the Church. The vast majority of European clerics and kings sided with Anaclete's rival, Innocent

---

[122] Alexander of Telese, *Ystoria Rogerii*, 19; *Roger II*, ed. Loud, 75.

[123] A marginal entry in a manuscript of the Chronicle of Romuald of Salerno reports that on Christmas Day the prelates of Calabria, Apulia and Capua had consecrated Roger, placed a crown on his head and ordered everyone to call him king, and that they had done so at the Pope's command: *Ystoria Rogerii*, 343–4. Falco, from neighbouring Benevento, reports that in 1130 Roger demanded that the pope crown him king: Falcone de Benevento, *Chronicon Beneventanum*, ed. Edoardo D'Angelo (Florence, 1998), 106. Anaclete did not, however, perform the ceremony, which instead devolved to a papal legate, who, on Christmas Day 1130, performed the deed – although, Falco stressed, it was the archbishop of Palermo who put the crown on Roger's head: Falcone, *Chronicon*, 108.

[124] Hartmut Hoffmann, 'Langobarden, Normannen, Päpste. Zum Legitimationsproblem in Unteritalien', *Quellen und Forschungen aus italienischen Archiven und Bibliotheken* 58 (1978), 137–80, at 172–6; Houben, *Roger II. von Sizilien*, 54. See also Loud, *Church in Norman Italy*, 255–9.

92   3. BECOMING KING

II.[125] Anaclete, by contrast, was reviled as an antipope who had violently
usurped the *cathedra* of St Peter. Therefore, Roger's royal title was the gift of
a schismatic. To his opponents, Roger's kingship was as illegitimate as the
person who had bestowed it upon him.[126]

Roger's backing for Anaclete had grave repercussions. In the mid-1130s, he
nearly lost his kingdom when Emperor Lothar III swept through southern Italy
in an attempt to depose him.[127] To make matters worse, in 1139 Roger took
Innocent II captive. Roger did not release the pope until he had confirmed his
royal title and Anaclete's privileges.[128] There, too, Roger followed established
custom. In 1059, Robert Guiscard had received recognition from Nicholas II in
return for promising to drive the pope's rival from Rome, but only after he had
inflicted a devasting defeat on the pontiff's forces.[129] At the same time, that
precedent only reinforced the image of Roger as illegitimate and tyrannical.
Incarcerating popes was really quite uncouth. Understandably, Alexander of
Telese therefore passed over such unsavoury matters. The decision may have
been easier because an earlier clash between Roger and the Holy See signalled
that even the pope could not defy the will of God. To thwart Roger's planned
conquest of Apulia, his opponents had persuaded Honorius II to threaten the
duke with excommunication. In response, Roger sent envoys to the pope,
patiently explaining that Apulia was his by right. He even offered to do homage
for it. To no avail. Undeterred, Roger sent further embassies, but finally
determined that he had no choice but to pursue his claims by force. That he
did, and was promptly excommunicated. However, once Roger had vanquished most of his foes, Honorius relented, lifted the sentence and enfeoffed
him with Apulia.[130] Like the Sicilians, the pope was unable to prevent Roger
from acquiring what was his by right. All he could do was recognise and
execute the divine will. By implication, the precise identity of the pope confirming Roger's kingship was of little consequence. He merely enacted
a decision that had already been made by an authority far higher than his.

Alexander's take on kingship was aimed an audience that consisted mostly
of Roger's inner circle. He had embarked upon compiling the *Ystoria* at the
behest of the king's sister.[131] He concluded it with a lengthy address to Roger,

---

[125] I. S. Robinson, *The Papacy, 1073–1198. Continuity and Innovation* (Cambridge, 1990),
     69–76, 382–6.
[126] Helene Wieruszowski, 'Roger II of Sicily. *Rex tyrannicus* in twelfth-century political
     thought', *Speculum* 38 (1963), 46–78.
[127] Houben, *Roger II. von Sizilien*, 71–3.
[128] Houben, *Roger II. von Sizilien*, 74.
[129] Loud, *Age of Robert Guiscard*, 186–94.
[130] Alexander of Telese, *Ystoria Rogerii*, 10–5; *Roger II*, ed. Loud, 68–72. For the context, see:
     Markus Krumm, 'Bound by loyalty: conflict, communication and group solidarity in
     twelfth-century Southern Italy', *HSJ* 30 (2018), 107–31.
[131] Alexander of Telese, *Ystoria Rogerii*, 1; *Roger II*, ed. Loud, 63.

urging the king to continue doing God's work and to 'subjugate to your own rule fortifications, impregnable cities and the stronger and impregnable towns'.[132] The *Ystoria* served and sought to shape the self-representation and self-legitimation of the Hauteville king. Roger humbled the mighty and protected the poor, and he was doing God's bidding by amassing many lands and riches. Yet Alexander was also aware that power required moral purpose. Hence the emphasis on Roger's stern and rigorous justice. Hence, too, the lengthy exhortation to continue doing justice that took up most of the *Ystoria*'s concluding section. But such references were far outnumbered by ones that focussed on Roger's ruthless pursuit of power. Unlike 'Gallus', Alexander never described his protagonist actually *doing* justice. By contrast, he reported in detail how Roger prepared a campaign, how he conducted sieges or how he led his men into battle. Virtue and violence sat uneasily together.

Alexander's view was certainly not shared by the rulers of the Holy Roman Empire or by their peers in Constantinople. Lothar III, Conrad III, Frederick Barbarossa, John and Manuel Komennos led campaigns against Roger and his heirs, or at least lent their backing to those rebelling against him.[133] Even Alexander could not pass over the deep hostility towards Roger's claims from within southern Italy. Most of the *Ystoria* is taken up with recounting the numerous plots and machinations spun against Roger, the rebellions he had to put down and the opponents he defeated. What to Alexander may have been evidence of divine backing, to many of the king's subjects and neighbours it provided the very grounds on which he ought to be resisted. Roger had overturned established custom, defied popes and emperors and ruled his people with harsh brutality. He was a tyrant, not a king.

The Sicilian example therefore points to a broader problem. How could one prevent a king from turning into a tyrant? Alexander seems to have been aware that the question might be posed in relation to Roger. In his account, the king's innate suitability prevented him from allowing rigour to lapse into oppression. Even so, Alexander added a lengthy exhortation urging Roger to restore peace and to enforce the law. Others may well have thought that simple remonstration, while laudable, was by no means enough. More forceful mechanisms were called for, such as the joint rulership envisaged by the Sicilians' eleventh-century forebears. Collective governance allowed rulers to be guided and restrained. That was probably also precisely why Roger and his court were keen to end the practice. They may not have objected to the principle, but they remained wary of the degree to which it empowered the king's opponents and

---

[132] Alexander of Telese, *Ystoria Rogerii*, 90; *Roger II*, ed. Loud, 127.

[133] Paul Magdalino, *The Empire of Manuel I. Komnenos, 1143–80* (Cambridge, 1993), 38–9, 50–6; Ralph-Johannes Lilie, *Byzantium and the Crusader States 1096–1204*, transl. J. C. Morris and Jean E. Ridings (Oxford, 1993), 102–3, 113–14; John B. Freed, *Frederick Barbarossa: the Prince and the Myth* (New Haven, CT, 2016), 52–7, 113–19; *Roger II*, ed. Loud, 33–4, 39, 50, 60–1.

94   3. BECOMING KING

rivals. The underlying question therefore remained unresolved: where was the line to be drawn between legitimate participation and rebellious insurrection? If kingship was created by God, how could mere mortals demand a say in its exercise? In the absence of a Samuel or Nathan, who would decide whether someone opposing Roger was a second David or another Jeroboam?[134]

These questions were closely tied to a further set of issues: who determined whether a ruler was a legitimate king or a tyrant? This was a matter of particular concern in relation to new kingships. 'Gallus' and Roger constructed their accounts so as to downplay the role of whoever conferred, suggested or confirmed a royal title. At Gniezno, Otto's gift of a crown was framed as resulting from the emperor's inability to respond adequately to the Polish duke's lavish generosity. Boleslaw's kingship was not created, but merely recognised by Otto. In Palermo, in 1130, pope and people alike were deprived of agency. Both examples reflect the potential implications of an act of confirmation. In Poland, Otto's successors had to be denied a right of oversight. In Sicily, nobles and pontiffs had to be prevented from demanding a say in the affairs of the realm. At the same time, Vincent Kadlubek, the anonymous author of the *Vita* of St Stanislas or the compilers of the legends of St Stephen had no difficulty embracing or accepting the role of the *populus*. That each addressed distinctive audiences goes some way towards explaining their different approaches. But that merely reinforces the fact that, even within a shared framework, different readings could be placed upon common norms and values. How did high medieval observers negotiate this tension?

---

[134] Jeroboam led a rebellion against Solomon's son Rehoboam because of the latter's oppressive taxation and his refusal to take the counsel of his people. Jeroboam later revived the cult of the Golden Calf, thereby further incurring divine anger: 1 Kings 11–13.

4

Conferring Kingship

Recognition was sometimes solicited and sometimes offered unasked. Sometimes it was given by the people, more commonly by someone from outside the realm. Whichever path was chosen, the relationship between the ones confirming and the ones claiming a royal title had to be negotiated. Who could legitimately participate in this process? How did they and how did later observers define the relationship between the recipient of a crown and the person or people authorising its possession?

4.1 Popes, Emperors and Mighty Neighbours

The royal office was a duty, created so that anyone exercising it would enact the will of God. As it entailed so much worldly power, it also brought with it temptations, and required kings of sufficient moral fervour to fortify them against the lures and snares of secular might. They had to be cajoled and coerced into accepting the throne, but their virtuous disposition and innate capability was easily discernible both to their people and to outside observers. Men greedy for the throne, by contrast, were desirous not of fulfilling their duties, but of exerting power over others. They also shied away from seeking proper recognition. To German observers, this had marked out as tyrannical Boleslaw I[1] and Roger II.[2] The first violated the rights of the empire by seizing the title and insignia of kingship, and the latter usurped the title of 'king'. Similar accusations were made in eleventh-century France when Rodulfus Glaber dismissed Duke Conan's claim to the kingship of Brittany.[3] It even penetrated works of fiction. In twelfth-century England, Geoffrey of Monmouth, writing about the rule of Vortigern (the archetypal bad king of

---

[1] Wipo, *Gesta Chuonradi*, in *Wiponis Opera*, 31–2; *Annales Quedlinburgenses*, ed. Martina Giese, MGH SSrG (Hanover, 2004), 522. This section draws on Björn Weiler, 'Crown-giving and king-making in the west, c. 1000 – c. 1250', *Viator* 41 (2010), 57–88, at 72–5 and 78–9.

[2] Otto of Freising and Rahewin, *Gesta Frederici, seu rectius Cronica*, ed. Franz-Josef Schmale, transl. Adolf Schmidt (Darmstadt, 1965), i.3, pp. 126–7.

[3] Rodulfus Glaber, *Historiarum libri quinqui*, in *Rodulfus Glaber: Opera*, ed. and transl. John France, Neithard Bulst and Paul Reynolds (Oxford, 1989), 58–9.

96   4. CONFERRING KINGSHIP

the pre-Saxon past), stressed that he had lusted after, plotted to gain and eventually usurped the throne.[4] Only tyrants *desired* a crown. Only tyrants laboured and schemed to get it. Only tyrants refused to have their claims scrutinised by others.

In order to be valid, kingship had to be confirmed by someone who materially was a disinterested party and did not act under duress. This had been one of the problems facing Roger II. Geoffrey of Monmouth's account of Vortigern played on that same theme. Vortigern had not seized the throne straightaway. Instead, he had at first appointed in Constans a particularly inept ruler whom he had subsequently murdered. When nobody was willing to crown Constans – a former monk – Vortigern 'himself performed the role of bishop and placed the crown on Constans' head with his own hands'.[5] Kingship was tainted if those confirming or conferring it were of a dubious moral disposition, or if they usurped the prerogatives of others. In twelfth-century England, the coronation of Henry II's eldest son had to be repeated because it had been performed by the archbishop of York, not that of Canterbury, who had been forced into exile by the king.[6] Kingship had to be recognised by someone in a position persuasively to confirm that the claimant's motives were pure.

Moreover, it had to be recognised by someone whose authority exceeded that of one's rivals, and who acted free from fear or obeisance. Ideally, this would be someone who would not derive any claims of political overlordship from his involvement, and who possessed the moral or political authority to defend its legitimacy against possible detractors. Thus, while in Sicily God may have predestined Roger II for the throne, and while the people may have pushed him into claiming a throne, he still was eager to ensure recognition from the pope. Roger's was a common strategy.[7] Not everyone sought recognition through the formal giving of a crown. After 1143, the rulers of Portugal simply styled themselves king in their correspondence with the curia, and did so until 1178, when the papal chancery at last relented and addressed them as kings in return.[8] In many cases, approaching the papacy was made easier by the

[4] Geoffrey of Monmouth, *The History of the Kings of Britain. An Edition and Translation of De gestis Britonum [Historia Regum Britanniae]*, ed. Michael D. Reeve, transl. Neil Wright (Woodbridge, 2007), 122–3.

[5] Geoffrey of Monmouth, *History of the Kings of Britain*, 118–19.

[6] Anne Heslin [Duggan], 'The coronation of the Young King in 1170', *Studies in Church History* 2 (1965), 165–78; Matthew Strickland, *Henry the Young King, 1155–1183* (New Haven, CT, 2016), 78–94. See also below, Chapter 9.

[7] See also below, Chapter 10.

[8] Robinson, *The Papacy*, 302–3. See also Kurt Villards Jensen, 'Crusading at the fringe of the Ocean: Denmark and Portugal in the twelfth century', in *Medieval History Writing and Crusading Ideology*, ed. Tumoas M. S. Lehtonen and Kurt Villards Jensen with Janne Malkki and Katja Ritari (Helsinki, 2005), 195–206; Johannes Fried, *Der päpstliche Schutz für Laienfürsten. Die politische Geschichte des päpstlichen Schutzprivilegs für Laien*

II. CREATING KINGSHIP 97

fact that the bishops of Rome lacked the means to turn a largely honorific role into one of real political significance. What they *did* possess was the moral clout with whose aid unwanted attention might be seen off. It was with this in mind that the kings of Hungary approached the *curia* in order to bypass the claims of both the German and the Byzantine emperors – Emperor Henry III (1039–56) had at one point seized the Hungarian royal insignia,[9] and in the 1050s, the Byzantine emperor, Constantine X Monomachos, may have sought to impose his authority by offering a crown.[10] Approaching the successor of St Peter provided a way of sidestepping the awkward consequences of dealing with powerful neighbours. In this regard, papal king-making was no different from the prestige to be derived from securing papal recognition for a saint's cult, a monastic foundation or a war of conquest. Prestige accrued because of the Roman pontiff's idealised position as standing above the fray and rivalries of secular politics. It also projected power, not least because getting papal confirmation was an expensive business.[11] Only the truly wealthy could afford to gain approval from the see of St Peter.

The papacy remained the preferred source of recognition for a claim to kingship even when pontiffs sought to convert symbolic capital into hard political currency. In 1318 it was by approaching the *curia* that the barons and clergy of Poland revived Polish kingship,[12] and it was to the papal court that the Scottish barons and clergy turned with the Declaration of Arbroath in 1320 to win recognition of Scottish sovereign kingship.[13] The papacy's role was recognised even by those in competition with it. In 1251, Henry III of England (1216–1272) prepared to secure a papal mandate confirming that nobody could be elected or crowned ruler of Scotland without Henry's

---

(*11.–13. Jhdt.*), Abhandlungen der Heidelberger Akademie der Wissenschaften: Philosophisch-historische Klasse (Heidelberg, 1980), 140–2; Benedict G. E. Wiedemann, 'The kingdom of Portugal, homage and papal "fiefdom" in the second half of the twelfth century', *JMedH* 41 (2015), 432–45; Simon John, 'The papacy and the establishment of the kingdoms of Jerusalem, Sicily and Portugal: twelfth-century papal political thought on incipient kingship', *Journal of Ecclesiastical History* 68 (2017), 223–59.

[9] *Register Gregors VII.*, ii.13.

[10] Zoltán J. Kosztolnyik, 'The Monomachos crown, domestic intrigue and diplomatic reality prevalent at the Hungarian court during the mid-eleventh century', *Chronica. Annual of the Institute of History, University of Szeged* 1 (2001), 30–44.

[11] Wiedemann, 'The kingdom of Portugal'.

[12] For a short survey: Percy Ernst Schramm, 'Das polnische Königtum. Ein Längsschnitt durch die polnische Geschichte (im Hinblick auf Krönung, Herrschaftszeichen und Staatssymbolik)', in his *Könige und Päpste*, vol. 4, 570–92; Paul W. Knoll, *The Rise of the Polish Monarchy: Piast Poland in East Central Europe, 1320–1370* (Chicago, 1972). See also the case of Serbia: Burian, 'Die Krönung des Stephan Prvovencani'.

[13] Walter Bower, *Scotichronicon*, ed. and transl. D. E. R. Watt et al., 9 vols. (Aberdeen, 1987–96), vol. 7, 4–9. See also an earlier, seemingly parallel case, Benedict G. E. Wiedemann, '"Fooling the court of the Lord Pope": Dafydd ap Llywelyn's petition to the curia in 1244', *Welsh History Review* 28 (2016), 209–32.

98   4. CONFERRING KINGSHIP

permission.[14] The king of England aimed to exercise a function that the *curia* increasingly viewed as its prerogative. Still, he could not openly dispute that right. Likewise, in the 1040s, after Henry III had seized the Hungarian royal crown, he presented it to the pope.[15] In the later twelfth century, the imperial court protested when Innocent III sought to provide Lewon II of Armenia with a crown. In the end, it settled for a compromise: the new crown was presented by imperial envoys and had an imperial eagle affixed to it.[16] Those who desired to curtail or prevent access to royal power appealed to papal authority as frequently as those who sought to claim or establish royal status.

Some popes sought to derive political influence from their king-making role.[17] Papal–Hungarian relations during the pontificate of Gregory VII (1073–85) illustrate the point.[18] Already in October 1074, barely a year into Gregory's pontificate, King Solomon had been chided for taking his kingdom in fief from the emperor, not the Holy See.[19] In April 1075, Gregory returned to the matter. He attempted to make peace between Géza and his brother, and to give Hungary a king, not a kinglet (*at rex ibi, non regulus fiat*),[20] that is, one recognised by Gregory, not his imperial adversary. When, in the end, Ladislaus I succeeded, Gregory tried yet again to assert papal prerogatives. In 1077, he ordered his correspondents to ensure that Ladislaus send emissaries to Rome

---

[14] *Anglo-Scottish Relations 1174–1328. Some Selected Documents*, ed. and transl. E. L. G. Stones (London, 1965), no. 9.

[15] *Register Gregors VII.*, ii.13.

[16] Claudia Naumann, *Der Kreuzzug Kaiser Heinrichs VI.* (Frankfurt am Main, Berlin and Bern, 1994), 30–42, 204–10, and Peter Halfter, *Das Papsttum und die Armenier im frühen und hohen Mittelalter. Von den ersten Kontakten bis zur Fixierung der Kirchenunion im Jahre 1198* (Cologne, Weimar and Vienna, 1996), 189–244. For the negotiations see Tschamtschean, a roughly contemporary Armenian chronicler, as cited by A. H. Petermann, 'Beiträge zu der Geschichte der Kreuzzüge aus armenischen Quellen', in *Abhandlungen der königlichen Akademie der Wissenschaften zu Berlin aus dem Jahre 1860* (Berlin, 1861), 81–186, at 150, 152–5. For the wider background: Rudolf Hiestand, 'Precipua tocius christianissimi columpna – Barbarossa und der Kreuzzug', in *Friedrich Barbarossa: Handlungsspielräume und Wirkungswesen des staufischen Kaisers*, ed. Alfred Haverkamp (Sigmaringen, 1992), 51–108; Peter Halfter, 'Die Staufer und Armenien', in *Von Schwaben bis Jerusalem. Facetten staufischer Geschichte*, ed. Sönke Lorenz and Ulrich Schmidt (Sigmaringen, 1995), 187–208. See also the comparable debate concerning Bulgaria: James Ross Sweeney, 'Innocent III, Hungary and the Bulgarian coronation: a study in medieval papal diplomacy', *Church History* 42 (1973), 320–34.

[17] *Regestum Innocentii III Papae super negotio Romani Imperii*, ed. Friedrich Kempf, Miscellanea Historiae Pontificiae xii (Rome, 1947), nos. 14, 29, 136.

[18] See also: Rudolf Schieffer, 'Gregor VII. und die Könige Europas', *Studi gregoriani per la storia della Libertas Ecclesiae* 13 (1989), 189–211; H. E. J. Cowdrey, *Pope Gregory VII, 1073–1085* (Oxford, 1998), 443–8.

[19] *Register Gregors VII.*, ii.13. Similar commands – to give the papacy its due – had been directed to Solomon's rival, Duke Géza, in March 1074 and 1075: ibid. i.58, ii.63.

[20] *Register Gregors VII.*, ii.70.

to acknowledge his obligations towards the Holy See.[21] Viewed in this context, the dogged yet low-key fashion in which the rulers of Portugal had pursued their royal title seems considerably less peculiar. While papal authorisation was still sought, papal authority could be bypassed, reduced or even challenged.

This type of evasive action was not limited to papal king-making. Shortly after receiving that papal-imperial crown, Lewon II received one from the Byzantine emperor. Faced with the choice of alienating either his immediate neighbour or those whose support he needed to keep that neighbour at bay, Lewon simply wore both crowns.[22] His example also stands as a warning against viewing the power relations in evidence too rigidly. Anyone making a king had as much to gain from the exchange as the person who had approached him. Besides, not every act of receiving a crown inevitably resulted in a prolonged battle to define just what this meant for the relationship between king and king-maker. For claims of overlordship to be made, conditions had to allow them to be voiced. In Hungary, Gregory VII had been able to arrogate to himself the right to choose a king because there was a succession dispute, and because one candidate had approached him to invalidate the claims of another. German emperors, similarly, had been able to intervene because a disputed succession had forced rival candidates to muster support from beyond the realm. Foreign rulers did not usually involve themselves, unless they had been called upon to do so.

Sometimes, being the junior partner in a relationship could carry considerable benefits. Powerful backers provided leverage in dealing with hesitant prelates and nobles, and could serve to intimidate rivals. This was the strategy chosen on the death of Boleslaw I,[23] and in Denmark during the 1150s.[24] Comparable calculations had probably motivated Ioannitsa of Bulgaria in 1204, when he offered his support to the crusaders assembled outside Constantinople in return for recognition of his royal title.[25] Other advantages might also accrue. In 1195, the ruler of Cyprus was anointed king by imperial emissaries, and became a vassal in return.[26] According to at least one German source, the king had been taken captive by Richard I of England during the Third Crusade, and had been released only after paying a hefty ransom. The

---

[21] *Register Gregors VII.*, iv.25.

[22] Petermann, *Beiträge*, 152–3; *La Chronique attribuée au connéetable Smbat*, transl. Gérard Dédéyan (Paris, 1980), 72–3. In fact, one contemporary chronicler claimed that the Caliph at Baghdad, too, sent Lewon gifts for this coronation: Petermann, *Beiträge*, 152.

[23] Wipo, *Gesta Chuonradi*, 47–9.

[24] Otto of Freising and Rahewin, *Gesta Frederici*, ii.5, pp. 290–1; Odilo Engels, 'Friedrich Barbarossa und Dänemark', in *Friedrich Barbarossa*, ed. Haverkamp, 353–85.

[25] Robert de Clari, *La Conquête de Constantinople*, ed. and transl. Peter Noble (Edinburgh, 2005), 76–9.

[26] *Annales Marbacenses Qui Dicuntur (Cronica Hohenburgensis cum Continuatione et Additamentis Neoburgensibus)*, ed. Hermann Bloch, MGH SSrG sep. ed. (Hanover and Leipzig, 1907), 67; *Gesta episcoporum Halberstadensium*, MGH SS 23 (Hanover, 1874), 112.

100   4. CONFERRING KINGSHIP

emperor responded by imprisoning Richard I, and releasing him only after he had paid an even heftier ransom. Thus, the English king was made to atone for the indignity he had inflicted upon the emperor's man.[27] Declaring someone to be a king also incurred a duty to come to his assistance, to defend him against foes and to punish those who shamed or humiliated him.[28] Hence dependent status was not necessarily rejected by the 'subservient' party.

Moreover, being asked, or at least being perceived as able to give a crown signalled power, moral rectitude and political legitimacy. There was no point in asking a weak ruler, one notorious for his moral failings or one whose own legitimacy was in question. This may explain the curious crown-giving bonanza that occurred in Germany after 1198. Two rival claimants had been chosen for the imperial throne. One took the opportunity to confer a royal title on the duke of Bohemia.[29] His rival responded by holding a festive diet at Cologne, where he solemnly crowned the relics of the three magi.[30] In other cases, writers invented episodes when the eminence of their protagonist was demonstrated by his making of kings. The early thirteenth-century *Morkinskinna* is the most detailed such account. Its author, an anonymous Icelander, dealt at some length with the adventures of King Sigurd, who in 1107–10 had embarked on a crusade to the Holy Land. The story of Sigurd's exploits is a long catalogue of honours. While wintering in England, he was received splendidly and honourably,[31] and when he arrived in the Holy Land,

---

[27] *Historia de expeditione Friderici*, in *Quellen zur Geschichte des Kreuzzugs Kaiser Friedrichs I.*, ed. A. Chroust, MGH SS sep. ed. (Berlin, 1928), 104–5.

[28] See also the parallel case of Wales: in 1240, King Henry III gave Dafydd ap Llewellyn a 'lesser kind of crown, called a garland, as *insignum* of the principality of North Wales, and Dafydd declared himself to be in everything subject to the king of England: diadema minus, quod dicitur garlonde insigne principatus Northwalliae, per omnia tamen subiciens se regi Angliae', *Annals of Tewkesbury*, in *Annales Monastici*, ed. H.R. Luard, 5 vols. (London, 1864–9), vol. 1, 43–182, at 115. For the Welsh view, which does not mention the crown, *Brut y Tywysogyon or The Chronicle of the Princes. Peniarth Ms. 20 Version*, transl. Thomas Jones (Cardiff, 1955). This probably served to strengthen his position in relation to the other Welsh princes: Huw Pryce, 'Negotiating Anglo-Welsh relations: Llewellyn the Great and Henry III', in *England and Europe in the Reign of Henry III (1216–1272)*, ed. Björn Weiler with Ifor Rowlands (Aldershot, 2002), 13–30, *passim* and at 21–2 on the act of Gloucester; R. R. Davies, *The Age of Conquest. Wales, 1063–1415* (originally published as *Conquest, Coexistence and Change. Wales 1063–1415*) (Oxford, 1987; repr. 1991), 239–50.

[29] *Arnoldi Chronica Slavorum*, ed. Johann M. Lappenberg, MGH sep. ed. (Hanover, 1869), 219; *Annales Marbacenses*, 74.

[30] Bernd Ulrich Hucker, *Kaiser Otto IV.* (Hanover, 1990), 22–35, 95–101, 567–70.

[31] *Morkinskinna. The Earliest Icelandic Chronicle of the Norwegian Kings (1030–1157)*, translated with introduction and notes by Theodore M. Andersson and Kari Ellen Gade (Ithaca, NY, 2000), chapters 61–3, pp. 313–25 for Sigurd's campaign; chapter 61, p. 314 for his reception at the court of King Henry. I am grateful to Haki Antonsson for this reference. On the text see Theodore M. Andersson, *The Sagas of Norwegian Kings (1130–1265). An Introduction* (Ithaca, NY, 2016), 51–74; Ármann Jakobsson, *A Sense of*

II. CREATING KINGSHIP   101

King Baldwin had the streets of Jerusalem decked out with carpets and precious stones, hosted a most splendid banquet in the king's honour and presented him with a relic of the Holy Cross.[32] The account of Sigurd's crusade ends with a lengthy report on his glamorous sojourn at the Byzantine court. In between, the king and his band conquered several castles in Spain, and generally wreaked havoc upon Muslims and unfaithful Christians.[33] In the course of their travels, they also reached Sicily, where Sigurd received a splendid welcome from Roger II. During a feast lasting several days, Roger most willingly waited on the Norwegian king. On the seventh day, Sigurd repaid this service by leading Roger to the throne and installing him as king.[34]

We can be fairly certain that Sigurd did not engage in king-making. Roger had barely entered his teens when Sigurd would have visited Sicily, and Sigurd was, in fact, dead by the time Roger did become king (he died in March 1130). What matters is the anonymous author's concern with and representation of Sigurd's fame as reflected in the many splendid receptions he was given, and in the fact that he bestowed a royal title upon someone known for his might. Roger 'was a powerful monarch', who 'conquered all of Apulia and subdued a large number of islands in the Mediterranean. He was called Roger the Great.'[35] There was no claim to Norwegian lordship over Sicily. Instead, the tale of Sigurd's Sicilian sojourn served as testimony to the power of Norwegian kings, and it was to a domestic Norwegian audience that this message was communicated. Notably, the episode inverts the imagery employed in Gallus Anonymus' account of Boleslaw I's elevation in 999/1000.[36] In the *Gesta Principum Polonorum*, the crown-giving had been embedded in a narrative of parity between Boleslaw and Otto III. In *Morkinskinna* it served to highlight the superiority of Sigurd. He had merited the right to enthrone Roger because

---

Belonging: Morkinskinna and Icelandic Identity, c. 1220 (Odense, 2014). The episode goes well beyond what other contemporary or near-contemporary sources report: Theodoricus Monachus, *Historia*, 65–6; *Ágrip a Nóregskonungasgum. A Twelfth-Century Synoptic History of the Kings of Norway*, ed. and transl. M. J. Driscoll (London, 1995), 71–5; *Fagrskinna. A Catalogue of the Kings of Norway*, transl. Alison Finlay (Leiden and Boston, 2004), chapters 87–9, pp. 255–7. See also: Ármann Jakobsson, 'Image is everything: the Morkinskinna account of King Sigurðr of Norway's journey to the Holy Land', *Parergon* 30 (2013), 121–40; Scheel, *Skandinavien und Byzanz*, vol. 2, 641–50, 1040–63. *Chronique d'Ernoul et de Bernard le Trésorier*, ed. Louis de Mas Latrie (Paris, 1871), 13–14, by contrast, claimed that the king of France crowned Roger II.

[32] *Morkinskinna*, chapter 61c, pp. 321–2.

[33] *Morkinskinna*, chapter 61, pp. 316–20.

[34] *Morkinskinna*, chapter 61a, pp. 320–1. The story was taken up and expanded a few decades later in Snorri Sturluson's *Heimskringla*, which added that Sigurd granted Roger the right that there should always be a king of Sicily, although in the past there had been only counts or dukes: Snorri Sturluson, *Heimskringla: History of the Kings of Norway*, transl. Lee M. Hollander (Austin, TX, 1964), 385.

[35] *Morkinskinna*, chapter 61b, p. 321.

[36] See above, Chapter 3.

102   4. CONFERRING KINGSHIP

of his rectitude, martial exploits, wealth and might. Kingship was a personal accolade, but so was the ability to make kings. Just as the claim of an aspirant to a throne needed confirmation from someone of undisputed moral integrity, so conferring a crown could garner prestige only by awarding it to someone truly deserving of that honour.

Such might also have been the thinking behind an episode which purportedly took place during the Fourth Crusade. According to Robert de Clari (d. 1216), the army assembled outside Constantinople was approached by Ioannitsa of Bulgaria, who wished for its leaders to make him king. He followed well-established practice. Ioannitsa's predecessor had contacted the crusading armies of Frederick Barbarossa and Henry VI, as had Lewon II of Armenia.[37] In 1195, in the midst of Emperor Henry VI's preparations for his crusade, envoys from Cyprus arrived, requesting that the emperor send two archbishops to anoint their newly established ruler.[38] In Ioannitsa's case, the crusaders refused. While Robert gave no reason for their decision, his account of Ioannitsa's rise to power is suggestive. Ioannitsa had started out as the keeper of an imperial horse farm. To avenge an insult from a palace servant, he embarked on a career of plunder and raiding.[39] Robert de Clari's version of events points to the importance of standing. All the new kingships discussed here were awarded to descendants of already well-established rulers. Boleslaw I was the scion of a long line of princes, as were Roger II, and St Stephen. Just as possessing power greater than any of one's people denoted individual probity, so a dynasty's longevity signified familial suitability. In Robert's account, Ioannitsa failed to meet so basic a criterion. Hence he could not legitimately be made king. And Ioannitsa's alleged motivation – revenge – certainly did not conform to expectations of a king's requisite moral rigour. Choosing a corrupt, lowborn and violent oppressor of his people would reflect as badly upon those granting or confirming his royal status as on the tyrant whose greed and ambition they had failed to thwart.

4.2 Courtiers, Nobles and Bishops

Similar expectations applied within the realm. There, it is worth pausing to consider the genre of texts we most frequently have to work with, their likely audience and the social group to which the majority of their authors belonged. Most relevant information comes from regnal histories. Many had been

---

[37] Hiestand, 'Precipua tocius christianissimi columpna'.

[38] *Annales Marbacenses*, 67.

[39] Robert de Clari, *La Conquête de Constantinople*, ed. and transl. Peter Noble (Edinburgh, 2005), 65, pp. 78–81. See also, generally, Francesco Dall'Aglio, 'L'immagine della Bulgaria in occidente al tempo della quarta crociata', *Annuario Istituto Romeno di Cultura e ricerca Umanistica* 5 (2003), 79–103; Dall'Aglio, 'The second Bulgarian kingdom and the Latin empire of Constantinople: a general overview', *Palaeobulgarica* 37 (2013), 9–17.

II. CREATING KINGSHIP

written by members of the court. The Anonymous Notary described himself as the notary of King Bela; Cosmas was a canon at Prague Cathedral; Sven Aggesen's uncle had been archbishop of Lund.[40] If not the king, then members of his entourage, and those whose task it was to counsel him, were frequently addressed by such works. Sven dedicated his writings to Archbishop Absalon of Lund,[41] Theodoric the Monk the *Historia de Antiquitatibus* to Archbishop Eystein of Trondheim[42] and Gallus Anonymus the *Gesta Principum* to Archbishop Martin of Gniezno and to Bishop Paul of Poznan, as well as the ducal chaplains.[43] That audience was chosen for a reason. 'Gallus' stressed the responsibility of prelates to offer the king advice. Indeed, many of these accounts established models for how the relationship between counsellor and kings should unfold. The image painted by Saxo Grammaticus in book five of the *Gesta Danorum*, of the relationship between the legendary King Frothi III and his confidant Erik, provided a blueprint for dealings between the archbishops of Lund and the Danish kings. Until he secured Erik's services, Frothi had been a most foolish and inept ruler. By taking Erik's advice, he became one of the most successful of early Danish kings (and a great lawgiver) while Erik acquired fame and riches.[44] Both the people giving and the ones receiving good advice gained from the exchange.

The attention of that particular audience of officials, high-ranking churchmen and court clerics was coveted in part because history was considered a medium appropriate to teaching them. Through knowledge of the past they would learn how to use their position for the good of the realm. The connection comes fully to the fore in Sven Aggesen's *Lex Castrensis*, Law of the Retainers (*c.* 1181–2). Ostensibly an account of the legal customs of the royal court as they had been under King Knud the Great (r. 1014–35), it treated matters ranging from seating arrangements[45] to the king's duty to remain loyal

---

[40] *The Works of Sven Aggesen, Twelfth-Century Danish Historian*, transl. Eric Christiansen (London, 1992), 1–2. See Lars Boje Mortensen, 'The Nordic archbishoprics as literary centres around 1200', in *Archbishop Absalom of Lund and His World*, ed. Karsten Frijs Jensen and Inge Skovgaard-Petersen (Roskilde, 2000), 133–57 . This section expands upon examples from Björn Weiler, 'Tales of first kings and the culture of kingship in the west, c. 1050–1200', *Viator* 46:2 (2015), 101–28, at 118–26, but pursues rather different questions.

[41] *Brevis Historia*, in *Scriptores Minores*, ed. Gertz, vol. 1, 94–5.

[42] Theodoricus Monachus, *Historia*, 1.

[43] *Gesta Principum Polonorum*, 2–3, 110–11, 210–11. For a fuller discussion of the putative audience of these texts see Weiler, 'Tales of first kings', 118–27.

[44] Saxo Grammaticus, *Gesta Danorum: the History of the Danes*, ed. Karsten Frijs-Jensen, transl. Peter Fisher, 2 vols. (Oxford, 2015), v.3.8–12, 22–6, vol. 1, pp. 278–85, 296–301.

[45] *Lex Castrensis*, in *Scriptores Minores*, ed. Gertz, vol. 1, 73–5. On the text: Mia Münster-Swendsen, '"Auf das Gesetz sei das Land Gebaut": Zum Zusammenhang rechtlicher und historischer Diskurse im hochmittelalterlichen Dänemark', in *Macht und Spiegel der Macht*, ed. Vercamer and Kersken, 85–102.

104   4. CONFERRING KINGSHIP

to his men.[46] Yet the *Lex* was also a lament on the decline of Danish political culture. The wise and righteous order of Knud had been abandoned when kings ceased to enforce the law. Knud himself had set a dangerous precedent. While campaigning abroad, Sven recounts, Knud had killed one of his retainers in a fit of rage. When his men realised what had happened, they convened to discuss the matter. They faced a dilemma. If, as the law demanded, they executed the king for his crime, justice would have been served, but they would be leaderless and would be driven from these foreign lands. On the other hand, pardoning Knud threatened to set an example that might encourage others to commit heinous deeds in turn. Eventually, Knud's followers decreed that the royal throne was to be placed in their midst, that Knud had to prostrate himself in front of it and that he was to await judgement while in this position. Only once Knud had made sufficient atonement was he pardoned and only then was he raised onto the throne by his men. Subsequently, it was decided that anyone else committing comparable acts would either be put to death or exiled.[47] Under King Niels (1104–38), however, a powerful noble killed one of his peers. As a direct result, the law was softened to allow compensation to be paid. From then on, Sven complained, the rigour of justice ceased to prevail in Denmark.[48]

Sven had been a prominent figure in the Danish Church, and was a regular participant in royal campaigns.[49] He was member of the very section of society that, in the *Lex Castrensis*, had been called upon to restore the right order of the world. The king had forfeited the right to occupy the seat of power and justice. Like a true penitent (visualised by him lying prostrate on the floor), Knud had to submit himself to judgement by his people, before being reinstated to his former rank. That he did not simply reoccupy the throne, but was led to it by the assembled men, only served to reinforce the point. He was king through and by the consent of his people.[50] Moreover, this was not the end of the remedial measures taken. The law was strengthened, and Knud's authority was fully restored only after everyone present had loudly acclaimed the decision reached. Kingship, Sven seems to imply, existed independently of the king. It was not his to do with as he wished. The ruler was the source of law, but was also bound by it. It fell to the leading men of the realm to enforce the law, and

---

[46] *Lex Castrensis*, in *Scriptores Minores*, ed. Gertz, vol. 1, 74–5.

[47] *Lex Castrensis*, in *Scriptores Minores*, ed. Gertz, vol. 1, 78–81.

[48] *Lex Castrensis*, in *Scriptores Minores*, ed. Gertz, vol. 1, 84–7.

[49] Michael Winterbottom, 'Karsten Friis-Jensen's preliminary findings towards a new edition of Sven Aggesen', in *Historical and Intellectual Culture*, ed. Heebøll-Holm, Münster-Swendsen and Sønnesyn, 295–316.

[50] This echoed a point made by Sven when he introduced the *Lex Castrensis*: it had not been compiled by Knud personally. Rather, the king had convened an assembly of great men, and asked those most prudent and wise among them to collate customs for his court: *Lex Castrensis*, in *Scriptores Minores*, ed. Gertz, vol. 1, 66–72.

II. CREATING KINGSHIP

to do so alongside the king. If the monarch was too weak or if he had himself committed a crime, his leading subjects had to ensure that the right order of the realm be maintained.[51] The *Lex Castrensis* provided a definition of good royal lordship directed as much towards the king's advisors as towards the monarch himself.

The Danish example is unusual because the need for oversight and the limits of royal power were made explicit in relation to a monarch who otherwise conformed to an ideal type of royal lordship. The closest parallel is the Anonymous Notary's account of the election of Álmos as leader of the Hungarians.[52] The Hungarians set out to conquer Pannonia. Realising that they would not be able to complete the journey without 'a duke and ruler', the Seven Leaders, 'noblemen by birth and strong in war, firm in their faithfulness', picked Álmos to fulfil that role. They then swore a five-part oath. They and their progeny would always elect as their lord a member of Álmos' lineage; all land and booty would be divided between them; the Leaders and their heirs would always advise their lord and participate fully in the *honor regni*, the honour and business of the realm; anyone seeking to sow discord would pay for this with his blood; if Álmos, any of the Leaders or one of their descendants violated these terms, he would be cursed for all eternity.[53] The Notary's account defined baronial participation in the king's governance as rooted in a time well before the existence of the realm over which the Árpáds came to rule. It was also the very source and origin of their power.

We do not know when the Notary wrote – the *Gesta* is commonly dated to somewhere between *c.* 1200 and *c.* 1230. Therefore, it is impossible to determine whether it echoed or foreshadowed the Golden Bull. Certainly, the Notary linked the Seven Leaders directly to his own time. The *Gesta*, as the preface stated, recorded the origins of Hungary's dukes and kings and nobles.[54] When first introducing the leaders, the Notary pointed out that they were those, 'who right up to the present day are called the Hetumoger'. After recounting the oath, he listed the names of the leaders, linking them to current lineages among the Hungarian aristocracy. Evidently, the story of the election of Álmos was expected to resonate. The *Gesta* recounted an idealised past that provided guidance to its readers about how to handle the affairs of the present.

The *Gesta* furthermore points to a fundamental paradox in many of our materials. The Notary constructed an ideal past in which to anchor the rights of the aristocracy. He also sketched a history devoid of resistance and conflict.

---

[51] Sven reflected a broader consensus: Saxo Grammaticus, *Gesta Danorum*, i.2.1–2, pp. 20–3. See also Thomas Foerester, "'. . . um in der Gerechtigkeit nicht weniger stark wie in der Schlacht zu erscheinen". Königtum und Recht in den Gesta Danorum des Saxo Grammaticus', in *Macht und Spiegel der Macht*, ed. Vercamer and Kersken, 103–18.

[52] See Chapter 3.

[53] *Anonimi Gesta Hungarorum*, 16–19.

[54] *Anonimi Gesta Hungarorum*, 1–4.

106   4. CONFERRING KINGSHIP

Hungarian history consisted of little more than a sequence of wise and prudent lords. The Seven Leaders therefore claimed a right that their descendants had never exercised. There was no need for them to do so.[55] The Notary's image of concord and amity may well have been all the more forceful as a reminder of why such tranquillity existed. His example also suggests that just because an author wrote about the right to restrain the monarch did not mean that he demanded it to be exercised at once. In fact, the relative ease with which the issue was discussed, suggests that the underlying principles were deemed to be self-evident.[56] Kingship (and leadership) was conditional upon power being exercised for the common good, and at the behest and in consultation with a ruler's leading subjects.

At the same time, once a precedent had been established, it could inspire concrete action. In 1222, Andrew II of Hungary conceded to the demands of his nobles and issued the Golden Bull. Many of its clauses dealt with the kind of grievances common to such documents: rules of inheritance, the farming of royal estates and the rights of nobles and freemen in relation to the monarch.[57] All that was, however, framed as a return to an ideal *status quo ante*. Andrew promised to reinstate the good old laws of St Stephen.[58] In this, the Golden Bull invoked a long tradition. From *c.* 1085, a sequence of saints' lives had focussed on Stephen's succession, reforms and missionary activities.[59] An important theme in this cult was Stephen's collation and promulgation of law. That was reinforced under King Coloman (1095–1116), whose path to the throne had been circuitous, to say the least. Initially destined for a career in the Church, and at one point even a bishop, Coloman was forced into exile. He returned to Hungary and seized the throne. Membership of the Church normally (though not necessarily) barred a would-be claimant from succeeding to the throne, and so Coloman found himself in a position of precarious legitimacy. Worse still, he overrode the claims of his brother Álmos, who had been his predecessor's chosen heir, and then managed to fall out both with the armies of the First Crusade, and with Emperor Henry IV.[60] This context may explain

---

[55] Lászlo Veszprémy, 'Umwälzungen im Ungarn des 13. Jahrhunderts: vom "Blutvertrag" zu den ersten Ständeversammlungen', in *Macht und Spiegel der Macht*, ed. Vercamer and Kersken, 383–402, at 387–92.

[56] See, similarly, letters of advice to kings: Weiler, 'Clerical admonitio'.

[57] For examples, see the case studies assembled in *Album Elemèr Mályusz* (Brussels, 1976).

[58] *The Laws of the Medieval Kingdom of Hungary*, vol. 1, 34.

[59] Klaniczay, *Holy Rulers*, 123–34; László Veszprémy, 'Royal saints in Hungarian chronicles, legends and liturgy', in *The Making of Christian Myths in the Periphery of Latin Christendom (c.1000–1300)*, ed. Lars Boje Mortensen (Copenhagen, 2006), 217–36, at 224–32.

[60] Albert of Aachen, *Historia Ierosolomitana. History of the Journey to Jerusalem*, ed. and transl. Susan B. Edgington (Oxford, 2007), 45–48, 59–60; Nora Berend, *At the Gate of*

II. CREATING KINGSHIP 107

why, *c.* 1100, he convened an assembly of nobles and prelates to revise the laws of Hungary.[61] Like the first king, he compiled and improved the customs of the realm, and did so with the advice and counsel of his people. In taking this approach, Coloman helped reinforce the status of Stephen's legislative endeavours as the foundation of good kingship. He purported not to revise the law, but to restore it.

Together, Coloman's efforts and those of the early twelfth-century hagiographers helped create a political-textual community grounded in the laws of St Stephen.[62] Good kings not only kept the law, but sought also to ensure that it aligned with the customs of Hungary's first king. This did not rule out innovation, but new clauses were framed as expurgating later emendations, or as putting an end to abuses that weak kings had allowed to take root – echoing the trajectory sketched by Sven Aggesen in the *Lex Castrensis*. In 1222, we find innovation and reform cloaked in an invocation of St Stephen. The first clause in the Golden Bull stipulated that an annual assembly be held on the feast of Stephen, at the old royal capital of Székesfehérvár.[63] In a striking parallel to the Blood Oath recorded by the Anonymous Notary, the Golden Bull granted the nobility a right to take up arms against and replace kings who violated its provisions. The image of St Stephen as lawgiver and ideal first king provided a conceptual framework for curtailing and challenging his successors.

The utilisation of St Stephen reflects a Europe-wide phenomenon. Similar concerns, though formulated under rather different circumstances, surface in the crusader states. The key figure here was Godfrey of Bouillon, the first ruler of crusader Jerusalem. What makes Godfrey's case unusual is the gradual development of his status as an ideal founder over the course of the twelfth century, and the sudden emergence in the thirteenth of his reputation as a lawgiver. In the 1120s, Fulcher of Chartres, himself a participant in the First Crusade and a leading figure in the kingdom's government, only recorded that, in 1099, Godfrey had been chosen as ruler because of his noble excellence,

---

Christendom: Jews, Muslims and 'Pagans' in Medieval Hungary, c. 1000–c. 1300 (Cambridge, 2001), 84–5; Paul Stephenson, *Byzantium's Balkan Frontier: A Political Study of the Northern Balkans, 900–1204* (Cambridge, 2000), 198–200.

[61] *Laws of the Medieval Kingdom of Hungary*, vol. 1, 24–6. For the context: Berend, Urbańczyk, Wiszewski, *Central Europe*, 217–20.

[62] Veszprémy, 'The invented eleventh century'. See also the symbolic significance of Stephen's supposed regalia: Péter László, 'The Holy Crown of Hungary, visible and invisible', *Slavonic and Eastern European Review* 81 (2003) 421–510; Nora Berend, 'The medieval origins of modern nationalism? Stephen of Hungary and El Cid of Spain', in *The Creation of Medieval Northern Europe: Essays in Honour of Sverre Bagge*, ed. Leidulf Melve and Sigbjørn Sønnesyn (Oslo, 2012), 219–45. On the concept of 'textual community': Stock, *Implications of Literacy*.

[63] *Laws of the Medieval Kingdom of Hungary*, vol. 1, 34. For the context: Berend, Urbańczyk and Wiszewski, eds., *Central Europe*, 425–30; Martin J. Rady, 'Hungary and the Golden Bull of 1222', *Banata* 24 (2014), 87–108.

108   4. CONFERRING KINGSHIP

military record, patient modesty and elegant manners.[64] On the occasion of
Godfrey's death in 1100, Fulcher penned a poem recounting how, through God's
will, Godfrey had been chosen as ruler of Jerusalem.[65] He did not otherwise
comment on his short reign. Soon, however, a myth developed that Godfrey had
refused to adopt the title of king.[66] Unlike in Hungary, however, there was no
royal effort to promote Godfrey's status as an ideal predecessor.[67]

All of this changed in the mid-thirteenth century, when John of Ibelin, lord
of Beirut, compiled the *Livre des Assises*, an account of the legal customs of the
realm. John had come to prominence during the struggles against Emperor
Frederick II and his attempts from the 1230s to assert royal authority in
Jerusalem.[68] The *Livre* presents an ideal of legal organisation, combined with
florid displays of learned jurisprudence. While not explicitly directed against
Frederick or his sons, it still aimed to enshrine in writing the supposed rights of
the aristocracy of Outremer in relation to its kings. Of particular significance in
this context is the prologue, which places the *Livre*'s provisions in their
imagined historical context. After the crusaders had conquered Jerusalem,
John explains, Godfrey convened an assembly of prelates, barons and other
wise men, and asked them to define the laws by which the kingdom should be
ruled. These, readers would subsequently find recorded.[69] The *Livre* used a key
element of the ideal type of the first king – the founder of monarchy and giver
of laws. It did so independently of any indigenous traditions. John of Ibelin
attributed to Godfrey the ancient customs he purported to record, in large
measure because codifying them was what first kings were supposed to have
done. The new image of Godfrey served to legitimise resistance towards the
power of his successors and attempts to curtail and channel it. What links
John's approach to the other examples discussed is the invocation of pan-
European models of what first kings (or rulers) were meant to do, and the
fashioning of them as a means with which to help shape the affairs of the
present.

---

[64] Fulcher, *Historia*, 307–8.
[65] Fulcher, *Historia*, 350–1.
[66] Guibert of Nogent, *Dei Gesta Per Francos et cinq autres textes*, ed. R. B. C. Huygens,
CCCM (Turnhout, 1996), 317–18; Charles Kohler, 'Histoire anonyme des rois de
Jérusalem (1099–1187)', *Revue d'Orient Latin* 5 (1897), 211–53, at 232; *Peregrinationes
tres: Saewulf, John of Würzburg, Theodericus*, ed. R. B. C. Huygens with a study on the
voyages of Saewulf by John H. Pryor, CCCM (Turnhout, 1994), 125. Simon John, *Godfrey
of Bouillon: Duke of Lotharingia, Ruler of Latin Jerusalem, c. 1060–1100* (London and
New York, 2018), 181–5.
[67] Anette Güntzel, 'Godfrey of Bouillon: the stylization of an ideal ruler in universal
chronicles of the 12th and 13th centuries', *Amsterdamer Beiträge zur älteren
Germanistik* 70 (2013), 209–22; John, *Godfrey of Bouillon*, 229–43.
[68] On John and the historical context see: Peter W. Edbury, *John of Ibelin and the Kingdom
of Jerusalem* (Woodbridge, 1997), 24–103.
[69] John of Ibelin, *Le Livre des Assises*, ed. Peter W. Edbury (Leiden, 2003), 51–2.

II. CREATING KINGSHIP 109

Within a regnal community, accounts of the foundation of kingship, or of the deeds of a paradigmatic ruler, provided a canvas onto which later generations could project concerns about the present, and with which they might chart a course for the future. The phenomenon was by no means limited to new realms. The conditionality of royal power, the need for the ruler to be overseen and his performance to be assessed by the ruled, simply appears to have found different conduits in polities whose regnal status remained uncontested. We may, for instance, find evidence of an ideal *status quo ante* in need of restoration. Often, that was associated with a particular ruler. Yet in the absence of a founding hero of monarchy, the precise identity of that ideal forebear changed from generation to generation. In England, he was usually associated with a ruler's predecessor but one.[70] The key exception was Henry I (d. 1135). By the late twelfth century he had, in some circles at least, emerged as the ideal type of a just and righteous king.[71] In Germany, an ideal predecessor or ancestor was invoked, without any reason being necessarily given as to why he might be worth emulating. In the 1040s, Bern of Reichenau likened Emperor Henry III to Charlemagne. A century later the *Annals of Pöhlden* described Lothar III as a worthy heir of Constantine, Charlemagne and Otto I.[72] Importantly, none of these three was stylised as the founder of a monarchy. Constantine seems to have been remembered primarily because his wife Helena found a relic of the True Cross[73] and because he was the first Christian Roman emperor.[74] He was invoked to define the royal office only in the most general terms. The relative lack of engagement with founding figures may reflect the fact that, in established realms, the figure of the first king was of far less significance than in ones that had been newly created. The unbroken sequence of rulers testified to the legitimacy of royal lordship.

---

[70] Björn Weiler, 'Kings and sons: princely sons and the structures of revolt in Europe, c. 1170–1280', *Historical Research* 82 (2009), 17–40, at 22–4. See also the figure of Edgar, paired with his advisor St Dunstan: William of Malmesbury, *Gesta Pontificum Anglorum*, ed. and transl. Michael Winterbottom, 2 vols. (Oxford, 2007–8), vol. 1, 34–5, 258–9; Eadmer, *Historia Novorum in Anglia*, ed. Martin Rule (London, 1884), 3.

[71] Alan Cooper, 'Walter Map on Henry I: the creation of eminently useful history', *The Medieval Chronicle* 7 (2011), 103–14. For a more hostile view: Matthew Paris, *Chronica Majora*, ed. Henry R. Luard, Rolls Series, 7 vols. (London, 1872–4), vol. 5, 286–7.

[72] *Die Briefe des Abtes Bern von Reichenau*, ed. Franz-Josef Schmale (Stuttgart, 1961), no. 26 (Charlemagne); *Annales Palidenses*, MGH SS 16 (Hanover, 1859), 77 (Constantine, Charlemagne, Otto I). See also, below, Chapter 9.

[73] Marianus Scotus, *Chronicon*, MGH SS 17 (Hanover, 1861), 525; Hermann of Reichenau, *Herimanni Augiensis Chronicon*, MGH SS 5 (Hanover, 1844), 79.

[74] Bernold of Reichenau, *Chronicon*, MGH SS 17 (Hanover, 1861), 407; *Annales Magdeburgenses*, MGH SS 16 (Hanover, 1859), 119. Godfrey of Viterbo was more concerned with his illegitimate lineage: Godfrey of Viterbo, *Speculum Regum*, MGH SS 22 (Hanover, 1872), 81. Matters were more complicated in relation to Charlemagne. A fuller study of the image of legendary kings in high medieval Germany remains a desideratum, as would one of the image of Charlemagne.

Many regnal histories offered, or claimed to offer, the first full narrative of a community's origins. Not infrequently, they included an account of how indigenous royal or quasi-royal lordship had first been established. Ultimately, having kings or king-like dukes served to reinforce a community's distinctiveness. If only such men could be kings as were mightier than others, then the people over whom they ruled would not be subject to any monarchs other than their 'own', that is, kings who had been chosen by and from among them. Consequently, challenges to political distinctiveness often centred on the legitimacy of that first ruler. This necessitated that stories of the origins of kingship be fashioned in such a way so as to allow them to conform to shared European norms. Such practical necessities may have been reinforced by an impetus to construct a community's past in a manner that conformed to common models of literary composition. Perhaps for that very reason we often find echoes of developing approaches, for instance, in biblical exegesis. That the idea of oversight was not new bears reiterating. Still, from *c.* 1180, the inherent sinfulness of the royal office as a secular institution, resulting in a need for the ruled to ensure that the rulers abide by the law, became a popular theme in interpretations of the Bible.[75] The parallels with Sven Aggesen and the Anonymous Notary are evident. Such similarities may have reflected the lack of an indigenous tradition of regnal history in Latin. They could also have been shaped by the rhetorical conventions at which authors and patrons wanted to be seen to excel. Danes and Poles may not have been Romans, but they certainly could write like them. At the same time, the goal remained to ascertain distinctiveness, to show that Norwegians, Danes, Poles, Hungarians and Bohemians possessed a long and venerable history, independent of and equal to that of their neighbours. Such distinctiveness extended to modes of political organisation. In recording how their forebears had established ideal practices of oversight and governance under Álmos and Knud the Great, Sven and the Notary recorded a model of how they thought their realms should be governed. They may also have implied that Danes and Hungarians were better at upholding common norms than their immediate neighbours.

Most of these examples, though written by clerics, centred on the aristocracy or the king's immediate lay followers and clerical advisors as the ones charged with providing oversight. What about the broader Church? With the partial exception of Sicily, ecclesiastical institutions (as opposed to individuals) were granted only a limited role. In Hungary, Stephen's crown may have been bestowed by the pope, but then an archangel had instructed him to do so, while in Poland the initiative rested with Otto III. To some extent, the lack of references to the Church simply reflected the antiquity of the institution of

---

[75] This condenses an argument made more fully in Weiler, 'Tales of first kings', 124–6; Weiler, 'Thinking about power', at 18–23. For developments in biblical exegesis: Buc, 'Exègése et pensée politique', and '*Principes gentium dominantur eorum*'.

rulership. In Poland, there always had been dukes. Even Piast's son simply replaced a dynasty that had turned out to be unworthy. In Hungary, Stephen may have been the first king, but he was the descendent of dukes, who, as the anonymous notary explained, had initially been chosen when the Magyars were still pagans. At most, Lisa Wolverton has suggested, in Bohemia, Libuše may have foreshadowed the later *ecclesia*, just as Samuel (who had anointed Saul and David) foreshadowed the medieval Church.[76] Given that kingship and conversion were intrinsically linked, an institution that pre-dated the acceptance of Christianity could, by definition, not have been sanctioned by the Church. Moreover, a central feature of the institution of kingship was the establishment of an autochthonous ecclesiastical organisation. Otto III had granted Boleslaw all the rights pertaining to the imperial Church in his domains, and Stephen had established dioceses only after he had become king. This had implications for the role of the Church in the creation of kingship. Normally, inaugurating the king signified ecclesiastical leadership within the realm.[77] However, if, as Gallus Anonymus seems to imply, ecclesiastical institutions had been under the authority of foreign kings when kingship was first established, that would have undermined a theme central to these narratives. Kingship had been earned through the virtuous exercise of overweening might. An act of recognition merely acknowledged that fact. An absence of references to the Church was thus rooted both in the nature of the texts recording the emergence of kingship, and the circumstances under which it unfolded.

Once we venture beyond the immediate moment when kingship was created, and turn to the installation of subsequent rulers, we find that practices in new kingdoms fell into line with those followed elsewhere in Latin Europe. In Poland, oversight was central to the cult of St Stanislas. Similar claims were staked by the archbishops of Canterbury in England, Reims in France, Cologne in Germany, Santiago de Compostela in Castile and by the bishops of St Andrews in Scotland. Moreover, just as with the narrative codification of oversight, it is also in new realms that we find pan-European developments applied earlier, or at least more forcefully.[78] An especially salient example

---

[76] Wolverton, *Cosmas of Prague*, 120. See also above, Chapter 3.

[77] See below, Chapters 8 and 9.

[78] See, for a useful case study of the process of appropriation, the parallels between the account by 'Gallus' of Boleslaw I and William of Poitiers' of William the Conqueror: Elisabeth van Houts, 'The writing of history and family traditions through the eyes of men and women: the Gesta Principum Polonorum', in *Gallus Anonymus and His Chronicle in the Context of Twelfth-Century Historiography from the Perspective of the Latest Research*, ed. Krzysztof Stopka (Krakow, 2010), 189–203; van Houts, 'The echo of the conquest in the Latin sources: Duchess Matilda, her daughters and the enigma of the Golden Child', in *The Bayeux Tapestry: Embroidering the Facts of History*, ed. Pierre Bouet (Caen, 2004), 135–54.

survives from Norway. In 1161, Magnus Erlingsson had been enthroned as king. Yet there were problems. Unlike his rivals and predecessors, he was not the son of a king, and could only claim royal descent through his mother. He was also underage. Both were among the most common reasons why candidates might be dismissed by electors, or why their claim to the throne was challenged. Worse still, Magnus was not an underage son of a king claiming his inheritance, but an underage pretender. Additional measures had to be taken. It is in this context that Magnus' becoming the first king of Norway to be formally crowned should be understood. Moreover, the ceremony had been authorised and witnessed by two papal legates. In addition, Magnus issued two charters. In one of them, the so-called 'coronation oath', he vowed to remain an obedient son of the Church, to do justice to all his people, but especially to widows and orphans, in accordance with the law of the land, and to heed the advice of Archbishop Eystein of Nidaros in conducting the affairs of his realm.[79] The list of promises differs little from the one that Gallus Anonymus had constructed for Boleslaw I, or from coronation charters and oaths as they survive from England, Germany or the Holy Land.[80] Magnus simply undertook to do what good kings were supposed to do. In a second document, Magnus swore to abide by the archbishop's counsel: it was Eystein, who, through divine inspiration, had presided over his coronation and made him king. Magnus would remain obedient to him in all matters pertaining to the realm.[81] While it was not unusual for archbishops to guide a king, that they had such a role enshrined in a royal charter certainly was. Normally, coronation oaths and charters promised virtuous rule in fairly generic terms. At most, they might single out specific abuses, or promise to restore the good old laws of a particular predecessor.[82] Magnus' grant, by contrast, enshrined the formal oversight of his governance.

Ultimately, the coronation charter had little lasting impact. After King Sverrir had seized the throne from Magnus, he did not renew it, and the archbishop was exiled.[83] Still, while Eystein's might have been a particularly brazen attempt to profit from his role in Magnus's elevation, the attempt itself was not unusual. A generation later, Archbishop Adolf of Cologne would attempt something quite similar. In 1198, the German princes had elected two rival candidates for the imperial throne. Adolf claimed that, as he was to perform the coronation, it fell to him to determine who should be

---

[79] *Latinske Dokument til Norsk Historie fram til År 1204*, ed. and transl. Eirik Vandvik (Oslo, 1959), no. 10. See also Odd Sandaaker, 'Magnus Erlingssons Kroning: ein "politiserande" Sagatradisjon?', *Historik Tijdskrift* 77 (1998), 181–96.

[80] See Chapter 9.

[81] *Latinske Dokument*, no. 9.

[82] See Chapters 7 and 8.

[83] Anne Duggan, 'The English exile of Archbishop Øystein of Nidaros (1180–3)', in *Exile in the Middle Ages*, ed. Laura Napran and Elisabeth van Houts (Turnhout, 2004), 109–30.

II. CREATING KINGSHIP 113

crowned.[84] He sought to exploit a well-documented practice, where the prelate presiding over an election or inauguration quizzed the candidates either before or as part of formal proceedings. As a rule, this was a highly ritualised performance, with its outcome settled well in advance.[85] In 1161 and 1198, by contrast, Eystein and Adolf sought to turn a largely ceremonial role into one where they alone would determine that outcome, or where they could derive from it the formal right to the continuing oversight of the king's governance.

While ultimately unsuccessful, their efforts nonetheless foreshadowed future developments. By the early thirteenth century, the leader of a kingdom's episcopate was expected to act as guardian of the just governance of the realm. In England, the cult of Thomas Becket was transformed. The archbishop had been martyred not for his defence of the liberty of the Church, but because of his insistence on the just governance of the realm.[86] His successors were expected to reprimand and restrain the king whenever he threatened to violate the secular customs of the realm or the rights of his people. Still, this was more a moral expectation than a definite rule. Once more it was in a 'new' kingdom that a bishop's duty of oversight was first turned into a formal duty. In 1231, the Golden Bull was reissued and revised. The new version instituted an annual assembly, which the Hungarian prelates were required to attend 'to hear complaints of the humble and confirm liberties which may possibly have been violated'. Moreover, should it transpire that the palatine, the king's deputy and chief officer, 'badly manage the affairs of the king and kingdom, they shall petition us to install a more suitable person of our choice in his place'.[87] It fell to the prelates to oversee royal governance, to act as representatives of the people against the king's agents. By making the king, they also became guarantors of his just governance. Moreover, by assuming the throne, kings accepted a textual tradition of rulership that led all the way back to the Old Testament. The kings of Israel could flourish only if they heeded the law of God, and the prophets and priests entrusted with collating and enforcing it. In the same vein, medieval kings could succeed only if they heeded the lessons conveyed to them by their prelates and priests. The latter were mediators between God and men, and they were keepers of communal memory, of the history and customs of the realm.

---

[84] Franz-Reiner Erkens, *Der Erzbischof von Köln und die deutsche Königswahl* (Siegburg, 1987), 17–40; Hugo Stehkämper, 'Über das Motiv der Thronstreit-Entscheidungen des Kölner Erzbischofs Adolf von Altena 1198–1205: Freiheit der fürstlichen Königswahl oder Aneignung des Mainzer Erstkurrechts?', *Rheinische Vierteljahresblätter* 67 (2003), 1–20.

[85] See Chapters 8 and 9.

[86] Kay Brainerd Slocum, *Liturgies in Honour of Thomas Becket* (Toronto, 2004); Phyllis B. Roberts, *Thomas Becket in the Medieval Latin Preaching Tradition. An Inventory of Sermons about Thomas Becket c. 1170 – c. 1400* (Steenbruggen, 1992), nos. 53, 142.

[87] *Laws of the Medieval Kingdom of Hungary*, vol. 1, 38.

114   4. CONFERRING KINGSHIP

They preserved knowledge of how things had been, and so of how they should be. There was no need for the role of prelates to be anchored in the moment when a royal title had first been created. It was woven into the very fabric of kingship.

Everyone participating in the process of king-making derived from it an increase in or at least confirmation of their status and standing. That was true of kings, courtiers, nobles and prelates as well as of popes, emperors and neighbours. Consequently, those overseeing the installation of a king derived from their involvement a responsibility to counsel, and if necessary to restrain the ruler. Furthermore, every means by which power could be gained also helped establish the conceptual framework within which it could be challenged. The dynamic applied both to kings and to the people who made them. Ultimately, the brazenness of Eystein and Adolf provided their rivals with the moral justification to dismiss their claims and to invalidate their efforts. Just as kings should not seek power out of a desire to rule over others, so those who recognised their titles, who elected and who inaugurated them, had to be of good moral standing.

Accounts of first kings, and of the creation of rulership, enshrined general principles by rooting them in a pivotal moment of the communal past. Naturally, the path to kingship in Piast Poland had, by force of context and circumstance, to be different from that taken in Armenia, Bohemia, Portugal or Sicily. Still, although each experience was different, rulers resorted to similar means by which to obtain a crown or assert their right to one. The kings themselves as well as the ones recording their deeds evaluated royal pretensions with reference to a set of norms that were easily understood across the Latin west. The imagery of Sigurd's crowning of Roger II contained so many parallels with Otto's of Boleslaw because both events were described in relation to a shared set of expectations as to how a royal title was granted or obtained, of what made a king a king.

Counts and dukes became kings once they were deemed too powerful to be mere princes. Such thinking reflected practical needs. Great responsibility required great power. Yet might also had to be channelled and, if possible, curtailed. It had to be exercised for the good of the people, not that of the ruler. It was not an opportunity for self-enrichment. Consequently, rulership in general, and kingship in particular, remained contractual. If a ruler failed to heed the norms and obligations of his office, it fell to his people to ensure that he did. Recognising a title in turn was embedded in a closely related set of norms. The moral standing of the person awarding or granting royal status was inextricably linked to that of the one claiming or receiving it. Each reflected the other, and could enhance as well as weaken. Moreover, authorising royal status carried with it a responsibility to ensure that so elevated a rank was not bestowed upon a tyrant or usurper. Moral suitability needed to be ascertained. Recognition also called for a promise of protection. Being approached to offer it demonstrated that one possessed both the willingness and the ability to provide it. In principle, these mutually dependent expectations militated against one party gaining an undue advantage over the other. In practice, the legitimacy of the parties involved lay in the eye of the beholder. The question of who should perform the part of a Saul or Nathan was not so much answered as it was avoided. Individuals and communities may have claimed for themselves a particular role in the king-making process, but they could do so only to the extent that their peers and rivals would let them. It became imperative to create as broad a consensus as possible. It became equally important to devise tools and mechanisms that demonstrated that the way agreement had been reached, and that the motivation of those privy to it, also adhered to these same norms.

PART III

Succession

Once royal status had been recognised, it had to be passed on to the next generation. Only then did it become more than an individual accolade. Even in established polities, antiquity and hence legitimacy were expressed through a community's unbroken sequence of rulers. In terms of importance, securing a royal succession therefore almost matched the creation of kingship itself. In practice, passing the throne from one ruler to the next was also when ideal and reality diverged to a greater extent and more frequently than during most other stages of the king-making process. This was partly the result of coincidence, of matters beyond the control of any one individual. But there also were norms and expectations that could be given contradictory and mutually exclusive readings. How did actors and observers resolve these tensions? What tools did they have at their disposal to do so?

Approaching these questions from a transeuropean perspective makes visible patterns that remain hidden from view when each realm is viewed in isolation. For instance, patrilineal succession, the practice of an eldest son following his father onto the throne, is still considered to be the standard mode of passing the crown from one generation to the next. Any deviation is taken to indicate a crisis or at least to denote something out of the ordinary.[1] Yet during

---

[1] See, for instance, the contributions to *Die mittelalterliche Thronfolge im europäischen Vergleich*, ed. Matthias Becher (Ostfildern, 2017) and Frédérique Lachaud and Michael Penman, eds., *Making and Breaking the Rules: Succession in Medieval Europe, c. 1000–c.1600 /Établir et abolir les normes: la succession dans l'Europe médiévale, vers 1000–vers 1600* (Turnhout, 2008). For specific case studies: Sverre Bagge, 'Die Herausbildung einer Dynastie. Thronfolge in Norwegen bis 1260', in *Idoneität – Genealogie – Legitimation. Begründung und Akzeptanz von dynastischer Herrschaft im Mittelalter*, ed. Cristina Andenna and Gert Melville (Cologne, 2015), 257–72; Erich Hoffmann, *Königserhebung und Thronfolgeordnung in Dänemark bis zum Ausgang des Mittelalters* (Berlin and New York, 1976); Andrew W. Lewis, 'Anticipatory association of the heir in early Capetian France', *American Historical Review* 83 (1978), 906–27; Lewis, *Royal Succession in Capetian France: Studies on Familial Order and the State* (Cambridge, MA, 1981); Bart Jaski, *Early Irish Kingship and Succession* (Dublin, 2000); Immo Warntjes, 'Regnal succession in early medieval Ireland', *JMedH* 30 (2004), 377–410; Cyril Toumanoff, 'The Albanian royal succession', *Le Muséon* 97 (1984), 87–94; T. M. Charles-Edwards, 'Dynastic succession in early medieval Wales', in *Wales and the Welsh in the Middle Ages: Essays Presented to J. Beverley Smith*, ed. Ralph Griffiths and Philipp Schofield (Cardiff, 2011), 70–88; Jerry R. Craddock, 'Dynasty in dispute: Alfonso X el Sabio and the succession to

118   III. SUCCESSION

the eleventh and twelfth centuries it occurred in only 54 out of roughly 160 successions – a third of the total.[2] Father–son succession might have been normative, but it most certainly was not the norm. Even when a throne had passed to a king's son under seemingly straightforward circumstances, the act may on closer inspection reveal itself to have been a moment of considerable uncertainty.[3] A ruler, may, for instance, have cast aside the claims of one son in favour of another, as had happened in England in 1087. A succession may also have come about because a son had taken up arms against and deposed his father, as in Germany in 1105. Or it could mean that one sibling had killed or overthrown his brothers, as in Hungary and León in the 1070s. A smooth succession from father to son was very rare indeed.

This has wider implications. First, attention needs to shift from rulers to the elites of the realm. A succession was not something kings could decide on their own. The agreement of princes and prelates had to be sought whenever a ruler attempted to settle his inheritance while still alive. Moreover, because successions were inherently fragile, settlements might not last or could be disputed. Elites would frequently be called upon to fill a vacancy, choose between aspirants and devise a transition that, ideally, would prevent unrest and civil war. In the absence of a king, it fell to them to decide on a suitable successor. Their role has been noted in general terms,[4] but it has not been explored in any

---

the throne of Castile and Leon in history and legend', *Viator* 17 (1986), 197–219; Ulrich Schmidt, *Königswahl und Thronfolge im 12. Jahrhundert* (Cologne and Vienna, 1987); Armin Wolf, ed., *Königliche Tochterstämme, Königswähler und Kurfürsten* (Frankfurt/Main, 2002).

[2] The rather fraught case of Norway does not substantially alter the overall picture, given the number of claimants who were (or claimed to be) sons of kings. See below, Chapter 5, 'Crisis, Suitability and Right'.

[3] See, for instance, Alheydis Plassmann, '[...] et clauses thesaurorum nactus est, quibus fretus totam Angliam animo subiecit suo [...]. Herrschernachfolge in England zwischen Erbschaft, Wahl und Aneignung (1066–1216)', in *Die mittelalterliche Thronfolge*, ed. Becher, 193–227; generally: Matthias Becher, 'Die mittelalterliche Thronfolge im europäischen Vergleich. Einführende Überlegungen', in *Die mittelalterliche Thronfolge*, ed. Becher, 9–19, at 12–13. Capetian France was no exception. See, for instance, Richer of St Remi, *Histories*, transl. Justin Lake (Cambridge, MA, 2011), vol. 2, 224–5; Rodulfus Glaber, *Historiarum libri quinqui*, 104–5; Suger, *Vie de Louis VI le Gros*, ed. and transl. Henri Waquet (Paris, 1929), 38; Rigord, *Histoire de Philippe Auguste*, ed. and transl. Elisabeth Carpentier, Georges Pon and Yves Chauvin (Paris, 2006), 136–9. In fact, so proverbial was the instability of French royal rule that the eleventh-century monks of St Emmeram in Regensburg deemed it plausible that the keeper of the relics of St Denis, deciding that the French had proven incapable of protecting them, had given the saint's remains to the emperor, who then deposited them with the Regensburg monks: *Die jüngere Translatio S. Dionysii Aeropagitae*, ed. and transl. Veronika Lukas, MGH SSrG sep. ed. (Wiesbaden, 2013), 308–459. See also Lewis, 'Anticipatory succession'.

[4] Becher, 'Die mittelalterliche Thronfolge', 17–18; Becher, 'Dynastie, Thronfolge und Staatsverständnis im Frankenreich', in *Der frühmittelalterliche Staat*, ed. Pohl and Wieser, 183–99.

III. SUCCESSION   119

depth regarding the stages that precede a formal election. Both conceptually
and practically, I propose, prelates and nobles played a far more significant part
than most current scholarship suggests. Second, kings and people did not act in
a normative void. Recent discussions have limited themselves to pointing out
that there was no strict distinction between suitability and hereditary right,
often without considering what suitability might have entailed.[5] Still less
interest has been shown in the broader moral framework within which the
process unfolded. Karl Ubl's study of childless kings remains an important
exception.[6] He pointed to the importance of *memoria*, of the liturgical commemoration of the late ruler, as a factor in determining how a succession was
prepared.[7] His approach can be taken further by considering the particular
relationship between the monarch and the divine, and of the king's office as
that of a keeper of the realm. In the absence of a ruler, that role devolved, at
least temporarily, to 'the people' – or rather, to the kingdom's elites. Finally,
any settlement remained provisional. Kings could propose an heir, but whatever agreement was reached during their lifetime needed to be confirmed after
their death. Any analysis of the process of succession therefore ought to take
into account how a putative successor was prepared for the moment of
transition. Much hinged on the success of these efforts: the *memoria* of the
late king, the welfare of his dependants, as well as the peace and tranquillity of
the realm – in fact, its very existence. Still, while this aspect has been recognised
as significant in relation to the biography of individual rulers, it has not so far
been conceptualised as part of the broader succession process.[8] What then did
a moral process of succession entail? What was the role of the people? And
what were the steps rulers could take to prepare their chosen heir for it?

[5] This is especially striking in the otherwise erudite and thoughtful contributions to *Die
mittelalterliche Thronfolge*, ed. Becher. Likewise, most of the equally insightful chapters in
Idoneität – Genealogie – Legitimation, ed. Andenna and Melville, treat the content of
idoneitas only in passing. The chapters by Andenna, Peltzer and Burkhardt, discussing
later medieval examples, are partial exceptions. At most, like the editors (17), the majority
of authors limit themselves to mentioning in passing that suitability manifested itself in
relation to an otherwise unspecified corpus of virtues. For a fuller discussion of what
suitability entailed see above, Chapter 3, and below, Chapters 5–10.

[6] Karl Ubl, 'Der kinderlose König. Ein Testfall für die Ausdifferenzierung des Politischen im
11. Jahrhundert', *HZ* 292 (2011), 323–63.

[7] For the concept of *memoria*: Otto Gerhard Oexle, 'Die Gegenwart der Lebenden und der
Toten. Gedanken über Memoria', in *Gedächtnis, das Gemeinschaft stiftet*, ed. Karl Schmid
and Joachim Wollasch (Munich and Zurich, 1985), 74–107; Karl Schmid and
Joachim Wollasch, eds., *'Memoria'. Der geschichtliche Zeugniswert des liturgischen
Gedenkens im Mittelalter* (Munich, 1984).

[8] See, for useful case studies, Matthew Strickland, 'On the instruction of a prince: the
upbringing of Henry, the Young King', in *Henry II: New Perspectives*, ed.
Christopher Harper-Bill and Nicholas Vincent (Woodbridge, 2008), 184–214; Jonathan
R. Lyon, 'Fathers and sons: preparing noble youths to be lords in twelfth-century
Germany', *JMedH* 34 (2008), 291–310.

5

Duties, Norms and Process

In the early decades of the eleventh century, Bishop Thietmar of Merseburg (d. 1018) recounted what would turn out to be a pivotal episode in the history of the East Frankish realm.[1] In December 918, an ailing King Conrad I, the first non-Carolingian to rule east Francia, called together his followers and relatives. He left no children. His brother Eberhard was his closest surviving male relative. The question as to who would succeed him to the throne had therefore become urgent.[2] Conrad seems to have defied the expectations of everyone present when he nominated his most bitter and persistent foe, Duke Henry of Saxony. Henry, Conrad announced, 'was most suitable to the task. [Those present] should also commend Conrad's soul and the multitude of his surviving blood relations and dependants to Henry's protection. And they should give their consent to this without delay.'[3] A few weeks later, the princes did as requested, electing the duke as their king.

Thietmar's account points to the moral expectations surrounding the succession process, in both east Francia and Latin Europe at large. As regards the former, he drew on a narrative tradition that had begun to take shape just over a generation after Henry's succession in 919.[4] There was, for instance,

---

[1] The best introductions in English to Thietmar remain *Ottonian Germany*, ed. David A. Warner (Manchester, 2001), 1–64 and Sverre Bagge, *Kings, Politics, and the Right Order of the World in German Historiography c. 950–1150* (Leiden, 2002), 95–188. In addition: Markus Cottin and Lisa Merkel, eds., *Thietmars Welt. Ein Merseburger Bischof schreibt Geschichte* (Merseburg, 2018); Heinrich Lippelt, *Thietmar von Merseburg. Reichsbischof und Chronist* (Cologne, 1973); Hans-Werner Goetz, 'Die Chronik Thietmars von Merseburg als Ego-Dokument: ein Bischof mit gespaltenem Selbstverständnis', in *Ego Trouble. Authors and Their Identities in the Early Middle Ages*, ed. Richard Corradini (Vienna, 2010), 259–70.

[2] Hans-Werner Goetz and Simon Elling, eds., *Konrad I. – Auf dem Weg ins deutsche Reich?* (Bochum, 2006); Wolfgang Giese, *Heinrich I.* (Darmstadt, 2008), 58–61.

[3] Thietmar, *Chronicon*, transl. Werner Trillmich (Darmstadt, 1974), i.8, pp. 10–13; *Ottonian Germany*, ed. Warner, 72–3.

[4] It has triggered a rich secondary literature: Johannes Fried, 'Die Königserhebung Heinrichs I. Erinnerung, Mündlichkeit und Traditionsbildung im 10. Jahrhundert', in *Mittelalterforschung nach der Wende 1989*, ed. Michael Borgolte, HZ Beiheft 20 (Munich, 1995), 267–318; Matthias Becher, 'Von den Karolingern zu den Ottonen. Die Königserhebungen von 911 und 919 als Marksteine des Dynastiewechsels im Ostfrankenreich', in *Konrad I.*, ed. Goetz and Elling, 245–64. Antoni Grabowski, *The*

122   5. DUTIES, NORMS AND PROCESS

a common emphasis on suitability. Conrad favoured his erstwhile rival because Henry, as opposed to Conrad's brother Eberhard (or any other of the other great men of the realm), was the one most capable of doing justice and of wielding royal power. According to Liudprand of Cremona (c. 970), Conrad had designated Henry because he was not driven by the lust to govern, *regnandi cupiditas*, or a desire to be placed above others, *praesidendi ambitio*. Indeed, at first Henry had rejected the offer of the throne. Even when he was eventually persuaded to accept it, he did so *non ambitiose*, not out of ambition.[5] In this, Liudprand portrayed the king as following St Augustine's precept that power should be assumed in order to serve, not to lead (*ut prosit, non presit*). The ideal leader remained hesitant, and relented only in order to do justice and to protect the common good. Henry's suitability was rooted both in the fact that he was mightier than any other prince and in his moral disposition.

Moreover, fate was on his side. According to Widukind of Corvey, writing *c.* 970, while Conrad and Eberhard possessed the means to rule, Henry possessed *fortuna*.[6] The term could denote luck. It also had connotations of divine blessing.[7] In some respects, Conrad resembled Saul, who had held the throne

---

Construction of Ottonian Kingship. Narratives and Myths in Tenth-Century German History (Amsterdam, 2018), 47–83, offers a refreshing take by focussing on the normative principles invoked. Ditto, Philippe Buc, 'Noch einmal 918–919: of the ritualized demise of kings and of political rituals in general', in *Zeichen, Rituale, Werte: Internationales Kolloquium des Sonderforschungsbereichs 496 an der Westfälischen Wilhelms-Universität Münster*, ed. Christine Witthöft and Gerd Althoff (Münster, 2004), 151–78.

[5] Liudprand of Cremona, *Antapodosis*, ed. P. Chiesa, in *Liudprandi Cremonensis Opera Omnia*, CCCM 156 (Turnhout, 1998), 43–4. On Liudprand: Jon N. Sutherland, *Liudprand of Cremona. Bishop, Diplomat, Historian* (Spoleto, 1988); Nikolaus Staubach, 'Historia oder Satira ? – Zur literarischen Stellung der Antapodosis Liudprands von Cremona', *Mittellateinisches Jahrbuch* 24–5 (1989–90), 461–87; Robert Levine, 'Liudprand of Cremona: history and debasement in the tenth century', *Mittellateinisches Jahrbuch* 26 (1991), 70–84. Similarly Adalbert of Magdeburg in his continuation of Regino of Prüm, *Chronicon cum continuatione Treverensi*, ed. Friedrich Kurze, MGH SS sep. ed. (Hanover, 1890), 156.

[6] Widukind of Corvey, *Die Sachsengeschichte*, in *Quellen zur Geschichte der sächsischen Kaiserzeit*, ed. and transl. Albert Bauer and Reinhold Rau (Darmstadt, 1977), i.25, pp. 26–7; English translation: Widukind of Corvey, *Deeds of the Saxons*, transl. Bernard S. Bachrach and David S. Bachrach (Washington, DC, 2014), 38. On Widukind: Helmut Beumann, *Widukind von Korvey. Untersuchungen zur Geschichtsschreibung und Ideengeschichte des 10. Jahrhunderts* (Weimar, 1950); Beumann, 'Historiographische Konzeption und politische Ziele Widukinds von Corvey', in his *Wissenschaft vom Mittelalter. Ausgewählte Aufsätze* (Cologne and Vienna, 1972), 71–108; Gerd Althoff, 'Widukind von Corvey. Kronzeuge und Herausforderung', *FmSt* 27 (1993), 253–72; Bagge, *Kings, Politics*, 23–79.

[7] Dieter von der Nahmer, '"Fortuna atque mores". Zu Widukind I 25 und zur Bedeutung dieser Paarformel für die Rerum gestarum saxonicarum libri tres', in *Studi Medievali* 3rd series 53 (2012), 313–56; Hans-Werner Goetz, 'Fortuna in der hochmittelalterlichen Geschichtsschreibung', *Das Mittelalter* 1 (1996), 75–89.

III. SUCCESSION   123

of Israel through divine favour, until God bestowed his blessing on David instead. The *Annals of Quedlinburg* (which equally stressed Henry's *fortuna*) suggest a similar parallel: Conrad had been granted the throne because of his faith, and had been richer and more powerful than anybody else as a result.[8] According to the Old Testament, David and Solomon enjoyed untold riches and unrivalled power as long as they remained devout servants of the Lord. Likewise, that Conrad had waged war on Henry might have mirrored Saul's persecution of David, as does the fact that, on his deathbed, Conrad recognised Henry as his rightful heir, just as a defeated Saul had finally recognised David (1 Samuel 26:25). However, medieval writers could draw upon the Old Testament without suggesting that the precise sequence of biblical events was replicated in the present. For instance, unlike David, Henry had not been raised to the throne in opposition to Conrad, but at the latter's behest and only after the king's death. Most accounts also stressed Conrad's good character. Even Widukind – a Saxon writing in praise of a Saxon dynasty – described the old king as 'a brave and powerful man, effective both in managing the kingdom and in prosecuting war. He was generous and cheerful, and outstanding in all of the virtues.'[9] Conrad was not a bad ruler, but simply one whom *fortuna* had forsaken. Henry therefore resembled David because he had become king not by descent, but because of his virtue and might.

By the time Liudprand and Widukind were writing, Henry's lineage had firmly established itself on the East Frankish throne. In 962, Henry's son Otto even revived the title of Roman emperor. From this later vantage point, Henry was a first king: he had founded a new and glorious line of rulers.[10] Yet these accounts also transcend the historically contingent.[11] In particular, they point

---

[8] *Annales Quedlinburgenses*, ed. Martina Giese, MGH SSrG sep. ed. (Hanover, 2004), 454.

[9] Widukind of Corvey, *Sachsengeschichte*, i.25, pp. 26–7; *Deeds of the Saxons*, 39. Similarly, according to Adalbert of Magdeburg, Conrad was 'in everything mild-mannered, prudent, and a lover of the divine faith': Regino of Prüm, *Chronica*, 156.

[10] The aspect was reinforced by a strong regional perspective in the sources, most of which originated in Saxony. Widukind embedded his account in a history of glorious Saxon exploits, including their (putative) participation in the campaigns of Alexander the Great and their conquest of Britain: Widukind of Corvey, *Sachsengeschichte*, i.2, 8, pp. 20–3, 26–9; *Deeds of the Saxons*, 5–6, 10–12. Henry's kingship marked the point from whence the Saxons ruled the Franks, rather than being ruled by them. His elevation also elevated his people. For Thietmar, Henry's kingship mattered because he founded the see of Merseburg, thereby providing a bishopric for the descendants of Julius Caesar's army, who, Thietmar claimed, had first settled the area: Thietmar, *Chronicon*, i.2–3, pp. 4–7; *Ottonian Germany*, ed. Warner, 68–9.

[11] See also, though focussing on particular realms rather than transeuropean patterns: Warntjes, 'Regnal succession'; T. M. Charles-Edwards, 'Dynastic succession in early medieval Wales', in *Wales and the Welsh in the Middle Ages: Essays Presented to J. Beverley Smith*, ed. Ralph Griffiths and Philipp Schofield (Cardiff, 2011), 70–88; Martyn J. Rady, 'Election and descent in medieval Hungarian kingship', in *Élections et pouvoirs politiques du VIIe au XVIIe siècle: actes du colloque réuni à Paris 12 du 30*

124   5. DUTIES, NORMS AND PROCESS

towards a threefold responsibility on the part of ruler and ruled alike: to ensure continuing peace and tranquillity, the well-being of the king's dependants and followers and his own salvation.[12] All overlapped, and constituted the essential framework within which a royal succession unfolded. In appointing Henry, Conrad ensured that peace prevailed, that bloodshed was avoided, and that his *memoria* continued through his dependants and relatives. How a ruler readied the realm for his succession therefore shed light on the legitimacy of his reign.

5.1 *Memoria*, Continuity and Peace

Successions were moments of crisis. Few worse calamities could befall a realm than the absence of a king. When, in Sven Aggesen's *Lex Castrensis*, the Danes allowed Knud to atone for murdering one of his retainers, they worried above all that, if they punished the king as the law demanded, they would be unable to fight off their enemies. The absence of a ruler also heralded a breakdown of law and justice.[13] After the murder of Count Charles the Good of Flanders in 1127, Walter of Trier lamented, peace had been upturned, the tranquillity of the realm disturbed, honesty and fidelity extinguished. War, unrest and turmoil now ruled the land.[14] Precisely because the king (or the king-like ruler) was supposed to be more powerful than any of his subjects, a disputed or open succession brought to the fore men's ambitions that he had previously suppressed. In the 1030s, after Casimir of Poland had been forced into exile, 'Gallus' recounted the disastrous consequences for the realm:

> the neighbouring kings and dukes had been riding roughshod over the portion of Poland nearest to each of them . . . Yet at the same time . . . her own inhabitants were doing even more ghastly and senseless things to her. For serfs rose against their masters, and freedmen against nobles, seizing power for themselves, reducing some in turn to servitude, killing others, and raping their wives and appropriating their offices in most wicked

---

novembre au 2 décembre 2006, ed. Corinne Péneau (Pompignac, 2008), 383–90. Note, though, the important exception of Thomas Foerster, 'Neue Herrschaft in neuen Reichen. Geneaologie, Identität und die Ursprünge weiblicher Nachfolge im 12. Jahrhundert', in *Idoneität – Geneaologie – Legitimation*, ed. Andenna and Melville, 139–66.

[12] See also, for a slightly different reading, Bernd Schneidmüller, 'Zwischen Gott und den Getreuen. Vier Skizzen zu den Fundamenten mittelalterlicher Monarchie', *FmSt* 36 (2002), 193–224.

[13] See also Sigebert of Gembloux, *Chronica – Continuatio Gemblacensis* (s.a. 1147), MGH SS 6 (Hanover, 1844), 389: 'Cunradus rex Heinricum filium suum Aquisgrani in regem sublimat, ne post decessum suum regnum absque principe remaneret, et aliqua rerum perturbatio moveretur'.

[14] *Vita Caroli comitis auctore Waltero archidiacono Treverensi*, MGH SS 12 (Hanover, 1856), 542. See also: Leo of Vercelli, *Versus de Ottone et Henrico*, ed. Karl Strecker, MGH Poetae Latini Medii Aevii (Berlin, 1939), 480–3; *Vita Heinrici IV. Imperatoris*, ed. Wilhelm Wattenbach, MGH SS sep. ed. (Hanover, 1876), 9–11.

III. SUCCESSION

fashion. ... In the end foreigners and her own people had between them reduced Poland to such desolation that she was stripped of almost all her wealth and population.[15]

By failing to secure his succession, or by choosing as his heir someone who failed to maintain justice and peace, and who did not protect those who could not protect themselves, a ruler would leave his people exposed to the whims of greedy men and hostile neighbours. Rather than being a guardian of peace and justice, he would, in death, open the gates to tyrants and invaders.

This turmoil was especially felt by ecclesiastical institutions. Communities like Corvey and Merseburg, being either royal foundations or the recipients of lavish royal patronage, relied on the king's protection. Churches and monasteries were also most likely to have to provide for a populace whose livelihood, lives and limbs were under threat when public order collapsed. All of this helps explain their concern for a smooth and peaceful transition. But then members of the aristocracy faced similar threats. Rivals might no longer be restrained by fear of royal intervention. They would be free to ravage the lands of their foes, attack their religious foundations and seize by force goods, property and men. There were good reasons why, the moment William the Conqueror breathed his last in 1087, the nobles in attendance abandoned the royal corpse and rushed home to fortify their castles.[16] Concern for the continuing well-being of the kingdom at large was therefore closely intertwined with that for a ruler's family and entourage. Until the very close of our period, effective governance meant the establishment, balancing and utilisation of networks. These were never hermetically sealed, but rather constituted overlapping and interlocking spheres of influence. Still, those involving the king were of particular importance. A royal connection lent authority to interactions with other groups and individuals, and offered protection and access to patronage. But networks were temporary, dependent on the interaction between individuals.[17] Moreover, new kings, even if from within the same kin group, would normally bring associations of their own. Therefore, in order to preserve the peace and to satisfy a moral duty of care towards his dependants, a good king would see to it that they were provided for under his successor, that their rights and privileges would be maintained and their lands protected. These concerns, we might speculate, were perhaps why, in Thietmar of Merseburg's account, Conrad I had begun his speech designating Henry with a request that the duke offer protection to 'the multitude of [Conrad's] surviving blood relations and dependants'.[18]

---

[15] *Gesta Principum Polonorum*, i.19, pp. 78–9.

[16] Orderic Vitalis, *The Ecclesiastical History of Orderic Vitalis*, ed. and transl. Marjorie Chibnall, 6 vols. (Oxford, 1969–80), vol. 4, 94–5.

[17] For a particularly important case study, see: Lyon, *Princely Brothers and Sisters*.

[18] Thietmar, *Chronicon*, i.8, pp. 10–13; *Ottonian Germany*, ed. Warner, 72–3.

126 5. DUTIES, NORMS AND PROCESS

When Conrad I nominated Henry as his successor, Thietmar reported, he commended his soul to Henry's care. This points to a third aspect of royal succession, and one that has often been overlooked: ensuring the deceased king's liturgical commemoration.[19] It is, of course, difficult to fathom the motivation of individuals at a distance of several hundred years. Still, impending death tends to focus the mind, especially when account would have to be rendered for one's deeds. Orderic Vitalis, writing in the 1130s, made this a central theme in recounting William the Conqueror's death in 1087. The account, which runs to almost forty pages in the modern printed edition,[20] reflected Orderic's own ambivalent attitude towards the king.[21] At first glance, the chronicler established William as a model of a king dying well, when, in fact, he offered a warning on the transience of earthly power. The Conqueror was humble, showed contrition and sought to make amends for his transgressions. Feeling death approaching, William sent lavish gifts to the clergy of Mantes, to compensate for the churches he had previously destroyed.[22] He then called together his court and recounted his deeds. He had won the English throne through divine blessing, and had been victorious in many battles against 'the men of Exeter and Chester and Northumbria, against the Scots and Welsh, Norwegians and Danes'. However, while 'ambitious men rejoice in such triumphs', the king explained, 'fear and dread now clutch me and gnaw at my heart when I consider what cruel brutality was unleashed in these conflicts'. He therefore pleaded with the priests in attendance to pray on his behalf, and asked that the riches he had accumulated be distributed among the poor. William urged the clergy to remember that he had never harmed the Church. He sold no ecclesiastical offices, always combated simony and in appointing bishops and abbots sought to promote only the worthiest candidates. The king pointed out that he had 'further

---

[19] Childless kings seemed especially eager to obtain salvation and commemoration through lavish patronage of new foundations: Ubl, 'Der kinderlose König'. See also: Bernd Schneidmüller, 'Die Kathedrale also Braut Christi: Heinrich II. und die Bamberger Domweihe 1012', in *1000 Jahre Kaiserdom Bamberg*, ed. Norbert Jung and Wolfgang F. Reddig (Petersberg, 2012), 32–45; Schneidmüller, 'Die einzigartig geliebte Stadt: Heinrich II. und Bamberg', in *Kaiser Heinrich II. 1002–1024*, ed. Josef Kirmeier, Bernd Schneidmüller and Stefan Weinfurter (Stuttgart, 2002), 30–51; Stefan Weinfurter, 'Bamberg und das Reich in der Herrscheridee Heinrichs II', *Bericht des Historischen Vereins für die Pflege der Geschichte des ehemaligen Fürstbistums Bamberg* 137 (2001), 53–82; Eric C. Fernie, 'Edward the Confessor's Westminster Abbey', in *Edward the Confessor: the Man and the Legend*, ed. Richard Mortimer (Woodbridge, 2009), 139–50.

[20] Orderic Vitalis, *Ecclesiastical History*, vol. 4, 80–109. David Bates, *William the Conqueror* (New Haven, CT, 2016), 474–90. On Orderic: Charles C. Rozier, Daniel Roach, Giles E. M. Gasper and Elisabeth van Houts, eds., *Orderic Vitalis: Life, Works and Interpretations* (Woodbridge, 2016); Marjorie M. Chibnall, *The World of Orderic Vitalis* (Oxford, 1984).

[21] I am grateful to Abigail Monk for this point.

[22] Orderic Vitalis, *Ecclesiastical History*, vol. 4, 80–1.

III. SUCCESSION   127

enriched the nine abbeys of monks and one of nuns that my ancestors founded in Normandy', that, in his time as duke, 'seventeen abbeys of monks and six of nuns were built' and that he freely and generously confirmed charters and grants for these institutions. Such lavish acts of piety ought to translate into intercession after his death.

William proceeded to admonish his sons (only two of whom were present),

> to keep the company of good and wise men and obey their precepts in all things if you wish to prosper long and honourably. The teaching of the holy philosophers is to know good from evil, preserve justice in all things, shun evil with determination, be merciful and helpful to the sick and poor and law-abiding, overthrow and punish the proud and wicked, refrain from harming the humble, be a devout worshipper in the Church, cherish the service of God above all riches, and obey the divine law by night and day . . .[23]

Like a truly good king, he recounted the basic principles of his office, exhorting his successors to abide by them.[24]

Yet William remained hesitant to endorse his sons. He lamented having appointed Robert, the eldest, as his heir in Normandy. As this had been done with the agreement of the counts and barons of Normandy, he had no right to rescind the grant, even though he knew 'for certain that any province subjected to [Robert's] rule will be most wretched'. Moreover, he named no heir for the kingdom of England:

> For I did not come to possess such a dignity by hereditary right, but wrested the kingdom from the perjured king Harold with bitter strife and terrible bloodshed . . . I treated the native inhabitants of the kingdom with unreasonable severity, cruelly oppressed high and low, unjustly disinherited many, and caused the death of thousands by starvation . . . In mad fury I descended upon the English of the north like a raging lion, and ordered that their homes and crops with all their equipment and furnishings should be burnt . . . I dare not transmit the government of this kingdom, won with so many sins, to any man, but entrust it to God alone . . . I hope that my son William . . . [may] bring lustre to the kingdom if such is the divine will.[25]

The king merely expressed the hope that, God willing, the younger William might enhance the glory of the English crown. Here, the time and context of writing become important. Orderic composed his account two generations after the events recorded, in full knowledge of the ensuing disputes between the Conqueror's sons (Robert, William and Henry), William II's less than

---

[23] Orderic Vitalis, *Ecclesiastical History*, vol. 4, 90–3.
[24] See also the parallel narrative premise underpinning the *Libellus* of St Stephen of Hungary: *Libellus de institutione morum*, ed. Joseph Balogh, in *Scriptores Rerum Hungaricarum*, vol. 2, 619–20.
[25] Orderic Vitalis, *Ecclesiastical History*, vol. 4, 92–5.

128   5. DUTIES, NORMS AND PROCESS

exemplary rule in England, the wars between Henry and Robert Curthose and the devastation those had wreaked upon Normandy. In Orderic's rendering, only once Henry had seized the English throne in 1100, and after he had defeated and imprisoned Robert (in 1106), did order and stability return. The Conqueror's handling of his succession both foreshadowed this fraught history and legitimised Henry's rise to power.[26]

This context heightens a pervasive sense of ambiguity in Orderic's account. The Conqueror may have repented, given money to the poor, released prisoners[27] and, in facing his end, given 'sound and practical advice to all who consulted him about the affairs of the kingdom'.[28] However, 'when the just ruler fell, lawlessness broke loose', while 'those whose whole aim is to plunder and steal were left free by the death of the just judge'.[29] That was not supposed to happen. A good death would have been like that of Emperor Henry IV in 1106, who the previous year had been deposed and exiled by his son. The emperor's passing, a variant of Sigebert of Gembloux's chronicle reports, was lamented so greatly that the people clandestinely scooped up the soil from his grave to disperse it over their fields. They did so partly because they hoped that this would make harvests more fertile, partly because they and various 'poor clerics' believed that Henry had been sanctified by the manner of his death.[30] The people were not meant to face lawlessness and unrest, fear for their lives or seek refuge in their castles. In Orderic's rendering, William had known that on his death turmoil would befall the realm. He had regretted not being able to deprive Robert of Normandy, refused to nominate William for the English throne and warned that releasing his brother, Bishop Odo of Bayeux, from prison would be 'the cause of death and grievous harm to many'.[31] He had ruled firmly, even brutally, and it was partly his guilty conscience about the blood he had shed that prevented him from settling the succession in the manner befitting a truly good king. Endowing churches and setting free prisoners was not enough. Even seizing a throne through divine benevolence was insufficient, if it coincided with killing one's subjects.

Orderic's ambivalence towards William shaped how he reported events after the Conqueror's death. The moment the king had breathed his last, the royal carcass was abandoned. The servants stripped away whatever valuables they could grab, and the nobles took refuge in their castles. It therefore fell to a low-

---

[26] Orderic's contemporary, Hermann of Tournai, claimed that the success of King Stephen in 1135 was divine punishment for the fact that Henry I had abducted his wife (Matilda's mother) from a nunnery: Herman de Tournai, *Liber de Restauratione S. Martini Tornacensis*, MGH SS 14 (Hanover, 1883), 282; Eadmer, *Historia Novorum*, 121–6.
[27] Orderic Vitalis, *Ecclesiastical History*, vol. 4, 96–101.
[28] Orderic Vitalis, *Ecclesiastical History*, vol. 4, 100–1.
[29] Orderic Vitalis, *Ecclesiastical history*, vol. 4, 102–3.
[30] Sigebert of Gembloux, *Chronica*, MGH SS 6, 371–2, variant d.
[31] Orderic Vitalis, *Ecclesiastical History*, vol. 4, 100–1.

III. SUCCESSION   129

ranking knight to escort the king's remains to Caen, where the funeral rites were administered, and to do so at his own expense.[32] That, too, was a parodic inversion of what was supposed to happen. When Valdemar I of Denmark died in 1182, Saxo Grammaticus reports, the peasants abandoned their fields not out of fear, but in order to carry the king's bier, 'so that they could perform a last dignified service for him'.[33] Valdemar's remains were carried by peasants out of love, not because the great men of the kingdom had fearfully hastened to their fortified places. In Normandy, even William's funeral, Orderic recounts, did not go smoothly. First, a local man, Ascelin fitzArthur, objected loudly to the site of the duke's burial. He claimed that it occupied the place of his family home, which William had violently seized from his father. 'Therefore', Ascelin declared, 'I lay claim to this land, and openly demand it, forbidding in God's name that the body of this robber be covered by earth that is mine or buried in my inheritance.' After the attending nobles and prelates hurriedly scrambled together money to purchase the plot, they tried to bury the king. However,

> when the corpse was placed in the sarcophagus, and was forcibly doubled up because the masons had carelessly made the coffin too short and narrow, the swollen bowels burst, and an intolerable stench assailed the nostrils of the bystanders and the whole crowd.

Even the thick cloud of frankincense could not sweeten the smell, and so the priests rushed through the remainder of the ceremony with unholy speed.[34] Orderic concluded:

> All who beheld the corruption of that foul corpse learnt to strive earnestly through the salutary discipline of abstinence to earn better rewards than the delights of the flesh, which is earth, and will return to dust.[35]

What are we to make of this? Orderic drew on two literary models in particular. One is the Old Testament, 2 Maccabees 9, where Antiochus, on planning to attack Jerusalem and enslave the Jews, was struck by a horrible disease that involved a most penetrating stench. He vainly sought to make amends by promising to turn Jerusalem into the equal of Athens, to rebuild the Temple and even to convert to Judaism. He claimed to have acted for the

---

[32] Orderic Vitalis, *Ecclesiastical History*, vol. 4, 102–7. For the context of the royal corpse being stripped of its possessions, though focussing on the later Middle Ages, Michail A. Bojcov, 'Die Plünderung des toten Herrschers als allgemeiner Wahn', in *Bilder der Macht in Mittelalter und Neuzeit. Byzanz, Okzident, Russland*, ed. Michail A. Bojcov and Otto Gerhard Oexle (Göttingen, 2007), 53–118.

[33] Saxo Grammaticus, *Gesta Danorum*, xv.6.11, pp. 1492–3.

[34] Orderic Vitalis, *Ecclesiastical History*, vol. 4, 106–7.

[35] Orderic Vitalis, *Ecclesiastical History*, vol. 4, 108–9.

130   5. DUTIES, NORMS AND PROCESS

common good, appointed a successor and begged those in attendance to remember him.[36] Even without being replicated exactly, the biblical precedent nonetheless reinforced the inherent ambiguity of William's rule. The Conqueror had committed many abominable acts, for which his endowment of churches and monasteries, and all the amends he sought to make, compensated only partially. The biblical model was closely entwined with a literary tradition that contrasted worldly splendour with the uncertainty that, after death, would face even the wealthiest and most powerful.[37] The king's decomposing remains signalled the transience of secular wealth. Ascelin's complaints, placed so prominently, echoed the very transgressions to which William had confessed and for which he had sought to atone. Indeed, Orderic's account was framed by memories of William's unjust acts. It opened with the clergy of Mantes receiving belated compensation for the duke's destruction of their churches, and it concluded with the dispute over William's burial plot, which had similarly been seized by unjust and violent means. The humiliations inflicted upon the king's remains suggested that his atonement had only just begun.

Orderic's account was, of course, rather different from Thietmar's or Widukind's. He focussed firmly on the extended preparations for William's departure from this life, and the moral lessons to be drawn from them and from the events that followed. Settling, or rather refusing to settle, the succession was only part of a broader set of measures taken by the dying king. William's main concern was for his soul, and the goal was to make amends for the blood he had shed, the suffering he had inflicted and the livelihoods he had destroyed. The extent and manner of his atonement were exemplary. But, or so Orderic seemed to imply, they were also insufficient. That the Conqueror failed to settle his succession stemmed from these past misdeeds and added new ones to the ledger. William refused to nominate an heir because he had acquired and kept the English throne through violence. But because he failed to name an heir, he unleashed potentially even greater suffering. The humiliations inflicted upon the king's mortal remains reflected this failure and were its immediate consequence. William's entourage, all too aware of the unrest about to unfold, fled from the king's side to fortify their castles, and it fell to a motley group of prelates and knights to perform a duty that should have been that of William's successor: to ensure that proper burial be offered for the king's remains, and to procure the prayers and intercession that he so evidently required.

[36] I am grateful to Mayke de Jong for pointing out this parallel.

[37] Lothar Bornscheuer, *Miseriae Regum. Untersuchungen zum Krisen- und Todesgedanken in den herrschaftstheologischen Vorstellungen der ottonisch-salischen Zeit* (Berlin, 1968), 116–19; Peter Christian Jacobsen, 'Das Totengericht Kaiser Heinrichs II. Eine neue Variante aus dem Echternacher "Liber aureus"' *Mittellateinisches Jahrbuch* 33 (1998), 53–8.

III. SUCCESSION   131

Once we look beyond obvious differences between Orderic and the Saxon chroniclers, familiar themes nonetheless emerge. A succession was a moment of crisis. This all the more so, if, as in England, no heir had had been chosen, or if, as in Normandy, he was deemed ill-suited for the task. Uncertainty gave rise to unrest. A truly good king therefore sought to prepare for the moment of transition. He might not always succeed, but, like Conrad and unlike William, he ought to try. His responsibility for the welfare of the realm, in this regard at least, extended beyond the grave.[38] Moreover, for those wielding power greater than that of any of their people, it was all too easy to succumb to the snares and temptations of their office. Justified warfare could shade into the shedding of innocent blood, firm rigour into tyranny and unbridled force into grave injustice. Rulers could guard themselves by governing with wisdom and by heeding the advice of prudent men. And they could atone for their transgressions by securing the prayers of pious monks and clerics. But it also fell to their heirs to ensure continuing commemoration and a return to the right balance between rigour and mercy. Picking the right successor – one both willing and able to care for his predecessor's salvation – was a matter of political and personal urgency.

The moral obligations surrounding the transition from one ruler to the next extended to the king's successor and to his leading subjects. They are essential to an understanding of how high medieval Europeans sought to come to terms with the reality of royal successions. Importantly, they were not concerned with abstract legal principles.[39] Instead, the writings of contemporaries crystallised a set of moral expectations that permeated the succession process. The fervency with which observers upheld this normative framework, and the ease with which its component strands were woven even into passing references to a king's succession, reflected the severity of the crisis that a king's demise could herald. They also echo the frequency with which such crises nonetheless

---

[38] This even applies to seeming exceptions like Edward the Confessor (d. 1066) and Emperor Henry II (d. 1024): Edwina Bozóky, 'The sanctity and canonisation of Edward the Confessor', in *Edward the Confessor*, ed. Mortimer, 173–86; Renate Klauser, 'Der Heinrichs- und Kunigundenkult im mittelalterlichen Bistum Bamberg. Idee und Wirklichkeit', in *Bericht des Historischen Vereins für die Pflege der Geschichte des ehemaligen Fürstbistums Bamberg* 95 (1956), 1–211. See generally, Klaniczay, *Holy Rulers*.

[39] Not without reason did Bernd Kannowski, 'The impact of lineage and family connections on succession in medieval Germany's elective kingdom', in *Making and Breaking the Rules*, ed. Lachaud and Penman, 13–22, exclude any narrative sources when discussion the legal framework of imperial succession. They reveal a rather different image: Björn Weiler, 'Suitability and right: imperial succession and the norms of politics in early Staufen Germany', in *Making and Breaking the Rules*, ed. Lachaud and Penman, 71–86. For valiant but ultimately unsuccessful attempts to deduce legal principles from narrative sources, see George Garnett, *Conquered England: Kingship, Succession and Tenure, 1066–1166* (Oxford, 2007). See also the poignant remarks by Becher, 'Die mittelalterliche Thronfolge', 17–18.

132   5. DUTIES, NORMS AND PROCESS

occurred and the extent to which nobles and clergy shared in the responsibility for an orderly transition. Their representations of the past show how actors and observers sought to shape a reality that all too often threatened to undermine the very foundations on which the existence of the realm, the peace and tranquillity of its people and the eternal salvation of its rulers rested.

5.2 Crisis, Suitability and Right

The anonymous *Historia Norwegie* from *c.* 1170–5 (though possibly conceived as early as 1152–3)[40] recorded the history of Norwegian kings from their mythical origins in Sweden to the reign of Olaf Haraldson (d. 1030). The *Historia* ordered time via the sequence of rulers. Most striking is the image it paints of an orderly succession:

> King Yngve, who, according to a great many was the first ruler of the Swedish realm, became the father of Njord, whose son was Frøy. . . . Frøy engendered Fjolne, who was drowned in a tun of mead. His son, Sveigde, is supposed to have pursued a dwarf into a stone and never to have returned, but this is plainly to be taken as a fairy-tale. He sired Vanlande, who died in his sleep, suffocated by a goblin, of the demonic species known in Norway as 'mare'. . . . Dag . . . was killed by the Danes in a royal battle . . . while he was trying to avenge the violence done to a sparrow. This man engendered Alrek, who was beaten to death with a bridle by his brother Eirik. Alrek was father to Agne, whose wife dispatched him with her own hands by hanging him on a tree with a golden chain near a place called Agnafit.[41]

The narrative continues along these lines in dealing with the kings proper settling in Norway. Østeyn, nicknamed 'Fart', bequeathed the throne to his son Halvdan Gold-Lavisher and Food-Niggard, 'since, whereas he bestowed gold on his retainers, he weakened them with hunger at the same time',[42] who fathered Gudrød the Hunter-King. And so on. Writing about a past for which he had only fragmentary information, the anonymous author constructed a strict sequence of son succeeding father. There was no disruption in the line of kings. They might drown in barrels of mead, disappear into stones in the pursuit of dwarves or be suffocated by goblins, but they were still succeeded by their sons. The pattern was broken only when the author reached the reign of Harald Fairhair in the late ninth century – when, in short, he entered historical time. While the sixteen sons attributed to Harald may have been a symbolic rather than

---

[40] *Historia Norwegie*, 217–23.
[41] *Historia Norwegie*, 74–7. The excerpt condenses the rather more elaborate genealogy surviving in *Yinglinga Saga*, on which: Andersson, *Sagas of Norwegian Kings*, 79–80.
[42] *Historia Norwegie*, 78–9.

III. SUCCESSION   133

an accurate number (other sources counted twenty),[43] the dynastic wars of the eleventh century were rooted partly in the sheer number of Harald's progeny.[44] The author did not, however, fashion the dynastic history of Norway as one of decline from a golden age to a less than exemplary present. Instead, the *Historia* constructed a narrative of regnal continuity, culminating in the kingdom's conversion to Christianity, probably with an eye to the establishment in 1151 of Nidaros (Trondheim) as an archbishopric, the *sine qua non* of a community's regnal status.[45] Past stability was not an ideal against which contemporary reality could be measured and found wanting, but the assertion of a tradition that reinforced the antiquity and hence distinctiveness of the kingdom of Norway.

It also was an image that stood in marked contrast to the reality of Norwegian politics. This was certainly true of the *Historia*'s narrative once it dealt with historical as opposed to legendary kings, but it was truer still of the period when it was written. If we follow Snorri Sturluson's thirteenth-century *Heimskringla*, between the death of Olav Tryggvason in 1000 and 1177, when Sverrir Sigurdsson claimed the throne, nineteen kings ruled. The number is somewhat inflated by the occasional practice of co- or shared kingship. Even so, only six of these kings died of illness or old age.[46] Two met their death while plundering or attacking foreign lands.[47] The remaining eleven were killed while fighting over the throne. In 1135, Magnus Sigurdsson survived being castrated and blinded by his rival Harald Gilli,[48] but was eventually killed in 1139 during a battle against Harald's sons;[49] Harald had in the meantime met his end while fighting Sigurd Slembidjakn, extramarital progeny of Magnus Barelegs;[50] Sigurd's claim to the throne ended when he was tortured to death by the sons of Harald Gilli,[51] two of

---

[43] *Historia Norwegie*, 80–1, 138, 196–9.
[44] Sverre Bagge, *From Viking Stronghold to Christian Kingdom: State Formation in Norway, c. 900 – 1350* (Copenhagen, 2010), 25–53; Bagge, 'Die Herausbildung einer Dynastie. Thronfolge in Norwegen bis 1260', in *Idoneität – Genealogie – Legitimation*, ed. Andenna and Melville, 257–72. See also, for the transformation of dynastic memory, the important article by Sverrir Jakobsson, 'The early kings of Norway, the issue of agnatic succession and the settlement of Iceland', *Viator* 47 (2016), 171–88.
[45] In fact, the last entry in the *Historia* recorded the arrival of the kingdom's first bishops. *Historia Norwegie*, 104–5, 205–17.
[46] Snorri Sturluson, *Heimskringla. History of the Kings of Norway*, transl. Lee M. Hollander (Austin, TX, 1964, repr. 1999), 599 (Magnus the Good, 1047), 663 (Magnus Haraldson, 1066), 667 (Olaf the Gentle, 1093), 701 (1116, Olaf Magnusson), 705 (1122, Eystein), 714 (1130, Sigurd).
[47] Snorri, *Heimskringla*, 655, 686: Harald Hardrada while invading England (1066), and Magnus Olafson (Barelegs) when plundering Ireland (1103).
[48] Snorri, *Heimskringla*, 723.
[49] Snorri, *Heimskringla*, 745.
[50] Snorri, *Heimskringla*, 733.
[51] Snorri, *Heimskringla*, 748–9.

134   5. DUTIES, NORMS AND PROCESS

whom died fighting each other,[52] and the third while doing battle with yet another claimant, Håkon Sigurdsson,[53] who himself fell while fighting Magnus Erlingsson, the first claimant to the throne not a king's son;[54] Magnus saw off challenges from Sigurd Sigurdsson (grandson of Harald Gilli),[55] and another alleged son of Sigurd Haraldsson's,[56] before dying in battle against Sverrir, who claimed Sigurd Haraldsson as his father.[57] Sverrir, finally, was the first Norwegian king in seventy years to die of old age.[58] At precisely the point when the author of the *Historia Norwegie* postulated as a rule a clear succession from father to son, Norway was plunged into dynastic turmoil.

In their ferocious violence, the dynastic politics of high medieval Norway were exceptional. Elsewhere in western Europe, castrating, blinding or otherwise maiming one's rivals had long fallen out of fashion. In fact, when, early in the thirteenth century, English chroniclers wanted to paint King John of England as a tyrant, they blamed him for the murder of his nephew and putative rival, Arthur of Brittany.[59] Norway was, however, less unusual as regards a highly unstable line of succession. In England, between the beginning of the eleventh century and 1216, an eldest son inherited the throne only twice.[60] Three times it passed to a younger brother,[61] three times within the wider family[62] and twice it was won by conquest.[63] Violent succession disputes erupted in 1035, 1066, 1100, 1135, 1199 and 1216. Even a transition from father to son could contain its share of strife. In 1189 Richard I led a revolt against his father Henry II, who died soon after having been forced into a humiliating defeat, and in 1216 the infant Henry III had to be hurriedly crowned at Gloucester because Westminster was occupied by a rival claimant to the throne. Similarly, in Germany, the direct succession from father to son occurred a mere five times between *c.* 1000 and 1200 (out of ten

---

[52] Snorri, *Heimskringla*, 763 (1155, Sigurd Haraldson), 766 (1156, Eystein, an illegitimate son).

[53] Snorri, *Heimskringla*, 785.

[54] Snorri, *Heimskringla*, 796 (1161).

[55] Snorri, *Heimskringla*, 803 (1163).

[56] Snorri, *Heimskringla*, 820 (1177).

[57] *Saga of King Sverri*, chapter 4, p. 4.

[58] *Saga of King Sverri*, chapters 180–1, pp. 230–3 (1202). It seems, though, that Snorri might himself have been somewhat confused. Note the heroic efforts by modern historians to disentangle the genealogy of twelfth-century Norwegian kings, visualised by Scheel, *Skandinavien und Byzanz*, 1198.

[59] J. C. Holt, 'King John and Arthur of Brittany', *Nottingham Medieval Studies* 44 (2000), 82–103.

[60] Richard I in 1189, Henry III in 1216.

[61] Aethelred in 978; Henry I in 1100; John in 1199.

[62] Edward the Confessor in 1042; Stephen in 1135; Henry II in 1154.

[63] Knut (1016) and William I (1066).

III. SUCCESSION   135

successions).[64] The pattern was replicated almost everywhere in Europe, apart from France, where an unbroken (though not always uncontested) line of sons followed their fathers between 987 and 1328. In short, dynastic instability was a recurring feature in the regnal politics of high medieval Europe. Why was this so?

In Norway, the relative looseness of rules of inheritance may have played a major part. Illegitimacy was no bar to the throne.[65] In other realms, out-of-wedlock progeny rarely stood a chance. Tancred, illegitimate nephew of William of Sicily, claimed the throne in 1189, but was eventually overthrown by the forces of his aunt Constance and her husband, Emperor Henry VI.[66] In fact, outside Scandinavia, the last claimant reputedly born out of wedlock to win and keep a throne had been William I of England in 1066. The emphasis on legitimate birth did, of course, limit the pool of potential candidates for the throne.[67] In theory, this should have curtailed the room for violent succession disputes. In practice, it did not. There was, for instance, little agreement as to how the strength of a hereditary claim was to be assessed. For example, would the son of a predeceased older brother have a better claim than a younger brother? Precisely that question was posed in England, when King John succeeded his brother Richard. Some of the Breton aristocracy wary of John maintained that his nephew Arthur had a stronger claim (as Arthur's father Geoffrey had been John's elder brother).[68] Similarly, there was no established consensus that kingship was not to be shared among a ruler's progeny. The number of Norwegian kings in the twelfth century partly suggests as much. That a principle of hereditary succession had been accepted (or was propagated) as normative did not mean that a ruler's death usually coincided with the swift and smooth elevation of his eldest son.

Moreover, by limiting the pool of legitimate successors, premature death – through illness, accident or war – increased the risk of a disputed succession. In Sicily, Roger II outlived four of his five sons, all of whom had survived into adulthood.[69] Warfare also took its toll. In 1154, the son of William I of Sicily

---

[64] Conrad II to Henry III (1038), Henry III to Henry IV (1053), Henry IV to Henry V (1105) and Frederick I to Henry VI (1190). Henry VI had his son acclaimed as king in 1195, but on his death the German princes elected his cousin Otto and his brother Philipp.

[65] Bagge, *From Viking Stronghold*, 47–50; Bagge, 'Herausbildung einer Dynastie'. Generally, see Sara McDougall, *Royal Bastards. The Birth of Illegitimacy, 800–1230* (Oxford, 2017), which does not, however, discuss the Norwegian case.

[66] Bates, *William the Conqueror*, 16–24.

[67] Janet Martin, 'Calculating seniority and the contests for succession in Kievan Rus', *Russian History/Histoire Russe* 33 (2006), 267–81; Cherie Woodworth, 'The birth of the captive autocracy: Moscow, 1432', *Journal of Early Modern History* 13 (2009), 49–69.

[68] Holt, 'King John and Arthur'.

[69] Romuald of Salerno, *Chronica*, 230–1.

136   5. DUTIES, NORMS AND PROCESS

was killed by an arrow when looking out of the window of a besieged castle.[70] In 1131 Philipp, who only two years earlier had been crowned king of France during his father's lifetime, was riding through the outskirts of Paris when he crossed paths with a 'devilish pig' (*porcus diabolicus*). The king's horse was so perturbed by the encounter that it threw off its rider, who promptly broke his neck.[71] In 1184, Henry VI, eldest son of Emperor Frederick Barbarossa, narrowly escaped an even more hideous death. During an assembly at Erfurt, the floor of the building where the gathering was held suddenly collapsed. Several participants drowned in the latrine beneath. Henry survived only because he had been sitting in a window, conversing with the archbishop of Mainz.[72] Just over a decade later, his brother Conrad was less fortunate. In 1196, in a gruesome testimony to both the sexual violence of aristocratic life and medieval dental hygiene, Conrad had tried to rape a woman, who defended herself by biting Conrad in the chest. The wound turned black, and Conrad died three days later.[73] Just as commonly, fathers died suddenly and unexpectedly. As with royal heirs, riding, hunting and feasting accidents abounded. In 1047, Magnus the Good of Denmark was killed when his horse was startled by a hare and he was impaled on a tree trunk 'from which spikey shoots happened to protrude'.[74] In 1143, the horse of King Fulk of Jerusalem threw off its rider. As Fulk lay prostrate on the ground, his saddle fell on his head and his 'brains gushed forth from both ears and nostrils'.[75] The kingdom of Jerusalem was especially prone to such mishaps: between 1185, when Baldwin IV died, and 1192, the throne passed successively to Baldwin's nephew, his sister-in-law, her second husband, her

---

[70] Hugo Falcandus, *Il regno di Sicilia*, transl. Vito Lo Curto (Cassino, 2007) (reprinting the Latin edition of *La Historia o Liber de Regno Sicilie e la Epistola ad Petrum Panormitane Ecclesie Thesaurium di Ugo Falcando*, ed. G. B. Siragusa (Rome, 1897)), 136–7.

[71] *Chronique de Saint-Pierre-le-Vif de Sens, dite Clarius: Chronicon Sancti Petri Vivi Senonensis*, ed. and transl. Robert-Henri Bautier, Monique Gilles and Anne-Marie Bautier (Paris, 1979), 196; Suger, *Vie de Louis VI le Gros*, ed. and transl. Henri Waquet (Paris, 1929), 266 (*porcus diabolicus*). Similarly, Hugh (II) of France had died falling of a horse: Rodulfus Glaber, *Historiarum libri quinqui*, 152–3.

[72] The episode was widely reported, and was even commemorated in some atrociously bad poetry: *Chronica S. Petri Erfordensis Moderna*, in *Monumenta Erphesfurtensia saec. xii, xiii, xiv*, ed. Oswald Holder-Egger, MGH SS sep. ed. (Hanover and Leipzig, 1899), 193; *Annales Zwetlenses*, MGH SS 9 (Hanover, 1851), 542; *Chronica Reinhardsbrunnensis*, MGH SS 30 (Hanover and Leipzig, 1896), 542; *Annales Aquenses*, MGH SS 24 (Hanover, 1879), 38. The fullest modern account can be found in Thomas Foerster's forthcoming biography of Henry VI.

[73] Conrad of Scheyern, *Annales*, MGH SS 17(Hanover, 1861), 631; Hansmartin Schwarzmaier, 'Konrad von Rothenburg, Herzog von Schwaben. Ein biographischer Versuch', *Württembergisch Franken* 86 (2002), 13–36. I am grateful to Thomas Foerster for these references. I have also borrowed his line about dental hygiene and sexual violence.

[74] Saxo Grammaticus, *Gesta Danorum*, x.22.6, pp. 784–5.

[75] William of Tyre, *Chronicon*, 710–11.

III. SUCCESSION   137

sister-in-law and her brother-in-law. The next king of Jerusalem died in 1197, when, after a night of heavy feasting, he decided to urinate out of a castle window. He lost his balance, and fell to his death.[76] And then there were the rulers who died in war. In 1103, the death of Erik the Good while on crusade threw the Danish royal succession into disarray, and Emperor Henry VI's demise in 1196 that to the German throne. Each left behind heirs deemed unfit to rule, either because of their tyrannical proclivities (Denmark) or because they were still toddlers (Germany). The list could be continued, but the point has been made: premature and sudden deaths abounded, and frequently cast into doubt the prospect of an orderly succession.

In a system where regnal continuity was dependent on a clear and undisputed sequence of rulers, the premature demise of either the king or his most likely heir was both more common and more dangerous than many medieval writers tend to admit or their modern readers tend to imagine. Many rulers died without heirs, without male heirs, with several potential heirs or with one still under age. In each scenario, it normally fell to the kingdom's leading elites to pick a successor. The inevitable dangers of lacking a king meant that a ruler's decision could be challenged and overturned, that a hereditary line of succession could be broken. Biological accidents could bring to the fore the ambitions of relatives and nobles who sought (or found themselves called upon) to fill the vacancy. In most such cases, rivalries erupted over who would exercise power on behalf of the heir. In some instances, the claims of an heir already chosen were even set aside. This happened in England in 1135 and in Germany in 1198. There was a reason why Suger of St Denis so happily contrasted the smooth succession of Capetian kings (the French royal dynasty, named after Hugh Capet, its first member to be king of west Francia) with the chaos and turmoil to be witnessed among their English and German peers.[77]

Even so, maintaining a dynastic link was important. In England in 1066, Tom Licence has recently suggested, Edward the Confessor may have sought to establish Edgar Aetheling as his successor because he, unlike other claimants, was a member of the royal house of Wessex.[78] Other options were available. Sverrir of Norway claimed that he had experienced a vision in which St Olaf, the patron saint of Norway, revealed to him that he was in fact of royal stock and urged him to seize control of the realm.[79] Sverrir clearly was no usurper.

---

[76] *Chronique d'Ernoul et de Bernard le Trésorier*, ed. M. L. de Mas Latrie (Paris, 1871), 309–10.

[77] Suger, *Histoire de Louis VII*, in Suger, *Oeuvres*, ed. Françoise Gasparri, 2 vols. (Paris, 1996–2001), vol. 1, 156–60.

[78] Tom Licence, 'Edward the Confessor and the succession question: a fresh look at the sources', ANS 39 (2017), 113–28. But see also Stephen Baxter, 'Edward the Confessor and the succession question', in *Edward the Confessor*, ed. Mortimer, 77–118.

[79] *Saga of King Sverri*, 11. See also, generally: Lars Lönnroth, 'Sverrir's dreams', *Scripta Islandica* 57 (2007), 97–110.

138   5. DUTIES, NORMS AND PROCESS

He was both of royal descent and selected by heaven to restore peace among his people. More commonly, candidates or their supporters argued that they had been designated as successor by the late king, even if this meant overriding the rights of an existing heir.[80] Seizing the throne of León in 1072, Alfonso claimed that his brother had nominated him as king, and in 1152 in Germany partisans of Frederick I employed a whole gamut of reasons as to why his kingship was legitimate, including that he had been designated by his predecessor, Conrad III. Frederick, he had allegedly declared, was more capable of pacifying the realm than Conrad's infant son.[81] A familial relationship either existed already or it had to be established. It any event, it was an essential precondition for claiming the throne. Writing in the 1170s, the Danish chronicler Sven Aggesen could claim that, 'no son succeeded his father to the throne for a space of many centuries. It passed to grandsons, or nephews, who, to be sure were sprung from royal stock on the one side.'[82]

Heredity and family connections played a central role in thinking about kingship and succession. Yet we also encounter a striking divergence between norms and practice. Norway provided an especially colourful example, but in thirteenth-century Germany, chroniclers also stressed the direct succession from father to son as a norm, whereas in reality the principle of hereditary succession was honoured mostly in its breach.[83] It was invoked even by those who sought to overturn it. When Pope Innocent III felt called upon to settle the German Double Election of 1198, he rejected one candidate at least in part because he was the descendant of a long line of tyrants.[84] Gerald of Wales, writing in the early thirteenth century, dismissed the Norman claim to the English throne partly because the Normans had failed to abide by due principles of inheritance. They were 'rulers, not

[80] *Liber Eliensis*, ed. E. O. Blake, Camden Third Series 92 (London, 1962), 285–6.

[81] *Carmen Campodoctoris*, in *Chronica Hispana Saeculi XII*, ed. Emma Falque, Juan Gil and Antonio Maya, CCCM (Turnhout, 1990), 99–108, at 106; Otto of Freising, *Gesta Frederici*, ii.2, pp. 284–7.

[82] Sven Aggesen, *Brevis Historia*, in *Scriptores Minores*, ed. Gertz, vol. 1, 106–7; English translation: *The Works of Sven Aggesen, Twelfth-Century Historian*, transl. Eric Christiansen (London, 1992), 55.

[83] Björn Weiler, 'Tales of trickery and deceit: the election of Frederick Barbarossa (1152), historical memory, and the culture of kingship in later Staufen Germany', *JMedH* 38 (2012), 295–317.

[84] *Regestum Innocentii III Papae super negotio Romani Imperii*, ed. Friedrich Kempf, Miscellanea Historiae Pontificiae xii (Rome, 1947), nos. 3, 5, 8, 9, 18, 29. See also Cristina Andenna, 'Cesarea oder viperea stirps? Zur Behauptung und Bestreitung persönlicher und dynastischer Idoneität der späten Staufer in kurialen und adligen Diskursen des 13. Jahrhunderts', in *Idoneität – Genealogie – Legitimation*, ed. Andenna and Melville, 189–256; and Kai Hering, '"Fridericus primus [...] natus ex clarissima progenie Carolorum". Genealogie und Idoneität bei den frühen Staufern', in *Idoneität – Genealogie – Legitimation*, ed. Andenna and Melville, 305–28.

III. SUCCESSION

succeeding each other by lineal descent, but rather through inversion, acquiring violent domination by killing their own and slaughtering their relatives'.[85] Heredity had become a key condition for claiming the throne. It could be rejected only by acceptance of the principle, but inverting its meaning. Someone who claimed the throne as part of his inheritance had also been bequeathed the morals of his ancestors. The hereditary principle had become a means through which its own logic could be subverted.

Moreover, it existed alongside the equally potent imperative of suitability. Hence Conrad chose Henry as his successor, while the Conqueror was hesitant about confirming the succession of William II in England and regretted Robert Curthose's in Normandy. Across western Europe, subjects frequently found themselves called upon to choose between rival claimants to the throne. In such circumstances, a discourse of suitability could be invoked. It was easy to find biblical precedent for doing so. In the Old Testament, it was David not Jonathan who succeeded Saul. The pattern repeated itself with David and Solomon.[86] Later tradition had it that Pippin claimed the throne in 751 because he, rather than the Merovingians, possessed the *virtus*, the power and suitability to rule.[87] The model was followed by the Capetians in 987[88] and alluded to by Widukind of Corvey in his record of the events of 918. Similarly, the *Encomium Emmae Reginae* described the death of Edmund Ironside in 1016 as an act of divine judgement. Rather than letting the kingdom suffer in divisions and separation, it was now united under the rule of King Knud.[89] The underlying reasoning in all these instances remained the same. A new ruler had been brought onto the throne because his predecessor or rivals had proven themselves unfit to govern. He possessed the means, skills and willingness to rule; they did not. Hereditary succession was meant to be normative, but it was not meant to be practised invariably.

Still, suitability could not be invoked without justification. There had to be a pressing need for dynastic precedent to be set aside. Suitability could establish precedent. When recounting Henry I succeeding Conrad in 919, the *Annals of Quedlinburg* (*c.* 1025) emphasised that Conrad, too, had held the

---

[85] Gerald of Wales, *De Principis Instructione Liber*, 718–19.

[86] Isidore of Seville, *Isidori Hispalensis Episcopi Etymologiarum*, ed. W. M. Lindsay, Scriptorum Classicorum Bibliotheca Oxoniensis, 2 vols. (Oxford, 1911), ix.3; Pseudo-Cyprianus, *De xii Abusivis Saeculi*, 42–5; St Augustine, *De Civitate Dei*, xvii.20.

[87] *Einhardi Vita Karoli Magni*, ed. and transl. Reinhold Rau, 3 vols. (Darmstadt, 1955–60), vol. 1, 168–9.

[88] Richer, *Historia*, vol. 2, 154–66; Yves Sassier, '"La royauté ne s'acquiert pas par droit héréditaire". Réflexion sur la structure du discours attribué à Adalbéron de Reims en faveur de l'élection de Hugues Capet', in *Élections et pouvoirs politiques*, ed. Péneau, 341–50.

[89] *Encomium Emmae Reginae*, ed. Alistair Campbell, with a supplementary introduction by Simon Keynes (Cambridge, 1998), 14. I am grateful to Ann Williams for this reference.

140   5. DUTIES, NORMS AND PROCESS

throne on account of his virtue.[90] That being so, there was no break with but rather a reinforcing of precedent. More commonly, circumstances demanded that strict hereditary lines be set aside. This was especially the case when a putative heir was variously underage (as in Germany in 983, 1152 and 1198), a woman (England in 1135) or not resident in the realm (Jerusalem in 1118). Almost by definition, in these scenarios an heir lacked the resources and networks or the concrete experience that would allow him or her to confront those who might seek to profit from the uncertainty surrounding a vacant throne.[91] Instead, powerful male relatives had to step in. They alone could restore peace and public order. In Alexander of Telese's recounting, when Duke William of Apulia died in 1126, he left his lands without a protector. Robbers and thieves began to act with impunity. Nobody dared to travel the roads, and even peasants lacked the courage to till their fields. Without Roger II stepping in, the duchy would have suffered unimaginable crimes.[92] Unlike his rivals, Roger acted, and proved himself to be God's chosen instrument by dint of the fervour with which he restored public order. When King Baldwin I of Jerusalem died without issue in 1118, the barons of the Holy Land faced a similar dilemma. His brother Eustace had remained in Lotharingia, while a recent abortive campaign into Egypt had left the realm exposed to and under threat from hostile neighbours. According to William of Tyre, the precarious military situation, combined with Eustace's prolonged absence, resulted in the election of Baldwin's eponymous cousin, the count of Edessa. The dangers facing the realm did not brook any delay. It was therefore paramount, the barons and clergy claimed, that someone be chosen who could command the armies of Palestine and administer the affairs of the realm.[93] In fact, one of the reasons Albert of Aachen – the chronicler closest in time to the events described – gave for the election was that Baldwin 'was an undaunted knight who had often endured many perils in battles for the safety of Christians, and ... had kept the lands of Edessa vigorously defended from all enemy attack'.[94] Faced with the choice between maintaining traditional patterns of

---

[90] *Annales Quedlinburgenses*, 454. Likewise, Adalbert of Magdeburg emphasised that Conrad had become king because the preceding royal *stirps* (clan) had died out. Regino of Prüm, *Chronica*, 155.

[91] For underage rulers, see: Thilo Offergeld, *Reges pueri: das Königtum Minderjähriger im frühen Mittelalter* (Hanover, 2001); Thomas Voghtherr, '"Weh dir, land, dessen König ein Kind ist." Minderjährige Könige um 1200 im europäischen Vergleich', *FmSt* 37 (2003), 291–314. In the case of female heirs see, however, Thomas Foerster, 'Neue Herrschaft in neuen Reichen'.

[92] Alexander of Telese, *Ystoria Rogerii*, 8–9.

[93] William of Tyre, *Chronicon*, 548–51.

[94] Albert of Aachen, *Historia Ierosolomitana*, 872–3. See also Hans Eberhard Mayer, 'The succession to Baldwin II of Jerusalem: English impact on the East', *Dumbarton Oaks Papers* 39 (1985), 139–47.

III. SUCCESSION   141

inheritance and selecting a capable and experienced leader, the custodians of the security of the realm could justify a break with dynastic continuity. In practice, family relationship and suitability were not so much polar opposites as the twin pillars on which a claim to the throne commonly rested. Kings had to be related to their predecessors and they had to be more suitable than their rivals.[95] Baldwin II was cousin to his predecessor and Roger seized the possessions of his nephew. In an inversion of the argument put forth by Gerald of Wales and Innocent III, heredity could even be an expression of suitability. Around 1200, Gislebert of Mons inserted an entirely fictional account of the election of Frederick Barbarossa as king of the Romans in 1152 into a history of the counts of Hainaut. He recounted how, after Conrad III had died, the German princes assembled to choose a successor. However, 'because so many princes disagreed about the election of so great an honour', they entrusted it to four of the most powerful among them, including Duke Frederick (Barbarossa) of Swabia. All four desired to become emperor, and Frederick, 'astute and vigorous', convinced each of the others that they should compete for the crown, but that they should also 'entrust the whole election to him alone'. The day of the election having arrived,

> the three declared that they had yielded the entire election to the duke of Swabia alone. With everyone listening and not contradicting, Frederick said that he was born of emperors and that he knew no one better to rule the Empire, and therefore he chose himself for the height of such great majesty.[96]

That is, Frederick invoked both suitability – he knew no one more suitable of ruling the realm – and heredity – he was, after all, the descendant of emperors. Gislebert echoed the self-representation of Barbarossa's court. Conrad III, Frederick's backers claimed, had designated him as his heir because he was the most suitable, but also because he was a member of the same *stirps*, the same clan.[97] This, more than outright rejection of one discourse in favour of

---

[95] Stefan Weinfurter, 'Idoneität – Begründung und Akzeptanz von Königsherrschaft im hohen Mittelalter', in *Idoneität – Genealogie – Legitimation*, ed. Andenna and Melville, 127–38.

[96] Gislebert of Mons, *La Chronique de Gislebert de Mons*, ed. Léon Vanderkindere (Brussels, 1904), 92–4; translation: Gilbert of Mons, *Chronicle of Hainaut*, transl. and intro. Laura Napran (Woodbridge, 2005), 54–5. Weiler, 'Tales of trickery and deceit', 295–8; Bernd Schneidmüller, 'Mittelalterliche Geschichtsschreibung als Überzeugungsstrategie: eine Königswahl des 12. Jahrhunderts im Wettstreit der Erinnerungen', *Heidelberger Jahrbücher* 52 (2008), 167–88. Note also the very similar language used in England in 1126 when Henry I designated his daughter Matilda as heiress 'since her grandfather, uncle and father had been kings, while on her mother's side the royal lineage went back for many centuries': William of Malmesbury, *Historia Novella*, ed. Edmund King, transl. K. R. Potter (Oxford, 1998), 6–7.

[97] Otto of Freising, *Gesta Frederici*, ii.1, pp. 284–5.

142   5. DUTIES, NORMS AND PROCESS

another, was how the relationship between suitability and right was commonly established.

Claiming the throne normally required one or more of three steps to be taken: overturn a decision already made, cast aside relatives who might have a closer family relationship with the deceased ruler and face down rivals. Any of these ran (or could be portrayed as running) counter to fundamental principles of good governance. Royal power ought to be offered, not sought. And it had to be conferred free of fear or favour, and solely because a candidate was able to perform the duties of kingship. Depriving relatives of their inheritance hardly fitted this image. Unsurprisingly, therefore, *how* a ruler had become king could be used to justify resistance. The manner of either designation or enthronement could be dismissed as illegitimate. In such a case, the candidate opposed had never been king in the first place. Rivals became mere usurpers and disturbers of the peace. Those taking up arms against them not only fought to claim what was rightfully theirs, but also to restore the proper order of the realm. They acted at the behest of heaven, as when St Olaf himself had urged Sverrir to claim the Norwegian throne. They intervened to free the people from the tyranny of evil kings, as William the Conqueror claimed he had done in 1066,[98] or Emperor Henry VI when he took control of Sicily in 1194.[99] They stepped forward to remedy an act of tyranny, because a successor had been imposed improperly or had turned out to be unsuited to the task. Such was the reasoning proposed by the German princes who in 1077 deposed Emperor Henry IV.[100] And they fought usurpers who failed to maintain the peace, as was argued by the supporters of Valdemar I in Denmark and of Matilda in England.[101]

Once a throne had been occupied, amends for the questionable means by which it had been taken could be made. Henry I of east Francia refused to

---

[98] See, most recently, Bates, *William the Conqueror*, 210–17; but see also: Ian Howard, 'Harold II, a throneworthy king', in *Harold II*, ed. Owen-Crocker, 34–52; N. J. Higham, 'Harold Godwinesson: the construction of kingship', in *Harold II*, ed. Owen-Crocker, 19–34.

[99] Peter of Eboli, *Book in Honour of Augustus (Liber ad Honorem Augusti) by Piedro da Eboli*, transl. Gwenyth Hood (Tempe, AZ, 2012), 118–19.

[100] Gerd Althoff, *Heinrich IV.* (Darmstadt, 2006), 228–52; I. S. Robinson, *Henry IV of Germany, 1056–1106* (Cambridge, 1999), 204–5; Daniel Brauch, 'Heinrich V. und sein Vater in den Jahren 1098–1103', in *Heinrich V. in seiner Zeit. Herrschen in einem europäischen Reich des Hochmittelalters*, ed. Gerd Lubich (Cologne, Weimar and Vienna, 2013), 61–80; Michaela Muylkens, *Reges geminati. Die Gegenkönige in der Zeit Heinrichs IV.* (Husum, 2011). On the level of hostility engendered by Henry and the moral failings attributed to him: Althoff, *Heinrich IV.*, 261–72; Gerd Althoff, ed., *Heinrich IV.* (Ostfildern, 2009), especially the contributions by Gerd Althoff, Matthias Becher, Hermann Kamp, Christel Meier and Steffen Patzold.

[101] On Matilda, see below, this chapter. Saxo Grammaticus, *Gesta Danorum*, xii.8.2, pp. 894–5.

III. SUCCESSION 143

receive unction.[102] Ladislaus I of Hungary (who had seized the throne from his brother Solomon) abstained from wearing a crown for seven years.[103] Henry I of England (who had pre-empted and later imprisoned his oldest brother) issued a charter of liberties and recalled the archbishop of Canterbury from exile.[104] Principles of just rule had to be reasserted, and adherence to them had to be demonstrated. Yet refusing unction or not wearing a crown worked only if a ruler was able not just to take, but also to keep the throne. To get to that stage, the royal dignity had to be conferred in a process – sometimes an election, sometimes a form of designation – that reflected and reinforced the moral framework of succession. That framework reflected the frequency with which either an open or a disputed succession could occur. It also took account of the dangers a disputed succession would pose to a ruler's *memoria*, his successor's legitimacy and the welfare of the realm. This framework was not a rigid template. It upheld a set of shared norms that was open to interpretation and different weighting. It was combined with a series of mechanisms to determine which interpretation was most appropriate for a given situation. Which one that turned out to be reflected precedent, the requirements of that particular moment and the skills, means and power of the actors involved. The framework thus did not prevent, but certainly offered ways of negotiating the uncertainty surrounding a vacant throne.

5.3   Succession as Moral Process

It was probably in 1099 that Duke Wladyslaw of Poland decided to settle his succession. He was fifty-six years old, only a little younger than Henry I of England would be when he designated his heir in 1126,[105] or Louis VI of France when he announced his in 1129.[106] He certainly qualified as advanced in age. William the Conqueror died before reaching sixty,[107] Emperor Henry IV when he was fifty-five and Henry V at thirty-eight. The time had clearly come to pick an heir. An added complication was that Wladyslaw had not initially been destined for the throne. When his brother Boleslaw II had been exiled after murdering Stanislas of Kraków, Wladyslaw had acted as regent for his underage nephew, Mieszko III, and had become duke only after Mieszko's

---

[102] Liudprand, *Antapodosis*, 43–4.
[103] *Legenda sancti Ladislai regis*, in *Scriptores Rerum Hungaricarum*, ed. Szentpétery, vol. 2, 517–18.
[104] C. Warren Hollister, *Henry I* (New Haven, CT, 2001), 108–12, 117–18.
[105] Judith Green, *Henry I: King of England and Duke of Normandy* (Cambridge, 2006), 20.
[106] *Chronique de Saint-Pierre-le-Vif de Sens*, 124; *La Chronique de Morigny*, ed. Léon Mirot (Paris, 1909), 56.
[107] Bates, *William the Conqueror*, 33, for William the Conqueror's likely birth in 1028. William A. Aird, *Robert 'Curthose', Duke of Normandy (c.1050–1134)* (Woodbridge, 2011), 58; Orderic Vitalis, *Ecclesiastical History*, vol. 2, 356–7, vol. 3, 98–9, vol. 4, 92–3.

144   5. DUTIES, NORMS AND PROCESS

premature death.[108] To ensure the tranquillity of the realm and his own *memoria*, Wladyslaw had to ensure a smooth and legitimate succession. In 1099, he therefore divided his lands between Zbigniew, his oldest but illegitimate son and Boleslaw III, his legitimate younger son, but kept for himself the chief cities of the realm. The settlement was announced not long after the cathedral at Gniezno had been consecrated, and after Boleslaw and Zbigniew had returned from a successful campaign in Pomerania.[109]

By granting lands to both Zbigniew and Boleslaw, Wladyslaw reflected broader European conventions. Fathers were supposed to provide for all their progeny. In 1063, King Fernando I of León announced how, on his death, his domains should be divided among his sons. Alfonso was to become king of León, with authority over his brothers, who respectively received Castile and Galicia, while his daughters were put in charge of certain nunneries.[110] Similar practices are observable in France, Sicily and Germany.[111] Yet Wladyslaw's decision also reflects features rooted deeply in contemporary Polish politics. He failed to designate one heir as holding authority over the other. In Sicily, by contrast, Roger II had declared that, just as with Alfonso in León, Roger of Apulia preceded his brothers in rank. He was clearly expected to be treated as their overlord. The same was true in England. Henry II decided to divide his lands between Henry, who would be king, Richard, who would become count of Poitou, Geoffrey, who received Brittany and John, who was granted Ireland.[112] At most, the fact that Wladyslaw reserved for himself the chief cities of the realm may suggest that he intended to continue exercising some oversight. If that was indeed the case, then it probably reflected the particular challenges of this precise moment. Zbigniew, initially destined for the Church, had been abducted by his father's Silesian opponents, before allying himself with them and with the duke of Bohemia, another inveterate foe. He only returned to Poland *c.* 1096.[113] Moreover, by 1099 Boleslaw was about to come of age (he had been born

---

[108] *Gesta Principum Polonorum*, i.29, pp. 100–3. Zbigniew Dalewski, 'Boleslaw Wrymouth's penance and Gallus Anonymus' chronicle', in *Gallus Anonymus*, ed. Stopka, 125–40.

[109] *Gesta Principum Polonorum*, ii.7, pp. 132–3. Whether Zbigniew's illegitimacy was indeed a factor remains a matter of debate. McDougall, *Royal Bastards*, does not discuss the Polish case, but provides essential background reading.

[110] *Historia Silense*, ed. Justo Perez de Urbel and Atilano Gonzalez Ruiz-Zorilla (Madrid, 1959), 204–5. On the text: Richard Fletcher, 'A twelfth-century view of the Spanish past', in *The Medieval State. Essays Presented to James Campbell*, ed. J. R. Maddicott and D. M. Palliser (London, 2000), 147–61.

[111] Lewis, *Royal Succession*, 155–71; Hugo Falcandus, *Il regno di Sicilia*, 136–7; Arnold of Lübeck, *Chronica*, 151–2.

[112] John Gillingham, 'At the deathbeds of the kings of England, 1066-1216', in *Herrscher- und Fürstentestamente im westeuropäischen Mittelalter*, ed. Brigitte Kasten (Cologne, Weimar and Vienna, 2008), 509–30.

[113] *Gesta Principum Polonorum*, ii.4–5, pp. 120–9.

III. SUCCESSION 145

c. 1086). Neither of his sons could be ignored, and their rivalry was likely to come to a head soon. One way of pre-empting a prolonged dispute was to ensure continuing oversight through their father, while, simultaneously, providing both Zbigniew and Boleslaw with lands commensurate with their status. Governing lands on their own, but under Wladyslaw's watchful eye, they would also be challenged to demonstrate their ability to rule. There might even have been some hope that conflict between the brothers could be avoided. Wladyslaw's announcing the settlement after the siblings had returned from a jointly led campaign could suggest as much.

The settlement of 1099 provides an ideal point of entry for exploring how actors and observers fashioned the process of designation as a tool for determining a successor's legitimacy. He should, of course, be pious, just and warlike, but such qualities reinforced rather than substituted for the manner in which he had been installed as heir. That process was all the more important, when as in Wladyslaw's case, the proposed settlement collapsed. Then, the ability to define the legitimacy of the process meant defining the legitimacy of the claimant, as the next section will explore, and as will emerge in subsequent chapters. What follows therefore sets the scene. It outlines how one particular observer established legitimacy by stressing the process through which a throne was ultimately secured. That observer was none other than 'Gallus'. He began writing *c.* 1110, with the memory of Wladyslaw's proposal still fresh, and he did so while at – or at least in close proximity to – the heart of the ducal court. Indeed, the aftermath of the 1099 settlement was not to reach its gory conclusion until just before 'Gallus' began compiling the *Gesta*.[114] From that later vantage point, Wladyslaw's proposal provided a tool for explaining and evaluating subsequent developments. Whether the events of 1099 unfolded exactly as reported by 'Gallus' is therefore less important than the significance that he attached to the process by which a successor should be picked. For that to have legitimising power, it needed to be fashioned as an archetype that combined all the elements required to make a settlement legitimate. It also had to reflect the specific circumstances and challenges of the Polish case.

This, then, is how 'Gallus' reported the events of 1099:

> Now when their father was asked by the magnates which of his sons more distinguished himself in sending and receiving embassies, in calling up and levying an army and in the manifold affairs of so great a realm, he is said to have replied: 'As an old and infirm man it is my duty to divide the realm between them and to judge matters for the present. However, to set one before the other, or to grant them excellence and wisdom, is not something in my power, it belongs to God Almighty. Still, I can reveal to you the one desire of my heart: that after my death I would have you all with one accord obey the one who is wiser and better in defending the

---

[114] See also below, Chapter 10.

146   5. DUTIES, NORMS AND PROCESS

land and striking the foe. But in the meantime, let each of them keep the part of the realm as it has been divided between them. . . . But in the last resort, if both of them prove unfit, or if they should happen to fall out with each other, he who sides with foreign nations and brings them in to the destruction of the realm, should be deprived of rule and forfeit his inheritance. And let him possess the throne of the kingdom by perpetual right who better provides for the honour and advantage of the land.'[115]

Wladyslaw's request that the magnates reject whichever son allied himself with foreign foes both hinted at Zbigniew's past misdeeds and foreshadowed the ones he was yet to commit. In 1102, he once again collaborated with the Bohemians.[116] Boleslaw, by contrast, abided by his father's wishes. In the 'Gallus' version of events, he alone met the criteria set out by the magnates and by Wladyslaw. Boleslaw, not Zbigniew, repeatedly proved himself capable of 'striking the foe and defending the land', of 'receiving and sending embassies' and of providing 'for the honour and advantage of the land'. Other elements in the narrative of 'Gallus' point in the same direction. Boleslaw had, for instance, been conceived only after Wladyslaw and his wife had embarked upon a campaign of rigorous fasting, praying and almsgiving, and after their having donated the golden statue of a child to the shrine of St Gilles.[117] The circumstances of Boleslaw's birth echoed the portents and visions announcing an ideal or first king. Clearly, he would rule with celestial backing. Even so, the rivalry between the brothers could not be ignored.[118] For the narrative strategy of 'Gallus' to work, Boleslaw's personal suitability had to be beyond doubt and the process of his succession beyond dispute.

Like Conrad I, Wladyslaw left the choice of his successor to the people and to God. Indeed, the extent to which the initiative was portrayed as resting with the Polish aristocracy merits exploration. Wladyslaw had begun to settle his succession at the behest of the magnates. They, 'Gallus' reported, had demanded a ruler and had defined his chief duties. Yet they had not initially claimed for themselves a right to choose the duke. That remained Wladyslaw's prerogative. He had devolved the decision to them, but had also outlined the criteria that were to guide them in making it. This marks a striking departure from how 'Gallus' reported earlier successions. Siemowit, the first Polish duke, had simply been put in place by 'the king of king and duke of dukes' (i.e. God). On his death, he had been succeeded by his eldest son, who had been followed

---

[115] Gesta Principum Polonorum, ii.8, pp. 132–5.

[116] Przemysław Wiszewski, Domus Bolezlai: Values and Social Identity in Dynastic Traditions of Medieval Poland (c. 966–1138) (Leiden and Boston, 2010), 258–301 offers a fuller summary of Gallus's account.

[117] Gesta Principum Polonorum, i.30, pp. 104–5. See also: van Houts, 'The writing of history', 101–3.

[118] Dalewski, 'Boleslaw Wrymouth's penance'.

III. SUCCESSION 147

by his and so on.[119] Boleslaw I had assumed power on his father's death,[120] as did Mieszko II[121] and Boleslaw II.[122] In each instance, the succession was clear. There was no dispute, and hence no process of election. The case of 1099 apart, 'Gallus' recorded only two departures from this pattern, and alluded to a third. Mieszko II's son Casimir had been exiled. In the chronicler's eyes, the act was one of great perfidy, perpetrated by traitors fearing that Casimir might punish them for having unjustly expelled his mother.[123] The second exception was Boleslaw II, who, 'Gallus' implied, might have been deposed for ordering the mutilation and death of St Stanislas.[124] And there was of course the son of Piast, who expelled a ruling duke.[125] The succession to Wladyslaw was therefore the first in which the magnates were legitimately called upon to choose their ruler. This need not mean that what happened in 1099 was an innovation. Almost anywhere in Europe, a new king had to be chosen by the nobles and prelates. In Poland, we may assume, Casimir's and Boleslaw II's exile would not have occurred without a vote among the leading figures of the realm. More likely, the seeming departure from previous norms reflected the particular circumstances of 1099. For the first time in the realm's history, one brother competed with the other for the right to rule. In this context, descent and inheritance alone proved insufficient grounds on which to base a choice. In their stead, the act of election – one, moreover, based on suitability – became the means with which full legitimacy could be ascertained. It did not, however, supersede descent. Inheritance and suitability, confirmed by an act of election, became the twin pillars on which Boleslaw's right to the throne rested.

However, without Wladyslaw's recommendation, neither the process of election nor its outcome would have carried much weight. It was therefore of paramount importance that the duke's decision was made solely for the common good. And so it was. Wladyslaw, 'Gallus' stressed, acted of his own volition, but at the behest of his people. His decision was not born of weakness. Like a truly good ruler, he sought to assuage his people's fear of civil strife, and did so by attempting to stifle the incipient rivalry among his progeny. There may even have been a penitential aspect to Wladyslaw's approach. Unlike William the Conqueror, he may not have gained the throne through violent conquest; he had, however, obtained it only after his brother had been exiled for heinous crimes and after his nephew's death. By passing the decision to God and to his people, Wladyslaw displayed the penitent humility of a pious ruler. This had an added advantage. Responsibility for the breakdown of

---

[119] *Gesta Principum Polonorum*, i.3–4, pp. 22–9.
[120] *Gesta Principum Polonorum*, i.6, pp. 30–1.
[121] *Gesta Principum Polonorum*, i.17, pp. 72–3.
[122] *Gesta Principum Polonorum*, i.22, pp. 86–9.
[123] *Gesta Principum Polonorum*, i.18, pp. 74–5.
[124] *Gesta Principum Polonorum*, i.27, pp. 96–7.
[125] See above, Chapter 3.

148   5. DUTIES, NORMS AND PROCESS

relations between his sons rested all the more clearly with Zbigniew, retrospectively justifying Wladyslaw's caution, the decision of the magnates and Boleslaw's rule. Evidently, Zbigniew was driven by ambition and greed, not concern for the honour of his realm or the welfare of his people. Boleslaw, by contrast, acted as a duke should act. That was why the magnates, who had acted in accordance with the general precepts that his father had laid out for them, had chosen him.

All available steps had been taken to secure the throne for Boleslaw. He was the legitimate son of a duke, had proven himself capable of ruling like one and had been chosen freely by his people. Even so, his claim was disputed. Even 'Gallus' could not pass over Zbigniew's challenge.[126] To overcome this problem, he presented a subtly crafted narrative highlighting the process through which Boleslaw had come to rule the Poles. He may even have alluded to earlier episodes in Polish history. The *Deeds of the Princes of the Poles* opened with a duke refusing to perform his duties, in this case, to host strangers seeking sustenance. They were welcomed by a peasant, Piast, whose son, in turn, replaced the duke who had been so neglectful of his duties. The origins of Piast rule rested on the family's willingness to abide by the obligations of the ducal office. A similar emphasis marked the origins of Polish kingship. In the rendering of 'Gallus', Boleslaw I had received a crown because he was virtuous and king-like. It is thus worth noting that 'Gallus' dated the events of 1099 as occurring just after the dedication of a new cathedral at Gniezno – the very place where Polish kingship had begun in 999/1000, and where mysterious strangers had predicted the great future of the son of Piast.[127]

There were further echoes of the Piast origin myth. Piast had welcomed these strangers, who had planned to attend the haircutting of the duke's eldest son – presumably, some sort of rite of transition from boyhood to adolescence or adulthood. On leaving, they predicted a great future for this son. The episode reverberated in the account by 'Gallus' of Boleslaw's knighting, which also marked his coming of age.[128] During the ceremony, an unnamed individual, speaking 'from the spirit of prophecy', announced that, 'on this day, the good Lord has visited the kingdom of Poland . . . Until now Poland was trodden down by her enemies, but this young lad (*istum puerulum*) will restore her as she was in times of old.'[129] However implicitly, the description by 'Gallus' of Wladyslaw's succession invoked a recurring theme in his writing: the Piasts owed their standing to their ability and

---

[126] See also below, Chapter 10.
[127] See above, Chapter 3.
[128] See below, Chapter 6.
[129] *Gesta Principum Polonorum*, ii.20, pp. 154–5.

III. SUCCESSION   149

willingness to act righteously. Boleslaw III alone would follow in their footsteps.

'Gallus' offered at once a record of the Polish past and a guide to virtuous rule in the present. In Boleslaw I, history provided a precedent against which subsequent rulers could be measured. It also showed how crises had come about and how they could be handled.[130] Once 'Gallus' turned to events within living memory, he focussed on how reality could be made to align with normative expectations. In Boleslaw III's case, how Wladyslaw's settlement had been proposed was essential to the legitimacy of his claim. At the same time, recording Wladyslaw's efforts did not serve merely propagandistic ends. When the duke left the decision on his succession to the Polish nobility and clergy, he broke with established precedent, but potentially also created a new one. In Poland just as in Norway, on entering historical time the ideal sequence of father following son was honoured chiefly in the breach. Until 1099, however, no record seems to have survived (or at least none to have been available to 'Gallus') on how a succession dispute ought to be handled. 'Gallus' remedied that situation.

Something like the process described by 'Gallus' surfaces across the Latin world. Suitability had to be ascertained. Yet there also had to be a family connection. Furthermore, a succession, in the event of more than one claimant appearing, ought to be decided free of fear or favour, and had to be authorised by the people. Both premises underpinned accounts of Conrad I's deathbed. He recommended that Henry become his heir, while he left the decision to the princes. In England in 1087, the Conqueror suggested that the English might want to consider his son William for the throne. All of this served to meet and to reinforce the moral responsibilities surrounding the succession and the royal office itself. Rulership was too onerous a duty to be handed over to someone who lacked the means or the morals to wield it for the benefit of all. Equally, kingship was not simply in the ruler's gift. The moral responsibility for the well-being of the realm extended to the 'people'. Ultimately, it was they who had to choose a successor. Kings might guide their decision, but could not determine it.

In this regard, the Polish case also leaves questions unanswered. No evidence survives to record Zbigniew's perspective or that of his supporters. However, a near contemporary of 'Gallus', Cosmas of Prague, provides us with a glimpse of what that might have been. In his rendering, Boleslaw bribed the Bohemians with ten sacks of gold.[131] Duke Vladislav of Bohemia, when

---

[130] Grischa Vercamer, 'Das Bad des Königs – beschreibt Gallus Anonymus ein genuin piastisches/polnisches Ritual? Überlegung zu Ehre und Herrschaftsvorstellung bei den frühen Piasten (Bolesław I. und Bolesław III.) aufgrund des Kapitels 1,13', *FmSt* 43 (2009) 349–72; Dalewski, 'Boleslaw Wrymouth's penance'.

[131] Cosmas of Prague, *Chronica*, 179; *Chronicle of the Czechs*, 199–200.

150   5. DUTIES, NORMS AND PROCESS

meeting one of his rivals, exclaimed that he did not want to be compared to
Boleslaw, 'who summoned his brother Zbigniew with evil intentions ... and
deprived him of his eyes on the third day'.[132] Accusations of venality and
tyranny could easily be levelled at the protagonist of the 'Gallus' narrative. He
had sought to buy his throne and had cruelly mutilated his brother, and he had
done so under the pretext of providing him with a safe conduct. He had seized
the throne by force and could not be considered a just ruler. Cosmas' comments point to the fact that norms were open to interpretation. They had to be
weighed up. Where, for instance, would descent rank in relation to suitability?
The issue was not discussed in the Polish case, but could it be that Zbigniew's
status as older son was undermined by his illegitimate birth? Or did Boleslaw's
suitability outweigh his status as the younger brother? These were precisely the
questions that electors and subjects had to ponder. Asking them became all the
more pressing if, as frequently happened, a decision made during a ruler's
lifetime had to be revisited after his death. What did this mean for the process
of succession? How could rivals and their respective backers utilise norms? Did
they really even share a common framework?

5.4 Disputed Norms

To address these issues, let us shift the focus to England in the reign of William
the Conqueror's youngest son, Henry I (r. 1100–1135).[133] In 1122, Henry's sole
legitimate son drowned. Three years later, Henry's nephew William Clito, son
of his older brother Robert, also died.[134] The king's second marriage had
remained childless, which left Henry's daughter Matilda as his sole progeny
not born out of wedlock.[135] Other putative claimants included the king of
Scotland (related to Henry's first wife) and Henry's nephew Stephen of Blois
(son of William the Conqueror's daughter Adela). If the king wanted his
daughter to succeed, measures had to be taken to secure the throne for her.
Henry duly had the barons and clergy confirm Matilda as his heiress not once,
but twice. Yet Matilda never became queen of England. In 1135, the English
decided to offer the throne to Stephen instead, and Matilda's efforts to reclaim
her inheritance remained unsuccessful. In the end, she had to resign her claim
to her son Henry. At the same time, Stephen's grip on the crown was by no
means secure. A stalemate prevailed until 1153, when the English barons
forced Henry to accept Stephen as king, and Stephen to designate Henry as

[132] Cosmas of Prague, Chronica, 205; Chronicle of the Czechs, 222–3.
[133] The section on Stephen and Matilda is based on Weiler, 'Kingship, usurpation', which
has, however, been updated and revised for this book.
[134] Green, Henry I, 193–5; Hollister, Henry I, 309–10; Karl Leyser, 'The Anglo-Norman
succession 1120–1125', ANS 13 (1990–1), 225–42.
[135] Henry was the father of at least 18 illegitimate children. Kathleen H. Thompson, 'Affairs
of the state: the illegitimate children of Henry I', JMedH 29 (2003), 129–51.

III. SUCCESSION   151

his heir.[136] The civil war caused enough suffering for modern historians to label these years the 'Anarchy of Stephen's Reign'.[137] Because fronts remained hardened, an almost unparalleled wealth of sources survives in which contemporaries sought to come to terms with the events unfolding around them. We can hear a multiplicity of voices. What did they have to say?

Perhaps the most sophisticated commentator on Henry I's efforts was William of Malmesbury, whose *Historia Novella* was written between 1138 and 1142.[138] In his rendering, Matilda was both truly worthy of her claim and a last resort. She had been reluctant to come to England. She had not desired the throne, but was an obedient daughter who did her father's bidding. Yet her status was precarious. Henry, William claimed, had proposed her as heiress only because he did not have a legitimate son.[139] The key event in having Matilda established as successor was an assembly at London around Christmas 1126. Having bestowed Shropshire on his second wife, and,

> in grief that the woman did not conceive ... [Henry] was, with good cause, thinking anxiously about the successor to his throne. After deliberating long and deeply on this matter he then, at this same council, bound the nobles of all England, also the bishops and abbots, by the obligation of an oath that, if he himself died without a male heir, they would immediately and without hesitation accept his daughter Matilda ... as their lady. He said first what a disaster it had been for the country that fortune deprived him of his son William, who would have claimed the kingdom as of right. As it was, he said, his daughter remained, in whom alone lay the legitimate succession, since her grandfather, uncle and father had been kings, while on her mother's side the royal lineage went back for many centuries.[140]

Matilda's claim rested on three pillars: designation, consent and descent. Henry nominated her, while the barons and clergy vowed to 'defend the English realm on her behalf against all'.[141] Indeed, so important was their consent that William inserted a separate chapter naming everyone who had

---

[136] Edmund King, *King Stephen* (New Haven, CT, 2010), 279–81.

[137] *The Anarchy of King Stephen's Reign*, ed. Edmund King (Oxford, 1994); Hugh M. Thomas, 'Miracle stories and violence in King Stephen's reign', *HSJ* 13 (1999), 111–24; Thomas, 'Violent disorder in King Stephen's England: a maximum argument', in *King Stephen's Reign: 1135–1154*, ed. Graeme J. White and Paul Dalton (Woodbridge, 2008), 139–70.

[138] On Malmesbury's shifting attitude towards Matilda: Kirsten A. Fenton, *Gender, Nation and Conquest in the Works of William of Malmesbury* (Woodbridge, 2008), 51–2.

[139] William of Malmesbury, *Historia Novella*, ed. Edmund King, transl. K. R. Potter (Oxford, 1998), 4–7.

[140] William of Malmesbury, *Historia Novella*, 19–22.

[141] John of Worcester, *The Chronicle of John of Worcester*, ed. and transl. R. R. Darlington, P. McGurk and Jennifer Bray, 3 vols. (Oxford, 1995–8), vol. 3, 166–7.

152   5. DUTIES, NORMS AND PROCESS

been present in 1126,[142] and Henry had the oaths repeated in 1131.[143] Just as significant was Matilda's royal pedigree. William traced Matilda's English ancestry back to the ninth century.[144] The focus probably reflected William's preoccupations and the circumstances of Henry's succession. In the *Gesta Regum*, the chronicler had included a prophecy attributed to Edward the Confessor. After three foreign rulers, English and Norman would be united once more.[145] This initially referred to Henry's son (who was had probably been alive when William wrote the passage).[146] It applied equally to Matilda (their mother, a Scottish princess, was descended from the Wessex kings of England). Moreover, when Henry had seized the English throne, William stressed that Henry, unlike his siblings, had been born in the purple, that is, after his father had been crowned king of England.[147] Being born the son of a king had predestined Henry to become one himself. All of this reinforced Matilda's right to be England's next ruler. Unlike Robert of Gloucester, she was the legitimate offspring of kings; unlike David of Scotland, she was of English royal stock; unlike Stephen of Blois, she was the daughter of a ruling monarch, not merely the grandchild of one. And unlike all of them, she had been nominated by her father and accepted by the great men of England.

William's account was designed to discredit Stephen without necessarily backing Matilda. The chronicler noted further that in 1126 'there was a noteworthy contest, it is said, between Robert [of Gloucester] and Stephen [of Blois], who as rivals in distinction strove with each other for the honour of swearing first, the one claiming the prerogative of a son, the other the rank of a nephew'.[148] Having been the first among the laity to accept Matilda, and having jostled with his cousin for the privilege of doing so, Stephen's perjury was all the greater. Moreover, the episode evoked an infamous precedent. Harold Godwinson, too, had sworn to accept William of Normandy as the future king of England, only to usurp the throne once Edward the Confessor had breathed his last.[149] William was not alone in drawing this parallel. Henry of Huntingdon, in recording Stephen's election, used the very phrase – *regni diadema . . . invasit*, he invaded the crown of the realm – which he had earlier

---

[142] William of Malmesbury, *Historia Novella*, 19–22. See also, for the list of reputed attendants, *Regesta Regum Anglo-Normannorum 1066–1154*, ed. H. W. C. Davis, H. A. Cronne and Charles Johnson, 4 vols. (Oxford, 1913–69), vol. 2, no. 1715.

[143] William of Malmesbury, *Historia Novella*, 19–22.

[144] William of Malmesbury, *Historia Novella*, 19–22.

[145] William of Malmesbury, *Gesta Regum*, ii.226, pp. 414–15; Hugh M. Thomas, *The English and the Normans. Ethnic Hostility, Assimilation and Identity 1066–c.1220* (Oxford, 2003), 56.

[146] Malmesbury, *Gesta Regum*, v.419, pp. 758–9.

[147] William of Malmesbury, *Gesta Regum*, v.390, pp. 709–11.

[148] William of Malmesbury, *Historia Novella*, 8–9.

[149] William of Poitiers, *The Gesta Guillelmi of William of Poitiers*, ed. and transl. R. H. C. Davis and Marjorie Chibnall (Oxford, 1998), 100–3.

III. SUCCESSION   153

employed to describe Harold's conduct.[150] There was little to distinguish King
Stephen from the archetypal usurper in the Norman tradition of English
history. Henry's terminology was carefully chosen: the term *regnum invadere*,
to invade the realm, denoted the unjust ruler, the usurper and the tyrant.[151]
Stephen acted in violation of natural law, but in perjuring himself, he also acted
Deum temptans,[152] contrary to divine law and spurning the will of God.[153] To
his enemies, the king was a perjurer and usurper. His succession therefore
remained invalid. Unlike Stephen and his supporters, those backing Matilda
fulfilled their oaths. Her claim was legitimate because the circumstances of her
designation were beyond reproof.

How did Stephen's backers respond? They certainly recognised the parallels
with Harold. Even the *Liber Eliensis*, otherwise supportive of the king, used an
account of Harold's coronation to describe Stephen's.[154] Averting allegations
of perjury and usurpation became a primary concern for his allies. To this end,
they employed a variety of strategies. They questioned the legitimacy of the
1126 oath, argued that Stephen had in fact been designated by Henry I and
insisted that the circumstances in 1135 demanded that he, rather than Matilda,
wear the crown. The 1126 oath was unlawful, forced upon the barons by the
king. The promise, made under duress, invalidated Matilda's claim.[155] Thus,
although Stephen had participated in the meeting, neither he nor his electors
were guilty of perjury. This line of reasoning was not without its risks. In 1196
Emperor Henry VI had extracted an oath from the German princes to elect his
infant son Frederick as king and heir presumptive. However, once the emperor
died, these promises were quickly disregarded. The ensuing turmoil came to
pitch the late emperor's brother, Duke Philip of Swabia, against his cousin,
Count Otto of Poitou. Philip soon faced accusations of perjury, as he had been

---

[150] Henry of Huntingdon, *Historia Anglorum*, 384–5; 699–703.
[151] Cf. for instance: *Sancti Leonis Magni Sermones Inediti*, PL 56, col. 1151; Hincmar of
Rheims, *De Fide Carolo Regi Servanda*, PL 125, col. 965; Rodulfus Glaber, *Historiarum
libri quinqui*, 24–7; *Lamperti Monachi Hersfeldensis Annales*, ed. Oswald Holder-Egger,
transl. Adolf Schmidt (Darmstadt, 1973), 70, 87; *Annales Patherbrunnenses. Eine verlorene Quellenschrift des zwölften Jahrhunderts, aus Bruchstücken wiederhergestellt*, ed.
Paul Scheffer-Boichorst (Innsbruck, 1870), 151; *Innocentii Pontificis Romani Epistolae
et Privilegia*, PL 179, col. 53; Helinand of Froidmont, *Chronicon*, PL 212, col. 824. See also
above, Chapter 4.
[152] Henry of Huntingdon, *Historia Anglorum*, 699–701.
[153] William of Newburgh, *Historia Rerum Anglicarum*, ed. Richard Howlett, in *Chronicles of
the Reigns of Stephen, Henry II and Richard I*, vols. 1 and 2 (London, 1884–5), vol. 1,
32–3.
[154] *Liber Eliensis*, 246–7.
[155] Gervase of Canterbury, *The Historical Works of Gervase of Canterbury*, ed.
William Stubbs, 2 vols. (London, 1879), 93. This reflected Canon Law. Cf., for instance,
Corpus Iuris Canonici I: Decretum Magistri Gratiani, ed. Emil Friedberg (Leipzig, 1879),
d.2 c. xxii q. ii, iii, vii. R. H. Helmholz, *The Spirit of Classical Canon Law* (Athens, GA,
1996), 164–72.

154   5. DUTIES, NORMS AND PROCESS

the one who reputedly instigated young Frederick's original election.[156] Although the oath had been performed under duress, the duke's opponents argued, Philip had been so eager to comply that this excuse could not apply to him. Pope Innocent III, called upon to arbitrate, concurred. The princes' oath had been forced from them. They were within their rights to choose another king, as long as they did so freely. Philip, however, was bound by his earlier promise, as he had contravened the oath not because of the pangs of conscience, but because of his lust for power.[157] Even if an oath was invalid, it could only be broken with pure motives. Innocent was schooled in the finer points of canon law and the product of later intellectual developments, yet his objections to Philip present, albeit in a more refined form, the very principles alluded to by William of Malmesbury. Even if Henry I had coerced his barons into accepting Matilda, the fact that Stephen had so willingly done his bidding invalidated the reason he later gave for having disregarded them. His actions were tainted by the fact that he pursued his own advantage.

Moreover, denying that the 1126 oath was valid did not necessitate Stephen holding the throne instead. A somewhat different argument line of reasoning was therefore also employed: Henry I himself had designated Stephen as his heir. He may have forced the barons to accept Matilda in 1126 and 1131, but with death approaching, Henry had realised his error, declared Matilda unfit to rule and requested that Stephen be accepted as his heir instead.[158] Stephen was cleared of perjury, while even her own father had denied Matilda's suitability. One should not underestimate the effectiveness of this stratagem. Archbishop William of Canterbury could only be persuaded to consecrate Stephen after he had been assured that Henry I had indeed chosen him to be king.[159] That witnesses to back this claim could be named left Matilda's partisans little room for manoeuvre.[160] All William of Malmesbury could offer in response was to advance a counterclaim: Robert of Gloucester had been with the king to the end. When asked about the choice of his successor, Henry had confirmed Matilda's designation.[161]

---

[156] *Annales Marbacenses Qui Dicuntur*, ed. Hermann Bloch, MGH SS sep. ed. (Hanover and Leipzig, 1907), 69. For the background cf. Peter Csendes, *Heinrich VI.* (Darmstadt, 1993), 171–8; Heinrich Mitteis, *Die deutsche Königswahl. Ihre Rechtsgrundlagen bis zur Goldenen Bulle*, 2nd ed. (Brünn, Munich and Vienna, 1944; repr. Darmstadt, 1987), 113–41; Bernd Ulrich Hucker, *Kaiser Otto IV.* (Hanover, 1990), 22–35.

[157] *Regestum Innocentii III Papae*, no. 29.

[158] *Liber Eliensis*, 244–5.

[159] *Gervase of Canterbury*, 94. See also *Gesta Stephani*, ed. K. R. Potter and R. H. C. Davis (Oxford, 1976), 8–9.

[160] John of Salisbury, *Historia Pontificalis. Memoirs of the Papal Court*, ed. and transl. Marjorie Chibnall (London, 1956), 83–6; *The Letters and Charters of Gilbert Foliot*, ed. Adrian Morey and C. N. L. Brooke (Cambridge, 1967), no. 26.

[161] William of Malmesbury, *Historia Novella*, 23–5.

III. SUCCESSION

155

Designation certainly gave Stephen a right to the throne, but the English still lacked a reason to offer it to him. This contextualises the *Gesta Stephani*'s account of the calamities that had befallen the realm after Henry's death: England,

> formerly the seat of justice, the habitation of peace, the height of piety, the mirror of religion, became thereafter a home of perversity, a haunt of strife, a training-ground of disorder, and a teacher of every kind of rebellion.

The public peace was shattered, and no one remained to uphold justice and control the lawlessness of a kingless people. Amidst this turmoil, Stephen of Blois, the late king's favourite nephew, arrived and quickly made his way to London, where he attended an assembly of magnates and prelates. They decided to elect a king,

> who, with a view to re-establishing peace for the common benefit, would meet the insurgents of the kingdom in arms and would justly administer the enactments of the laws.[162]

As the most suitable candidate for this task, Stephen was chosen.[163] Henry's death had allowed evil and greedy men to pursue their desires without fear of reprisal. Only a strong king could restore tranquillity, and only Stephen had the means and skills to undertake the task. He had been motivated by concern for the welfare of his uncle's subjects, and it was they who offered him the crown, rather than he who sought it.

The problem was, of course, that the very same concepts could just as easily be applied to discredit Stephen. A number of Angevin sources (thus named after Matilda's husband, the count of Anjou) use almost identical imagery to emphasise just how immoral his actions had been. John of Worcester's account is typical:

> After Henry's burial, and with Stephen as king, it was not long before there was much discord throughout England and Normandy, and the bonds of peace were torn apart. Each man rose against his fellow. ... Each man plundered the goods of others. The strong violently oppressed the weak. ... When all should have been at peace through fear of the king, who should be as a roaring lion, there is in many places ... depopulation and devastation.[164]

Not only was Stephen a perjurer and usurper, but he also proved himself incapable of performing his duties. The outbreak of hostilities, the oppression

---

[162] Orderic Vitalis in lamenting the death of Henry I used a similar terms: Orderic Vitalis, *Ecclesiastical History*, vol. 6, 450–3.

[163] *Gesta Stephani*, 6–9.

[164] John of Worcester, *Chronicle*, vol. 2, 216. Cf. also *The Peterborough Chronicle 1070–1154*, ed. Cecily Clark (Oxford, 1958), 54–5.

156   5. DUTIES, NORMS AND PROCESS

of the poor and powerless, rather than ending with the election of a new king, came to the fore more fully. In the words of William of Newburgh, Stephen did not reign, but merely assumed the *name* of king.[165] Instead of oppressing the oppressors, Stephen depended on them. Not only was he incapable of ruling the realm, but his kingship was the very root of its sufferings. Having Stephen as king and having no king at all came to mean the same thing: in those days, there was no king, and everyone did as they pleased.[166]

As much as the parlous state of affairs seemed to necessitate Stephen's actions in 1135, so his inability to deal with them justified the defiance of his opponents. The dangers posed by the absence of a monarch could serve to justify taking the throne, but they could only be used effectively if the new ruler proved himself successful. Angevin supporters such as William of Newburgh and Osbert de Clare employed the very terminology used to back Stephen's claims to highlight the challenges overcome by King Henry II on his arrival in England. England, which had been without justice, was restored to its former glory, while the oppressors now became the oppressed.[167] He revived the peace and the rigour of law.[168] Matilda's partisans responded to Stephen's claims by portraying him as someone who, in every respect, violated the very principles of royal lordship. The Angevins did not dispute the values on which Stephen's backers based his claim. They denied his ability to conform to them. Claiming the throne on the grounds of necessity and suitability alone meant treading a dangerous path.

The English experience highlights limitations in the moral process of succession. It could work only once agreement had been achieved, or at least once a candidate had shown sufficient strength to subdue his opponents or to cajole them into submission. On its own, it was a tool with which crises could be handled, but not one with which they could always be avoided. Agency rested with individuals and groups utilising a framework consisting of loosely defined norms, and of the processes that communicated adherence to them. A legitimate claimant must have the means and the character to serve the welfare of the people and the realm. Descent could be invoked, but was insufficient to secure the throne, just as suitability could be used to justify a claim only if it could be demonstrated. In this regard, Matilda and Stephen both fell short. Each was unable to act like a king because each lacked the resources. A desire to do good

---

[165] William of Newburgh, *Historia*, vol. 1, 51–3.
[166] William of Newburgh, *Historia*, vol. 1, 69–70. This echoes the identical verses in Judges, 'In those days there was no king in Israel; everyone did what was right in his own eyes'(17:6 and 21:25). See also Gilbert Foliot: after the death of Alexander the Great, Gilbert explained, his children each assumed the crown, and began to reign in their own regions. History now repeated itself, as could be seen in the sufferings of the English nation: *Letters and Charters of Gilbert Foliot*, no. 26.
[167] *The Letters of Osbert of Clare, Prior of Westminster*, ed. E. W. Williamson (Oxford, 1929), no. 38. I am grateful to Brian Briggs for this reference.
[168] William of Newburgh, *Historia*, vol. 1, 101–2.

III. SUCCESSION 157

could not compensate for an inability to overcome one's rivals. Concord could not be reached until other claimants were forced to withdraw in favour of the strongest among them. The dispute was thus not about different norms, but about who was better suited to uphold them.

These commonalities extended to the issue of hereditary right and the moral responsibility of the ruler to establish his successor. As regards the former, Matilda clearly held the better cards, even though attempts were made to weaken her hand. John of Salisbury, for instance, alleges that Stephen's allies argued that she was illegitimate, as her mother had been a nun abducted by Henry I.[169] The accusation did not catch on in England,[170] but then, it would seem that, as far as the English barons and clergy were concerned, a succession that ensured the continuity of a functioning royal line mattered more than one that adhered to strict patterns of descent. In 1153 Stephen's eldest son Eustace died. Subsequently, the great men of the realm forced a settlement upon the king and Matilda's son Henry. Stephen must adopt the latter as his son and heir, while Stephen's surviving son must do homage to Henry. In return, Henry must accept Stephen as king and promise to protect the estates of his son.[171] In consequence of that recognition of the legitimacy of Stephen's kingship, the grants he made and the privileges he offered also remained valid. In this way, leading subjects sought to protect their own gains as much as the continuing prosperity of Stephen's progeny. They also maintained an unbroken sequence of legitimate kings. And they fulfilled a moral obligation of their own by ensuring a smooth succession on Stephen's death.

Their efforts set them apart from both Henry I and Stephen. The reputation of the former was transformed partly because Henry II, on coming to the throne, set aside much of what he had promised at Winchester. Instead, he established his grandfather's reign as the ideal *status quo ante* that it was his duty to restore.[172] However, with the partial exception of William of Malmesbury, those writing during the mid and late 1130s took a rather different view of the Conqueror's son. Henry emerged as a cruel and greedy tyrant,[173] who even blinded his own relatives.[174] Some writers insinuated that the late king's

---

[169] John of Salisbury, *Historia Pontificalis*, 83.
[170] See, though, Herman de Tournai, *Liber de Restauratione*, 282.
[171] *Gesta Stephani*, 240–1; William of Newburgh, *Historia*, vol. 1, 90–1.
[172] Cooper, 'Walter Map on Henry I'; Weiler, 'Kings and sons', 22–3.
[173] See, for instance, John of Worcester, *Chronicle*, vol. 3, 198–203; Judith Collard, 'Henry I's dream in John of Worcester's chronicle (Oxford Corpus Christi College, MS 157) and the illustration of twelfth-century English chronicles', *JMedH* 36 (2010), 105–25; Claude Carozzi, 'Die drei Stände gegen den König: Mythos, Traum, Bild', in *Träume im Mittelalter. Ikonologische Studien*, ed. Agostino Paravacini Bagliani and Giorgio Stabile (Stuttgart and Zürich, 1989), 149–60. Generally: Alan Cooper, '"The feet of those that bark shall be cut off": timorous historians and the personality of Henry I', *ANS* 23 (2001), 47–67.
[174] Henry of Huntingdon, *Historia Anglorum*, 699–700.

158   5. DUTIES, NORMS AND PROCESS

governance had helped bring about the turmoil after his death. Hermann of
Tournai suggested that the civil war was divine punishment for Henry's having
abducted Matilda's mother from a nunnery.[175] Henry of Huntingdon represented the late king's death as a gruesome affair, appropriate to that of a tyrant:

> the corpse was cut all over with knives, sprinkled with a great deal of salt,
> and wrapped in ox hides, to stop the strong pervasive stench, which was
> already causing the deaths of those who watched over it. It even killed the
> man who had been hired for a great fee to cut off the head with an axe and
> to extract the stinking brain, although he had wrapped himself in linen
> cloths around his head: so he was badly rewarded by his fee. He was the
> last of many whom King Henry had put to death. ... See, I say, the
> outcome of events, upon which final judgement always depends.[176]

Moreover, Henry had indeed passed away in a state of gluttony (from a surfeit
of lampreys), but also while filled with 'anger and ill-feeling, which were said by
some to have been the origin of the chill in his bowels and later the cause of his
death'.[177] There was no time for him to display the contrition of William the
Conqueror or to enact the pious passing of Conrad I. It is likely that Henry of
Huntingdon wrote the account around 1139, just as the conflict between
Matilda and Stephen began to break fully into the open. Even more than in
the Conqueror's case, the manner of the king's passing provided a commentary
on his reign, and foreshadowed the suffering that his sins would unleash upon
his people. Because he had acted as a tyrant, the settlement that he had hoped
to prepare fell apart as soon as, after his death, 'the frank views of the people
came out'.[178] In 1153, by contrast, the leading men of the realm ensured that
whatever agreement was reached reflected the expectations of the moral
process of succession, and secured peace and tranquillity for the kingdom at
large.

Stephen was no better than Henry. In 1152, Henry of Huntingdon reported,
he had sought to secure the succession of his son Eustace by having him
crowned during his lifetime. While not an unusual practice in a broader
European context (about which more in the next chapter), it was unprecedented in post-Conquest England. Worse still, Stephen proceeded in truly
tyrannical fashion. He called together the prelates of England, and demanded

---

[175] Herman de Tournai, *Liber de Restauratione*, 282.
[176] Henry of Huntingdon, *Historia Anglorum*, 702–3. See also: Dietrich Lohrmann, 'Der
Tod König Heinrichs I. von England in der mittellateinischen Literatur Englands und
der Normandie', *Mittellateinisches Jahrbuch* 8 (1972), 90–107. On the funeral practice:
Alexandre Bande, *Le cœur du roi. Les Capétiens et les sépultures multiples XIIIe–XVe siècles*
(Paris, 2009), 51–9; Romedio Schmitz-Esser, *Der Leichnam im Mittelalter.
Einbalsamierung, Verbrennung und die kulturelle Konstruktion des toten Körpers*
(Ostfildern, 2014), 213–20, 633–51.
[177] Henry of Huntingdon, *Historia Anglorum*, 490–1.
[178] Henry of Huntingdon, *Historia Anglorum*, 700–1.

III. SUCCESSION 159

that they crown Eustace king. When they refused, he incarcerated them, but ultimately had to relent in face of their steadfast resistance.[179] The bishops could point to a decree from Pope Celestine III no less, who a decade earlier had mandated that there could be no change to the English crown, as it was still under dispute.[180] Far from settling his son's succession so as to bring about peace and tranquillity, Stephen's actions threatened to renew the turmoil that had plagued England for almost two decades. The barons and clergy, on the other hand, lived up to the expectations that Henry I and Stephen had so obviously failed to meet.

In some respects, their proposed settlement contains many of the features encountered in east Francia in 918. Conrad I had faced a powerful opponent in Henry of Saxony, who was also the son of his erstwhile rival for the throne. Unlike Stephen, however, in facing defeat, Conrad had not sought to install his brother Eberhard. That would only have prolonged the suffering of his people. Instead, he had nominated Duke Henry, in the expectation that he was going to safeguard the possessions of Conrad's family and followers. This is not to say that the English prelates and aristocracy were familiar with events in Saxony two centuries before. Rather, they were forced to take upon themselves a task that consecutive kings had been incapable of shouldering.

That they did so during the king's lifetime was unusual, but so were the conditions under which they acted. They attempted to end a war that had been raging for nearly two decades. Yet the basic principle that the people had to give their consent remains in evidence across the high medieval west. They had to determine which interpretation prevailed, and how to weigh up competing claims of suitability and right. That was certainly the case when a throne was vacant, but it was also a requirement when a ruler sought to install or nominate an heir. Conrad I, William the Conqueror and Wladyslaw alike had couched their choice of successor in terms of a suggestion, to be pondered and ratified by the leading men of the realm. Even Henry I had twice asked for Matilda to be acknowledged as his heir, and, in however heavy-handed a fashion, Stephen had likewise sought the consent of the clergy for Eustace to be crowned. Indeed, the electoral element was integral to the moral process of succession. Kings could not represent a community of the realm if they lacked subjects to lead, and they could not rule without men willing to fight on their behalf or to assist them with advice and counsel. How, then, was the principle of consent applied in practice?

---

[179] Henry of Huntingdon, *Historia Anglorum*, 758–9. David Crouch, *The Reign of King Stephen, 1135–1154* (Harlow, 2000), 245–6.
[180] John of Salisbury, *Historia Pontificalis*, 85–6; Henry of Huntingdon, *Historia Anglorum*, 758 n. 163.

160   5. DUTIES, NORMS AND PROCESS

5.5 Kings and People

A distinction must be drawn between the role of the people in a ruler's lifetime and after his death. Regarding the former, the narrative sources suggest that the process could be initiated only by the king. Most western emperors, for instance, were described as simply presenting their son to an assembly of princes, and having him either confirmed as heir or elected king.[181] When Philipp I of France was crowned king during his father's lifetime in 1059, he was elected first by his father, then by the leading secular magnates and finally by the knights and people at large.[182] Accounts of a similar sequence survive from England, Sicily, Denmark, Castile, Hungary and Portugal.[183] The people convened at the king's command, and followed his lead. It seems as if their agency was accepted only in moments of crisis or when established customs were overturned. Henry I of England may have commanded his barons and clergy to accept Matilda as queen. Yet that he should have felt the need to solicit their agreement twice suggests that the unusual prospect of a female succession necessitated that the people's consent be both public and repeated. Only rarely was the full decision left to the people, and then only if the authority to choose had explicitly been delegated to them by the ruler. Poland in 1099 would be one such example.

This image of royal dominance may not have reflected reality, but it did reflect a complex set of expectations. There was, for instance, the premise that royal authority was divinely ordained. Old Testament precedent suggests that

---

[181] See, for instance, the designations of Otto III (983) (*Die deutsche Königserhebung im 10.–12. Jahrhundert*, ed. Walter Böhme, 2 vols. (Göttingen, 1970), vol. 1, nos. 80, 81), Henry III (1026) (ibid., vol. 1, nos. 152 (Wipo, who, unusually, claimed that Conrad II acted at the behest of the princes in making his son king), 153–162), Henry IV's son Conrad (1076) (ibid., vol. 1, nos. 202–4), Conrad III's son Henry (1147) (ibid., vol. 2, nos. 74–8), and Henry VI (1169) (ibid., vol. 2, nos. 114–22).

[182] *Ordines Coronationis Franciae. Texts and Ordines for the Coronation of Frankish and French Kings and Queens in the Middle Ages*, ed. Richard A. Jackson, 2 vols. (Philadelphia, PA, 1995–2000), vol. 1, 228–32. See also the coronation of Philipp (he who later had a fatal encounter with a possessed pig) in 1129: *Chronicon Sancti Petri Vivi Senonensis*, 124.

[183] William of Malmesbury, *Historia Novella*, 19–22; Roger of Howden, *Chronica Magistri Rogeri de Houdene*, ed. W. Stubbs, Rolls Series, 4 vols. (London, 1868–71), vol. 4, 90–1; Ugo Falcando, *Il regno di Sicilia*, 188–9. For an English translation: *The History of the Tyrants of Sicily by 'Hugo Falcandus'*, transl. Graham A. Loud and Thomas Wiedemann (Manchester, 1998), 137. Sven Aggesen, *Brevis Historia*, in *Scriptores Minores*, ed. Gertz, vol. 1, 121, 125, 127, 129. See, though, Saxo Grammaticus, *Gesta Danorum*, xiv.33.1–2, pp. 1244–7, where, in 1165, the nobles had proposed that Valdemar's son Knud be declared his heir, to which first the king agreed and then the whole assembled army (see also below, Chapter 6). *Historia Compostellana*, ed. Emma Falque Rey, CCCM 70 (Turnhout, 1988), 84–5; *Legenda S. Stephani*, in *Scriptores Rerum Hungaricarum*, ed. Szentpétery, vol. 2, 381; Monica Blöcker-Walter, *Alfons I. von Portugal* (Zürich, 1966), 151.

III. SUCCESSION   161

the choice of a king's successor rested with God. The people might be invited to consent to His decision, but they could not initiate the process of choosing a king. When the Israelites rejected the tyranny of Solomon's eldest son, they were nonetheless rebels who defied the will of God. Of course, the Bible provided a framework to be interpreted and adapted. Kings could still be deposed because they proved to be tyrants, or because they had never really been kings in the first place. It was the people's call to make, as long as they did God's bidding. But Old Testament precedent also points to a practical problem. Arranging one's succession demonstrated power in the sense that, by necessity, it was publicly enacted. Resistance constituted a grave challenge to the king's authority. It would be mounted only in the most exceptional of circumstances. This was perhaps what Stephen had banked on in 1152. Instead, his inability to have Eustace crowned laid bare the weakness of his grip on power, and may have encouraged the unusual step taken in 1153. Equally important proved to be the premise that the only valid election was a unanimous one. Dissent, especially when expressed in public, invalidated both process and candidate.[184] Being unable to secure sufficient backing would have denoted either a lack of authority on part of the king, or of legitimacy and suitability on his heir's. A flawed process provided a means by which to dispute royal status, and hence by which to unravel any decisions that a king might have sought to put in place. That rulers took the lead should therefore only be read as evidence of royal authority to the extent that they were able to muster the backing of many or even most of their subjects. The people played a walk-on part not because their consent did not matter, but because it ought to be given freely and without debate. Their agreement could be deemed valid only if there was nothing to report beyond the decision itself.

In practice, accepting an heir was always conditional, even if, by its very nature, the narrative record tends to obscure that particular aspect. There were few exceptions. In 1053, Hermann of Reichenau reported, Emperor Henry III asked the German princes to accept his infant son, the future Henry IV, as king after his death. They consented, but did so on condition that Henry IV first prove himself to be a just and equitable ruler.[185] Hermann died in 1054, and his

---

[184] See, generally, Timothy Reuter, 'Assembly politics in western Europe from the eighth century to the twelfth', in his *Medieval Polities and Modern Mentalities*, ed. Janet L. Nelson (Cambridge, 2006), 193–216. Though note also the criticism of Reuter's model by Leidulf Melve, 'Assembly politics and the "rules of the game" (ca. 650–1150)', *Viator* 41 (2010), 69–90; Melve, 'Performance, argument, and assembly politics (ca. 1080 – ca. 1160)', *Super alta perennis* 10 (2010), 85–108. See also below, Chapters 7, 8 and 10.

[185] *Herimanni Augiensis Chronicon*, ed. Georg Heinrich Pertz, MGH SS 5 (Hanover, 1844), 133. On the text most recently, Walter Berschin and Martin Hellmann, eds., *Hermann der Lahme: Gelehrter und Dichter, 1013–1054* (Heidelberg, 2015). On the episode: Robinson, *Henry IV of Germany*, 21–2. On how Henry might have proved himself to be a good king without being king, see below, Chapter 6.

162   5. DUTIES, NORMS AND PROCESS

account is thus not blighted by foreknowledge of Henry's turbulent reign. It offers a rare glimpse of expectations that otherwise remained unspoken or at least unrecorded. Designation and acclamation did not secure Henry IV's rule. They constituted a down payment, so to speak, of future loyalty, provided the boy grow up to be a just and righteous lord.

The record's relative silence on conditions for support reflects what we know to have happened during 'proper' elections – those, that is, taking place after a ruler's death. If consent was to be freely given, it could not be bartered for or bargained with. Any suggestion of corruption would invalidate the process at large.[186] This makes a rare example of negotiating that survives from late twelfth-century Germany all the more valuable. In 1195/6, Emperor Henry VI tried to have his infant son Frederick elected king.[187] According to the *Annales Marbacenses*, the most detailed source for the proceedings, Henry also proposed that succession should henceforth be by hereditary right, 'as in France'.[188] Other chroniclers added that several princes had demanded a change in inheritance laws, so that imperial fiefs could be passed on to female heirs. In response, Henry proposed that the same apply to the imperial dignity.[189] The whole episode poses problems. There is, for instance, no documentary evidence to confirm that patterns of inheritance were in fact changed, while most surviving narratives were written at least a generation after the event.

Flying in the face of the evident injunction against doing so, emperor and princes nonetheless bartered. The princes' demands were understandable, given that, over the previous generation, their ranks had repeatedly been thinned by catastrophe. In 1167, disease had ravaged the imperial army in Italy. Several thousands were supposed to have died, including the archbishop of Cologne, his and the king of Bohemia' brothers, the dukes of Swabia and

---

[186] See below, Chapter 7.

[187] The election has triggered a rich literature, far in excess of the existing evidence. See, by way of introduction: Schmidt, *Königswahl*, 225–60; Ernst Perels, *Der Erbreichsplan Heinrichs VI.* (Berlin, 1927); Peter Csendes, *Heinrich VI.* (Darmstadt, 1993), 171–8; Wolfgang Stürner, *Friedrich II.*, 2 vols. (Darmstadt, 1992–2000), vol. 1, 41–8; Ludwig Vones, 'Confirmatio Imperii et Regni. Erbkaisertum, Erbreichsplan und Erbmonarchie in den politischen Zielvorstellungen Kaiser Heinrichs VI.', in *Stauferreich im Wandel. Ordnungsvorstellungen und Politik in der Zeit Friedrich Barbarossas*, ed. Stefan Weinfurter (Stuttgart, 2002), 312–34; Ulrich Schmidt, '"Ein neues und unerhörtes Dekret": der Erbreichsplan Heinrichs VI.', in *Kaiser Heinrich VI. Ein mittelalterlicher Herrscher und seine Zeit* (Göppingen, 1998), 61–81. I am grateful to Thomas Foerster for his advice on this episode.

[188] *Annales Marbacenses*, 67–8.

[189] *Chronica Reinhardsbrunnensis*, MGH SS 30, 556–8; *Gesta Episcoporum Leodiensium abbreviata*, MGH SS 25(Hanover, 1880), 132. Other accounts mention the opposition of the archbishop of Cologne, but not Henry's plan to turn the empire into a hereditary monarchy: *Die deutsche Königserhebung*, ed. Böhme, vol. 2, nos. 123–31.

III. SUCCESSION   163

Zähringen, Duke Welf VII and the counts of Nassau, Sulzbach and Tübingen, to name but some of the most high-ranking casualties.[190] The death toll resulted in a fundamental reordering of the imperial aristocracy. In 1184, several dozen leading nobles drowned in an Erfurt latrine. In 1190, Frederick Barbarossa's crusade ended with the death of the emperor, his son and of numerous other participants.[191] Just as kings were expected to provide for their progeny and for their *memoria*, so magnates were of course supposed to provide for their own. Moreover, Henry was about to embark on a crusade, which provided further impetus to settle his succession. In fact, some chroniclers explicitly link his efforts to the proposed campaign.[192] There was thus good reason to tackle the problem of inheritance and succession on both a regnal and an aristocratic level. That the German princes deemed the king's request to have his son accepted as heir to be the appropriate moment at which to state their demands would suggest that they followed well-established precedent, however rarely recorded it is.

At the same time, that they cast aside their earlier agreement within a year highlights how preliminary such deals could prove to be. Indeed, the role of the people became a rather different one after a king's death. This was so in part because in most instances even an heir who had already been designated still needed to be elected in order to become king. This was after all why, as Henry of Huntingdon lamented, in 1135 all those who had initially accepted Matilda as Henry's heir now backed Stephen. It was also why the German princes, once news of Henry VI's death reached them, had the opportunity to elect a king in young Frederick's stead. Their earlier agreement was valid only until a new ruler had been chosen. Until that point, they could revise and revisit past decisions. This step provided a safeguard against forced concessions – an argument central to Stephen's claim in 1135/6, and Philipp of Swabia's in 1198. A putative heir sometimes also proved unsuitable for the throne. After the death of King Erik the Good in 1103, the Danes decided not to offer the crown to his son, because he had turned out to have all the makings of a tyrant while acting as regent during Erik's crusade.[193] It was also after a ruler's death that matters of suitability and right had to be pondered, especially when there were several putative heirs, as in Jerusalem in 1118. The electoral dimension of the succession process was necessary precisely because successions were often disputed. It became a tool for safeguarding and protecting the peace and tranquillity of the realm.

---

[190] Freed, *Frederick Barbarossa*, 343–5.

[191] *Historia de expeditione Friderici imperatoris*, in *Quellen zur Geschichte des Kreuzzuges Kaiser Friedrichs I.*, ed. A. Chroust, MGH SS sep. ed. (Hanover and Berlin, 1928), 92–3; *Epistola de morte Friderici imperatoris*, ibid., 176.

[192] *Chronica Reinhardsbrunnensis*, 558; *Ottonis de Sancto Blasio Chronica*, ed. Adolf Hofmeister, MGH SS sep. ed. (Hanover and Leipzig, 1912), 71.

[193] Saxo Grammaticus, *Gesta Danorum*, xii.8.2, pp. 894–5.

164   5. DUTIES, NORMS AND PROCESS

Notably, the convention of electing a king prevailed even when no crisis loomed. Knud VI of Denmark had been confirmed as his father's successor during the latter's lifetime in 1165 and was crowned king in 1170. Nevertheless, on his father's death in 1182, he had to present himself to successive regional assemblies for them to elect him king.[194] In England, Henry II was similarly acclaimed before he could be crowned in 1154.[195] Kings could become kings only with the consent of their people. Just as the Israelites had been asked repeatedly whether they wanted to have a king, so the leading subjects of the realm had to confirm that they were willing to submit to the authority of their chosen ruler. They also ensured the continuity of the realm and satisfied moral obligations of their own. Princes and prelates had to ensure that the best candidate was chosen, one who would not invite foreign invasions, who would not oppress his people and who had both the material means and the moral disposition to lead his kingdom. By participating in the making of a ruler, elites shared in the moral responsibility underpinning his office.

Moreover, in practical terms, there was little point in choosing a ruler who would become lazy and indulgent, who would favour one faction over others or who would bring about civil unrest. In this sense, the practice of election highlights the fragility of the overall succession process. Because a ruler had to be chosen on his predecessor's death, powerful subjects and relatives might feel called upon to utilise that moment to advance their own ambitions, to propose that experience and suitability trumped direct descent. Equally, elections provided a means by which the exercise of royal power could be directed. Claimants had to demonstrate that they would be good kings: that they sought to serve, not merely to lead. It likewise forced rulers to ensure that their heirs would satisfy the demands and expectations of their people. Subjects might be compelled to accept an heir, but acceptance given under such circumstances was never binding. For a succession to unfold as planned, it was not enough just to designate heirs, or even to have them publicly accepted. They had to be readied for the moment when claims would have to be validated by the kingdom's elites.

[194] Saxo Grammaticus, *Gesta Danorum*, xvi.1.1, pp. 1494–5.
[195] William of Newburgh, *Historia*, vol. 1, 101.

6

Designating an Heir

Succession was a process, not an event. It normally unfolded in several stages. Each led up to, but also depended upon the others. All were provisional: heirs could die or earlier agreements might be rescinded after a ruler's death. For these reasons, successors might be nominated at birth, during early childhood or once they reached maturity.[1] Sometimes they were confirmed more than once. St Stephen of Hungary was declared a putative heir when he was born, and then again when he reached adulthood.[2] Emperor Henry IV was designated at birth, at age three or four and again on his father's death.[3] And Knud VI of Denmark was confirmed as heir when he was two years old, was crowned when he turned seven and was elected again when he finally followed Valdemar I on the Danish throne.[4] Just how a designation unfolded could also vary. Sometimes an heir apparent was crowned, sometimes elected and sometimes knighted. Several of these steps could be combined, or could be performed over the years as an heir grew up. Each signalled that he had either completed or was about to commence yet another stage towards proving his suitability and towards ascertaining the right to rule.

---

[1] Henry I of east Francia, for instance, designated his son Otto only in 936, when Otto was twenty-three (Widukind of Corvey, *Die Sachsengeschichte*, i.41, p. 60). On which see also Johannes Laudage, 'Hausrecht und Thronfolge. Überlegungen zur Königserhebung Ottos des Großen und zu den Aufständen Thankmars, Heinrichs und Liudolfs', *Historisches Jahrbuch* 112 (1992), 23–71. Likewise, in 1065 Fernando I of León divided his inheritance when his sons were in their mid to late twenties (*Historia Silense*, ed. Justo Perez de Urbel and Atilano Gonzalez Ruiz-Zorilla (Madrid, 1959), 205). On the other hand, Wladyslaw of Poland settled his succession when his sons were about to come of age, as did William the Conqueror with Robert Curthose in 1066 (Orderic Vitalis, *Ecclesiastical History*, vol. 2, 356–7, vol. 3, 98–9, vol. 4, 92–3).

[2] *Legenda S. Stephani*, in *Scriptores Rerum Hungaricarum*, ed. Szentpétery, vol. 2, 381.

[3] Hermann of Reichenau, *Chronicon*, 129, 132–3; *Annales Augustani*, MGH SS (Hanover, 1839), 126; Lampert of Hersfeld, *Annales*, ed. Oswald Holder-Egger, transl. Adolf Schmidt (Darmstadt, 1973), 63, 66; *Annales S. Disibodi*, MGH SS 17 (Hanover, 1861), 19.

[4] Saxo Grammaticus, *Gesta Danorum*, xiv.33.1–2, pp. 1244–7, xiv.40.12, pp. 1322–3.

166   6. DESIGNATING AN HEIR

6.1 The Promise of Good Governance

Sometimes, an heir was crowned during his father's lifetime. The practice was common in France and Germany[5] and was successfully adopted in Denmark in 1170.[6] Still, while copied in Sicily in 1151,[7] England in 1152 and 1170[8] and Jerusalem in 1183,[9] it never became universal. When coronations did occur, they often happened at an early age. Most German kings had their sons enthroned between the ages of one and nine.[10] A similar pattern is evident in France.[11] Occasionally, crownings followed on from a previous designation. In England, Henry II's eponymous son had been acclaimed as heir at the age of six in 1161, and Valdemar I's in 1165 when he was two, before both were crowned in 1170.[12] While there were no firm rules as to when a coronation

[5] *Annales Aquenses*, MGH SS 24 (Hanover, 1879), 685-6; *Chronica Regia Coloniensis (Annales Maximi Colonienses)*, ed. Georg Waitz, MGH sep. ed. (Hanover, 1880), 120; *Ruotgers Lebensbeschreibung des Erzbischofs Bruno von Köln: Ruotgeri Vita Brunonis archiepiscopi Coloniensis*, ed. Ingrid Ott, MGH SS sep. ed. NS (Hanover, 1951), 43; *Annales Colbazienses*, MGH SS 19 (Hanover, 1866), 714; *Annales Magdeburgenses*, MGH SS 16 (Hanover, 1859), 180. Lewis, *Royal Succession*, 46; Andrew W. Lewis, 'Anticipatory association of the heir in early Capetian France', *American Historical Review* 83 (1978), 906-27; Ivo of Chartres, *Correspondence I*, ed. Jean Leclerq (Paris, 1949), nos. 65-6; Orderic Vitalis, *Historia Ecclesiastica*, vol. 6, 390.

[6] Saxo Grammaticus, *Gesta Danorum*, xiv.40.12, pp. 1322-3; *Annales Lundenses*, in *Danmarks Middelalderlige Annaler*, ed. Erik Korman (Copenhagen, 1980), 85.

[7] John of Salisbury, *Historia Pontificalis. Memoirs of the Papal Court*, ed. and transl. Marjorie Chibnall (London, 1956), 69; Hugo Falcandus, *Il regno di Sicilia*, 26-9; Hugo Falcandus, *History of the Tyrants*, 59; Romuald of Salerno, *Chronica*, ed. Giousue Carducci and Vittorio Fiorini (Città di Castello, 1909-35), 231.

[8] Anne Duggan, 'The coronation of Henry the Young King in 1170', *Studies in Church History* 2 (1968), 165-78; Matthew Strickland, *Henry the Young King, 1155-1183* (New Haven, CT, 2016), 40-4, 78-94.

[9] Strickland, *Henry the Young King*, 41; Bernard Hamilton, *The Leper King and His Heirs. Baldwin IV and the Crusader Kingdom of Jerusalem* (Cambridge, 2000), 207-9; William of Tyre, *Chronicon*, 1058-9.

[10] Otto II in 961 (aged six, *Die deutsche Königserhebung*, ed. Böhme, vol. 1, nos. 62-79); Otto III in 983 (aged three, ibid., vol. 1, nos. 80-90); Henry III in 1026 (aged nine, though repeated two years later, ibid., vol. 1, nos. 152-81); Henry IV (three times: at birth, aged four, and on his father's death, when aged six: ibid., vol. 1, nos. 182-201); Conrad (III) in 1075 and 1087 (aged one and twelve, ibid., vol. 1, nos. 202-10); Henry (VI) in 1147 (aged nine, ibid., vol. 2, nos. 74-6); Henry VI in 1165 (aged four, ibid., vol. 2, nos. 114-122); Frederick II in 1196 (aged two, ibid., vol. 2, nos. 123-31). See, however, Liudolf (aged sixteen, ibid., vol. 1, nos. 54-61), and Henry V in 1098/9 (aged seventeen/eighteen, ibid., vol. 1, nos. 266-80), though in the latter case, the coronation followed Henry's elder brother rebelling against their father, and being deposed as a result. Said brother had been one when first nominated, and twelve the second time round.

[11] Rodulfus Glaber, *Historiarum Libri quinqui*, 50-1; Richer, *Histories*, vol. 2, 164-6; Lewis, 'Anticipatory association', at 907-11; Strickland, *Henry the Young King*, 40-4.

[12] Strickland, *Henry the Young King*, 41-2; Saxo Grammaticus, *Gesta Danorum*, xiv.33.1, pp. 1244-5. In Germany, likewise, heirs were sometimes re-crowned when they came of age

III. SUCCESSION   167

should occur, there were nonetheless practical reasons why an heir should be chosen at so young an age. When, in 1165, the Danish magnates approached Valdemar I about making his son Knud VI co-ruler, Saxo Grammaticus recorded them as arguing that 'in this way the lords would have a personage whose rank and title they could have recourse to if Fortune should bring about a change in the matter of the king's life'.[13] Having an heir apparent provided a promise of continuity and stability, a source of authority and leadership should misfortune befall the king. The need for a backup, so to speak, might have been felt with particular urgency in Denmark, where Valdemar had emerged victorious – indeed as the sole surviving claimant – from a prolonged struggle for the throne only in 1157.[14]

It is partly for this reason that the Danish case stands out for both the detail and the range of the surviving evidence.[15] As with most heirs, Knud VI's succession unfolded in phases. There was the initial nomination, followed by a coronation, the coming of age and the acclamation on his father's death. Of these, the first two will be of particular interest, and it is in relation to them that a comparatively rich record remains. Saxo Grammaticus, writing in the early thirteenth century, fashioned the latter parts of his *Gesta Danorum* as an account of the rulership of Knud's father, Valdemar I, and of the king's close relationship with Saxo's patron, Archbishop Absalon of Lund. In addition, a number of shorter annals from the thirteenth century reveal how the event was understood by later observers, while several hagiographical texts provide useful context for the coronation in 1170. Knud's case therefore brings together the perspectives of those close to the king, of the contemporary local clergy and of subsequent generations. This range of viewpoints is unusual,[16] but they allow broader questions to be asked. Why was crowning a successor attempted in the first place? Why did it take root in some realms but not others? And what was the relationship between these early stages of nominating an heir and his subsequent preparation and training?

(Henry III and Conrad (III)), or when they succeeded to the throne as sole ruler (Henry IV).

[13] Saxo Grammaticus, *Gesta Danorum*, xiv.33.1, pp. 1244–5.
[14] For the political context: Lars Kjaer, 'Political conflict and political ideas in twelfth-century Denmark', *Viking and Medieval Scandinavia* 13 (2017), 61–100.
[15] I am grateful to Lars Kjaer and Erik Niblaeus for their comments on an earlier draft of this section.
[16] The *Chronicon Sancti Petri Vivi Senonensis* was rather more representative of the genre when it simply stated that in 1128, his father having called together the magnates of the realm, Philipp was anointed king by the archbishop of Reims. *Chronique de Saint-Pierre-le-Vif de Sens, dite Clarius: Chronicon Sancti Petri Vivi Senonensis*, ed. and transl. Robert-Henru Bautier, Monique Gilles and Anne-Amrie Bautier (Paris, 1979) 124. See also Johanna Dale, *Inauguration and Liturgical Kingship in the Long Twelfth Century. Male and Female Accession Rituals in England, France and the Empire* (Woodbridge, 2019), 105–29.

168   6. DESIGNATING AN HEIR

As for 1165, Saxo's account is both terse and disingenuous. The nobles, concerned

> over the unpleasant, dangerous disturbances and other difficult circumstances which the state of Denmark was suffering, ... resolved to decree royal honours to Knud, Valdemar's son, in order that they might recognize him as his father's present colleague in authority as well as the future holder of his crown.[17]

Saxo rather downplayed the novelty of what was proposed. While Danish kings had hitherto assigned quasi-regal authority and power to their favourite heirs, they had not normally installed them as co-rulers. For instance, Erik the Good, the son of Sven Estrithson, had appointed his older, but illegitimate, son Harald as co-regent when he went on crusade.[18] Yet on Erik's death another king had been chosen in Harald's stead. In fact, Saxo himself explained,

> the custom had been for Sven [Estrithson]'s sons each to take his turn over the succession to the crown according to precedence in age, the older always having the next in line as his heir to the throne.[19]

In 1134, the convention of choosing Sven's progeny had to come to an end with the murder of Niels, the last of his sons, but the tradition of electoral kingship was maintained. Valdemar himself had been acclaimed and elevated by the Danish nobles. In 1165, however, a radical departure was proposed: 'the monarch', Saxo recorded one objection, 'was keen to make hereditary a throne which had hitherto been subject to the vicissitudes of election'.[20] Succession through the will of the people was to be replaced by succession through inheritance. Just as in any European monarchy, an electoral element was, of course, maintained: the nobles *requested* that Knud become king. Still, henceforth the Danes would no longer have the right to dismiss a useless and inept claimant in favour one more virtuous and suitable.[21] Knud's elevation constituted a far greater expansion of royal power than Saxo's sparse account suggests.

The event fits within a broader European pattern. For example, it foreshadowed Henry VI's efforts in Germany a generation later. Unlike there, however, Valdemar's efforts took root. They did so partly because Valdemar lived long enough for Knud to come of age and claim the crown. But Saxo also depicted the *process* of elevation as having been conducted in a manner that left no room for criticism. Valdemar's son was raised to the throne legitimately because he was chosen freely by the people, because circumstances demanded

---

[17] Saxo Grammaticus, *Gesta Danorum*, xiv.33.1, pp. 1244–5.
[18] Saxo Grammaticus, *Gesta Danorum*, xii.3.6, pp. 876–7; xii.6.5, pp. 884–5.
[19] Saxo Grammaticus, *Gesta Danorum*, xii.8.2, pp. 894–5.
[20] Saxo Grammaticus, *Gesta Danorum*, xiv.33.4, pp. 1246–9.
[21] Saxo Grammaticus, *Gesta Danorum*, i.22, 3.1, pp. 22–3.

III. SUCCESSION   169

that he was and because he had been bequeathed an illustrious pedigree. Ever since the death of Erik the Good in 1103, Saxo suggested, both the Danes and their leaders had shown that ancient customs could no longer be upheld. Far from choosing the most suitable leader, they had elevated corrupt, inept and bloodthirsty ones. Erik the Memorable, for instance, had his older brother Harald murdered, and drowned his nephew Björn as well as ten of Björn's relatives, both adults and children, before himself being stabbed to death at an assembly.[22] The *Chronicon Roskildense* lamented the immense bloodshed at the Battle of Fodevig (which ended in the death of Niels' son Magnus),[23] and Saxo remarked that 'no other war was more prolific in squandering bishops' blood'.[24] At the same time, Saxo painted a clear contrast with the direct line of Erik the Good's legitimate descendants. While other royals lapsed into inept or murderous tyranny, Erik's son Knud Lavard and Knud's son Valdemar upheld traditions of good rule, moral rectitude and rebuttal of enemies of faith and realm. In some respects, Knud VI's succession therefore held out the promise of a return to the good old days of Erik. The promise took centre stage five years later, when Knud was crowned and anointed king.

The act of 1170 constituted an even greater innovation. Previously, the royal title had been conferred either in an assembly of the Danish nobles, or by foreign rulers, most commonly the Holy Roman emperor.[25] Valdemar himself had visited the court of Frederick Barbarossa to have his claim confirmed.[26] Danish kings had not, however, been anointed, and nor is there evidence for a formal coronation ceremony. This changed after 1170. While Knud was never able to have an heir crowned, partly because he had no children, his brother Valdemar II (r. 1202–1241) had two of his sons installed as co-rulers, an example emulated by his successors in turn.[27] Equally lasting was the innovation of anointing and crowning. Indeed, it was so successful that a thirteenth-century continuation of the *Chronicon Roskildense* could only make sense of the proceedings in 1170 by claiming that Valdemar had been consecrated king, robed in purple and crowned by the archbishop of Lund in

---

[22] Sven Aggesen, *Brevis Historia*, in *Scriptores Minores*, ed. Gertz, vol. 1, 134–7; Sven Aggesen, *Short History*, in *The Works of Sven Aggesen, Twelfth-Century Historian*, transl. Eric Christiansen (London, 1992), 70–1; *Chronicon Roskildense*, in *Scriptores Minores*, ed. Gertz, vol. 1, 30–1; Saxo Grammaticus, *Gesta Danorum*, xiv.1.2, 4, 13, ii. pp. 972–5, 982–3.

[23] *Chronicon Roskildense*, in *Scriptores Minores*, ed. Gertz, vol. 1, 28–9.

[24] Saxo Grammaticus, *Gesta Danorum*, xiii.11.11, ii. pp. 968–9.

[25] Erich Hoffmann, *Königserhebung und Thronfolgeordnung in Dänemark bis zum Ausgang des Mittelalters* (Berlin and New York, 1976), 56–80.

[26] Saxo Grammaticus, *Gesta Danorum*, xiv.8.1–4, pp. 1032–7; Odilo Engels, 'Friedrich Barbarossa und Dänemark', in *Friedrich Barbarossa: Handlungsspielräume und Wirkungsweisen des staufischen Kaisers*, ed. Albrecht Haverkamp (Sigmaringen, 1992), 353–85.

[27] Hoffmann, *Königserhebung und Thronfolgeordnung*, 116–19, 128–9.

170   6. DESIGNATING AN HEIR

1157.[28] The son could not receive unction unless the father had also done so. In hindsight, Knud's coronation turns out to have been a pivotal moment in the development of Danish kingship. Why was this so?

Once more, Saxo provides the most detailed account. Valdemar, he reports, had sent envoys to Rome to secure the canonisation of his father, Knud Lavard, who had been killed in 1131. On hearing that the request had been granted, the king determined to combine celebrations of his father's sanctification with his son's enthronement:

> Valdemar issued a proclamation summoning all the Danish nobility to Ringsted, where he would institute divine honours for his parent and royal honours for his son ... he believed that he himself would enjoy a notably large increase in fame, if on a single day he presented one of them with an altar, the other with a crown, the kingdom to the boy in his childhood while the common religion sanctified the other's spirit. The monarch reckoned that nothing else in the world would afford him greater pleasure than to see his son endowed with the emblems of his own sovereignty while he himself was still alive.[29]

The ceremony itself was recorded only in passing: 'the bones of Valdemar's father were being consigned to the altar and the king's son, Knud, after being consecrated, was being handsomely enthroned in the royal purple at the age of seven'.[30]

The coronation of 1170 was a demonstration of might. In Saxo's words, Valdemar expected that it would bring him pleasure, and 'a notably large increase in fame'. He was at the height of his power. In 1168/9, the island of Rügen had been conquered after a campaign that had lasted over ten years,[31] Valdemar's eponymous second son was born in 1170 and the king embarked on a codification of Danish law.[32] The festivities celebrated that power and communicated it to rivals both foreign and domestic. For example, Valdemar demonstrated parity with, perhaps even superiority to, the king of Norway, who had been the first Scandinavian ruler to undergo a full coronation ceremony (though as yet without anointing).[33] In Saxo's rendering, keeping

---

[28] *Chronicon Roskildense*, in *Scriptores Minores*, ed. Gertz, vol. 1, 33. I am grateful to Lars Kjaer for this reference.

[29] Saxo Grammaticus, *Gesta Danorum*, xiv.40.1, pp. 1312–13.

[30] Saxo Grammaticus, *Gesta Danorum*, xiv.40.12, pp. 1322–3.

[31] Saxo Grammaticus, *Gesta Danorum*, xiv.25.1–3, pp. 115–49. Kurt Villads Jensen, *Crusading at the Edges of Europe. Denmark and Portugal c.1000 – c. 1250* (Abingdon, 2017), 153–63, which does not, however, mention either translation or coronation. The same is true of Ane L. Bysted, Carsten Selch Jensen, Kurt Villads Jensen and John H. Lind, *Jerusalem in the North. Denmark and the Baltic Crusades, 1100–1522* (Turnhout, 2004), 67–76.

[32] *Annales Ripenses*, in *Danmarks Middelderliger Annaler*, 258.

[33] See below, Chapter 9.

III. SUCCESSION   171

up with the Norwegians proved a major benefit of young Knud's elevation.[34] Another putative addressee was Frederick Barbarossa, who had initially sided with Valdemar's rivals,[35] then forced Valdemar into accepting him as overlord, and who later lent his support to Knud's opponents.[36] By having Knud crowned in Denmark, Valdemar departed from established custom and sidelined the emperor. Moreover, when Valdemar approached the pope, he contacted Alexander III, whose election in 1159 had been bitterly opposed by Frederick.[37] In fact, the emperor had sent envoys to solicit (and had initially received) Valdemar's backing for an imperial anti-pope.[38] In 1170, Valdemar thus acted in defiance of his powerful southern neighbour, but in obedience to the Roman Church.

Of even greater significance was the translation of the relics of St Knud Lavard. To combine the settlement of a royal succession with the commemoration or celebration of a saint or particular religious feast day was not unusual.[39] Henry II of England had his eldest son crowned during a parliament after Easter,[40] Roger II had his sons knighted at Christmas,[41] Frederick Barbarossa his at Pentecost[42] and Wladyslaw his on the feast of the Assumption of Mary.[43] The date heightened the solemnity of the occasion and

---

[34] Saxo Grammaticus, *Gesta Danorum*, xiv.41.1–3, pp. 1322–5. The *Annals of Lund* have little to add to the image: under the year 1171 (!), they record the martyrdom of Thomas Becket, and Knud's translation. The day, according to the *Annals*, filled the Danes with great joy, partly because the king's father was recognised (*autorizatur*), and partly because his son Knud was anointed king. The ceremony took place in the presence of several prelates from Sweden and Denmark, as well as a Norwegian representative, who, on that day, proclaimed that a peace had been agreed between the kings of Norway and Denmark: *Annales Lundenses*, 58–9.

[35] Saxo Grammaticus, *Gesta Danorum*, xiv.8.1–4, pp. 1032–7.

[36] Saxo Grammaticus, *Gesta Danorum*, xvi.3.5, pp. 1504–7.

[37] Freed, *Frederick Barbarossa*, 303–48; Knut Görich, *Friedrich Barbarossa. Eine Biographie* (Munich, 2010), 389–441.

[38] Saxo Grammaticus, *Gesta Danorum*, xiv.28.1–22, pp. 1192–1213 (28.1.5 for lands in Italy). Generally: Engels, 'Friedrich Barbarossa und Dänemark'; Freed, *Frederick Barbarossa*, 274–5, 439–42; Görich, *Friedrich Barbarossa*, 163–4. Thomas Riis, 'The significance of 25 June 1170', in *Of Chronicles and Kings: National Saints and the Emergence of Nation States in the High Middle Ages*, ed. John D. Bergsagel, David Hiley and Thomas Riis (Copenhagen, 2015), 91–102, views the imperial dimension as dominating events in 1170.

[39] The topic merits a study of its own. In the meantime, see: Jürgen Petersohn, ed., *Politik und Heiligenverehrung im Hochmittelalter* (Sigmaringen, 1994); Antonsson, *St. Mágnus of Orkney*; Klaniczay, *Holy Rulers*.

[40] Roger of Howden, *Gesta Henrici II: the Chronicle of the Reigns of Henry II and Richard I AD 1169-1192, Known Commonly under the Name of Benedict of Peterborough*, ed. William Stubbs, 2 vols., Roll Series (London, 1867), vol. 1, 4–6.

[41] Alexander of Telese, *Ystoria Rogerii*, 84.

[42] Gislebert of Mons, *Chronicle of Hainaut*, 156.

[43] *Gesta Principum Polonorum*, ii.18, pp. 152–3.

172   6. DESIGNATING AN HEIR

underscored the connection between royal status and its divine origins.[44] Moreover, the religious ceremony served to highlight a king's accomplishments and to focus attention on particular functions of the royal office. In 1063 Fernando I of León used the festive translation of the relics of St Isidore of Seville to announce how he envisaged his domains to be divided after his death.[45] This took place at León, which, fittingly, had not only been the site of his coronation,[46] but was also in the process of being rebuilt as a royal necropolis for Fernando and his dynasty. The combination of translation and designation came about because, during a recent campaign against his Muslim neighbours in the south, Fernando had retrieved the remains of St Justa, whom he intended to have transferred to León Cathedral. However, while his emissaries were visiting her shrine to collect the remains, none other than St Isidore of Seville appeared to one of them in a vision, demanding that his body also be reinterred at León. They gladly obliged.[47] By the mid-eleventh century, Isidore had become something akin to a patron saint of Christian Iberia. The translation of his relics therefore testified to Fernando's religious zeal – attested to by the saint, no less – and numerous conquests. It granted the king a status as guardian and protector of the faith far exceeding that of his neighbours, rivals and peers.[48] Yet it was also an exhortation to and a promise on behalf of his heirs. They would remain devout sons of the Church, its fierce and valiant defenders.

Comparable events are recorded across the high medieval west. It seems, for instance, that in 1161 Henry II of England had simultaneously pursued the canonisation of Edward the Confessor, by then established as a paragon of royal justice and peacekeeping, and the coronation of his

[44] Dale, *Inauguration and Liturgical Kingship*, 141–57.
[45] *Historia Silense*, 205.
[46] *Historia Silense*, 182.
[47] *Historia Silense*, 197–201.
[48] This role continued well into the thirteenth century. See, for instance, *Historia translationis Sancti Isidori*, in *Chronica Hispana saeculi xiii*, ed. Luis Charlo Brea, Juan A. Estévez Sola and Rocío Carande Herrero, CCM (Turnhout, 1997), 119–79, at 148–60. For modern studies: Patrick Henriet, 'Mahomet expulsé d'Espagne par Isidore de Séville. Sur la postérité moderne d'un épisode hagiographique rejeté par les bollandistes', in *Vitae Mahometi. Reescritura e invención en la literatura cristiana de controversia*, ed. Cándida Ferrero Hérnandez and Oscar de la Cruz Palma (Madrid, 2014), 255–76; Francisco Prado-Vilar, 'Lacrimae rerum: San Isidoro de León y la memoria del padre', *Goya: Revista de Arte* 329 (2009), 195–221; C. J. Bishko, 'The liturgical context of Fernando I's last days according to the so-called *Historia Silense*', in his *Spanish and Portuguese Monastic History 600–1300* (Aldershot, 1984), VII: 47–58; Emma Falque Rey, 'De Sevilla a León: el último viaje de San Isidor', *Anuario de Historia de la Iglesia Andaluza* 9 (2016), 11–31; J. J. Williams, 'León: the iconography of the capital', in *Cultures of Power: Lordship, Status, and Process in Twelfth-Century Europe*, ed. T. N. Bisson (Philadelphia, PA, 1995), 231–58. I am grateful to Simon Doubleday, Francisco Prado-Vilar and Jamie Woods for their advice.

III. SUCCESSION   173

eldest son.[49] At Aachen in July 1215, Frederick II decided to repeat his coronation as king of the Romans. The ceremony once complete, he took the cross. The day after his crowning, he participated in a festive translation of the relics of St Charlemagne. His involvement was framed as one of penitential humility. He did not transfer the relics with his own hands, as Frederick Barbarossa had done in 1165, but aided the craftsmen in hammering shut the saint's sarcophagus.[50] Frederick placed himself not only in the tradition of his father and grandfather – both of whom had died on crusade – but also of the first western emperor, who by the thirteenth century had been transformed into an inveterate battler of Muslims and pagans, a crusader *avant la lettre*.[51] Frederick's participation marked a promise to be a forceful defender of the realm and of Christendom at large. All these occasions had in common the fact that, precisely because they highlighted the divine underpinnings of royal power, they also served to propagate a particular understanding of the king's office. Might could be celebrated only because it had been wielded in exemplary fashion and for the common good.[52] Embracing

[49] Duggan, 'Coronation'; Strickland, *Henry the Young King*, 39–40. On the cult of Edward the Confessor in the mid-twelfth century: John P. Becquette, 'Aelred of Rievaulx's *Life of Saint Edward, king and confessor*: a saintly king and the salvation of the English people', *Cistercian Studies Quarterly* 43 (2008), 17–40; John E. Lawyer, 'Aelred of Rievaulx's "Life of St. Edward the Confessor": a medieval ideal of kingship', *Fides & Historia* 31 (1999), 45–65.

[50] *Reineri Annales*, MGH SS 16 (Hanover, 1859), 651–80, at 673. The connection between translation and coronation was overlooked by Jürgen Petersohn, 'Kaisertum und Kultakt in der Stauferzeit', in *Politik und Heiligenverehrung*, 101–46, at 115–16.

[51] Surprisingly, a credible study of the place of Charlemagne in high medieval Germany remains a desideratum. In the meantime, see Knut Görich, 'Herrschen mit dem heiligen Karl?: die Staufer, Karl der Große und Aachen', *Rheinische Vierteljahresblätter* 82 (2018), 23–36.

[52] The connection applied even when it was drawn implicitly, and not necessarily by the king, as when, in 1220, Archbishop Stephen Langton of Canterbury interrupted the second coronation of King Henry III to announce the canonisation of St Hugh of Lincoln: Daniel Baumann, *Stephen Langton. Erzbischof von Canterbury im England der Magna Carta* (Leiden and Boston, 2009), 256–7. There, it was the promise to abstain from the tyrannous acts of King John that mattered. Hugh's cult built partly on his forceful admonition of monarchs and the fervour with which he had protected the liberties of his see and of the people at large. *Magna Vita Sancti Hugonis. The Life of St Hugh of Lincoln*, eds. and trans. Decima L. Douie and David Hugh Farmer, 2 vols. (Oxford, 1961–85), vol. 1, 65–72, 112–19, vol. 2, 99–105; Gerald of Wales, *The Life of St Hugh of Avalon, Bishop of Lincoln 1186–1200*, ed. and transl. Richard M. Loomis (New York and London, 1985), 28–9; *The Metrical Life of St Hugh of Lincoln*, transl. Charles Garton (Lincoln, 1986), 36–9. See also Ryan Kemp, 'Hugh of Lincoln and Adam of Eynsham: Angevin kingship reconsidered', *HSJ* 30 (2018), 133–57. It might even be worth speculating whether the translation of the remains of Thomas Becket that year should not also be viewed in this light: Richard G. Eales, 'The political setting of the Becket translation of 1220', *Studies in Church History* 30 (1993), 127–39. His cult had, after all, begun to centre on his forceful resistance to tyranny as such, not merely in relation to the Church: Kay Brainerd Slocum,

174   6. DESIGNATING AN HEIR

or appropriating the saintly and the supernatural was always embedded in an exhortation to perform the duties and to act in recognition of the origins of the royal office. This was all the more important in the context of a coronation or the settlement of a succession.

Royal authority was contingent upon virtuous governance. The conceptual link was central to the proceedings at Ringsted in 1170. St Knud Lavard had been the only legitimate son of Erik I. He eventually became duke of Schleswig, but in 1131 was murdered by his cousin Magnus.[53] As early as 1146, Valdemar had unsuccessfully sought to secure his father's canonisation. Only by the late 1160s was he able to secure sufficient backing to approach the papal court again.[54] The festivities were therefore partly a celebration of the unity between king and prelates, newly restored and now made manifest. Knud's cult also centred on themes of good rulership. He had been a victim of royal tyranny: unjustly accused, persecuted and finally slain by those far less deserving of the crown.[55] He was the good king who never was. That, at least, was the image painted by the extant materials for the liturgy of St Knud Lavard. We do not know whether these had been composed specifically for the proceedings in 1170. It has been suggested that they were, but they have also been dated to c. 1180–1200, though still drawing on materials written from c. 1135 onwards.[56] The precise date of origin is, however, less significant than the fact that the liturgical texts established a tradition asserting dynastic continuity and the virtuous exercise of power. The liturgy stressed that Knud Lavard was the scion

---

Liturgies in Honour of Thomas Becket (Toronto, 2004), 171–3, 186, 196, 213–15, 220–1, 229–30, 278, 299, 300, 301, 313–14; Phyllis B. Roberts, *Thomas Becket in the Medieval Latin Preaching Tradition. An Inventory of Sermons about Thomas Becket c. 1170 – c. 1400* (Steenbruggen, 1992), nos. 53, 142.

[53] John Bergsagel, 'Between politics and devotion: the canonizations of Knud Lavard and Edward the Confessor', in *Political Plainchant? Music, Text and Historical Context of Medieval Saints' Offices*, ed. Roman Hankeln (Ottawa, 2009), 49–58; and the essays by Bergsagel, Jensen, Lind and Petersen in *Of Chronicles and Kings*, ed. Bergsagel, Hiley and Riis.

[54] Antonsson, *St. Mágnus of Orkney*, 133–9.

[55] It is worth noting that, in later Danish accounts Knud Lavard's translation was paired with the martyrdom of an even more famous victim of royal tyranny: Thomas Becket. *Annales Lundenses*, in *Danmarks Middelalderliger Annaler*, 58–9 (coronation, canonisation, Becket); *Dansk-svenske annaler 916–1265*, in ibid., 13 (1171: Becket, canonisation, coronation); *Dansk Tekst Årborg 1074–1265*, in ibid., 18 (1171: Becket, canonisation, coronation); *Annales Waldemarii*, in ibid., 78 (1171: Becket, canonisation; 1172: coronation); *Annales Sorani vet.*, in ibid., 90 (1171: Becket and translation; 1172 coronation); *Annales 980–1286*, in ibid., 270 (1170: conversion of Rügen, translation of Knud, birth of Valdemar II; 1171: Becket; 1172: Knud is crowned (sole entry)); *Annales Essenbecenses*, in ibid., 277 (1170: coronation; 1171: Becket and translation); *Annales 1098–1325*, in ibid., 320 (1171: Becket, translation and coronation).

[56] Michael Chesnutt, 'The medieval Danish liturgy of St Knud Lavard', in *Bibliotheca Arnamagnaeana xlii: Opuscula XI*, ed. Britta Olrik Fredericksen (Copenhagen, 2003), 1–160, at 54–7.

III. SUCCESSION   175

of Erik the Good, a faithful and pious ruler. During his reign, law and justice flourished, Denmark abounded in people and the people in food. Erik was loved by his subjects, established hospices for pilgrims and provided succour to paupers. Knud Lavard followed in his father's footsteps. He proved to be a just judge, equipped with innate virtue, a loyal servant of his king and an even more faithful protector of his people and of the Christian faith. Even though he never desired the throne, Knud's exceptional qualities nonetheless aroused his cousin's murderous jealousy.[57] He died a martyr because he was a just and pious lord.

Accounts of the translation reinforce this message. Once Valdemar came of age, they report that he made the pagans adopt Christianity, turned the faithful towards peace and offered protection to the lovers of it. He transformed hatred into love, pain into joy, war into peace and hardship into abundance.[58] With the help of the archbishops Eskil of Lund and Stephen of Uppsala, he petitioned the pope to have his father's sanctity recognised.[59] In ensuring appropriate commemoration of Knud Lavard, Valdemar fulfilled his duty to secure the continuation of the royal line, the stability of the realm and the tranquillity of his people. He demonstrated that he had been bequeathed both his father's illustrious pedigree and his innate virtue. He won the throne because he was the descendant of kings, and because he both possessed the means and displayed the moral character to act like one.[60]

Canonisation and coronation communicated interlocking ideals. Because Valdemar emulated his virtuous forebears, the right order of the world had been restored, so that peace and public order prevailed. By contrast, the years

[57] Chesnutt, 'Medieval Danish liturgy', 90–1 (Erik), 93–5 (Knud's virtuous conduct), 99–102 (plotting and martyrdom), 119–21 (Knud's virtuous conduct). For the historical context: Kjaer, 'Political conflict and political ideas'; Bysted, Jensen, Jensen and Lind, *Jerusalem in the North*, 38–43.

[58] Chesnutt, 'Medieval Danish liturgy', 120–1.

[59] Chesnutt, 'Medieval Danish liturgy', 120–3. See also the account of Valdemar in Sven Aggesen, *Brevis Historia*, in *Scriptores Minores*, ed. Gertz, vol. 1, 138–9. An insightful glimpse of the rather complex background to these events is provided by Mia Münster-Swendsen, 'Banking on – and with – the Victorines: the strange case of Archbishop Eskil's lost deposit', in *Denmark and Europe in the Middle Ages, c1000–1525. Essays in Honour of Professor Michael H. Gelting*, ed. Kerstin Hundahl, Lars Kjaer and Niels Lund (Farnham, 2014), 91–110. For the extent to which these values shared a framework with the self-representation of Knud Lavard's and Valdemar's rivals, see Kjaer, 'Political conflict', 76–96. See also Jensen, *Crusading at the Edges*, 163–6 for some of the values espoused. For the cultivation of a dynastic past by Valdemar and his descendants: Lars Kjaer, 'Runes, knives and Vikings: the Valdemarian kings and the Danish past in comparative perspective', in *Denmark and Europe in the Middle Ages*, 255–67.

[60] Notably, when Valdemar was himself first proposed for the throne, it was because of his father's virtue and his descent from Erik: Saxo Grammaticus, *Gesta Danorum*, xiv.2.2, pp. 984–5. On the reputation of Erik see also Haki Antonsson, *Damnation and Salvation in Old Norse Literature* (Woodbridge, 2018), 60–2.

176   6. DESIGNATING AN HEIR

between Erik's death and Valdemar's succession became a shameful interlude, overcome by the restoration of a rightful line of good and pious kings. Simultaneously, the festivities pointed to just how precarious peace and tranquillity actually were. In 1170, Knud VI was seven, a year older than Knud Lavard had been when Erik I died in 1103. Just as Erik's legacy was squandered by his brothers and their heirs, so Valdemar's and Knud Lavard's would be at risk, unless steps were taken to ensure that peace and justice, so recently restored, endured. In this regard, the events of 1170 justified and legitimised so unprecedented a step as the crowning and anointing of the king's heir. Yet this was no mere power grab. On the contrary, by embedding this innovation in the context of a cult that commemorated a paragon of just and righteous rule, and of a man who himself had been the victim of royal tyranny, Knud VI was exhorted be a just and pious king himself. At Ringsted, just as at León and Aachen, the religious underpinnings of royal power were stressed in order to define its purpose, and to remind the king that his standing was contingent upon the performance of his duties.

This context set the Danish experience apart from Sicily's and England's. Roger II had used his son's coronation in 1151 to assert that he, not the pope, exercised control over the Sicilian Church. To John of Salisbury, that the ceremony even took place marked Roger as a tyrant and usurper.[61] In England, Henry the Young King's enthronement was firmly embedded in a display not of pious fervour, but of unbridled royal might. Easter had been celebrated at Windsor, where the king of Scotland and his brother had been present, as well as 'all of the noble and great men of England, bishops as well as earls and barons'.[62] From thence, the court proceeded to London, where Henry's coronation was preceded by the announcement of a reform of shire administration.[63] The enthronement demonstrated the extent of the king's reach both within his realm and beyond. It enacted royal power that was overwhelming, unencumbered and in no need of authorisation by the exiled archbishop of Canterbury, Thomas Becket. It was an act of defiance, designed to spite Becket and to isolate him with a display of backing from the kingdom's nobles, neighbours and prelates.[64] That the Young King rebelled against his father a few years later would have done little to legitimise a practice that was increasingly associated with murder and bloodshed. By contrast, the Danish king succeeded at least in part because the proceedings celebrated royal power not as an end in itself, but as a means to advance the common good.

---

[61] John of Salisbury, *Historia Pontificalis*, 69.
[62] Roger of Howden, *Chronicle of the Reigns*, vol. 1, 4.
[63] Roger of Howden, *Chronicle of the Reigns*, vol. 1, 4–6.
[64] Other factors also came into play. William I of Sicily died when his son was about twelve years old, that is, perhaps too young to have already been designated king. That son then died without legitimate male children.

III. SUCCESSION   177

Events at Ringsted in 1170 point to broader themes: the act of designation created a means by which principles underpinning the moral framework discussed in the previous chapter could be rehearsed. How precisely that was done, which duties and functions were emphasised, how they were ranked and ordered, was conditioned by the particular moment in time, the circumstances out of which a particular act emerged, the traditions to which it responded, and, of course, the kind of ceremony performed. Hence the emphasis on the defence of the faith in León, just governance in 1170 or crusading at Aachen in 1215. Sometimes, a broader set of qualities was invoked, as in Poland in 1099, when the magnates were called upon to choose as their duke the candidate who distinguished himself 'in sending and receiving embassies, in calling up and levying an army and in the manifold affairs of [the] ... realm'.[65] But then Wladyslaw's settlement coincided with his sons coming of age, with their receiving lands and territories of their own and with their return from a jointly led campaign. These variations were not departures from, but rather reinforced common European expectations of the royal office, of what kings should do and the qualities they ought to possess. They also permeated the other stages of preparing an heir for the throne.

Accepting or endorsing the crowning of an heir constituted a provisional promise at best. Just like any form of designation, it helped identify an heir, and certainly helped strengthen his case. Where underage heirs are concerned, however, designation and acclamation mattered above all because they initiated a period of training for kingship. The young ruler still had to learn what it meant to be a just and pious lord. This conditionality foreshadowed the extended period of a king's inauguration.[66] Enthronement was contingent upon the ruler proving that he deserved to wear the crown. In the case of designated heirs, the key difference was that they had their fathers to guide them. If kings lived long enough, if their heirs survived and provided royal offspring did not turn out to be oppressors, there was every chance that chosen successors would be able to forge the networks necessary for the successful exercise of the royal office, and to demonstrate that they had the means and disposition to wield a king's power. They would have a headstart over their rivals. But to gain that, they first had to be trained.

6.2   Training for Kingship

When Knud VI was crowned in 1170, he may not have noticed the reference to Knud Lavard's education in the saint's *Passio*. Knud, it recorded, was given into the care of Skjalm, 'who was most valiant among the Danes'.[67] Saxo

---

[65] *Gesta Principum Polonorum*, ii.8, pp. 132–5.
[66] See Chapter 10.
[67] *In passione*, in *Vitae Sanctorum Danorum*, ed. M. C. Gertz (Copenhagen, 1908–12), 190.

178   6. DESIGNATING AN HEIR

Grammaticus fleshed out this skeletal report: Skjalm was 'a man of the most brilliant and incorruptible merit, who had been allotted the administration of Zealand and also of Rügen, which he himself had made tributary'. The provision for King Erik's eponymous younger son, by contrast, 'was more superficial, because this child was of meaner birth, and he was therefore consigned to the charge of less influential tutors'.[68] Neither the hagiographical sources nor Saxo, however, outline the *content* of Knud's education. At most, the description of Skjalm as valiant, brilliant, a man of great honour and standing, gives an indication of the qualities he was supposed to foster in his charge. Knud Lavard's time in Skjalm's entourage does, however, reflect common practices. Royal sons frequently spent time in another household as part of their upbringing. Roger, oldest son of William I of Sicily, had been tutored by Archdeacon Walter of Céfalu,[69] Mieszko III of Poland by King Ladislaus of Hungary,[70] Sverrir of Norway's eldest son by his trusted follower Gudlaug Vali[71] and the future Alfonso VII of Castile by Count Peter of Trava.[72] Yet most writers remained reticent about what precisely a king's education entailed.[73] Indeed, what follows is the first systematic sketch of an heir's training and preparation for kingship as it was practised across high medieval Europe.

Saxo, when recounting the deeds of Valdemar I, recorded his quasi-miraculous birth,[74] mentioned in passing that, as an infant, he was considered a candidate for the throne[75] and then resumed his narrative once Valdemar

---

[68] Saxo Grammaticus, *Gesta Danorum*, xii.6.5, pp. 884–5.

[69] Hugo Falcandus, *Il regno di Sicilia*, 133.

[70] *Gesta Principum Polonorum*, ii.29, pp. 172–3.

[71] *Saga of King Sverri*, chapter 62, p. 82.

[72] *Historia Compostellana*, ed. Emma Falque Rey, CCCM 70 (Turnhout, 1988), 85.

[73] This has posed real problems for modern biographers of medieval kings, and explains why relatively little work has been done on the education of kings (and of noble elites) in a high medieval context. Key exceptions are: Aurell, *Lettered Knight*, 44–50 (tutors and households), 50–55 (ecclesiastical institutions); Lyon, 'Fathers and sons'; Matthew Strickland, 'On the instruction of a prince: the upbringing of Henry, the Young King', in *Henry II. New Interpretations*, ed. Christopher Harper-Bill and Nicholas Vincent (Woodbridge, 2007), 184–214. The evidence becomes richer for the later Middle Ages: Werner Paravacini and Jörg Wettlaufer, eds., *Erziehung und Bildung bei Hofe. 7. Symposium der Residenzen-Kommission der Akademie der Wissenschaften in Göttingen* (Stuttgart, 2002).

[74] Saxo Grammaticus, *Gesta Danorum*, xiii.7.3, pp. 940–3. Quasi-miraculous, because he was born a week after his father's murder, which Saxo took to be a sign of divine favour towards Knud Lavard's kin. See the similar rendering of the births of Boleslaw III and Philipp Augustus: *Gesta Principum Polonorum*, i.31, pp. 106–9, ii.1, pp. 116–17; Rigord, *Histoire*, 120–3; William C. Jordan, '"Quando fuit natus": interpreting the birth of Philip Augustus', in *The Work of Jacques LeGoff and the Challenges of Medieval History*, ed. Miri Rubin (Woodbridge, 1997), 171–88. See also above, Chapter 3.

[75] Saxo Grammaticus, *Gesta Danorum*, xiv.2.1, pp. 982–5.

III. SUCCESSION 179

was 'for the first time of a proper age to take part in armed conflict'.[76] Suger of St Denis, writing about Louis VI and Louis VII, and Rigord, treating Philipp Augustus of France, similarly skirted over the kings' early years, and moved instead straight from birth to first military encounters.[77] At most, an infant ruler's early exploits were enumerated in order to suggest that they foreshadowed future greatness. Boleslaw III 'did not indulge in silly games, the way children usually like to play, but he did his best as much a boy could to imitate vigorous and martial deeds'.[78] The future Roger II often started fights involving bands of followers when playing with his older brother Simon. Roger always led his side to victory, and frequently taunted Simon with the pointed suggestion that he, not Simon, ought to succeed their father. Roger would make his brother either a bishop or pope. 'And hence', Alexander of Telese commented, 'I believe that through these insulting words he foretold that he already intended to be truly the ruler after his father, and . . . to extend his lands far and wide, as he was to do following his victories.'[79] Long before they ever assumed power, Boleslaw and Roger demonstrated their bravery, ambition and ability to rule, be it by imitating knights or by bullying their unfortunate elder siblings.

Once the record picks up again, martial exploits predominate. The first deed of Louis VI reported by Suger was a successful campaign against King William Rufus of England.[80] Frederick Barbarossa appeared in action for the first time just after he had come of age, when he took it upon himself to wage war on his father's behalf. To this end, he attacked the count of Wolfratshausen, single-handedly capturing one of the count's allies.[81] Boleslaw III not only led his companions into battle against anyone attacking Wladyslaw's domains,[82] but also displayed great bravery and skill in tackling wild beasts. While still a *puer* – a boy, denoting that he had not yet come of age – he killed a boar[83] and a – 'Gallus' explicitly noted – mating bear.[84] The expectation that future kings

---

[76] Saxo Grammaticus, *Gesta Danorum*, xiv.4.1, pp. 1006–7. The same pattern applied to Saxo's treatment of Knud VI.

[77] Suger, *Vie*, 4; Suger, *Histoire de Louis VII*, in *Oeuvres*, ed. and transl. Françoise Gasparri, 2 vols. (Paris, 1996–2001), vol. 1, 157–8; Rigord, *Histoire*, 120–3.

[78] *Gesta Principum Polonorum*, ii.9, pp. 134–5.

[79] Alexander of Telese, *Ystoria Rogerii*, 7; *Roger II*, ed. Loud, 65. See also the very similar depiction of Zbigniew in the *Gesta Principum Polonorum*, ii.17, pp. 152–3.

[80] Suger, *Vie*, 8–11.

[81] Otto of Freising, *Gesta Frederici*, i.27, pp. 180–3. On the episode: Freed, *Frederick Barbarossa*, 42; Görich, *Friedrich Barbarossa*, 63, 67. See also Suger's list of all the great men captured by Louis VI during his first campaign: Suger, *Vie*, 8–10.

[82] *Gesta Principum Polonorum*, ii.12–13, pp. 138–9.

[83] *Gesta Principum Polonorum*, ii.11, pp. 136–7.

[84] *Gesta Principum Polonorum*, ii.12, pp. 138–9. Compare a similar story about killing a bear as token of martial prowess, relating to Godfrey, the future king of Jerusalem: Albert of Aachen, *Historia Hierosolymitana*, 142–5. On the political and military importance of the hunt: Thomas F. Allsen, *The Royal Hunt in Eurasian History* (Philadelphia, PA, 2006), 124–40, 160–4, 213–22.

180   6. DESIGNATING AN HEIR

participate in martial exploits could pose problems. Hunting was one activity where similar skills could be acquired and demonstrated. Another was tournaments. When Henry the Young King lamented that he could not acquire knightly skills because there were no wars to be fought in England, he embarked upon the tournament circuit instead.[85]

Hunting and tournaments did, however, require princes to be, of 'a proper age to take part in armed conflict', as Saxo had put it.[86] The expectation reflected practical needs. 'Gallus' marvelled that 'even before [Boleslaw] was able to mount or get off a horse by himself, he would march against the enemy at the head of knights, against the wishes of his father or at times without his knowledge'.[87] In other words, princes had to reach a degree of physical maturity, which they normally did in their early teens, before they could embark on knightly pursuits. Louis VI of France was 'hardly twelve or thirteen years old' when he led his first campaign,[88] and Boleslaw III – who, as we have seen, was knighted at the age of thirteen – led attacks into enemy territories 'when he had still not attained the rank of knighthood'.[89] Physical fitness was supposed to coincide with mental readiness. Boleslaw was 'a boy by age, an old man in capability' when leading his first raids,[90] and Louis VI fought the English when 'valour was growing, maturing, and beginning to flourish in the spirit of this young man, and he could no longer endure hunting and the amusements of boys'.[91]

Knightly pursuits allowed future kings to demonstrate that they excelled at martial tasks. And excel at them they did. They were more courageous, more forceful and more successful than their peers. They certainly were more accomplished than their rivals. Valdemar 'completely vanquished' one of his competitors, who not only sided with the murderers of Knud Lavard, but who, 'despite extraordinary eloquence, was in fact totally disorganised in his conduct'.[92] Successful military leadership required courage as well as discipline, and the ability to inspire, direct and control armed men. Roger II led his band of brawling boys, Boleslaw his companions, Frederick his father's men and Louis his people. Leadership furthermore had to be tempered by adherence to moral norms. Louis VI 'showed so much zeal in forming virtuous habits, and his graceful body was growing so tall that his future reign held immediate promise that the kingdom would be honourably enlarged, fostering hope that our prayers

---

[85] *History of William Marshal*, ed. A. J. Holden, transl. S. Gregory, notes by D. Crouch, 3 vols. (London, 2002), ll. 2391–576.

[86] Saxo Grammaticus, *Gesta Danorum*, xiv.4.1, pp. 1006–7. The same pattern applied to Saxo's treatment of Knud VI.

[87] *Gesta Principum Polonorum*, ii.9, pp. 134–5.

[88] Suger, *Vie*, 4; *Deeds of Louis the Fat*, 24.

[89] *Gesta Principum Polonorum*, ii.12, pp. 138–9.

[90] *Gesta Principum Polonorum*, ii.13, pp. 138–9.

[91] Suger, *Vie*, 6; *Deeds of Louis the Fat*, 25.

[92] Saxo Grammaticus, *Gesta Danorum*, xiv.4.1, pp. 1006–7.

III. SUCCESSION   181

for the protection of the churches and the poor would be answered'.[93] Coming of
age also meant being able to distinguish right from wrong. Or, as the *Vita* of
Emperor Henry IV (d. 1106) phrased it, it meant reaching 'that measure of age
and mind in which [the king] could discern what was honourable, what shameful, what useful, and what was not'.[94]

Putative kings therefore demonstrated their innate moral qualities early on.
Frederick Barbarossa rejected as shameful the suggestion that he charge a hefty
ransom for his noble prisoner, instead releasing him without payment.[95]
Valdemar pursued his father's canonisation as soon as he came of age. Louis
VI 'became a renowned and spirited defender of his father's kingdom. He took
care that the churches prospered and zealously sought peace for those who
prayed, those who toiled, and the poor.'[96] Princes knew how to balance power
with moral rectitude. They demonstrated suitability, and thereby acquired
a following of their own. Barbarossa's erstwhile captive became one of King
Frederick's earliest supporters[97] and Valdemar's bested opponent his close
ally.[98] Martial exploits and proficiency in warlike endeavours enabled heirs
and heirs apparent to show that they could exercise leadership. They could and
would offer patronage to their dependants and justice to their people. They
possessed both the means and the moral disposition to rule.

Still, sources reveal little about the actual training received. St Stephen was
'nourished with a royal education',[99] and Valdemar, once of sufficient age,
decided 'to serve a soldier's apprenticeship',[100] while Frederick Barbarossa 'had,
as was common, been trained in knightly games'.[101] There was little mention of
teachers, just as there was none of a prince's literary education. Suger, for instance,
noted that Louis VI had been raised at St Denis not in his *Deeds* of the king, but in
an account of the abbey's rebuilding.[102] Both omissions, I suggest, are connected.
Neither reflects actual practice. Future kings proved their suitability by demonstrating that they were innately capable of acting like kings. Even when they
sought out adventures or submitted themselves to training, they did so out of their
own volition, not as directed by their fathers, instructors or regents. Boleslaw III
was explicitly described as so eager to wage war that he proceeded even over
Wladyslaw's objections or without his knowledge. Louis VI and Henry IV were

[93] Suger, *Vie*, 4; *Deeds of Louis the Fat*, 24.
[94] *Vita Heinrici IV Imperatoris*, 14.
[95] Otto of Freising, *Gesta Frederici*, i.27, pp. 182–3.
[96] Suger, *Vie*, 14; *Deeds of Louis the Fat*, 29.
[97] Freed, *Frederick Barbarossa*, 79–80; Görich, *Friedrich Barbarossa*, 90.
[98] Saxo Grammaticus, *Gesta Danorum*, xiv.14.1–3, pp. 1052–5.
[99] *Legenda S. Stephani*, in *Scriptores Rerum Hungaricarum*, ed. Szentpétery, vol. 2, 381:
      'crevit infans regali nutritus educatu'.
[100] Saxo Grammaticus, *Gesta Danorum*, xiv.4.1, pp. 1006–7.
[101] Otto of Freising, *Gesta Frederici*, ii.27, pp. 180–1.
[102] Suger, *Gesta Sugerii Abbatis*, in Suger, *Oeuvres*, vol. 1, 54–155, at 138.

182 6. DESIGNATING AN HEIR

similarly depicted as naturally coming to an age where, without further instruction, they could distinguish right from wrong, while Frederick Barbarossa dismissed the dishonourable suggestions of his men *ex innata nobilitate*, out of innate nobility of character.[103] In fact, moral disposition was meant to be discernible from birth. As the *Vita* of St Ladislaus of Hungary put it, the infant showed that he would in future be king.[104] Just as a virtuous disposition would become apparent in infancy, so too would an evil or malicious character. Aethelred II revealed his future depravity when, during his christening, he defecated into the baptismal font.[105] Bernard of Clairvaux, on first beholding the young Henry II of England only had to glance at the boy to be able to pronounce: 'From the devil he has come, and to the devil he will go.'[106] Education and training could foster and nourish, perhaps even cloak, but not remedy a future ruler's character.

The emphasis on natural, inherited characteristics reflects the basic premise that kings would not be ready to rule if they could not discern by themselves what was right and what was wrong. This did not mean that they were infallible. Seeking out wise and prudent counsel was the mark of a good ruler. But they would know, rather than needing to be told, that advice and guidance were required. The theme also reflects conventions of genre. Most of these accounts sought to represent a future king as conforming already in his youth to an ideal type of noble and aristocratic behaviour. That certainly involved showing due reverence to the Church: Louis VI, Suger stressed, was a devout friend of the Church of St Denis.[107] Above all, however, heirs apparent had to be able to ward off enemies, oppress the oppressors and defend by arms those who could not protect themselves. Lords and kings existed to wield the sword of worldly justice, to ensure a righteous peace, where necessary by engaging in bloodshed and violence. These activities were prohibited to their clerical peers and subjects, at least in theory. This reasoning underpinned Roger II's supposed taunting of his brother,[108] or Cardinal Peter Damian's warning to the margrave of Tuscany that he should focus on punishing evildoers, and leave being merciful to priests.[109] It was also why Sverrir of Norway, initially ordained a priest, abandoned the clerical life once he came of age: he was too unruly and got into too many fights.[110] It is therefore most often in accounts of royal saints, of kings who had initially been destined for the Church or ones renowned for their piety, that a love of learning was recorded. Emperor Henry II (d. 1024) had spent his childhood at

[103] Otto of Freising, *Gesta Frederici*, ii.27, pp. 182–3.
[104] *Legenda S. Ladislai*, in *Scriptores Rerum Hungaricarum*, ed. Szentpétery, vol. 2, 515–16.
[105] William of Malmesbury, *Gesta Regum*, ii.164, pp. 268–9.
[106] Gerald of Wales, *De Principis Instructione*, 700–3. See also ibid. 702 n. 348.
[107] Suger, *Vie*, 4.
[108] Alexander of Telese, *Ystoria Rogerii*, 7; *Roger II*, ed. Loud, 65.
[109] *Briefe Peter Damian*, nos. 66–7.
[110] *Saga of King Sverri*, 2–3.

III. SUCCESSION   183

Hildesheim, where he was nourished and educated in literature,[111] Robert the
Pious of France (d. 1031) was well versed in and dedicated to the study of
letters[112] as well as of the liberal arts from an early age[113] and Sverrir had been
five years old when he became the foster son of Bishop Hroi in the Faroe
Islands, who 'put him to books'.[114] In most cases, however, accounts of a ruler's
deeds made little reference to his literary education because they sought to
construct an ideal type of secular lordship.

That was not the only factor at play. Instruction established a hierarchy.
Teachers held authority over their students, resembling that between a new
king and those confirming or conferring his title. Yet rulers were supposed to
act unencumbered by ties except for those established through the loyal and
faithful service of their subjects. And they were, of course, meant to owe
obedience and to be subservient only to God. In combination, these features
help explain why accounts of a king's education and training are often allusive,
veiled and sparse. Even when referenced, the relationship between teacher and
pupil was normally downplayed, and framed so as to maintain hierarchies.
When, in 997, Gerbert of Aurillac was asked to tutor Emperor Otto III, he went
to considerable lengths to stress the moral and intellectual superiority of his
imperial charge.[115] Alternatively, writers insisted that they acted at the king's
behest when offering instruction. The initiative rested firmly with the ruler.
Even in the twelfth century, when giving unsolicited advice became a marker of
pious fervour, instruction remained embedded in a rhetoric of solicitous
praise. Good rulers knew where to get and how to appreciate good counsel,
and that receiving and endorsing it denoted moral excellence.[116]

Such protestations of subservience communicated what writers, their peers
and audiences thought should be. They were rhetorical exercises.[117] They

[111] *Die Vita Sancti Heinrici regis et confessoris und ihre Bearbeitung durch den Bamberger Diakon Adelbert*, ed. Marcus Stumpf, MGH SSrG (Hanover, 1999), 229.
[112] Helgaud of Fleury, *Vie de Robert le Pieux*, ed. Robert-Henri Bautier and Gilette Labory (Paris, 1965), 60.
[113] Richer of Saint-Rémi, *Histories*, vol. 2, 226–7.
[114] *Saga of King Sverri*, 2.
[115] Gerbert d'Aurillac, *Correspondance*, ed. P. Riché and J. P. Callu, 2 vols. (Paris, 1993), vol. 2, no. 187. See also, for the context, Heinrich Zimmermann, 'Gerbert als kaiserlicher Rat', in *Gerberto: Scienza, storia e mito. Atti del Gerberti Symposium (Bobbio 25–27 Iuglio 1983)* (Piacenza, 1985), 235–54.
[116] *Die Briefe des Abtes Bern von Reichenau*, ed. Franz-Josef Schmale, Veröffentlichungen der Kommission für geschichtliche Landeskunde in Baden-Württemberg Reihe A: Quellen 6 (Stuttgart, 1961), no. 31; *Diplomatari i Escrits Literaris de l'Abbat i Bisbe Oliba*, ed. Eduard Junyent i Subirà and Anscari M. Mundó, Institutut d'Estudis Catalans: Memòries de la Secció Històrico-arqueològica 44 (Barcelona, 1992), Textos literaris no. 16. See also Weiler, 'Clerical admonitio'.
[117] See, for instance, *Aurea Gemma Oxonienses*, in *Die Jüngere Hildesheimer Briefsammlung*, ed. Rolf de Kegel, MGH Epistolae: Briefe der Deutschen Kaiserzeit (Munich, 1995), no. 134.21.

184 6. DESIGNATING AN HEIR

could not wholly cloak the fact that instructing the king signalled virtue and hence standing within the realm. Gerbert may have protested his inferiority, but he and the people collating his letters nonetheless ensured that the correspondence with the emperor was preserved. Requests to offer advice, to instruct the king or his chosen heir marked out teachers as excelling in the study of letters and morals, and was testimony to their intellectual and religious preeminence as well as that of their relatives, patrons, pupils and peers. It was probably for this reason that Saxo mentioned Knud Lavard being given into the care of Skjalm, who was, after all, the grandfather of Saxo's patron Absalon.[118] Knud's relationship with Skjalm foreshowed that between Valdemar and Absalon, and formed part of restoring the norms and conventions of the glorious days of King Erik the Good. It was perhaps for that same reason that, Sven Aggesen recounted, Knud VI was taught by Absalon.[119]

It is therefore often in texts recounting the deeds of those called upon to teach an heir, or in ones written by them, that reference to instruction is made. When detailing his efforts to rebuild the abbey church, Suger mentioned that the infant Louis VI of France had been tutored at St Denis.[120] William of Palermo and Peter of Blois had taught King William II of Sicily 'the basic arts of versification and literature', before their erstwhile protégé turned to 'abject books in imperial leisure'.[121] More commonly, being charged with teaching the king or his heir signalled excellence and status. That pre-eminence was then passed onto to a teacher's charge. When Henry II asked William Marshal to act as tutor for his son, the request testified to William's elegance and knightly skill. Through his instruction, 'the young king's reputation increased, along with his eminence and the honour paid to him; he also acquired the quality of valour'.[122] The twelfth-century Vita of St Anno of Cologne recorded that the archbishop had been entrusted with the education of the infant Henry IV. The pupil would subsequently show little gratitude for this favour (beneficium). Even so, through his instruction Anno ensured that the boy was suitable for holding royal power.[123] The archbishop honoured the king by giving him the benefit of his instruction. Similar themes surface in accounts of other saintly prelates. When the future Bishop Otto of Bamberg accompanied a Salian princess to the Polish ducal court, his wisdom and piety were so cherished that many nobles entrusted their sons to his tutelage,[124] and when Anselm of

[118] Saxo Grammaticus, Gesta Danorum, 884 n. 20.
[119] Sven Aggesen, Lex Castrensis, in Scriptores Minores, ed. Gertz, vol. 1, 64.
[120] Suger, Gesta Sugerii Abbatis, in Suger, Oeuvres, vol. 1, 138.
[121] Peter of Blois, Opera Omnia, ed. J. A. Giles, 4 vols. (Oxford, 1846–7), vol. 1, no. 66.
[122] History of William Marshal, ll. 1935–58 (quotation at 1952–4).
[123] Vita Annonis Minor. Die jüngere Annovita, ed. and transl. Mauritius Mittler (Siegburg, 1975), 18.
[124] Ebonis Vita S. Ottonis Epsicopi Babenbergensis, ed. Jan Wikarjak and Kasimierz Liman, Monumenta Poloniae Historica Series Nova (Warsaw, 1969), 10.

III. SUCCESSION   185

Bec first visited England in the 1080s, his advice and teaching were sought by
the 'courts of noblemen'. Even William the Conqueror,

> who had seized England by force of arms and was reigning at that time –
> although he seemed stiff and terrifying to everyone because of his great
> power – nevertheless unbent and was amiable with Anselm, so that to
> everyone's surprise he seemed an altogether different man when Anselm
> was present. The good report of Anselm thus became known in every part
> of England, and he was beloved by everyone as a man to be revered for his
> sanctity.[125]

Saintly men instructed their audiences and the sons given into their care in
proper moral conduct. They taught them how to use power, and how to acquire
the ethical outlook that enabled rulers and princes to become good kings.

To benefit fully from such instruction, a knowledge of letters was needed. In
1161, Peter of Blois, writing on behalf of Archbishop Rotrou of Rouen, urged
Henry II of England to provide his eldest son with a literary education. His letter
offers perhaps the fullest programmatic statement on the subject to survive from
high medieval Europe. Literature, Peter declared, provided a compendium of all
useful knowledge: how to govern the state; how to erect, destroy and rebuild
castles; how to wage war; how justice, reverence for the law and the peace of
liberty could be nurtured; and how the friendship of neighbouring nations could
be won. Henry, who had himself been trained in letters since early adolescence,
provided a most glorious example. As a result of this education, he went on to be
wise in governance, perceptive in judgements, cautious in commands and
circumspect in counsel. The bishops of the realm therefore implored Henry to
ensure that his son be trained to act in a like fashion. An illiterate king was like
a navigator without oarsmen or a bird without feathers. Julius Caesar had been
so well versed that he could dictate four letters at once, thereby greatly strengthening the laws of Rome. The power of innate virtue, if exercised in conjunction
with philosophy, would increase understanding and discernment fourfold.
Aristotle's teaching had made Alexander even greater. Solomon had treasured
wisdom above riches and beauty. For how could a king rule according to divine
law, if he could not discern that law? In order to discern it, he would have to be
proficient in letters. Peter continued to list kings whose throne had been blessed
and whose realms flourished because they had been well versed in literature:
David, Josiah, Constantine, Theodosius and Justinian. Peter added a warning:

---

[125] Eadmer, *Vita St Anselmi*, ed. and transl. Richard W. Southern (Oxford, 1962), 56–7. See
also the *Life* of St Theodgar: *Vitae Sanctorum Danorum*, 15; William FitzStephen, *Vita
Sancti Thomae Cantuariensis Archiepiscopi et Martyri*, in *Materials for the History of
Thomas Becket*, ed. J. C. Robertson, Rolls Series, 7 vols. (London, 1875–85), vol. 2, 22. For
context: Helmuth Kluger, 'Bischof und König in Dänemark um das Jahr 1100', *in Die
früh- und hochmittelalterliche Bischofserhebung im europäischen Vergleich*, ed. Franz-
Reiner Erkens (Cologne, Weimar and Vienna, 1998), 321–42.

186   6. DESIGNATING AN HEIR

the continuation of both realm and dynasty depended upon kings abiding by divine law. When David had asked God for wisdom, the Lord had promised that his kingdom and his line would be blessed provided they enforced divine law. Yet if they defied the will of God, He would unleash upon them righteous anger and great fury. The history of the kings of Israel showed how, from Saul and his son Jonathan onwards, kings had concluded their days well and had reigned in glory as long as they did God's bidding. But once they veered from the path of righteousness, they died by the sword. Worse still, the failings of kings rebounded upon their people. David's presumption resulted in a great pestilence, killing 70,000 people, and Jeroboam's rent Israel asunder. Finally, if a ruler did not heed the law of God, the throne would pass to foes, lesser men and aliens. Therefore, Henry II was urged, his son ought to be instructed in letters. Armed with wisdom, he would vanquish evil and give a shining example to others.[126]

Peter of Blois had little to say about what exactly should be read in this course of literary instruction. The emphasis on models from the Bible offers an indication of the role of history within the young prince's instruction, as does an emphasis on the practical needs to be served. Literature provided a storehouse of useful information about warfare, governance and justice. Such utility extended to moral lessons. A knowledge of letters enhanced the innate virtue of princes and provided them with the means of fathoming God's will. Illiterate kings, by contrast, endangered the welfare of their people, both in this world and the next. Moreover, Peter pointed out, the Old King had himself been trained in letters from an early age. That was no mere flattery. Henry's father, the count of Anjou, had been a patron of William of Conches, whose *Dragmaticon* became a popular treatise on the natural world, and Count Fulk Rechin of Anjou was reputed to have written a history of the comital house.[127] On the English side, Henry's uncle had been a patron of William of Malmesbury and Geoffrey of Monmouth; the king's grandmother had commissioned William of Malmesbury to write the *Gesta Regum*; and his mother had been the recipient of a copy both of William's *Gesta Regum* and of the Latin *Kaiserchronik*.[128] Literary patronage was very much a family tradition.

[126] Peter of Blois, *Opera Omnia*, vol. 1, no. 67. On Henry the Young King's education see Strickland, 'On the instruction of a prince'.

[127] Nicholas L. Paul, 'The chronicle of Fulk le Rechin: a reassessment', *HSJ* 18 (2006), 19–36; William of Conches, *A Dialogue on Natural Philosophy: Translation of the New Latin Critical Text with a Short Introduction and Explanatory Notes*, transl. Italo Roca (South Bend, IN, 1997). See also Nicholas Vincent, 'The great lost library of England's medieval kings? Royal use and ownership of books, 1066–1272', in *1000 Years of Royal Books and Manuscripts*, ed. Kathleen Doyle and Scot McKendrick (London, 2013), 73–112.

[128] Johanna Dale, 'Imperial self-representation and the manipulation of history in twelfth-century Germany: Cambridge, Corpus Christi College MS 373', *German History* 29 (2011), 557–83; Björn Weiler, 'William of Malmesbury, Henry I, and the *Gesta Regum Anglorum*', *ANS* 31 (2009), 157–76; Jean-Guy Gouttebroze, 'Robert de Gloucester et l'écriture de l'histoire', in *Histoire et littérature au Moyen Âge*, ed.

III. SUCCESSION   187

Henry II followed suit. As Peter of Blois explained to the archbishop of Palermo, in the king's household, 'every day is school, in the constant conversation of the most literate and discussion of questions'.[129]

The expectation that rulers commission and collect learned texts, that they listen to, engage and converse with scholars and writers, was by no means peculiar to England. In the eleventh century, King Sancho of Navarre commissioned letters and treatises from Bishop Oliba of Vic and Abbot Bern of Reichenau provided materials for the imperial library of Henry III.[130] In twelfth-century Denmark, Valdemar I and Knud VI collated accounts about the weapons of their forebears, the laws of Knud the Great and ancient inscriptions.[131] In the crusader states William of Tyre singled out King Baldwin III of Jerusalem as enjoying conversations with learned men and the study of history.[132] In fact, history appears to have been a popular subject in the instruction of rulers. Around 1040 Wipo composed the *Gesta Chuonradi* for Emperor Henry III. It used the deeds of Henry's father to construct an ideal image of kingship. Around 1125, William of Malmesbury dedicated his *Gesta Regum Anglorum* to Henry I's likely successors and their advisors. In the early thirteenth century Giles of Paris penned an account of the deeds of Charlemagne for the edification and instruction of the future Louis VIII.[133] The imperial palace at Hagenau, a residence favoured by both Frederick Barbarossa and Henry VI, was so famed for its library that Godfrey of Viterbo celebrated its holdings in verse. The emperor's book chests preserved 'for him the best authors and the tales of the saints. If you want to read chronicles, the hall will offer them to you. There you will find law and sciences, and every poet. The great Aristotle, Hippocrates and Galen give you worthy counsel in this house, and teach you what to avoid.'[134] No book catalogue has survived from twelfth-century Hagenau, but the subjects covered in Godfrey's

---

Danielle Buschinger (Göppingen, 1991), 143–60. For putative antecedents see also: David R. Pratt, 'Kings and books in Anglo-Saxon England', *Anglo-Saxon England* 43 (2014), 297–377.

[129] Peter of Blois, *Opera Omnia*, vol. 1, no. 66.

[130] *Diplomatari i Escrits Literaris*, Textos literaris no. 16; *Die Briefe des Abtes Bern*, no. 27.

[131] Kjaer, 'Runes, knives and Vikings', 256–7: Saxo Grammaticus, *Gesta Danorum*, preface 2.5, pp. 12–13, vii.10.3, pp. 514–15 (inscriptions commissioned by Halfdan to commemorate his father's deeds, sparking Valdemar's interest); xi.3.1, pp. 790–1 (the knife of Harald Hadrada); Sven Aggesen, *Lex Castrensis*, in *Scriptores Minores*, ed. Gertz, vol. 1, 64 (Knud VI being consulted about commissioning a copy of the *Lex Castrensis*). See also Erik Petersen, ed., *Living Words and Luminous Pictures. Medieval Book Culture in Denmark* (Copenhagen, 1999).

[132] William of Tyre, *Chronicon*, 715 (I am grateful to Matthew Strickland for this reference).

[133] Wipo, *Gesta Chuonradi*, 2–3; Weiler, 'William of Malmesbury, Henry I'; Marvin Colker, 'The "Karolinus" of Aegidius Parisiensis', *Traditio* 29 (1973), 199–326.

[134] Godfrey of Viterbo, *Denumeratio regnorum imperio subiectorum*, in *Littérature Latin et histoire du Moyen Âge*, ed. Leopold Delisle (Paris, 1890), 41–50, at 48–9, ll. 148–56. I am grateful to Thomas Foerster for this reference.

188 6. DESIGNATING AN HEIR

list do not diverge much from those viewed as essential by Peter of Blois: history, law, theology, medicine and natural philosophy. Other evidence also suggests that the Staufen emperors were avid collectors, and even producers, of texts. Henry VI wrote vernacular poetry,[135] Frederick Barbarossa travelled with a collection of books when campaigning in Italy,[136] Burgundino of Pisa claimed to have conversed with the emperor about natural philosophy[137] and Hugh of Honau, a court cleric, drew on the imperial library at Hagenau in his study of Aristotle.[138]

None of this necessarily meant that Frederick Barbarossa and his peers were avid readers.[139] They were, however, supposed to surround themselves with men who were. Literary court culture most likely unfolded in conversation, discussion and the studying of excerpts, perhaps even in translation.[140] That much is suggested by Peter of Blois' description of the court of Henry II. Likewise, Burgundino discussed 'the nature of things and their causes' with Frederick.[141] Baldwin III 'easily surpassed all the other princes of the realm in liveliness of mind and flourishing speech', and sought relaxation from public affairs by 'eagerly imbibing readings (*lectiones*). In particular, he enjoyed listening to histories, and diligently explored the deeds and *mores* of ancient kings and of the greatest of the princes; he was refreshed by the tales of, above all, literate men, but also by those of prudent laymen.'[142] It was perhaps in this context that many of the texts discussed in previous chapters reached the ears of rulers: not through active reading, but through interlocutors who expounded the moral principles on which the royal office rested and who recounted exemplary deeds. Literary culture was to some extent performative, enacted and played out before an elite audience.

These efforts met practical needs. As William of Malmesbury had claimed of Henry I of England, it was because of his reading history that the king learned

---

[135] Elke Ukena-Best, 'Die Lyrik Kaiser Heinrichs VI. und König Konrads (Konradin)', in *Dichtung und Musik der Stauferzeit*, ed. Volker Gallé (Worms, 2011), 147–73.

[136] *Die Urkunden Friedrichs I.*, ed. Heinrich Appelt, MGH Diplomata (Hanover, 1975–90), no. 534; Freed, *Frederick Barbarossa*, xxiii.

[137] Peter Classen, *Burgundio von Pisa: Richter, Gesandter, Übersetzer* (Heidelberg, 1974), 28–9, 77. See also Florian Hartmann, 'Wie sag ich's dem Kaiser? Friedrich Barbarossa als fiktiver Kommunikationspartner in der italienischen Rhetoriklehre', in *Friedrich Barbarossa*, no editor (Göppingen, 2017), 32–47.

[138] Nikolaus Martin Häring, 'The Liber de homoysion et homoeysion by Hugh of Honau', *Archives d'histoire doctrinale et littéraire du Moyen Âge* 34 (1967), 129–253, at 131–2. See also generally: Peter Ganz, 'Friedrich Barbarossa: Hof und Kultur', in *Friedrich Barbarossa*, ed. Haverkamp, 623–50, especially at 637–9.

[139] Ganz, 'Friedrich Barbarossa', 638.

[140] Henry Bainton, 'Literate sociability and historical writing in later twelfth-century England', *ANS* 34 (2011), 23–40.

[141] Némésius d'Émèse, *De natura hominis. Traduction de Burgundio de Pise*, ed. G. Verbeke and J. R. Moncho (Leiden, 1975), 1.

[142] William of Tyre, *Chronicon*, 714–15.

III. SUCCESSION   189

'how to ride his subjects with a lighter rein as time went on'.[143] Knowledge of the past also served to justify, guide or initiate concrete political action. When pondering whether to claim a royal title, Roger II of Sicily appointed a commission of scholars to research the ancient history of kingship in Sicily.[144] Valdemar I, when confronted with mysterious inscriptions near Blekinge, 'sent men ... to make a closer investigation of the rows of characters there, and then copy the twiggy outlines of the letters'.[145] Scholars helped illuminate the past for the benefit of ruler and realm. As experts on history, they also enabled monarchs to perform a most basic duty: to recognise, recover and restore good law. Knud VI commissioned Absalon of Lund to gather the legal customs of Knud the Great (who himself had brought together wise men to compile them),[146] St Stephen of Hungary convened scholars to collate law,[147] and at Roncaglia in 1158 Frederick Barbarossa called upon judges and lawyers to define imperial rights in Italy.[148] Yet that was possible only because the ruler sought the company of wise and prudent men, of whose expertise he could readily avail himself.

Their counsel further supported the monarch in his role as keeper and protector of the faith. While rulers did not usually engage in settling theological disputes, they certainly were called upon to resolve others, especially when the matter at hand touched upon royal privileges or the king's prerogatives. In the 1160s, the monks of Battle Abbey, a community originally endowed by William the Conqueror, disputed the rights of the bishop of Chichester to exercise oversight of them. Partly because it involved a royal charter, the case was ultimately decided by the king himself.[149] In 1167 Pope Alexander III requested that Louis VII of France help resolve a clash between the canons and the archbishop of Reims.[150] This religious dimension called for familiarity with basic principles of theology and doctrine. As Peter of Blois had explained, kings could only abide by divine law if they knew what it was. Therefore, they had to be made aware of how it applied to the art of governance. Hence Oliba of Vic advising his king on marriage laws and auguries, Burgundino of Pisa discussing 'the nature of things' with Frederick

---

[143] William of Malmesbury, *Gesta Regum*, v.390, pp. 710–11.
[144] Alexander of Telese, *Ystoria Rogerii*, 23.
[145] Saxo Grammaticus, *Gesta Danorum*, preface 2.5, pp. 12–13. For context: Kjaer, 'Runes, knives and Vikings'.
[146] Sven Aggesen, *Lex Castrensis*, in *Scriptores Minores*, ed. Gertz, vol. 1, 64.
[147] *Legenda maior*, in *Scriptores Rerum Hungaricarum*, ed. Szentpétery, vol. 2, 384; Sven Aggesen, *Lex Castrensis*, in *Scriptores Minores*, ed. Gertz, vol. 1, 66–7.
[148] Görich, *Friedrich Barbarosssa*, 307–9.
[149] Nicholas Vincent, 'King Henry II and the monks of Battle: the Battle Chronicle unmasked', in *Belief and Culture in the Middle Ages. Essays in Honour of Henry Mayr-Harting*, ed. Richard Gameson and Henrietta Leyser (Oxford, 2001), 264–86.
[150] *Alexandri III epistolae et privilegia*, PL 200 (Paris, 1855), no. 470. I am grateful to Emily Wood for this reference.

190   6. DESIGNATING AN HEIR

Barbarossa[151] or the emperor writing to the abbot of Tegernsee, requesting that, as he had a talented scribe in his community, a missal and a volume of 'letters and gospels according to the order of clerics' be produced for his perusal.[152] Knowledge of literature was essential for just and righteous government, but it was dependent on and required a court that attracted wise and learned men.

The expectation reflects a widely held assumption that erudition signalled and served to disseminate moral knowledge.[153] The premise was central to Peter of Blois' advice, which formed itself part of a venerable tradition of letters in which clerics demonstrated their grasp of epistolary style, classical literature, the Bible and current theology, all employed in exhorting royal audiences to strive even harder in their pursuit of moral excellence.[154] Learning provided the tools with which such truths could be uncovered. The court of David I of Scotland (r. 1124–1153) was famed for its purity and learning. It was because of the time he had spent in David's service that St Ailred of Rievaulx 'acquired from the best of leaders the royal virtues which later he was to describe in writing for the consolation of the faithful'.[155] Similar connotations surrounded courtly conduct.[156] Outward appearance denoted inner virtue. Key aspects of *curialitas* included *mansuetudo* and equanimity of mind. Both were rooted in biblical precept and the writings of Cicero and Seneca. *Mansuetudo* most commonly relates to a demonstrative refusal to display one's rank in interacting with those of lesser status. For royal accessibility to function, it was essential that the people know that they could lay their grievances before the king without fear. When, in 1024, the future emperor Conrad II halted his coronation procession to do justice to a widow, an orphan and an exile, he practised *mansuetudo*.[157] So did Boleslaw I of Poland when he 'did not stir from the spot' until he had finished listening to the complaints of peasants, widows and orphans,[158] or Henry I of England, who allowed himself to be

---

[151] Classen, *Burgundio von Pisa*, 77.

[152] *Die Tegernseer Briefsammlung des 12. Jahrhunderts*, ed. Helmut Plechl and Werner Bergmann, MGH Epistolae (Hanover, 2002), no. 164.

[153] See, fundamentally, C. Stephen Jaeger, *The Envy of Angels. Cathedral Schools and Social Ideals in Europe, 950-1200* (Philadelphia, PA, 1994).

[154] Weiler, 'Clerical *admonitio*'.

[155] Walter Daniel, *The Life of Ailred of Rievaulx*, ed. and transl. F. M. Powicke (London, 1950), 3. See also F. M. Powicke, 'The dispensator of King David I of Scotland', *Scottish Historical Review* 23 (1925), 34–40.

[156] Foundational: Jaeger, *Origins of Courtliness*; Josef Fleckenstein, ed., *Curialitas. Studien zu Grundfragen der höfisch-ritterlichen Kultur* (Göttingen, 1991). See, though, Weiler, 'Royal virtue', and Rüdiger Schnell, '"Curialitas" und "dissimulatio" im Mittelalter: zur Independenz von Hofkritik und Hofideal', *Zeitschrift für Literaturwissenschaft und Linguistik* 41 (2011), 77–138.

[157] Wipo, *Gesta Chuonradi*, 26; *Deeds of Conrad II*, 70. See also, below, Chapter 4.

[158] *Gesta Principum Polonorum*, i.9, pp. 48–9.

III. SUCCESSION   191

thronged by petitioners seeking redress.[159] Haughty and arrogant kings did
not make for just rulers. Equanimity of mind, by contrast, denoted that
a monarch was guided by reason, not fear, anger, hatred or lust. Enmity and
greed held no sway over him. Serene demeanour and the absence of airs
signalled that he had taken the moral framework of kingship to heart.

Courtliness also greased the wheels of elite conduct. Knowing how to behave
in the presence of great and mighty subjects, treating them with the respect
they felt they deserved and not allowing gestures or miens to betray actual
thought or feeling were essential when forging alliances, settling disputes,
gaining agreement and enforcing concord (unless their display was used
precisely because it was so unusual).[160] William of Malmesbury painted
a clear contrast between Earl Robert of Gloucester on the one hand, and, on
the other, King Stephen and Matilda. Where Stephen was polite but untrustworthy, prone to succumb to exultation and despair, deceitful and fickle, and
where Matilda was haughty and disdainful, Robert displayed a truly regal
demeanour that implicitly established him as more deserving of the throne
than either his cousin or his sister.[161] Stephen's fickleness and Matilda's
arrogance carried with them real political costs. His untrustworthiness
deprived the king of the backing he needed fully to establish his claim. Any
support he did obtain was as unreliable as his own promises. Matilda squandered her best chance to occupy the throne when she so alienated the citizens
of London with her haughty attitude that they drove her from the city.
Through their brutish and uncourtly behaviour, both king and empress
revealed an inner disposition that made them unfit to rule.

Curialitas could not be practised without training in literature. Celebrating
ease of manners and not allowing status or fortune to deflect from pursuing
what was right drew on both classical Roman and patristic precedent. They
were prominent themes in Cicero's writings on friendship and on duties and
Gregory the Great's *Pastoral Care*.[162] *Curialitas* was further embedded in

---

[159] Walter Map, *De Nugis Curialium*, v.6, pp. 470–3.
[160] See, for instance, Gerd Althoff, 'Empörung, Tränen, Zerknirschung. "Emotionen" in der
öffentlichen Kommunikation des Mittelalters', *FmSt* 30 (1996), 60–79; Althoff, 'Der
König weint: rituelle Tränen in öffentlicher Kommunikation', in '*Aufführung*' und
'*Schrift*' in *Mittelalter und früher Neuzeit*, ed. Jan Dirk Müller (Stuttgart, 1996),
239–52; Althoff, 'Tränen und Freude: Was interessiert Mittelalter-Historiker an
Emotionen?', *FmSt* 40 (2016), 1–11. Equally important was the role of wit and irony:
Katrin Beyer, *Witz und Ironie in der politischen Kultur Englands im Hochmittelalter*
(Würzburg, 2012).
[161] Björn Weiler, 'Kingship, usurpation and propaganda in twelfth-century Europe', *Anglo-
Norman Studies* 23 (2001), 299–326.
[162] Winterbottom, 'The transmission of Cicero's De Officiis'; J. G. F. Powell, 'The manuscripts and text of Cicero's Laelius de Amicitia', *Classical Quarterly* 49 (1998), 506–18, at
507; Richard W. Clement, 'A handlist'. See also: Jaeger, *Envy of Angels*, 193–5, 279–80;
Sita Steckel, *Kulturen des Lehrens im Früh- und Hochmittelalter: Autorität,*

192   6. DESIGNATING AN HEIR

a demonstrative display of erudition. Learning conveyed both refinement and
moral rectitude. Peter of Blois' advice to Henry II provides a case in point.
Henry and his court were expected to know about the basics of Roman history,
the legal reforms of Justinian, the fortunes of Alexander's world empire and the
trajectory of Israelite history. The latter included reference even to characters
as obscure as Jeroboam (who was otherwise rarely mentioned except in biblical
commentaries).[163] A less extensive but still impressive range of references
featured in letters sent by Oliba of Vic to the king of Navarre and by Bern of
Reichenau to successive emperors. In a like vein, works of history commissioned by or aimed at a royal audience often put on display the refined Latinity
of their authors. William of Malmesbury, Godfrey of Viterbo and Vincent
Kadlubek composed narratives that defied easy reading. They demanded
contemplation, meditation and extrapolation, and had been composed
respectively for Queen Matilda of England, Emperor Henry VI and the Piast
duke of Kraków. Royal recipients were expected to appreciate complex and
difficult texts, thereby demonstrating their erudition, refinement and good
character. That the rhetorical fireworks on display seem likely to have exceeded
the literary skills of their nominal recipients mattered less than the expectation
that the latter would recognise (and reward) the accomplishment evident in
the former.

A literary education was about more than just being able to read.[164] It
provided its recipients with an essential set of tools without which they
would not be able to govern, and therefore constituted a central part of the
education that kings could bestow upon their chosen heirs. When Emperor
Henry II spent time at Hildesheim and Louis VI of France at St Denis, it not
only testified to the piety and devotion of their fathers, but also constituted an
attempt to ready their sons for assuming the reins of power. Their exposure to
books gave them access to the basic knowledge they needed to divine God's
will. It aided them in choosing wise and prudent counsellors, in drawing
fruitful lessons from their erudition and in interacting in a refined and elegant
manner with their subjects. Yet learning was to provide prospective rulers with

---

Wissenkonzepte und Netzwerke von Gelehrten (Cologne, Weimar and Vienna, 2010),
171–81.

[163] Weiler, 'Whatever happened to Jeroboam? Narratives of kingship and the Bible'
(forthcoming).

[164] Before the thirteenth century, it was also unlikely to have extended to actual writing,
partly perhaps because that was too menial a task. See, for instance: Hartmut Hoffmann,
'Eigendiktat in den Urkunden Ottos III. und Heinrichs II.', *DA* 33 (1988), 390–423;
Walter Koch, 'Zusammenarbeit bei der Ausfertigung der Urkunden in der Kanzlei
staufischer Herrscher', in *La collaboration dans la production de l'écrit médiéval*, ed.
Herrad Spilling (Paris, 2003), 411–18; Nicholas Vincent, 'The personal role of the kings
of England in the production of royal letters and charters (to 1330)', in *Manu propria.
Vom eigenhändigen Schreiben der Mächtigen (13.–15. Jahrhundert)*, ed. Claudia Feller
and Christian Lackner (Vienna, 2016), 171–84.

III. SUCCESSION 193

a basic grasp rather than in-depth knowledge. When Peter of Blois described himself as having instructed the future king of Sicily in 'the *basic* arts of versification and literature' (emphasis mine),[165] he probably gave a fairly accurate impression of what a royal education entailed. Even so, there was a lot to take in. Kings had to know enough to be able to grasp the complexity of historical precedent, and to understand the principles underpinning legal custom and the doctrines of the faith. All this they had to know sufficiently well to be able to convene and preside over debates, to navigate the pitfalls of conflicting and divergent laws and resolve disputes and ecclesiastical rivalries, while also setting an example to their people in displaying serenity and equanimity of mind in just the right combination of erudition, virtue and refinement. That Frederick Barbarossa, with his notoriously weak grasp of Latin,[166] assembled so veritable a treasure at Hagenau, that he commissioned his uncle Otto of Freising, taught at Paris, to compile an account of his deeds and that he sought the company of scholars like Burgundino, may indicate just how important the expectation was that a ruler act as patron of and have some grounding in matters of literature.

Training in letters played an integral role in preparing heirs for the succession. It reinforced the sense of obligation and duty that marked them out as worthy of the throne and the moral principles they were supposed to uphold. An ability to follow and engage in learned discourse was essential for a ruler like Knud VI to realise the promise of good governance that had been so integral to his coronation. Because it equipped them with some of the technical expertise needed to rule effectively, it marked out Louis VI or Baldwin III as deserving and capable of holding authority over their people. Yet there were reasons that militated against instruction being reported in detail. Rulers should be judges and warriors, not priests. Literature existed alongside and was, in the imagination of many a clerical writer, subsidiary to the ability to wield the sword of secular justice. A literary education also established hierarchies to a far greater extent than training in warfare and hunting. Anno of Cologne, Absalon of Lund and Suger of St Denis could expect to derive far greater benefits from their role in the king's upbringing than William Marshal could ever hope to receive for instructing the king's son in riding a horse and wielding a lance.

The relative scarcity of evidence should therefore not be mistaken for evidence of absence. It does, however, underscore the extent to which conventions of writing can make it difficult to grasp fully what training a ruler entailed. The phenomenon was even more pronounced regarding the role of women. Female relatives were by no means as marginal as the surviving record implies. Occasionally, they even took full charge of an heir's education:

[165] Peter of Blois, *Opera*, vol. 1, no. 66.
[166] Freed, *Frederick Barbarossa*, 33–4.

194   6. DESIGNATING AN HEIR

Wladyslaw's wife Judith ensured that Zbigniew was sent to Gandersheim for further instruction.[167] In this, she might have followed family tradition. Her mother had overseen the education of Emperor Henry IV.[168] Moreover, wives, daughters, sisters and mothers acted as conduits through which both patterns of advice-giving and knowledge of history circulated. Otto of Bamberg was able to educate the sons of the Polish nobility only because he had travelled in Judith's entourage.[169] Women commissioned or received works of history. They often did so to maintain the memory of their husbands and relatives, as when Queens Edith and Emma of England commissioned biographies of their deceased spouses,[170] or when Roger II's sister instructed Alexander of Telese to put into writing the deeds of her brother.[171] Then marriage politics came into play. With notable exceptions, it was far more common for a wife than for a husband to move to a foreign realm. Henry I of England, for example, was married first to a Scottish princess and then to a Flemish noblewoman; Emperor Henry III to a daughter of the duke of Aquitaine; William I of Sicily to a Navarrese princess; Wladyslaw I to a German one. And so on. Many of these new arrivals requested or received accounts of a community's history.[172] Acquiring knowledge of the past was not, of course, an exclusively female concern. It was, however, one of particular relevance for many royal women, and fed, either directly or indirectly, into the education of future kings.

This interest in history and advice-giving points to the political role of queens. In most realms where anointing and crowning was practised, spouses were consecrated alongside their husbands, or at the point of marriage.[173] They shared in the sacral status of the royal office, but also in its duties and obligations. Queen consorts might not be expected to wield the sword of justice themselves, but they were certainly supposed to know how it ought to be handled.[174] That much is suggested by the ease with which queens could, at least initially, act as regents after their husband's death or in his absence. Agnes of Poitou, widow of Emperor Henry III (d. 1056) and Margarete of Navarre, widow of William I of Sicily (d. 1166) were natural guardians of their sons, and

---

[167] *Gesta Principum Polonorum*, ii.4, pp. 122–3; van Houts, 'The writing of history', at 195.
[168] Berthold of Reichenau, *Chronicon*, 181.
[169] *Ebonis Vita S. Ottonis*, 10. See also, generally, van Houts, 'The writing of history', 193–6.
[170] Van Houts, 'The writing of history', 197.
[171] Alexander of Telese, *Ystoria Rogerii*, 2.
[172] Van Houts, 'The writing of history', 197.
[173] Dale, *Inauguration and Liturgical Kingship*, 88–94.
[174] Amalie Fößel, *Die Königin im mittelalterlichen Reich* (Stuttgart, 2000), 153–221; Carsten Woll, *Die Königinnen des hochmittelalterlichen Frankreich 987–1237/8* (Stuttgart, 2002). See also the case studies compiled in Claudia Zey, ed., *Mächtige Frauen. Königinnen und Fürstinnen im europäischen Mittelalter* (Stuttgart, 2015); and the thoughtful comments by Florian Trautmann, 'Thronfolgen im Mittelalter zwischen Erbe und Wahl, zwischen Legitimität und Usurpation, zwischen Kontingenz und (konstruierter) Kontinuität', in *Die mittelalterliche Thronfolge*, ed. Becher, 449–66, at 452–4.

III. SUCCESSION 195

freely exercised the functions of the royal office on their behalf. While they faced challenges, those centred less on their qualification than on the absence of indigenous networks and family alliances with which rivals could be kept at bay.[175] For our purposes, this means that, with the possible exception of training in actual warfare, the role of mothers in the education of heirs probably reinforced, rather than being fundamentally distinct from, other parts of an heir's preparation for kingship.

The early stages of an heir's training can therefore be summed up as beginning at age five to seven. Around then, he was either given into the household of trusted secular leaders or of ecclesiastical advisors, or received training at court. Much of this instruction focussed on gaining a grounding in literature, broadly interpreted as including law, history, natural philosophy and theology. Once an heir was physically mature enough, training in warfare and hunting assumed a more prominent role. The precise weighting of one in relation the other is difficult to ascertain, largely because it depended on the preferences of an heir as much as those of his father's court. Both literary training and martial skills were, however, requirements, and both served to prepare an heir for a time when he would have to demonstrate suitability as well as descent. Literary instruction centred on appropriate moral lessons and principles, the foundations of just rule and the ability to converse in a courtly manner. Military training fostered valour and leadership, and helped an heir develop networks and alliances of his own. All this was, however, merely laying the foundations. Putative successors still had to show that they could apply basic skills and abstract principles in practice.

6.3   Knighting and Marriage

Normally on reaching their early or mid-teens, though sometimes sooner, heirs were entrusted with territories of their own, with diplomatic missions or with leading military campaigns. At times, these commissions coincided with a formal ceremony marking their coming of age, though what precise form that took varied. Knud VI was awarded lands when he married the daughter of the duke of Saxony,[176] and in Jerusalem Baldwin III marked his assumption of

---

[175] Anne Foerster, *Die Witwe des Königs. Zu Vorstellung, Anspruch und Performanz im englischen und deutschen Hochmittelalter* (Ostfildern, 2018), 94–110; Fößel, *Die Königin*, 317–71; Robinson, *Henry IV*, 27–37; Althoff, *Heinrich IV.*, 44–51; Christina Wötzel, 'Agnes von Poitou – Ehefrau Kaiser Heinrichs III., Mutter Heinrichs IV., und Kaiserin (1024–1077)', in *Kaiser Heinrich III.: Regierung, Reich und Rezeption*, ed. Jan Habermann (Gütersloh, 2018), 57–82; Annkristin Schlichte, *'Der gute König'. Wilhelm II. von Sizilien (1166–1189)* (Tübingen, 2005), 13–21; Emily Joan Ward, 'Anne of Kiev (*c*.1024–*c*.1075) and a reassessment of maternal power in the minority kingship of Philip I of France', *Historical Research* 89 (2016), 435–53.

[176] Saxo Grammaticus, *Gesta Danorum*, xiv.55.1, pp. 1420–1.

196   6. DESIGNATING AN HEIR

full regal power with the festive wearing of a crown.[177] In other kingdoms, a knighting ceremony was preferred. Grants of lands, military commissions or diplomatic initiatives often clustered around, but occasionally preceded, such festivities. Boleslaw III held the duchy of Wroclaw 'before he attained the rank of knighthood',[178] Louis VI of France led campaigns and was granted noble titles even before he was knighted in 1098,[179] Henry IV received Bavaria aged four,[180] and Henry VI was active in Namur and Hainaut before he became a knight.[181] In this way, heirs could prove their mettle and acquire the networks they needed to rule. Royal knighting ceremonies therefore rarely involved only the king's chosen heir. When Roger II of Sicily dubbed his two eldest sons in 1135, he awarded the belt of knighthood to another forty young men,[182] and when Wladyslaw made Boleslaw a knight, he also 'gave arms to many of his young companions'.[183] Heirs forged their skills alongside their future companions and prospective counsellors.

That sons acted under parental guidance provided an opportunity for fathers to intervene, should their progeny misstep. King Sverrir of Norway was especially prone to berating his eldest son, Sigurd. On one occasion, Sigurd had allowed himself to be surprised by hostile forces. As punishment, he was demoted to serving alone as sentry for the king's army.[184] On another, he had sought refuge in a church to hide from battle and was publicly chided by his father.[185] Sverrir's stern demeanour might have been unusual, but what mattered was that transgressions could be pointed out and remedied under a father's watchful eye.[186] Successors were eased into the practice of ruling.

---

[177] William of Tyre, *Chronicon*, 777–8.
[178] *Gesta Principum Polonorum*, ii.13, pp. 138–9. See the parallel case of Louis the Fat of France, as described by Abbot Suger of St Denis: Suger, *Vie de Louis VI*, 14–42, 68–80.
[179] Orderic Vitalis, *Ecclesiastical History*, vol. 4, 264–5; Augustin Fliche, *Le règne de Philippe 1er, roi de France (1060–1108)* (Paris, 1912), 78–86.
[180] *Annales Altahenses Maiores*, ed. Wilhelm Giesebrecht and Emund Oefele, MGH SS sep. ed., 2nd edition (Hanover and Leipzig, 1890), 49.
[181] *Chronica Regia Coloniensis*, 323.
[182] Alexander of Telese, *Ystoria Rogerii*, 84.
[183] *Gesta Principum Polonorum*, ii.18, pp. 152–3.
[184] *Saga of King Sverri*, chapter 130, pp. 160–1.
[185] *Saga of King Sverri*, chapter 164, pp. 212–13.
[186] Lyon, 'Fathers and sons'. It also provided an opportunity to deflect blame. See, for instance, Saxo Grammaticus, *Gesta Danorum*, xv.1.2, pp. 1446–7: 'Valdemar, meeting his troops at Flaster . . . told them that it was not his plan to challenge the enemy's large forces with such a paltry band, seeing that on a military venture a king must inevitably win either maximum renown or maximum disgrace. For this reason he preferred to entrust supreme command of the expedition to Absalon and his own son, Cnut, who would return with a modicum of praise if they handled the affair successfully, but with only a small share of blame if things went badly.' Also, ibid., xv.6.2, pp. 1486–7: 'because [Valdemar] thought it would be difficult to attack a castle, he preferred that the assault be conducted under someone else's leadership rather than his own, in case his efforts did

III. SUCCESSION   197

Ideally, they learned how to negotiate the intricacies and pitfalls of regnal politics, and how to pursue gain without alienating their people. Nonetheless, their fathers' oversight provided a check, a means to revise and an authority to which to appeal. This period of quasi-apprenticeship furthermore offered a ruler's subjects the chance to assess an heir's suitability. Hence perhaps the conditions put forth by the German princes when electing Henry IV in 1053: their loyalty was contingent on the young boy turning out to be a just king.[187] Hence also the decision of the Danish nobles not to elect Erik I's son Harald as king. While acting as his father's regent, Harald

> had earned himself the people's supreme loathing . . . His superintendence had turned to malicious ill-treatment . . . The result of this was that all hated his vile tyranny and had not the slightest intention of handing the kingdom to its despoiler; it would be intolerable, they believed, to repay his cruelties with indulgence, his wringing grasp with preferment.[188]

And hence perhaps also the extraordinary emphasis placed on royal justice in 1165 and 1170, when Valdemar's innovations deprived the Danes of precisely the kind of prerogative that they had until then exercised.

Formal ceremonies marked an important stage in this process,[189] and usually occurred between ages twelve and twenty.[190] They signalled a boy's entry into adulthood and his ability to perform the secular functions of rulership. Many had already proven their mettle, and knighting marked not so much their coming of age, as yet another stage in their preparation for kingship. They received the belt of knighthood because they were ready, as Alexander of Telese phrased it, 'to exercise [their] rights as lords'.[191] The connection was made explicit by Gallus Anonymus. In 1099, Boleslaw III's elevation was interrupted when Boleslaw led an expedition against the Pomeranians, who had invaded Poland, and it was immediately followed by another against the Cumans, who were preparing to raid the duchy.[192] Not

not turn out in accordance with his wishes and the glory of so many successful enter-prises of the past was dimmed'. One remains surprised that Knud did not at some point rebel against his father.

[187] Hermann of Reichenau, *Chronicon*, 133.

[188] Saxo Grammaticus, *Gesta Danorum*, 894–5.

[189] There were, however, different types of knighting. See Max Lieberman, 'A new approach to the knighting ritual', *Speculum* 90 (2015), 391–423; Björn Weiler, 'Knighting, homage, and the meaning of ritual: the kings of England and their neighbours in the thirteenth century', *Viator* 37 (2006), 275–300; Zbigniew Dalewski, 'The knighting of Polish dukes in the early Middle Ages: ideological and political significance', *Archivum Poloniae Historiae* 80 (1999), 15–43.

[190] Henry of Huntingdon, *Historia Anglorum*, vi.37, pp. 402–3. See also the important remarks by Emily Joan Ward, 'Child kingship and notions of (im)maturity in north-western Europe, 1050–1262', *ANS* 40 (2018), 197–211.

[191] Alexander of Telese, *Ystoria Rogerii*, 8; *Roger II*, ed. Loud, 66.

[192] *Gesta Principum Polonorum*, ii.19, pp. 154–5.

198   6. DESIGNATING AN HEIR

unlike one ruler conferring a crown upon another, the ceremony merely acknowledged what was obvious already. Boleslaw was made a knight because he already acted like one.

The relationship between knighting and kingship seems to follow a similar pattern, though with regnal variations. In Germany, sons were crowned soon after they had been elected king, but were not knighted until they reached maturity.[193] In other realms, knighthood could be a precondition for kingship. In the so-called *ordo* of St Louis from *c.* 1250, dubbing the king preceded the coronation.[194] The practice was not peculiar to France. In 1125, Alfonso I of Portugal took the insignia of knighthood from the altar of the cathedral of Zamora and made himself a knight before the coronation proper was performed.[195] Similarly, in 1199, following the death of Richard the Lionheart, the mother of his nephew Arthur sought to safeguard her son's claims by having King Philipp Augustus of France dub him a knight.[196] And in 1216 the partisans of Henry III had the young boy hurriedly knighted before bringing him to Gloucester for a makeshift coronation.[197] Knighting in these instances did not, however, necessarily denote coming of age: while Arthur was thirteen, Henry III was only nine. Instead, it demonstrated readiness to perform the duties of kingship.

Knighting – or other ways of signalling that an heir had come of age – marked a qualitative shift, not least because of how it unfolded. A performative act played out before the leading men of the realm, it was frequently combined with tackling issues of major concern, in which the new knight and ruler *in spe* would henceforth be expected to engage. The dubbing of Frederick Barbarossa's son Henry VI in 1184 may serve as example. A diet had specifically been called for the occasion. It was a lavish affair. So much wine and food was transported to Mainz, one chronicler recounted, that the ships delivering provisions blocked traffic on the Rhine; the ceremonial offices of butler, marshal and chamberlain were performed only by dukes and kings; so numerous were the princes and prelates in attendance that a veritable tent city arose

---

[193] Henry VI had thus been crowned aged five in 1169 (*Chronica Regia Coloniensis*, 120; *Annales Pegavienses*, MGH SS 16 (Hanover, 1859), 260), but was not knighted until fifteen years later (Arnold of Lübeck, *Chronica Slavorum*, ed. Johann M. Lappenberg, MGH SS 21 (Hanover, 1869), 151–3; Gislebert of Mons, *Chronica*, 155–7; *Annales Marbacenses*, 54).

[194] Jacques Le Goff, Éric Palazzo, Jean-Claude Bonne and Marie-Noël Colette, eds., *Le sacre royal à l'époque de Saint Louis d'après le manuscrit Latin 1246 de la BNF* (Paris, 2001).

[195] Monica Blöcker-Walter, *Alfons I. von Portugal* (Zürich, 1966), 20–2, 151. See also José Mattoso, 'À propos du couronnement des rois portugais', in *L'espace rural au Moyen Âge, Portugal, Espagne, France (XIIe-XIVe siècle), Mélanges en l'honneur de Robert Durand*, ed. Monique Bouron and Stéphanie Boissellier (Rennes, 1999), 133–46.

[196] *Chronica Magistri Rogeri de Houdene*, ed. W. Stubbs, 4 vols. (London, 1868–71), vol. 4, 86–7.

[197] *History of William Marshal*, ll. 15287–346.

III. SUCCESSION   199

outside Mainz to house them.[198] In fact, another chronicler added, over 70,000 knights had been present,[199] while a third observed that they had come from all lands between the Balkans and Spain.[200] The highlight of the proceedings was Henry's knighting with that of his younger brother. The event also offered an opportunity for the young king to demonstrate his skills as ruler. First, a dispute had broken out between the count of Hainault and the duke of Namur. It was settled only through Henry's intervention. Then the abbot of Fulda complained that his honorific seat to the emperor's left had been taken by the archbishop of Cologne. This was no small matter. At stake was the abbot's ability to demonstrate proximity to the emperor, to solicit grants and privileges both for himself and his dependants and hence his standing within the community of the realm. Given just how illustrious an audience had assembled at Mainz, pressing home this point was important. A right not claimed was a right forfeited.[201] The metropolitan faced similar pressures. He was, after all, the leader of the German Church, the emperor's close confidant and had crowned Henry king. He therefore threatened to break up the assembly by departing early. In the end, considerable brinkmanship was required of both the emperor and his son. Neither dispute was intended to challenge imperial authority, but context and occasion demanded that count and duke, abbot and archbishop each use the opportunity to defend their status. Other matters proved less contentious. Barbarossa created a king of Sardinia[202] and envoys from the count of Flanders sought an alliance,[203] while, once the knighting had been performed, the emperor and his two sons, together with many of the princes, presented lavish gifts to prisoners, to those who had pledged to go on crusade and to male and female entertainers. The festivities concluded with tournaments in which Henry and his brother were said to have led 20,000 knights.[204]

[198] Arnold of Lübeck, *Chronicon Slavorum*, 151–2. See also, for a summary of sources: RI IV.2.4 no. 2762, in *Regesta Imperii Online*: www.regesta-imperii.de/regesten (accessed 21 May 2019). For context: Gerd Lubich, 'Das Kaiserliche, das Höfische und der Konsens auf dem Mainzer Hoffest (1184). Konstruktion, Inszenierung und Darstellung gesellschaftlichen Zusammenhalts am Ende des 12. Jahrhunderts', in *Staufisches Kaisertum im 12. Jahrhundert. Konzepte – Netzwerke – Politische Praxis*, ed. Stefan Burkhardt, Thomas Metz, Bernd Schneidmüller and Stefan Weinfurter (Regensburg, 2010), 277–93.

[199] Gislebert of Mons, *Chronique*, 157; *Annales Marbacenses*, 54.

[200] Otto of St Blasien, *Ottonis de Sancto Blasio Chronica*, ed. Adolf Hofmeister, MGH SSrG (Hanover, 1912), 37. See also *Chronica Regia Coloniensis*, 133.

[201] For the context: Hans-Werner Goetz, 'Der "rechte" Sitz: Die Symbolik von Rang und Herrschaft im hohen Mittelalter im Spiegel der Sitzordnung', in *Symbole des Alltags, Alltag der Symbole. Festschrift für Harry Kühnel zum 65. Geburtstag*, ed. Gertrud Blaschitz, Helmut Hundsbichler, Gerhard Jaritz and Elisabeth Vavra (Graz, 1992), 11–47.

[202] *Annales Aquenses*, MGH SS 24, 39.

[203] Gislebert of Mons, *Chronique*, 162.

[204] Arnold of Lübeck, *Chronica Slavorum*, 151–3; Gilbert of Mons, *Chronica*, 155–62.

200   6. DESIGNATING AN HEIR

Like Knud's coronation in 1170, events at Mainz were a celebration of might
and promised good governance for the future. Kingship was created, while the
number and rank of those attending testified to the sway that both Henry and
his father held across Christendom. The proceedings demonstrated not only
that Henry had what it took to be a warlike king, but also that he respected the
limitations within and the purpose for which power ought to be wielded. Both
were symbolically expressed by a festive crown-wearing.[205] The ceremony,
reserved for high religious feast days and especially important secular events,
made manifest the religious underpinnings of royal rule. It involved a solemn
Mass, and visualised the direct relationship between kingship and the
divine.[206] At Mainz, the connection was reinforced when the diet occurred at
Pentecost – one of the most important dates in the liturgical calendar – and by
the religious service opening the proceedings. The knighting, relegated to
the second day, was subsidiary to the moral functions of the royal office,
which the martial skills celebrated ought to aid, but not to rival. In fact, their
display was carefully circumscribed: no weapons were used in the tournaments
fought by Henry and his men,[207] echoing provisions of the Third Lateran
Council that had banned those who died during tournaments from receiving
church burial.[208] Fighting was a tool, to be employed only when needed, and
never for amusement or sport. Moreover, the knighting was followed by
carefully targeted displays of generosity. Henry and his parents gave horses,
precious garments, gold and silver to prisoners and to those who had taken the
cross (as well as to the minstrels present). The princes followed suit, not only to
honour Frederick and his son, but also to heighten their own fame.[209] Emperor
and king set an example, and encouraged others to do good as well. Equally, the
disruption caused by the duke of Namur and the abbot of Fulda presented an
opportunity as much as a challenge. The grander the festivity, the more likely it
would be utilised for precisely this kind of confrontation. Inauguration ceremonies – and, marking his entry into adulthood, Henry's knighting was a kind
of inauguration – were especially prone to such displays. How a ruler handled
disruptions should demonstrate his ability and willingness to perform the
duties of kingship, and serve to show that he possessed the mindset of someone

---

[205] Arnold of Lübeck, *Chronica Slavorum*, 151: 'Quod coronatus Heinricus in regem'. For
the terminology: Dale, *Inauguration and Liturgical Kingship*, 136–40. See also Gislebert
of Mons, *Chronique*, 156. On the practice: Hans-Walter Klewitz, 'Die Festkrönungen der
deutschen Könige', *ZSRG* 59 (*Kanonistische Abteilung* 28) (1939), 45–96; separate
reprint (Darmstadt, 1966); Carlrichard Brühl, 'Fränkischer Krönungsgebrauch und das
Problem der "Festkrönungen"', *HZ* 194 (1962), 265–326; Brühl, 'Kronen- und
Krönungsgebrauch im frühen und hohen Mittelalter', *HZ* 234 (1982), 1–31.

[206] See also below, Chapter 9.

[207] Gislebert of Mons, *Chronique*, 157.

[208] *Decrees of the Ecumenical Councils*, ed. and transl. Norman P. Tanner, 2 vols. (London
and Washington, DC,1990), vol. 1, 200.

[209] Gislebert of Mons, *Chronique*, 156–7.

III. SUCCESSION   201

who would not allow anger, fear or favour to shape the exercise of his duties.[210]
In Mainz, Henry, assisted by his father, passed the test with ease.

The proceedings set the scene for the next few months. Four weeks later,
Henry attended a meeting with the count of Flanders at Gelnhausen,[211]
shortly after a truce between the count and the king of France had been
agreed. By the end of July, he was at Erfurt, where he negotiated with envoys
from the duke of Poland[212] and settled a dispute between the archbishop of
Mainz and the landgrave of Thuringia.[213] In other words, Henry distinguished himself 'in sending and receiving embassies, in calling up and
levying an army and in the manifold affairs of [the] … realm'.[214] Henry's
coming of age did not materially change his duties – he had fought wars and
been engaged in diplomatic missions before – but it still marked a shift. At
Erfurt, he acted as his own agent, unsupervised by his father. Such autonomy
was important, and seems to have been associated with formally coming of
age. Hence, Louis VI received the territory of the Vexin on occasion of his
knighting, and Wladyslaw divided up lands between his sons just as they were
about to be made knights. The practice also puts into perspective the revolt of
Henry the Young King in England in 1173. A draft letter, written by
a member of his entourage, gives some indication of the reasoning behind
the uprising. Henry was not allowed to hear cases in court or select his own
counsellors, and had members of his household appointed and dismissed at
his father's whim. Aged eighteen, and crowned king three years earlier, he
had not yet been declared of age. He was prevented from developing
a following of his own, from demonstrating both his right and his capacity
to rule. Demonstratively, therefore, at the outset of his rebellion Henry had
himself made a knight.[215] Autonomy was important because it allowed
a putative heir to exercise patronage, do justice, administer lands, reward
friends and followers and so much else that was required for his claim to be
realised. But for that to happen, a formal recognition of the transition from
adolescence to manhood was needed.

The act also prepared an heir for the next stage on his path to kingship:
marriage. In October 1184, Henry VI attended a diet at Augsburg, where his
betrothal to Constance, the aunt of the king of Sicily, was announced.[216] We do
not know when negotiations for the union had begun, but it is conceivable that
they had been underway by, or had been embarked upon just after, the Mainz

---

[210] See also below, Chapter 10.
[211] RI IV.3, no. 2f. Accessed 24 May 2019.
[212] *Annales Aquenses*, 38; *Chronica S. Petri Erfordensis moderna*, 193.
[213] *Chronica Reinhardsbrunnensis*, MGH SS 30 (Hanover and Leipzig, 1896), 542.
[214] *Gesta Principum Polonorum*, ii.8, pp. 132–5.
[215] *Le recueil des historiens des Gaules et de la France* 16 (Paris, 1814), 643–8.
[216] *Annales Marbacenses*, 55; Otto of St Blasien, *Chronica*, 39; *Annales Augustani*, 9.

202   6. DESIGNATING AN HEIR

diet.[217] By the thirteenth century, an expectation had developed that male spouses were to have been knighted before they could be married. In 1251, Alexander III was knighted on the eve of his wedding,[218] and the future Edward I was in 1254, prior to his marriage to Eleanor of Castile.[219] In the eleventh and twelfth centuries, matters had been more fluid, though the expectation remained that both partners had reached adulthood by the time they married. Knud VI, for example, had been betrothed while still an infant. When his first wife died in childhood, another union was arranged.[220] His new fiancée stayed at the Danish court for several years before the wedding,[221] but the ceremony did not take place until 1177, when Knud turned fourteen.[222] Marriage required that both partners were old enough to consent.[223] Even more clearly than knighting, it signified that an heir had come of age.

Ideally, the choice of spouse reinforced the moral dimension of kingship. Queens were supposed to be exemplars of regal virtues themselves – not least perhaps because of their pivotal role in passing these on to the next generation. Elvira, the wife of Roger II, was 'distinguished by the grace of religion and the generosity of almsgiving'.[224] Ingeborg, sister of Knud VI and unhappily married to Philipp Augustus of France, was 'beautiful, a holy maiden, and adorned by virtue', as well as a solace to her people.[225] Boleslaw III's mother Judith had 'always performed acts of charity towards the poor and those in captivity', and redeemed many Christians sold as slaves.[226] So far, so formulaic. Occasionally, a more complex image emerges. Wipo's account of Gisela, married to Emperor Conrad II, is unusual in its relative detail. 'Held in esteem above all these

[217] Heinz Wolter, 'Die Verlobung Heinrichs VI. mit Konstanze von Sizilien im Jahre 1184', *Historisches Jahrbuch* 105 (1985), 30–51.

[218] Matthew Paris, *Chronica Majora*, vol. 5, 267–8.

[219] *Annals of Burton*, in *Annales Monastici*, ed. H. R. Luard, 5 vols. (London, 1864–9), vol. 1, 193–500, at 323; Matthew Paris, *Chronica Majora*, vol. 5, 449–50; *Diplomatic Documents Preserved in the Public Record Office 1101–1272*, ed. Pierre Chaplais (London, 1964), nos. 271, 273; Jofré de Loaysa, *Crónica de los Reyes de Castilla Fernando III, Alfonso X, Sancho IV y Fernando IV (1248–1305)*, ed. and transl. Antono García Martinez (Murcia, 1982), 82–3.

[220] Saxo Grammaticus, *Gesta Danorum*, xiv.30.1, pp. 1228–9; xiv.37.4, pp. 1264–5. Joachim Ehlers, *Heinrich der Löwe. Eine Biographie* (Munich, 2008), 184.

[221] Saxo Grammaticus, *Gesta Danorum*, xiv.54.13, pp. 1402–3.

[222] Saxo Grammaticus, *Gesta Danorum*, xiv.55.1, pp. 1420–1. Henry I of England's daughter Matilda was eight when betrothed to Emperor Henry V and sent to Germany, with the wedding conducted when she turned twelve: Elisabeth van Houts, *Married Life in the Middle Ages, 900–1300* (Oxford, 2019), 68–70, 89–90.

[223] Van Houts, *Married Life*, 234–9.

[224] Alexander of Telese, *Ystoria Rogerii*, 59; *Roger II*, ed. Loud, 104. See, generally, Jörg Rogge, 'Mächtige Frauen? Königinnen und Fürstinnen im europäischen Mittelalter (11.–14. Jhdt.)', in *Mächtige Frauen*, ed. Zey, 437–57.

[225] Rigord, *Gesta*, 320–1, 362–3.

[226] *Gesta Principum Polonorum*, ii.1, pp. 116–17.

III. SUCCESSION 203

[Conrad's officials] because of her prudence and counsel', she was of noble stock – a descendant of Charlemagne's, no less. Moreover, while

> characterized by such great nobility and a most becoming appearance, she was marked by no arrogant pride; fearful in the service of God, assiduous in prayers and almsgiving . . . She was liberal of character; distinguished by ingenuity; avid of glory, but not of praise; loving of modesty; patient of womanly labour; not at all extravagant in useless matters, but abundantly generous in the honourable and useful; rich in estates; qualified through experience to administer well the highest dignities.

She was Conrad's 'necessary companion'.[227] Queens, by providing succour to the poor and powerless, by being patrons of the Church and an example of virtue to others, performed essential functions of kingship. In Gisela's case, many of her qualities reflected both biblical precepts of how rulers should act and the demeanour that Cicero and Seneca had sketched as necessary if one were to wield power over others. Good wives strengthened their husbands' claim to suitability.

Wipo praised Gisela for her ingenuity and experience, which enabled her to direct unspecified higher matters. She was well equipped to offer advice and counsel, and to be the king's necessary companion. Yet he also remains curiously reticent about what that may have involved in practice. The only episode where Gisela played an active part occurred during the rebellion of Ernst, her son from a previous marriage. Forced to choose between love for her son and love for her husband, she sided with Conrad.[228] And Wipo was quite exhaustive when it came to describing the role of the queen. Sometimes a more active role can be surmised. It seems, for instance, that Gertrude – Knud VI's fiancée – was from the outset part of Valdemar's inner circle. During a feast she noticed that one of the retainers was acting in a suspicious manner, and alerted Valdemar to what turned out to be a plot to kill the king.[229] An especially rich example survives in the *Gesta Stephani*, an anonymous account of the reign of Stephen of Blois in England, produced in two stages *c*. 1140–54. In 1141, Stephen had been captured at the Battle of Lincoln, and had been imprisoned by the partisans of his rival Matilda. The *Gesta* narrated subsequent events so as to establish a careful contrast between Stephen's seemingly successful rival, and his queen, also called Matilda. The account reveals just how far much royal

---

[227] Wipo, *Gesta Chuonradi*, 24–6; *Deeds of Conrad II*, 69. Generally: Kurt-Ulrich Jäschke, '"Tamen virilis probitas in femina vicit": Ein hochmittelalterlicher Hofkapellan und die Herrscherinnen – Wipos Äußerungen über Kaiserinnen und Königinnen seiner Zeit', in *Ex ipsis rerum documentis. Beiträge zur Mediävistik. Festschrift für Harald Zimmermann zum 65. Geburtstag*, ed. Klaus Herbers, Hans Henning Kortüm and Carlo Servatius (Sigmaringen, 1991), 429–48.
[228] Wipo, *Gesta Chuonradi*, 43–4; *Deeds of Conrad II*, 85.
[229] Saxo Grammaticus, *Gesta Danorum*, xiv.54.13, pp. 1402–3.

204   6. DESIGNATING AN HEIR

women were expected to operate within the same moral framework as their male relatives.

Pointedly, the author refused to call either woman by her name. Henry I's daughter was simply 'the countess' (she was married to the count of Anjou), and Stephen's wife 'the queen' (to minimise confusion, I will follow his example). Rank denoted moral suitability. The countess simply was not fit to be queen. Her support was hollow and morally suspect. Many of Stephen's partisans had gone over to her side only reluctantly and because they feared that the king's fortunes could not be revived. The countess' backers, on the other hand, included 'effeminate men [*viri molles*], whose endowment lay rather in wanton delights than in resolution of mind'.[230] I will return to the importance of morally upright supporters in the next chapter. Being supported by wanton and greedy men was a sure sign that a claimant lacked the morals required to perform the duties of kingship. Second, she behaved in a greedy and arrogant fashion:

> she at once put on an extremely arrogant demeanour instead of the modest gait and bearing proper of the gentle sex, began to walk and speak and do all things more stiffly and more haughtily than she had been wont, to such a point that soon, in the capital of the land subject to her, she actually made herself queen of all England and gloried in being so called.

Unlike good rulers, the countess did not practise *mansuetudo* – she certainly did not cast aside the loftiness of her rank. Instead, she delighted in becoming ever more inaccessible. Neither did her pretensions match the reality of her position: she was reluctantly called 'queen of all England', when, in fact, she only ruled London. Like Vortigern and other tyrants, she usurped a title of which she was evidently unworthy.[231]

Other episodes further highlighted the countess' lack of suitability. When she met Bishop Henry of Winchester, who reluctantly accepted her claim, he also handed over 'the royal crown, which she always most eagerly desired'.[232] Good rulers, we may recall, did not seek the royal title, but had it thrust upon them. Worse was yet to come: 'Then she, on being raised with such splendour and distinction to this pre-eminent position, began to be arbitrary in all that she did.' Erstwhile followers of Stephen saw their royal grants revoked. Through 'reckless innovation' they were deprived of their possessions and inheritance. Others, 'she drove from her presence in fury after insulting and threatening them'. Not that the countess' partisans fared any better: she treated them rudely, 'rebuffing them by an arrogant answer and refusing to hearken their words . . . she no longer relied on their advice, as she should have done,

---

[230] *Gesta Stephani*, 118–19.
[231] See also Weiler, 'Rex renitens', for further examples.
[232] *Gesta Stephani*, 118–19.

III. SUCCESSION   205

but arranged everything as she herself saw fit and according to her own arbitrary will'.[233] The Londoners had an especially unpleasant experience. They had initially invited her, 'and when the citizens thought they had attained to joyous days of peace and quietness and that the calamities of the kingdom had taken a turn for the better, they found themselves confronted with demands for exorbitant demands of money'. When asking for leniency, the countess 'blazed into unbearable fury'.[234] Finally, when the queen requested mercy for her husband, 'she was abused in harsh and insulting language'.[235] In the end, the Londoners put an end to the countess' pretensions. When she called a large and festive assembly, expecting to gain their backing in claiming the throne, the citizens rebelled, and the countess took flight. Her bid for the throne had failed.

The *Gesta*'s account paints a mirror image of how William of Malmesbury had portrayed Stephen's treatment of Matilda's partisans: he was haughty, humiliated them in public and made promises he had no intention of keeping.[236] The *Gesta*'s highly gendered language notwithstanding, the countess failed not because she was a woman, but because she failed to act like a king. She strove for the wrong kind of masculinity. Instead of being gentle and kind, she became erratic and rude. She treated even her own followers with haughty disdain. Far from heeding the advice of wise and prudent men, she followed her own inadequate counsel and surrounded herself with scoundrels and brigands. Instead of maintaining the law and enforcing justice, she employed arbitrary means to enrich herself and her followers. Few things were more frowned upon than claimants who acted as if the realm were theirs to do with as they wished.[237] New rulers were also supposed to be forgiving to erstwhile rivals and opponents. At least, they were meant to listen patiently to petitions from their people, not shout at them in blazing fury. The queen's treatment was truly unbecoming of a righteous ruler. She had, in fact, asked for very little: that her husband be released from 'his filthy dungeon' – an especially humiliating treatment – and that Eustace, their son, be allowed to inherit the lands that she had brought into their marriage. By refusing this request, the countess was threatening to deprive Eustace of his inheritance, and the queen of her dowry. That, with Stephen in captivity, Eustace was a quasi-orphan and the queen a quasi-widow hardly needed spelling out. The countess did not deserve to wear the crown.[238]

The *Gesta* had much less to say about the queen, but the contrast between the two women was all the more powerful for it. Unlike the countess, she adopted

---

[233] *Gesta Stephani*, 120–1.
[234] *Gesta Stephani*, 120–3.
[235] *Gesta Stephani*, 122–3.
[236] See below, Chapter 10.
[237] See Chapters 7–10.
[238] Even William of Malmesbury was aghast at this decision, and viewed it as the root of the misfortunes that subsequently befell the empress' cause: *Historia Novella*, 98–100.

206   6. DESIGNATING AN HEIR

the right kind of masculinity. The queen was 'a woman of subtlety (*astuti pectoris*) and a man's resolution'. After the countess had denied her request, she 'brought a magnificent body of troops' to lay waste to the surroundings of London. With the countess unwilling to aid the Londoners, they formed an alliance with the queen instead.[239] On entering the capital, the queen 'forgetting the weakness of her sex and a woman's softness ... bore herself in a virile and virtuous fashion;[240] everywhere by prayer or price she won over invincible allies'. She urged the king's men to join her, and she 'humbly besought the Bishop of Winchester', imploring him 'with great earnestness' to set free her husband. Thus, the prelate 'might gain her a husband, the people a king, and the kingdom a champion'.[241] Unlike the countess, the queen recognised the importance of consent, of appealing to what was right and of casting aside the haughtiness of rank. Stephen would reign not for private gain, but to be a king to his people and a champion to the realm. Unlike the countess, he would place the common good above private gain. The countess had drawn to her side men who were either reluctant in their loyalty or lustful and depraved, and she dismissed from her presence wise, virtuous, and prudent counsellors. The queen, by contrast, listened to 'men of war and inferior to none in military matters or any good quality'. She also proved herself a capable commander. She had led the skirmishes that had brought the Londoners to heel, and managed to assemble over a thousand men to confront the countess and her allies in a decisive battle at Winchester.[242] There, the countess' brother was captured. He was eventually exchanged for Stephen, and the countess withdrew to her estates in Anjou.

Once her husband regained the throne, the *Gesta* made no more mention of the queen. Still, for a decisive moment, we can see her forge alliances, put pressure on the undecided and prepare for war. She emerges as a political and military leader (and one more capable than her spouse). Unlike the countess, she adhered to the moral framework of rulership. She took wise and prudent counsel, acted for the common good, and did not allow sorrow or rage to cloud her judgement. These normative expectations existed independently of gender. The queen succeeded because she acted like a capable ruler. The countess failed because she lacked the character and inner disposition required to wear the crown. Or at least that was how the author of the *Gesta* saw it.[243] This is not to say that gender-specific expectations did not exist, but rather that they

---

[239] *Gesta Stephani*, 122–4.

[240] I have revised Potter's translation of *viriliter sese et virtuose continere* as 'with the valour of a man'. The Latin conveys a rather more nuanced image.

[241] *Gesta Stephani*, 126–7.

[242] *Gesta Stephani*, 128–31.

[243] It was a view shared by William of Malmesbury, who also established a contrast between Matilda's haughtiness, and Robert of Gloucester's exemplary, noble and serene demeanour, his love of justice, martial prowess, piety and ease of manners: William of Malmesbury, *Historia Novella*, 70–9, 83–7, 97–109.

III. SUCCESSION 207

amplified essential royal virtues. By looking after the sick and incarcerated, the enslaved and impoverished, queens defended those who could not defend themselves. When they acted as counsellors and deputies, as representatives of royal power, they were also expected to uphold the right order of the realm, to ensure that justice was done, that equity prevailed and that prudent advice was given. The choice of spouse reflected, and ideally reinforced, a king's suitability to rule.[244]

A successful union heralded a continuation of the royal line. It also offered opportunities to strengthen and expand networks.[245] Marrying heiresses or female relatives of erstwhile rivals could be an act of peacemaking, as when Valdemar I took as his wife the half-sister of one of his opponents.[246] We have also seen that rulers often favoured foreign brides. Such alliances might have entailed an expectation of future backing. When Stephen of Blois pursued the coronation of his son Eustace, he also negotiated for him a marriage with a Capetian princess.[247] Wladyslaw of Poland assured himself of the backing of his imperial in-laws before campaigning in Pomerania.[248] Other matches established parity, as in those between the ruling families of the eastern and western empires,[249] or between branches of the Polish Piasts and the rulers of Kievan Rus.[250] Securing a spouse from distant lands suggested that a regnal community was part of a wider family of Christian nations. It was thus evidence of Valdemar II's success, that, while his father and brother had married German princesses, he took wives from Bohemia and Portugal, and married off a daughter to the king of France.[251] In the thirteenth century, Sturla Thordarsson even invented an extensive bridal

---

[244] Surprisingly little work has been done on how the trope of the bad queen relates to the normative foundations of kingship. See, in the meantime, Ármann Jakobsson, 'Queens of Terror: Perilous women in Hálfs saga and Hrólfs saga kraka', in *Fornaldarsagornas struktur och ideologi*, ed. Ármann Jakobsson, Annette Lassen and Agnata Ney (Uppsala, 2003), 173–89; Philippe Buc, 'Italian hussies and German matrons: Liudprand of Cremona on dynastic legitimacy', *FmSt* 29 (1995), 207–25.

[245] See, generally: Martin Aurell, ed., *Les stratégies matrimoniales: (IXe–XIIIe siècle)* (Turnhout, 2013); Tobias Weller, *Die Heiratspolitik des deutschen Hochadels im 12. Jahrhundert* (Cologne, Weimar and Vienna, 2004).

[246] Saxo Grammaticus, *Gesta Danorum*, xiv.14.2, pp. 1054–5.

[247] *Gesta Stephani*, 225–6.

[248] *Gesta Principum Polonorum*, ii.1, pp. 116–17.

[249] Görich, *Friedrich Barbarossa*, 167–8; Franz Hermann Tinnefeld, 'Byzanz und die Herrscher des Hauses Hohenstaufen', *AfD* 41 (1995), 105–28; Karl-Heinz Rueß, ed., *Die Staufer und Byzanz* (Göppingen,2013).

[250] *Gesta Principum Polonorum*, iii.23, pp. 158–9 nn. 2–3; Christian Raffensperger, *Reimagining Europe*.

[251] George Conklin, 'Ingeborg of Denmark, queen of France, 1193–1223' in *Queens and Queenship in Medieval Europe*, ed. Ann Duggan (Woodbridge 1997), 39–52. See also Colette Bowie, *The Daughters of Henry II and Eleanor of Aquitaine: A Comparative Study of Twelfth-Century Royal Women* (Turnhout, 2014).

208   6. DESIGNATING AN HEIR

quest, in which Håkon IV of Norway came to pick a Castilian princess as his spouse.[252] Foreign alliances signified that the fame of king and people had spread well beyond the confines of the realm.

Wedding festivities were a manifestation of power. Alongside knighting, crowning or the formal designation of an heir, they ranked among the most public stages in readying him for the succession. A sizable public was therefore required. Valdemar I 'summoned the foremost citizens of Denmark and Sweden to grace the royal wedding of his son'.[253] Wealth and standing were displayed. Boleslaw III – who was duke already when he married Zbyslava of Kiev in 1105, but remained lodged in a succession struggle with his brother – marked his wedding with lavish generosity:

> So for eight days before the wedding and as many after the octave of the wedding the warlike Boleslaw did not cease handing out gifts, to some pelts and cloaks lined with furs and worked with orphrey, to the magnates mantels and gold and silver vessels, to some cities and castles, to others villages and estates.[254]

When Henry VI married Constance of Sicily in January 1186, the ceremony similarly projected imperial power.[255] The nuptials took place on the eve of the feast of St Charlemagne,[256] and were followed by a festive crown-wearing. With the patriarch of Aquileia and the archbishop of Vienne acting as consecrating prelates, and with two cardinals present, Frederick Barbarossa elevated Henry VI to the rank of Caesar – an unprecedented appropriation of Roman and Byzantine models, which meant that he was raised to the status of co-emperor – and Constance was crowned queen.[257]

---

[252] Gudbrand Vigfusson, ed., *Icelandic Sagas and Other Historical Documents Relating to the Settlements and Descents of the Northmen on the British Isles*, Rolls Series (London, 1887–94), vol. 4: *The Saga of Hacon and a Fragment of the Saga of Magnus*, transl. G. W. Dasent, 302–3, 311–15. *Chronicle of Alfonso X*, transl. Shelby Thacker and José Escobar (Lexington, KY, 2002), 32–3 for a more sober account. For the context: Bruce E. Gelsinger, 'A thirteenth-century Norwegian–Castilian alliance', *Medievalia et Humanistica* NS 10 (1981), 55–80.

[253] Saxo Grammaticus, *Gesta Danorum*, xiv.55.1, pp. 1420–1. See, generally, van Houts, *Married Life*, 64–74.

[254] *Gesta Principum Polonorum*, ii.24, pp. 160–1.

[255] *Annales Aquenses*, 39; *Annales Marbacenses*, 56. Generally: Görich, *Friedrich Barbarossa*, 520–4.

[256] Csendes, *Heinrich VI.*, 61. See, though, Thomas Foerster, *Kaiser Heinrich VI.* (forthcoming), 76–7, who suggests the anniversary of the destruction of Crema in 1160.

[257] *Annales Parmenses maiores*, MGH SS 18 (Hanover, 1863), 665; Paul Scheffer-Boichorst, *Annales Patherbrunnenses, eine verlorene Quellenschrift des zwölften Jahrhunderts; aus Bruchstücken wiederhergestellt* (Innsbruck, 1870), 178; *Annales Romani*, MGH SS 5 (Hanover, 1849), 479; Ralph de Diceto, *Ymagines Historiarum*, in *Radulfi de Diceto Opera Historica*, ed. William Stubbs, Rolls Series, 2 vols. (London, 1876), vol. 2, 39.

III. SUCCESSION 209

The festivities were of such splendour that they were reported in Italy, Germany, England, France and Belgium.[258]

But that was not all. That the ceremony took place in Milan, at the commune's request, denoted a remarkable shift in relations between townspeople and emperor. After having been locked in conflict for almost three decades, they had settled their differences only in 1183. Both the invitation and its acceptance made visible this profound transformation in the political landscape of Lombardy.[259] The wedding furthermore occurred during the final stages of a prolonged Italian sojourn. Frederick had travelled south in September 1184, not long after Henry's knighting.[260] The visit took him, among other places, to Pavia, Verona, Faenza, Bologna, Treviso and Reggio, many of which were Milan's erstwhile allies.[261] Frederick's itinerary was a celebration of imperial might restored and of a concord newly won between the ruler and his people. At Cremona, he was seated on a stage specifically erected for him outside the cathedral, overlooking the town's main square.[262] At Verona he presided over a diet jointly with the pope,[263] while the citizens of Bergamo greeted his arrival with a most solemn procession.[264] He was also called upon to act as keeper of the peace and guardian of justice. While approaching Lodi in January 1185, the emperor was petitioned by the citizens of Crema, who asked for succour against the Cremonese. The latter made matters worse by attacking properties belonging to the men of Crema during Frederick's stay in Piacenza a few weeks later. The challenge to imperial authority was such that it could not go unpunished, and Frederick assembled an army of Lombard urban militia and imperial knights that successfully brought the Cremonese to heel.[265]

The festivities at Milan formed a ceremonial highpoint in the restoration of concord and imperial authority in Italy. Emperor and king acted as peacemakers, guardians of the Church and keepers of the law. Henry's nuptials were accompanied by a general amnesty, lavish donations to religious houses and, immediately after the wedding, military campaigns into Campania and in the vicinity of Rome. Barbarossa, the *Annales Marbacenses* report, returned to Germany, having brought all of Italy

---

[258] See the list of sources in RI IV.2.4, no. 2953.
[259] Görich, *Friedrich Barbarossa*, 520–4.
[260] *Annales Ratisponenses*, MGH SS 17 (Hanover, 1861), 589.
[261] Johannes Codagnelli, *Annales Placentini*, ed. Oswald Holder-Egger, MGH sep. ed. (Hanover and Leipzig, 1901), 12; *Annales Placentini Ghibellini*, MGH SS 18 (Hanover, 1863), 465.
[262] *Annales Cremonenses*, MGH SS 31 (Hanover, 1903), 6.
[263] Johannes Codagnelli, *Annales Placentini*, 12; *Annales Stadenses*, MGH SS 16 (Hanover, 1859), 350.
[264] Johannes Codagnelli, *Annales Placentini*, 12.
[265] *Die Urkunden Friedrichs I.*, ed. Heinrich Appelt, no. 895; *Annales Cremonenes*, 6; *Annales Aquenses*, 39; Johannes Codagnelli, *Annales Placentini*, 12.

210   6. DESIGNATING AN HEIR

into his grace.[266] The events also marked a final stage in paving the way for Henry's succession. The Mainz diet in 1184 had reinforced his status as king and heir designate in Germany. His wedding in Milan, and the alliance with the kings of Sicily (another erstwhile foe), established Henry as future ruler of Italy. Moreover, while Barbarossa was still in robust health – so much so, in fact, that a few years later he would embark on a crusade – he was also well into his sixties (he had been born in 1122). Most of his peers had died at a much younger age. In some ways, Henry's knighting and subsequent marriage therefore marked the point after which not much more could be done to safeguard his claim, or to prepare for the moment, when, after Frederick's death, he would face the German princes. He had received about as thorough a training in the business of kingship as possible. He had been taught his letters, had been given a good grounding in philosophy and theology, was an accomplished leader of men, had settled conflicts across the realm and had been given the opportunity to acquire networks of allies and friends. Unlike William the Conqueror a century earlier, Frederick had ensured that he met the moral expectations surrounding the succession. He had appointed a capable heir who would safeguard peace and tranquillity, ensure the continuity of the realm and see to the liturgical commemoration of his forebears.

Frederick's was also an unusual case. Henry was one of the very few sons in high medieval Europe to succeed to the throne (and in Germany, the first to do so since 1105/6), and among the fewer still whose fathers lived long enough to see them reach maturity. The generation of rulers succeeding c. 1180–90 was almost unique in this regard. In England in 1189, Richard the Lionheart was the first son to follow his father onto the throne since 1087, and in 1182 Knud VI the first legitimate son to succeed in Denmark since 1080. That each died relatively young, succeeded by their brothers, only underlines just how exceptional their cases were. In this regard, the sequence of stages outlined here – from designation, through training and education, to adulthood and marriage – was therefore an ideal type, which, like most ideal types, rarely existed in real life. Nevertheless, by tracing these stages it becomes possible to see why their absence mattered. That Henry I's daughter Matilda or Henry VI's son Frederick had not been properly prepared for their future role may have been a major factor contributing to their eventual failure. In Matilda's case, both her gender and her marriage complicated matters. There were, of course, female rulers who did succeed. Personality and chance played their part, but so did structures, conventions and traditions. Urraca of Castile outlived her male rivals, quickly divorced her first husband (who was eyed suspiciously by her Castilian subjects) and proved politically more astute than Matilda. Melisende of Jerusalem ruled through her husbands, at a time when her subjects were

---

[266] *Annales Marbacenses*, 56.

III. SUCCESSION 211

desperate for the military backing that foreign kings could bring, and in a society where noblewomen exercised a greater degree of influence than in the Latin west as a whole.[267] In the Anglo-Norman realm, by contrast, Matilda's husband Geoffrey of Anjou remained unacceptable as king, and Matilda faced male relatives who had the track record, resources and networks that allowed them to bid for the throne. Frederick's election as king had been a grudging concession. That Henry VI died soon after allowed those hostile to the 1196 settlement to reopen the matter. Even a combination of designation, election and coronation did not guarantee a smooth succession.

What happened in England in 1135/6 and Germany in 1197/8 reflected the specific challenges, context and circumstances of a particular moment. But they also point to structural features. Underage rulers and female heirs often lacked the opportunity to acquire a reputation for military skills, and to build the networks needed to subdue opponents and to see off rivals. Matilda's foreign marriages – first to Emperor Henry V, then to the count of Anjou – placed her outside the community of the realm, and marked an important difference between her and Urraca of Castile, Melisende of Jerusalem or Constance of Sicily. Frederick (II) was simply too young for established loyalties to survive the rupture of the emperor's death. Similar challenges were faced by absent heirs, such as the surviving brother of Godfrey I and Baldwin I in Jerusalem.[268] Because they lacked experience, reputation and networks, they were also perceived as unprepared for the political challenges a succession entailed, or to meet those that otherwise faced the realm. Choosing a king who was present, had a record of successful governance and at least some family relationship with his predecessor could prove more beneficial to the interests of the realm.

All these were reasons given by Otto of Freising to explain why, on the death of Conrad III in 1152, Frederick Barbarossa was elected king instead of Conrad's underage son. Frederick's many virtues were well known, and he was related to Conrad as well as to Conrad's chief rival. He was the candidate most likely to end the rivalry between the lineages.[269] Conrad himself had recognised that his son was too young to be elected king.[270] Fearing civil war, the princes therefore elected a king who was suitable and capable of averting

---

[267] Bernard Hamilton, 'Women in the crusader states: the queens of Jerusalem, 1100–1190', in *Medieval Women. Dedicated and Presented to Professor Rosalind M. T. Hill on the Occasion of her Seventieth Birthday*, ed. Derek Baker (Oxford, 1978), 143–174; Sarah Lambert, 'Queen or consort: rulership and politics in the Latin East, 1118–1228', in *Queens and Queenship*, ed. Duggan, 153–169; Alan V. Murray, 'Women in the royal succession of the Latin Kingdom of Jerusalem (1099–1291)', in *Mächtige Frauen?*, ed. Zey, 131–62.

[268] See below, Chapters 7 and 8.

[269] Otto of Freising, *Gesta Frederici*, ii.1, pp. 284–5.

[270] Otto of Freising, *Gesta Frederici*, i.71, pp. 280–1.

212   6. DESIGNATING AN HEIR

unrest. The needs of the realm justified breaking the line of succession.[271] Saxo
Grammaticus attributed the same rationale to the Danes when they first
pondered, but then decided against, making the infant Valdemar king. While
his father's many excellent deeds boded well for the boy's ability to rule, 'his
son's years were not yet ripe enough for royal command, and ... it was no
advantage to the Dane to serve in the army of an immature leader'.[272] Saxo's
comment tallies with the emphasis on physical readiness for combat, encountered in the account by 'Gallus' of Boleslaw III. It also reflects the link between
physical, mental and moral maturity so central to both a king's military and to
his literary education. To be a good ruler, one had to be old enough, experienced and successful.

Arguments like the ones reported by Otto and Saxo reflected the extent to
which, well into the thirteenth century, the individual king acted both as manifestation of the community of the realm and as its keeper. Administration and
bureaucracy could only compensate to some extent for the absence of a ruler
capable of waging war, doing justice and settling disputes.[273] Mere rumours of the
king's death could trigger unrest and rebellion.[274] Even in England, Sicily and
Aragon, realms with the perhaps most developed judicial-fiscal apparatus in the
high medieval west, the personality of the king, his ability to navigate factions at
court, to provide military leadership, to balance rigour with generosity and to be
seen as preserving the rights and liberties of his leading subjects while also
maintaining justice and peace, were at the very least as important as
a functioning apparatus of tax collectors and estate managers.[275] The same
tools, employed by different kings, could become both means of oppression and
cause for celebration. Because so much depended on the individual holding the

---

[271] In reality, matters were more complicated: Weiler, 'Tales of trickery and deceit',
299–301; Werner Goez, 'Von Bamberg nach Frankfurt und Aachen: Barbarossa's Weg
zur Königskrone', *Jahrbuch für fränkische Landesforschung* 52 (1992), 61–72;
Stefanie Dick, 'Die Königserhebung Friedrich Barbarossas im Spiegel der Quellen –
Kritische Anmerkungen zu den "Gesta Frederici" Ottos von Freising', *Zeitschrift der
Savigny-Stiftung für Rechtsgeschichte (Germanistische Abteilung)* 121 (2004), 200–37.

[272] Saxo Grammaticus, *Gesta Danorum*, xiv.2.2., pp. 984–5. Saxo claimed that the ruler
chosen – and other kings since Niels – acted as regents for Valdemar. Ibid. p. 984 n. 24,
p. 1083, n. 104. They were thus not kings, but regents, and could be deposed once
Valdemar came to claim his right.

[273] See also the thoughtful comments, though largely focussing on the later Middle Ages, by
Frédérique Lachaud and Michael Penman, 'Introduction: Absentee Authority across
Medieval Europe', in *Absentee Authority Across Medieval Europe*, ed. Lachaud and
Penman (Woodbridge, 2017), 1–19.

[274] See the examples collated by Florian Hartmann, 'Das Gerücht vom Tod des Herrschers
im frühen und hohen Mittelalter', *HZ* 302 (2016), 340–62.

[275] Catherine A. Rock, 'Fouke le Fitz Waryn and King John: rebellion and reconciliation', in
*British Outlaws of Literature and History: Essays on Medieval and Early Modern Figures
from Robin Hood to Twm Shon Catty*, ed. Alexander L. Kaufman (Lexington, KY, 2011),
67–96; Bisson, *Tormented Voices*; Schlichte, *Der 'gute König'*.

III. SUCCESSION 213

reins of power, minority governments were especially prone to accusations of favouritism and factionalism, as well as challenges from disgruntled barons, disappointed rivals and covetous neighbours.[276] Expressing fears of unrest and disorder was thus not mere artifice, but reflected the moral responsibility on the part of the kingdom's elites to ensure the continuing tranquillity of the realm. Kings could guide them in meeting that responsibility, even if there was no direct heir, if he was underage or if the heir was a woman. However, for that guidance to carry weight, it had to be given with death approaching.

6.4   Deathbed Designation

Deathbed designation was implicit for a son who had been knighted, entrusted with lands or put in charge of castles, men and courtiers – who had, in short, regularly been presented as a king in waiting, whose status as heir and successor was therefore beyond doubt. Matters were rather different when the throne was vacant, when the claims of an heir had to be set aside or rivals needed to be overcome. Then, designation or otherwise acting like an heir became both useful and necessary. In England, Harold Godwinson in 1066 and Stephen of Blois in 1135 claimed that Edward the Confessor and Henry I respectively had designated them as heirs on their deathbeds.[277] In 1072, Alfonso, in seizing the throne of León, asserted that his brother had nominated him as successor.[278] In Germany in 1152, partisans of Frederick Barbarossa maintained that he had been chosen as heir by his dying predecessor, Conrad III.[279] All these claims emerged during a disputed or open succession. Harold had to fend off the king of Norway and the duke of Normandy, and Stephen his cousin Matilda. Alfonso's brother had been murdered and Alfonso had to swear an oath affirming that he had not been complicit in his killing. The 1152 election marked the first time in the German kingdom's history when an eldest son was sidelined in determining his father's succession. Indeed, so unusual was Frederick Barbarossa's elevation that, from the beginning of the thirteenth century, a considerable corpus of legends began blossom around it.[280] The

---

[276]   This was certainly case with Otto III and Henry IV in Germany, William II and Frederick II in Sicily, Alexander II and Alexander III in Scotland, Henry III in England, Louis IX in France and Magnus Erlingsson in Norway. A partial exception was Baldwin III in Jerusalem. See, generally, Thilo Offergeld, *Reges pueri: das Königtum Minderjähriger im frühen Mittelalter* (Hanover, 2001); Christian Hillen and Frank L. Wiswall, 'The minority of Henry III in the context of Europe', in *The Royal Minorities of Medieval and Early Modern England*, ed. Charles F. Beem (New York, 2008), 17–66; and Emily Ward's forthcoming study of royal minorities in the twelfth and thirteenth centuries.

[277]   Harold: *The Gesta Guillelmi of William of Poitiers*, ed. and transl. R. H. C. Davis and Marjorie Chibnall (Oxford, 1998), 100–1; Stephen, *Liber Eliensis*, 285–6.

[278]   *Carmen Campodoctoris*, 106.

[279]   Otto of Freising, *Gesta Frederici*, ii.2, pp. 284–7.

[280]   Weiler, 'Tales of trickery and deceit'.

214   6. DESIGNATING AN HEIR

examples discussed in the previous chapter follow the same trajectory. On his
deathbed, Conrad I appointed not his brother, but his chief rival. William the
Conqueror's sons embarked upon twenty years of intermittent warfare before
the succession was finally settled in favour of the youngest among them. Even
then, Henry I lay claim to a kind of designation. According to William of
Malmesbury, when Henry complained about being mistreated by his elder
siblings, the Conqueror had intimated that he, too, would one day be king.[281]

Two possible reasons may explain why deathbed designation was so important: its public nature and the normative expectations surrounding the death of
a good king. Ideally, a ruler's death was not a private moment. He would pass
away surrounded by friends, family and followers, make amends for past
transgressions and confirm the identity of his successor. The king's soul
would be depart in peace – at least in part because sins had been confessed,
and because he had ensured the well-being of his people and dependants. The
ideal reflected both precedent and necessity. Bad kings died lonely and
defeated, while good ones were given the opportunity to ensure a peaceful
transition of power. According to the Old Testament, Saul had died by his own
hand, accompanied only by his shield bearer (1 Samuel 31:2–6), while David
summoned Solomon, and instructed him in the duties of kingship, before
passing away peacefully (1 Kings 2). The biblical model forms part of the
backdrop before which Widukind of Corvey, Thietmar of Merseburg and
Orderic Vitalis painted their highly stylised accounts of the deaths of Conrad
I of east Francia and of William the Conqueror.[282]

The ideal reflected common practice. Hugo Falcandus, almost certainly
a contemporary and in any case a close observer of the inner workings of the
Sicilian royal court, described the death of William I in 1166 thus:

> As he was still lying on his deathbed, he summoned the great men of the
> court, and in the presence of the archbishops of Salerno and Reggio, he
> told them his last wishes, deciding that his elder son William was to reign
> after him. He wanted [his youngest son] Henry to be satisfied with the
> principality of Capua, which he had granted him a long time ago, and he
> told the queen to undertake the care and administration of the entire
> realm, which is commonly called *balium*, until the boy should reach such
> discretion as should be sufficient to govern affairs wisely. He ordered the
> bishop-elect of Syracuse, Caid Peter, and the notary Matthew ... to

---

[281] William of Malmesbury, *Gesta Regum*, v.390, pp. 710–11.
[282] Peter Christian Lohrmann, 'Das Totengericht Kaiser Heinrichs II. Eine neue Variante
aus dem Echternacher "Liber aureus"', *Mittellateinisches Jahrbuch* 33 (1998);
Stuart Airlie, 'Sad stories of the death of kings: narrative patterns and structures of
authority in Regino of Prüm's chronicle', in *Narrative and History in the Early Medieval
West*, ed. Ross Balzaretti and Elizabeth M. Tyler (Turnhout, 2006), 105–31. See also
Gerald of Wales, *De Principis Instructione*, 196–233, 234–317.

III. SUCCESSION   215

remain ... *familiares* of the court, so that the queen should decide what
ought to be done on the advice of these men.[283]

Hugo's account reflects the specific circumstances of 1166. William's sons were
under age, with William II born in 1153. While close enough to reaching
maturity that a regency government would be in place for only a few years, it
was nonetheless required. Worse still, in 1161 there had been a failed coup, led
by two of William's relatives.[284] By confirming the succession of William II, his
father sought to pre-empt the recurrence of such moves. Leadership of the
regency council was entrusted to his widow, not his relatives, in an attempt to
prevent the not uncommon practice of uncles claiming to act as regents for
their nephews before seizing the throne for themselves.[285] But Margaret was
a Navarrese princess with few indigenous networks at her disposal. Hence
William decreed that she be assisted by leading members of his court: Caid
Peter, a convert from Islam, who had been among his most trusted military
leaders; Matthew of Ajello, who later became chancellor of the kingdom of
Sicily and had risen to prominence since the coup of 1161; and Richard Palmer,
an Englishman, who, alongside the other two, formed a triumvirate of William
I's closest confidants. Their presence potentially protected Margaret against
plots and intrigues, but also ensured a continuity of governance essential for
the minority not to be plagued by unrest. The regency could, however,
function authoritatively only because it had been put in place by the king in
the presence of the leading men of court and realm. They were called upon to
confirm and enforce his decision. The presence of the archbishops of Reggio
and Salerno – leading ecclesiastical figures who were not part of the proposed
regency – and the fact that they were singled out by Hugo suggests efforts to
secure an elite backing as broad as possible.

   Hugo's account stresses that the wider populace was excluded. The late
king's regime had been so unpopular that his death was kept secret, lest the
news inspire violence. Both the fear of imminent strife and the exclusion of the
people at large are attested to across the Latin west. When Emperor Otto III
died in Italy in 1002, his entourage kept his death secret until a large enough
army could be assembled to escort his remains safely back across the Alps.[286]
In 1087 the witnesses to William the Conqueror's final hours rushed home to
fortify their castles in fear of the impending peril.[287] The king's death was
a moment of crisis. For that very reason, the role of the people was carefully

---

[283] Hugo Falcandus, *Il regno di Sicilia*, 188; *History of the Tyrants*, 137.
[284] Hugo Falcandus, *Il regno di Sicilia*, 132; *History of the Tyrants*, 110.
[285] As happened in Denmark in 1103, or Germany in 1198: *Continuatio Admuntensis*, MGH
     SS 9 (Hanover, 1851), 588–91; *Chronica Regia Coloniensis*, 162–3; *Annales Marbacenses*,
     71–3.
[286] Thietmar, *Chronicon*, iv.50, pp. 166–7.
[287] Orderic Vitalis, *Ecclesiastical History*, vol. 4, 94–5.

216   6. DESIGNATING AN HEIR

circumscribed. In 1087, they first made an appearance at William the Conqueror's funeral, and elsewhere they emerged only to lament the demise of a truly good king.[288] By that stage, the matter of a succession had already been resolved or had at least come into the open.

Until then, however, it was a matter of concern first and foremost for those immediately touched by the king's death. Hence Conrad addressing the 'first among the people',[289] or William the Conqueror convening the leading men of Normandy.[290] It was perhaps also why a deathbed designation carried particular weight in an open or disputed succession. There was no record of the last wishes of Valdemar I or Frederick Barbarossa concerning their succession. In fact, Saxo describes Valdemar as trying to conceal his final illness from his son.[291] But then there was no need for them to be recorded. By the time of their passing, Frederick and Valdemar had had ample opportunity to ensure that Knud VI and Henry VI were ready to assume power. In 918, by contrast, as well as in 1066, 1087, 1135, 1152 and 1166, such certainty was lacking. The deathbed was a ruler's final opportunity to ensure an orderly transition of power. That he was supposed to act unencumbered by worldly cares reinforced the legitimising force of any designation he might offer. A dying ruler was expected to ready himself to meet his maker. Or, as the prophet Isaiah said to King Hezekiah: 'Put your house in order, for you will not live' (Isaiah 38:1).[292] A king would no longer be driven by fear or favouritism, and would nominate the successor most capable of holding the reins of power.

Other conditions also had to be met. The dying ruler had to have been a good king. There was not much advantage to be had from being designated by a corrupt and greedy one. The premise formed a defining theme in accounts of Conrad I's designation of Henry I – who, Saxon writers stressed, was a good man.[293] Furthermore, an act of designation had to be framed in terms of aiding the common weal or of recognising a claim that was otherwise indisputable. This was the approach chosen by Otto of Freising when recounting Frederick Barbarossa's designation at the hands of Conrad III:

> after he had commended to duke Frederick the regalia [imperial insignia, but also imperial properties] together with his only son, also called Frederick. For [Conrad] was a prudent man and had little hope that his son, who was very young, would be chosen as king. He therefore judged it to be of greater benefit for both the public and the private good, if his

---

[288] Sigebert of Gembloux, *Chronica*, 371–2, variant d; Saxo Grammaticus, *Gesta Danorum*, xv.6.11, pp. 1492–3.

[289] Thietmar, *Chronicon*, i.8, pp. 10–11; *Ottonian Germany*, ed. Warner, 72–3.

[290] Orderic Vitalis, *Ecclesiastical History*, vol. 4, 90–3.

[291] Saxo Grammaticus, *Gesta Danorum*, xv.6.7, pp. 1490–1.

[292] See also Gerald of Wales, *De Principis Instructione*, 248–9.

[293] Widukind of Corvey, *Sachsengeschichte*, i.25, pp. 26–7; *Deeds of the Saxons*, 39. See above, Chapter 5.

III. SUCCESSION 217

brother's son should succeed him, who had already amply demonstrated his many virtues.[294]

Moved by concern for the welfare of his people, Conrad III settled his succession. At the age of seven, his son was simply too young. Pushing for his elevation ran a high risk of inciting unrest and rebellion, and would have meant betraying Conrad's responsibility not only for the peace of the realm, but also for the welfare of his son. Conrad was able to make this kind of choice because he was himself a good king. Even though racked by illness – likely, Otto mused, brought on by Italian doctors bribed by the king of Sicily – Conrad nonetheless convened a diet at Bamberg, where he died. He was mourned by many, and the canons of Bamberg Cathedral even defied the wishes of his relatives and had him buried next to Emperor Henry II, who, Otto emphasised, was soon after canonised by the pope.[295] Conrad died an exemplary death and merited burial among saints. He displayed equanimity of mind in the face of adversity, and did not allow personal matters to interfere in settling the affairs of the realm. Moreover, the ailments plaguing Conrad were caused not by past transgressions, or by gluttonous wrath, but by the sinister plots of perfidious foes. His designation of Frederick Barbarossa reflected both Conrad's accomplishments, and those of the heir he chose as guardian of his son and keeper of his people.[296]

Even when a dynastic line was disrupted, the continuity of the realm had to be maintained. That was best accomplished by electing the putative ruler most capable of warding off foreign foes. The duty was also expressed symbolically. In 1152, Conrad III handed over the imperial insignia. We will return to them more fully in Chapter 9. They included both physical representations of royal duties – crown, sceptre, sword, and so on – and royal estates. The former signified the existence of a community of the realm that transcended the lifespan of an individual king. The latter added to the resources at a ruler's disposal. Passing these on communicated to officials, household knights, castellans and others that authority over them had been handed to a designated heir. Yet because insignia denoted the community of the realm,

---

[294] Otto of Freising, *Gesta Frederici*, i.71, pp. 280–1.
[295] Otto of Freising, *Gesta Frederici*, i.71, pp. 278–81.
[296] It is not quite clear how far Otto modelled this passage on events in 918. That Conrad had nominated Henry, rather than his brother, was well known. Otto himself recorded this in his earlier *Chronica* (Otto of Freising, *Chronica sive historia de duabus civitatibus*, ed. Walther Lammers, transl. Adolf Schmidt (Darmstadt, 1960), 454–5). It was also recorded in the anonymous imperial chronicle from *c.* 1125 (Ekkehard of Aura, *Ekkehardi Uraugiensis Chronica*, MGH SS 6 (Hanover, 1844), 175). In addition, the autograph copy of Liudprand of Cremona's *Antapodosis* was kept at Freising (Steffen Patzold, 'Wie bereitet man sich auf einen Thronwechsel vor? Überlegungen zu einem wenig beachteten Text des 11. Jahrhunderts', in *Die mittelalterliche Thronfolge*, ed. Becher, 127–57). However, any references remain implicit.

218   6. DESIGNATING AN HEIR

not the personal property of the king, the transfer still had to be confirmed. The nominated heir acted merely as custodian. He was by no means assured the right to don the regalia himself. In 1125, one chronicler reported that Henry V had called the great men of the realm to his deathbed, where he entrusted both the imperial insignia and his wife to Duke Frederick of Swabia, 'as if he were his heir' (emphasis mine).[297] Even so, they proceeded to elect not him, but Lothar of Saxony.

In this context, an important variation on deathbed designation needs to be considered; namely, the claim to restore a legitimate line that had insidiously been disrupted. Rather than linking himself to an immediate predecessor, someone aspiring to the throne might instead seek to establish a connection with a forebear, whose implicit quasi-designation of the contender simultaneously delegitimised his rivals. In 1066, William the Conqueror asserted designation by Edward the Confessor, with Harold consequently a mere usurper,[298] and after 1154, Henry II similarly declared Stephen's reign to be illegitimate, with Henry I as the ideal ancestor whose line was now restored.[299] Elsewhere, more elaborate but nonetheless recognisably similar strategies were employed. The coronation of Knud VI in 1170 completed the restoration of the line of Erik the Good and healed the break in the tradition of just kingship marked by the murder of Knud Lavard. Otto of Freising's account of Barbarossa's succession provides another case in point. Like other partisans of the Staufen family, the chronicler regarded Lothar's election in 1125 as illegitimate. In their eyes, it was the root of the dynastic rivalries that had beset Germany ever since, which only Barbarossa would be able to heal. In 1125, the favourite, entrusted with the imperial insignia by a dying Henry V, had been none other than Frederick's eponymous father. When the majority of the princes wanted to elect him, Otto reports, the archbishop of Mainz conspired to elect Lothar, who 'placed his own interests above the common weal'. Goaded by the prelate, the new king attacked his rival's wider family, thrusting the realm into turmoil.[300] While Conrad's election in 1138 partially remedied that break, only Barbarossa's in 1152 fully mended it. He was Frederick's son, and he was related to Lothar's family. He therefore held out the prospect of restoring the peace and tranquillity that had been disrupted ever since the wishes of Henry V had been ignored.[301] While none of these examples involve

---

[297] *Frutolfs und Ekkehards Chroniken und die anonyme Kaiserchronik*, ed. and transl. Franz-Josef Schmale and Irene Schmale-Ott (Darmstadt, 1972), 374–5.

[298] George Garnett, 'Coronation and propaganda: some implications of the Norman claim to the throne of England in 1066', *TRHS*, 5th series, 36 (1986), 91–116.

[299] *Select Charters 1066–1307*, ed. William Stubbs (Oxford, 1913), 157–8.

[300] Otto of Freising, *Gesta Frederici*, i.16–17, pp. 156–9.

[301] Otto of Freising, *Gesta Frederici*, ii.2, pp. 284–7, where he explicitly portrayed the Staufen as part of the Salian royal line (Frederick's grandfather had been married to Henry V's sister).

III. SUCCESSION   219

a deathbed designation as such, they nonetheless follow a similar trajectory. A connection with a predecessor was sought, be it through family relationship or by dint of a claimant's virtue and the promise to preserve the legacy of an illustrious forebear. That quasi-designation brought to an end a period of unrest caused because the right order of the world had been disturbed. It ensured the revival and hence the continuity of the community of the realm. The claimant invoking this line of succession established himself as the legitimate heir and descendant if not in blood, then in spirit, of a truly exemplary king.

Just receiving or claiming designation was not enough. Heirs had duties. When Sverrir of Norway was told that he was the son of a king,

> this information caused him much anxiety, and his mind wavered greatly. To contend for the kingdom ... seemed difficult; and, yet, supposing he were a king's son, it seemed contemptible that he should do nothing more than a plain yeoman's son would do.[302]

Being the rightful heir king demanded that one also act like one. Both willingness and ability had to be demonstrated. There was, for instance, the taking under one's protection of one's predecessor's family and dependants. In 918, Conrad I had specifically commended these groups into Henry's care, as had Henry V in 1125 when he entrusted Frederick with his widow 'as if he were his heir', and Conrad III in 1152, when he asked Frederick Barbarossa to take care of his son. Alongside ensuring the liturgical commemoration of one's forebear, and more than any other act, this established a quasi-familial link between ruler and heir. Guardianship of one's dependants and responsibility for one's soul conferred a degree of personal responsibility far greater than that involved in the handing over insignia, or the naming of an individual as capable occupant of the royal throne. These were duties that *sons* ought to perform.

While caring for a predecessor's *familia* established a personal relationship, taking charge of his *memoria* expressed concern for the continuity of the realm. Endowing and confirming gifts to commemorate one's forebears was an act of filial piety. In 1060, Philipp I of France marked his accession to the throne with a series of charters ensuring the liturgical commemoration of his father,[303] as did Louis VI in 1108.[304] Immediately after his coronation, Conrad

---

[302] *Saga of King Sverri*, chapter 4, p. 4.

[303] *Recueil des Actes de Philippe Ier, Roi de France (1059–1108)*, ed. M. Prou and M. H. d'Arbois de Jubainville (Paris, 1908), nos. 2–5. See also Dale, *Inauguration and Liturgical Kingship*, 165–6. See also Bernd Schneidmüller, 'Die gegenwart der Vorgänger. Geschichtsbewußtsein in den westfränkisch-französischen Herrscherurkunden des Hochmittelalters', in *Hochmittelalterliches Geschichtsbewußtsein im Spiegel nichthistoriographischer Quellen*, ed. Hans-Werner Goetz (Berlin, 1998), 217–35.

[304] *Recueil des Actes de Louis VI, roi de France (1108–1137)*, ed. Robert-Henri Bautier and Jean Dufour, 4 vols. (Paris, 1992–4), vol. 1, nos. 19–20.

III confirmed donations made by Henry IV and Henry V,[305] and initiated an annual memorial Mass for the former.[306] Other charters refer to Henry IV and Henry V as grandfather and uncle,[307] while Conrad II – the first Salian emperor – was described as 'forefather' (*abavus*).[308] Gifts reinforced a dynastic connection, even if it had been interrupted. They communicated claims to continuity, and through their omission highlighted illegitimate breaks. One of Conrad's earliest charters, for example, issued a few weeks after his coronation in 1138, confirmed grants to the abbey of Stavelot and Corvey made by named predecessors: the kings Sigebert, Dagobert, Chlodwig and others, as well as the emperors Charles, Louis, the three Ottos, Conrad [II] and the three Henrys.[309] Tellingly, Lothar III was omitted from the list, even though he had confirmed these same privileges a decade earlier.[310] The right sequence of kings had been restored, and so had the continuity of the realm. Similarly, in 1147 Conrad III marked the anniversary of his coronation with a donation designed to support prayers on behalf of his predecessors in general, and in particular on behalf of Henry IV and Henry V. Once again, Lothar was omitted.[311] Commemoration constructed lines and patterns of legitimate succession. It was not an apolitical act.

While charters and donations communicated adherence to abstract norms,[312] they could legitimately be issued only once a candidate had been elected and enthroned. No less public but equally incisive as a means of claiming quasi-designation, and one that could be performed sooner, was to take charge of a predecessor's funeral. Normally, this was another task undertaken by a ruler's kin. When Henry II of England died in 1189, his eldest son Richard hastened to Fontrevault to take charge of the proceedings. This was all the more necessary, as only a few weeks earlier Richard, in open rebellion against his father and allied with the king of France, had inflicted a humiliating

---

[305] *Die Urkunden Konrads III. und seines Sohns Heinrich*, ed. Friedrich Hausmann, MGH Diplomata (Vienna, Cologne and Graz, 1969), no. 3. Generally: Thomas Zotz, 'Königtum und Reich zwischen Vergangenheit und Gegenwart in der Reflexion deutscher Herrscherurkunden des Hochmittelalters', in *Hochmittelalterliches Geschichtsbewußtsein im Spiegel nichthistoriographischer Quellen*, ed. Goetz (Berlin, 1998), 237–55, at 249–54.

[306] *Urkunden Konrads III.*, no. 4.

[307] *Urkunden Konrads III.*, nos. 2, 8, 16, 20, 43–5, 47–8, 54, 75, 80, 89, 117, 130, 139, 211.

[308] *Urkunden Konrads III.*, nos. 5, 7, 43, 117.

[309] *Urkunden Konrads III.*, no. 5.

[310] *Die Urkunden Lothars III. und der Kaiserin Richenza*, ed. Emil von Ottenthal and Hans Hirsch, MGH Diplomata (Berlin, 1927), no. 13.

[311] *Urkunden Konrads III.*, no. 176. See also, no. 43 (for Conrad II and Henry IV at Speyer).

[312] There has been a rich tradition of German scholarship on the use of charters as means for communicating political values, helpfully summarised by Herwig Wolfram, 'Political theory and narrative in charters', *Viator* 26 (1995), 39–52. For recent case studies: Krieg, *Herrscherdarstellung*; Dale, *Inauguration and Liturgical Kingship*, 159–90.

III. SUCCESSION   221

defeat upon Henry. Indeed, their relationship was so fraught that, Roger of Howden reports, the king's corpse began to bleed when Richard approached it. Only once the funeral obsequies had been completed did Richard proceed to England to claim the throne.[313] In 1214 the funeral for William the Lion of Scotland similarly framed the inauguration of his son Alexander II.[314]

A funeral's being supposedly overseen by a ruler's heir helps explain some of the extraordinary steps taken by some claimants. One of the most colourful examples is that of body- (or rather corpse-) snatching perpetrated by Henry, duke of Bavaria and future emperor. When Otto III's remains were escorted back to Germany for burial at Aachen in 1002, Henry gathered his troops and lay in wait for the emperor's corpse. As soon as the procession entered Bavaria, he not only took charge of the imperial remains, but also demanded that those accompanying them should choose him as their next king. Most demurred. The archbishop of Cologne even sought to thwart Henry's ambition by hiding the Holy Lance.[315] Against the will of the attendant nobles and prelates, Henry nonetheless organised a particularly splendid burial for Otto's intestines. It was only at the behest of a close relative that he allowed the funeral procession to leave Bavaria, but not without first repeating his request to each of the great men accompanying it that they elect him king.[316]

Henry was unusual in his persistent efforts, but the desire to oversee the funeral of his predecessor was not. In 1135, Stephen hurried across the Channel to seize the throne as soon as he heard of his uncle's demise. When the remains of Henry I arrived at Reading Abbey, Stephen personally helped carry the bier with the royal corpse, and saw to it that a solemn mass was said for the king. Soon after, he was crowned king.[317] In Norway, Sverrir hastened to Bergen to be present at the funeral of Magnus Erlingsson, the king whose

---

[313] Roger of Howden, *Gesta Henrici II: the Chronicle of the Reigns of Henry II and Richard I AD 1169-1192, known commonly under the name of Benedict of Peterborough*, ed. William Stubbs, 2 vols., Roll Series (London, 1867), vol. 2, 71.

[314] Johannis de Fordun, *Chronica Gentis Scotorum et Gesta Annalia*, ed. William F. Skene, 2 vols. (Edinburgh, 1872), vol. 1, 280-1 (translation, vol. 2, 275-6). See also below, Chapter 9.

[315] Gunter Wolf, 'Die Heilige Lanze, Erzbischof Heribert von Köln, und der "secundus in regno" Pfalzgraf Ezzo', *Zeitschrift für Kirchengeschichte* 104 (1993), 23-7. On the artefact: Peter Worm, 'Die Heilige Lanze. Bedeutungswandel und Verehrung eines Herrschaftszeichens', *Arbeiten aus dem Marburger Hilfswissenschaftlichen Institut* (2000), 179-216; Percy Ernst Schramm, 'Die "Heilige Lanze", Reliquie und Herrschaftszeichen des Reiches und ihre Replik in Krakau. Ein Überblick über die Geschichte der Königslanze', in Percy Ernst Schramm (with others), *Herrschaftszeichen und Staatssymbolik. Beiträge zu ihrer Geschichte vom dritten bis zum sechzehnten Jahrhundert*, 3 vols. (Stuttgart, 1954-6), vol. 2, 492-537; Franz Kirchweger, ed., *Die Heilige Lanze in Wien: Insignie, Reliquie, 'Schickalsspeer'* (Vienna, 2005).

[316] Thietmar, *Chronicon*, iv.50-1, pp. 165-8.

[317] *Chronicle of John of Worcester*, vol. 3, 215-16; William of Malmesbury, *Historia Novella*, 29-30.

222   6. DESIGNATING AN HEIR

throne he had taken. He not only gave a speech during the proceedings, but 'the burial-place of King Magnus was put in careful order by King Sverrir; coverlets were spread over the tombstone, and a railing set up around it'.[318] Finally, in Jerusalem William of Tyre made much of the symbolism surrounding the passing of power from Baldwin I to Baldwin II. The latter was entering the city from one gate, while the bier with the remains of the former arrived by another. Baldwin attended the funeral, and was elected king shortly thereafter.[319] In each instance, taking a leading role in a predecessor's burial established a claimant as quasi-heir, as someone willing to ensure the commemoration of their forebear and as capable of maintaining the continuity of the realm. Henry and his peers clearly met the expectations inherent in the moral framework of succession.

Royal burials were public affairs. Ideally, the king died surrounded by the chief men of the realm, but even if that was not possible, sufficient time was allowed to elapse for as many of them as possible to convene for the interment of his remains. On the death of Wladyslaw in 1102, the presiding archbishop delayed the funeral for five days in order to secure a large enough audience.[320] Especially in the case of an open succession, the proceedings created an opportunity to deliberate on how the throne was to be filled and how the imminent crisis could be averted. For example, in 1002 Otto's burial coincided with a decision by those present to support the duke of Lotharingia.[321] In 987, whereas the king of west Francia had died at Senlis and wanted to be buried at Reims, it was decided to hold the obsequies at Compiègne instead, in order 'to forestall the possibility that a large number of the magnates would refuse to attend the funeral because of the length of the journey and would leave without reaching a decision on what was best for the kingdom'.[322] A king's funeral brought together the very men a claimant had to convince that he was most suited for the throne. Taking charge of the proceedings meant staking a claim that, even without engaging in an act as extreme as Henry of Bavaria's, could not be ignored.

Oversight of a royal funeral was therefore often a demonstration of power. Sverrir of Norway made the point with brutal poignancy.[323] Immediately after

---

[318] *The Saga of King Sverri*, chapter 97, p. 122.
[319] William of Tyre, *Chronicon*, 548–50. See also, for Anglo-Saxon England, Nicole Marafioti, *The King's Body. Burial and Succession in Anglo-Saxon England* (Toronto, 2014), especially 81–124. And for Poland: Zbigniew Dalewski, 'Begräbnis des Herrschers. Ritual und Streit um die Thronfolge im Polen des früheren Mittelalters', *FmSt* 43 (2009), 327–47.
[320] See below, Chapter 10.
[321] Thietmar, *Chronicon*, iv.54, pp. 171–2.
[322] Richer, *Histories*, vol. 2, 206–9.
[323] David Brégaint, 'Staging deaths: King Sverre or a usurper's path to the throne', *Medievalista online* 23 (2018), https://journals.openedition.org/medievalista/1591 (accessed 30 January 2020), at 6–7.

III. SUCCESSION
223

Magnus' funeral, he called an assembly, where Sverrir explained that he had been sent by God to free the people from tyranny, to avenge the injustices inflicted on Sverrir's kin by Magnus and his father and to humble the proud. Just as God had defeated Satan and expelled him from heaven, just as Saul roamed his lands 'possessed by an unclean spirit' once he had defied the will of God, so Sverrir's proud and haughty opponents had been laid low. Worst among them had been Magnus' father who, while not even of royal kin, had nonetheless made his son king, and arrogated to himself the dignity of earl. Sverrir conceded that many of the people present remained hostile to him. Some even claimed that he had sold his soul to the devil – a bad bargain indeed, he retorted, to sell one's soul for a kingdom so torn by strife, and a foolish thing to say. Sverrir concluded: 'I would now warn King Magnus's men, who have been present at this meeting, to withdraw from the town before the third day from this time.'[324] They could either live free by accepting Sverrir as king, or die in defence of tyranny.

Sverrir's speech encapsulates many of the themes encountered in this and previous chapters. He did not seek the throne, but assumed it out of duty and in order to free the people from the tyranny of cruel and haughty usurpers. There certainly was not much material gain to be had. Sverrir returned to the theme many years later, as he sat dying (he had refused to lie down): 'The kingdom has brought me labour and unrest and trouble, rather than peace and a quiet life.'[325] Material concerns were clearly not what had motivated him. At Bergen, Sverrir also likened himself implicitly to David. One of only two direct biblical references in the entire speech was to Saul, who had been driven to madness after defying the will of God (resulting in David's kingship). The other was to Christ in the desert. This needs to be read alongside one of Sverrir's earlier dreams, in which he had been crowned by the prophet Samuel, who had also anointed David to replace Saul.[326] Moreover, like David, Sverrir was of humble stock and was merely an instrument of divine justice. As he explained to the men of Bergen: 'God sent from the outlying islands a mean and lowly man to bring down their pride. I was that man.' Simultaneously, he restored a rightful line of kings, interrupted by Erling's machinations. Even the speech Sverrir gave during the funeral reflected these themes: '[Magnus] was hard to me and my men; may God forgive him now for all his transgressions. Yet he was an honourable chief in many respects, and adorned by kingly descent.'[327] Like

---

[324] *Saga of King Sverri*, chapter 99, pp. 124–5.
[325] *Saga of King Sverri*, chapter 180, p. 231. See also, generally, Ármann Jakobsson, 'King Sverrir of Norway and the foundations of his power: kingship ideology and narrative in Sverrissaga', *Medium Aevum* 84 (2015), 109–35, especially 112–21.
[326] *Saga of King Sverri*, chapter 10, pp. 11–12.
[327] *Saga of King Sverri*, chapter 97, p. 122. See further the character sketch of Magnus, ibid., chapter 98, pp. 122–3, which focussed on his jovial demeanour, love of drinking bouts,

224   6. DESIGNATING AN HEIR

Conrad I in east Francia and Lothar III in Germany, Magnus was a good man, though perhaps not quite up to the task that had been thrust upon him by his father's lust for power. Sverrir, by contrast, was the rightful descendant of kings. He had shown that he acted with divine blessing, and that he possessed the martial skills as well as the moral character needed to wear the crown. He was able to succeed, even though he lacked the support and training that kings were otherwise meant to provide for their heirs. This only underlined his innate suitability.

Sverrir presented himself as conforming to an ideal type. His designation came not from his father, but from the prophet Samuel as well as from his father's erstwhile followers. When the latter first requested that he act as their leader, they and Sverrir followed the spirit of the moral process outlined earlier. Their approach was made freely and unprompted, on grounds both of his descent and his suitability. He himself showed due hesitation.[328] More importantly, when Sverrir felt death approaching, he died an exemplary death. That included sending a letter to his surviving son Håkon, 'touching the ordering of the kingdom'. Subsequently, Sverrir addressed 'all those present, and said: "I call you all to witness, that I know of no son alive except only Håkon, though hereafter men come forward desirous of raising strife in the land, and call themselves my sons".'[329] The letter conformed to the paradigm of a good death, where the ruler, in the mould of a dying David instructing Solomon, rehearsed to his heir the principles of good governance. It also expressed the expectation that Håkon would follow his father's advice, and rule as a just and pious king. It was, if not a promise of, then an exhortation to future good governance. Sverrir's speech reflected the dynastic history of twelfth-century Norway, where royal promiscuity combined with a relaxed approach towards illegitimate descent had resulted in a veritable plethora of royal progeny jostling for the throne.[330] It is somewhat ironic that Sverrir should have ruled out a recurrence of his own path to the throne. But then this was about ensuring the continuity of a dynastic line, securing the peace and tranquillity of the realm and Sverrir's commemoration. The king explicitly confirmed Håkon's status as his sole surviving son. That he did so just before receiving last unction also

---

generosity, ease of manners and the fact that he was popular because he was not a descendant of Harald Gilli. Both mark a striking contrast with Sverrir's speech at the burial of Earl Erling a few years earlier. There, he recounted that the archbishop of Nidaros had claimed that those dying while fighting Sverrir would go to heaven. Hence there was no reason to mourn the earl, who would now become a great saint. Unless, that is, the archbishop was unfairly biased. Sverrir then proceeded to list Erling's many crimes. Hence, he concluded, it might be best to pray for him, after all: ibid., chapter 38, pp. 49–51; Brégaint, 'Staging deaths', 5–6.

[328] See below, Chapters 7 and 8.

[329] *Saga of King Sverri*, chapter 180, p. 231; Brégaint, 'Staging deaths', 7–9.

[330] See above, Chapter 5.

III. SUCCESSION 225

obliged Sverrir's companions to defend his acknowledged heir against putative rivals, and thereby to limit the room for challenges to be brought. Sverrir did his best to ensure that, on facing the great men of Norway, Håkon would encounter no obstacle to having his kingship confirmed.

There is nothing in *Sverrisaga* about the training received by Sverrir's sons, beyond the frequent admonitions he had offered to his firstborn, and a note to the effect that he had given him into fosterage to a trusted ally.[331] However, Håkon had been an active participant in royal campaigns, even leading troops separately from his father. He had been prepared for the succession as thoroughly as possible. At the same time, the fact that he only emerged as putative heir after his elder brother's death in 1200 serves to highlight the inherent fragility of the succession process. Heirs could die before they were ready. There could even be no heir at all. There also was no certainty that a favoured successor would indeed be chosen by the great men of the realm. All a ruler could do was pave the way for him. He could do so, as Sverrir had done, by designating him on his deathbed. He could also have him elected and confirmed as successor early on, as Valdemar had done in Denmark or Frederick Barbarossa in Germany. If given sufficient time, he might even have him undergo basic instruction in letters, as Peter of Blois had proposed for the eldest son of King Henry II of England, or training in the arts of governance, as in the case of Boleslaw III in Poland. None of these guaranteed a smooth succession. But they certainly stacked the cards in favour of a monarch's chosen heir. To win the game, he still had to convince the magnates and prelates that he was ready to be king. He had to be elected.

---

[331] *Saga of King Sverri*, chapters 130, 164, pp. 160–1, 212–13.

PART IV

Election

There could be no king who had not been chosen by the people. Even William the Conqueror, having defeated Harold at Hastings, waited until the English offered him the throne before he had himself crowned.[1] The people's freedom to choose was, however, circumscribed by norms as well as needs. As a rule, they were expected to choose the king's eldest son, or at least another close relative, and certainly one from among the royal *stirps*, however loosely defined. They also had to pick a ruler capable of defending the realm and of humbling the mighty, and powerful enough to terrorise or, preferably, cajole his opponents into accepting him, but without becoming a tyrant. The only state of affairs worse than having no king was having one who turned into an oppressor or who proved useless in the face of foreign and domestic foes. Finally, candidates were meant to possess certain qualities, and should have displayed those well in advance of their election. In 1131, the barons of Jerusalem picked Count Fulk of Anjou to be their king. The *Chronica de Gestis Consulum*, the Angevin house chronicle, mentioned the event only in the most cursory way: Baldwin II of Jerusalem had sent envoys to France to find a husband for his daughter, suitable (*idoneus*) to rule as his successor. Fulk, who lacked a wife, was chosen on the advice of King Louis of France, the bishops and many discerning men.[2] The royal dignity did not come to Fulk unexpectedly. Only a few pages earlier, and clearly aware of the subsequent course of events, the *Chronica* had enumerated his numerous qualities. Fulk was an honourable man, strenuous in arms, devout in his faith, favourably inclined towards the servants of God, was generous to his friends, yet oppressive to those of an evil mind or otherwise hostile towards him. Because of these attributes Fulk had quickly acquired unequalled fame.[3] He had acted like a king before he ever wore a crown.

Much of this will look familiar. The ability to behave in a regal fashion was necessary for the status of kingship to be bestowed. Boleslaw I of Poland and Roger II of Sicily became kings because they acted like kings. Comparable qualities marked out contenders as throne-worthy in Iberia, Germany and

---

[1] William of Poitiers, *Gesta Guillelmi*, ii.28–9, pp. 144–51.
[2] 'Elegerunt itaque, consilio Ludovici regis et episcoporum et multorum peritorum, Fulconem Andegavensem, qui uxorem carebat.' *Chronica de Gestis*, 69.
[3] *Chronica de Gestis*, 67.

228   IV. ELECTION

Normandy.[4] These character traits, furthermore, reflect the model rulers of the Bible and antiquity, and the expectations formulated by writers like Cicero, Seneca, Augustine and Gregory I, as refined and shared by their medieval readers. Yet these attributes were also open to interpretation. In 1131, the men of Jerusalem were fortunate in that their king was alive. He could take the initiative in choosing a husband for his daughter and a ruler for his people. More commonly, a late king's subjects found themselves confronted not with the need to assess absolutes, but with a choice between claimants who showed strengths and weaknesses in a variety of combinations. How did they go about ensuring that the best person was chosen? What could be done if it turned out that the wrong person had been elected? And who were 'the people'? How did they actually vote?

In tackling these questions, we will encounter more than the usual share of challenges. Even though an electoral element was ubiquitous across the Latin west, once it came to actually writing about it, the topic proves to have been of concern mostly to German authors. That partly reflects their perception of domestic political structures. In the 1150s, Otto of Freising could claim that in Germany kings were elected, rather than chosen by hereditary succession.[5] A generation later, Henry VI sought to establish hereditary succession 'in the manner of the French', that is, as something supposedly unlike what was practised in Germany.[6] At the same time, Otto's statement was very much a case of special pleading. He had to explain why Conrad III was succeeded by his nephew, not his son. Tellingly, even in the thirteenth century, just as hereditary succession ceased to prevail in practice, contemporary authors nonetheless portrayed it as an ideal to be upheld.[7] This should warn against taking the image painted by German authors at face value.[8] Moreover, once set alongside examples from Denmark, England, France, Jerusalem, Norway and Poland, few of the features highlighted in the German sources prove to be unusual.

While the imbalance in the medieval evidence can be corrected by adopting a broadly comparative perspective, the same is not possible as regards modern scholarship. Because the medieval evidence is richest in Germany, elections have not been studied in any detail for other parts of Latin Europe (and even then mostly by German academics or those trained in the German tradition).[9] It is largely absent from discussions of royal successions in England,[10] France[11]

---

[4] For further examples, see Weiler, 'Kingship in dynastic chronicles'.
[5] Otto of Freising, *Gesta Frederici*, ii.1, pp. 284–5.
[6] *Annales Marbacenses*, 67–8.
[7] Weiler, 'Tales of trickery and deceit'.
[8] Weiler, 'Suitability and right'.
[9] Hoffmann, *Königserhebung und Thronfolgeordnung*.
[10] George Garnett, *Conquered England: Kingship, Succession and Tenure, 1066–1166* (Oxford, 2007).
[11] See, however, the important exception of Lewis, 'Anticipatory succession'.

IV. ELECTION 229

or the crusader kingdom of Jerusalem.[12] Simultaneously, precisely because of its geographical focus, German scholarship has found little reception among modern historians studying other parts of Europe.[13] Yet there is much to be learned. In his classic study of imperial elections, last revised in 1944, Heinrich Mitteis highlighted the variety of terms employed by medieval authors, and used that to construct a model where an election extended from nomination to coronation.[14] Like succession, it was a process, not an event. This does not mean that Mitteis' conclusions should be adopted unquestioningly. His juxtaposition of electoral to hereditary succession, and his desire to trace indisputable rules of electoral procedure, even to identify a legally precise moment at which a vote would be considered complete and binding, defy the complexities of the surviving evidence. His work remains, however, the most comprehensive treatment of the process anywhere in medieval Europe. It cannot be ignored.

Mitteis set the tone for most subsequent research on medieval elections. However, as Steffen Patzold has pointed out,[15] much of the German debate developed within conceptual parameters first established in the nineteenth century. It postulated a clear opposition between electoral and hereditary succession, and often centred on the question of when exactly hereditary succession ceased to be and election became normative.[16] This, as we have seen from previous chapters, creates a false dichotomy, certainly as far as the central Middle Ages are concerned. In addition, there has been a tendency to seek to derive from narrative sources a set of clearly defined legal norms.[17] The approach poses several problems. First, its evidential basis is exceptionally

[12] Except in relation to specific successions: Mayer, 'The succession to Baldwin II'; Alan V. Murray, 'Dynastic continuity or dynastic change? The accession of Baldwin II and the nobility of the kingdom of Jerusalem', *Medieval Prosopography* 13 (1992), 1–28; Murray, 'Women in the royal succession'.

[13] See, for instance, Mitteis, *Die deutsche Königswahl*; Schmidt, *Königswahl und Thronfolge*; and the essays collected in Reinhard Schneider, ed., *Wahlen und Wählen im Mittelalter* (Sigmaringen, 1990), which, strikingly, while treating elections in a variety of contexts – of bishops and popes, in German and Italian towns, of the lower clergy or among guilds – contains not a single chapter focussing on royal elections outside the medieval German realm. *Die mittelalterliche Thronfolge*, ed. Becher, follows a similar pattern.

[14] Mitteis, *Die deutsche Königswahl*, 47–59.

[15] Steffen Patzold, 'Königserhebungen zwischen Erbrecht und Wahlrecht? Thronfolge und Rechtsmentalität um das Jahr 1000', *DA* 58 (2002), 467–507.

[16] See, most recently, Kannowski, 'The impact of lineage', following Armin Wolf, whose collected papers have been published in his *Verwandschaft – Erbrecht – Königswahlen* (Frankfurt/Main, 2013).

[17] See, for instance, Ulrich Reuling, *Die Kur in Deutschland und Frankreich. Untersuchungen zur Entwicklung des rechtsförmlichen Wahlaktes bei der Königserhebung im 11. und 12. Jahrhundert* (Göttingen, 1979); Reuling, 'Zur Entwicklung der Wahlformen bei den hochmittelalterlichen Königserhebungen im Reich', in *Wahlen und Wählen*, ed. Schneider, 227–70.

230   IV. ELECTION

weak. The most recent study of election procedures in high medieval Germany, for instance, largely relied on just three accounts, two of them stretching to a couple of sentences at most.[18] Second, little attention was paid to questions of authorship, audience or purpose of composition, let alone to a key fundamental methodological problem. As far as chronicles and other narratives are concerned, pointing out the moral meaning of events was frequently at least as important as providing an accurate depiction of what had actually happened. Delineating precise legal norms was certainly not what most of these texts were meant to provide. Finally, legal – and for that matter moral – principles provided not a rigid template, but a framework, to be adapted as circumstances demanded and opportunity allowed. At most, surviving accounts allow us to see how individual authors and their communities envisaged an ideal election to unfold. Their efforts offer helpful insights into contemporary horizons of expectation and the principles that writers as well as their readers, peers and patrons deemed to be important. However, they should certainly not be read as if they had been penned by modern students of constitutional law.

Moreover, given the preoccupations of recent scholarship, important aspects of the election process have rarely been touched upon. For example, very little work has been done on the moral framework of elections. The key exception is a foundational article by Walter Maleczek, published in 1990.[19] Ranging chronologically from the late Roman republic to the thirteenth century, and covering episcopal and papal elections, decision-making in Italian communes and German imperial elections, Maleczek traced shifting notions of how a 'sensible result' ('vernünftiges Ergebnis') could be achieved. Three of his findings open up especially fruitful paths of enquiry. First, since late antiquity, unanimity had been central for an election to be legitimate. Only that would accurately reflect God's will. Dissent invalidated any decision reached. Campaigning or canvassing were to be frowned upon. In fact, in 1215 the Fourth Lateran Council decreed that the ideal election was one where an assembly decided on a candidate unanimously and spontaneously, without prior debate or consultation.[20] Even when a majority vote was deemed legitimate, either it had to result in compromise or the minority would eventually have to fall in line with the majority.[21] Unanimity still remained the goal. Second, a major variation on this theme was the premise that the *sanior pars* – the better, wiser or more mature party – ought to prevail, though how precisely it could be identified remained a matter of

---

[18] Reuling, 'Zur Entwicklung der Wahlformen': Wipo, Thietmar of Merseburg and Otto of Freising.
[19] Walter Maleczek, 'Abstimmungsarten. Wie kommt man zu einem vernünftigen Wahlergebnis?', in *Wahlen und Wählen im Mittelalter*, ed. Schneider, 79–134.
[20] Maleczek, 'Abstimmungsarten', 85–7.
[21] Maleczek, 'Abstimmungsarten', 95–7, 101–17.

IV. ELECTION 231

debate. In some ways, the principle seems to have been more important than its practical application.[22] Medieval attempts to define who that *sanior pars* was point to the premise (which was not fully spelled out by Maleczek) that the motivation of those voting was at least as important as the number of votes cast. Third, there were evidently rival discourses, different ways of defining what a legitimate outcome would be and what constituted due process. Was it the vote of the *sanior pars*? The majority? A compromise? What precisely did unanimity mean?

The twin poles of unanimity and probity were central to the normative framework of elections, and will form the focus of Chapter 7. Just as in the case of succession, process mattered not as a set of concrete rules, but as a means by which to assess and demonstrate the suitability not only of the claimants themselves, but also of those doing the choosing. Taking this more comprehensive approach enables us to tackle questions left either unanswered or unasked even by Maleczek. How could adherence to norms be demonstrated? How could it be enforced? Who determined which set of approaches was most appropriate at a given moment, and how should those be interpreted? In seeking to provide answers, Chapter 8 addresses another gap in current scholarship: the social experience of elections. Historians have explored modes of voting and have sought to delineate concrete rules and procedural norms. But they have not considered how those could be implemented in practice. That something was postulated as an ideal did not mean that it actually happened. Just as little attention has been paid to the relationship between organising and planning an election and the moral framework to which it was supposed to conform. How strictly, for instance, was the ban on campaigning and canvassing enforced? How were decisions prepared? Who was involved in reaching them? How were they communicated to the wider community of the realm?

---

[22] Maleczek, 'Abstimmungsarten', 117–26.

7

Unanimity and Probity

After the death of King Erik the Memorable of Denmark in 1137, Saxo Grammaticus recounted,

> no one was so convinced of his own descent or courage that he dared to seek or to seize it. Neither Sven, Erik's son, nor Knud, Magnus's son, nor Valdemar, Knud's son, was yet old enough to assume the crown. Christiern, however, who had helped avenge the father of Valdemar, declared that this boy was eminently suited for the kingship. But his mother, observing that the royal office, beset with a multitude of harsh perils, could only be handled with difficulty even by adults and would be disastrous for a young lad, refused to surrender the boy to Christiern's request, saying that such an employment was the prerogative of his elders. Finally, when the other persistently repeated his demand, she forced him to swear an oath that he would never allow the election of Valdemar to the monarchy.[1]

It is hard not to empathise with Valdemar's mother. After all, her husband, the father of her unborn child, had been murdered because of mere rumours that he desired the throne. Her implacable hostility to seeing Valdemar engage in the business of kingship also proved prescient. In 1137 a perilous conflict was avoided, but a few years later Sven, Knud and Valdemar did compete for the throne. Bloodshed ensued. Knud was slain during a feast hosted by Sven, and Sven subsequently fell in battle against Valdemar. It took almost twenty years for Erik's succession to be settled. And Denmark was by no means unusual. In 1002, Margrave Ekkehard of Meißen was murdered while campaigning for the imperial crown; in 1066, Harald Hardrada and Harold Godwinson lost their lives in pursuit of the English throne; in 1112, after yet another failed attempt to become duke of Poland, Zbigniew was blinded by his brother; and in 1125, a victorious Lothar III began persecuting his defeated Staufen rivals. Claiming the throne was a dangerous business. It was not to be embarked upon lightly.

Seeking the crown was a matter of concern not only for the candidate in question. In Saxo's rendering, the initiative for Valdemar's kingship emanated not from his family, but from among his father's erstwhile allies. This comes as

---

[1] Saxo Grammaticus, *Gesta Danorum*, xiv.2.1, pp. 982–5.

233

234   7. UNANIMITY AND PROBITY

no surprise. An election inevitably pitched men of great power against each other. Mere lords did not make it to the royal finishing line. However, those great men did not act in isolation. Each formed part of a web of dependants, friends, relatives and allies. These networks were key both to the success of a bid for the royal throne and to one being made in the first place. Backers had to be won, the loyalty of allies and family secured. Neighbours and peers needed to be sounded out. They also could develop a dynamic of their own. When the Birkibeinar, his father's erstwhile followers, first offered the Norwegian throne to Sverrir, he demurred. In fact, he contemplated going on pilgrimage to Jerusalem to avoid becoming embroiled in the turmoil of Norwegian politics. However, the Birkibeinar kept watch on him, and eventually presented Sverrir with a stark choice. He must either take charge of them or be killed by them along with all his relatives. Their reasoning was as follows: the Birkibeinar had lost everything in the service of Sverrir's father. Their fathers and brothers had been killed and their lands had been seized. If they could not persuade Sverrir to take the throne, their only option was to wipe out Sverrir and his clan in order to curry favour with King Magnus and his father. Sverrir had a moral obligation both to his father and to his father's loyal supporters. In refusing to assume leadership of his desolate band of followers, he would betray not only their many services, but also his own and his family's honour.[2] Failure to claim the throne was an abrogation of the very duties that came with being one of the leading men of the realm.

Twelfth-century Norwegian royal politics were especially violent. The link between loyalty and patronage was not, however, unusual. Followers provided services for a variety of reasons. Family tradition and the absence of other sources of patronage certainly mattered, as did normative expectations of who could rightfully demand their loyalty. Provided one had a choice, nobody liked to serve a tyrant. Equally, connections that had formed over a generation or more could develop normative force: this was what one's forebears had done. Alongside and frequently interspersed with these, there existed pragmatic concerns: the ability to count on the backing of someone more powerful, who could assist in pursuing property claims and warding off rivals, who would help arrange advantageous marriages and secure favourable court hearings and who might offer support in the peaceful settlement of disputes, or armed assistance if required.

This broader framework is key to understanding why the choice of king mattered, and why an entourage might exert pressure on candidates. The standing of princes was in part dependent on the size of their household and affinity. If they could not protect their own, then these might look elsewhere.[3] Crucially, if a claimant had reasonable expectations of being able to succeed to

---

[2] *Saga of King Sverri*, chapter 9, pp. 9–11.
[3] Görich, *Friedrich Barbarossa*, 141.

IV. ELECTION

the throne, then the prospects for his followers also improved. They would be in possession of a most valuable asset: direct access to the royal person. On the other hand, a rival, perhaps with overlapping and disputed aspirations, gaining the crown or the ear of the king became a worrying prospect indeed. A candidate's chances of success had to be good enough for his bid to be a risk worth taking. The only course of events worse than a rival's patron succeeding was for one's own to be humiliated or to alienate the king ultimately chosen. Finally, even if the widespread premise that a king be more powerful than all the other princes did not always reflect reality, a successful candidate nonetheless received the crown because he had been able to forge alliances with other leading nobles and prelates. Those needed to be maintained, but they also provided a powerful means by which to take on anyone who rejected the outcome of an election, and even to settle old scores. In most medieval realms, this would not result in murder and exile. It could, however, mean that old disputes were revived and renegotiated, that the succession to fiefs and lands could become more difficult, that favoured ecclesiastical candidates would fail to succeed – and so on. A claimant's success or failure, and the honour or shame he incurred in the process, had immediate repercussions for his friends, family and followers. While being asked to stand for election could therefore be a sign of prestige, rejecting the invitation could also prove prudent. In 1125, several sources report that Count Charles the Good of Flanders had been approached about becoming a candidate for the German throne. Having consulted his nobles (who strongly advised against it), Charles declined. Yet the fact that he had been approached served to highlight the count's reputation for justice, martial prowess and piety.[4]

Alongside pragmatic concerns, there were moral and ethical ones. At least in theory, kingship was not in the gift of the people. The royal office had been ordained by God, and God would ensure that the most suitable and legitimate candidate would hold it. Unless, that is, the people merited punishment. Saxo Grammaticus explicitly linked the famine blighting Denmark during the rule of King Oluf, which ended only on Oluf's death, with the Danes' rebellion and the killing of St Knud Lavard.[5] Generally, though, all its connotations of divine sanction notwithstanding, being God's angel of vengeance was unlikely to be a label that most kings would have been keen to embrace – unless, as in the case of Sverrir, it was to undo injustice and to humble lowborn yet haughty usurpers like Erling. Hence the frequency with which visions and portents foretold that a particular claimant would be king because of his great virtue and

---

[4] Matthias Becher, 'Karl der Gute als Thronkandidat im Jahr 1125. Gedanken zur norddeutschen Opposition gegen Heinrich V.', in *Heinrich V. in seiner Zeit. Herrschen in einem europäischen Reich des Hochmittelalters*, ed. Gerhard Lubich (Cologne, Weimar and Vienna, 2013), 137–50.

[5] Saxo Grammaticus, *Gesta Danorum*, xii.1.2–4, pp. 864–7; xii.2.2–3, pp. 868–71.

236   7. UNANIMITY AND PROBITY

inherent suitability.[6] Even Emperor Henry II, or so Thietmar of Merseburg claimed, had been chosen unanimously, not least because of a vision, experienced by an unnamed priest. In it, a voice from heaven had ordained that Henry be king.[7] Exercising the royal office constituted a moral as well as a political duty. The king had to maintain the right order of the world, and had to do so not only by punishing evildoers, maintaining the peace and protecting the Church, but also by acting as moral exemplar. Moreover, with the exception of Denmark and Norway, once a king had been installed, he was difficult to be rid of again. It was paramount to choose a ruler who not only had the material means to exercise his office, but also the requisite moral outlook. Chapter 8 will discuss what this meant for conducting an election. Here, the focus will be on the normative framework of elections and the efforts taken to meet both practical needs and moral expectations. At its core were the expectation of unanimous consent and a deep concern for the probity both of claimants to the throne, and of those determining which of them would occupy the throne.

7.1   The Right Kind of Unanimity

Kingship may have been a gift from God, but it required the consent of the ruled.[8] Both demanded that a unanimous decision was reached. Dissent denoted that the divine will had been defied, whether because an unsuitable person had been chosen or because greedy and corrupt men resisted their Creator. There were normative as well as practical reasons underpinning this set of assumptions. Kings ought to be elected because they were suitable to occupy the throne, not because they promised to serve the worldly goals of their supporters. Unanimity also heightened the authority of the ruler. By backing his succession, the electors undertook to support him in the governance of the realm and to defend his claims against foes at home and abroad. This mattered even if there was no rival: inevitably, successions were moments of crisis. Erstwhile confidants were eager to secure position and status; those

---

[6]   William of Tyre, *Chronicon*, 427; *Anonymi Gesta Hungarorum*, 13–15; *Saga of King Sverri*, 2; *Gesta Principum Polonorum*, 6–9; *Legenda maior*, in *Legenda S. Stephani*, in *Scriptores Rerum Hungaricarum*, ed. Szentpétery, vol. 2, 379; Alexander of Telese, *Ystoria Rogerii*, 84–7; Albert of Aachen, *Historia Ierosolimitana*, 446–51.

[7]   Thietmar, *Chronicon*, v.2, pp. 194–7; *Ottonian Germany*, ed. Warner, 206–7. Similarly, Adelbert of Bamberg reported that St Wolfgang had appeared to Henry in a vision, and foretold his elevation: *Die Vita sancti Heinrici regis et confessoris und ihre Bearbeitung durch den Bamberger Diakon Adelbert*, ed. Marcus Stumpf, MGH SSrG (Hanover, 1999), 227–9.

[8]   Or, as explained in a letter sent on behalf of Frederick Barbarossa to Pope Eugenius in early 1152, Frederick had been granted royal dignity by God, who, not long after the death of his predecessor, had moved the princes, as well as the people at large, to confer the crown on him. *Briefbuch des Abts Wibald*, no. 349.

IV. ELECTION 237

who under the previous ruler had felt unfairly treated now expected their grievances to be heard and rectified; conflicts that had been held at bay by the old king burst out into the open.[9] The ruler needed the backing of his subjects just as much they needed that of the king. A smooth election served the interests of both.

High medieval writers therefore placed considerable value on succession through unanimous election. As the Danish chronicler Sven Aggesen put it, 'it was the primeval custom of our forefathers that, when kings were raised to the throne, all the Danes came together in a body at Isøre, so that royal inaugurations should be enhanced by the consent of all'.[10] Indeed, most accounts of royal successions stressed the unanimous nature of the event, whether in France, Hungary, Jerusalem, England or Germany.[11] Despite his corpse-snatching antics, even Henry II, Thietmar of Merseburg claimed, was elected unanimously,[12] and 'according to the divine will'.[13] Yet unanimity alone was not enough. It had to be the right *kind* of unanimity, and it could be achieved over time. The distinction between legitimate and illegitimate consent was at the heart of Bishop Thietmar of Merseburg's account of the imperial election of 1002.[14] Thietmar wrote within a few years of the events he recorded. He had either observed some of them himself, or, as a leading member of the Saxon aristocracy, had access to close relatives who had done so. Moreover, he compiled his *Chronicon* in part as a guide for his successors on how to engage in the politics of the realm. This did not prevent Thietmar from imposing his own interpretation on the matters at hand. He was, for instance, a staunch supporter of Henry II, who had not only re-established Merseburg, but had also appointed Thietmar its bishop. Yet Thietmar's interpretation of what happened was embedded in, and to some extent subordinate to, a detailed description of how he and his peers navigated the choppy waters of imperial politics. He offers one of the most detailed accounts to survive from the European Middle Ages of what politics meant in practice: of how the business of the realm was conducted, of the tools and mechanisms employed in its pursuit, of the challenges to be faced and opportunities to be seized. What then does he have to say about issues of unanimity and probity?

---

[9] See also below, Chapter 10.

[10] Sven Aggesen, *Brevis Historia*, in *Scriptores Minores*, ed. Gertz, vol. 1, 124–7; *Short History*, in *The Works of Sven Aggesen*, transl. Eric Christiansen, 65.

[11] See, for instance, Richer, *Histories*, vol. 2, 222–3; *Legenda S. Ladislai regis*, in *Scriptores Rerum Hungaricarum*, ed. Szentpétery, vol. 2, 518; Otto of Freising, *Gesta Frederici*, ii.1, pp. 284–5; Rigord, *Histoire*, 122–5.

[12] Thietmar, *Chronicon*, v.11, pp. 204–5; *Ottonian Germany*, ed. Warner, 213.

[13] Thietmar, *Chronicon*, v.2, pp. 194–7; *Ottonian Germany*, ed. Warner, 206–7.

[14] Partly because of Thietmar's treatment, the 1002 election has triggered an especially rich literature, most of it concerned with arguing whether or not hereditary lines of succession prevailed. For a comprehensive survey of that literature, and for an equally insightful critique, see Patzold, 'Königserhebungen'.

238   7. UNANIMITY AND PROBITY

Otto III's death without heirs opened wide the pool of potential successors. Duke Henry of Bavaria made his move early, but his efforts proved at first fruitless. In fact, we know of at least four other claimants. Most of those accompanying Otto's corpse, for instance, had not taken kindly to Henry's antics.[15] When pressed by the duke, the archbishop of Cologne declared that 'he would freely assent to whomever the better and greater part of the entire people inclined'.[16] That, as matters stood, would not be Henry. The prelate's emphasis on the 'greater and better part of the entire people' suggested that a divisive election could be countenanced, as long as the *sanior pars* agreed on a candidate. In fact, most of the prelates and princes escorting the emperor's remains chose to support Hermann of Swabia, while during Otto's funeral at Aachen others promoted the candidacy of the duke of Lotharingia.[17] In addition, Otto's Italian subjects elected a king of their own in the person of Arduin.[18] Meanwhile, the leading men of Saxony convened to discuss the state of the realm. In the course of their deliberations, Margrave Ekkehard of Meißen 'wanted to exalt himself over them'.[19] And, indeed, casting aside the views of his peers, he proceeded to claim the throne for himself.

The situation was serious. The proliferation of candidates heralded unrest and civil strife. Measures therefore had to be taken to ensure a peaceful resolution. In Saxony, about which Thietmar was much better informed than other parts of the realm, successive meetings took place. Nobles and prelates sought to narrow down the number applicants and to choose one behind whom they could all rally. Similar conventions probably took place across the realm.[20] They served to scrutinise candidates, but also allowed observers like Thietmar to assess the motivation of those backing a particular claimant and to comment on the validity of the proceedings. Just as in the case of designation, an election was a moral process. Only those who remained fully aware of the grave responsibility they were about to shoulder (or which they were asking a claimant to shoulder), who acted for the common good and not their private interests, could legitimately claim the throne and only they could legitimately raise one of their peers to the royal dignity. Other aspects of the

---

[15] See above, Chapter 6.
[16] Thietmar, *Chronicon*, iv.50, pp. 166–7; *Ottonian Germany*, ed. Warner, 187–8.
[17] Thietmar, *Chronicon*, iv.54, pp. 170–1; *Ottonian Germany*, ed. Warner, 188–9.
[18] Thietmar, *Chronicon*, iv.54, pp. 170–1; *Ottonian Germany*, ed. Warner, 188–9.
[19] Thietmar, *Chronicon*, iv.52, pp. 166–9; Eduard Hlawitschka, 'Merkst Du nicht, daß Dir das vierte Rad am Wagen fehlt? Zur Thronkandidatur Ekkehards von Meißen (1002) nach Thietmar, *Chronicon*, iv.c.52', in *Geschichtsschreibung und geistiges Leben im Mittelalter. Festschrift für Heinz Löwe zum 65. Geburtstag*, ed. Karl Hauck and Hubert Mordek (Cologne and Vienna, 1978), 287–311, at 297–9; Stefan Weinfurter, *Heinich II. Herrscher am Ende der Zeiten* (Regensburg, 1999), 36–41.
[20] Althoff, *Kontrolle der Macht*, 114–20. See also below, Chapter 8.

IV. ELECTION 239

election – even the desire for unanimity and concord – could reinforce, but could not substitute for this most essential moral requirement.

Thietmar approached the issue by sketching a series of contrasts – between Henry and his rivals, and between Henry and his eponymous father. Indeed, he opened his account of the 1002 election by juxtaposing the two dukes. When first mentioning the younger Henry's election, Thietmar recorded a vision experienced by an unnamed priest:

> after the death of Otto III, a certain venerable father had a revelation from heaven. A voice said to him: 'Do you recall, brother, how the people sang, "Duke Henry wants to rule, but God is unwilling?" Now, however, Henry must provide for the care of the kingdom by the divine will.' Everything pertaining to divine or human matters promoted him to the kingdom before others contemporary with him, whether they were willing or not.[21]

The verses cited by the heavenly voice referred to a failed bid for the throne by Henry's father. When Emperor Otto II died in 983, the elder Henry, having been exiled for a previous rebellion, hastened to Saxony. On Palm Sunday 984, shortly after he had taken control of the infant Otto III, Henry convened a diet at Magdeburg, to which he called 'all the leading men of the region ... in the course of negotiations, [he] demanded that they submit to his power and raise him to the kingship.' Some, Thietmar reports, did Henry's bidding willingly. Others employed an elaborate ruse and declared that they would be happy to swear fealty to Henry, but only if their king (Otto III) allowed them to do so. Undeterred, Henry called another meeting at Quedlinburg. While his followers acclaimed him as king, many nobles convened elsewhere to organise resistance. Moreover, while the list of Henry's opponents included leading Saxon nobles and clerics, the duke was backed by the dukes of Poland and Bohemia, traditional enemies of his people. After Quedlinburg, Henry's campaign quickly unravelled. Hurrying to Bavaria, he was able to secure the support of many Bavarian bishops, but a meeting with the archbishop of Mainz proved unsatisfactory. Henry even had to agree to return the infant king to his mother. By the end of June 984, he submitted.[22] Not only did he surrender his claim, he also repented of having raised it in the first place. On his deathbed, Thietmar reports, the duke summoned his son and advised him: 'Go quickly to your homeland, put your government in order, and never oppose your king. I much regret ever having done so myself.'[23]

The differences between Henry the elder's bid and his son's reinforced the legitimacy of Henry II's claim. Where the father had acted out of ambition and a desire to rule, the son was compelled by heaven to seek the throne; where the former had sought to disinherit his nephew, the latter was among Otto's most

---

[21] Thietmar, *Chronicon*, v.2, pp. 194–7; Warner, *Ottonian Germany*, 206–7.

[22] Thietmar, *Chronicon*, iv.1–8, pp. 114–23; *Ottonian Germany*, ed. Warner, 149–55.

[23] Thietmar, *Chronicon*, iv.20, pp. 134–7; *Ottonian Germany*, ed. Warner, 165.

240   7. UNANIMITY AND PROBITY

loyal servants; and where the elder Henry's ambitions had failed because of a lack of backing even from among his fellow Saxons, the younger was elected by the leading men of the realm. Moreover, the younger Henry's supporters gave their consent unanimously and freely. It came from the right people and for the right reasons. While Henry II was chosen for the benefit of his people, those endorsing his father had been driven by greed and a lust for power. They had assisted the elder Henry from fear or because they had viewed doing so as an opportunity to extend their own domains. Their support denoted a lack of principles.

The chronicler was careful not to paint Henry II's domestic rivals as archetypal villains. Just like the emperor's father – who, on his deathbed, had been allowed to repent – they were described as decent men, though blinded by ambition or led astray by evil counsellors. Hermann 'was a God-fearing and humble man. Seduced by many who were pleased by his mildness, he armed himself against Henry.' Dietrich was 'a wise man experienced in warfare, to whom the larger part of the people would incline'.[24] The partial exception was Ekkehard, who initially backed Henry but then could no longer restrain his ambition. He arrogated to himself a ceremonial position normally reserved for the king. Seeing, furthermore, that he would make no headway in Saxony, he travelled westwards to consult with Duke Hermann and others, insisting along the way, and with varying success, that he be received as king. However, when staying at Pöhlde, Ekkehard and his entourage were attacked, and Ekkehard was killed.[25] The margrave's hubris became his undoing.

Thietmar's circumspection reflects the fact that overcoming Dietrich and Hermann took some effort. They were received in grace, not defeated in battle.[26] They might have listened to bad advisors, and clearly lacked the moral outlook necessary to become king. However, they ultimately submitted to the rightfully chosen ruler. They possessed *some* of the virtues of a truly good king, but their qualities were no match for those of Henry, who excelled 'in everything pertaining to divine and human matters'. In a like vein, Thietmar never explicitly stated who voted for Henry II. The duke was chosen not in the regions over which he ruled already – Saxony and Bavaria – but in Mainz, well outside his domains. This set him apart from other candidates – chief among them Dietrich, who remained in Lotharingia, and Ekkehard, who could not even get the backing of the Saxons. There clearly were some who did not vote for Henry. However, even they ultimately came to side with him. In fact, Henry spent the months after his inauguration visiting and winning over

---

[24] Thietmar, *Chronicon*, v.3, pp. 196–7; *Ottonian Germany*, ed. Warner, 207.

[25] Thietmar, *Chronicon*, v.4–6, pp. 196–201; *Ottonian Germany*, ed. Warner, 208–10.

[26] Weinfurter, *Heinrich II.*, 53–4. Concerning Hermann's attack on Strasbourg and the demand to divide the realm between him and Henry, see also *Die St Galler Annalistik*, ed. and transl. Roland Zingg (Ostfildern, 2019), 186.

IV. ELECTION   241

some of the men who had been absent from his election or who had otherwise
failed to back him. In Thuringia, he received the homage of the duke and his
men,[27] before moving to Merseburg, where he met an assembly of the Saxons.
After the king had vowed to uphold their laws, the duke handed the imperial
lance to Henry, the people acclaimed the new king and did homage to him.[28]
Unanimity could be established gradually. What mattered was that those who
attended an election agreed to it without dissent. Winning over those who had
been absentees, even opponents of a ruler, was something to be undertaken
once a king had been enthroned.[29]

Furthermore, unanimity alone was not enough to ensure that rulership was
either successful or legitimate. Just as important were the moral standing and
the motivation of electors and elected. Henry the Elder, when claiming the
throne in 984, and Hermann of Swabia in 1002 followed evil counsel.[30] In
Hermann's case, Thietmar noted, the men urging him to claim the throne did
so because they hoped to profit from his well-known mildness. To be a truly
successful claimant, one had to be both closely related to one's predecessor and
morally superior to one's rivals. The point was made most explicitly when
Thietmar dealt with elections outside Germany. After the death of Otto III, the
Lombards proceeded to elect their own king in Arduin, who 'was more familiar
with the arts of destruction than those of government, and by the judgement of
God, those who elected him subsequently learned so for themselves'.[31] When
he 'seized the bishop of Brixen by the hair, as this prelate was saying things that
displeased him, and revealed his unbridled rage to all by forcing him to the
ground like a common cowherd', the Italians called upon Henry to rid them of
their tyrannous ruler.[32] Also in 1002, the Bohemians deposed their duke –
a tyrant who had castrated one brother and tried to suffocate another in

---

[27] Thietmar, *Chronicon*, v.14, pp. 206–9; *Ottonian Germany*, ed. Warner, 214–15.
[28] Thietmar, *Chronicon*, v.15–17, pp. 208–11; *Ottonian Germany*, ed. Warner, 215–17. On
      Merseburg see also Walter Schlesinger, 'Die sogennante Nachwahl Heinrichs II. in
      Merseburg', in *Geschichte in der Gesellschaft. Festschrift für Karl Bosl zum 65.
      Geburtstag*, ed. Friedrich Prinz, Franz-Josef Schmale and Ferdinand Seibt (Stuttgart,
      1974), 350–69.
[29] See below, Chapters 8 and 10.
[30] Concerning the former, see also the *Annals of Quedlinburg*: immediately after young Otto
      had been crowned king at Aachen on Christmas Day 983, Henry took possession of his
      nephew to act as his guardian. Soon, however, 'stimulated by the goad of increasing greed,
      and enticed by the wicked words of certain men, he tyrannically seized the throne. In that
      act of pride, it was revealed that he desired both to be called king and to be consecrated
      king. Although he managed to be called king by a few, he did not succeed in being
      consecrated king because he was prevented by God and by the decision of the faithful,
      who did not give their consent to him, but rather supported the lawfully elected and
      anointed king.' *Annales Quedlinburgenses*, 470–3; English translation: *Ottonian Germany*,
      ed. Warner, 154 n. 23.
[31] Thietmar, *Chronicon*, iv.54, pp. 170–1; *Ottonian Germany*, ed. Warner, 190.
[32] Thietmar, *Chronicon*, v.24, pp. 218–19; *Ottonian Germany*, ed. Warner, 221.

242 7. UNANIMITY AND PROBITY

a bathtub. Unanimously, they elected in his stead Wlodowej, a shameless drunk.[33] While Arduin and Wlodowej had been chosen with the free consent of all, their lack of morals set them apart from Henry and his rivals. Dietrich, and Hermann may not have been as suitable for the throne as Henry, but their virtuous disposition still far surpassed that of their Lombard and Bohemian counterparts. Inevitably, therefore, Arduin and Wlodowej did not last. Arduin found himself hunted and deposed, and eventually became a monk.[34] On Wlodowej's death, the exiled duke returned, and killed both his remaining brothers and all those who had supported his deposition.[35] Unanimity without morality led to bloodshed and tyranny.

The moral dimension of choosing a king was especially important when it came to challenging a ruler who had already been accepted and enthroned. Emperor Henry IV (r. 1056–1106) faced a total of five anti-kings, three of them his sons. In each case, care was taken to ensure a semblance of unanimity and to portray the election of his opponent as conforming to idealised norms. The best documented of these challenges is the one mounted by Rudolf of Rheinfelden in 1077.[36] His succession broke with precedent on a number of fronts. Previously, no eastern Frankish king had formally been deposed. There had, of course, been rival claimants, but they were all members of the royal *stirps*. Rudolf was not. Every care was therefore taken to present Rudolf's elevation as conforming to an ideal type of how an election should proceed. As in 1002, character and unanimity took centre stage. Lampert of Hersfeld, writing contemporaneously with events, dealt extensively with events leading up to Rudolf's election (though he stopped writing just before it happened). In his account, moves to replace Henry can be dated back to 1073.[37] That year, having recently rebelled, the Saxons agreed to a meeting at Gerstungen with a delegation of princes and prelates acting on the king's behalf, among them Rudolf of Rheinfelden, duke of Swabia. Once the emperor's representatives heard of the accusations against their lord, Lampert reports, they were horrified and agreed that the Saxons were to be reprimanded not for having defended their women and children by force, but for having put up with the king's tyranny for so long. The Saxons wanted to elect a new king at once, but decided to delay until they had lured Henry away from their lands. More specifically, they would have chosen Rudolf of Rheinfelden, but for the fact that the duke refused. He would not agree to his own elevation unless an assembly

---

[33] Thietmar, *Chronicon*, v.23, pp. 216–9; *Ottonian Germany*, ed. Warner, 221.

[34] Thietmar, *Chronicon*, vii.24, pp. 378–9; *Ottonian Germany*, ed. Warner, 323; Rosa Maria Desi, 'La double conversion d'Arduin d'Ivrée: Pénitence et conversion autour de l'An Mil', in *Guerriers et moines. Conversion et sainteté aristocratiques dans l'Occident médiéval (IXe – XIIe siècle)*, ed. Michel Lauwers (Antibes, 2002), 317–48.

[35] Thietmar, *Chronicon*, v.29, pp. 222–5; *Ottonian Germany*, ed. Warner, 224–5.

[36] On Rudolf: Muylkens, *Reges geminati*, 18–204.

[37] Muylkens, *Reges geminati*, 71–92.

IV. ELECTION 243

of *all* princes were to consent and declare that he could do so without breaking his oath of loyalty to the king.[38] With this, Lampert set the scene for the events unfolding three years later. Around Easter 1076, several princes and bishops convened to discuss the state of the realm. They were especially aggrieved by Henry's brutality and fickleness. Moreover, their concerns were shared by all the princes, or so Lampert asserted.[39] A year later, after Henry had (temporarily) been excommunicated by the pope, the princes gathered again, this time at Forchheim in Franconia. The ranks of the rebels had swelled considerably. No longer limited to just the Saxons, they now included the dukes of Bavaria, Swabia and Zähringen, and the archbishop of Mainz as well as the bishops of Metz and Würzburg, leading figures from the southern and western heartlands of the realm.[40]

Lampert repeatedly stressed the broad backing received by Henry's opponents. The Saxons had convinced even the king's emissaries that their actions were justified. In 1076 and 1077 almost all the German princes sided with those who sought to depose Henry. The motivations of both the electors and of their preferred nominee were also beyond rebuke. They did not act out of greed or lust for domination. If anyone had succumbed to the temptations of power, then it was the king. The election was therefore undertaken as a last resort, and only because a corrupt and evil ruler had left his subjects no choice. For these reasons, all possible care was taken to ensure that every step of the election process conformed to how a king *should* be chosen. Berthold of Reichenau, writing before 1088, reports that on 15 March a great number of the leading men of the realm convened. After lengthy discussion, everyone present agreed to elect Rudolf of Rheinfelden king: first the archbishop of Mainz, then the other prelates, followed by the nobles and 'all the people', who confirmed the decision by performing their oath of loyalty to the new king. The election, the chronicler emphasised, 'truly was not heretical, since it was lawfully carried out according to the general agreement and with the approval of all the people, electing a man who did not desire the office, but was unwilling and compelled to accept it'. Eleven days later, on 26 March, Rudolf entered Mainz, where he was 'approved, anointed, and ordained as the just king, ruler and defender of the whole kingdom of the Franks by those same bishops and by an assembly of all the people'.[41] The image persisted well into the twelfth century. According to Paul of Bernried, whose *Vita Gregorii VII* was written *c.* 1128,

---

[38] Lampert von Hersfeld, *Annales*, 202–5. On Lampert see: Tilman Struve, 'Lampert von Hersfeld', *Hessisches Jahrbuch für Landesgeschichte* 19 (1969), 1–123; 20 (1970), 32–142; Bagge, *Kings, Politics*, 231–311.
[39] Lampert von Hersfeld, *Annales*, 350–3. Muylkens, *Reges geminati*, 94–127.
[40] Lampert von Hersfeld, *Annales*, 418–21.
[41] *Bertholds and Bernolds Chroniken*, ed. and transl. Ian Stuart Robinson (Darmstadt, 2002), 141; English translation: *Eleventh-Century Germany. The Swabian Chronicles*, transl. I. S. Robinson (Manchester, 2008), 167. Muylkens, *Reges geminati*, 129–58.

244   7. UNANIMITY AND PROBITY

the assembled princes desired to reach a unanimous decision. They feared that any dissension among them would only aggravate further the many evils that had befallen the realm already.[42] In other words, Rudolf consented to his election only at the urging of prelates, princes and the people at large.[43] He was a most suitable candidate for the throne – humble, hesitant to assume power and forced into action by the tyrannous deeds of Henry IV and the pleas of his people. His election was beyond reproach because it was unanimous, undertaken as a last resort and through electors who acted solely for the common good.

These were, of course, partisan accounts. Yet Henry IV's supporters notably focussed their response not on the manner of Rudolf's elevation, but on that of his death in 1080, as a consequence of having lost his right hand in battle. According to the *Vita Heinrici IV*, this was a warning to all those who contemplated perjury: the right hand was, after all, the one with which Rudolf had sworn fealty to Henry.[44] The *Annals of Augsburg* stressed the association of Forchheim with Pontius Pilate, the archetypal false judge.[45] The most explicit reference to the election came in a letter by Wenrich of Trier. He described Gregory VII as supporting the tyrannous and treacherous usurpation of the throne by someone who placed a bloody and violent crown on his own head.[46] Whether or not Rudolf's election had been unanimous was less significant than the motivations underpinning it. By stressing Rudolf's treacherous end, by emphasising the association between the meeting at Forchheim and the judgement of Pontius Pilate and by describing the duke as someone who violently usurped the throne, these accounts invalidated the electoral process by subverting its claim to morality. The Forchheim assembly, it might be inferred, conformed to the letter, but not the spirit of how a king should be chosen. Defying his lord and betraying his oath of loyalty, Rudolf could not conceivably have been a just and pious ruler.

---

[42] Paul of Bernried, *Vita Gregorii VII*, in *Pontificum Romanorum qui fuerunt inde ab exeunte saeculo 9 usque ad finem saeculi 13 Vitae ab aequalibus conscriptae*, ed. I. M. Watterich, 2 vols. (Leipzig, 1862), vol. 1, 529–32. English translation: *The Papal Reform of the Eleventh Century: Lives of Pope Leo IX and Pope Gregory VII*, transl. I. S. Robinson (Manchester, 2004), 64–82. On the text: Walther Berschin, *Biographie und Epochenstil im lateinischen Mittelalter*, IV/2 (Stuttgart, 2001), 452–4.

[43] A like image is painted in Bruno of Merseburg's Saxon War, written *c.* 1085: *Brunos Buch vom Sachsenkrieg*, ed. Hans-Eberhard Lohmann (Leipzig, 1937), 85–6. On Bruno see: David. S. Bachrach, 'Bruno of Merseburg and his historical method, c.1085', *JMedH* 40 (2014), 381–98; Wolfgang Eggert, 'Wie "pragmatisch" ist Brunos Buch vom Sachsenkrieg?', *DA* 51 (1995), 543–53.

[44] *Vita Heinrici IV Imperatoris*, 19. See also Frutolf of Michelsberg, *Chronica*, ed. Franz-Joseph Schmale and Irmgard Schmale-Ott (Darmstadt, 1972), 94–5; Sigebert of Gembloux, *Chronica*, MGH SS 6, 364.

[45] *Annales Augustani*, MGH SS 3, 129.

[46] Wenrich of Trier, *Epistolae sub Theodoerici episcopi Virdunensis nomine composita*, ed. K. Francke, MGH Libelli 1 (Hanover, 1891), 280–99 at 294. Generally: Robinson, *Henry IV of Germany, 1056–1106*, 204–5.

IV. ELECTION   245

A similar emphasis on unanimity predicated on motivation surfaces elsewhere in Latin Europe. Events in England after 1135 may serve as example.[47]
Matilda had twice been confirmed as her father's heir, each time in a public
assembly and by all the prelates and barons present. Yet, on her father's death,
the throne was claimed Stephen of Blois, who was also elected unanimously.[48]
In 1153, the Treaty of Winchester, unanimously agreed by barons, clergy and
the rival pretenders to the throne, stipulated that Stephen remain king during
his lifetime, but that he adopt Henry as his successor.[49] We are thus dealing
with multiple acts of unanimous decision-making, none of them quite final.
Far more significant was the motivation of those giving their consent.
Stephen's partisans dismissed Matilda's claim because the oaths sworn to
accept her as queen had been forced. Moreover, on his deathbed Henry had
designated Stephen as his successor. Unanimity mattered (which was, after all,
how Stephen had been chosen), but it remained invalid if it had not been freely
reached. It could also be overridden if circumstances required that a more
suitable and powerful ruler be chosen (though he, too, had to be a unanimous
choice). In turn, Matilda's supporters questioned the moral foundations on
which Stephen's initially unanimous election rested. Henry of Huntingdon
stressed that Stephen's kingship was based on perjury. That his election had
been unanimous, that all those who had earlier sworn to accept Matilda then
elected Stephen, merely revealed the depravity of the English. In fact, God
censured those backing the usurper. Archbishop William of Canterbury, who
had crowned the king, died within a year. In a parallel with Thietmar's
portrayal of Arduin, Henry pointed out that the bishop of Salisbury was
subsequently persecuted by the very tyrant he had helped create.[50]
A candidate not suitable to hold the power of a king, or one chosen for the
wrong reasons, would be an oppressor of his people. Even a unanimous
decision had to be overturned if it had evidently been immoral in the first
place.
    One means of gauging the moral suitability of candidate and electors was to
consider the rationale underpinning their actions. This was a central feature in
Thietmar's carefully crafted contrast between Henry II, his father and his
rivals. William of Malmesbury pursued a similar line, describing Stephen as

> a man of extraordinary energy but lacking in judgment, active in war, of
> extraordinary spirit in undertaking difficult tasks, lenient to his enemies
> and easily appeased, courteous to all: though you admired his kindness

---

[47] See also above, Chapter 5.
[48] *Gesta Stephani*, 12–13; Richard of Hexham, *De gestis regis Stephani*, in *Chronicles of the Reigns of Stephen, Henry II, and Richard I*, ed. Richard Howlett, 4 vols. (London, 1884–9), vol. 2, 139–78, at 144–5.
[49] *Gesta Stephani*, 239–41.
[50] Henry of Huntingdon, *Historia Anglorum*, 701–3.

246　　　　　　　　　7. UNANIMITY AND PROBITY

in promising, still you felt his words lacked truth and his promise fulfilment.[51]

Like Thietmar, William did not paint a caricature of tyranny. Instead, he sketched the decline of a man who had some qualities of a good king, but not enough of them. Once elected, Stephen abandoned the advice of the wise and prudent men who, at first, had foolishly sided with him, and squandered the treasure inherited from Henry I. As a result, he attracted 'a class of men full of greed and violence, who cared nothing for breaking into churchyards and plundering churches', as well as those 'who hated King Henry's peace because under it they had but a scanty livelihood'.[52] Given that he had such supporters, it did not take long for 'the poison of malice, long nurtured in King Stephen's mind' to burst forth.[53] Both gradual and inevitable, his decline was rooted in the inability to act like a king.

William's account highlights the mutually reinforcing relationship between poorly qualified candidates and their supporters. Just as evil princes surrounded themselves with evil men, so those lacking the exemplary virtues of Henry II attracted followers who sought to exploit their generosity and mildness. While good kings valued truthful counsel, weak kings shunned anyone who might chastise them. Those truly capable of ruling would recognise when they were being led astray, and mend their ways accordingly. Tyrants and those unfit to be king, on the other hand, did not. Therefore, the motivations of the men choosing a king inevitably reflected the virtue and character of their favoured candidate.

At the same time, writers could take great care to exculpate actors for backing the wrong claimant. In 1118, William of Tyre reports, some of the barons in the crusader kingdom of Jerusalem initially decided not to support Baldwin II, the cousin of Baldwin I, but the late king's brother, Eustace. That, they declared, was what ancient law and custom demanded.[54] In the end, Eustace abandoned his claim. The nobles who had invited him might have been mistaken, but they still upheld basic norms of royal power. Eustace was the last surviving brother of the first ruler of crusader Jerusalem. In the absence of other male heirs, he should be considered next in line. His supporters were misguided, not evil, and ultimately ended up supporting Baldwin anyway. William of Malmesbury also excused the actions of some of Stephen's initial backers. The king had vowed to restore the governance of the English Church to the ideal *status quo ante* of William the Conqueror's reign. In fact, it was only because of these promises that Bishop Henry of

---

[51] William of Malmesbury, *Historia Novella*, 28–9.
[52] William of Malmesbury, *Historia Novella*, 32–3.
[53] William of Malmesbury, *Historia Novella*, 44–5.
[54] William of Tyre, *Chronicon*, 549–50.

IV. ELECTION 247

Winchester and the archbishop of Canterbury had accepted him. The archbishop had even forced Stephen to swear a solemn oath enshrining his promises.[55] Stephen similarly won over many nobles by vowing to be approachable and generous – not qualities commonly associated with Henry I.[56] However, once enthroned, his character flaws surfaced and he broke each of these commitments. Stephen both alienated those who at first had sided with him, and convinced the ones who had remained aloof to revive Matilda's claims.[57] William distinguished carefully between the motivation of Stephen's supporters who later switched sides, and of the king and his most loyal backers. The former tried to act for the good of the realm, but were duped by a king as charming as he was duplicitous. The latter sought to enrich themselves by exploiting the flawed character of an illegitimate and inept ruler. Those misguided in their decision would realise the error of their ways, while corrupt and evil men would continue down their nefarious path.

A unanimous election was essential for a king to become the legitimate ruler of his people. Yet it could be achieved over time, had to occur for the right reasons, had to be conducted by the right kind of people and had to result in the elevation of the right kind of person. Hence the extraordinary lengths to which the partisans of Rudolf of Rheinfelden and Stephen of Blois went in ensuring that their actions conformed to an ideal type of how a king should be chosen. Even that, however, might not be enough to persuade people inherently hostile to a particular candidate – especially if he proved unable to achieve unanimity even once elected and enthroned. Similarly, once agreement had been reached, the public process of electing a king – the behaviour expected of the successful claimant and of the electors – was designed to demonstrate that the right person had been chosen, for the right reasons and by the right people. But to get to that stage, and for that final display to be credible, further steps had to be taken. Because bad people elected bad kings, it was paramount that the probity of the candidates themselves was ascertained, which then testified to the righteous thinking of their backers. Having gained certainty about a candidate's moral suitability enabled the electors to assure themselves and a wider public of attendants, dependants and commentators, that they had, in good conscience, chosen the most suitable person for the throne. How someone seeking the throne demonstrated his moral backbone and virtuous disposition, during and in the lead up to the election, therefore highlights both the moral framework and the practical requirements of kingship.

---

[55] William of Malmesbury, *Historia Novella*, 28–9.
[56] Cooper, 'The feet of those that bark'.
[57] William of Malmesbury, *Historia Novella*, 28–31, 44–7.

248   7. UNANIMITY AND PROBITY

7.2 The Right Kind of Probity

As a rule, good kings were hesitant about assuming power.[58] Albert of Aachen reported that Baldwin II of Jerusalem was unsure whether to agree to his own election, as he felt that his county of Edessa already provided him with sufficient worldly goods.[59] Implicitly, Baldwin accepted the throne not for earthly gain, but in order to defend the beleaguered realm against its many foes. Rudolf of Rheinfelden's supporters also insisted that he had been reluctant to be king. According to Lampert of Hersfeld, he refused to be elected unless all the princes agreed,[60] and Berthold asserted that his election had been canonical, at least in part because Rudolf had to be forced into accepting the throne.[61] The duke's hesitation helped establish a clear contrast – both moral and procedural – between his kingship and that of Henry IV. Rudolf's reluctance publicly demonstrated that he did not desire the throne, but acted only at the behest of his people. The pattern was repeated across the Latin west. In Hungary, the *Legenda S. Ladislai Regis* recorded that St Ladislaus, lacking any desire for honour or worldly goods had been chosen unanimously.[62] In 1125, several chroniclers report, Lothar III had been elected king of the Romans despite being unwilling to assume power.[63] Hesitation could also be expressed through rejecting the appurtenances of royal power. Henry I of east Francia in 919 refused royal unction;[64] St Ladislaus abstained from wearing a crown and had it respectfully carried before him instead;[65] in the crusader states a legend developed that Godfrey had refused to adopt a royal title.[66] Good kings were reluctant kings.

Bad ones, by contrast, lusted after the royal crown, and worked hard to obtain it. This was true not only of the abortive attempts described by Thietmar. In 1138, Otto of Freising asserts, Duke Henry of Saxony failed to succeed to the throne because of his haughty and supercilious demeanour, and the fear that he might abuse his power to further his personal affairs over the

---

[58] See above, Chapters 3–5. For the phenomenon generally, Weiler, 'The *rex renitens*', on which the section on reluctance is loosely based.

[59] Albert of Aachen, *Historia Hierosolimitana*, 872–3.

[60] Lampert von Hersfeld, *Annales*, 350–3.

[61] *Bertholds and Bernolds Chroniken*, 141; *Eleventh-Century Germany*, 167. The image persisted into the twelfth century: Paul of Bernried, *Vita Gregorii VII*, i.529–32.

[62] *Legenda S. Ladislai regis*, in *Scriptores Rerum Hungaricarum*, ed. Szentpétery, vol. 2, 518.

[63] *Kaiserchronik eines Regensburger Geistlichen*, MGH Deutsche Chroniken 1 (Hanover, 1895) 387, ll. 16954–70; Godfrey of Viterbo, *Pantheon sive memoria saecularum*, PL 198, col. 986.

[64] Thietmar, *Chronicon*, i.8, pp. 10–13; *Ottonian Germany*, ed. Warner, 97; Liudprand of Cremona, *Antapodosis*, 43–4; Widukind of Corvey, *Die Sachsengeschichte*, i.26, p. 39.

[65] *Legenda S. Ladislai regis*, in *Scriptores Rerum Hungaricarum*, ed. Szentpétery, vol. 2, 517–18.

[66] William of Tyre, *Chronicon*, 430–2; Guibert of Nogent, *Dei Gesta Per Francos*, 317–18; *Histoire anonyme*, 232; *Peregrinationes tres*, 125. See also Chapter 3 above.

IV. ELECTION 249

business of the realm.[67] In 1141, the *Gesta Stephani* described Matilda as lusting for the royal crown and turning into a tyrant the moment she had it in her possession.[68] Rodulfus Glaber dealt at length with the succession to the kingdom of Burgundy in the 1030s. Its ruler, Rudolph III, lacked a legitimate male heir, which incited the ambitions of two of the chronicler's least favourite figures: Count Odo of Blois and Emperor Conrad II. Odo, descendant of Theobald the Deceiver, thus called for having invited the duke of Normandy to a feast and murdering him,[69] 'sought by force rather than flattery to seize the government of [Rudolf's] realm while he was still living. He offered many gifts to the magnates if they would accept him as king. But it was all in vain ...'[70] Undeterred, Odo pursued his claim, and even accepted the offer of the Lombard crown from the citizens of Milan, only to be defeated and killed in battle.[71] Conrad was no less perfidious a character. He represented what Rodulfus considered to be a common evil of the age. After Henry II's death, 'many of the magnates sought to interpose themselves, seduced by the brilliance of the royal crown rather than moved by a desire to foster the public weal and rule with justice. Foremost amongst them was Conrad ...'[72] In fact, when describing a heresy detected at Monteforte in Lombardy, Rodulfus reported that the devil bragged that Conrad had only been able to seize the throne with his help.[73] No wonder that Conrad's son feared for his father's soul.[74] Both count and emperor were driven by ambition and a lust for power. Royal might ceased to be a tool and became an end in itself. Odo and Conrad lacked the motivation and the moral probity truly to be kings.

Tyrants usurped the throne rather than waiting for it to be offered to them. They schemed to obtain what those truly deserving of so great an honour accepted only warily.[75] The moral dimension centred on the duties of kingship.

---

[67] Otto of Freising, *Gesta Frederici*, i.23, pp. 168–9.
[68] See above, Chapter 6.
[69] Rodulfus Glaber, *Historiarum libri quinqui*, 162–5.
[70] Rodulfus Glaber, *Historiarum libri quinqui*, 160–1.
[71] Rodulfus Glaber, *Historiarum libri quinqui*, 160–3.
[72] Rodulfus Glaber, *Historiarum libri quinqui*, 170–1.
[73] Rodulfus Glaber, *Historiarum libri quinqui*, 178–9.
[74] Rodulfus Glaber, *Historiarum libri quinqui*, 250–1.
[75] For related examples see: Wenceslaus I of Bohemia (935): *Gumpoldi Vita Vencezlai Ducis Bohemiae*, MGH SS 4, 219; Mieszko II of Poland (1030): *Annales Quedlinburgenses*, 364–7; Harold II of England (1066): *The Gesta Guillelmi of William of Poitiers*, 100–1; *The Gesta Normannorum Ducum of William of Jumieges, Orderic Vitalis and Robert of Torigni*, ed. and transl. Elisabeth M. C. van Houts, 2 vols. (Oxford,1995), vol. 2, 158–61; Henry of Huntingdon, *Historia Anglorum*, 384–9; 'The Brevis relatio de Guilelmo nobilissimo comite Normannorum*, written by a monk of Battle Abbey', ed. Elisabeth M. C. van Houts, *Camden Miscellany* 34 (1997), 1–48, at 28–9; Baldwin of Edessa (1098): Matthew of Edessa, *Armenia and the Crusades, Tenth to Twelfth Centuries: the Chronicle of Matthew of Edessa*, transl. Ara Edmond Dostourian (Lanham, MI, 1993), 221–2; Henry I of England (1100): Walter Map, *De Nugis Curialium*, 468–72; Matthew Paris, *Chronica*

250   7. UNANIMITY AND PROBITY

As Rodulfus had complained, none of the princes seeking to succeed Henry II did so because they wanted to be just rulers. Instead, they were driven by greed and a desire for the trappings of worldly might. Rashness and a lust for power, openly displayed, disqualified a candidate from legitimately ruling his people. The moral underpinnings are familiar ones. Kings had been granted immense power by God, but great power brought with it great responsibility. It also brought with it many temptations, and it took a man of exemplary virtue to uphold the former and withstand the latter. Anyone of a weak disposition would follow in the footsteps of Stephen of Blois, break their promises and bring about great misery. Those already evil would emulate Arduin of Ivrea, who beat bishops as if they were common servants, or the dukes of Bohemia, who were either lascivious drunkards or who maimed and murdered their own siblings. There was thus something distinctly pragmatic about this moral imperative. Displaying reluctance and insisting, however passively, that others encourage and cajole one into assuming power helped ensure that the king eventually chosen was at least aware that his new status was an office, a duty and a privilege, not a means by which to enrich himself or his backers.

The pragmatic dimension becomes even more marked once attention shifts from the ruled to the ruler. All the reluctant kings so far encountered faced several rivals, or even sought to displace a monarch who had already been enthroned. Lothar III's election in 1125 was so contentious that it remains the best documented such event in high medieval Europe;[76] Henry I of east Francia was chosen king over his predecessor's brother;[77] Godfrey became ruler of Jerusalem in competition with his fellow crusader, Count Raymond of Toulouse.[78] Each faced an added impetus to prove and demonstrate suitability, to show that they were indeed those most deserving of the crown. That does not, however, exhaust the practical advantages to be drawn from a public display of hesitation. Sverrir of Norway may serve as an example. Not only was his rival Magnus Erlingsson already firmly entrenched and in control of most of the realm, he had also won papal backing. The reasons Sverrir gave for his reluctance therefore merit consideration. First, when the Birkibeinar initially approached him, he suggested they approach Birgi instead. The latter had three

---

Majora, vol. 2, 130–1; Philipp of Swabia (1198): *Continuatio Admuntensis*, 588–91; *Chronica Regia Coloniensis*, 162–3; *Annales Marbacenses*, 71–3. See also, above, Chapters 3 and 4.

[76] Orderic Vitalis, *Ecclesiastical History*, vol. 6, 360–7; John Kinnamos, *Deeds of John and Manuel Comnenus*, transl. Charles M. Brand (New York, 1976), 72–3. See also below, Chapter 8. Generally, Schneidmüller, 'Mittelalterliche Geschichtsschreibung'.

[77] See above, Chapter 5.

[78] Raymond d'Aguilers, *Le 'Liber' de Raymond d'Aguilers*, ed. John Hugh Hill and Laurita L. Hill (Paris, 1969), 152; for an English translation: Raymond d'Aguilers, *Historia Francorum qui ceperunt Iherusalem*, transl. John Hugh Hill and Laurita L. Hill (Philadelphia, PA, 1968) 130; Albert of Aachen, *Historia Hierosolymitana*, 444–7.

IV. ELECTION   251

sons, whose claims were no weaker than those of Magnus. Sverrir further
suggested that the Birkibeinar ask Birgi to nominate one of them to be their
leader. Second, the Birkibeinar were a ragtag bunch: they had little in common
save 'poverty and trouble'. They lacked wealth, standing and allies. Little could
be accomplished by leading them. Third, Sverrir possessed neither the means
nor the experience to be their lord. He was little known, of uncertain parentage,
incapable of enterprise and utterly unfamiliar with the laws and customs of the
land.[79] The Birkibeinar would have none of this. They did not, however, force
Sverrir to assume leadership until after they had followed his advice. But then
Birgi also refused their offer. His sons, he explained, were too young and, being
Swedes, would never be accepted as kings in Norway. Furthermore, once told of
Sverrir's initial refusal, Birgi insisted that the Birkibeinar try again: nothing
would come of their endeavours unless Sverrir became their leader. Birgi also
procured a letter from King Knud of Sweden, and added one of his own, both
promising to lend whatever backing they could to Sverrir and his men. Only
then did the Birkibeinar return to Sverrir, confronting him with a stark choice
between leadership and death.[80] Moreover, in the evening after he finally
accepted command of them, Sverrir had a dream in which he was accosted by
the prophet Samuel, who anointed him and promised God's backing for his
endeavours.[81] Sverrir now had no choice but to claim the throne.

Sverrisaga combines the moral and the practical in exemplary fashion.
Sverrir did not seek power, but had it thrust upon him. His hesitation secured
much needed support and reinforced the loyalty of his men. By suggesting that
the Birkibeinar approach Birgi, Sverrir not only ensured that Birgi reinforced
the strength of Sverrir's claim – he, rather than Birgi's sons, would best be
suited to lead the band – but also got Birgi and King Knud to pledge their
support. By insisting that they still wanted Sverrir to be their leader, the
Birkibeinar forswore the right to abandon him, even though he was poor of
means, ill-equipped for enterprise and unfamiliar with the laws and customs of
the land. The episode echoed 1 Samuel 8. Samuel listed all the rights a king
would have over the Israelites. He could tax them, turn some of them into
slaves, others into servants, and they would have no escape from the yoke thus
placed upon them. Only after the Israelites repeated that they still wished to
have a king did the prophet pick one for them. *Sverrisaga* also foreshadowed an
account penned by Walter Bower in the fifteenth century, which ultimately fed
into Shakespeare's *Macbeth*. In book five of the *Scotichronicon*, composed
about 1440, Bower recounted how in the eleventh century, Malcolm, the
rightful king of Scotland, had fled to England. There, he was met by
Macduff, a leading nobleman, who tried to convince him to return home

[79]   *Saga of King Sverri*, chapter 8, pp. 8–9.
[80]   *Saga of King Sverri*, chapter 9, pp. 9–11.
[81]   *Saga of King Sverri*, chapter 10, pp. 11–12.

252   7. UNANIMITY AND PROBITY

and to assume the kingship of the Scots. Malcolm, however, feared that this
was a trap laid by his enemies, and therefore decided to test Macduff. He began
by explaining that he would not be able to restrain his lustful desires. Macduff
sought to assure him that this would not pose a problem. He listed several
earlier kings with unrestrained libido who nonetheless had been able to secure
their subjects' loyalty. But Malcolm still declared himself unworthy. Once
chosen king, he would not only ravish the wives and daughters of his nobles,
but would also rob them of their riches and treasures. Again Macduff found
past precedent to point out that this was common behaviour for kings.
However, when Malcolm then protested his lack of faith, that he could not
be trusted and frequently broke his word, Macduff decided that he could not
support Malcolm's claim any longer and left. Malcolm, now convinced that
Macduff's mission was no ruse, set out after him, revealed that all he had told
him had been a ploy and happily travelled back to Scotland.[82] A show of
reluctance served as a public confirmation of universally held beliefs about the
duties of kingship. It also provided a mechanism for the prospective ruler to
assure himself of the support of his putative subjects. There was no point in
accepting an election if the offer was made halfheartedly, or if the electors were
unwilling to lend the candidate their full backing.

While nobody should desire the throne, refusing it could be construed as an
act in defiance of the divine will. As Gregory the Great had explained, one must
not refuse such responsibility when it was offered. While some faked humility
to escape these obligations, they in fact committed the sins of pride and
disobedience.[83] The concept was employed widely by Anglo-Norman chroniclers. In 1099, they claimed, Duke Robert of Normandy, eldest son of William
the Conqueror, had been offered the crown of Jerusalem. However, he rejected
the offer, hoping for greater gains and an easier life back in England and
Normandy. In fact, Robert was so afraid of having to assume the throne that he
secretly abandoned the crusaders' camp. This, at least, was the version of
events related by William of Malmesbury, Henry of Huntingdon and Ralph
Niger.[84] Robert's defeat and incarceration at the hands of his youngest brother
in 1106 resulted from his defiance of God's will. There is no factual basis to this
tale. Crusading texts and those from the Holy Land list only Godfrey and
Count Raymond as putative rulers of Jerusalem.[85] Robert's refusal was rooted

---

[82] Walter Bower, *Scotichronicon*, vol. 3, 3–17. K. D. Farrow, 'The historiographical evolution
      of the Macbeth narrative', *Scottish Literary Journal* 1 (1994), 5–23. I am grateful to Simon
      Taylor and Michael Brown for these references.
[83] Gregory the Great, *Regula Pastoralis*, i.148–50.
[84] William of Malmesbury, *Gesta Regum Anglorum*, vol. 1, 702–3; Henry of Huntingdon,
      Historia Anglorum, 442–3; Radulfus Niger, *Chronica: eine englische Weltchronik des 12.*
      Jahrhunderts, ed. Hanna Krause (Frankfurt/Main, et al., 1985), 260–1.
[85] Petrus Tudebodus, *Historia de Hierosolymitano Itinere*, ed. John and Laurita L. Hill
      (Paris, 1977), 142; Raymond d'Aguilers, *Le 'Liber'*, 152; Albert of Aachen, *Historia*

IV. ELECTION

253

in the concerns of later English writers. By refusing to rule Jerusalem, he forfeited the right to govern England.[86] Worse still, Robert's actions were rooted not in pious humility, but in a lust for worldly pleasure. William of Malmesbury claimed that he had refused the kingdom 'not from any consideration of modesty ... but through fear of its insoluble difficulties'. More poignantly, Robert 'returned home, expecting to be free to devote himself to pleasure and delight'.[87] Henry of Huntingdon asserted that Robert refused the crown 'because of the labour involved'.[88] The duke hesitated to accept the throne not because he was wary of the moral challenges that holding so much power entailed, but because he feared the ardours of governance.

Just as unanimity had to be reached for the right reasons and with the right people, so reluctance had to be displayed with the right inner disposition, and on the right grounds. Simply refusing a throne because the task was too difficult meant rejecting God's will. The only course of action even more despicable was to feign reluctance – though even then there was room for interpretation. Gislebert of Mons' account of Frederick Barbarossa's succession in 1152 provides a case in point. Frederick had tricked several nobles who lusted after the throne. He met each of them privately, declaring that he did not want to be king himself. But it would be more suitable if he cast their vote in their stead and on their behalf. Each agreed, and transferred his vote to Frederick. During the election, each of the aspirants declared that that he had placed his in Frederick's hands. Frederick then simply nominated himself.[89] The episode reveals much about the relationship between motivation and action in the display of reluctance. Frederick clearly desired the throne – he did, after all, develop an elaborate ruse to seize it. He still emerged as the more suitable candidate because he revealed as false the pretence of his rivals' humility. He tricked the tricksters. On the other hand, a leader might project humility but then prove himself unworthy of the throne. In 1134 the Danes chose Erik the Memorable as their king. Erik initially refused the honour. He wanted to exact revenge on Niels first – and revenge, he felt, would be unworthy of a king. To some extent, Erik was acting like an ideal

Ierosolimitana, 446–55; Robert the Monk, *Historia Iherosolimitana*, ed. Damien Kempf and Marcus G. Bull (Woodbridge, 2013), 101; Baldric of Bourgeuil, *Historia Ierosolimitana*, ed. Steven Biddlecombe (Woodbridge, 2014), 112–13.

[86] The episode had a long life in English historical memory. It was, for instance, invoked when, on Christmas Day 1256, Earl Richard of Cornwall was offered the crown of the Holy Roman Empire. According to Matthew Paris, those attending the Christmas parliament urged Richard not to repeat the mistake made by Robert of Normandy: Matthew Paris, *Chronica Majora*, vol. 5, 601–3. See also, for his general reception of the story about Robert, with some emendations not found in Matthew's sources: Matthew Paris, *Historia Anglorum*, ed. Frederick Madden, 3 vols. (London, 1866–9), vol. 1, 149–50.

[87] William of Malmesbury, *Gesta Regum*, vol. 1, 702–3.

[88] Henry of Huntingdon, *Historia Anglorum*, 442–3.

[89] Gislebert of Mons, *Chronique*, 92–4; *Chronicle of Hainaut*, 54–5. See also above, Chapter 5.

254   7. UNANIMITY AND PROBITY

ruler. However, when his forces entered Jütland, they were routed in battle by Niels' allies. Erik therefore returned and accepted the royal title, now intent on exacting even fiercer revenge.[90] Far from strengthening his claim, Erik's hesitation had weakened it. He pretended to have the inner disposition of a good king, but lacked the resources of one. There was no point in rejecting an honour if one lacked the means to perform the duties it entailed.

Displays of reluctance had to be recognised and accepted by the electors, who had to play their part and seek to overcome it. There was no guarantee that they would do any of these things. In 1103, Ubbe refused the Danish throne and suggested that his brother Niels occupy it instead. To Saxo, this testified to Ubbe's sagacity, and he berated the Danes for not realising that Ubbe 'was shunning the burden by a pretence of unskillfulness'. They should have persisted, as only a truly wise man would prefer a private life to taking on the burdens of the realm.[91] Like Valdemar's mother, Ubbe had realised the dangers inherent in bidding for the throne. Unlike the Birkibeinar, however, the Danes did not see through Ubbe's ruse, and picked a less suitable king instead. They had failed in their duties and therefore became the architects of their own misfortunes. By voting for Niels, they proved that they could no longer be entrusted with choosing their king.[92]

Equally, rivals and subjects had to accept that reluctance did signify suitability. There was no guarantee that they would. In Germany in 1125, Archbishop Adalbert of Mainz wanted to make Duke Lothar of Saxony king, but could not do so without possessing the imperial insignia. He therefore held an assembly in which the throne was offered to Duke Frederick of Swabia, who handed the insignia to the princes and, to show his reluctance, refused the crown, presumably in the expectation that he would be pressured into accepting it. Instead, Adalbert announced that, as Frederick had refused the throne, Lothar should occupy it instead.[93] The episode was recorded over a century later by Albert of Stade. It reflects the myths that had begun to surround the famously contentious 1125 election. Albert's account also echoes a popular type of anecdote, normally recounted in relation to Frederick Barbarossa, about his tricking his way to the throne.[94] Many of these borrowed from another well-known episode in the election of Pope Alexander III in 1159, the most detailed account of which survives in a letter by Arnulf of Lisieux. Having been elected, Alexander III gave the required display of humility by rejecting the insignia of his office. His rival, Victor III, immediately jumped onto the papal throne, grasped the insignia and

---

[90] Saxo Grammaticus, *Gesta Danorum*, xiii.8.2–4, pp. 947–51.
[91] Saxo Grammaticus, *Gesta Danorum*, xii.8.2–3, pp. 894–7.
[92] See also above, Chapter 6, and below, Chapter 8.
[93] *Annales Stadenses*, MGH SS 16, 322.
[94] Weiler, 'Tales of trickery and deceit'.

IV. ELECTION   255

proclaimed himself pope.[95] The archbishop and Victor broke the rules. They exploited the expectation that Conrad and Alexander display due hesitation before assuming power. Unlike Frederick Barbarossa, they did not have a legitimate cause for doing so. They certainly lacked the backing of their people. Thus, both Lothar's kingship and Victor's pontificate were morally stained from the outset.

Like any symbolic act, the display of humility was precarious and its meaning malleable. Whether it was going to be perceived as legitimate or not, as undertaken sincerely or under false pretences, remained for audiences to decide. Yet describing the act and its performance was also a popular vehicle through which to convey meaning. Indeed, many of the examples discussed were written several decades after the events recorded. They are unlikely to have been based on eyewitness testimony, but rather employed the gesture of a candidate's unwillingness to come to terms with an unexpected course of events, to hint at how those subsequently unfolded or to pass judgement on the actors involved. For Gislebert and others, trickery may have served to explain Frederick Barbarossa's unexpected succession in 1152, not least because it reflected his reputation as wily and not wholly trustworthy. For Saxo, the inability of the Danes to choose the right king strengthened the case for hereditary succession, which was introduced in 1165.[96] And to William of Malmesbury and Henry of Huntingdon, Robert Curthose's refusal to bear the burden of ruling Jerusalem legitimised his dispossession at the hands of Henry I. A candidate unwilling to take the throne provided a convenient shorthand with which to convey moral, if not always historical, truths.

Still, the trope of the reluctant king would not have been credible had reluctance not been what good rulers were supposed to show before accepting the throne. Writers may have been concerned with communicating ethical norms rather than the exact course of events, but in order for that to work, their accounts needed to seem plausible.[97] There were, after all, good reasons why a display of humility and hesitation could prove advantageous. Beyond garnering support, there was the public nature of the act and the particular context in which it was normally performed. Successful

[95] *The Letters of Arnulf of Lisieux*, ed. Frank Barlow, Camden Series Third Series 61 (London,1939), nos. 28–9.

[96] Notably, Saxo's account conflated several events in dealing with Erik the Memorable, whose defeat in Jütland, for instance, had actually taken place three years before his election. Saxo Grammaticus, *Gesta Danorum*, vol. 2, p. 946 n. 47.

[97] Authors might also have drawn on clerical models, where the demonstrative display of hesitation and reluctance was deeply ingrained in the ritual context of papal or episcopal elections. But then the practice might easily be transferred from one sphere to the other, given that in either case power had been granted by and therefore ultimately derived from god. See Weiler, '*Rex renitens*', 18–26 and above, Chapter 2. On the interplay between clerical and secular elections, Reinhard Schneider, 'Wechselwirkungen von kanonischer und weltlicher Wahl', in *Wahlen und Wählen*, ed. Schneider, 135–71.

256   7. UNANIMITY AND PROBITY

claimants did not demur in closed meetings, but in large assemblies that brought together as many of the leading men of the realm as possible. This was as true when new kingships were created as when an already established royal title was claimed. Rudolf of Rheinfelden expressed his hesitation before ever larger groups of princes, Ubbe to the Danes who had come together to choose a king and Frederick of Swabia before the princes and prelates who had convened for that same purpose. Hesitation also had to be well-timed to be effective. It was normally displayed during the final stages of the election process. Otherwise, the archbishop of Mainz' ruse would not have worked, nor would have Victor III's usurpation. Only once a decision had been made, could a display of reluctance credibly be performed. There would have been little point in rejecting a dignity for which one had not even been chosen. The act signalled virtue only if it was performed at a moment when power was within one's reach. In being offered a crown, a candidate already demonstrated that he had the power and means to claim it. Now he had to show that he deserved it.

Through their presence, participants attested to the virtue of the new ruler. They were, however, complicit if they picked a king unsuitable for the role or if they later betrayed their initial choice. Reluctant kingship reflected on the moral disposition of the electors as much as that of the king. This narrative function was closely entwined with broader structural patterns. Notably, a display of hesitation occurred almost exclusively when there was a disputed succession or when a new kingship was created. In 919, Conrad I was succeeded not by his brother Eberhard, but by Duke Henry of Saxony. In Jerusalem in 1118, Baldwin I was succeeded not by his brother, but by an eponymous cousin. Rudolf of Rheinfelden in 1077 and Sverrir of Norway a century later claimed the throne in opposition to powerful rulers. Hesitation required that there were rivals who had to be overcome at least in part through demonstrating adherence to ideals of royal governance. Reluctance was not normally on display when a leader could claim divine designation – as with Emperor Henry II in 1002 – or when his claim rested on restoring a legitimate line of succession – as with William the Conqueror in 1066 or Valdemar I of Denmark in 1146. Of course, suitability still had to be demonstrated. Yet, if there were several claimants with equally valid claims, or if someone more powerful had to be overcome, it became essential that no accusations of ambition or greed could be levelled at a king or his electors. Public reluctance provided a convenient shorthand with which to communicate that a royal title had been accepted for the common good, at the behest of the people, that it had been offered by men of probity and good repute, and in such a manner as to ensure that rejecting their approach would have equalled defying the will of God.

So far, we have focussed on how the moral probity of the prospective king could be established. We have also seen that candidates for the throne were not

IV. ELECTION   257

free agents. They were embedded in a complex web of expectations and norms as well as of practical needs and obligations. By asserting their own suitability, they asserted that of their dependants and backers. Simultaneously, we have to contend with the fact that normally very little is said about the motivation of electors – except when it was decried as immoral. Rare indeed are statements like Otto of Freising's about those voting for Frederick Barbarossa in 1152: they elected him not only because of his outstanding valour and great energy, but also because he was related to two prominent families in the realm, the Welfs and the Staufen. The first produced great dukes; the second, emperors. Through the election of Frederick, the rivalry between the two dynasties would be ended and their forces combined for the benefit of the realm. This, Otto stressed, had been the consideration when Frederick's election was celebrated.[98] Debates as such are recorded even more rarely, with Thietmar's account of 1002 an important exception.[99] Frequently, observers do not even name the electors. Such relative silence reflects the importance of amicable unanimity. Both ruler and process derived their legitimacy from the fact that the great men and the prelates had acted in unison. Somewhat ironically, electors proved their moral probity by conducting an election in such a way to render reports of their role redundant.

The absence of evidence can thus be revealing. On an elementary level, the best means electors had of demonstrating that their motives were pure was to stress that they elected the right candidate and for the right reasons. A display of unanimity and, if appropriate, of royal reluctance went some way towards satisfying the requirement. But other steps also needed to be taken. Campaigning for the throne and negotiating over one's vote were frowned upon. Both did still happen, as we will see. But they did not normally form part of the publicly visible process of choosing a king. Only tyrants, usurpers and anyone lacking sufficient qualification for the throne campaigned. Henry II may have taken Otto's funeral cortege captive and demanded that he be crowned king, but in the end a celestial vision and Henry's undeniable suitability sufficed to ensure his succession. Henry's father, by contrast, as well as Hermann of Swabia and Ekkehard of Meißen actively campaigned for the throne, and even tried to force the people to vote for them. Odo of Blois tried to win over the Burgundians with threats and promises in order to secure the throne. Good kings did no such thing. If their claim was undisputed, they simply stated it and had it unanimously approved.

If conditions were posed, they were carefully circumscribed. Bruno of Merseburg's account of Rudolf of Rheinfelden's election in 1077 offers an illuminating vignette. Otto of Northeim, a leading Saxon noble, did not want to elect Rudolf, unless he first promised to restore Otto's honour – code for his

---

[98] Otto of Freising, *Gesta Frederici*, ii.2, pp. 284–7.
[99] See Chapter 8.

258   7. UNANIMITY AND PROBITY

rights, privileges and standing. On hearing of Otto's demands, the papal legate attending the assembly intervened: a king was to be chosen for the benefit of all, not for that of a single person. If, in fact, Rudolf had made such promises prior to being elected, this would constitute simony, the sale of spiritual services for money. The sole exception were urgent abuses, but those had to be framed in terms of general principle, and had to be identified as such by the assembled prelates.[100] The link between concrete material promises and simony is especially worth noting. Being a gift from God, the royal office could not be sold or bought. The legate's intervention also reflects practical needs. Kings should be beholden not to powerful men but to the community of their subjects. In fact, it is striking how reticent contemporary or near-contemporary observers were about specific promises made to individual electors. Often they can be surmised only from grants issued and initiatives undertaken by rulers soon after their election. When kings were forced to make promises, they related to the general affairs of the realm, were issued to a particular group of people who spoke on behalf of the community as a whole and tended to be combined with the inauguration ceremony itself. In other words, every care was taken to ensure that, in the public performance of an election, those choosing a king be seen to act not for their own benefit, but for that of the people and the realm at large. It was by meeting that expectation, alongside the unanimity of their decision, that they demonstrated probity and ensured the legitimacy of their chosen king. Their performance attested to the fact that they had adhered to the moral framework for choosing a ruler.

But to get to that stage, several steps had to be taken. Electors had expectations of their own to meet. Like kings, they were embedded in networks of friends, family and followers. Supporting a candidate should thus bring with it rewards that went beyond upholding the common good. Disputes had to be settled, rivals kept at bay, injustices rectified. Furthermore, voters still had to narrow down a range of applicants. How did they do that? Who were they? What challenges did they face? What steps did they take to ensure that, even in the case of a disputed succession, a semblance of unanimity was achieved and probity demonstrated? Even once all these issues had been clarified, there remained the problem that every succession was a moment of crisis. How did electors and candidates ensure that events did not spiral out of control? And how did they negotiate the inevitable clash between norm and reality? Bartering, campaigning and deal-making *did* take place. Votes were bought, alliances were forged and supporters needed to be won. How were these embedded in a process whose legitimacy depended on avoiding precisely such dealings?

---

[100] Bruno of Merseburg, *Saxonicum Bellum*, 85–6.

8

Choosing a King

Elections were both essential and elusive. Few writers dealt with them in detail, and even then only if they occurred during a time that authors or at least their parents and grandparents could recall, or if there was something extraordinary about them. 'Gallus' may have traced the Piast dukes of Poland back to their mythical origins, but he first touched on the procedure for choosing a duke when recounting the events of 1099, just over a decade before he commenced writing.[1] Cosmas of Prague recorded the deeds of the Bohemians from the fall of the Tower of Babel to the early twelfth century. But the first election that he explicitly described as such happened in 1037. Such reticence did not imply that elections were something novel. Cosmas remarked that the new duke's attendants distributed coins among the waiting crowds, 'just as they always do in the election of a duke'.[2] It just so happened that the 1037 succession was the first for which Cosmas had sources to draw upon. A similar pattern is evident in the Middle High German *Kaiserchronik* (c. 1140). It only moved from generally noting the fact of an election to a reasonably in-depth account of one when it came to that of Lothar III in 1125.[3] Elections were assumed to have happened in the past, but how precisely they unfolded often proved elusive.

Authors also limited themselves to recounting what was widely visible. Cosmas focussed on the manner of acclamation, and the *Kaiserchronik* on Lothar's reluctance. They did not know, or chose not to reveal, much about how that stage had been reached. The omission points to an inherent tension between the normative framework of elections and how a ruler was in fact chosen. It will form a recurring theme throughout this chapter. Furthermore, events in 1037, 1099 and 1125 demanded attention because something unusual had happened or was triggered by them. In 1037, the burial of Duke Oldrich was interrupted when his older brother Jaromir unexpectedly arrived. Jaromir had been blinded, deposed and kept in chains by his younger sibling. On reaching Prague, the former duke halted the proceedings to give a speech at Oldrich's coffin, before placing his youngest brother on the ducal throne. Jaromir then

---

[1] See Chapter 5.
[2] Cosmas of Prague, *Chronica*, 78; Cosmas of Prague, *Chronicle of the Czechs*, 106.
[3] *The Book of Emperors*, 378.

260   8. CHOOSING A KING

insulted a prominent aristocratic faction. Its leader responded by sending 'his executioner: when the blind man [i.e. Jaromir] went out to purge his belly in the night, he pierced him through with the sharpest dagger, from his posterior all the way to his inner stomach'.[4] The 1037 election may not have been unusual, but the events surrounding it certainly were. They required recording because, even by Bohemian standards, they were exceptionally violent. Less spectacularly, but no less significantly, the Polish settlement of 1099 fell apart within a few years, resulting in a civil war that continued into the time when 'Gallus' was working on the *Gesta*. Lothar's elevation similarly heralded a period of considerable unrest. The context and consequences of an election inevitably determined what was remembered and therefore what could be recorded.

At the same time, because so little was known about ancient practices, the moment when a ruler was chosen presented writers with an opportunity to fashion an ideal with which to comment on the present, and with which to promote what should be over what was. Saxo Grammaticus provides an especially colourful example. After the death of the mythical King Frothi III, he recounts, the Danes picked his successor by way of a poetry competition.[5] This stands in striking contrast to the rather more sordid considerations that Saxo believed to have motivated their eleventh- and twelfth-century descendants. Whereas the Danes of yore, 'filled with a desire to echo the glory when noble braveries had been performed, alluded in the Roman manner to the splendour of their nobly wrought achievements with choice compositions in a poetical manner',[6] the kingdom's modern inhabitants were characterised by their sluggishness regarding matters of religion and learning.[7] The imagined election of Frothi's successor highlighted standards of virtue and literacy that Saxo's contemporaries were in dire need of emulating. Saxo was not the only one to realise the potential of election narratives as a vehicle for communicating fundamental principles. In the Anonymous Notary's *Gesta Hungarorum*, the Blood Oath denoted the origins of a communal Hungarian past. In Theodoric the Monk's version of the Norwegian past, a marked contrast was

---

[4] Cosmas of Prague, *Chronica*, 77–9 (quotation at 79); Cosmas of Prague, *Chronicle of the Czechs*, 105–8 (quotation at 107–8).

[5] Saxo Grammaticus, *Gesta Danorum*, vi.1.1, pp. 354–7: 'they therefore decided that the man most suitable to take up the sceptre would be someone who could attach to Frothi's new burial-mound an elegy of praise glorifying him, one which would leave a handsome testimony of the departed king's fame for later generation'. On Frothi see also above, Chapter 4. Indeed, book six of the *Gesta Danorum* focussed on the appreciation that the ancient Danes had habitually shown for poetry, and its effectiveness as a political tool (ibid., 354 n. 1). A key figure was Starkath, who not only composed a poem about Danish wars in Sweden (ibid, viii.1.1, pp. 532–3), but also berated King Ingiald for indulging in unpatriotic luxury. Naturally, he did so in the form of two long poems: ibid, vi.9.2–20, pp. 424–47.

[6] Saxo Grammaticus, *Gesta Danorum*, Preface i.3, pp. 4–7.

[7] Saxo Grammaticus, *Gesta Danorum*, Preface i.1, pp. 2–3.

IV. ELECTION   261

established between kings who had been chosen by the people and those who murdered their way onto the throne. After the death of Harald Fairhair, his son Erik, who had killed several of his brothers, was simply recorded as succeeding. Because of Erik's tyranny, 'the Norwegians recalled Håkon and made him their king'.[8] He proved to be a just and pious ruler, 'who reigned in peace for 19 years', before being killed in battle by his nephews.[9] Håkon's relatives, by contrast, merely acceded to the throne, and were themselves expelled by Håkon the Evil. It was during his reign that Olaf Tryggvason was 'proclaimed king' by all the people.[10] Olaf brought Christianity to Iceland and the Shetlands, and built the first churches in Norway. And so the pattern continued. Virtuous rulers were chosen by the people. Tyrants and usurpers simply seized the crown. Election was a mark of virtue.

The high medieval evidence therefore presents us with something of a dilemma, yet one that conforms to the pattern established in the previous chapter. The best election was one that did not merit recording.[11] The relative lack of detail also suggests that many observers had not been privy to the process in its entirety. Idealised depictions like Saxo's and Theodoric's, passing allusions as in the *Kaiserchronik* and accounts of especially contentious occasions like the one recorded by Cosmas allow us to sketch a horizon of expectations. They reveal what contemporaries deemed feasible and what they thought should happen (or should have happened). They also offer glimpses of the social realities surrounding the electoral process. The exclusion of unwanted witnesses would be one example. So would be the emphasis on public consent, on the presentation of the new ruler to the people at large for acclamation and the importance attached to that act as the foundation on which legitimate rulership rested. More will emerge as this chapter progresses. We can fill some of the remaining gaps by considering the context of what was said, and of the social realities reflected in it. And then there are other types of materials, notably letters, that allow us to flesh out the often sparse narrative record. Taken together, and approached in this fashion, enough evidence survives to sketch a pattern of the election not as an event, or a set of legal norms, but as an extended process.

8.1 Preparing

In the summer of 1125, important news reached the chancery of Bishop Otto of Bamberg. Emperor Henry V had died on 23 May 1125. In the weeks that

---

[8] Theodoricus Monachus, *Historia*, 6; *An Account of the Ancient History of the Norwegian Kings*, transl. David and Ian McDougall, introduction by Peter Foote (London, 1998), 5.
[9] Theodoricus Monachus, *Historia*, 9–10; Theodoricus Monachus, *An Account*, 7.
[10] Theodoricus Monachus, *Historia*, 17–18; Theodoricus Monachus, *An Account*, 14.
[11] See, for example, *Annales Aquenses*, 686; *Annales Pegavienses*, 260; Rigord, *Histoire*, 122–5; Roger of Howden, *Gesta*, vol. 2, 79–83; Saxo Grammaticus, *Gesta Danorum*, xiv.33.1, pp. 1244–5.

262   8. CHOOSING A KING

followed, a group of princes and prelates who had been present at the emperor's funeral invited the great men of the realm to convene at Mainz on 24 August to elect a new king. They announced their efforts in a series of letters, but only the one sent to Bamberg survives. The signatories explained that so important and urgent a matter as the election of a king could not be decided in Otto's absence. They therefore requested that he attend the Mainz diet so that, guided by the Holy Spirit, they could reach a decision. The authors assured the bishop that they had no preferences themselves and had no secret designs that could shape their decision. However, in light of the oppressions recently suffered by the Church, they hoped to choose a ruler who would provide for both Church and realm, act within the limits of the law and nourish them and the people with tranquillity. They also offered a safe conduct lasting four weeks, and requested that Otto come attired in a noble fashion, not dressed like a pauper.[12]

These were the opening shots in a notoriously fraught succession. Henry V was the first emperor in over a century to have died without any direct heirs – his closest relative was his nephew, Duke Frederick of Swabia – and without having designated a successor.[13] Moreover, relations between leading nobles, notably the dukes of Saxony and Swabia, had been fraught for some time. The so-called Investiture Contest – the recent oppression of the Church alluded to in the letter – complicated matters further. The term refers to a series of clashes between popes and kings across Latin Europe. They related to how prelates were appointed and how they were inaugurated – their investiture. The issue at stake was where precisely the line ought to be drawn between a prelate's worldly power – his role as landholder and secular lord – and his spiritual authority – the right, in the succession of St Peter, to bind and to loosen the faithful in his diocese. Matters were aggravated by a group of especially headstrong pontiffs and of equally stubborn emperors. Further complications arose because in Germany, more so than in other realms, the dispute was embedded in a series of local and regional conflicts. Nobles and prelates switched allegiances based not solely on their support for one ideal of episcopal power over another, but in order to thwart or to gain an advantage over their rivals. Consequently, whereas in most European realms the issue, if it arose at all, had been settled in the early decades of the twelfth century, in the Empire a compromise was not reached until 1122.[14]

---

[12] *Codex Udalrici*, ed. Klaus Nass, MGH Briefe, 2 vols. (Wiesbaden, 2017), no. 348. The letter is undated. Its modern editor dated it cautiously to some point between May and August, though one may safely assume that it was sent soon after the funeral. This would also fit the general pattern of preparation that the following paragraphs will outline.

[13] This had last occurred in 1024, after the death of Henry II. Henry V had supposedly passed the royal insignia to Frederick; for this, and why it might not have been enough, see Chapter 6.

[14] Thomas Kohl, *Streit, Erzählung und Epoche: Deutschland und Frankreich um 1100* (Stuttgart, 2019); Jörg Bölling, *Zwischen Regnum und Sacerdotium: Historiographie,*

IV. ELECTION 263

The 1125 letter had been composed with these troubles very much in mind. By taking charge of the emperor's obsequies, its signatories could claim a degree of moral authority and responsibility for the welfare of the realm that exceeded that of their peers. Moreover, their number included a combination of leading churchmen, Henry's relatives, staunch allies and erstwhile opponents. It was headed by the archbishops of Cologne and Mainz, the two most prominent figures in the German episcopate. They often oversaw the election and competed for the right to crown the king. The only other high-ranking secular clerics involved were the bishops of Worms and Speyer, from the economic heartlands of the realm along the middle and upper Rhine valley. The abbot of Fulda, Ulrich of Kemenaten, presided over one of the oldest and wealthiest abbeys in the German realm. The secular princes included the two leading contenders for the throne: Duke Lothar of Saxony (eventually Lothar III) and Duke Frederick of Swabia. Lothar had been one of Henry V's chief opponents.[15] Frederick, by contrast, was not only Henry's nephew, but had also acted as his regent in Germany while the emperor campaigned in Italy in 1116. Through marriage, Frederick was furthermore related to the dukes of Bavaria.[16] Convening the assembly to choose Henry's successor was about the only issue on which Lothar and Frederick managed to agree. Count Berengar of Sulzbach, the third prince listed, was a landholder in Franconia and the Bavarian palatinate, and had been among the emperor's closest confidants. In 1105, he had persuaded Henry to depose his father; he had been one of the emperor's representatives in negotiations with the papal court in 1111/12 and 1122; he remained a regular attendant at Henry's court until the end.[17] Finally, Godfrey of Calw, count palatine of the Rhine, had been another one of Henry V's trusted allies. He had repeatedly accompanied the emperor on Italian campaigns, and had been one of the signatories to the Concordat of Worms, which ended the Investiture Contest in Germany.[18] The list of senders was carefully calibrated to avoid favouring one particular party, but the signatories

---

Hagiographie und Literatur im Sachsen der Salierzeit (1024–1125) (Ostfildern, 2017); Ludger Körntgen, 'Der Investiturstreit und das Verhältnis von Religion und Politik im Frühmittelalter', in *Religion und Politik im Mittelalter: Deutschland und England im Vergleich*, ed. Ludger Körntgen and Dominik Waßenhoven (Berlin, 2013), 89–115.

[15] Wolfgang Petke, 'Kaiser Lothar von Süpplingenburg in neuerer Sicht', in *Konrad von Wettin und seine Zeit*, ed. Cornelia Kessler, Ute Werner and Ilsetraut Danne (Halle/Saale, 1999), 113–28. A full and modern biography of Lothar remains a desideratum.

[16] Hansmartin Schwarzmaier, '*Pater imperatoris*. Herzog Friedrich II. von Schwaben, der gescheiterte König', in *Mediaevalia Augiensia. Forschungen zur mittelalterlichen Geschichte*, ed. Jürgen Petersohn (Stuttgart, 2001), 247–84.

[17] Jürgen Dendorfer, 'Die Grafen von Sulzbach', in *Hochmittelalterliche Adelsfamilien in Altbayern, Franken und Schwaben*, ed. Ferdinand Kramer and Wilhelm Störmer (Munich, 2005), 179–212, at 209–10.

[18] Wilhelm Kurze, 'Adalbert und Gottfried von Calw', *Zeitschrift für württembergische Landesgeschichte* 24 (1965), 241–308.

264   8. CHOOSING A KING

were also powerful enough to communicate the gravity of the occasion, and to exert pressure on men like the bishop of Bamberg to attend speedily, in the right frame of mind and suitably attired.[19]

Given how contentious Henry's succession was likely to prove, the probity of both process and voters proved a major concern. The letter's signatories protested that they had no ulterior motive in calling together the electors, and no favourites. The ultimate decision rested with God, who, they hoped, would inspire the princes and prelates once assembled. Even the list of tasks facing the new king was generic: he was to pacify the realm, bring tranquillity and justice and end the oppression of the Church. It was no different from the list of qualities attributed to Fulk of Anjou before he became king-designate of Jerusalem in 1131, or, for that matter, from any other general description of royal duties. Such formulaic vagueness was in all likelihood intentional. Being general and unspecific in the expectations of the new king, while remaining rooted in a well-established tradition of defining royal duties, served to reinforce the non-partisan nature of the signatories' efforts. Agreeing on a new ruler was likely to prove difficult, but in order for a decision to be reached, it had to be for the common good, not factional interests.

The letter furthermore offers glimpses of the practical measures to be taken in preparing an election. Someone had to convene the community of the realm. There also was a degree of advance deliberation. The signatories had to determine how that community could be constituted, how a procedure could be devised that ensured that the throne was filled unanimously and with probity and who should conduct it. That matters were left not solely in the hands of either archbishop suggests a degree of mistrust and a desire to help shape the process, rather than being confronted with it. It was also deemed appropriate that as broad as possible a range of electors participate. The greater the number of backers for the result, the more likely it was to endure. However, it was not just their presence that was required. So were their advice and counsel, as the letter explicitly noted. There seems to have been a sense that choosing Henry's successor would take time and that it would require wide and thorough consultation. It would not be an easy decision to make. The safe conduct of four weeks issued to Otto of Bamberg suggests just how difficult the letter's authors might have anticipated negotiations to prove.

That three months elapsed between Henry's death and the planned election was by no means unusual. Just how long it took to prepare an election varied between kingdoms and depended on the political context of each succession. In 1118, Baldwin II of Jerusalem was chosen within days of his predecessor's

---

[19] See also the not dissimilar group of people who, in 1101, were sent to invite Baldwin of Edessa to become ruler of Jerusalem: Albert of Aachen, *Historia Ierosolimitana*, 528–9. They included: Bishop Robert of Ramla, Godfrey I's steward and chamberlain, and several knights.

IV. ELECTION 265

death. In England, William Rufus died on 2 August, and his brother Henry I was crowned on 5 August 1100. Similarly, Henry died on 1 December 1135, and Stephen was crowned on 22 December. There were good reasons for such haste. In 1118, the kingdom of Jerusalem faced the threat of an attack from Egypt; in 1100, Henry acted to prevent his older brother Robert from claiming the English throne; Stephen proceeded with similar speed to pre-empt moves by his cousin Matilda. Rapid seizure of the throne was necessary to prevent rivals from claiming it. Having too long a vacancy was fraught with risk. After Emperor Lothar III died in December 1137, the partisans of his erstwhile rival Conrad (who had been elected anti-king in 1127) pre-empted an assembly called to Mainz for May 1138 by holding one in March at Koblenz instead.[20] They succeeded in part because they were able to rush Conrad to Aachen, where he was crowned and consecrated. Generally, though, considerable time elapsed between a king's death and his successor's election. In 1002, Otto III died on 23 January, and Henry II was not crowned until 7 June. But then Otto's remains had had to be transported across the Alps for burial at Aachen (a distance of over 1,500 kilometres) before the coronation ceremony could be conducted. In 1024, Henry II died on 13 July, and the election of his successor began seven weeks later, on 4 September 1024. The three months envisaged in 1125 were therefore by no means unusual.[21]

In the Empire, so long a vacancy was also necessary on grounds of geography, logistics and politics. If we take the 1125 election as starting point, the distance from Magdeburg (a centre of power in Saxony) to Mainz (where the election was held) was about 400 kilometres. Assuming a travel speed of *c.* 20–30 km a day (not unreasonably slow for what would have been a suitably festive and hence slow-moving entourage),[22] this would have taken a fortnight to three weeks. Any stops to consult, win allies and so on would have increased the journey time. To this should be added at least the same amount of time again to prepare: to gather men and resources and procure equipment, but also to consult with followers and neighbours before setting out. Even Bamberg was still a little less than a week's journey from

[20] Schmidt, *Königswahl und Thronfolge*, 77–85; Gerd Lubich, 'Beobachtungen zur Wahl Konrads III. und ihrem Umfeld', *Historisches Jahrbuch* 117 (1997), 311–39.
[21] Figures are more difficult to come by in many other realms. In England, two months passed between the Battle of Hastings and William the Conqueror's coronation in 1066, Stephen's death on 25 October and Henry II's coronation on 19 December 1154, Henry II's death on 6 July and Richard I's coronation on 3 September 1189. Those did not, however, involve an act of election. In Sicily, the centrality of Palermo militated against lengthy preparations. We have no reliable records on this issue from Hungary and most of Iberia.
[22] Martina Reinke, 'Die Reisegeschwindigkeit des deutschen Königshofes im 11. und 12. Jahrhundert nördlich der Alpen', *Blätter für deutsche Landesgeschichte* 123 (1987), 225–51, at 235–40. While the average speed was about 43 km a day, the vast majority of royal journeys progressed at about 23 km a day.

266   8. CHOOSING A KING

Mainz (240 km),[23] which partly explains the four-week safe conduct granted
to the bishop in 1125. Furthermore, a kingdom's economic and political
geography mattered. In England, as a first step towards claiming the throne,
Henry I, Stephen and Henry II hurried to seize the royal treasury at
Winchester (just over 100 km from Westminster), while many of the succession debates in the crusader kingdom took place in Jerusalem, with Palermo
playing a similar role in Sicily.[24] The relative concentration of the resources
and machinery of power meant that a sufficient number of the great men of
the realm would already have been in a particular place. A kingdom's size also
needs to be taken into account. England, for instance, was considerably
smaller than the duchy of Bavaria before 1156 (when it still included most
of modern Austria).[25] The geographical dimension was even more striking in
the case of Norway. The archbishopric of Nidaros (Trondheim) was over
600 km from Bergen, a royal centre under Magnus Erlingsson. Värmland,
where Sverrir first encountered the Birkibeinar, was 570 km from Trøndelag,
where he was proclaimed king, and so almost 1,000 km from Bergen. In
England, by contrast, the distance between Dover (a key entry point) and
Winchester was a mere 200 km, and even York was only 350 km from
Winchester. Furthermore, these figures do not take into account terrain.
Unlike England, Norway has mountain ranges. In fact, sailing along the
coast would often prove faster than land travel.[26] In consequence, kings
could therefore be chosen at any of four major regional assemblies, and
then had to win the support and acceptance of others – perhaps one reason
why we should avoid pinning just one specific date to the election of
a Norwegian king. In Sverrisaga, for example, Sverrir was described as
being elected king in the Vik,[27] accepted by the men of Selbu and
Gaulardale,[28] and at Eyra, near Nidaros.[29] It was not until much later that
he was crowned. The account covering the period between these early
acclamations and the king's formal inauguration occupied over a hundred
of the saga's chapters (out of a total of 182).[30] A realm's physical geography,

---

[23] Travel by ship could speed up journey times. In 1152, it took Frederick Barbarossa three
days to get from Bamberg to Mainz. See below, Chapter 10.

[24] Peter of Eboli, Liber in Honorem, 91–5; Hugo Falcandus, Il regno di Sicilia, 132.

[25] Using modern borders (with all the provisos that entails), 130,345 km² for England
compared to 154,429 km² (70,550 [Bavaria] and 83,879 [Austria]). I am grateful to Levi
Roach for this observation. It is worth keeping in mind, however, that borders were fluid,
and that modern Bavaria contains regions not part of the medieval duchy.

[26] Dagfinn Skre, 'Norjvegr – Norway: from sailing route to kingdom', European Review 22
(2014), 33–44. I am grateful to Alex Woolf for this reference, and for his help with the
Norwegian case more generally.

[27] Saga of King Sverri, chapter 11, pp. 12–13.

[28] Saga of King Sverri, chapter 14, p. 17.

[29] Saga of King Sverri, chapter 16, p. 20.

[30] Saga of King Sverri, chapter 123, pp. 154–5.

IV. ELECTION 267

size, communication networks and distribution of power centres determined just how long in advance an election had to be planned.

Furthermore, electoral assemblies were large public events. They posed considerable logistical challenges. Provisions, accommodation and venues for the several stages of the election process had to be procured. In 1024, the imperial chaplain Wipo reported, the princes and prelates chose a place between Worms and Mainz (probably Kamba), 'which could accommodate a very large crowd because of its flatness'.[31] While numbers are difficult to come by, we can get a sense of the size of the crowds in attendance from the *Narratio de electione Lotharii*. One of the most detailed accounts of a royal election to survive from the central Middle Ages, it covers events at Mainz in 1125.[32] Without offering precise figures, the *Narratio* listed the *types* of attendant at Mainz: a papal legate, archbishops, bishops, abbots, priors, secular clergy, monks, dukes, margraves, counts and diverse other nobles. At one point, it noted that twenty-four bishops remained by the time the assembly concluded. The only prelates mentioned specifically were the archbishop of Mainz (who convened the meeting), the bishop of Basle (who stayed with the duke of Swabia), the bishop of Regensburg and the archbishop of Salzburg (who persuaded the duke of Bavaria to back Lothar) and the new bishop of Brixen, who had been elected and consecrated immediately prior to the election. No other imperial diet, the anonymous author stressed, had attracted as many participants. The *Narratio* went on to describe how the Saxons stayed on one side of the Rhine, by its banks, with many splendid castles (presumably wooden), and just above them the duke of Austria and his men, while the duke of Swabia, together with the bishop of Basle, stayed on the other side of the river.[33] While this juxtaposition reflected political divisions, it also suggests that key participants were not actually lodged in Mainz. This would not have been unusual. In 1184, when Frederick Barbarossa had his two eldest sons knighted at Mainz, most of those attending also stayed in tents and wooden buildings outside the town,[34] and in 1234 a diet at Frankfurt was similarly concluded outside rather than within the city walls.[35]

---

[31] Wipo, *Gesta Chuonradi*, 13; *Deeds of Conrad II*, 60–1.
[32] Originally perhaps based on an eyewitness account, the text was repeatedly rewritten over the next few decades. Heinz Stoob, Zur Königswahl Lothars von Sachsen im Jahre 1125', in *Historische Forschungen für Walter Schlesinger*, ed. Helmut Beumann (Cologne and Vienna, 1974), 438–61, argued for a date *c.* 1130–3, but Schneidmüller, 'Mittelalterliche Geschichtsschreibung' has convincingly argued for a later date of *c.* 1160.
[33] *Narratio de electione Lotharii Saxoniae ducis in regem Romanorum*, MGH SS 12 (Hanover, 1856), 510.
[34] Arnold of Lübeck, *Chronicon*, 151–2; Gislebert of Mons, *Chronicon*, 157; *Annales Marbacenses*, 54; Otto of St Blasien, *Chronicon*, 37; *Chronica regia Coloniensis*, 133.
[35] *Annales Erphordenses*, in *Monumenta Erphesfurtensia saec. XII. XIII. XIV.*, ed. Oswald Holder-Egger (Hanover, 1899), 80–116, at 84–6.

268   8. CHOOSING A KING

The list of titles and functions in the *Narratio* masks the scale of the entourage accompanying these men. It is, however, possible to offer an informed guess about this wider following. A start can be made by taking into account the size of the royal court. It provides a useful benchmark against which to surmise princely and episcopal entourages. Reliable estimates for Germany put its average size at about 1,000 people. These would have included household knights, clerks, scribes, chaplains and servants, as well as key advisors, visiting dignitaries and so on.[36] The so-called *Constitutio Domus Regis* from England, a thirteenth-century redaction of a text probably dating from *c.* 1135/6, listed royal servants such as the keepers of the royal larder and those in charge of various breeds of hunting dog. It also noted the allowance for the king's bakers, which estimated that bread for 700 people would be provided each day.[37] To these would have to be added officials, who were not all included in the text, as well as visitors, nobles and prelates in attendance, envoys, messengers and so on. Feasibly, the English court would routinely have included close to a thousand people.[38] Numbers for smaller kingdoms are difficult to come by, though a recent estimate puts the later medieval Swedish royal court at about 300 people.[39] Kings travelled with a considerable entourage, numbering in the hundreds, perhaps even thousands.

Princely and episcopal entourages would probably have been smaller, though the size of a following was a marker of status and resources. Magnates were expected not to outdo the king, but they may well have sought to outdo each other. It is also unlikely that most princes would have brought their entire household with them. Estates needed to be administered in their absence, rivals kept at bay and so on. They would, however, have been accompanied by neighbours and peers. The *Narratio* asserts that, when no amicable settlement could be reached, the archbishop of Mainz asked the Bavarians, Swabians, Saxons and Franks to nominate ten men each to choose a suitable candidate.[40] This would have been credible only if a sizable number of lords and nobles from each respective region had been in attendance. Princes would furthermore have brought an armed escort, both for protection (in 1002 Ekkehard of Meißen had been murdered while travelling to an electoral assembly) and to demonstrate status. Appearing as a prince, not

---

[36] Johannes Laudage, 'Der Hof Friedrich Barbarossas: eine Skizze', in *Rittertum und höfische Kultur der Stauferzeit*, ed. Johannes Laudage and Yvonne Leiverkus (Cologne, Weimar and Vienna, 2006), 75–92.

[37] *Dialogus de Scaccario. The Dialogue of the Exchequer; Constitutio Domus Regis. The Disposition of the King's Household*, ed. Emilie Amt and S. D. Church (Oxford, 2007), 200.

[38] Stephen D. Church, 'Some aspects of the royal itinerary in the twelfth century', *Thirteenth Century England* 11 (2007), 31–45.

[39] J. B. L. D. Strömberg, 'The Swedish kings in progress – and the centre of power', *Scandia: Tidskrift for Historisk Forskning* 70 (2004), 167–217.

[40] *Narratio de electione*, 510.

IV. ELECTION 269

a pauper (as the bishop of Bamberg had been exhorted), meant a suitably martial display. Baldric's *Life* of Archbishop Albero of Trier (who was to play a major role in the 1138 imperial election) even claimed that the prelate enjoyed intimidating his fellow-metropolitan at Mainz by having armed men beat their drums and shouting in martial fashion whenever he sailed up the Rhine.[41]

The fraught nature of the 1125 election made such warlike displays even more likely. In fact, the *Narratio* reports that the dukes had brought sizable contingents of knights, as had the archbishop of Mainz. It does not say how many armed men there were. Gislebert of Mons, when recounting the festivities surrounding the knighting of Frederick Barbarossa's sons in 1184, listed the number of armed men that accompanied each of the leading princes. The duke of Bohemia was said to have brought 2,000 knights, the duke of Austria 500, the duke of Saxony 700, the count palatine of the Rhine and the landgrave of Thuringia over 1,000 each.[42] The figures may be slightly exaggerated, but they fit a general pattern. Knut Görich has estimated that in 1158 the duke of Swabia – by no means the wealthiest of the German princes – contributed 600 knights to Frederick Barbarossa's Italian campaign, and another 1,500 in 1162.[43] Even when approached with caution, these estimates offer some indication of the resources at the disposal of leading secular lords. Entourages of 200 to 300 for each of the great princes seems a cautious but not unrealistic guess. Comparable numbers of followers would have accompanied leading prelates, though other clerical communities may have been present as part of a patron's entourage. All in all then, it is plausible that several thousand people plausibly attended the meeting at Mainz, with 8–10,000 a perhaps not unrealistic estimate. Of course, not all of them would have participated in the election, but housing, provisioning and even entertaining so large a group required preparation. Even a smaller gathering would have necessitated considerable advance preparation on the part of both host and visitors, and thus helps account for the considerable time that could pass between a ruler's death and the choosing of his successor.

Then there were political factors to take into account. Prospective candidates had to sound out their chances or had to be convinced to put themselves forward. Failure was always possible. The dangers of pursuing the throne were many. At best, claimants might find themselves humiliated. At worst, as in Knud Lavard's case and, in fact, that of most Norwegian rulers of the twelfth

---

[41] Baldric of Trier, *Gesta Alberonis Auctore Balderico*, in *Lebensbeschreibungen einiger Bischöfe des 10.–12. Jahrhunderts*, transl. Hatto Kallfelz (reprinting the Latin from MGH SS 8, 243–60) (Darmstadt, 1973), 604–5; an English translation is available in *A Warrior Bishop of the Twelfth Century. The Deeds of Albero of Trier, by Balderich*, transl. Brian A. Pavlac (Toronto, 2008), 71.
[42] Gislebert of Mons, *Chronique*, 156.
[43] Görich, *Friedrich Barbarossa*, 140.

270   8. CHOOSING A KING

century, they would be slaughtered by their rivals. There was a considerable incentive for princes to ensure that pursuing the throne was feasible, or that doing so would at least not end in public embarrassment. It was far preferable to follow in the footsteps of Charles of Flanders, whose reputation was heightened by having been offered but then refusing the throne. However, as a result the evidence for anyone sounding out their chances can be difficult to come by. Sometimes, though, we *can* catch glimpses of the preparations taken to bid for the throne. In 1197, Burchard of Ursberg reports, Philipp of Swabia had been on his way to meet his brother Henry VI in Sicily when news reached him of the emperor's death. He hastened back to Germany and wintered at Hagenau. There, he took soundings with his brother's men, and began soliciting supporters for an imminent election.[44] Simultaneously, the archbishop of Cologne began to look for a candidate to champion, and initially bribed the duke of Zähringen to seek the throne, before settling on Otto, the nephew of the king of England.[45]

Widespread reticence makes all the more useful a sequence of extant letters about the kingship of Italy. After the death of Emperor Henry II in 1024, several Lombard princes contacted King Robert of France and Duke William of Aquitaine about claiming the Italian throne. Probably in mid-1025, William approached Bishop Leo of Vercelli,[46] a leading ecclesiastic in northern Italy. 'The Italians', William claimed, 'have persuaded my son and myself to intervene in the affairs of the kingdom of Italy and have sworn that in all good faith they will do what they can to secure for us the kingdom and the Roman Empire.' The duke therefore requested that Leo aid his own and his son's efforts.[47] At roughly the same time, Count Fulk of Anjou intervened on the duke's behalf with King Robert of France. As the king had not accepted the Lombards' offer of a crown, they had approached William, who accepted it on his son's behalf. Fulk requested that the king intervene with the duke of Lotharingia to dissuade him and others from throwing in their lot with

---

[44] Burchard of Ursberg, *Burchardi Praepositi Urspergensis Chronicon*, ed. Oswald Holder-Egger and Bernhard von Simson, MGH SS sep. ed., 2nd edition (Hanover and Leipzig, 1916), 76.

[45] Burchard of Ursberg, *Chronicon*, 79–80. For a slightly different emphasis, *Annales Marbacenses*, 71–3. For both see: Bernd Schütte, 'Das Königtum Philipps von Schwaben im Spiegel zeitgenössischer Quellen', in *Philipp von Schwaben: Beiträge der internationalen Tagung anlässlich seines 800. Todestages*, ed. Andrea Rzihacek and Renate Spreitzer (Vienna, 2010), 113–28; Robert Gramsch-Stehfest, 'Außenseiterchancen: die Königswahl von 1198, die Zähringer und das Netzwerk der Reichsfürsten in staufischer Zeit', in *Die Zähringer: Rang und Herrschaft um 1200*, ed. Jürgen Dendorfer, Heinz Krieg and R. Johanna Regnath (Ostfildern, 2018), 187–212.

[46] On Leo: Heinrich Dormeier, 'Un vescovo in Italia alle soglie del mille. Leone di Vercelli "Episcopus imperii, servus sancti Eusebi"', *Bolletino storico vercellese* 28:53 (1999), 37–74.

[47] *The Letters and Poems of Fulbert of Chartres*, ed. and transl. Frederick Behrens (Oxford, 1976), no. 103.

IV. ELECTION 271

Conrad II of Germany.[48] Probably in the autumn, a passing reference in a letter to Fulbert of Chartres reveals, William started making plans for a journey to Italy, to ensure that his son's bid could indeed be pursued successfully or, as Fulbert's correspondent put it, honourably and safely.[49] Thereafter, however, the project quickly fell apart. Leo of Vercelli ended up siding with Conrad,[50] and William complained bitterly to the margrave of Turin about the treachery of the Lombards.[51]

These letters played on familiar themes. The count of Anjou stressed that William and his son had given in to the entreaties of the Lombards, much against their will and on condition that all the Italian margraves agreed to his elevation.[52] Reluctance was shown and unanimity was sought. When William ultimately admitted that the bid had failed, he stressed that he abandoned the project because of the immoral demands made by the Italians, namely, that he depose certain bishops, and appoint those more pliable to the interests of his Italian backers.[53] William's son would become king only to do what was just and serve the needs of the realm, not those of his supporters. The Lombards had failed to live up to expectations of probity and threatened to undermine the legitimacy of William's endeavour. Still, considerable advance negotiations had taken place. At least some Italian nobles and bishops had approached first the king of France, and then the duke of Aquitaine. William, in turn, had taken soundings among his allies and contacts in Lombardy, while also trying to secure the backing of his own king back in France. This was not just a matter of keeping Conrad II at bay. When writing to the margrave of Tuscany, William stressed that several men had sought to exploit his absence in order to sow unrest in Aquitaine or otherwise utilise it for nefarious purposes.[54] In order to be able to bid for the throne, a candidate had to ensure that his domains remained at peace. Finally, just accepting the throne was not enough. William set out for Italy to verify that a bid could indeed succeed, that he did truly have the support he was promised. The offer of being elected was only the beginning, not the end point of pursuing a crown.

Though unusually well documented, William's case was by no means unique.[55] His son was a ruler from outside the realm that he was invited to

---

[48] *Letters of Fulbert*, no. 104.
[49] *Letters of Fulbert*, no. 109.
[50] *Letters of Fulbert*, no. 113.
[51] *Letters of Fulbert*, no. 111.
[52] *Letters of Fulbert*, no. 104.
[53] *Letters of Fulbert*, no. 113.
[54] *Letters of Fulbert*, no. 111.
[55] Martin Aurell, 'Le refus de la royauté d'Aragon par Raimond Bérenger IV selon Guillaume de Newburg', in *Figures de l'autorité médiévale: mélanges offerts à Michel Zimmermann*, ed. Pierre Chastang, Patrick Henriet and Claire Soussen Max (Paris, 2016), 33–44.

272   8. CHOOSING A KING

rule. Until the thirteenth century, most European kings originated from among a kingdom's aristocracy, though there were exceptions. In 1125, Baldwin of Flanders was invited to claim the German throne. In 1131, the count of Anjou became king of Jerusalem. After the death of William II, Emperor Henry VI became ruler of Sicily by right of his wife Constance. In such circumstances, it was of paramount importance to ensure that the promised support did in fact exist. The new king was much more dependent on the good will and backing of the leading nobles of the realm. In these cases the sounding out of followers and putative subjects is better recorded, partly because travel was involved, and partly because inviting someone to claim the throne garnered prestige for the lord contacted (especially if he turned down the offer). It is, for instance, conceivable that William of Tyre's account of the 1118 election in Jerusalem reflected just the kind of preliminary exploration also undertaken by William of Aquitaine in 1025. Eustace was approached, he was willing in principle, but when he set out to investigate the possibility of claiming the throne, events had made his bid obsolete. Eustace and William turned back when they found a king already chosen in their place.

While the efforts of foreign rulers are better documented, the basic principle that choosing a king required advance negotiations equally applied when a king was chosen from among a kingdom's aristocracy. In the mid-eleventh century, Wipo recounted the preparations for the election of Conrad II, in 1024: 'The expedient of letters and envoys made it possible to weigh private counsels and the opinion of individuals as to the man to whom each would consent, to whom he would object, or whom he wanted for his lord'.[56] Wipo was unusual in making specific reference to these advance negotiations. In most cases, preparations were overshadowed by the election itself. They were further obscured by the opprobrium associated with soliciting votes or demanding rewards in return for one's backing. We are thus fortunate to have Thietmar of Merseburg. In 1002, the succession to Otto III was discussed at Regensburg (when Henry II demanded that he be chosen as king), Aachen (during Otto's funeral) and at several meetings in Saxony. On first hearing of Otto's death, the Saxon bishops and princes convened at Frohse[57] and then again at Werla.[58] Similar gatherings seem to have taken place elsewhere – hence the candidacy, for instance, of Hermann of Swabia. Ekkehard of Meißen, after seeing his ambitions come to naught in Saxony, set out 'to the western regions where he could speak to Duke Hermann and other leading men regarding the realm and its welfare'.[59] Considering that Ekkehard insisted that he be received in a quasi-regal fashion at Paderborn and Hildesheim, he

---

[56] Wipo, Gesta Chuonradi, 13; Deeds of Conrad II, 60.
[57] Thietmar, Chronicon, iv.52, pp. 166–9; Ottonian Germany, ed. Warner, 188–9.
[58] Thietmar, Chronicon, v.3, pp. 196–7; Ottonian Germany, ed. Warner, 207.
[59] Thietmar, Chronicon, v.4, pp. 196–9; Ottonian Germany, ed. Warner, 208.

IV.   ELECTION   273

was presumably looking to win allies, not cast his vote for Hermann.[60] Well in advance of the formal election, therefore, the leading princes and prelates of the realm got together with their neighbours and followers to decide on how to proceed.

We can glimpse similar mechanisms in later texts. Written in the second half of the twelfth century, the *Vita* of Bishop Meinwerk of Paderborn (d. 1036) reports that, after the death of Emperor Henry II, the Saxons again convened at Werla to discuss whom they would support as king.[61] In England in 1135, the *Gesta Stephani* recount, the Londoners convened in the city upon Stephen's arrival to discuss the need for a king. Writing *c.* 1230, Snorri Sturluson reported how, *c.* 1160, some of the great men of Norway assembled to deliberate as to which of several potential candidates they should support, before proceeding to Bergen to conduct a formal election.[62] Each gathering took place well in advance of the formal election and involved only those from a particular region. A key issue seems to have been identifying putative candidates. In 1160 the Norwegian lords approached three nobles who refused the offer, before they settled on Magnus Erlingsson. Similar concerns drove the Saxons who met in 1002. They wanted to support just one candidate, but were undecided as to which one. In this respect, meetings also served to weed out claimants. It was at Frohse that Ekkehard of Meißen realised that he did not have the backing even of the Saxons, and it was at Werla that the latter decided to support Henry II. In other instances, assemblies could be used to sound out candidates. In England in 1135, the Londoners may have elected Stephen king, but he still had to be formally chosen and anointed. Stephen was therefore approached by Archbishop William of Canterbury, who raised doubts about the legitimacy of his claim. Only once those had been assuaged did the metropolitan consent.[63] The nature of William's concerns merits consideration. First, he insisted that a proper electoral assembly needed to be called. "'For'", he said, "just as a king is chosen to rule all, and, once chosen, to lay the commands of his sovereign power on all, assuredly in like manner it is fitting that all should meet together to ratify his accession and all should consider in agreement what is to be enacted and what rejected.'"[64] William insisted that unanimity be secured for Stephen's accession.[65] Like the Saxon meeting at

---

[60] *Ottonian Germany*, ed. Warner, 209 n. 22.
[61] *Vita Meinwerci episcopi Patherbrunnensis. Das Leben Bischof Meinwerks von Paderborn*, ed. and transl. Guido M. Berndt (Paderborn, 2009), 222–3. On the text: Hagen Keller, 'Meinwerk von Paderborn und Heimrad von Hasungen: Spätottonische Kirchenmänner und Frömmigkeitsformen in Darstellungen aus der Zeit Heinrichs IV. und Friedrich Barbarossas', *FmSt* 39 (2005), 129–50.
[62] Snorri Sturluson, *Heimskringla*, 'The Saga of Magnus Erlingsson', 789–90.
[63] *Gesta Stephani*, 8–13.
[64] *Gesta Stephani*, 10–11.
[65] *Gesta Stephani*, 12–13.

274   8. CHOOSING A KING

Frohse a century earlier, those in England and Norway sought to ascertain the suitability of a prospective ruler.

Once approached, a candidate held meetings with his men and neighbours. In 1125, Galbert of Bruges reports, the wiser among the German prelates discussed the various princes and lords in neighbouring regions, seeking a candidate who was 'noble both in descent and morals'. They eventually settled on Count Charles of Flanders. When envoys from the archbishop of Cologne arrived, informing Charles of the decision, he took counsel 'with the nobles and peers of his lands'.[66] Galbert wrote under the shadow of Charles's subsequent murder. He established a clear contrast between those present who loved the count as if he was their father and who were thus worried that his elevation might damage the realm, and those who saw the offer of the imperial crown as an opportunity to rid themselves of their lord. Galbert's is not a notarial record of events. Even so, his account is indicative of the kind of debates that are at least likely to have taken place, and that often made necessary a delay between the death of a king and the choice of his successor. Candidates had to be found and recruited, just as much as claimants had to assure themselves of the backing of their people. The election was the culmination, not the starting point, of a prolonged process of consultation and deliberation.

Part of these preparations included settling conflicts and forging alliances. Advance consultation also provided an opportunity for candidates to canvass, cajole and coerce putative backers. According to the *Vita* of Meinwerk of Paderborn, in 1024 the Saxons may have convened at Werla to pick a favoured candidate, but what really mattered was that the bishop had struck a deal that greatly expanded the estates of his Church.[67] Such exchanges may have formed part of the process of negotiating, but are difficult to disentangle from the ordinary structures of diets and assemblies. In 1125, the king-making was preceded by the election and consecration of the bishop of Brixen. Even an event like the knighting of Frederick Barbarossa's eldest son in 1184 was but one among a whole range of issues dealt with during the festive diet accompanying it. In general, when we do have evidence for bargaining, it often remains vague, and candidates seem to have been reticent about making concrete promises. Very rare indeed are passages like one in the *Vita* of Burchard of Worms (1000–25), written not long after the bishop's death, that in 1002 Henry II won over the prelate by promising to secure for him a castle held by one of Burchard's rivals.[68] Once again it is Thietmar who has

---

[66] Galbert of Bruges, *De multro, traditione, et occisione gloriosi Karoli comitis Flandriarum*, ed. Jeff Rider, CCCM (Turnhout, 1994), 10–13; Becher, 'Karl der Gute als Thronkandidat'.

[67] *Vita Meinwerci*, 222–5.

[68] *Vita Burchardi episcopi Wormatiensis*, MGH SS 4, 836.

IV. ELECTION 275

most to say about such dealings. The episode in question involved his uncle, Margrave Liuthar, and great-uncle, Rikbert. Between the meetings at Frohse and Werla, Liuthar and Rikbert travelled to Bamberg in Franconia (a distance of about 300 km), where they met up with Duke Henry. Rikbert had been deprived of his fief by Otto III, and at Bamberg 'he received the duke's favour and the hope of retaining and increasing his benefice'. While Liuthar did not do homage to Henry (as the Saxon nobles had agreed not to pick a king until meeting at Werla), he nonetheless advised the duke to send a knight to Werla to meet up with his cousins Adelheid and Sophie (daughters of Otto II). When the Saxons convened, Henry's emissary 'revealed his commission to the whole assembly and promised many good things to those who helped his lord obtain the throne'. Instantly, the majority of attendants agreed to back Henry.[69]

Thietmar's episode was carefully constructed. It was framed by the unsuccessful bid of Ekkehard of Meißen, and opened by recounting how Hermann of Swabia had been led astray by evil men, while Dietrich of Lotharingia confidently awaited his own election. Thietmar established a contrast between Henry and his rivals. Whereas Ekkehard sought to bluster his way onto the throne, Henry stayed aloof and acted only in response to Saxon approaches. Unlike Hermann, he did not lend his ear to evil men. And while Dietrich simply expected to be made king, Henry ensured that he was. Significantly, neither Liuthar and Rikbert nor Henry were described as bargaining for the throne. Obviously, Rikbert wanted to have his fiefs restored, and Liuthar did what good lords were supposed to do: he intervened with someone more powerful. Henry, as we know, clearly desired the throne. Still, according to Thietmar, he did not actually *promise* that Rikbert's fiefs would be restored. He merely gave Rikbert reason to hope that this would happen. Meanwhile Liuthar adhered to the decision, reached at Frohse, that the Saxons would pick their preferred candidate only at Werla. Similarly, Henry's emissary did not make concrete, but only very general promises – 'many good things' would come to the Saxons in exchange for backing Henry. No bartering took place.

A similar degree of reticence emerges from the letters exchanged between William of Aquitaine and Leo of Vercelli. When the duke first approached the bishop, he shared news of his son's elevation and offered: 'You may rest assured that if you will promote our cause, you will never have seen such good days as those in which you help us to attain that honour, for all that is mine will indeed be yours.'[70] William never specified what these rewards might be. When, later in the year, Leo demanded a wondrous mule, a precious bridle and marvellous hangings (tapestries), this, as much as William's response, appears to have been a joke, the precise meaning of which is lost in the mists of

---

[69] Thietmar, *Chronicon*, v.3, pp. 196–7; *Ottonian Germany*, ed. Warner, 207–8.
[70] *Letters of Fulbert*, no. 103.

276   8. CHOOSING A KING

time.[71] It is, of course, conceivable that details would have been hashed out by messengers – after all, in 1002 Henry had sent an emissary, not a missive, to the Saxons at Werla. Still, just as Thietmar fashioned an account that clearly exculpated Henry and his relatives from the suspicion of selling or buying the throne, so William of Aquitaine was hesitant to commit to writing the concrete material benefits that he would make available to his backers.

Such circumspection resembles events during Rudolf of Rheinfelden's election, when Count Otto of Northeim was reprimanded for demanding that his personal grievances be addressed so as to secure his vote. Kingship was a gift from God, and should be neither awarded nor acquired for material gain. Only tyrants or those lacking the moral stature required of a king did campaign openly – as they did in Rodulfus Glaber's depiction of Odo of Blois or Thietmar's account of Ekkehard of Meißen. Moral opprobrium did not, of course, mean that no campaigning took place. Sources clearly suggest otherwise. It does mean, however, that the process of negotiation is frequently discernible only once a king had been enthroned. Even then, the relevant exchanges are often indistinguishable from what kings were supposed to do anyway: confirm the grants of their predecessor, reform the realm, settle disputes and so on.[72] The Gesta Stephani is representative of how these actions were often framed. Once Stephen had been elected and crowned, 'all the chief men of the kingdom accepted him gladly and respectfully, and having received very many gifts from him and likewise enlargement of their lands[,] they devoted themselves wholly to his service by voluntary oath, after paying homage'.[73] Stephen's generosity may well have included rewards for supporters. It also conformed to well-established precedent.[74] In the specific context of 1135/6, generosity was displayed in an attempt to shore up Stephen's kingship by winning over those who had not attended his election and coronation. A somewhat stronger indication of a connection between royal largesse and pre-electoral bargaining is provided by a charter for the bishop of Bamberg, issued by Frederick Barbarossa immediately after his coronation in 1152. He granted the advocacy of the abbey of Niederaltaich to the bishop. Not only had Conrad III died at Bamberg, and it was in all likelihood there that Frederick decided to claim the throne, but a later document refers to Frederick discussing the affairs of the realm with the bishops of Bamberg and Würzburg in the days between Conrad's death and his election. It is therefore highly plausible that the transfer of Niederaltaich – a wealthy Benedictine house with rich estates bordering Bohemia – was among the

[71] Letters of Fulbert, nos. 112–13.
[72] A methodological problem exemplified by Siegfried Haider, Die Wahlversprechungen der römisch-deutschen Könige bis zum Ende des 12. Jahrhunderts (Vienna, 1968). See also below, Chapter 10.
[73] Gesta Stephani, 12–13.
[74] See below, Chapter 10.

IV. ELECTION 277

promises made in return for the bishop's backing.[75] Even so, any suggestion of a direct link between the prelate's vote and the gifts he received was carefully avoided.

Taken together, these examples suggest that Henry II and William of Aquitaine were unusual only in that a record of their pre-electoral campaigning survives. The relative absence of evidence for a practice likely to have been fairly common only serves to reinforce the importance of the moral framework within which bartering took place. Furthermore, the spiritual and moral opprobrium associated with purchasing and selling a divinely sanctioned office had implications for the kind of promises that kings did make once elected. They were not conditions that candidates accepted to secure the throne, but confirmations of generally valid principles. Consequently, the public enactment of the relationship between ruler and ruled sought to uphold the premise of the king as keeper and guardian of the realm. Just as Henry and Liuthar had, in Thietmar's rendering, made sure that none of their interactions could be construed as selling or buying votes, so a king had to be elected freely and solely because he was the most suitable and rightful claimant. They met widely held expectations. But for those to be met, time was needed. Many of these preparatory meetings can only be surmised. They were rarely reported, partly because the election itself was deemed more significant, partly because the subject matter called for a limited audience. But they set an important precedent, and shaped how the election itself was conducted and organised.

8.2 Convening

The venue for choosing a king was rarely fixed. Denmark, where, according to Saxo and Sven Aggesen, kings were habitually chosen at Isøre,[76] remains an exception, not least because – in the absence of a coronation ceremony before 1170 – election and inauguration frequently coincided. The position of Nidaros (Trondheim) in Norway was similar. Until the introduction of a coronation ceremony in the 1160s, the final election at Nidaros also marked the beginning of a king's reign over all of Norway.[77] In most realms, however, choosing a king and enthroning him remained distinct events, as did the sites where each took place. Sometimes, politics and geography helped determine which location was picked. In smaller kingdoms, or those with dominant urban centres, chief cities were preferred, as when Louis VII of France convened the French nobles and prelates at Paris to have his son Philipp confirmed

---

[75] Haider, *Wahlversprechungen*, 66–7; Görich, *Friedrich Barbarossa*, 100; Freed, *Frederick Barbarossa*, 73.
[76] Sven Aggesen, *Brevis Historia*, in *Scriptores Minores*, ed. Gertz, vol. 1, 124–7; Sven Aggesen, *Short History*, in *The Works of Sven Aggesen*, transl. Eric Christiansen, 65; Saxo Grammaticus, *Gesta Danorum*, xi.10.2, pp. 824–5 n. 32.
[77] Brégaint, *Vox regis*, 36–7.

278   8. CHOOSING A KING

as his successor[78] or when Roger II designated his at Palermo.[79] Just as frequently, the circumstances of a bid for the throne decided where a king was chosen. In 987, Richer of Saint-Rémi reported, the archbishop of Reims took drastic measures to ensure that a sufficient number of nobles would be present to elect a new ruler of the western Franks. The king had died at Senlis, and had wanted to be buried at Reims, but it was decided to hold the funeral at Compiègne instead (a distance of roughly thirty-five kilometres from Senlis instead of 130) because too many magnates might baulk at having to travel that far.[80]

Securing a large enough audience was a common concern. It certainly trumped considerations like the kind of traditional voting site postulated by later writers in Denmark. Henry I, for instance, had his daughter designated as heiress during a Christmas parliament in London in 1126,[81] and had the oaths renewed during a meeting at Northampton in 1131.[82] Henry II had his eponymous son elected in London, whereas his grandson Henry III was chosen as king in Winchester. There was no clear pattern. In Germany, Henry II and Lothar III had been elected at Mainz; Conrad II between Worms and Mainz; Henry III at Minden; Henry IV at Goslar; Rudolf of Rheinfelden at Forchheim; Conrad III at Konstanz; his son at Frankfurt, as had been Frederick Barbarossa; Henry VI at Bamberg; and Frederick II at Würzburg.[83] The priority seems to have been to bring together either as large a group of electors as possible or one likely to support a particular candidate. At most, confirmations of an heir seem to have taken place in a ruler's territorial heartlands (Minden, Goslar, Bamberg, Würzburg), often combined with assemblies that would ensure a suitable audience, such as the ones meeting at Christmas or Easter, or those called either before a king's departure for or on his return from campaign. Vacancies, on the other hand, were filled in close proximity to the territories of leading churchmen who then took a prominent role in conducting the election (Frankfurt or Mainz).

The role of prelates in determining an election site raises the question of who actually participated in choosing a king. Unfortunately, most accounts do not name the electors. Exceptions occur when the decision became disputed. In 1198, Burchard of Ursberg reported, Philipp of Swabia had secured the backing of the bishop of Strasbourg, the duke of Saxony, the margrave of Meißen, the archbishops of Hamburg and Magdeburg and many other princes and

[78] Rigord, *Histoire*, 122–3.
[79] Romuald of Salerno, *Chronica*, 222.
[80] Richer, *Histories*, vol. 2, 206–9.
[81] William of Malmesbury, *Historia Novella*, 6–9.
[82] William of Malmesbury, *Historia Novella*, 18–21.
[83] *Die deutsche Königserhebung*, vol. 1, no. 153 (Henry III); ibid., vol. 1, no. 182 (Henry IV); ibid., vol. 1, no. 122 (Conrad II); ibid., vol. 2, no. 74 (Henry (VI); ibid., vol. 2, no. 79 (Frederick I); ibid., vol. 2, no. 114 (Henry VI); ibid., vol. 2, no. 124 (Frederick II).

IV. ELECTION 279

prelates.[84] As regards the 1125 election, the *Narratio* lists the archbishop of Mainz, the leading candidates for the throne and the forty electors chosen by the princes – though none of them is identified by name. Richer's report of the 987 election at Compiègne was no different. The archbishop of Reims presided over the gathering, with the only other individuals mentioned being Charles of Lotharingia (who left the meeting on realising he would not prevail) and Hugh Capet.[85] Wipo is a rare exception. He named the archbishops of Mainz, Cologne, Trier and Salzburg and the bishops of Metz, Strasbourg, Würzburg, Bamberg, Konstanz, Augsburg, Regensburg and Freising, together with 'many other bishops and abbots from these regions'. The absence of prelates from northern Germany and Saxony should be noted. Alongside the ecclesiastical princes, he included the dukes of Saxony, Istria, Bavaria, Swabia, Lotharingia, the Ripuarians, Kuno of Worms (nominally duke of Franconia) and the duke of Bohemia.[86] Most of the realm was represented, though Wipo did not list secular princes below the rank of duke and skirted over the role of abbots. Listing everyone present, he explained, might have made his work unreadable. He also sought to provide a potted biography for each of the ecclesiastical princes, and purported not have enough information about the Saxon prelates. Taken together, these accounts give us a sense of just how wide the field of electors could be. Especially if there were several candidates, if the heir was a woman or under age, an election was too momentous an occasion not to bring together as many of the great men of the realm as possible.

This did not mean that everyone who really mattered participated. Not infrequently, a ruler, once enthroned, had to win the backing of those who had not been party to his initial election. Henry II did not at first have the support of the archbishop of Cologne,[87] and had to visit Saxony after his coronation to secure the backing of the Saxons.[88] When recounting Stephen's elevation to the English throne in 1135, neither the *Gesta Stephani* nor William of Malmesbury list the electors. It is, however, possible to identify certain patterns. There was no fixed set of voters. Even in Germany, a college of electors, a narrowly defined group whose duty it was to choose a king, was first

---

[84] Burchard of Ursberg, *Chronicon*, 76, 79. The 1198 Thronstreit has triggered an exceptionally rich literature. Useful for immediate orientation: Thomas Zotz, '*Werra magna et dissensio nimis timenda oritur inter principes Theutonicos de imperio*. Der Thronstreit zwischen Philipp von Schwaben und Otto von Braunschweig 1198–1208', *Zeitschrift für Württembergische Landesgeschichte* 69 (2010), 17–36; Peter Csendes, 'Die Doppelwahl von 1198 und ihre europäischen Dimensionen', in *Staufer und Welfen: zwei rivalisierende Dynastien im Hochmittelalter*, ed. Werner Hechberger and Florian Schuller (Regensburg, 2009), 156–71; Hucker, *Kaiser Otto IV.*, 47–99.
[85] Richer, *Histories*, vol. 2, 222–3.
[86] Wipo, *Gesta Chuonradi*, 9–12; *Deeds of Conrad II*, 58–9.
[87] Lantbert of Deutz, *Vita Heriberti, Miracula Heriberti, Gedichte, liturgische Texte*, ed. Bernhard Vogel, MGH SSrG sep. ed. (Hanover, 2001), 162–3.
[88] Weinfurter, *Heinrich II.*, 52–3. See also below, Chapter 10.

280   8. CHOOSING A KING

mentioned in the 1220s, was not invoked in practice until 1273 and was enshrined as a binding rule only in 1356.[89] And there were unofficial actors as well. During the English succession struggles after 1135, the citizens of London played a decisive role that was never formalised.[90] Peter of Eboli assigned a similar part to the citizens of Palermo on the death of William II of Sicily.[91] For most of the period under consideration, then, the electors varied, but were generally the leading men of the realm, on occasion interspersed with social groups who were not usually granted a say in regnal politics.

Not every vote carried equal weight. In the case of some archbishops – like those of Lund, Nidaros, Canterbury, Mainz and Cologne – their role was often, though not always, linked to their convening or presiding over an election. Another factor was the particular status of spiritual lords within the realm, the role of ecclesiastical institutions as keepers of communal memory and the self-perception of bishops as guardians of the kingdom's religious and moral welfare. Alone among the electors, prelates could not claim the throne.[92] This did not mean that they did not support or encourage particular candidates, or that they were not guided by political and material considerations. Some of them clearly were, and were, in fact, expected to be. Hence the emphasis in the *vitae* of Burchard of Worms and Meinwerk of Paderborn on the grants they had solicited in return for backing a successful candidate, or the bishop of Bamberg receiving Niederaltaich. Wipo's list of prelates present in 1024, and the potted biographies he provided for them, also point to dynastic networks and to transregional connections that fundamentally shaped the political role of bishops. The archbishop of Trier, for instance, was the uncle and guardian of the duke of Swabia; that of Salzburg the brother of the margrave of Meißen; the bishop of Augsburg that of Henry II. Many had also been transplanted from other regions. The archbishop of Mainz originally hailed from Bavaria. Bishops could represent overlapping, sometimes even competing networks. Family connections as well as a prelate's obligations towards his see and its patrons firmly anchored him in local and regional associations of rivals, benefactors and allies. These connections made prelates essential members in any coalition a putative ruler might seek to assemble. Because they straddled sometimes divergent, even competing networks, they

[89] Franz-Reiner Erkens, 'Anmerkungen zu einer neuen Theorie über die Entstehung des Kurfürstenkollegs', *MIÖG* 119 (2011), 376–81.

[90] Jean A. Truax, 'Winning over the Londoners: King Stephen, the Empress Matilda and the politics of personality', *HSJ* 8 (1996), 42–62. See also below, Chapter 9, for the coronation of Richard I in 1189.

[91] Peter of Eboli, *Liber ad Honorem*, 94–5.

[92] Saxo, for example, dismissed Sverrir of Norway not only as of low birth, but also because he was a priest: Saxo Grammaticus, *Gesta Danorum*, xiv.53.1, pp. 1390–1. See, though, the example of Coloman of Hungary, discussed in Chapter 3.

IV. ELECTION   281

could also act as mediators and peacemakers. In 1138, the *Vita* of Albero of
Trier reports, the prelate – once a bitter opponent of Henry V – ensured that
the Saxons supported Conrad III.[93] Combined with the material resources at
their disposal, this made bishops formidable players in electoral politics.[94]

Ecclesiastical institutions also served as keepers of communal memory.
They preserved a record of past practices, helped perhaps by the fact that
episcopal elections were far more frequent than regnal ones. How monks chose
their abbots and cathedral canons their bishops provided useful examples of
how to conduct an election.[95] Given that on average eighteen to twenty years
passed between the choosing of one king and the next, having access to
a record of previous elections was both useful and necessary. Steffen Patzold
has recently unearthed an especially striking example. The library of Freising
Cathedral contained the autograph of Liudprand of Cremona's *Antapodosis*,
a history of emperors Otto I and Otto II, written in the late tenth century.
When a new emperor was to be elected in 1024, either the bishop himself or
one of his clerics produced a summary of accounts of earlier elections as
recorded by Liudprand.[96] We know this because a series of marginal annota-
tions in the manuscript pointed specifically to electoral procedures. We do not
know whether the scribe collated this information for his own benefit, or that
of the bishop, his peers or noble patrons. His compilation is, however, suggestive. Someone evidently felt the need to find out just how a king was chosen
in the past. He was able to do because he had access to works of history.
Liudprand's text, in turn, was available because the bishopric of Freising
possessed a degree of institutional longevity far greater than that of a noble
household, or even of a private library like that which Frederick Barbarossa
and Henry VI would in the following century assemble at Hagenau.[97]
Conceivably, Weingarten, a centre of dynastic memory for the Welfs, and

---

[93] *Gesta Alberonis*, 586–7.
[94] Dominik Waßenhoven, 'Bischöfe als Königsmacher?: Selbstverständnis und Anspruch
      des Episkopats bei Herrscherwechseln im 10. und frühen 11. Jahrhundert', in *Religion
      und Politik im Mittelalter*, 31–50; Waßenhoven, 'Swaying bishops and the succession of
      kings', in *Patterns of Episcopal Power*, ed. Körntgen and Waßenhoven, 89–110; Patzold,
      'Königserhebungen'.
[95] Weiler, '*Rex renitens*', 24. Indeed, there was considerable overlap between ecclesiastical
      and secular practices. For example, the hierarchical order of voting and the use of delegate
      votes can be observed in clerical as well as royal elections: Malaczek, 'Abstimmungsarten',
      99–100; Schneider, 'Wechselwirkungen von kanonischer und weltlicher Wahl'. The
      former even constituted a central plank of the 1059 papal election decree:
      Norbert Gussone, *Thron und Inthronisation des Papstes von den Anfängen bis zum 12.
      Jahrhundert* (Bonn, 1978), 239–41.
[96] Steffen Patzold, 'Wie bereitet man sich auf einen Thronwechsel vor? Überlegungen zu
      einem wenig beachteten Text des 11. Jahrhunderts', in *Die mittelalterliche Thronfolge*, ed.
      Becher, 127–57.
[97] See above, Chapter 6.

282   8. CHOOSING A KING

Ripoll, which performed a similar function for the counts of Barcelona, as well as bishoprics like Bamberg, Lund, Prague and Rochester would also have served as repositories of such records of historical precedent. In the 1160s the monks of Durham Cathedral compiled historical examples that helped illuminate precedent for the conflict between Becket and Henry II,[98] while Nicholas Paul has pointed to the importance of dynastic monastic foundations as a source for aristocratic crusading memory.[99] They not only preserved the *memoria* of ancestors, but also provided practical guidance. Alternatively, if a community lacked the holdings of a long-established seat like Durham or Freising, clerics might themselves put quill to parchment. Thietmar wrote his *Chronicon* specifically so that his successors would be aware of the political processes in which they were expected to participate. Ecclesiastical institutions, acting either on their own accord or at the behest of patrons, functioned as repositories of procedural and historical precedent.

The moral and religious dimension of the bishop's office should not be overlooked. Since at least the ninth century, an integral part of episcopal self-perception had been the role of prelates as keepers of the community's spiritual well-being.[100] In theory, if not always in practice, they performed this function by advising and counselling, admonishing and reprimanding rulers. When we do have accounts of the election process, it often fell to bishops to assess the moral character of claimants. In 1125, the archbishop of Mainz required that the three leading candidates – Lothar of Saxony, Leopold of Austria and Frederick of Swabia – first promise that they would willingly accept and support whomever the princes chose as king. Supposedly, this would ensure a unanimous election and demonstrate the candidates' moral suitability.[101] A claimant who refused to support the verdict of princes and prelates risked the welfare of the realm, and revealed himself to be driven by ambition and greed. Indeed, the *Narratio* asserted, the duke of Swabia repeatedly proved his lack of moral probity. First, he was reluctant to accept the outcome of the election in advance. Second, when he lost, he began plotting against the successful candidate.[102] The metropolitan was vindicated. He had protected the princes from choosing as their king a man so evidently unsuited for the royal office.

It was perhaps for similar reasons that, in 1135, the archbishop of Canterbury took it upon himself to verify the legitimacy of Stephen's bid for

---

[98] Simon MacLean, 'Recycling the Franks in twelfth-century England: Regino of Prüm, the monks of Durham, and the Alexandrine Schism', *Speculum* 87 (2012), 649–81.

[99] Nicholas L. Paul, *To Follow in Their Footsteps. The Crusades and Family Memory in the High Middle Ages* (Ithaca, NY, 2012), 299–303.

[100] Ryan Kemp, 'Images of Kingship in bishops' *vitae* and *gesta*: England and Germany in the long twelfth century' (PhD thesis, Aberystwyth University, 2019), chapter 1.

[101] *Narratio de electione*, 510.

[102] *Narratio de electione*, 510–11.

IV. ELECTION 283

the throne. In Sicily, Walter, the late king's chancellor played on these expectations. After the death of William II in 1189, he urged the archbishop of Palermo to take the lead in assessing the various candidates:

> kind father, light of the kingdom, glory of the clergy,
> beneficial counsel, shepherd and honor of the city,
> road of peace, love of reason, constancy of truth,
> provide for the widowed realms through your counsels,
> give counsel so that they do not perish.[103]

It was the metropolitan's duty to offer advice, to act as keeper of the well-being of the realm and as guardian of truth and reason. Peter of Eboli, who penned these lines, was being deeply ironic. His account of the 1189 election was designed to invalidate its outcome. In his view, the chancellor plotted to have an easily malleable man installed as king. Through flattery, Walter steered an inept and easily swayed archbishop towards choosing precisely that kind of man. Walter and the archbishop adhered to the letter, but not the spirit, of the principle that leaders of a kingdom's Church should offer guidance in choosing a king and of their responsibility for the moral and spiritual well-being of the realm.[104]

Archbishops were by no means expected to remain neutral. When the prelates and nobles of west Francia had to elect a king in 987, they had to choose between Charles of Lotharingia and Count Hugh of Paris. The archbishop of Reims opened the proceedings. He outlined the difficult choice before the assembled magnates and carefully weighed up the qualities of the two candidates. Charles might be more closely related to the late king, but he lacked the virtuous character required of a ruler. Charles should be chosen only if one wished misfortune upon the realm. Hugh, on the other hand, was 'a man famed for his deeds, his nobility, and his wealth, whom you will find a guardian not only of the common weal but also of your private property'.[105] The archbishop clearly viewed his role not as that of an arbiter between competing claims, but as a judge determining suitability. As in Germany in 1125, in England in 1135 and in Sicily in 1189, how he expressed his partisanship was rooted in the moral obligations of his office. The presiding prelate had to ensure that both the process of choosing the king and its outcome adhered to the normative framework of kingship.

---

[103] Peter of Eboli, *Liber ad Honorem*, 98–9.
[104] See, for a comparable example, Albert of Aachen's portrayal of Daimbert of Pisa, patriarch of Jerusalem, plotting to prevent Baldwin I from taking control of Jerusalem: *Historia Ierosolimitana*, 522–3.
[105] Richer, *Historiae*, 220–1. For the context: Yves Sassier, "'La royauté ne s'acquiert pas par droit héréditaire'. Réflexion sur la structure du discours attribué à Adalbéron de Reims en faveur de l'élection de Hugues Capet', in *Élections et pouvoirs politiques du VIIe au XVIIe siècle: actes du colloque réuni à Paris 12 du 30 novembre au 2 décembre 2006*, ed. Corinne Péneau (Pompignac, 2008), 341–50.

284 8. CHOOSING A KING

What of the relationship between secular and ecclesiastical electors? Most sources were produced by clerical actors, which partly explains why they feature quite so prominently. But we can still see that, in practice, matters were more complicated. When, in 1099, the victorious crusading army proceeded to elect a ruler of Jerusalem, the secular leaders did so without consulting the clergy.[106] Until the later twelfth century, narratives from Denmark and Norway subsumed prelates under the general bracket of electors. However, all three realms either lacked a particularly dense ecclesiastical organisation or it was only beginning to form. According to William of Tyre, in 1099 the secular princes had been left to their own devices because the clerics had convened separately to elect a patriarch of Jerusalem. While eight Danish dioceses had been in place by *c.* 1100, in Sweden a diocesan organisation had not fully developed until the 1170s. Norway – by far the largest of the Scandinavian realms – only had three episcopal sees.[107] Bishoprics there may have been too dispersed for their occupants to be closely involved in many of the preparatory meetings discussed. This did not prevent prelates from assuming a prominent part in electoral politics, of course. In 1135, Saxo Grammaticus reported, Bishop Rike of Schleswig had earned the favour of King Erik of Denmark by supporting him in his bid for the throne.[108] When Oluf raised an army against Erik, it was Archbishop Eskil of Lund who thwarted the rebels' assembly at Arnedal,[109] though he later cast his lot with Knud, another challenger.[110] Yet all these cases involved prelates providing military and political backing once a ruler had already been enthroned, not in the lead-up to the assembly choosing him. A further contributing factor may have been that, before the later twelfth century, most Scandinavian realms lacked a formal coronation ceremony. We may be dealing with narrative conventions, but those did not originate in a vacuum. At least in theory, in these realms prelates remained an important but by no means the decisive group in choosing a king.

In polities with an already well-established diocesan organisation, the relationship also remains difficult to ascertain. It seems that clerical and secular voters were kept separate, at least once the formal process commenced. Accounts of the election of Rudolf of Rheinfelden in 1077 report that the clergy deliberated separately from the princes.[111] Wipo recorded only secular princes as having been involved in discussions about the several aspirants to the throne.[112] In 1037, it was Jaromir, the former duke of Bohemia, who

---

[106] William of Tyre, *Chronicon*, 422–4.
[107] Birgit Sawyer and Peter Sawyer, *Medieval Scandinavia: From Conversion to Reformation, 800–1500* (Minneapolis, 1993), 108–10.
[108] Saxo Grammaticus, *Gesta Danorum*, xiv.1.12, pp. 982–3.
[109] Saxo Grammaticus, *Gesta Danorum*, xiv.2.6, pp. 986–7.
[110] Saxo Grammatcius, *Gesta Danorum*, ix.3.3, pp. 998–9.
[111] Berthold, *Chronica*, 292.
[112] Wipo, *Gesta Chuonradi*, 16.

IV.   ELECTION   285

initiated the choice of his successor.[113] And in 1137, it was Christiern, a former retainer of Knud Lavard's, who persuaded the Danes to elect Erik as their king.[114] Once a formal decision had been reached, however, clerical leaders took the lead in announcing it. In 1024, the first person to vote was the archbishop of Mainz, followed by 'the other archbishops and men in holy orders', before first Conrad's eponymous cousin and then the remaining nobles voiced their assent.[115] When, in 1059, King Henry I of France had his son elected king, he was the first to vote, but was followed by a papal legate; by the archbishops, bishops, abbots and other clergy; and only then by the secular princes.[116] And in 1077, the first to cast their vote for Rudolf of Rheinfelden had been the papal legates, followed by the ecclesiastical leaders, with the laity last.[117] All these instances, it is worth stressing, relate to the public enactment of a decision that had already been agreed upon. The act of voting constituted the culmination of a process of negotiation and debate. It demonstrated unanimity and thereby established the legitimacy of both candidate and electors.

This division of roles did not mean that lay princes played a marginal or even subordinate part. Bishops could not become kings. That reinforced their status as moral arbiters, but also limited the weight they carried in the decision-making process. Moreover, most members of the episcopacy were the nephews and uncles, brothers, sons and cousins of lay magnates. They were deeply embedded in aristocratic networks and princely political culture. They were not an entirely separate caste. A more fruitful approach would be to suggest that princes and prelates formed part of a larger cross-section of elites, constituting distinct yet closely entwined pillars on which rested the successful selection of a ruler as well as the successful exercise of the ruler's office. The clergy provided guidance on precedent, assessed the moral calibre of the candidates proposed and generally ensured the legitimacy of proceedings. They participated in preparing and calling an election, and could take an important role in directing proceedings or sounding out candidates. They confirmed and guided the electors, but did not decide for them.

In tracing the stages of the electoral process thus far, we have seen how complex was the interaction between the norms and expediency. An emphasis

---

[113] Cosmas of Prague, *Chronica*, 78; Cosmas of Prague, *Chronicle of the Czechs*, 106.
[114] Saxo Grammaticus, *Gesta Danorum*, xiv.2.2, pp. 984–5.
[115] Wipo, *Gesta Chuonradi*, 18–19.
[116] *Ordines Coronationis Franciae*, ed. Jackson, vol. 1, 231.
[117] Berthold, *Chronica*, 292. Paul of Bernried, on the other hand, gave the princes the first vote: Paul of Bernried, *Vita Gregorii VII*, vol. 1, 531–2. Prelates voting first would conform to a general pattern: for instance, in 1130, Roger II had first the clergy and then the barons decide that he should adopt the title of king of Sicily: Alexander of Telese, *Ystoria Rogerii*, 23–4. See, generally, Maleczek, 'Abstimmungsarten', 98–101, whose only secular examples of the practice are, however, from Germany.

286   8. CHOOSING A KING

on unanimity often cloaked a considerably more contentious reality. The stress
on moral probity seemingly clashed with more mundane concerns over access,
patronage and power. Yet we also witnessed considerable overlap between the
two. Nobody liked supporting a ruler whose word could not be trusted, who
favoured his own men to the disadvantage of his erstwhile peers or who
threatened to turn into a tyrant. Equally, a divided election heralded turmoil
and unrest. And no king could perform his duties effectively without the
backing of his people. This context helps explain the extensive preparations
taken before an election could occur. They were all the more called for when, as
so often happened, no clear line of succession existed. Yet that problem could
be tackled only once all the preparations had been taken, once candidacies had
been declared, supporters won and once the princes and prelates of the realm
at last convened to choose their king.

8.3 Choosing

When they finally got together, electors did not proceed straight to a vote.
Discussion and debate moved from preparatory and regional meetings to the
community of the realm. For many this may also have presented the first
opportunity to interrogate rival candidates, or to consult and negotiate with
their peers from across the kingdom. Such private gatherings were integral to
the process. In 1024, Wipo reported that the particular area where the election was
held had been chosen because its flatness would accommodate a large crowd, but
also because 'some island retreats were nearby, thus making it safe and suitable for
the consideration of secret matters'.[118] Isøre similarly provided several smaller
islands close to the assembly site.[119] Deliberations were conducted by only a small
circle of participants. The vast majority of attendants would know that they took
place, but would not know what was being discussed. What reports of these
discussions we do have are therefore often highly stylised, designed to reinforce –
or question – a candidate's legitimacy. Still, they allow us to trace what should,
even if they do not necessarily reveal what actually did, happen.

Wipo's account of Conrad II's election provides a case in point.[120] After
Henry II's death, the princes and prelates exchanged envoys and letters in the
lead-up to the election proper.[121] Once assembled, they began reviewing the
remaining candidates:

[118] Wipo, *Gesta Chuonradi*, 13; *Deeds of Conrad II*, 61.
[119] Saxo Grammaticus, *Gesta Danorum*, 824 n. 32. This reflects a general pattern in assembly
sites: Stefan Brink, 'Legal assembly sites in early Scandinavia', in *Assembly Places and
Practices in Medieval Europe*, ed. Aliki Pantos and Sarah Semple (Dublin, 2004), 205–16.
[120] On which see also Reuling, 'Zur Entwicklung der Wahlformen', 233–41;
Herwig Wolfram, *Konrad II. Kaiser dreier Reiche* (Munich, 2000), 60–3.
[121] Wipo, *Gesta Chuonradi*, 13. Reuling, 'Zur Entwicklung der Wahlformen', overlooked
this comment.

IV. ELECTION

a long disputation took place as to who ought to rule; and when age – too immature or, on the other hand, too greatly advanced – rejected one, untested valour, another; and a proven state of insolence, some others, few were chosen among many, and from the few two only were singled out. On them rested at last, in an instant of unity, the final examination of the greatest men, long contemplated with the utmost diligence.[122]

Those two were Conrad and his eponymous younger cousin. Wipo rehearsed their noble pedigree, which included leading members of the imperial aristocracy, a pope, the king of Burgundy and, of course, the Trojans. The cousins' suitability was demonstrated when they agreed that whichever between them should garner stronger backing from the princes would be supported by the other. They, the elder Conrad expounded, should not think better of themselves for being the sole remaining candidates, but ought to remember their forebears, 'who preferred to advance their glory with deeds rather than words'. They should thank God, the author of their good fortune. As no good man would pass judgement on himself, they should humbly accept that of the 'Franks, Lotharingians, Saxons, Bavarians and Alamanni'. Conrad also warned of the consequences if they mishandled so great an opportunity. They would acquire a reputation for 'baseness and jealousy, as though [they] were unable to uphold the high character of so great a position of command'. Once the younger Conrad agreed, they went before the princes, where the archbishop of Mainz voted first, and the younger Conrad, as first among the nobles, cast his vote for the elder. Once Conrad had been acclaimed, Henry II's widow handed over the imperial insignia[123] and preparations began for Conrad's coronation. Wipo ended his account with a list of Conrad's virtues:

> Truly, by the assent of God he was elected whose later acknowledgement by men had been foreseen by God. For he was a man of great humility, provident in counsel, truthful in statements, vigorous in deeds, not at all greedy, the most liberal of kings in giving. ... It was not, therefore, in accord with divine law for anyone on earth to fight him whom Omnipotent God had predestined to govern all.[124]

Wipo's report points to several levels of consultation. There was the exchange of letters and envoys in advance of the actual assembly. The venue between Worms and Mainz had been chosen because it provided ample opportunity for private meetings. The princes carefully deliberated before whittling down the list of putative candidates. They weeded out claimants because of age (being either too old or too young) and ensured that they possessed valour (martial prowess and rectitude) as well as a good character

---

[122] Wipo, *Gesta Chuonradi,* 15; *Deeds of Conrad II,* 61.
[123] On which see also: Hein H. Jonbloed, '"Wanburtich": Heinrichs II. Beteiligung and der Wahl von Kamba, 1024', *DA* 62 (2006), 1–63.
[124] Wipo, *Gesta Chuonradi,* 15–20; *Deeds of Conrad II,* 61–6.

288   8. CHOOSING A KING

(they would not indulge in insolent behaviour). The two chief rivals who emerged then got together and agreed that one would step aside in favour of the other.[125] In theory, none of this was supposed to happen. Electors were meant to be guided solely by the Holy Spirit. Yet in Wipo's rendering the process reinforced the legitimacy of Conrad's rule. The princes settled on a good ruler because so much care had been taken in picking the right person. Throughout, voters and candidates abided by strict standards of moral probity, and they reached amicable unanimity without searching for worldly glory. Indeed, at no point did Conrad try to win over his relative or any of the other men with any promise of material rewards. Instead, he upheld values of humility, truthfulness and generosity, all embedded in a sense of dutiful obligation to one's ancestors as well as to the realm. While, on one level, norms had therefore been violated, those transgressions actually upheld, celebrated and strengthened the moral framework within which Conrad and his people were supposed to operate.

Comparable episodes were recorded elsewhere in Latin Europe. In 1118, the barons of the crusader kingdom of Jerusalem had to choose a successor to Baldwin I. The late king had been a participant in the First Crusade and had followed his brother Godfrey onto the throne, but had left no heir. According to Albert of Aachen, writing between 1125 and 1150, as soon as Baldwin had been buried, members of the clergy demanded that a successor should be chosen, as it was 'useless advice [*non esse utile consilium*] for the place and people to lack for long a king and the comfort of a defender'. After some discussion, everyone settled on Baldwin of Edessa, the king's cousin, and another participant in the First Crusade, 'because he was an undaunted knight who had often endured many battles for the safety of Christians, and who had kept the land of Edessa vigorously defended from all enemy attack'. Baldwin accepted, albeit after some hesitation.[126] A slightly different version was recorded by William of Tyre. After Baldwin's death, many felt that, with numerous dangers facing the realm, they should elect the count of Edessa. Others, however, argued that the throne should be offered to Eustace, the youngest remaining brother of Godfrey. Moreover, Eustace was a pious man, of great repute, and likely to follow the model of his brothers, who had so successfully defended the realm. Some of the men backing Eustace set out to offer him the crown, which he accepted reluctantly. However, on reaching Apulia, news reached him that in the meantime the crown had been offered to Baldwin. Because he did not want to be the cause of discord in Christ's homeland, he returned to Lotharingia.[127]

---

[125] For the various types of meeting, see the typology developed by Gerd Althoff, 'Colloquium familiare – Colloquium secretum – Colloquium publicum. Beratung im politischen Leben des früheren Mittelalters', *FmSt* 24 (1990), 145–67.
[126] Albert of Aachen, *Historia Ierosolimitana*, 872–3.
[127] William of Tyre, *Chronicon*, 549–50.

IV. ELECTION   289

As in Germany in 1002 and 1125, the king's funeral provided the occasion
for discussions about the choice of his successor. As in 1024, the probity of
candidates was the most important question to consider. Moreover, both
Baldwin and Eustace were reluctant to assume the throne. The count's reasoning – he was content with the riches of Edessa and was concerned about
shouldering the duties of royal rule – foreshadowed that employed by Sverrir
of Norway, discussed in Chapter 6: given how much turmoil and labour being
king entailed, selling his soul for the royal crown would have been a bad
bargain indeed. Eustace also hesitated, and proved that he deserved his reputation for righteousness and piety when he chose to surrender an inheritance
that was his by right, rather than cause discord in the Holy Land. The men
electing a king were also driven by honourable motives. The clergy of
Outremer demanded a protector, and the great men of the realm took great
care to identify a candidate who was both of the right moral disposition and
capable of discharging his duties. Such righteous thinking even extended to
those who offered the throne to Eustace. They did so not out of greed or to
garner favours, but because they felt that fundamental principles of succession
needed to be upheld, especially as their favoured candidate was also a man of
good standing and honourable conduct.

The Jerusalem episode illustrates that debates revolved around reconciling
or even choosing between conflicting norms. Where, if we follow Wipo,
Conrad II had combined ancestry and suitability in exemplary fashion, in
1118 the barons and clergy of the Holy Land had to decide in favour of one or
the other. Similar dilemmas were discussed by Saxo Grammaticus. After the
death of Knud in 1042, Magnus of Norway claimed the Danish throne, which
had been promised to him by the late king. The Danes deliberated at length,
and then decided to honour Knud's promise: "'principles", they pleaded,
"deserved more concern than principalities"'.[128] Saxo did not agree. He saw
it as a 'half-way station to disaster', and felt vindicated by subsequent events. In
moving beyond the *stirps regia*, the Danes had failed to abide by the norms that
should guide the election of their rulers. They may have upheld an agreement
made by their previous king, but in the process they violated an even more
hallowed principle: that they should choose as their king not only someone
suitable, but someone of Danish stock and a member of the wider royal clan.
The account fits a broader pattern. Saxo often constructed deliberations either
in order to promote particular values or to highlight the recurring failure of the
Danes to perform their duties, resulting in the abolition of electoral succession
in 1165.[129] This was possible because each consultation involved the weighing

---

[128] Saxo Grammaticus, *Gesta Danorum*, x.21.4, pp. 776–9.
[129] We have already encountered their misreading of Ubbe's refusal to become king. Saxo
Grammaticus, *Gesta Danorum*, xii.8.3, pp. 894–7. See also above, Chapter 7. Generally:
Hermann Kamp, 'Tugend, Macht und Ritual: Politisches Verhalten beim Saxo

290 8. CHOOSING A KING

up of conflicting norms. In 1042, the question was whether to honour the promises made by the late king or to abide by the established customs of royal succession; in 1076, the Danes had to choose between the king's eldest son and the one most likely to offer rigorous justice;[130] in 1103, between an eldest son, who had already proven himself to be a tyrant, and the king's brother, who promised fair and equitable governance;[131] and in 1137, between Valdemar, who, while likely to become a capable ruler, was also still too young, and someone who could shoulder the burdens of kingship immediately.[132] Before a king could, it had to be determined according to which principle he *should* be chosen.

While Saxo berated the modern Danes for habitually making the wrong call, their decisions were also about shaping the realm's future governance. In 1076, he claimed, when asked to choose between the brothers Knud and Harald, many

> were frightened that these [Knud's previous exploits] might become even more severe, should he be invested with the kingdom . . . in like proportion they showed enthusiasm for Harald because they craved an easy life, . . . choosing for themselves a slothful ruler to govern them in preference to a valiant one. . . . Nevertheless, this mean-spirited attitude was glossed over with a spurious resemblance of reason, for they contended that Harald, being the elder, was owed a crown by simple law of nature.[133]

Should the Danes choose a king who might prove too rigorous in his pursuit of justice, or one who would prove lenient and easily handled, while also being the elder? Similar considerations were at play in 1042 and 1103. On each occasion, the issues at stake were not only who should be king according to what norms, but also what that decision heralded for the welfare of the realm, and for the relationship between people and monarch.

Saxo and the Danes were not the only ones to think along such lines. Peter of Eboli recounted machinations after the death of William II in 1189:

> Each one sought for himself a king someone he knew for a friend.
> This one sought a superior, that one an equal.
> This one asked a blood relation, that one a comrade.
> Each one sought a king for himself, this man or that man.[134]

Grammaticus', in *Zeichen, Rituale, Werte. Internationales Kolloquium*, ed. Gerd Althoff (Münster, 2004), 179–200; Thomas Riis, 'Saxo und die offizielle Königsideologie', in *Saxo and the Baltic Region. A Symposium*, ed. Tore Nyberg (Odense, 2004), 93–104.

[130] Saxo Grammaticus, *Gesta Danorum*, xi.10.1, pp. 822–3.
[131] Saxo Grammaticus, *Gesta Danorum*, xii.8.2, pp. 894–5.
[132] Saxo Grammaticus, *Gesta Danorum*, xiv.2.2, pp. 984–5.
[133] Saxo Grammaticus, *Gesta Danorum*, xi.10.1, pp. 822–3.
[134] Peter of Eboli, *Liber ad Honorem*, 94–5.

IV. ELECTION

The criteria according to which William's successor was to be chosen were designed to promote personal gain, not the common good. Everyone 'sought a king for himself'. The king's aunt Constance was ruled out because of her husband's alleged tyranny, and Roger of Andria was dismissed because of his sexual transgressions and profligate spending. Tancred of Lecce, by contrast, while physically repugnant, appealed because he would be easy to manipulate.[135] Peter was no neutral observer: the *Liber* was dedicated to Emperor Henry VI, who in 1194 deposed Tancred and put his wife Constance on the throne. But then one of the best narrative devices at his disposal was to focus on the consultations taking place. That the conversations he reported ran counter to what should be discussed on such occasions only reinforced the point. Tancred had been chosen not because he would uphold justice, defend the realm and protect the Church, but because he was weak and easily controlled. He was an usurper, not a rightful king.

In electing a ruler, the people chose not only an individual but also a style of governance. Danes and Sicilians played with that theme, but violated its underlying principles. Yet defining how and to what ends a king had been chosen could also provide a rhetorical tool for preserving the integrity of the realm. In 1199, Archbishop Hubert Walter of Canterbury crowned John king of England. Half a century later, Matthew Paris reimagined the event, and recorded a speech supposedly given by the metropolitan on that occasion. Nobody, Hubert explained, ought to be elected king who had not been unanimously chosen by the people. He should, moreover, have demonstrated through his many virtues that he was suited for so onerous an office. There was no reason why a succession ought to follow in line of descent. Neither Saul nor David had been of royal stock. They had been granted royal status because they were the most suitable and wise. Therefore, he should be elected king who was pre-eminent in strength and power within the realm, but who was also virtuous. As Richard had died without progeny, the archbishop argued, the assembled should choose John, the king's brother. When subsequently questioned about his statement, Hubert explained that he had deduced from prophecies and oracles that John would bring great disruption to the realm. To ensure that he lacked the means to do so, he decided to have John succeed by election rather than hereditary right.[136]

Nothing like the words attributed to Hubert was reported by John's contemporaries,[137] or in any of Matthew's sources. It was a fabrication entirely

---

[135] Peter of Eboli, *Liber ad Honorem*, 98–9.

[136] Matthew Paris, *Chronica Majora*, vol. 2, 454–5. Though, rather curiously, in his subsequent account of John's reign Matthew went to considerable lengths to dismiss the implications of Hubert's statement. A further exploration of Matthew's concept of kingship would prove a fruitful avenue of research.

[137] See, for the most detailed contemporary account, Gervase of Canterbury, *Gesta regum*, in *The Historical Works of Gervase of Canterbury*, vol. 2, 92.

292   8. CHOOSING A KING

of his own devising. But then, in this instance, Matthew's concern was with moral rather than historical truth. What mattered was not the actual course of events in 1199, but the lessons that could be drawn from John's reign. To Matthew, one of the key events of John's reign was Magna Carta, forced upon the king by his barons in 1215. It provided a blueprint for how the relationship between ruler and ruled should unfold, and for the right of the latter to exercise oversight of the former. Yet it could be valid only if the legitimacy of John's kingship rested on his meeting the conditions that had been placed upon him before he could occupy the throne. By choosing to have him succeed through election, not by hereditary right, the magnates ensure that John's authority became contingent upon his acting like a king, not a tyrant. Matthew may have spoken to the concerns of the mid-thirteenth century, but he invoked concepts, tools and mechanisms that were rooted much further back in time.[138]

Wipo, Albert, William, Peter and Matthew attributed strikingly similar concerns and practices to their protagonists. This despite the chronological span of their efforts, stretching from the eleventh to the thirteenth century; notwithstanding the fact that they were active in realms as diverse England, Germany, Jerusalem, Norway and Sicily; and even though they came from a variety of backgrounds. Matthew was a Benedictine monk, William a bishop, Wipo an imperial chaplain, and Albert a secular canon. We are evidently dealing with a set of norms and practices that points to transeuropean patterns of thought. This is not to say that the conversations recorded occurred as described. Apart from William (who was bishop of Tyre), none of these authors would have been privy to such gatherings, and most wrote several decades after the events recounted. They fashioned accounts that incorporated an ideal practice of election to communicate a particular interpretation of the past, to disparage or recommend a certain course of action or to root the concerns of the present in hallowed precedent.

In this regard, their efforts resemble episodes of kings hesitating before accepting the throne. The image of prelates and princes convening to select candidates provided a convenient shorthand, charged with potential meaning because it reflected shared expectations. Ideally, the great men of the realm would indeed discuss the suitability of candidates, and deliberations would be guided by concern for a claimant's honour, moral integrity and martial prowess. Electors would ensure that prospective kings had the right ancestry, were old enough to wear the crown and would not turn out to be tyrants and oppressors or prove useless as defenders of the realm. As representatives of the community of the realm, princes and prelates were supposed to direct royal power towards the common good. Assessing and interrogating candidates provided the perfect opportunity for them to do just that. Even if, as in the instances reported by Saxo and Peter, norms were violated, an audience still

[138] See above, Chapters 2–5.

IV. ELECTION

needed to know what should have happened for a transgression to be recognised. Only then could the right lessons be learned.

Most accounts stress the importance of private and confidential deliberation in the days immediately prior to the formal selection of a king. In 987, Charles, uncle of the recently deceased West Frankish monarch, sounded out his chances for election in a private conversation with the archbishop of Reims;[139] in 1024, the location for the electoral assembly had been chosen specifically to allow small groups to get together for private discussion; in 1118, leading members of the aristocracy of Outremer held private meetings in which they decided to back Eustace for the throne;[140] in 1189, Matthew, the chancellor of the kingdom of Sicily, sought a private conversation with the archbishop of Palermo in which he outlined the strengths and weaknesses of leading contenders for the throne.[141] Gatherings of this kind were essential in order to fashion the semblance of unanimity. While these conferences were held away from prying eyes and ears, they could only be conducted once a sufficient number of people had assembled. In that sense, they were still public. The great men were seen to be deliberating. They conscientiously discharged their duty to act on behalf and for the good of the community at large.

Their efforts legitimised the decision they ultimately reached. When the rebel princes convened at Forchheim in 1077, they did not proceed straight to promoting Rudolf's kingship. Instead, they first discussed the state of the realm. They only proposed to replace Henry with someone more suitable after the evidence clearly showed that the situation had been made intractable solely by the king's tyranny. Only then was Rudolf's kingship mooted, and only after his suitability had been ascertained was he chosen as king. Extensive and public deliberation, guided by demonstrative concern for the welfare of the realm, signalled the moral integrity of the process, of the chosen candidate and of those who had raised him to the throne. A decision had to be made and the reasoning behind it expounded and accepted. The public questioning as well as the symbolic endorsement of candidates by the leading prelates of the realm demonstrated that norms had been upheld. The process of election was less about voting than about proving that all this effort – the advance negotiations, the weighing-up of claims, the secret gatherings and private meetings – had indeed ensured that the decision reached was unanimous, that it was made for the right reasons, and that it resulted in the election of the right person.

[139] Richer, *Histories*, vol. 2, 214–15.
[140] William of Tyre, *Chronicon*, 549–50.
[141] Peter of Eboli, *Liber ad Honorem*, 98–9.

294   8. CHOOSING A KING

8.4 Accepting

If we know little about the deliberations and advance negotiations that accompanied the election of a king, we know even less about the actual process of voting. Here, even more than elsewhere, we depend on idealised renditions of reality. Worse, most chroniclers subsume the act in a general statement: the princes and prelates elected (*elegerunt*) a king.[142] The exceptions are few, with Wipo's account of 1024 among the most detailed:

> The Archbishop of Mainz, whose opinion had to be taken before all, asked by the people what was seemly to him, with a full heart and a happy voice, acclaimed and elected the elder Cuono [Conrad] as his lord and king, restorer and defender of the fatherland. The other archbishops and the remaining men of holy orders unhesitatingly followed him in this vote. The younger Cuono, who had been negotiating for a short time with the Lotharingians, returned suddenly and elected him as lord and king with the greatest good will. The King, taking him by the hand, made him sit beside him. Then, one by one, men from each of the several realms presented the same words of election again and again; there was a shout of acclamation by the people; all consented unanimously with the princes in the election of the King; all eagerly desired the elder Cuono. On him they insisted; him they placed without any hesitation before all the mighty lords; him they judged to be the most worthy of the regal power; and they demanded that there be no delay to his consecration.[143]

Wipo highlights a number of features. One of them was hierarchy. The order of voting denoted a prelate's position within the kingdom's Church. Hence the archbishop of Reims playing such a prominent role in 987, that of Mainz in 1024 and 1077 and that of Canterbury in 1135. Among secular leaders, an individual's ranking in the order of voting could convey complex messages. In 1024, the younger Conrad was the first among the secular princes to cast his vote for Conrad the Elder. The eagerness with which he embraced his erstwhile rival constituted a promise of future loyalty and ensured that the resulting election was indeed unanimous.[144] In England, William of Malmesbury described Stephen of Blois as competing to be the first among the laity to pledge fealty to Matilda as his future queen. Eagerness also expressed proximity to the ruler, perhaps even the expectation of future patronage. When

---

[142] Albert of Aachen, *Historia Ierosolimitana*, 446–7, 542–3, 872–3; Saxo Grammaticus, *Gesta Danorum*, xi.10.1, pp. 822–3; i.10.4–5, pp. 824–5; xii.8.3, pp. 894–7; xiv.2.2, pp. 984–5; *Annales Hildesheimenses*, 66; *Annales Palidenses*, 80. This is not a comprehensive list of examples.

[143] Wipo, *Gesta Chuonradi*, 19–20; *Deeds of Conrad II*, 65.

[144] On which see also Stefan Esders, '"Charles's stirrups hang down from Conrad's saddle": reminiscences of Carolingian oath practice under Conrad II (1024–1039)', in *Using and Not Using the Past After the Carolingian Empire, c. 900–c.1050*, ed. Sarah Greer, Alice Hicklin and Stefan Esders (London and New York, 2020), 189–99, at 190–3.

IV. ELECTION   295

erstwhile rivals and the king's closest relatives embraced a candidate, it was difficult for those of less exalted status to demur.

Sometimes votes were delegated. Obviously, princes and prelates voted in lieu of the people at large, and on behalf of their own networks of dependants and relatives. Occasionally, further steps were taken to emphasise this representative function. In 1125, the archbishop of Mainz supposedly insisted that the assembled princes select forty from their own ranks to vote in their stead.[145] Sverrisaga also reports that, after entering Nidaros, Sverrir nominated twelve men from each of the eight surrounding shires, who then acclaimed him as king on behalf of the region as a whole.[146] The process was central to anecdotes about Frederick Barbarossa tricking his way onto the throne.[147] The *Chronicon rhythmicum Austriacum*, probably written *c.* 1268, recounted how the German princes had convened to choose a king. Eventually, Frederick demanded to know what was taking them so long. When the princes lamented that, having searched to the ends of the earth, they could not find anyone who was of noble descent, generous, faithful, prudent and strong, he promised to find such a candidate for them, provided that the princes then elect that person. When they all agreed, Frederick nominated himself.[148] Delegation was embedded in what contemporaries thought feasible, plausible and practical in choosing a king. It served to reinforce the role of the electors as acting for the benefit of the community at large, reflected pragmatic needs and provided a means by which unanimity and concord could more easily be achieved.

Wipo points to yet another issue, though he does so in a rather veiled fashion: how to handle absentees. In 1024, the Lotharingians left when it transpired that Conrad the Elder was likely to succeed, while most Saxons had not attended in the first place. Significant absences were by no means unusual. In 1002, the archbishop of Cologne had avoided participating in Henry II's election (as had the Saxons), and most of the English barons and clergy had stayed away from Stephen's in 1135. Absences and early departures need not denote opposition. They could just as commonly be a means by which to ascertain status or of bartering for concessions. For this to work, certain conditions had to be met. One had to be of sufficient standing. Men like the archbishop of Cologne or the duke of Lotharingia were powerful enough for steps to have to be taken to solicit their backing. But dissent could not be voiced so strongly or so publicly that the validity of the whole process would be called into question. In 1002, a later *vita* of Heribert of Cologne asserted, the

---

[145] *Narratio de electione*, 510.
[146] *Saga of King Sverri*, chapter 16, p. 20.
[147] Gislebert of Mons, *Chronique*, 92–4; *Chronicle of Hainaut*, 54–5.
[148] *Chronicon rhythmicum Austriacum*, MGH SS 25(Hanover, 1880), 350–1. See also Georg Möser-Mersky, 'Das österreichische "Chronicon Rhythmicum"', *MIÖG* 73 (1965), 17–38.

296   8. CHOOSING A KING

archbishop declined to attend Henry II's election not because he had any misgivings about the duke of Bavaria, but because he was still overcome with grief over the death of Otto III.[149] In 1125, by contrast, these safeguards failed, and the assembly ended in a fracas. Frederick of Swabia left when it became apparent that Lothar would be elected king. This was so unusual that the event was recorded at Durham, St Denis, Constantinople and the Norman abbey of St Evroul.[150] Orderic Vitalis even claimed that the archbishop had threatened whichever candidate refused to accept the assembly's decision with beheading.[151] Frederick's dissent occurred at precisely the moment when the result of lengthy and secret deliberations, confirming the moral probity of the successful candidate and of the men choosing him, was about to be announced.[152] Worse, denying a candidate an unanimous election, and doing that in so public a fashion, called into question his ability to act like a king. The challenge was such that those who put their ambitions and worldly desires above the common good had to be brought to heel swiftly and decisively. In 1125, Lothar responded by seeking to dispossess the duke's family.[153] By mismanaging dissent, Frederick, Lothar and the archbishop caused the dispute to escalate to a point at which armed confrontation became inevitable.

Chapter 10 will treat in more detail how newly enthroned kings handled such situations. Sometimes small gestures would suffice. In 1138/9, the Saxons, initially excluded from Conrad III's election, were appeased when, at a subsequent assembly, the archbishop of Trier gave them a gift of thirty tuns of wine.[154] Normally, more elaborate steps had to be taken, and the king had to seek out the men who had been absent from his election. His presence communicated standing. Someone was clearly powerful enough that he could get away with waiting for the ruler to visit him before he offered his submission. Yet such encounters also required that the king demonstrate status – be it by performing his duties or by convening especially splendid and important meetings to coincide with them. In 1025, for example, Conrad II held his Christmas court in Saxony, where he solemnly confirmed the laws

---

[149] Lantbert of Deutz, *Vita Heriberti*, 162–3.

[150] *Die deutsche Königserhebung*, ed. Böhme, vol. 2, nos. 1–38.

[151] Orderic Vitalis, *Ecclesiastical History*, vol. 6, 364–5.

[152] See generally Timothy Reuter, 'Assembly politics in western Europe from the eighth century to the twelfth', in his, *Medieval Polities*, 193–216; Leidulf Melve, 'Performance, argument, and assembly politics (ca. 1080 – ca. 1160)', *Super alta perennis* 10 (2010), 85–108.

[153] *Narratio de electione*, 510–1; *Annales Magdeburgenses*, 183; Cosmas, *Chronica Boemorum*, 133; *Annales S. Pauli Virdunensis*, MGH SS 16, 501; Wolfgang Giese, 'Das Gegenkönigtum des Staufers Konrad 1127–1135', *ZSRG: Germanistische Abteilung* 95 (1978), 202–20. The ensuing conflict continued into the early reign of Frederick Barbarossa: Görich, *Friedrich Barbarossa*, 118–43.

[154] *Gesta Alberonis*, 586–7; *Warrior Bishop*, 55.

IV. ELECTION   297

and privileges of the Saxons before they acclaimed him as king.[155] It is, however, important to distinguish between the formal election and subsequent encounters, which were understood by contemporaries as falling into a rather different category.[156] When Henry II met the Saxons at Merseburg in 1002, Thietmar described them as requesting that the king grant and confirm their laws. Once Henry had done so, the assembled people, led by their duke, acclaimed him king. Even that was preceded by the 'humble devotion' with which the king was received on his arrival.[157] When Conrad II visited Minden in 1025, he was also met by many who had not been present at his election, and received them gracefully as his followers.[158] Comparable language was used by the *Gesta Stephani* when recounting Stephen's post-election traversing of England. He was 'greeted with an enthusiastic welcome', did justice and pacified the realm.[159] In other words, Henry, Conrad and Stephen were received as kings. There was no questioning their status. Those who had not participated in the election were still bound by its outcome. But they were powerful enough for the king to have had come to them to receive the promise of their fealty in person.

Yet offer it they must. A few months after the Birkibeinar had first made him king, Sverrir entered Nidaros (Trondheim), where he

> was received as befitted a king by the townsmen, who had the bells rung throughout the town and went in procession to meet him. He then caused the assembly to be called at Eyra, calling to it twelve men by name from each of the eight shires that lie within Agdanes. At this assembly of the eight shires, met together, the title King was given to Sverri, and ratified by the brandishing of weapons; land and liegemen were confirmed to him by oath in accordance with the old laws of the land.[160]

The initiative rested firmly with the king – unsurprisingly, as the assembly occurred just after his victory over the citizens of Nidaros. Sverrir even selected the men who would do the deliberating. Every measure had been taken to ensure the desired outcome. Moreover, the meeting resulted not in an election, but an acclamation. The men of Nidaros had already welcomed Sverrir like a king. They had rung church bells and greeted him in procession. Their acclamation merely underscored their submission. It was not constitutive of

---

[155] Wipo, *Gesta Chuonradi*, 29. See also *Annales Hildesheimenses*, 34.
[156] This goes against Mitteis, *Die deutsche Königswahl*, Malaczek, 'Zur Entwicklung', Reuling, 'Abstimmungen'. But also see, in the German context, Schlesinger, 'Die sogenannte Nachwahl'.
[157] Thietmar, *Chronicon*, v.15–6, pp. 208–11; *Ottonian Germany*, ed. Warner, 216–17. This reflects the ritual of *adventus*, on which see David A. Warner, 'Ritual and memory in the Ottonian "Reich". The ceremony of "Adventus"', *Speculum* 76 (2001), 255–83.
[158] *Annales Hildesheimenses*, 34.
[159] *Gesta Stephani*, 14–15.
[160] *Saga of King Sverri*, chapter 16, pp. 19–20.

298   8. CHOOSING A KING

Sverrir's kingship, which had originated in his election by the Birkibeinar. Still, proceeding in this fashion reinforced the probity and propriety of the townsmen's submission. No gifts were exchanged; no payments were made. Even the pretence that the men of Agdanes submitted out of their own volition was maintained. Everything unfolded 'according to the old laws of the land'.

The meeting conformed to broader European patterns. These gatherings provided an opportunity for agreement to be expressed. They did not, however, constitute a formal election. Furthermore, a semblance of voluntary action was required, as otherwise there would have been no amicable concord. And an agreement that was forced could be overturned as soon as circumstances allowed.[161] The electors were not, however, the only ones whose agreement was needed. At Eyra, the men selected by Sverrir conferred the title of king on him, but their decision was valid only once everyone had voiced their agreement. In 1024, Wipo reports, when the last vote had been cast, 'there was a shout of acclamation by the people; all consented unanimously with the princes in the election of the King'.[162] After Duke Bretislav of Bohemia had died in 1055, 'all of the Czech people great and small, by common counsel and like will, chose his firstborn son Spitihnev as their duke, singing Kyrie eleison, that sweet song'.[163] And in 1125, the *Narratio* reports, several of the laymen burst into shouts of 'Lothar should be king!' the moment the remaining princes had cast their vote.[164] As far as most chroniclers were concerned, the wider audience played a largely responsive role, relegated to acclaiming a decision already made.

Accepting that image unquestioningly would, however, underplay the many-layered significance of public consent. Bystanders were the dependants and relatives, the followers and friends, of the leading princes. Onlookers were the ones who had been brought together in the several meetings that Thietmar recorded for 1002. Their failure to act would have been held not only against them, but also against their lords who evidently had acted without the consent of their own men. Therefore, they could not claim to speak for the community of the realm, and that would call into question the validity of the whole election. Collectively, onlookers and bystanders could even exert pressure on the princes. That at least was the image conveyed by the *Narratio*. After the duke of Bavaria had departed with the duke of Swabia, it fell to the archbishop of Salzburg and the bishop of Regensburg, leading members of the former's entourage, to convince him to rejoin the remaining princes.[165] The prelates acted after the papal legate, who had attended the proceedings, had called

---

[161] See below, Chapter 5.
[162] Wipo, *Gesta Chuonradi*, 19–20; *Deeds of Conrad II*, 65.
[163] Cosmas of Prague, *Chronicon*, 103; Cosmas of Prague, *Chronicle of the Czechs*, 131.
[164] *Narratio de electione*, 511.
[165] *Narratio de electione*, 510–11.

IV. ELECTION 299

together the participating clergy. He warned them that whatever unrest ensued because of the disruption caused by Frederick would be the fault of those who had prevented a unanimous decision from being reached. They might not have a vote, but it was still morally incumbent upon them to ensure that the probity of the process could not be called into question.

Acclamation was no mere formality.[166] Its importance probably reflected discussions that the leading men themselves had held with one another and with their followers both before and during the electoral assembly – the letters and envoys referred to by Wipo, with whose aid private counsels could be weighed and the opinions of people solicited as to who should and who should not be king.[167] Presumably, under normal circumstances the twelve men from each of the eight districts called together at Eyra were supposed to have consulted with their peers before voting. Likewise, the forty nobles, whom the archbishop of Mainz had asked the laymen to elect in 1125, probably did not act in isolation from their peers. At some point, however, gathering the views of one's men was no longer possible. That was the case in 1024, when the two Conrads reached an agreement, or when, in 1125, the duke of Bavaria initially sided with his Swabian cousin. That made it all the more important for everyone to voice their agreement, including those who had not been privy to the final stage of deliberations. By acclaiming the new ruler, they confirmed not only the choice of candidate, but also that the process by which he was chosen had been conducted with due care and probity. Their consent established a promise of fidelity, of accepting the obligation of faithful service that the choice made by their leaders entailed. It served to confirm, even strengthen bonds between them and their leaders, and between them and the new king.

Acclamation was still not the end of the election process. The throne itself remained to be offered to and accepted by the successful candidate. That was the moment when the ritualised displays of reluctance discussed in Chapter 7 were performed. Good rulers stood back and consulted with their men. When the English offered the throne to William the Conqueror in 1066, he first took the advice of his Norman and French allies. Since he was not driven by the *libido regnandi*, the lust to rule, William explained, he saw no need for haste in assuming the English throne. He was eventually swayed by the unanimous counsel of the whole army.[168] Almost identical sentiments were ascribed to Baldwin of Edessa in 1118,[169] and it was after votes had already been cast in 1125 that, later tradition had it, both Frederick of Swabia and Lothar of Saxony waited to be talked into accepting the throne. This was the moment when rulers began to demonstrate that they had earned the title because they were

[166] Maleczek, 'Wahlformen', 88–95.
[167] Wipo, *Gesta Chuonradi*, 13; *Deeds of Conrad II*, 60.
[168] William of Poitiers, *Gesta Guillelmi*, 148–9.
[169] Albert of Aachen, *Historia Ierosolimitana*, 872–3.

300   8. CHOOSING A KING

capable of shouldering such grave responsibility. In exceptional circumstances, it was also when a final set of demands could be made.

Those were of a very particular kind.[170] Whether real or imagined, they could assume the status of foundational contracts that defined how the community of the realm ought to be governed. The Hungarian Blood Oath, discussed in Chapter 4, provides an especially striking example.[171] The imperative of moral probity, of choosing a ruler for the common good militated against making any other promises, at least in public. Even when men seemingly violated these rules, they were still portrayed as acting for the good of their dependants. Supposedly, that was what the bishops of Worms and Paderborn had done by enriching their sees before casting their votes. The principle also applied when norms were invoked to cloak a king's lack of suitability. In 1076, the Danes had to decide between Knud and Harald. The latter, Saxo Grammaticus claimed, enticed them with sweet promises: 'he undertook to abolish iniquitous laws and bring in ones that were as agreeable and mild as they could wish'. Swayed by such assurances, the Danes chose him.[172] Saxo made no secret of his opposition: Harald's elevation was reward for his laziness, and his acclamation the fruit of sugared lies.[173] The chronicler was not perturbed by Harald's promise to abolish iniquitous laws. That was what kings were supposed to do. Yet Harald had vowed to introduce new ones, aimed not at doing justice or reforming the realm, but at being agreeable to and soft on his people. Thus, he comprehensively failed in his duties. And still his offer was couched in terms that, even in Saxo's rendering, explicitly eschewed the prospect of a material *quid pro quo*.

The generic nature of these promises was shaped by three factors. First, the royal office was supposed to be in God's gift, with the electors acting solely under the guidance of the divine will. Second, a candidate who had to be reminded of the duties of his office would by definition be unworthy of the crown. Third, promises, in order to be valid, had to be granted out of a ruler's free volition. Just as there was to be no semblance of bribery, so there could be none of force. Even Magna Carta and the Golden Bull were framed as royal grants, as privileges freely issued by the monarch for the benefit of his people. Not only could a forced concession easily be cast aside, it also violated the premise that a king was raised to the royal dignity not only because he was suitable, but also because he was richer and more powerful than any of his people. A ruler who could be coerced into granting favours would be unable to restrain the mighty.

---

[170] Brun, *Saxonicum Bellum*, 85–6. See also: Paul of Bernried, *Vita Gregorii VII*, vol. 1, 530.
[171] *Anonymi Gesta Hungarorum*, 18–19. See also Chapters 3 and 4 above.
[172] Saxo Grammaticus, *Gesta Danorum*, i.10.4–5, pp. 824–5.
[173] Saxo Grammaticus, *Gesta Danorum*, xi.10.5, pp. 824–5.

IV. ELECTION 301

Choosing a ruler was shaped by a desire to align what should be with what was. The performance of election was about projecting and enacting legitimacy, and about demonstrating adherence to common values. The process sought to bring about the conditions in which such compliance could be enacted. Yet unanimity could often be secured only by engaging in actions that violated the imperative of probity. This tension reflected the fact that an election consisted of several stages, each addressing distinct, though at times overlapping publics. Audiences would normally include a putative claimant's confidants. They would also include the wider circle of a lord's dependants and armed men, as when Charles of Flanders consulted his followers about claiming the German throne, William the Conqueror his companions about having himself crowned or when the Birkibeinar offered Sverrir the choice between being their leader or becoming their victim. The public extended to men from particular regions coming together to decide which candidate they would support. Audiences also incorporated the semi-regnal public created by the prelates and princes who invited the bishop of Bamberg to prepare for the choice of Henry V's successor. Each was concerned with regional, local and institutional matters as well as with the business of the kingdom at large. The leading men of the realm had to satisfy the needs and expectations of their followers. They had to demonstrate that they could translate their part in the affairs of the realm into the political capital needed to protect, aid and enrich their entourage, and to outmanoeuvre their rivals. Consequently, when Otto of Northeim demanded redress before casting his vote for Rudolf of Rheinfelden, he probably did what was expected of him on such occasions. It was certainly what the bishop's *vita* found praiseworthy about Burchard of Worms, and it tallies with the attempts of Buris, recorded by Saxo, to translate his backing for the kingship of Knud VI into receiving large parts of Jütland.[174]

What mattered was that such concerns be dealt with before the final stages of the process commenced. An election's ceremonial high point was after all supposed to demonstrate that the local and personal had not impinged upon the needs of the community at large. Yet the effectiveness of this performance was contingent both upon how it was managed and upon the new ruler's subsequent actions. In a way, therefore, the duke of Zähringen's candidacy in 1198 and the plots spun by the Chancellor of Sicily in 1189 constitute evidence for the success of the moral framework for choosing a king, not its breakdown. In 1198, the archbishop of Cologne had evidently promoted someone unsuitable for the throne. In 1189, the chancellor sought to impose a weak and malleable king, the manner of whose appointment clearly indicated that he was not worthy of the crown. By contrast, successful kings overcame seeming violations of the moral framework of election. Henry II's reputation for sanctity easily outweighed his less than orthodox path to the throne, and

[174] Saxo Grammaticus, *Gesta Danorum*, xiv.33.2–3, pp. 1244–7. See also below, Chapter 10.

302 8. CHOOSING A KING

while even partisans of Frederick Barbarossa baulked at the circumstances of his election, they nonetheless concluded that his subsequent governance proved that he wore the crown legitimately.[175] They also framed their governance as enforcing, reviving or adhering to norms of what kings should do. The legitimacy of an election manifested itself in the new ruler's ability to prove that he was a just and pious keeper of his people. Somewhat paradoxically, therefore, even though the king took centre stage only once the decision in his favour had been reached, the responsibility for safeguarding the legitimacy of the process rested squarely upon his shoulders. He had to ensure not only that his own actions, but also those of the men who had raised him to the royal dignity were righteous. Thus, the tone was set for his inauguration.

[175] *Gesta episcoporum Halberstadensium*, 107; *Kaiserchronik eines Regensburger Geistlichen*, 397; *Chronicon Albrici monachi Trium Fontium*, 841.

PART V

Inauguration

Precisely when a king became king remains a matter of perspective. The day and date of the inauguration ceremony certainly carried weight.[1] However, just as important – in fact, to some observers far more significant – were the festivities surrounding it, notably the feast and procession. And, especially if there were rivals, just being enthroned was not enough. The new ruler still had to show that he was a capable and just governor of the realm. Like succession and election, the inauguration was a process.

This comes as no news to biographers of individual rulers.[2] It is not, however, an approach that has so far been adopted by historians working on king-making more generally. There, the emphasis remains firmly on enthronement, with the assumption that there was a particular moment, normally identified as the consecration, when a king was made. Relatively little attention has been paid to the other parts of the process. If discussed at all, they have largely been treated as distinctive from and hence as unrelated to the event of king-making.[3] By limiting their approach in this way, historians run several

---

[1] Dale, *Inauguration and Liturgical Kingship*, 179–80.

[2] See, for instance, Bates, *William the Conqueror*, 211–57 ('The Year of Victory'), 258–94 ('King of the English'); Görich, *Friedrich Barbarossa*, 93–116 ('Erhebung zum König'), 117–44 ('Neue Vertraute und alte Probleme'); Freed, *Frederick Barbarossa*, 60–88 ('King of the Romans'), 89–110 ('Itinerant Kingship'). See also the important case studies by Emilie M. Amt, *The Accession of Henry II in England: Royal Government Restored, 1149–59* (Woodbridge, 1997) and Graeme J. White, *Restoration and Reform 1153–65: Recovery from Civil War in England* (Cambridge, 2000).

[3] See, for instance, Klaus Herbers, 'Herrschernachfolge auf der Iberischen Halbinsel. Recht – Pragmatik – Symbolik', in *Die mittelalterliche Thronfolge*, ed. Becher, 231–52; Bagge, 'Herausbildung einer Dynastie'; Helene Basu and Gerd Althoff, eds., *Rituale der Amtseinsetzung. Inaugurationen in verschiedenenen Epochen, Kulturen, politischen Systemen und Religionen* (Würzburg, 2015), 41–60; Garnett, *Conquered England*; Paul Dalton, 'The accession of Henry I, August 1100', *Viator* 43 (2012), 79–109. See, by contrast: František Graus, 'Der Herrschaftsantritt St. Wenzels in den Legenden (Zum Quellenwert mittelalterlicher Legenden für die Geschichte I)', in *Osteuropa in Geschichte und Gegenwart: Festschrift für Günter Stökl zum 60. Geburtstag*, ed. Hans Lemberg, Peter Nitsche and Erwin Oberländer (Cologne and Vienna, 1977), 287–300; Plassmann, '[...] et clauses thesaurorum nactus est'; Ralph-Johannes Lilie, 'Erbkaisertum oder Wahlmonarchie? Zur Sicherung der Herrschaftsnachfolge in Byzanz', in *Die*

303

304   V. INAUGURATION

risks. Two merit particular attention. First, a focus on the inauguration ceremony, notably if it is reduced to crowning and anointing, gives us a rather
skewed perspective. That ceremony was a religious act. Inevitably, sources
stress the relationship between the monarch and the divine. The king was
raised above the other faithful. God had granted him power to wield over his
people. Mistaking this particular part of the inauguration for the whole,
scholars have allowed themselves to fall prey to several misconceptions. One
is that anointing and crowning was normative. It was not. Another, and one
ultimately more damaging, is to assume unquestioningly that the exalted
imagery of the inauguration was representative of how contemporaries
thought about royal power. When very little of it resurfaces in the practice of
rulership, the resulting tension has often been resolved by postulating a crisis
of royal sacrality.[4] That, we will see, would have come as a surprise to most
high medieval observers.[5] The various crises of power and sacrality that
historians have imagined for this period are rooted less in the medieval
evidence than in the selective manner in which it has been approached by
modern readers, and the preconceived notions that have shaped their interpretation of it.[6]

Second, just like the designation of an heir, enthronement did not signal
unconditional acceptance. For sure, the king derived considerable authority
from it. But how much and for how long was dependent upon performance.
Having been elected and inaugurated shortened the odds for success. But it
offered no guarantees. In this context, recent work by the Byzantinist Ralph-
Johannes Lilie will prove helpful. In an analysis of the reigns of ninety-four
emperors and empresses ruling Constantinople between 324 and 1453, he
demonstrated that an emperor who survived the first three years on the throne
was likely to die of old age, instead of being deposed or killed.[7] These findings

---

mittelalterliche Thronfolge, ed. Becher, 21–39, at 31–7. Part of the problem might well have
been the assumption that, because consecration and investiture were often viewed as
a constitutive element in the inauguration of bishops, the same must be true when it
came to the sacring and crowning of kings.
[4] Geoffrey Koziol, 'England, France, and the problem of sacrality in twelfth-century ritual',
in *Cultures of Power. Lordship, Status, and Process in Twelfth-Century Europe*, ed.
T. N. Bisson (Philadelphia, PA, 1995), 124–48; Teofilo F. Ruiz, 'Unsacred monarchy: the
kings of Castile in the late Middle Ages', in *Rites of Power. Symbols, Ritual and Politics since
the Middle Ages*, ed. Sean Wilentz (Philadelphia, PA, 1985), 109–45; Stefan Weinfurter,
'Idoneität – Begründung und Akzeptanz von Königsherrschaft im hohen Mittelalter', in
Idoneität – Genealogie – Legitimation, ed. Andenna and Melville, 127–38.
[5] The work of Ludger Körntgen is essential in this context: *Königsherrschaft und Gottes Gnade*;
'"Sakrales Königtum"; Herrscherbild im Wandel – ein Neuansatz in staufischer Zeit?', in
BarbarossaBilder: Entstehungskontexte, Erwartungshorizonte, Verwendungszusammenhänge,
ed. Knut Görich and Romedio Schmitz-Esser (Regensburg, 2014), 32–45.
[6] A fuller discussion follows in chapter 9.
[7] Ralph-Johannes Lilie, 'Der Kaiser in der Statistik. Subversive Gedanken zur angeblichen
Allmacht der byzantinischen Kaiser', in *Hypermachos: Studien zur Byzantinistik*,

V. INAUGURATION   305

cannot be mapped onto the political map of high medieval Latin Europe without some modification. Of the more than 160 successions during this period, only fifteen resulted in the ruler being killed, and two ended in depositions. Rarer still was a king's abdication, which occurred almost exclusively in the imagination of monastic scribes. Borivojc I of Bohemia, Harold Godwinson in England and Emperor Henry V became the subject of legends in which they resigned the throne or faked their own death in order to live out their days as humble and penitent monks. In real life, a lack of forced or voluntary abdications constitutes an important difference between Byzantine and Latin succession practices.

However, once coverage is extended to challengers, rival claimants and anti-kings, Lilie's model does work rather well, not least because the distinction between legitimate and illegitimate claims is a matter of perspective, and quite often rooted in hindsight. Success could be its own vindication. Crudely put, the major difference between a pretender and a legitimate monarch was that the latter survived, or at least that he outlasted his rivals.[8] That much is suggested by the examples of Valdemar I, Sverrir and Henry VI. Valdemar had been acclaimed king of Denmark in 1154, but did not become its sole ruler until the last of his rivals had been killed in 1157. Sverrir had become leader of the Birkibeinar in 1177, but King Magnus Erlingsson did not die in battle until 1184. It took Henry five years of campaigning before he could dislodge Tancred of Lecce from the throne of Sicily. Those who did not make it past that initial stage became usurpers and pretenders. Their careers were cut short or they surrendered after only a few years. The reigns of Harold Godwinson in England and Rudolf of Rheinfelden in Germany lasted respectively ten months and three years. Frederick of Swabia submitted to Emperor Lothar III in 1128, two years after he had been proclaimed king. Matilda's dreams collapsed three years after her return to England. Finally, kings who had not been able to overcome their main rivals within the first few years usually would have a rather troublesome reign. Emperor Henry IV's problems in Saxony began the year after he had come of age in 1065. His inability to resolve them plagued the remainder of his reign as well as that of his son. In England, Stephen of Blois was never able to establish his authority across the whole kingdom, especially after he had aggravated the earl of Gloucester to such an extent that in 1138 the magnate did his best to revive Matilda's claim. Success during these early stages of kingship was crucial.

Armenologie und Georgistik. Festschrift für Werner Seibt zum 65. Geburtstag, ed. Chrestos Staurakos (Wiesbaden, 2008), 211–34; see also his 'Erbkaisertum oder Wahlmonarchie?', 31.

[8] Using far more scholarly language, a similar point has been made by Michaela Muylkens for eleventh- and twelfth-century Germany: 'Rivalisierende Königsherrschaft als Form der Herrschaftsnachfolge', in *Die mittelalterliche Thronfolge*, ed. Becher, 163–91.

306   V. INAUGURATION

What was so special about this period? It was not, of course, a magic figure. Kings did not suddenly become secure on the morning of the first day of the thirty-seventh month of their reign. But the timeframe does reflect practicalities of power. New rulers needed to win over magnates and prelates who had remained aloof during the election, take control of the material resources of power and overcome rivals who would not accept initial defeat. A king would only fully be king once these challenges had been overcome. But they could not be dealt with all at once. And that took time. Factors as basic as the campaigning season – normally May through to October – determined how quickly a ruler could take control of the realm. With few exceptions, kings did not embark upon long-distance journeys during winter and early spring. The state of roads and passes militated against that, as did the need to provision a regal entourage. Seasonal conditions were a major factor that turned taking full possession of the material sources of power into an intermittent and hence extended process. They were closely entwined with the personal nature of royal lordship. Castles and estates had to be visited before they could be taken under one's control, officials needed to be appointed, networks forged and so on. Rulers had to get a sense of regions, rivalries and networks with which they may not have previously engaged. Furthermore, unrest often erupted during the months between a king's death and the election of his successor. In the absence of royal authority, rivals who had previously been restrained by the king's power would now seek to settle their grievances by force. The more ruthless among the great men of the realm could even feel encouraged to claim for themselves rights that had previously been held by the king. So would communities who saw an opportunity to assert their own standing in relation to princes, prelates and royal officials.

Simmering conflicts had a tendency of escalating, and seeing to them *successfully* was therefore a necessary precondition for legitimate governance. Tackling them also demonstrated that the current occupant was indeed the right man for the throne. At the same time, he would be able to give them his full attention only after he had extended his support within the realm, after he had subdued rivals and gained the backing of those who delayed endorsing him until he had shown that he was capable of ruling. That also took time. Furthermore, allies and followers needed to be rewarded. But that could mean disappointing powerful and mighty men. It inevitably disrupted existing networks. The ensuing tensions took time both to develop and to be resolved. If a ruler managed to negotiate these perils, if by the end conflicts had been settled, erstwhile opponents reconciled and integrated among the king's men, it would be easier to fight off even more perilous adversaries. If, by contrast, a ruler allowed discontent to breed, if he proved unable to bring opponents to heel, that was the moment to fill a vacuum created by a perhaps well-meaning but inept monarch, and maybe even to choose a better one instead.

What does this mean for a king's inauguration? Rulers were installed in a variety of ways. Sacring and crowning may be the best documented practices, but they were not the only ones. Furthermore, the inauguration ceremony formed part of a process that began with the election and concluded at some unspecified point during a king's early reign. In a way, it constituted a contract between king and electors, sealed during the installation ceremony and delivered upon once the ruler started exercising power. Inaugurating the king was therefore never just about him. It was also an attempt to shape and direct how he used his power, to assert the role of the realm's elites in its exercise and to demonstrate their standing both to the new ruler and to each other. Chapter 9 considers the ceremony itself. What did it entail? Who participated in it? How did it link the making of a king to the normative framework of royal power? Chapter 10 continues with the events following immediately thereafter. They merge seamlessly into the various steps a king could take to demonstrate suitability, and to fill abstract principles with concrete meaning. What were those? And what was the role of the elites in them?

9

Enthroning the King

In the 1180s, the English court cleric Gerald of Wales reported how a royal inauguration was performed at Tir Connail in Ulster:

> When the whole people of the land has been brought together in one place, a white mare is brought forward into the middle of the assembly. He who is to be inaugurated, not as a chief, but a beast, not as a king, but an outlaw, has bestial intercourse with her [*bestialiter accedens*] before all, professing himself to be a beast also. The mare is then killed immediately, cut up in pieces, and boiled in water. A bath is prepared for the man afterwards in the same water. He sits in the bath surrounded by all his people, and all, he and they, eat of the meat of the mare which is brought to them. He quaffs and drinks of the broth in which he is bathed, not in any cup, or using his hand, but just dipping his mouth into it around him. When this unrighteous rite has been carried out, his kingship and dominion have been conferred.[1]

Attempts have been made to link Gerald's account to fertility rites recorded in Vedic texts.[2] A more likely explanation is that Gerald either invented the ceremony, or that he drew on accounts from others who sought to discredit, and to garner English backing against, the local ruler.[3] The procedure certainly parodied the importance of the coronation feast, and underscored Gerald's general portrayal of Ulstermen as brutish and uncouth. Irish kingship was delegitimised, partly because of its seemingly pagan connotations, partly because of the lack of the civilised mores that English overlordship

---

[1] Gerald of Wales, *Giraldi Cambrensis Opera*, 8 vols., vol. 5: *Topographia Hibernica et Expugnatio Hibernica*, ed. J. F. Dimock, Rolls Series (London, 1867), 169. Translation: Gerald of Wales, *The History and Topography of Ireland*, transl. John J. O'Meara (Harmondsworth, 1982), 110. Whether *bestialiter accedens* should be translated as 'having bestial intercourse' is, however, a matter of debate (I am grateful to Josh Smith for this point).

[2] Jaan Puhvel, *Comparative Mythology* (Baltimore, 1987), 269–76. However David Fickett-Wilbar, 'Ritual details of the Irish horse sacrifice in *Betha Mholaise Daiminse*', *Journal of Indo-European Studies* 40 (2012), 314–43, has pointed out parallels in Old Irish saints' lives with which Gerald was unlikely to have been familiar.

[3] Robert Bartlett, *Gerald of Wales and the Ethnographic Imagination* (Cambridge, 2013), 12–15.

310   9. ENTHRONING THE KING

promised to offer. At the same time, Gerald's efforts point to the variety of
ways in which kings were inaugurated in high medieval Europe. The type
with which modern readers may be most familiar – involving a religious
service, during which the ruler was anointed with chrism (holy oil) and then
crowned – was practised in England, France, Sicily, Jerusalem and Germany,[4]
but only intermittently in Iberia.[5] It first occurred in Denmark in 1170. While
crowning was introduced to Norway in the 1160s, anointing was not added
there until 1247.[6] Other types of inauguration were common. In some Irish
texts, the new king was handed a hazel rod.[7] In thirteenth-century Scotland,
he was escorted to the graveyard of Scone Abbey, where he was placed on the
coronation stone, consecrated and acclaimed by the assembled nobles and
prelates, who then took off their cloaks and laid them before him.[8] And in
Portugal, Alfonso I became king by having himself declared a knight before

[4] Here, Carolingian precedent may have been key. Janet L. Nelson, 'Inauguration rituals' in
her *Rituals and Politics in Early Medieval England* (London, 1986), 283–308;
Carlrichard Brühl, 'Kronen- und Krönungsgebrauch im frühen und hohen Mittelalter',
HZ 234 (1982), 1–31.

[5] Thomas Deswarte, 'Liturgie et royauté dans les monarchies asturienne et léonaise (711–
1109)', *Cahiers de civilisation médiévale* 58 (2015), 279–90; Simon John, 'Royal inauguration and liturgical culture in the Latin kingdom of Jerusalem, 1099–1187', *JMedH* 43
(2017), 485–504; Herbers, 'Herrschernachfolge'; Ruiz, 'Unsacred monarchy'.

[6] On the slow spread of unction as part of the coronation ceremony, see Rudolf Schieffer,
'Die Ausbreitung der Königssalbung im hochmittelalterlichen Europa', in *Die mittelalter-
liche Thronfolge*, ed. Becher, 43–80. On Scandinavia, Erich Hoffmann, 'Coronations and
coronation ordines in medieval Scandinavia', in János M. Bak, ed., *Coronations. Medieval
and Early Modern Monarchic Ritual* (Berkeley, CA, 1990), 125–51. Other cases: Ioanna
Rapti, 'Featuring the king: rituals of coronation and burial in the Armenian kingdom of
Cilicia', in *Court Ceremonies*, ed. Alexander Beihammer, Stavroula Constantinou and
Maria Papani, 291–335; Marie Luise Burian, 'Die Krönung des Stephan Prvovencani
und die Beziehungen Serbiens zum Heiligen Stuhl', *AKG* 23 (1933), 141–51; Eric Fügedi,
'Coronation in medieval Hungary', *Studies in Medieval and Renaissance History* 3 (1980),
157–89.

[7] Elizabeth Fitzpatrick, 'Royal inauguration assembly and the Church in medieval Ireland',
in *Political Assemblies in the Early Middle Ages*, ed. Paul S. Barnwell and Marco Mostert
(Turnhout, 2003), 73–93, at 77–8.

[8] Johannis de Fordun, *Chronica Gentis Scotorum et Gesta Annalia*, ed. William F. Skene, 2
vols. (Edinburgh, 1872), vol. 1, 282–3 (1214), 294–5 (1249). See also Dauvit Broun,
'Contemporary perspectives on the inauguration of Alexander II', in *The Reign of
Alexander II, 1214–1249*, ed. Richard Oram (Leiden, 2005), 79–98; A. A. M. Duncan,
'Before coronation: making a king at Scone in the 13th century', in *The Stone of Destiny.
Artefact and Icon*, ed. Richard Welander, David J. Breeze and Thomas Owen Clancy
(Edinburgh, 2003), 139–68; John Bannermann, 'The King's Poet and the inauguration of
Alexander III', *Scottish Historical Review* 68 (1989), 120–49. On Scone, see David Rollason,
The Power of Place. Rulers and Their Palaces, Landscapes, Cities and Holy Places
(Princeton, NJ, 2016), 336–41. I am grateful to Matthew Hunter Hammond for his advice
on the Scottish materials.

V. INAUGURATION   311

taking (rather than having conferred upon him) the royal regalia from the altar of St Saviour's at Zamora.[9]

Indeed, for much of the period, it is unlikely that any two inaugurations looked exactly alike – even within the same kingdom. Iberia serves as an example. In Aragon, Ramiro I (1035–64) received unction and underwent a formal coronation, but then the practice fell into abeyance until Peter II travelled to Rome in 1204 to be crowned by the pope. His son James II succeeded to the throne without consecration again, while a form of self-coronation then prevailed from 1276 until the early fifteenth century. In Castile, Fernando I (1035–65) was crowned and consecrated, his son Sancho II crowned himself and (in 1072) Alfonso VI was not crowned at all. Alfonso VII received unction in 1111, but his heirs discontinued the practice until 1284, when it was temporarily revived.[10] Shifts in coronation practice frequently reflected moments of crises. In Castile, it had taken Sancho II seven years of fighting his brothers to become king. When he was murdered in 1072, his successor was directed to swear an oath that he had not been party to the killing. These circumstances may have made impossible a ceremony that, after all, echoed that of the consecration of a priest. In 1284, by contrast, it was precisely the context of Sancho IV's succession that necessitated a revival. He had deposed his father, and formal anointing may have been deemed to provide added legitimacy.[11] There was more than one path to the throne.

The Iberian kingdoms present an extreme case because of the variety of ceremonies in which their rulers were installed. But even in realms with seemingly more stable traditions of royal inauguration, subtle shifts and changes occurred. They militate against taking any one type of inauguration to be normative. Even so, variations should not blind us to just how many features were shared. Both differences and commonalties are therefore best traced by adopting a comparative perspective. That does, however, pose difficulties. Matters are not helped by the fact that many chronicle accounts are cursory. Most simply record that a ruler had been enthroned, where the event took place and, occasionally, which archbishop performed the rites.[12]

---

[9] Böckler-Walter, *Alfonso I.*, 151. On the act of self-coronation: Carlrichard Brühl, 'Les auto-couronnements d'Empereurs et des rois (xe–xixe s.)', *Acádemie des Inscriptions et Belles-lettres. Comptes rendues des séances de l'année 1984* (1984), 102–18; Jaume Aurell, *Medieval Self-Coronations: the History and Symbolism of a Ritual* (Cambridge, 2020).

[10] Schieffer, 'Ausbreitung der Königssalbung', 64–7. On Castile: Ruiz, 'Unsacred monarchy', 109–23. On Aragon: Damian J. Smith, *Innocent III and the Crown of Aragon. The Limits of Papal Authority* (Aldershot, 2004), 43–60; Bernard F. Reilly, 'Santiago and Saint Denis. The French presence in eleventh-century Spain', *Catholic Historical Review* 54 (1968), 467–83; Jaume Aurell, 'The self-coronations of Iberian kings: a crooked line', *Imago temporis. Medium Aevum* 8 (2014), 151–75.

[11] Jerry R. Craddock, 'Dynasty in dispute: Alfonso X el Sabio and the succession to the throne of Castile and León in history and legend', *Viator* 17 (1986), 197–219.

[12] Dale, *Inauguration and Liturgical Kingship*, 107–9.

312   9. ENTHRONING THE KING

We can also consult coronation *ordines*, texts purporting to record the liturgy used. But they are almost impossible to link to any particular ceremony.[13] This makes the three case studies that follow all the more important: Wipo's account of the coronation of Conrad II of Germany in 1024, Roger of Howden's of that of Richard I of England in 1189, and John de Fordun's of that of Alexander III of Scotland in 1249. They are the most detailed narrative record for specific royal inaugurations to survive from the central Middle Ages. They represent different types of genre, ceremony and purpose. Yet, read alongside each other, they demonstrate shared concerns, ideas and practices that both reflect and transcend the regnally specific and historically contingent.

9.1 Mainz (1024), Westminster (1189) and Scone (1249)

Wipo composed the *Gesta Chuonradi* (*Deeds of Conrad II*) around 1040, with much of his account of the 1024 election designed to establish Conrad as a model ruler. Similar intentions guided how he described the coronation. Taken together, his reports on election and inauguration account for nearly two thirds of the *Gesta*'s text. Wipo may even have been an eyewitness to the events described, though the evidence for that remains cursory.[14] He does, however, convey in unusual detail how the enthronement of an ideal ruler should unfold, and what its component parts could teach about the duties of kingship.

Once elected, and after Henry II's widow had handed over the imperial insignia, Conrad II and his entourage proceeded from the election site to Mainz, where the coronation took place. During the ceremony, the archbishop of Mainz rehearsed basic principles of good kingship. All power, he explained, had been granted by God, and God had installed the princes of the earth. He would forsake the ones who polluted their dignity with pride, envy, lust, avarice, anger, impatience or cruelty, as they would pollute their people in turn. The prelate continued by outlining Conrad's previous tribulations (he had fallen out with Henry II), which had been God's way of testing Conrad, of ensuring that he would truly be the vicar of God. The king should therefore always bear in mind that

---

[13] *Ordines Coronationis Franciae*, ed. Jackson. See, generally Dale, *Inauguration and Liturgical Kingship*; Janet L. Nelson , 'The rites of the Conqueror', *ANS* 4 (1982), 117–32, 210–21, Nelson, 'Ritual and reality in the early medieval *ordines*', in her *Politics and Ritual*, 329–40; Nelson, 'The second English *Ordo*', in her *Politics and Ritual*, 361–70.

[14] Wipo makes a passing reference, at the beginning of his account of the coronation, that could suggest he observed it in person: 'At no time have I found that God received such great praises from men on one day in one place' (Wipo, *Gesta Chuonradi*, 20; *Deeds of Conrad II*, 66). However, this may also be a rhetorical trope rather than evidence of eyewitness testimony.

V. INAUGURATION   313

It is great felicity to rule in this world, but the greatest is to triumph in Heaven. Although God requires many things of you, He wishes most of all that you render judgement and justice, and peace for the fatherland, which always looks to you; and [He wishes] that you be a defender of churches and clerics, the guardian of widows and orphans. With these and other good works your throne will be firmly established here and forever.[15]

Kingship had been created to maintain the peace, do justice and protect the Church, as well as those who could not protect themselves, notably widows and orphans. The archbishop further implored Conrad to show mercy to those who had wronged him in the past. The king was moved to tears, and, having been petitioned by dukes and prelates, pardoned all who had transgressed against him. The divine offices concluded and the coronation performed, Conrad led a procession out of the cathedral to his chamber, and then presided over a festive dinner.[16] The following morning, Conrad appointed key officers. Wipo did not go on to name the men who became 'mayor of the palace, ... chamberlains, ... stewards and cupbearers and other officials, although ... I neither remember nor have read that the ministries of any of his predecessors were provided for more suitably and honourably'. He did, however, identify Conrad's most trusted advisors: the bishops Bruno of Augsburg and Werinhar of Strasbourg, his vassal Werinhar and Conrad's wife Gisela.[17]

Wipo stressed the moral dimension of the royal office, and Conrad's inherent suitability for it. He even described Conrad as having been physically transformed: he led the procession to his chamber 'with an eager countenance and a noble step, as though he went higher "than any of the people from his shoulder and upward" [1 Samuel 10:23] and as if he had been transformed into a bearing not seen before in him'.[18] Yet the change related to Conrad's appearance, not his moral outlook. Wipo portrayed Conrad as performing the very duties of a king even before he had been consecrated as one. In a passage that in Wipo's rendering follows the account of the coronation, but that describes an incident preceding it chronologically, he recounted how three supplicants interrupted Conrad's procession: a peasant from Mainz, a young boy and a widow. When Conrad stopped to hear their grievances, several

[15] Wipo, *Gesta Chuonradi*, 23; *Deeds of Conrad II*, 67. See also: Volker Huth, 'Wipo, neugelesen. Quellenkritische Notizen zur "Hofkultur" in spätottonisch-frühsalischer Zeit', in *Adel und Königtum im mittelalterlichen Schwaben. Festschrift für Thomas Zotz zum 65. Geburtstag*, ed. Aandraes Bihrer, Margot Kälble and Heinz Krieg (Stuttgart, 2009), 155–68; Jacek Banaszkiewicz, 'Conrad II.'s theatrum rituale: Wipo on the earliest deeds of the Salian ruler (Gesta Chuonradi imperatoris cap. 5)', in *Central and Eastern Europe in the Middle Ages. A Cultural History*, ed. Piotr Górecki and Nancy van Deusen (London and New York, 2009), 50–81.
[16] Wipo, *Gesta Chuonradi*, 23–4; *Deeds of Conrad II*, 67–8.
[17] Wipo, *Gesta Chuonradi*, 24–6; *Deeds of Conrad II*, 68–9.
[18] Wipo, *Gesta Chuonradi*, 24; *Deeds of Conrad II*, 68.

314   9. ENTHRONING THE KING

princes urged him not to delay his coronation. Conrad responded by stating that it was better to do good than to hear about doing good.[19]

Widows, peasants, orphans and exiles were, of course, the very groups that the archbishop of Mainz had singled out as most in need of royal protection. They also feature prominently in the Bible in that role.[20] The eagerness with which Conrad delayed his coronation therefore demonstrated not only his preparedness to perform the duties of his office, but also his moral probity, the extent to which he viewed kingship as an opportunity to do good. All of this makes Wipo's a highly idealised version of events, designed not to paint an accurate picture of Conrad's coronation, but to establish the king as an exemplar of how royal lordship should be assumed. Even so, he points to important norms and common practices. They include the rehearsal of royal duties as part of the inauguration ceremony, the feast and procession, and the demonstrative performance of royal duties during the extended process of enthronement.

Roger, parson of Howden in Yorkshire, had been a cleric at the court of King Henry II of England (1154–89), and subsequently found himself in the employ of the bishop of Durham. He accompanied Richard I (1189–99) on the Third Crusade, and produced two chronicles: the *Gesta Henrici II*, taking events up to 1192, and the *Chronica*, begun not long thereafter and continuing up to 1201.[21] The *Gesta*'s report on Richard I's coronation in 1189 remains the richest such account to survive from the twelfth century,[22] and was plausibly penned within a few years of the events themselves. Richard had been in Normandy when his father died on 6 July 1189. His progress to England was slow. He did not arrive until 23 August, with the coronation taking place on 3 September. In the meantime, Richard settled affairs in Normandy, held a meeting with King Philipp of France and made preparations for his crusade. The delay was made possible by the fact that there was no feasible rival for the throne. It was made necessary because Richard had to oversee the burial of Henry II and because time was needed to assemble the great men of the realm in London. Roger provided a list of the most important bishops, abbots, earls and other barons in attendance, running to fifty-

---

[19] Wipo, *Gesta Chuonradi*, 26–7; *Deeds of Conrad II*, 70.

[20] See above, Chapter 2.

[21] On Roger: David Corner, 'The *Gesta regis Henrici Secundi* and *Chronica* of Roger, Parson of Howden' *Bulletin of the Institute of Historical Research* 56 (1983), 126–44; John Gillingham, 'Writing the biography of Roger of Howden, king's clerk and chronicler', in *Writing Medieval Biography, c. 750–1250. Essays in Honour of Frank Barlow*, ed. David Bates, Julia Crick and Sarah Hamilton (Woodbridge, 2006), 207–20; Gillingham, 'Two Yorkshire historians compared: Roger of Howden and William of Newburgh', *HSJ* 12 (2003), 15–37; Michael Staunton, *The Historians of Angevin England* (Oxford, 2017), 51–66.

[22] John Gillingham, *Richard I* (New Haven, CT, 1999), 107.

V. INAUGURATION   315

eight named individuals.[23] Each of them was, of course, accompanied by their own entourage. Thus, several thousand people are likely to have witnessed the proceedings. Indeed, financial records show that in the weeks preceding the coronation, nearly 2,000 pitchers had been ordered, almost 1,000 cups and over 5,000 dishes.[24] The king's inauguration was meant to be a most festive affair.

Celebrations began with a ceremonial procession into Westminster Abbey, led by clerics followed by abbots and four barons carrying candles. After them came John Marshal carrying the royal spurs and Godfrey de Luci with the royal cap; William Marshal, who brought the royal sceptre and the earl of Salisbury with the royal rod; David of Huntingdon, Robert of Leicester and John of Gloucester, with three splendid swords; six barons carrying a chest with the remaining regalia; William de Mandeville holding the royal crown in his hands; and then Richard, flanked by the bishop of Durham on his right and that of Bath on his left. Finally, the remaining participants, both lay and clerical, streamed into the church up to the altar (as Roger specifically notes). Once brought there, Richard swore that he would, throughout his life, pay due honour and reverence to God and His Church, exercise true justice for the people given into his hands and abolish bad law and perverse customs, but guard good ones.[25] Subsequently, the king took off the outer cloak he had worn on entering the church, and was clothed in royal garments and received the insignia carried during the procession. The handover unfolded in stages. Having been shod, and having been handed the sceptre and rod, Richard received unction from the archbishop of Canterbury. Having received the royal cloak, cap, spurs and mantle, he was led to the altar by the archbishop, where he was admonished against and prohibited on the part of God from assuming a worldly dignity unless he kept in mind the oaths he had sworn. Richard solemnly vowed that he would abide by them. Afterwards, Richard took the crown off the altar and was placed on the royal throne by the bishops of Durham and Bath. To conclude proceedings, a solemn Mass was celebrated,

---

[23] Roger of Howden, *Gesta*, vol. 2, 79–80. Bishops: the metropolitans of Canterbury, Troyes and York, and, from England, the bishops of Lincoln, Durham, Winchester, Exeter, Bath, Norwich, Chichester and Rochester; those of St David's, St Asaph and Bangor from Wales, and from Ireland those of Ferne and Enaghdun. Abbots: Galway, Westminster, St Albans, St Augustine's Canterbury, Hyde, Bury St Edmunds, Croyland, Battle, St Mary's York, Rievaulx, Holm and Mortemer-en-Lions, as well as the abbot of St Denis from France. Earls and nobles: Essex, Warenne, Warwick, Sussex, Oxford, Salisbury, Striguil, the king's brother John and David, earl of Huntingdon and brother of the king of Scotland. On Roger's account see Dale, *Inauguration and Liturgical Kingship*, 105–7. See also the comparable list for the coronation of Henry II in 1154 in Robert of Torigni, *The Chronicle of Robert of Torigny*, ed. Richard Howlett, in *Chronicles of the Reigns of Stephen, Henry II and Richard I* (London, 1889), vol. 4, 182.

[24] Gillingham, *Richard I*, 107 n. 27.

[25] Roger of Howden, *Gesta*, vol. 2, 81–2.

316   9. ENTHRONING THE KING

before Richard, carrying the sceptre in his right hand and the rod in his left, was escorted back to his chamber. Having laid down the insignia and crown, he attended a festive banquet, with everyone seated according to their rank.[26] However, the proceedings were overshadowed by anti-Jewish riots. Once those had been quelled, Richard received homage, issued a declaration of protection for his Jewish subjects and attended a church council at Pipewell,[27] where he appointed two new justiciars.[28]

Unlike Conrad II, Richard did not have to undergo a formal process of election. Still, his succession was by no means straightforward. Richard had repeatedly rebelled against his father,[29] and Henry II had died while seeking to put down the latest of these revolts. In fact, two days before his death, the late king had been forced into a humiliating agreement with Philipp Augustus. When Richard approached his father's corpse, it began to bleed 'as if his [the king's] spirit had been angered at his [Richard's] arrival'.[30] From the outset, therefore, Richard had to demonstrate suitability.[31] He did so by escorting Henry's remains to be laid to rest and by adopting measures that we would normally witness *after* a coronation. When he was inaugurated as duke of Normandy at Rouen, he also received absolution for having rebelled against his father.[32] In addition, Richard imprisoned the seneschal of Anjou in order to seize his father's treasure, and punished a group of knights who had betrayed both him and Henry.[33] On arriving in England, and just a few days prior to his coronation, he not only granted rich estates to John, but also celebrated his brother's marriage to the daughter of the earl of Gloucester.[34] Richard made arrangements to treat his father's servants well, to mend injustices and to assure himself of broad backing. He visited first Winchester, where he

[26] Roger of Howden, *Gesta*, vol. 2, 82–3. In the *Chronica*, Roger added some details: he pointed out that the crown was richly adorned with jewels; that Richard bent his knees when swearing the oaths at the beginning of the ceremony, and that he vowed to uphold good laws without fraud or bad intention; that the three spots on which he received unction denoted fame, fortitude and knowledge; that the crown was so heavy that it had to be sustained by two earls; that, during mass, Richard deposited one gold mark at the altar, as was customary during royal coronations; and that, during the coronation feast, the citizens of London served as cupbearers, and those of Winchester served the food. Roger of Howden, *Chronica*, vol. 3, 10–11.
[27] Roger of Howden, *Gesta*, vol. 2, 84–5, 87.
[28] Roger of Howden, *Gesta*, vol. 2, 87.
[29] Gillingham, *Richard I*, 76–100.
[30] 'ac si indignaretur spiritus ejus de adventu illius'. Roger of Howden, *Gesta*, vol. 2, 71. See also Gerald of Wales, *De Principis Instructione*, 694–5.
[31] See also Gillingham, *Richard I*, 104, who described this as a 'sustained exercise in image manipulation'.
[32] Ralph de Diceto, *Ymagines Historiarum*, in *Radulfi de Diceto Opera Historica*, ed. William Stubbs, Rolls Series, 2 vols. (London, 1876), vol. 2, 67.
[33] Roger of Howden, *Gesta*, vol. 2, 72.
[34] Roger of Howden, *Gesta*, vol. 2, 72, 78.

V. INAUGURATION   317

provided a suitable marriage for one of his closest allies, and then Salisbury, where he ordered an inventory of the late king's treasure to be produced.[35] Throughout, he was accompanied by leading prelates and magnates, who then escorted him to Westminster. Richard furthermore freed his mother Eleanor of Aquitaine, who had been kept in quasi-imprisonment by his father. The dowager queen sent messengers on his behalf across England, ordering that all those who had been imprisoned for offences against the (much hated) forest laws be set free, as well as others who had been held captive for a variety of crimes (though those guilty of felonies had to abjure the realm).[36] In addition, Richard restored estates and titles to everyone who had been dispossessed by his father.[37] Within a fortnight of his consecration, Richard not only appointed new justiciars, but also filled the long-vacant bishoprics of London, Winchester, Ely and Salisbury, and saw to it that his half-brother Geoffrey was elected archbishop of York.[38] Richard availed himself of the whole repertoire of symbolic and practical steps that combined made for an effective seizure of the reins of power. Simultaneously, he signalled that his reign would indeed offer a new beginning, and demonstrated his desire to act righteously and virtuously, to end the abuses of his father and to bring to justice men who had wronged the realm, its ruler and his people.

And it worked. According to Roger of Howden, Richard was viewed from the outset as a great improvement on Henry II: 'Those the father had exiled, the son recalled; whom the father kept in chains, the son allowed to depart unharmed; whom the father had afflicted with many punishments for reasons of justice, the son received in the cause of piety.'[39] William of Newburgh similarly commented on the great joy felt when the new king ended his father's habit of keeping bishoprics vacant,[40] while, in the early thirteenth century, Ralph of Coggeshall recounted the auspicious beginnings of Richard's reign. One hoped that he would become a mirror to all kings of the Norman people. When first seated on the throne, Ralph continued, Richard was affable to all, handled the affairs of religion kindly, eagerly granted just requests. He filled vacant bishoprics and abbacies with

---

[35] Roger of Howden, *Gesta*, vol. 2, 76–7.
[36] Roger of Howden, *Gesta*, vol. 2, 74–5. On forest laws see also Judith A. Green, 'Forest laws in England and Normandy in the twelfth century', *Historical Research* 86 (2013), 416–31. For a more critical view of the release of prisoners see William of Newburgh, *Historia Rerum Anglicarum*, ed. Richard Howlett, in *Chronicles of the Reigns of the Reigns of Stephen, Henry II and Richard I*, Rolls Series (London, 1884), vol. 1, 293.
[37] Roger of Howden, *Gesta*, vol. 2, 75.
[38] William of Newburgh, *Historia Regum Anglorum*, 300; Ralph of Coggeshall, *Chronicon Anglicanum*, ed. J. Stevenson, Roll Series (London, 1875), 28–9.
[39] Roger of Howden, *Gesta*, vol. 2, 76.
[40] William of Newburgh, *Historia Rerum Anglorum*, 300.

318   9. ENTHRONING THE KING

good and capable men, rightly kept what was his and eagerly confirmed privileges and charters of liberty, while all the payments he received in return were spent on preparing for his crusade.[41] Richard's long journey to the throne had been an extended demonstration of his suitability for it.

Wipo and Roger described inaugurations that involved sacring and crowning. Their accounts need to be set alongside John de Fordun's of the inauguration of King Alexander III of Scotland in 1249, the most detailed extant report of an inauguration that did not involve anointing. Almost nothing is known of John de Fordun beyond the sparse information recorded by Walter Bower, his fifteenth-century reviser and continuator. John was, in all likelihood, a secular priest of no particular standing. Not long before his death in 1363/4, he compiled a comprehensive history of Scotland. According to Bower, John travelled widely across Britain to collate materials, and modern scholars have identified several textual layers that plausibly suggest that he did indeed consult, copy and revise earlier, now lost sources. Two of John's works survive, though mostly in later redactions: the *Gesta Annalia* and the *Chronica Gentis Scotorum*.[42] The former contains his account of the enthronement of Alexander III in 1249. His father having died on 8 July, the prince – still a minor – was escorted to Scone Abbey for his enthronement on 13 July. He was met by the bishops of St Andrews and Dunkeld as well as by leading nobles, including Alan Durward (the justiciar) and the earl of Menteith. The earls of Fife and Strathearn escorted Alexander

> up to the cross which stands in the graveyard, at the east end of the church. There they set him on the royal throne, which was decked with silken cloths inwoven with gold; and the bishop of St Andrews, assisted by the rest, consecrated him king, as was meet. So the king sat down upon the royal throne – that is, the stone – while the earls and other nobles, on bended knee, strewed their garments under his feet, before the stone. Now, this stone is reverently kept in that same monastery, for the consecration of the kings of Albania [i.e. Scotland]; and no king was ever wont to reign in Scotland, unless he had first, on receiving the name of king, sat upon this stone at Scone, which, by the kings of old, had been appointed the capital of Albania.[43]

---

[41] Ralph of Coggeshall, *Chronicon Anglicanum*, 91.

[42] D. E. R. Watt, 'Fordun, John (*d.* in or after 1363)', *Oxford Dictionary of National Biography* (Oxford, 2004); www.oxforddnb.com/view/article/9875, accessed 16 July 2017. Stephen Boardman, 'Chronicle propaganda in fourteenth-century Scotland: Robert the Steward, John of Fordun and the "Anonymous Chronicle"', *Scottish Historical Review* 76 (1997), 23–43; Hans Utz, 'Erste Spuren von Nationalismus im spätmittelalterlichen Schottland. Forduns "Chronica Gentis Scottorum"', *Schweizerische Zeitschrift für Geschichte* 29 (1979), 305–29.

[43] John de Fordun, *Gesta Annalia*, vol. 1, 294 (translation, vol. 2, 290). See, generally, A. A. M. Duncan, 'Before coronation'.

V. INAUGURATION   319

Immediately after the enthronement, a Highland Scot stood up, and recited the
king's ancestry in Gaelic, all the way back to Gaithel Glas, son of Neoilus, king
of Athens, and Scota, the daughter of Pharaoh Chentres.[44]
As a narrator of an act of enthronement, John differs from Wipo and
Roger in a number of ways. First, he is unlikely to have had access to
eyewitness accounts. That is reflected in the extent to which he combined
the fantastic, the misleading and the probable. For instance, John stressed
that at Scone the bishop of St Andrews consecrated (*consecravit*) Alexander
III. The term implies the administering of unction.[45] However, in 1221,
Honorius III had refused a request from the Scottish king that his successors
receive unction,[46] and in 1251 the English royal chancery had pre-emptively
petitioned the papal curia to forbid a formal coronation ceremony taking
place in Scotland.[47] In fact, it was not until 1331 that Scottish kings received
the right to be anointed and crowned.[48] Second, the accession by no means
went smoothly.[49] It was preceded by a dispute over who should make
Alexander III a knight. In the event, that ceremony was not performed
until two years later.[50] John's image of timeless continuity cloaks a more
fragile reality. Yet other aspects of his account conform to patterns and
practices for which independent evidence exists. In early medieval Dál
Riata, a stone was used to symbolise the earth: a king was placed upon it
during his inauguration.[51] Comparable practices are attested in other Scots
kingdoms and in Gaelic literature.[52] Similarly, iconographic and archaeo-
logical sources confirm the general contours of John's account, especially

[44] John de Fordun, *Gesta Annalia*, vol. 1, 294–5 (translation, vol. 2, 290–1). See also
Bannerman, 'The King's Poet'.
[45] See the discussion in Dale, *Inauguration and Liturgical Kingship*, 132–3.
[46] Paul C. Ferguson, *Medieval Papal Representatives in Scotland: Legates, Nuncios, and
Judges-Delegate, 1125–1286* (Edinburgh, 1997), 87–8.
[47] *Anglo-Scottish Relations 1174–1328*, ed. Stones, no. 9; Marc Bloch, 'An unknown testimony on the history of coronation in Scotland', *Scottish Historical Review* 23 (1926),
105–6.
[48] Percy Ernst Schramm, 'Geschichte des Throns in England und Schottland', in his *Kaiser,
Könige und Päpste*, vol. 4, 270–83, at 281–3.
[49] Broun, 'Contemporary perspectives'.
[50] John de Fordun, *Gesta Annalia*, vol. 1, 293–5; Archibald A. M. Duncan, *Scotland. The
Making of the Kingdom* (Edinburgh, 1975), 554–5; Michael Brown, 'Henry the Peaceable:
Henry III, Alexander III and royal lordship in the British Isles, 1249–1272', in *England
and Europe in the Reign of Henry III (1216–1272)*, ed. Björn K. U. Weiler with Ifor
W. Rowlands (Aldershot, 2002), 43–66, at 48–9.
[51] Ewan Campbell, 'Royal inaugurations in Dál Riata and the stone of destiny', in *The Stone
of Destiny*, ed. Welander, Breeze and Clancy, 43–60, at 56–7.
[52] David H. Caldwell, 'Kinlaggan, Islay – stones and inauguration ceremonies', in *The Stone
of Destiny*, ed. Welander, Breeze and Clancy, 61–76; Stephen T. Driscoll, 'Govan: an early
medieval center on the Clyde', ibid., 77–84; Thomas Owen Clancy, 'King making and
images of kingship in Gaelic literature', ibid., 107–22.

320   9. ENTHRONING THE KING

the role of the earls, the location of the stone and the increasing centrality of Scone.[53]

Third, John's narrative served ends quite unlike those pursued by the English and German writers. Where Wipo had aimed to construct Conrad's succession as that of an ideal, and Roger Richard I's as that of a legitimate ruler, John's major concern was to highlight the antiquity of Scottish royal rule *per se*. The genealogy recited to Alexander III, which linked him back to ancient Egypt, established an unbroken line of Scottish leaders that pre-dated by several centuries that of their English neighbours, who claimed descent merely from Troy. And it stressed the distinctiveness of the Scottish monarchy, as its rulers were of Egyptian stock, not of defeated Trojans.[54] Hence also the emphasis on the unchanging pattern of Scottish royal inaugurations. In 1214, John claimed, the funeral for the late king was halted to escort Alexander II to Scone, where, following his enthronement and consecration by the bishop of St Andrews, the new king held a feast lasting three days, before resuming his father's funeral obsequies.[55] In 1165, William the Lion was escorted to Scone on his predecessor's death, and 'was raised to the king's throne' by the bishop of St Andrews and other prelates.[56] In 1153, Malcolm IV was simply made king at Scone,[57] as was David I in 1124.[58] In John's recounting, Alexander III's inauguration became the high point of Scottish royal lordship – perhaps not least, because he was the last medieval king of Scotland to be placed on the Stone of Scone (which Edward I had brought to Westminster in 1296).

Taken together, the accounts of Wipo, Roger and John highlight several themes. There was, for instance, Wipo's focus on royal virtue, on the inner disposition required of a just king: a lack of airs and a willingness to work for the common good. Many of the same qualities featured in Roger's account. Richard set free prisoners, restored goods unjustly seized by his father, imprisoned corrupt or treacherous officials and began filling the sees kept vacant by Henry II. Roger placed further emphasis on the right order of the world expressed through Richard's actions, and through the

---

[53] Duncan, 'Before coronation', *passim* and at 141–51.

[54] In fact, when recounting the death of David I in 1153, with which the *Chronica Gentis Scotorum* concluded, John de Fordun inserted a genealogy that closely resembled that read out at Alexander III's inauguration: John de Fordun, *Chronica Gentis Scotorum*, vol. 1, 251–3 (translation, vol. 2, 244–6). John similarly dates the arrival of the coronation stone in Scotland to the fourth century BCE, recounting versions linking it variously to Iberia, the Mediterranean or Egypt: *Chronica Gentis Scotorum*, vol. 1, 23–4 (translation, ii.23–4).

[55] John de Fordun, *Gesta Annalia*, vol. 1, 280–1 (translation, vol. 2, 275–6).

[56] John de Fordun, *Gesta Annalia*, vol. 1, 259–60 (translation, vol. 2, 255).

[57] John de Fordun, *Gesta Annalia*, vol. 1, 254 (translation, vol. 2, 249).

[58] John de Fordun, *Chronica Gentis Scotorum*, vol. 1, 230 (translation, vol. 2, 231).

coronation. John, finally, stressed the continuity of the realm, with the king being but the most recent in a long line of rulers. That provided both a source of prestige, and a normative framework to guide the king's actions.

The three chroniclers also point to the stages in which an enthronement unfolded (procession, inauguration, feast); the religious dimension (even when no unction was administered); an element of remonstration, of listing a king's duties and exhorting the new monarch to abide by them; the demonstrative exercise of royal duties immediately before and after the enthronement; and the appointment of officials and advisors. These lead to broader questions. If all other stages were omitted, which act would be sufficient on its own to convey royal status? The acclamation? The enthronement? The display of majesty? The demonstrative performance of royal duties? The answer implicitly given by most modern scholars is that it was the moment when a claimant was announced to be king, normally in a religious ceremony, and often marked by the handing over or taking possession of insignia of office: a stone, crown, or hazel rod.[59] While not without grounding in the evidence, this view still fails to capture a more fluid reality. In fact, were we to have posed the question to high medieval observers, they probably would not have understood it at all, or their answer would have varied depending on whom we asked, and when. Moreover, practices changed, as the Iberian case so strikingly illustrates. Seeking to pinpoint a particular moment of transition would presuppose a degree of ritual continuity that simply did not exist, and a degree of legal formalisation that did not emerge until the fifteenth century. In our sample, John made it clear that the ceremony at Scone was performed only *after* the title of king had already been bestowed upon a ruler. Yet it still mattered – hence the haste with which, for instance, Alexander II had been escorted to Scone. In England in 1189, Richard acted like a king – by granting lands, freeing prisoners, deposing corrupt officials – long before he was actually crowned. As regards 1024, Wipo did not distinguish between the stages of the king-making process, but portrayed them as a sequence of closely linked and overlapping acts. If one was more important to him than others, then it was the election and Conrad's enactment of just rule. Wipo referred to Conrad as king from the moment the archbishop of Mainz had cast his vote for him – that is, the beginning of the formal election. The coronation merely confirmed what already was. It is this medieval representation of royal inaugurations that will guide what follows.

---

[59] See most recently, and for a convenient summary of current scholarship, *Die mittelalterliche Thronfolge*, ed. Becher, and especially Trautmann, 'Thronfolgen' and Becher, 'Die mittelalterliche Thronfolge'.

322   9. ENTHRONING THE KING

9.2   The Continuity of the Realm

Sometimes election and coronation occurred in swift sequence,[60] as with Hugh Capet's inauguration in 987 and that of Conrad II in 1024.[61] Mere days passed between one and the other. At other times, the enthronement took place shortly after a predecessor's funeral, as with the inaugurations of Louis VI of France in 1108[62] and Baldwin II of Jerusalem in 1118.[63] In each of these scenarios, most of the great men of the realm would already have been assembled. Yet an unusually swift enthronement could also suggest greed and ambition. In 1066, William the Conqueror was said to have delayed his coronation because securing the peace was more important.[64] Sometimes, logistical requirements could cause a delay. Heirs might, for instance, be abroad, as was the case in England in 1154 and 1189. Similarly, in Denmark Valdemar II was campaigning in the Baltic when news reached him of the death of his brother Knud VI on 12 November 1202. Hastening home, 'after he [Valdemar] had been accepted as king to general agreement, he received the royal blessing from the venerable Archbishop Andrew of Lund on Christmas Day [six weeks later] and was gloriously raised to the throne in that city'.[65] Delays may also have been required when, even though an heir had already been chosen and designated during his predecessor's lifetime, a coronation was still meant to be preceded by a formal election, as in Denmark in 1182 and 1202. And then there was, of course, the desire to link the inauguration to particular dates. Important feasts like Pentecost and Christmas were favoured, as were All Saints and feasts associated with the Virgin.[66] Dates, Johanna Dale has shown, could be chosen to assert continuity. In 1152, Frederick Barbarossa was crowned on the same liturgical day, *Laetare* Sunday, as his predecessor Conrad III in 1138 and Conrad's predeceased eldest son Henry in 1147. And in 1154, Henry II had himself crowned king of England on the same liturgical feast day as Stephen.[67] While the timing of a predecessor's death obviously shaped the choice of dates available, the new ruler still possessed considerable

---

[60] See generally: Hermann Weisert, 'Zur Dauer der Königswahlen bis zu den Krönungen', ZSRG *(Germanistische Abteilung)* 115 (1998), 598–609.

[61] Richer, *Histories*, vol. 2, 222–5.

[62] Suger, *Vie de Louis VI*, 84–8.

[63] Albert of Aachen, *Historia Ierosolomitana*, 872–3; William of Tyre, *Chronicon*, 549–50.

[64] William of Poitiers, *Gesta Guillelmi*, 148–9. See also: Paul Dalton, 'After Hastings: William the Conqueror's invasion campaign, 15 October–25 December 1066', *Viator* 48 (2017), 139–78; Dalton, 'William the Peacemaker: the submission of the English to the duke of Normandy, October 1066–January 1067', in *Rulership and Rebellion in the Anglo-Norman World, c. 1066–c.1216. Essays in Honour of Professor Edmund King*, ed. Paul Dalton and D. E. Luscombe (Aldershot, 2015), 21–44.

[65] Arnold of Lübeck, *Chronica Slavorum*, 238; *Chronicle of Arnold*, 246–7.

[66] Dale, *Inauguration and Liturgical Kingship*, 141–58.

[67] Dale, *Inauguration and Liturgical Kingship*, 155.

V. INAUGURATION   323

agency. The precise date of an inauguration could serve to reinforce particular readings of the royal office, or to accentuate a claim to continuity. All of this was further conditioned by practical needs. Convening as many of the great men of the realm as possible took time, as did the preparations necessary for the festivities surrounding the enthronement. Just like the claiming of a royal title, the settlement of a succession or the choosing of a king, the act of enthronement derived legitimacy from the size and standing of its audience.

Sites of inauguration were by no means fixed either. John de Fordun's account emphasised the importance of Scone, which, in 1214, had been deemed significant enough for the Scottish nobles to have interrupted the funeral of William the Lion in order to escort his underage son there for his enthronement. In 1198, the German princes backing Otto IV hastened to secure Aachen as the site for the performance of his coronation. Yet the further back we go, the less standardised the choice of venue becomes.[68] Aachen did not begin to emerge as the regular coronation site of the German kings until 1028, when Conrad II had his son Henry III elected and crowned there.[69] The first English king to be crowned at Westminster was Harold in 1066.[70] In the crusader states, the early rulers were crowned at Bethlehem rather than Jerusalem.[71] In France Reims was accorded a similar function only from 1131. Even then challenges persisted. In the mid-twelfth century, the abbots of St Denis disputed the prominence of Reims, and in 1180/1 Philipp Augustus underwent another crown-wearing ceremony there, following his inauguration at Reims.[72]

Once a regular coronation site had emerged, however, recurring practice could beget new traditions. Scone, for instance, may have been designated as the capital of Alba by the mythical first rulers of Scotland, or so John de Fordun claimed, but the abbey had not been founded until the early twelfth century. In fact, it acquired particular prestige only towards the end of the fourteenth century, probably reflecting its association with coronation practices that could no longer be performed.[73] At other times, what began as a matter of political expediency could, in light of subsequent events, carry considerable symbolic weight. In 1066, Harold may have been crowned at Westminster only

---

[68] This contrary to Dale, *Inauguration and Liturgical Kingship*, 117.

[69] Rollason, *Power of Place*, 326; Percy Ernst Schramm, 'Die Königskrönungen der deutschen Herrscher von 961 bis um 1050', in his *Kaiser, Könige und Päpste*, vol. 3, 108–34.

[70] Rollason, *Power of Place*, 327.

[71] Hans Eberhard Mayer, 'Das Pontifikale von Tyrus und die Krönung der Lateinischen Könige von Jerusalem: Zugleich ein Beitrag zur Forschung über Herrschaftszeichen und Staatssymbolik', *Dumbarton Oaks Papers* 21 (1967), 141–232, at 150–64.

[72] Rollason, *Power of Place*, 329–30. On the context see also, Gabrielle M. Spiegel, 'The cult of Saint Denis and Capetian kingship', *JMedH* 1 (1975), 43–70.

[73] Richard Fawcett, 'The buildings of Scone Abbey', in *The Stone of Destiny*, ed. Welander, Breeze and Clancy, 169–81.

324   9. ENTHRONING THE KING

because circumstances required immediate action. Edward the Confessor had died without heirs, while the duke of Normandy and the king of Norway seemed poised to pursue their claims by force. A quick response was needed, and Westminster – the late king's recently completed foundation and burial place – would have seemed an appropriate venue. Most of the great men of the realm were already assembled, and using the abbey allowed Harold to perform the role of an heir who took charge of his predecessor's *memoria*. When an ultimately victorious William the Conqueror then legitimised his kingship by claiming continuity with Edward, it was likewise the abbey's association with the Confessor that may have motivated the choice of venue. Its appeal may have been enhanced further by the abbey's proximity to London, communicating both continuity and the new king's grip on the realm's most populous city. In other cases, the location of a kingdom's ecclesiastical centre could be a determining factor (Trondheim, Lund), the association with a favoured patron saint (Odense, Reims), or a community's legendary origins (Székesfehérvár).

Once such regular sites emerged, they expressed important political, religious and moral messages. Many inauguration sites stressed the continuity of a people and of a tradition of royal lordship that transcended the lifespan of any individual ruler. Around 1280 Simon de Kéza reported that Székesfehérvár had been where Árpad had first settled after conquering Hungary.[74] The inauguration site commemorated the origins of Magyar rule. It also linked the authority of the king back to the solemn promises about good lordship and shared government that Árpad was supposed to have made to the Seven Leaders. When recounting the events of 1024, Wipo invoked Charlemagne. On Conrad's approaching Mainz, his reception was such that even 'if Charlemagne had been present, alive, with his sceptre, the people would not have been more eager'.[75] Once the king had visited Aachen, where, Wipo stressed, the *archisolium*, the arch-throne, of the empire had been located since the days of Charlemagne, his demeanour and actions gave rise to a proverb: 'The saddle of Conrad has the stirrups of Charles'.[76] Conrad proved to be a worthy successor of Charlemagne because he conducted himself like an ideal king: 'His fame took strength from his virtues: every day he was held by all more outstanding than the day before for the fastness of peace, more dear for the grace of benevolence, more honoured for regal judgement.'[77] Aachen was a hallowed place because of its association with Charlemagne,[78] just as Scone

---

[74] Simon de Kéza, *Gesta Hungarorum*, ed. and transl. László Veszprémy and Frank Schaer (Budapest and New York, 1999), 82–3.
[75] Wipo, *Gesta Chuonradi*, 23; *Deeds of Conrad II*, 67.
[76] Wipo, *Gesta Chuonradi*, 28–9; *Deeds of Conrad II*, 72.
[77] Wipo, *Gesta Chunobradi*, 28; *Deeds of Conrad II*, 72.
[78] Knut Görich, 'Karl der Große – ein politischer Heiliger?', in *Religion und Politik im Mittelalter*, ed. Körntgen and Waßenhoven, 117–55. Werner Tschacher, *Königtum als lokale Praxis. Aachen als Feld der kulturellen Realisierung von Herrschaft. Eine*

V. INAUGURATION   325

derived its legitimacy from the imagined continuity that it represented with the
Albanian kings of yore and Székesfehérvár from its link with Árpad.
   Yet illustrious forebears also imposed moral obligations. They provided
a model against which suitability for the throne could be judged. Otto of
Freising employed the first Carolingian emperor as a lens through which to
read the history of contemporary Germany,[79] and the anonymous
Kaiserchronik (*c.* 1150) similarly established Charlemagne as ideal ruler against
whom to measure his successors.[80] In late twelfth-century Denmark, Sven
Aggesen used the court of Knud the Great (d. 1035) to fashion an ideal of
political organisation, and around 1200 Saxo Grammaticus constructed the
mythical Frothi III as a model against which to judge subsequent kings.[81] The
theme was also central to the *Gesta Principum Polonorum*.[82] Like Wipo's
Conrad, Boleslaw I displayed an earnest desire for justice.[83] He did not extract
forced labour from peasants,[84] and fought steadfastly in their defence. He
would rather defend a single chicken from being snatched by his enemies
than be seen idly feasting.[85] Through justice, fairness and piety, Boleslaw
'attained the heights of greatness. Justice, in that he decided cases in law
without respect to persons; fairness, for his concern and tact extended to
both princes and commoners; and piety, for he honoured Christ and his
Bride in every way.'[86] Later kings and dukes were judged against this model.

Verfassungsgeschichte (ca. 800–1918) (Stuttgart, 2010); Karlheinz Cosepius, 'Der
Aachener "Karlsthron" zwischen Zeremoniell und Herrschermemoria', in *Investitur-
und Krönungsrituale. Herrschereinsetzungen im kulturellen Vergleich*, ed.
Marion Steinicke and Stefan Weinfurter (Cologne, Weimar and Vienna, 2005), 359–75;
Dale, *Inauguration and Liturgical Kingship*, 117–27.

[79] Otto of Freising, *Gesta Frederici*, i.45, pp. 216–17 (Conrad III setting out on crusade from
Frankfurt, named after a ford discovered by Charlemagne when waging war against the
Saxons); iii.32, pp. 464–5 (Frederick invokes Charlemagne and Otto I as model when
beginning the siege of Milan); iii.49, pp. 492–3 (Guido of Biandrate does the same); iv.64,
pp. 644–5 (Frederick invokes the precedent of Justinian, Theodosius and Charlemagne to
convene an ecumenical council); iv.74, pp. 662–3 (the prelates backing Frederick to
depose Alexander III do the same); iv.86, pp. 712–13 (Frederick restores the derelict
palaces once built by Charlemagne to their former glory). This in addition to ii.3, pp.
286–7, where Otto explicitly states that, during the coronation, Frederick was placed on
Charlemagne's throne. See also: Gerhard Schwedler, 'Kaisertradition und Innovation. Die
Bezugsnahme Barbarossas auf andere Kaiser', in *Staufisches Kaisertum im 12.
Jahrhundert. Konzepte – Netzwerke – Politische Praxis*, ed. Stefan Burkhardt,
Thomas Metz, Bernd Schneidmüller and Stefan Weinfurter (Regensburg, 2010), 231–52.

[80] *Book of Emperors*, 326–31. See also Otto I (353–5).

[81] Saxo Grammaticus, *Gesta Danorum*, v.3.8–12, 22–6, pp. 278–85, 296–301. See also above,
Chapter 4.

[82] *Gesta Principum Polonorum*, i.6, pp. 32–5.

[83] *Gesta Principum Polonorum*, i.9, pp. 48–9. See also above, Chapter 3.

[84] *Gesta Principum Polonorum*, i.12, pp. 58–9.

[85] *Gesta Principum Polonorum*, i.15, pp. 64–5.

[86] *Gesta Principum Polonorum*, i.11, pp. 56–7.

326   9. ENTHRONING THE KING

In fact, 'Gallus' implied, Polish kingship lapsed because rulers had failed to abide by the exemplary standards of this particular forebear. The emphasis on precedent and antiquity surfaces throughout narratives of inauguration. We will discuss the coronation liturgy in more detail below, but it is worth noting the archaising imagery of the surviving sources. *Ordines* frequently looked back to models associated with Charlemagne or at least with reputable earlier rulers. Moreover, they drew extensively on each other, and on the liturgy for the enthroning of bishops. As a result, before the thirteenth century individual manuscripts can only in exceptional circumstances be linked to a particular coronation. At most, as Johanna Dale has shown, *ordines* for the German royal coronation, fashioned within the wider context of the imperial church and court, painted a somewhat different image of the relationship between the divine and the king than those conceived at the papal court.[87] Equally, one finds a far greater emphasis on the king's duties and obligations in the English coronation liturgy than in that of France, Sicily or Germany. Most anchored a coronation in time not by relating it to a concrete event, but by consciously copying and amplifying resonances with ancient precedent, with customs and forebears worth emulating. For example, the oath that, according to Roger of Howden, Richard I was asked to perform in 1189 can be traced back to the late tenth century. That it was associated with Edgar, one of the legendary 'good kings' of pre-Conquest English history, only reinforced its normative value.[88] Such demonstrative conservatism was a statement in its own right, not unlike the associations that accrued to inauguration sites and exemplary avatars of kingship. Together, they established a hallowed tradition, designed to lend force to the values and concepts of kingship for which they provided

---

[87] Johanna Dale, 'Inaugurations and political liturgy in the Hohenstaufen Empire, 1138–1215', *German History* 34 (2016), 191–213. See also, generally, Dale, *Inauguration and Liturgical Kingship*, 26–67; C. A. Bouman, *Sacring and Crowning* (Groningen and Jakarta, 1957); Erich Hoffmann, 'Coronations and coronation *ordines* in medieval Scandinavia', in *Coronations*, ed. Bak, 125–51; Percy Ernst Schramm, 'Ordines-Studien 2: Die Krönung bei den Westfranken und den Franzosen', *Archiv für Urkundenforschung* 15 (1938), 3–55; Schramm, 'Ordines-Studien 3: Die Krönung in England', *Archiv für Urkundenforschung* 15 (1938), 305–91; Schramm, 'Nachträge zu den Ordines-Studien 2–3', *Archiv für Urkundenforschung* 16 (1939), 279–86; Schramm, 'Das polnische Königtum. Ein Längsschnitt durch die polnische Geschichte (im Hinblick auf Krönung, Herrschaftszeichen und Staatssymbolik)', in his *Kaiser, Könige und Päpste* vol. 4, 570–92; Schramm, 'Die Königskrönungen der deutschen Herrscher von 961 bis um 1050', ibid. vol. 3, 108–34; Mirko Vagnoni, 'The sacrality of Queen in the Norman Sicily. The pattern of Ordo coronationis', *Mirabilia. Revista Eletrônica de História Antiga e Medieval* 17 (2013), 174–86; Rainer Elze, 'Eine Kaiserkrönung um 1200', in *Adel und Kirche. Festschrift Gerd Tellenbach*, ed. Josef Fleckenstein and Karl Schmid (Freiburg/ Br. and Basel, 1968), 365–373; Mayer, 'Das Pontifikale von Tyrus'.

[88] Mary Clayton, 'The Old English *promissio regis*', *Anglo-Saxon England* 37 (2008), 91–150; Pauline Stafford, 'The laws of Cnut and the history of Anglo-Saxon royal promises', *Anglo-Saxon England* 10 (1982), 173–90.

V. INAUGURATION 327

a convenient shorthand, and to reflect the distinction between the individual ruler and the community over which he presided.

In the view of the *Kaiserchronik*, for instance, imperial lordship originated in the foundation of Rome. There had been both good and bad emperors. Some followed in the footsteps of Julius Caesar (believed to have been the first emperor) and Charlemagne,[89] others in those of the archetypal tyrants Nero and Tarquin.[90] And there was, of course, a transfer of empire from Constantinople to Aachen.[91] Yet individual reigns were subsumed into the history of an empire that – while obviously dependent on the ability and willingness of each ruler to perform his duties – nonetheless transcended them. The anonymous author upheld a view common in twelfth-century Germany,[92] but by no means confined to it. A similar perspective was taken by John de Fordun, and it echoes the kind of thinking about royal continuity discussed above in relation to the moral framework of royal succession.[93] That was imagined as a steady sequence of sons following fathers, with a line of descent that was rooted in a remote yet reputable past. There had always been Danes, who made and unmade their kings as they saw fit, while in Bohemia the establishment of ducal rule occurred at the community's behest, and long after the latter had come into existence. More importantly still, while the people had bestowed the office of *leader* upon the person they deemed most suitable, the dignity of *kingship* had been granted by God. The king was the protector and guardian of the realm, but it was not his to do with as he pleased.[94]

What we are dealing with is, to use the technical term, a transpersonal concept of the state. While some modern scholars have argued that the concept did not emerge until several centuries later, it was nonetheless central to high medieval engagements with royal power.[95] Its practical implications are illustrated by another episode in Wipo's *Gesta*. During an assembly at Konstanz, Conrad II was receiving oaths of fealty from his Italian subjects when a dispute arose with the citizens of Pavia. The king demanded compensation for an imperial palace destroyed during the months between the death of Henry II and his own succession. The building, Wipo stressed, had been erected at the behest of Emperor Theodoric and had subsequently been embellished by Otto

---

[89] *Book of Emperors*, 73–9.

[90] *Book of Emperors*, 136–9 (Nero), 141–9 (Tarquin). See also: Jürgen Strothmann, 'Christus, Augustus und der mittelalterliche römische Kaiser in der staufischen Herrschaftstheologie', *AKG* 84 (2002), 41–65.

[91] The last Byzantine emperor listed was Constantine VI (d. 797; *Book of Emperors*, 316–17).

[92] Dale, 'Imperial self-representation'.

[93] See above, Chapter 5.

[94] See above, Chapters 3 and 4.

[95] Helmut Beumann, 'Zur Entwicklung transpersonaler Staatsvorstellungen', in *Das Königtum. Seine geistigen und rechtlichen Grundlagen*, ed. Theodor Mayer (Sigmaringen, 1956), 185–224, at 201–3. See also Jonathan R. Lyon, 'The medieval German state in recent historiography', *German History* 28 (2010), 85–94.

328   9. ENTHRONING THE KING

III. Its antiquity testified to its long-standing association with the empire. In response, the Pavesi claimed that they had done nothing wrong. The palace certainly belonged to the king, but with Henry II dead and no successor in place, the property lacked an owner, and they could therefore do with it as they saw fit. Conrad responded: 'even if the king had died, the kingdom remained, just as the ship whose steersman falls remains. They were public, not private buildings [*aedes publicae fuerant, non privatae*]'.[96] That is, the empire existed independently of who – or, indeed, whether anyone – occupied the throne. The king was merely the steward of the realm.[97]

Indeed, taking responsibility for the continuity of the realm was integral to every stage of the king-making process. When Roger II claimed the throne of Sicily, the royal title was a personal accolade, but his elevation also restored the Sicilians to their rightful place among the kingdoms of Europe, just as old as – or even more ancient than – those ruled by Roger's rivals in Byzantium and Germany. When St Stephen became king, the act marked the entry of the Hungarians into the community of Christian nations. Hence an archangel commanded the pope to give a crown to Stephen – notably, as the *Legend of St Stephen* stressed, because of the *people* over whom he ruled. At the same time, responsibility for the continuing welfare of the realm was shared by the kingdom's elites. Roger II acted at the behest of his people, and a succession could not be settled without the consent of the ruled. The king's inauguration was no exception. Just like the ruler, the princes and prelates received their authority from God. They merited their standing through both the deeds of their forebears and the divine will.[98] They held power in order to act as representatives of the people in choosing a king, and to ensure that the king did right. The inauguration symbolised and enacted their place within the community of the realm. It did so partly through the manner of their participation and partly through demonstrating that they had in fact chosen the right person. The princes acted as guardians of the realm. But they did so fully cognizant of the fact that, without a ruler, there could be no kingdom.

9.3   The Right Order of the World

In 1189, the procession entering Westminster Abbey was led by bishops followed by abbots and four barons holding candles. Members of the nobility

---

[96] Wipo, *Gesta Chuonradi*, 30; *Deeds of Conrad II*, 73. See for a somewhat different view as to the significance of Wipo's episode Hubert Anton, 'Anfänge säkularer Begründung von Herrschaft und Staat im Mittelalter. Historiographie, Herkunftssagen, politische Metaphorik (Institutio Traiani)', *AKG* 86 (2004), 75–122.

[97] Weiler, 'Thinking about power'; Stefan Weinfurter, 'Herrschen durch Gnade. Legitimation und Autorität des Königtums in ottonisch-frühsalischer Zeit', in *Forschungsbeiträge der Geisteswissenschaftlichen Klasse*, ed. Eduard Hlawitschka (Munich, 2009), 109–26.

[98] Weiler, 'Kingship and lordship', 103–23.

V. INAUGURATION 329

each carried one of the royal insignia, followed by two prelates escorting the king. During the feast following the coronation, citizens of London acted as cupbearers, and those of Winchester served the food.[99] The inauguration made manifest the right order of the world. Given the religious nature of the service, the clergy obviously took a lead role, but Roger of Howden structured the coronation as a transfer of kingship by both secular and ecclesiastical elites. Richard may have been escorted to the throne by the bishops and barons, but the tokens of his office – the crown, sword, spurs, sceptre and so on – were carried by the latter. The king was invested with power that ultimately derived from God, but that was also – both literally and figuratively – handed to him by his people.

Roger is unusually detailed in tracing the role of the laity during the religious segment of the king's inauguration. He is also unusual in that he granted the earls so prominent a role, where they were both preceded and followed by members of the clergy. Such symbolic intermingling is rare. Other elements in his account were not, however, uncommon. For instance, escorting the monarch to his consecration usually fell to secular elites. In 1214, the earls of Fife, Strathearn, Atholl, Angus, Menteith, Buchan and Lothian, together with the bishops of Glasgow and St Andrews, took charge of delivering the adolescent Alexander II to Scone,[100] with the earls of Strathearn and Fife also performing that role for Alexander III in 1251.[101] When Alfonso VI was crowned king of Galicia in 1111, it was leading nobles who acted as butler and steward during the coronation feast,[102] and the same happened when William Ironarm had been inaugurated as duke at Melfi in 1042.[103] The carrying of royal insignia and the performance of court offices demonstrated both standing in relation to one's peers and submission to one's king. The ambivalence is especially pronounced in the crown-wearing processions of high medieval German kings. In 1013, Boleslaw III of Poland had been forced to carry the emperor's sword: it was not an honourable act, but a sign of defeat and subservience.[104] On the other hand, during the Mainz diet of 1184 several leading members of the aristocracy competed for the right to do just that.[105] In the eyes of Lambert Waterloos, that the count of Flanders was allowed to carry the imperial sword

---

[99] Roger of Howden, *Chronica*, vol. 3, 10–11.
[100] John de Fordun, *Gesta Annalia*, vol. 1, 280–1 (translation, vol. 2, 275–6).
[101] John de Fordun, *Gesta Annalia*, vol. 1, 294–5 (translation, vol. 2, 290–1).
[102] *Historia Compostellana*, 106.
[103] Amatus of Montecassino, *Storia de' Normanni*, 97–8; *History of the Normans*, 76.
[104] Thietmar, *Chronicon*, vi.91, pp. 338–41; *Ottonian Germany*, ed. Warner, 298.
[105] Arnold of Lübeck, *Chronica*, 88; Gislebert of Mons, *Chronicon*, 156. Max Buchner, *Die Entstehung der Erzämter und ihre Beziehung zum Werden des Kurkollegs: mit Beiträgen zur Entstehungsgeschichte des Pairskollegs in Frankreich* (Paderborn, 1911), 134–43. See also Zbigniew Dalewski, 'Lictor imperatoris. Kaiser Lothar III., Sobeslav I. von Böhmen und Boleslaw III. von Polen auf dem Hoftag in Merseburg im Jahre 1135', *Zeitschrift für Ostmitteleuropaforschung* 3-4 (2001), 319–35.

330　　　　　　　　9. ENTHRONING THE KING

when Frederick Barbarossa wore his crown at the Christmas diet of 1152 raised the former above all the other princes.[106] In England in 1189, we may assume, submission and status were equally on display. The barons passed on the insignia with which the king was made. They conferred, and they accepted the ruler's authority to use the instruments of his office.

Unsurprisingly, the clergy dominated the religious stages of the inauguration. This was true even when there was no crowning or anointing. At Scone, the Stone of Destiny was brought to the abbey's altar for the king's enthronement. In Ireland, hazel branches were handed over by bishops, while Alfonso I of Portugal took the insignia of knighthood from the altar of St Saviour's at Zamora.[107] In fact, so important was their presence that sometimes forceful steps were taken to secure it. Sverrir of Norway had initially asked a papal legate to crown him. The legate had first agreed to perform the ceremony, but then refused on hearing of the king's falling out with the archbishop of Nidaros. Sverrir therefore decided to muster as many prelates as he could, but did so in his own idiosyncratic way. He began by confronting Bishop Nicholas of Stavanger with accusations of treason, and threatening him with unspecified harsh measures. The prelate meekly complied, helped assemble a group of bishops to elect a new occupant for the see of Bergen, and then presided over Sverrir's coronation.[108]

Normally, the ceremony was led by the head of the realm's Church, such as the bishop of St Andrews at Scone, the archbishop of Canterbury at Westminster or those of Trondheim and Reims in their respective cathedrals. Being able to perform the rite suggested that the prelate in question represented the kingdom's Church in its entirety. The prerogative was both highly desirable and defended with great vigour. In eleventh-century Castile, the city of León had been a recurring venue for royal ceremonies – perhaps not least because King Fernando I (d. 1065) had designated it as a royal necropolis.[109] It was therefore a major coup for the bishop (later archbishop) of Santiago de Compostela when in 1111 he managed to have the inauguration celebrated at his cathedral instead.[110] Other prelates forcefully defended their rights. After King Peter of Hungary had been deposed in 1041, Bishop Gerhard of Csanád,

---

[106] Lambert Waterlos, *Annales Cameracenses*, MGH SS 16, 523. On the context, see Görich, *Friedrich Barbarossa*, 185–95. Likewise, in 1184, Gislebert dwelled on how the count of Hainaut had been singled out for this honour, over many who were richer and more powerful: Gislebert, *Chronicon*, 156.

[107] Böckler-Walter, *Alfonso I.*, 151.

[108] *Saga of King Sverri*, chapter 123, pp. 154–5. This followed various earlier attempts, including the waging of war on prelates who refused to crown Sverrir: *Diplomatarium Norvegicum*, vol. 6, nos. 3 and 4 (accessed via www.dokpro.uio.no/dipl_norv/diplom_field_eng.html on 16 February 2021).

[109] *Chronica Naierensis*, 164–6. See also the special issue of *e-spania* 7 (2009): https://journals.openedition.org/e-spania/17958 and above, Chapter 6.

[110] *Historia Compostellana*, 105–6.

V. INAUGURATION

331

the leader of the Hungarian Church, refused to crown his successor, Samul Aba. When the king had himself crowned by the assembled clergy instead, their subservience triggered a furious response from the prelate, who warned of the evil ends that would befall the usurper.[111] In 1108, Suger reports, due to unspecified intrigues and dangers,[112] the coronation of Louis VI of France was performed at Orléans by the archbishop of Sens, rather than by the archbishop of Reims in his cathedral. Just after the ceremony had been completed, messengers from Reims arrived, seeking to halt the proceedings, as, they claimed, both apostolic privilege and ancient precedent demanded that it be performed only by the archbishop in his church.[113] The cathedral community's pre-eminence must take precedence over political expediency.

The right to place a crown on the king's head extended beyond the coronation to festive crown-wearing ceremonies that are attested across much of the Latin west.[114] The privilege was jealously guarded. In the 1120s, Henry I of England had worn his crown during Mass following the queen's coronation. With Archbishop Ralph of Canterbury old, weak and fast asleep, the bishop of Winchester had placed it on Henry's head. When someone nudged Ralph awake, and pointed out that the king was wearing his crown, the irate metropolitan interrupted the service and confronted Henry before the assembled prelates and magnates:

> furious that another man had anticipated a duty he should have carried out himself, he went up to the king, just as he was, in his holy pallium [a vestment bestowed by the pope as sign of archiepiscopal authority]. The king rose, out of respect for him. Ralph said: 'Who crowned you?' The king excused himself, saying he did not know. 'You have been crowned unlawfully,' Ralph said. 'Either you must take off your crown or I will not celebrate mass.' . . . Ralph therefore put out his hands to take off the crown, and the king began to untie the fastening at his chin; and Ralph was scarcely restrained by the united shouts and prayers of them all from bringing violence to bear on the king's head.[115]

There is much to savour in this anecdote: the king's inability to come up with a better excuse than pleading ignorance as to how the crown had landed on his head, the shouts and prayers of the audience which alone had prevented the prelate from – literally – tearing off said head, and Henry seeking in panic to

---

[111] *Legenda S Gerhardi Episcopi*, in *Scriptores Rerum Hungaricarum*, ed. Szentpétery, vol. 2, 500.

[112] Likely the putative rivalry of his half-brother Philippe: *Chronique de Morigny*, 56–8.

[113] Suger, *Vie de Louis*, 86–9. For the context: James Naus, 'The "Historia Iherosolimitana" of Robert the Monk and the coronation of Louis VI', in *Writing the Early Crusades: Text, Transmission and Memory*, ed. Marcus Bull and Damien Kempf (Woodbridge, 2014), 105–15.

[114] Dale, *Inauguration and Liturgical Kingship*, 136–41.

[115] William of Malmesbury, *Gesta Pontificum*, vol. 1, 210–13.

332   9. ENTHRONING THE KING

untie the knot under his chin that fastened the crown to his head. But the matter at hand was serious. At stake was the metropolitan's status as leader of the English Church. An archbishop of Canterbury had last administered unction and crowning in 1088, which was barely within living memory. In 1066, William the Conqueror had been crowned by the archbishop of York[116] and in 1100 Henry I by the bishop of Winchester. A right not exercised would soon lapse. Forceful steps had to be taken to defend it. In fact, so important was the prerogative to crown the king that Thomas Becket secured a papal mandate guaranteeing the archbishop of Canterbury's right to do so.[117] Being responsible for placing a crown on the royal head symbolised pre-eminence and leadership. That was the reason why the abbots of St Denis questioned the role of the archbishops of Reims,[118] and why the bishop of Santiago de Compostela, striving to have his see elevated to an archbishopric, so eagerly seized the opportunity to perform a coronation. Only those leading a kingdom's Church should enthrone its ruler.

The bishopric of Santiago de Compostela had been established as recently as 1095. Diego Gelmírez, its second occupant, found himself besieged by local aristocrats and Queen Urraca. In 1111, plans were mooted to crown the infant Alfonso VII king in opposition to his mother. Diego saw an opportunity to raise his standing and that of the community over which he presided. There had not previously been a tradition of crowning a king in Galicia, nor had Diego's predecessor participated in, let alone overseen, a royal inauguration elsewhere in Urraca's domains. The ceremony therefore served multiple ends. It asserted Alfonso's independence from his mother, staked a claim to his royal inheritance and cemented Santiago's pre-eminent role in the affairs of Galicia. The account in the *Historia Compostellana* focussed firmly on the prelate. Alfonso was relegated to a passive, almost supporting part. Diego was festively adorned in his pontifical garb. Diego conducted the boy to the altar. Diego anointed him. Diego put the crown on Alfonso's head. Diego placed the king on the throne. Diego read a most solemn Mass. Diego conducted the boy to the episcopal palace. Diego invited all the great men of Galicia to a most splendid feast.[119] Alfonso might wear the crown, but Diego clearly had made him king. The ceremony furthermore set a precedent when, on his mother's death, Diego crowned Alfonso king of León,[120] and it may have helped Santiago acquire

---

[116] William of Poitiers, *Gesta Guillelmi*, 146–7.

[117] *English Coronation Records*, ed. and transl. L. G. Wickham Legg (Westminster, 1901), 43–6.

[118] Roger of Howden, *Chronica*, vol. 2, 197.

[119] *Historia Compostellana*, 106. See also: Ermelindo Portera Silva, 'Diego Gelmírez y el trono de Hispania. La coronación real del año 1111', in *O século de Xelmírez*, ed. Fernando López Alsina, Henrique Monteagudo, Ramón Villares and Ramón José Yzquierdo Perrín (Santiago, 2013), 45–74.

[120] *Chronicon Adefonsi*, 150.

V. INAUGURATION   333

metropolitan status in 1120.[121] The circumstances were thus different from those in England and France. Diego initiated a tradition of overseeing the king's inauguration, rather than seeking to defend an established one. Events nonetheless unfolded according to a recognisable pattern: crowning made a king, but it also confirmed or even made leaders of the Church.

Leadership was, however, rooted in and needed to be backed up by collective action. Archbishops may have presided over the proceedings, but they acted alongside and in cooperation with their episcopal peers. A closer engagement with liturgical texts will prove fruitful. Fortunately, the *ordo* survives that was in all likelihood used when Roger II was crowned king of Sicily. Regrettably, it does not identify the participating clerics, referring simply to 'the archbishop' or 'one of the bishops'. Still, it exemplifies the extent to which coronations were the responsibility of the episcopacy as a whole. When the ruler entered the church, one prelate offered a prayer, while the king was accompanied by several other clerics, carrying the Gospels and relics. Once they reached the altar, the archbishop took over with another prayer, while the assembled clergy responded. Once the ruler had sworn his coronation oath and had been acclaimed by the people – all under the guidance of the metropolitan – another two bishops offered prayers before the archbishop anointed the king. Afterwards, bishops handed over each of the royal insignia, while the archbishop declaimed a prayer. After the metropolitan and the king had exchanged the kiss of peace, the clergy intoned the *Te Deum Laudamus*, and Mass was celebrated.[122] Coronations in England, France and Germany followed a similar pattern, with minor variations. In a twelfth-century English *ordo*, an unnamed bishop (rather than the metropolitan) asked the people whether they accepted the candidate as king,[123] while a short memorandum produced after the coronation of Philipp I of France in 1059 simply lists the bishops and abbots in attendance.[124] Far more important is that, in all of these texts, the archbishop and higher clergy acted in unison, each performing a distinctive part of the ceremony. The prospective king was presented to God, and reminded of his duties, by the community of the clergy of the realm.

That role reflects the moral obligations of bishops. Metropolitans, in overseeing an election, were meant to assess the moral stature of candidates. The same expectation surfaces in a king's inauguration. In either 975 or 979, St Dunstan, the archbishop of Canterbury, halted the coronation to present the prospective ruler with a letter. First, he made the candidate read out the

---

[121] *Epistolae Calixti II*, Patrologia Latina 163, no. 79. See also Luis Carlos Correia Ferreira do Amaral, 'As sedes de Braga e Compostela e a restauração da métropole galaica', in *O século de Xelmírez*, ed. López Alsina, Monteagudo, Villares and Yzquierdo Perrín, 17–44.

[122] Elze, 'Ordo for the coronation', 170–7.

[123] *English Coronation Records*, 31.

[124] *Ordines Coronationis Franciae*, vol. 1, 227–8.

334   9. ENTHRONING THE KING

promises contained in the letter. The king-to-be vowed to ensure that peace prevail among the Christian people of his realm, to ban robbery and other unjust actions, and to maintain justice and mercy. Next he had to swear a solemn oath that he would keep these promises. And only then did Dunstan allow the ceremony to resume and the coronation to take place.[125] The archbishop's demeanour may have been unusually forceful, but the principle that unction and coronation were contingent upon the king promising to be a just and faithful ruler was widely shared. Both the first and the second English *ordo* begin with the king, on entering the church, prostrating himself before the main altar. He is then raised up, and solemnly makes three promises: that his judgement will at all times offer peace to the Church and all Christians; that he will banish all iniquities and violence irrespective of the standing of the perpetrators; and that his judicial decrees will be guided by equity and mercy.[126] Similar undertakings are recorded elsewhere in Europe,[127] but only from the crusader kingdom of Jerusalem do oaths survive as separate documents, recorded independently of the liturgy itself.[128] Likewise, while in the English *ordines* the king was meant to make these promises unprompted, mainland practice was often closer to the example of St Dunstan. In Sicily, for instance, the archbishop posed three questions to the aspiring monarch: would he observe the Catholic faith and serve it in his actions and works? Was he willing to be a servant and defender of the Church? Would he defend the realm that had been given into his care and rule it with justice? Only once the future king had responded in the affirmative to each question, and only after he had added that he promised this, so God and all the saints help him, did the ceremony proceed.[129] The king was anointed only after

[125] *Memorials of St Dunstan, Archbishop of Canterbury*, ed. William Stubbs (London, 1874), 99–101. See also Clayton, 'Old English *promissio regis*'; Stafford, 'The laws of Cnut'. For the context see also: Warner, 'Comparative approaches'.

[126] *English Coronation Records*, 15, 30–1; H. G. Richardson, 'The English coronation oath', *TRHS* 23 (1941), 129–58; Richardson, 'The coronation in medieval England: the evolution of the office and the oath', *Traditio* 16 (1960), 111–202. Indeed, the sequence was still followed during the coronation of Elizabeth I and II in 1953: Lucinda May and Oonagh Gay, 'The Coronation Oath', House of Commons Library Standard Note SN/PC/00435 (I am grateful to Alex Woolf for this reference). See also *Regesta Regum Anglo-Normannorum 1066–1154*, ed. H. W. C. Davis, H. A. Cronne and Charles Johnson, 4 vols. (Oxford, 1913–69), vol. 3, nos. 270–1.

[127] *Ordines Coronationis Franciae*, vol. 1, 227–8; Elze, 'Ordo for the coronation', 171; Georg Waitz, ed., *Die Formeln der deutschen Königs- und der römischen Kaiserkrönung vom zehnten bis zum zwölften Jahrhundert* (Göttingen, 1872), 34–5. Note also the striking similarities with the Romano-German Pontifical: Cyrille Vogel and Reinhard Elze, eds., *Le Pontifical Romano-Germanique du dixième siècle*, 2 vols. (Vatican, 1963), 247–8.

[128] *Die Urkunden der lateinischen Könige von Jersusalem*, ed. Hans Eberhard Mayer with Jean Richard, MGH Diplomata, 4 vols. (Hanover, 2010), vol. 3, 1447–51.

[129] Elze, 'Ordo for the coronation', 171.

V. INAUGURATION

he had solemnly vowed to perform the duties of his office. It fell to the archbishop, in turn, and to his episcopal colleagues to ensure that he did make these promises.

The contractual understanding of kingship permeated the remainder of the ceremony and the rehearsal of royal duties continued. In Wipo's *Gesta*, the archbishop of Mainz preached a sermon in which he reminded Conrad of the duty to protect those who could not protect themselves and to show mercy to those who had wronged him in the past. At Westminster in 1189, the archbishop of Canterbury reminded Richard I of his obligations and asked him again to confirm that he was indeed willing to perform them. Only once Richard had confirmed again that he would strive to be a good king did the crowning occur. *Ordines* also describe a gradual transfer of power to the king, with each stage serving as a reminder of his duties. While much of this may seem repetitive to modern readers, repetition and reiteration was very much the point. The liturgy provided a continuous exhortation to be a good king, and an equally continuous rehearsing of the principles on which just rulership was built. The inauguration ceremony was designed in order to lodge knowledge of the duties of kingship firmly inside even the numbest royal skull.

The Sicilian *ordo* may stand in for others.[130] After the king had been anointed, he was handed sword, ring, cloak, cap and sceptre, before being crowned and then escorted from the altar to the throne. Each token of office was accompanied by an exposition of what it signified. The sword stood for the power that the king had been given by God in order to protect his Church and the faithful, destroy the enemies of the faith, assist and defend widows and orphans, lift up the desolate, humble the haughty and fight injustice, so that he might be a friend of justice and righteousness in the eyes of the Saviour. The ring symbolised the Christian faith, to remind the king of his obligations towards the Church and Christendom, which he should nourish so that he might find favour in turn before the king of kings. When being passed the sceptre, the *ordo* stipulates, the king also received the *regnum*, the realm. It further defines the sceptre as the rod of righteousness and equity, with which to nourish the righteous and humble the infidel, strike terror into those who had veered from the path of righteousness and guide them back into the fold. The king should heed the example of David, love the just and hate the iniquitous, so that he would be justified in receiving unction that raised him above those around him. With all the insignia handed over, the archbishop placed the *corona regni*, crown of the realm, on the king's head. It was to remind him that he shared in the ministry of his bishops (*et per hanc te participem ministerii nostri*): they were the shepherds and correctors of the inner soul (people's thoughts and actions). He was to take charge of outward actions by being

---

[130] On which see, most recently and magisterially, Dale, *Inauguration and Liturgical Kingship*.

336   9. ENTHRONING THE KING

a strenuous defender of the Church and the realm that God had given to him (*ecclesie defensor regnique a deo tibi dati*). The crowning was followed by further prayers, before the king was led away from the altar and placed on the throne, where he was yet again reminded of his duties: to honour the Church and be a protector and guardian of his people.[131]

The people did not simply choose Roger to be their king. Instead, they presented him to God as their choice for the ruler's office. His anointing and the investment with the royal insignia were framed by a series of prayers. After the people had given their assent, three bishops implored God to ensure that the king would rule his people with equity, justice and peace, that he would always be obedient to and be protected by God, and that the king would be wealthy through God's mercy and his kingdom rich in harvests.[132] These requests were repeated during the king's anointing. When chrism (the holy oil) was administered to his hands, the archbishop announced that the king was anointed as Samuel had anointed David, so that he might be a blessed and righteous king over the people which God had entrusted to his government. The accompanying prayer pleaded for abundant harvests and plentiful wine and oil, bodily health and worthy progeny for the king and that he may prove a protector of the fatherland, a patron of churches and shrines, an oppressor of rebels and hostile neighbours and amiable and generous to the good men of his kingdom. When the archbishop anointed the king on his head, shoulders and chest, he beseeched God to deem the ruler worthy of the royal dignity, and to make him a just and pious king, defender of the realm and protector of the Church.[133] Likewise, after the insignia had been handed over and the king was crowned, the archbishop offered a blessing: that God would accept the king as ruler over his people; that the people, who chose him as their king, would be governed wisely through the king's foresight and God's benevolence; that he may lack adversity and abound in good fortune; that peace may prevail in this world so that the king would find salvation in the next.[134] Only then was the ruler placed on his throne and the kiss of peace that concluded proceedings exchanged. All the people could do was to demonstrate that Roger promised to be a just ruler whom they had elected freely, and to request that God bestow his favour upon both the people and their chosen ruler.

The surviving twelfth-century English, French and German *ordines* pursue similar themes.[135] They conform to a pattern already evident in the selection of the coronation site and the invocation of a ruler's predecessors: the realm

---

[131] Elze, 'Ordo for the coronation', 174–5.
[132] Elze, 'Ordo for the coronation', 171–2.
[133] Elze, 'Ordo for the coronation', 172–3.
[134] Elze, 'Ordo for the coronation', 175.
[135] *Formeln*, 40–2; *English Coronation Records*, 35–9; *Ordines Coronationis Franciae*, 244–6.

V. INAUGURATION 337

existed through but independently of the individual king. Moreover, the inauguration enacted an idealised order of the world. The ruler being inaugurated had been chosen unanimously, as the one most suitable for the throne, eager to be a keeper and protector of his people. His subjects, with everyone assuming their proper place, collectively presented him to God to request divine approval for their choice, and for God to enable the monarch to be the good and just king that his subjects desired and that he promised to be. Kingship was not, however, the people's to give: only God could grant it. The ruler received the kingdom in trust, in order to guard and nourish the Church, defend widows and orphans and to see to the moral, spiritual and material well-being of his people. Royal authority was contingent on the ruler's willingness and ability to perform the duties for which he had received such power. Might and wealth were means to an end, supposedly both an incentive for and evidence of a ruler's willingness to do right by his people and by his Creator. As a twelfth-century English *ordo* put it, the crown's precious stones represented the virtues that, through the grace of God, should adorn the king.[136]

By invoking the kingship of Israel, the ceremonies of anointing and crowning placed the ruler in a tradition that transcended any particular medieval realm. In Sicily, the link had been made explicit when the archbishop likened the anointing of the king's hands to David's anointment by Samuel. In an Old Testament context, the act separated the ruler from his people. In the Book of Samuel, David had repeatedly refused to take violent action against Saul, who had, after all, been the Lord's anointed.[137] The Psalms also granted the king special status: 'Do not touch My anointed ones, And do My prophets no harm.'[138] Unction expressed a particular relationship with the divine, including that the person receiving it shared in the gift of prophecy. He would receive visions and instructions directly from God. In this regard, coronation *ordines* reflect those for the investiture of bishops. According to the Romano-German Pontifical, once a prelate had been chosen and the election duly been confirmed by the archbishop, the candidate underwent a process of interrogation not unlike that encountered by prospective kings. Only once the clergy and

---

[136] *English Coronation Records*, 34. See also *Selected Letters of Pope Innocent III*, no. 1. See furthermore the very similar symbolism invoked by Peter of Eboli in his account of Henry VI's imperial coronation: receiving unction on both hands meant that Henry could handle both the Old and the New Testament (i.e. be a pious ruler); the imperial sword denoted that Henry ruled both the Church and the world; the rod stood for the power of law, piety and equity; the ring for the pledge [of authority over] realms and the marriage with the Church; and the diadem for participation in the apostolic role: Peter of Eboli, *Liber ad honorem*, 122–3. Also Suger, *Vie de Louis*, 86–7: the sword denoted secular justice and the staff and sceptre the rod with which to defend the Church and the poor.

[137] 1 Samuel 24:6, 10; 26:9, 11, 16, 23.

[138] Psalms 105:15.

338   9. ENTHRONING THE KING

people had assented to his election did the formal investiture occur.[139] Both bishops and kings were anointed and thus awarded a religious status distinct from the vast majority of their subjects. Both owed fealty to God, who had entrusted them with the souls and the material well-being of the faithful. Yet, at least in the Sicilian *ordo*, the ruler also occupied an intermediate position.[140] His duties clearly were those of a secular lord: he was to wield the sword of justice in this world, vanquish the enemies of the faith and humiliate the haughty. He shared in the ministry of the clergy, but was not fully part of it. His position as keeper and guardian of the realm, and thus at the apex of its community, meant that he combined elements of worldly and spiritual power. That was possible only as long as everyone knew and acted according to their rightful place. In Sicily, this ordering of the realm was symbolised by the cooperation of the clergy, and in England in how kingship was transferred jointly by the barons and clergy. Collectively, ruler and ruled enacted how things should be.

9.4   Sacral Kingship

Kingship was rooted in the divine. Evidently, there was a numinous quality to the royal office. What does this mean exactly? To answer that question, the concept of 'sacral kingship' is frequently invoked. Yet its meaning is defined with as much success as jelly is nailed to a wall. In fact, when the early modernist Jens Ivo Engels tried to prise apart the meanings attached to the term by sociologists, anthropologists and historians, he concluded in evident frustration that the term was so vague that it ought to be discarded.[141] More recently, Johanna Dale, in a magisterial study of royal inaugurations in twelfth-century England, France and Germany, decided to avoid the term in favour of 'liturgical' kingship.[142] Why such reluctance to use the familiar phrase?

Several factors may have been at play: the concept's inherent fuzziness, the extent to which several different concepts were often lumped together and perhaps an instinctive reaction to the uncritical reception of anthropology

---

[139] *Le Pontifical Romano-Germanique*, vol. 1, 200–5. On which see most recently, Henry Parkes, 'Henry II, liturgical kingship, and the birth of the "Romano-German Pontifical"', *EME* 28 (2020), 104–41. See also, for the investiture of an abbot: Theodor Niederquell, 'Die Gesta Marcuardi', *Fuldaer Geschichtsblätter* 38 (1962), 173–99, at 180.

[140] See also, with emphasis on Germany, Schieffer, 'Mediator cleri et populi'.

[141] Jens Ivo Engels, 'Das "Wesen" der Monarchie? Kritische Anmerkungen zum "Sakralkönigtum" in der Geschichtswissenschaft', *Majestas* 7 (1999), 3–39. Similar concerns were expressed by Rory McTurk, 'Sacral kingship in ancient Scandinavia: A review of some recent writings', *Saga-Book* 19:2–3 (1975–6), 139–69; McTurk, 'Scandinavian sacral kingship revisited', *Saga-Book* 24:1 (1994), 18–32. I am grateful to Haki Antonsson for these references.

[142] Dale, *Inauguration and Liturgical Kingship*, 19–20.

V. INAUGURATION   339

among an earlier generation of historians. Let us begin with the last of these. Work on 'sacral kingship' often draws on practices of divine kingship in the pre-Christian west or in polytheist societies across the globe. Yet notions of divinity held rather different meanings in a religious universe inhabited by a multiplicity of deities. Each was subject to the course of time and hence to challenge and decline. This understanding of the divine was fundamentally different from that in a belief system centring on a single supernatural entity assumed to be omnipotent and omniscient.[143] One does not easily map onto the other. Consequently, accounts of sacral kingship in Java and Hawaii, Africa, America or south and south-east Asia, and even Rome, Greece and the ancient Near East, once consulted to look for parallels to and antecedents for the medieval west, helped encourage what one might term a maximalist understanding of 'sacral kingship'. The lines between the sacral and the divine become blurred. Sacrality, it seemed, turned kings into quasi-numinous beings, and it was this special status, not quite divine but certainly sacrosanct, that made it desirable for them to acquire the accoutrements of sacral royal lordship.[144] Kings aspired to be sacral because it granted them special, protected status.

Other concepts were added to the mix. In 1937, his reading of early anthropology convinced the Danish philologist Vilhelm Grønbech to postulate the idea of *Königsheil*: a pagan quasi-divine quality associated with the leaders of early Germanic tribes, which subsequently transmogrified into Christian royal sacrality.[145] In 1950, Karl Hauck added a kind of hereditary pagan sacrality, or *Geblütsheiligkeit*, which, despite František Graus' devastating

---

[143] Asfar Moin, *The Millennial Sovereign: Sacred Kingship and Sainthood in Islam* (New York, 2012); Greg Woolf, 'Divinity and power in ancient Rome', in *Religion and Power. Divine Kingship in the Ancient World and Beyond*, ed. Nicola Brisch (Chicago, 2008), 235–52; D. S. Levene, 'Defining the divine in Rome', *Transactions of the American Philological Association* 142 (2012), 41–81; Michael J. Puett, *To Become a God: Cosmology, Sacrifice and Self-Divinization in Early China* (Cambridge, MA, 2002). Generally, Franz-Rainer Erkens, ed., *Die Sakralität von Herrschaft: Herrschaftslegitimierung im Wechsel der Zeiten und Räume: fünfzehn interdisziplinäre Beiträge zu einem weltweiten und epochenübergreifenden Phänomen* (Berlin, 2002).

[144] See, for instance, Carl-Martin Erdsman, ed., *La Regalità sacra: Contributi al tema dell'VIII Congresso internazionale di storia delle religioni (Roma, aprila 1955)* (Leiden, 1959); Virginia M. Fields and Doris Reens-Budet, *Lords of Creation. The Origins of Sacred Maya Kingship* (London, 2005); John Pemberton and Funso S. Afolayan, *Yoruba Sacred Kingship: A Power Like That of the Gods* (Washington, DC, 1996); Henri Frankfort, *Kingship and the Gods. A Study of Ancient Near Eastern Religion as the Integration of Nature and Society* (Chicago, 1978); *Religion and Power*, ed. Brisch. See, however, more recently Eva Anagnostou-Loutides, *In the Garden of the Gods: Models of Kingship from the Sumerians to the Seleucids* (London, 2016).

[145] See for a fuller account of the development of the concept Eve Picard, *Germanisches Sakralkönigtum? Quellenkritische Untersuchungen zur Germania des Tacitus und zur altnordischen Überlieferung* (Heidelberg, 1991).

340   9. ENTHRONING THE KING

critique, was embraced by anglophone scholars, ensuring its continuing usage.[146] Underpinning both concepts was the belief in an inherent tension between paganism and Christianity, with royal sacrality a Christianised version of supposed pagan practices that it barely managed to tame, let alone conceal. The problem with this approach is that most practices and textual relics of supposedly pagan origin were, in fact, fundamentally Christian in provenance and meaning.[147] Even so, the supposed distinction between Germanic *Königsheil* and Christian sacrality became firmly entrenched in scholarly approaches. In a spirited defence of the idea of *Königsheil*, Walter Kienast still felt in 1978 that the concept merited rescuing,[148] while in 1982 Henry Myers would structure his study of medieval kingship as a recurring clash between supposedly Germanic and purportedly Christian antagonists.[149] Like the walking dead, the putrefying corpses of *Königsheil* and *Geblütsheiligkeit* continue to wander about, eager to devour the brains of anyone unfortunate enough to stray into their path.[150]

In the present context, these concepts formed an essential pathway through which a maximalist reading of sacrality was able to spread. Their impact was enhanced by a tendency to draw on early modern materials to illuminate medieval concepts. Yet that meant projecting back onto the medieval past readings of sacrality that would have been unthinkable before the Reformation. No high medieval king would have dared to issue statements like the one offered by James VI of Scotland to the English parliament in 1610: 'The State of MONARCHIE is the supremest thing upon earth: For Kings are not onely GOD's Lieutenants upon earth, and sit upon GOD's throne, but even by GOD himselfe they are called Gods.'[151] To most high medieval observers, early modern sacrality would have looked suspiciously

[146] Karl Hauck, 'Geblütsheiligkeit', in *Liber floridus. Mittellateinische Studien. Paul Lehmann zum 65. Geburtstag*, ed. Bernhard Bischoff (St Ottilien, 1950), 187–240; František Graus, *Volk, Herrscher und Heiliger im Reich der Merowinger: Studien zur Hagiographie der Merowingerzeit* (Prague, 1965); William A. Chaney, *The Cult of Kingship in Anglo-Saxon England: the Transition from Paganism to Christianity* (Oxford, 1970).

[147] Antonsson, *St Mágnus of Orkney*, 194–207.

[148] Walter Kienast, 'Germanische Treue und "Königsheil"', *HZ* 227 (1978), 265–324. Helpfully, at 278–305, Kienast listed all the source passages supposedly proving the practice's existence. To the present reader, they do little to strengthen his argument. See also Christoph Dartmann, 'Die Sakralisierung König Wambas. Zur Debatte um frühmittelalterliche Sakralherrschaft', *FmSt* 44 (2010), 39–58.

[149] Henry A. Myers, *Medieval Kingship* (Chicago, 1982), 7–22.

[150] Eduardo Fabbro, 'Conspicuous by their absence: Long-haired kings, symbolic capital, sacred kingship and other contemporary myths', *Signum. Revista da ABREM* 13:1 (2012), 22–45, gives some more recent examples.

[151] Cited after Glenn Burgess, 'The divine right of kings reconsidered', *EHR* 107 (1992), 837–61, at 837. It should, though, be noted that Burgess offered a spirited rejection of the idea of divine right of kings as absolutist. See, more recently, Ronald G. Asch, *Sacral*

V. INAUGURATION 341

like blasphemy.[152] Equally detrimental was a scholarly preoccupation with coronation liturgies, early modern ceremonial handbooks and ruler portraits in liturgical manuscripts.[153] Sacrality was reduced to and seen as rooted in the act of anointment.[154] Drawing primarily on such materials is like writing a history of US presidential politics by studying only the oath of office, the State Department's guide on protocol or the iconography of campaign logos. All three offer valuable insights, but none fully reflect the complex web of attitudes, expectations, practical requirements and conflicting interpretations of shared norms that surround the office and its occupants. Coronation liturgies inevitably stressed the relationship between the ruler and God. That was their point. In the same way as ruler images in liturgical texts, royal gospel books and similar devotional manuscripts, by their very nature they tend to project an exalted image of the relationship between the king and the divine.[155] But how representative are these materials of high medieval attitudes and practices?

Kingship between Disenchantment and Re-Enchantment: the French and English Monarchies 1587–1688 (Oxford, 2014).

[152] Indeed, a *vita* of Lanfranc, the first post-Conquest archbishop of Canterbury, recounted how one of the king's jesters, on seeing William I at table in full regalia, mockingly compared him to God. *Vita Lanfranci*, ed. Margaret Gibson, in *Lanfranco di Pavia e l'Europa de secolo xi*, ed. Giulio Donofrio (Rome, 1995), 639–715, at 708.

[153] See, for instance, Alain Boureau and Claudio Sergio Ingerflom, eds., *La royauté sacrée dans le monde chrétien. Colloque de Royaumont, mars 1989* (Paris, 1992); Francis Oakley, *Kingship. The Politics of Enchantment* (Oxford, 2006). The best surveys of the issue remain Fabbro, 'Conspicuously by their absence'; Johanna Dale, 'Conceptions of kingship in high medieval Germany in historiographical perspective', *History Compass* 16 (2018), 1–11. For useful case studies see Klaniczay, *Holy Rulers*; Mirko Vagnoni, 'Royal images and sacred elements in Norman-Swabian and Angevin-Aragonese kingdom of Sicily (1130–1343)', *Eikón. Imago* 2 (2013), 107–22; Vagnoni, 'The sacrality of the Queen'. Dale, *Inauguration and Liturgical Kingship*, constitutes a rare and important exception to this pattern.

[154] Jacques Le Goff, 'Aspects religieux et sacrés de la monarchie Française du Xe au XIIIe siècle', Boureau and Ingerflom, *La royauté sacrée*, 19–28, at 19.

[155] See, for instance, Robert Deshman, '"Christus rex et magi reges". Kingship and christology in Ottonian and Anglo-Saxon art', *FmSt* 10 (1976), 367–405; Steffen Patzold, '"Omnis anima potestatibus sublimioribus subdita sit": zum Herrscherbild im Aachener Otto-Evangeliar', *FmSt* 35 (2001), 243–72; Hagen Keller, 'Herrscherbild und Herrschaftslegitimation. Zur Deutung der ottonischen Denkmäler', *FmSt* 10 (1985), 290–311. For a more critical view: Bernhard Jussen, 'Richtig denken im falschen Rahmen? Warum das "Mittelalter" nicht in den Lehrplan gehört', *Geschichte in Wissenschaft und Unterricht* 67 (2016), 558–76, at 572. See also the points made by Körntgen, *Königsherrschaft*, 161–445. Many of these materials famously formed the starting point of Ernst Kantorowicz's investigation of the concept of the king's two bodies. On which see most recently Brett Edward Whalen, 'Political theology and the metamorphoses of The King's Two Bodies', *American Historical Review* 125 (2020), 132–45.

342   9. ENTHRONING THE KING

Many sceptics, instead of questioning the foundations on which the prevalent image of sacral kingship was based, focussed on moments when the claims of *ordines* failed to live up to reality, or when elements of the anointing ceremony were abandoned or revised. Teofilo Ruiz, for instance, proposed that, because Castilian kings forwent a ceremony of anointing, they secularised their polity and rejected the very ideas that were to give rise to the concept of 'sacral kingship'.[156] Geoffrey Koziol used moments of criticism, of royal performances of sacrality being inverted or mocked, to propose that the kings of England failed in their pursuit of 'sacral kingship'.[157] Finally, there is what by rights should be another recruit for the ghoulish troupe of *Königsheil* & co.: the supposed desacralisation of kingship in the wake of the Investiture Controversy.[158] In the twelfth century, the premise goes, a knightly-chivalric or even Romano-judicial vision of royal power replaced a Christocentric and sacral one.[159] Yet it was precisely during this and the following century that the evidence for the sacral underpinnings of royal lordship surfaced in an ever-expanding range of genres and media.[160] There is, in fact, no evidence at all to support the thesis that the Investiture Controversy had any impact on the sacral dimension of kingship. Far from receding or becoming less potent, representations of royal sacrality became ever more present, ever more exalted, and were put forth by an ever widening group of authors and agents.

We are therefore dealing with several interlocking misconceptions. First, as this book has amply demonstrated, the divine origins of the royal office were integral to high medieval concepts of kingship. Sacrality surfaces in theological writings, letters, charters and narrative sources. The future status of first kings was presaged by visions and miracles, and they had, at least in theory, been elevated to the royal dignity because of their willingness to execute the will of God. Securing the succession was a matter of personal responsibility towards one's relatives, dependants and people, and to God, and electors were supposed to be guided solely by the divine spirit in casting their votes. In this regard, inauguration ceremonies reinforced sacrality. But they did not *create* it.

---

[156] Ruiz, 'Unsacred monarchy'. See also: Peter Linehan, 'The king's touch and the dean's ministrations: aspects of sacral monarchy', in *The Work of Jacques Le Goff and the Challenges of Medieval History*, ed. Miri Rubin (Woodbridge, 1997), 189–206.

[157] Koziol, 'England, France'.

[158] Franz-Reiner Erkens, *Herrschersakralität im Mittelalter. Von den Anfängen biz zum Investiturstreit* (Stuttgart, 2006), 210–11.

[159] See, for instance, Bernhard Töpfer, 'Tendenzen zur Entskralisierung der Herrscherwürde in der Zeit des Investiturstreites', *Jahrbuch für Geschichte des Feudalismus* 6 (1982), 164–71. See also the critique by Körntgen, 'Sakrales Königtum' and 'Herrscherbild im Wandel'.

[160] Erkens, *Herrschersakralität*, 213–14; Jacques Le Goff, Éric Palazzo, Jean-Claude Bonne and Marie-Noël Colette, eds., *Le sacre royal à l'époque de Saint Louis d'après le manuscrit Latin 1246 de la BNF* (Paris, 2001); M. Cecilia Gaposchkin, *The Making of Saint Louis: Kingship, Sanctity, and Crusade in the Later Middle Ages* (Ithaca, NY, 2008).

V. INAUGURATION   343

Equally, where no unction was administered, this did not indicate that a religious dimension was absent. There were other ways in which the relationship between the divine and the king could be ascertained – for instance by having an enthronement take place in a church, the insignia being handed over by bishops or the ceremony being embedded in a religious service.

Second, just as the absence of crowning or anointing did not make the religious foundations of royal power any less important, so their presence did not turn kings into numinous beings. Indeed, we may safely assume that most medieval observers would have been sufficiently familiar with the Old Testament to know that, even in the Bible, the command not to touch the Lord's anointed was honoured mostly in the breach. Unction did not save Saul. Anointing had raised him above his people, but he forfeited his protected status once he defied the will of God. Indeed, the subsequent history of Israelite kingship is written in the blood of anointed rulers murdered by rebels, relatives and rivals.[161] Moreover, most twelfth-century clerics would have resisted the idea that anointing conferred a quasi-prophetic status upon the ruler. Even in the Old Testament, kings required reprimand and admonition, and coronation *ordines* were explicit in assigning responsibility for the interpretation of God's will to the clergy. At most, as in Sicily, the ruler might participate in their *ministerium*. In fact, *because* royal power had been granted by God, the king bore even greater responsibility to ensure that he fulfilled the duties and obligations that so elevated a status carried with it.[162] And those included looking for the advice of wise and learned men, seeking out prudent counsellors and virtuous advisors and heeding the admonitions of his clergy.

The high medieval rulers who celebrated, patronised or helped initiate the cults of martyred ancestors and predecessors would also have recognised that royal sacrality alone did little to prolong the royal lifespan. Killing the king was a bad thing, whether or not he had been anointed. If rulers had to be disposed of, then it was not as kings, but as usurpers of a dignity that God alone could bestow. They had already forfeited the right to the title and the authority it gave. Under such circumstances, anointing or crowning brought few advantages, as the disembodied spectres of Harold II of England, Rudolf of Rheinfelden or Magnus Erlingsson of Norway could testify. At best, to kill one's rival for the throne was deemed uncouth. Amends had to be made. In eleventh-century Hungary, Ladislaus I refused to wear his crown for seven

---

[161] See, for instance, the deaths of Ahaziah (2 Kings 9:22–28); Jehoash (2 Kings 12:1, 21; 2 Chronicles 24:25); Amon (2 Kings 22:1); Josiah (2 Kings 23:29); Nadab (1 Kings 14:20); Ela (1 Kings 16); Ahab (1 Kings 22); Jehoram (2 Kings 8); Zechariah (2 Kings 15:8–12); Shallum (2 Kings 15:14–17); Pekahiah (2 Kings 15:24); Pekah (2 Kings 16:9).

[162] Which, incidentally, is also how Burgess, 'Divine right of kings', understood sacrality to work in practice. It's just that the Stuart kings were rather less apt at expressing that view. In any case, the misfortunes of James VI's son rather prove my point that the protection offered by sacrality had its limits.

344   9. ENTHRONING THE KING

years because he had seized the throne from his brother. In León, the succession struggles after the death of Fernando I meant that anointing was suspended. And in 1066 William the Conqueror endowed a monastic foundation at the site of the Battle of Hastings, partly so as to atone for the bloodshed that had brought him to the throne.[163] But in each case the one who deposed his royal rivals still succeeded to the throne. Indeed, Ladislaus was eventually himself declared a saint. If anything, just as crowning and anointing became more common, so did the killing of kings. In later medieval England, John and Henry III faced assassination attempts, while Edward II, Richard II, Henry VI and Richard III died violent deaths either in battle or at the hands of their erstwhile subjects. That makes six out of the eleven kings ruling between 1199 and 1485. And few late medieval Scottish kings – the first to have received unction – died of natural causes. Crowning and anointing did not make the royal person sacrosanct.

The most fruitful approach towards royal sacrality is therefore also the simplest: to follow the sources. Kingship was rooted in the divine, they insist. Only God could bestow legitimate royal power. He did so at the behest of the people, and so as to reward those most capable of being shepherds and guardians of their flock. Sacrality manifested itself in remaining cognisant of these duties, which included the protection of the Church and ensuring the right order of the realm. It could mean healing scrofula, going on pilgrimage, ensuring that due veneration was paid to the saints, but also keeping the peace, defending the realm and protecting those who could not protect themselves. It involved knowing divine law, maintaining the *memoria* of one's predecessors, seeing to the spiritual well-being of one's people, listening to sage counsel and attending religious services.[164] How abstract concepts were translated into concrete political practice did vary between rulers and realms and over time. But wherever we have the evidence with which to trace how contemporaries conceptualised kingship, these principles underpinned how the relationship

---

[163] Bates, *William the Conqueror*, 286.
[164] See, for instance, Nicholas Vincent, 'The pilgrimages of the Angevin kings of England, 1154–1272', in *Pilgrimage. The English Experience from Becket to Bunyan*, ed. Colin Morris and Peter Roberts (Cambridge, 2002), 12–45; Vincent, 'King Henry III and the blessed Virgin Mary', *Studies in Church History* 39 (2006), 126–46; Aleksandre Twardaze, '"Das Leben des Königs Wachtang Gorgasali". Christliche Weltanschauung in Djuanschers Chronik aus dem 11. Jahrhundert', *AKG* 88 (2006), 45–74; Werner Tietz, '*Rex humillimus*. Heiligkeit bei Helgaud von Fleury', *Hagiographica* 4 (1997), 113–32; Stephen Marritt, 'Prayers for the king and royal titles in Anglo-Norman charters', *ANS* 32 (2009), 184–202; Thomas Callahan Jr, 'Sinners and saintly retribution: the timely death of King Stephen's son Eustace, 1153', *Studia Monastica* 18 (1976), 109–17; Charles Biskho, 'Liturgical intercession at Cluny for the king-emperors of Leon', *Studia Monastica* 3 (1961), 53–76; Terézia Kerny, 'Das Engelkrönungsmotiv in der Ikonographie König Stephans des Heiligen', *Acta Ethnographica Hungarica* 49 (2004), 313–42.

V. INAUGURATION   345

between rulership and the sacred was understood. They did not elevate the
king to a distinct spiritual sphere. In all likelihood, to most high medieval
observers, the sacral dimension of power was something quite self-evident and
almost quotidian. Because of that, they also approached it in a far more
pragmatic fashion than many a modern medievalist.[165]

The medieval evidence tallies with recent work in anthropology and in
the sociology of religion.[166] The meaning of sacrality could differ widely
depending on audiences and context. It was expressed differently during
ceremonies celebrating the bestowing of kingship, in liturgical texts
designed for the king's private contemplation, during crown-wearings, in
battle, assemblies, when settling disputes or when appointing bishops. It
provided a framework of meaning, the precise interpretation of which was
left to rulers and their subjects to articulate. Very different concepts of what
royal sacrality entailed could circulate even among the courtiers of Henry II
of England. Attitudes extended from a familiar emphasis on virtue and
responsibility to almost absolutist readings.[167] In contemporary Paris, new
ways of heightening royal sacrality were fashioned just as Ralph Niger and
Stephen Langton argued that the sacrality of the king's office necessitated
oversight by the ruled.[168] And sacrality was in the eye of the beholder. It
could only be conferred by others. Bestowing or confirming sacrality
acquired particular importance not only because it was a marker of status,
but also because it represented one's responsibility for the well-being of the
realm. Failing to perform one's role not only risked one's standing with the
community of the realm, but also constituted a betrayal of one's duties
before God. Hence the fervour with which successive archbishops of
Canterbury sought to control who placed a crown on the royal head, and
with which the monks of St Denis disputed the coronation rights of the
canons of St Remi. Sacrality ultimately meant that the right order of the

---

[165] Mine is rather more narrow definition than the one proposed by Antonsson, *St Mágnus of Orkney*, 199: '"Sacral kingship" is a concept that, if it is to signify anything, refers to the belief that the ruler stood in a supernatural relationship with the gods and was perceived as an intermediary between his people and the divine.' For another definition: Erkens, *Herrschersakralität*, 30–2. See also the important points made by Körntgen, *Königsherrschaft, passim*, and 447–50 for a concise summary.

[166] See, especially, David Graeber and Marshall Sahlins, *On Kingship* (Chicago, 2017), 377–463. Alan Strathern, *Unearthly Powers: Religious and Political Change in World History* (Cambridge, 2019), appeared too recently for its argument to be fully incorporated. See, however, ibid., 155–217, which applies the Graeber/Sahlins model in a broad global perspective, though one very much focussed on the period *c.* 1400–1800. R. Andrew Chesnut, *Devoted To Death: Santa Muerte, the Skeleton Saint* (Oxford, 2012); Robert A. Orsi, *Madonna on 115th Street: Faith and Community in Italian Harlem, 1880–1950*, 25th anniversary edition (London, 2010).

[167] Weiler, 'Thinking about power'.

[168] Buc, *L'Ambiguïté*.

346   9. ENTHRONING THE KING

realm was preserved. It did not set the king apart from his people, but reinforced the bonds between them.

9.5   The Crown as Symbol and Object

What does this mean for the place of the inauguration ceremony in the king-making process? There clearly was a numinous dimension to it. In the Sicilian *ordo*, the king's responsibility extended to ensuring good harvests – a concept that, by the twelfth century, was already somewhat archaic.[169] But then such conservatism tallies with the general structure of the coronation, with its emphasis on precedent and on the roots of the realm that transcended the individual ruler. One should not, of course, underestimate the emotional impact of these festivities. Inaugurations were rare events. Most onlookers would not experience them more than once or twice during their adult lives. The festivities marked an end of uncertainty, but also created new hopes and new anxieties. They were also truly grandiose occasions. Peter of Eboli's account of Henry VI's imperial coronation in 1194 conveys a sense of the sensual splendour on display:

> Balsam, frankincense, aloes, nutmeg, cinnamon, nard
> Customary for kings, amber of mild odor,
> Perfume the streets and houses and spread their scent throughout the city.
> The smoke of aromatic frankincense spirals everywhere;
> The road is clothed with sweet-smelling myrtle along with pinks;
> The lily flourishes next to the saffron-colored roses.
> The first house of the temple [i.e. Church] is adorned in fine linen and purple,
> The fiery wax candles shine like stars in their pine-wood holders. However,
> The interior house, where the table sparkles and also the Lamb [I.e. Christ],
> A work of much skillful labor, glows with purple in the golden place.
> There, by your office, [St] Peter, the pious hero is led in,
> Resplendent, and placed before the steps of the altar.[170]

On top of all this, the inauguration would ideally have brought together everyone who mattered. If not all, then most of the great princes and prelates of the realm would be in attendance, together with their entourage. Where a liturgy was performed, the continuous reiteration of the duties of kingship, and of the exceptional character of the act performed, would have reinforced the sense that something quite out of the ordinary was taking place.

A crowning furthermore constituted kingship in the sense that it marked an individual's succession to the throne, his assumption of the office with all the

---

[169] Marita Blattmann, "'Ein Unglück für sein Volk". Der Zusammenhang zwischen Fehlverhalten des Königs und Volkswohl in Quellen des 7. – 12. Jahrhunderts', *FmSt* 30 (1996), 80–102.

[170] Peter of Eboli, *Liber ad Honorem*, 122–3.

V. INAUGURATION 347

responsibilities that it entailed. In realms where coronations were practised, possession of the (or at least of a) crown mattered. A royal diadem remained the physical representation of the ruler's office as bestowed by God. From the thirteenth century, and especially in France and Hungary, it also communicated the numinous quality of kingship independently of the ruler. The office and the realm, but not the individual monarch, were sacralised.[171] Yet it would be mistaken to project later developments in one particular realm back in time and upon the whole of Europe. In practice, receipt of a crown was a token of sovereignty. That was the case in Hungary, where it was bestowed after an intervention from heaven, and in Armenia, where Lewon had to wear several diadems to avoid offending neighbours and putative allies.[172] The charters of Emperor Frederick Barbarossa convey a similar image. His actions were meant to preserve and enhance the honour of the imperial crown, while followers were rewarded for their loyalty towards and rebels punished because of their contempt for it.[173] The crown stood for the realm at large.

Given this symbolic significance, it was appropriate that it did not form part of a ruler's everyday garb. It was displayed only on special occasions, and in particularly festive contexts.[174] In England, for instance, the king wore the crown at Easter and Christmas and during the queen's coronation.[175] Comparable patterns have been traced for Hungary,[176] France, Sicily and the Iberian kingdoms.[177] For the Holy Roman Empire, Hans-Walter Klewitz has counted thirty-eight imperial crown-wearings between c. 1000 and 1235 (a by

---

[171] László, 'The Holy Crown'; Gábor Klaniczay, 'La royauté sacrée des Arpadiens dans l'historiographie hongroise médiévale et moderne', Comptes rendus. Académie des Inscriptions et Belles-Lettres 157 (2015), 595–619; Yves Sassier, 'La Corona regni: émergence d'une persona ficta dans la France du XIIe siècle', in La puissance royale: image et pouvoir de l'Antiquité au Moyen Âge, ed. Emmanuelle Santinelli and Christian-Georges Schwentzel (Rennes, 2012), 99–110.

[172] See above, Chapter 3.

[173] Urkunden Friedrichs II., vol. 1, nos. 30, 119, 188, 219; vol. 2, nos. 226, 244, 268, 288 (copying a charter of Conrad III's, Die Urkunden Konrads III., no. 29), 348, 372, 451, 456, 457, 463, 466, 489, 521; vol. 3, nos. 558, 613, 634, 640, 645, 664, 743, 748, 749, 750, 795; vol. 4, nos. 851, 930, 935, 938, 1025, 1026. See also Dale, Inauguration and Liturgical Kingship, 78–9.

[174] Schramm, Krönung in England, 57–9; Ernst H. Kantorowicz, Laudes regiae. A Study in Liturgical Acclamations and Medieval Ruler Worship (Berkeley, CA, 1943), 93; Dale, Inauguration and Liturgical Kingship, 136–41.

[175] The Peterborough Chronicle 1070–1154, ed. Cecily Clark (Oxford, 1958), 12; Martin Biddle, 'Seasonal festivals and residence: Winchester, Westminster and Gloucester in the tenth to the twelfth centuries', ANS 8 (1986), 51–72, at 51–2.

[176] Dušan Zupka, Ritual and Symbolic Communication in Medieval Hungary under the Árpád Dynasty (1000–1301) (Leiden, 2016), 176 (by the fourteenth century, the king of Hungary was allowed to wear the crown only four times a year).

[177] Carlrichard Brühl, 'Fränkischer Krönungsgebrauch und das Problem der "Festkrönungen"', HZ 194 (1962), 265–326, at 270 n. 2, 292–4.

348   9. ENTHRONING THE KING

no means comprehensive list). Of these, six occurred at Christmas, ten at
Easter, ten at Pentecost, seven on other feast days and five on miscellaneous
occasions, such as the consecration of a cathedral, the coronation of the king's
wife, or a meeting between emperor and pope.[178] When the duke of Bohemia
received a royal crown in 1158, the imperial privilege granting it stipulated that
he was allowed to wear it only on days when the emperor would also wear his,
that is at Easter, Pentecost and Christmas, in addition to the feast days of St
Wenzel and of St Adalbert of Prague.[179] The crown was special, signifying both
the continuity of the realm and the status of kingship. Receiving it was a very
memorable occasion indeed.

In some circumstances, donning the regalia denoted the restoration of the
king's authority and of the kingdom's honour. In 1162, Acerbus of Morena
claimed, Frederick Barbarossa wore his crown for the first time in three years.
He had vowed not to do so until Milan had finally been vanquished.[180]
Similarly, in England kings released from captivity festively wore theirs soon
after having been set free.[181] The crown denoted full and unblemished possession of the royal dignity. There also seems to have been an understanding that
wearing it signified adherence to higher moral values. This attitude underpinned the refusal of Ladislaus to wear a crown because he had expelled his
brother Solomon, and of King Edgar in England because of his past sexual
transgressions. They might be legitimate kings, but they had committed sins of
such gravity that they had to forswear at least temporarily the full display of
royal status. Both readings surface in William of Malmesbury's account of the
coronation of King Eadwig (r. 955–9). The monarch had conducted illicit
affairs simultaneously with his mistress Aelfgifu and with her daughter.[182]
Worse still, during his coronation the king absented himself from the feast,
'alleging necessities of nature', but in reality in order to consort with his female

[178] Hans-Walter Klewitz, 'Die Festkrönungen der deutschen Könige', *ZSRG* 59
(*Kanonistische Abteilung* 28) (1939), 45–96; separate reprint (Darmstadt, 1966), 65–6.
Klewitz should be read alongside the more systematic (but also rather rigid) distinctions
between festive crown-wearing, corroborative crown-wearing, co-crowning and 'walking under the crown' drawn up by Brühl, 'Fränkischer Krönungsgebrauch'. See also the
critique of both by Kurt-Ulrich Jäschke, 'Frühmittelalterliche Festkrönungen?
Überlegungen zu Terminologie und Methode', *HZ* 211 (1970), 556–88, especially at
565–9; and Brühl's response: 'Kronen- und Krönungsgebrauch'.
[179] *Urkunden Friedrichs I.*, vol. 1, no. 201. See also: Percy Ernst Schramm, 'Böhmen und das
Regnum: die Verleihung der Königswürde an die Herzöge von Böhmen (1085/6, 1158,
1198/1203)', in his *Kaiser, Könige und Päpste*, vol. 4, 516–39.
[180] *Acerbus of Morena*, in *Ottonis Morenae et continuatorum Historia Frederici I*, ed.
Ferdinand Güterbock (Hanover and Leipzig, 1930), 158–9.
[181] Knut Görich, 'Verletzte Ehre? König Richard Löwenherz also Gefangener Kaiser
Heinrichs VI.', *Historisches Jahrbuch* 123 (2003), 65–91.
[182] William of Malmesbury, *Saints' Lives. Lives of SS. Wulfstan, Dunstan, Patrick, Benignus
and Indract*, ed. and transl. M. Winterbottom and R. M. Thomson (Oxford, 2002), Vita
Dunstani, i.27, pp. 224–7.

V. INAUGURATION 349

companions. Eventually, St Dunstan went to search for him, and found the king 'sprawled between his whores, his crown flung off, some way away on the floor'.[183] Malmesbury painted a poignant image of the useless king, who, in order to satisfy carnal desires, rejected the duties and moral expectations of his office, and who ultimately was to lose his kingship just as he had once discarded his crown.[184]

The crown communicated royal status. It offered a visible shorthand for the duties and obligations of kingship, but neither the crown as symbol nor the individual object was associated with the numinous. Some of this did, of course, change over time. To this day, the Holy Crown of Hungary remains an expression of Hungarian statehood.[185] Similarly, by the thirteenth century the imperial insignia had come to express the continuity of imperial rule. This was so partly because of their association with Charlemagne. While evidently not the crown worn by the first post-Roman emperor in the west, the specimen still surviving in the Vienna Schatzkammer dates either from the reign of Conrad II (d. 1039) or that of Conrad III (d. 1152).[186] Thus, by the thirteenth century, an invented tradition had conferred upon it associations that established an image of continuity not unlike the numbering of rulers in the *Kaiserchronik*, discussed earlier. Yet it was not a sacred object. Before Richard of Cornwall decreed in 1262 that the imperial insignia be kept at Aachen, they had been pawned as surety for a loan.[187] In the 1260s Henry III of England similarly pawned the crown to repay loans from Italian moneylenders, and Richard's rival Alfonso X of Castile did the same thing to finance a planned campaign in north Africa.[188] As Jürgen Petersohn has argued concerning high medieval German kings, what mattered was that one had a crown that had legitimately been conferred and that was, if possible,

[183] William of Malmesbury, *Saints' Lives, Vita Dunstani*, i.27, pp. 226–7.
[184] William of Malmesbury, *Saints' Lives, Vita Dunstani*, i.28, pp. 228–31; ii.3, pp. 238–41.
[185] Péter, 'The Holy Crown', which is especially intriguing concerning the symbolic permutations and many travails of the crown after the Ottoman conquests and during the nineteenth century. See also Klaniczay, 'La royauté sacrée'.
[186] The debate has been ferocious. Perhaps its most level-headed summary is provided by Sebastian Scholz, 'Die "Wiener Reichskrone": Eine Krone aus der Zeit Konrads II.?', in *Grafen, Herzöge, Könige: der Aufstieg der frühen Staufer und das Reich (1079–1152)*, ed. Hubertus Seibert and Jörg Dendorfer (Ostfildern, 2005), 341–62. The earlier date had been proposed by Mechtild Schulze-Dörrlamm, *Die Kaiserkrone Konrads II (1024–1039). Eine archäologische Untersuchung zu Alter und Herkunft der Reichskrone* (Sigmaringen, 1991).
[187] Armin di Miranda, 'Richard von Cornwallis und sein Verhältnis zur Krönungsstadt Aachen', *Annalen des Historischen Vereins für den Niederrhein* 35 (1880), 65–92; Albert Huyskens, 'Der Plan des Königs Richard von Cornwallis zur Niederlegung eines deutschen Krönungsschatzes in Aachen', *Annalen des Historischen Vereins für den Niederrhein* 115 (1929), 180–204.
[188] William C. Jordan, *A Tale of Two Monasteries: Westminster and Saint-Denis in the Thirteenth Century* (Princeton, NJ, 2009), 104–5.

350   9. ENTHRONING THE KING

associated with one's predecessors.[189] In short, the evident significance of the crown as a symbol of royal status should not be misread as sacralising those wearing it.

Coronation *ordines* and narrative sources recounting a king's inauguration painted an image of timelessness that reflected fundamental assumptions about the royal office and about how things should be: the community of the realm acting in unison, with everyone in their proper place, and nobody driven by base motives. In this regard, inaugurations resembled elections. There, the final public act of choosing a king displayed unanimity and moral probity, irrespective of how a decision had in fact been reached. The enthronement likewise showed what kings should do. Yet, in the process, it limited itself to listing rather than defining. The king vowed to be a faithful son and guardian of the Church, a defender of the realm and protector of widows, peasants and orphans. But these were declarations of intent, not concrete actions that proved the sincerity of his intentions. Much of the remainder of the inauguration, and indeed much of the first few years of a ruler's reign, was taken up with demonstrating a willingness to apply and with attempts at defining these norms. The enthronement created a framework, the precise meaning of which was to be sketched out in what followed: the feast and procession, the appointment of officials, waging of war, doing justice, negotiating the conflicting demands of largesse and equity, balancing the common good against the needs of backers and allies. It was then that rulers truly became kings.

---

[189] Jürgen Petersohn, *Echte und falsche Insignien im deutschen Krönungsbrauch des Mittelalters? Kritik eines Forschungsstereotyps* (Frankfurt, 1993).

10

Beyond Enthronement

Once a throne had successfully been claimed, the hard work of keeping it began. The succession to Wladyslaw of Poland in 1102 provides a case in point. The duke had died at the beginning of June. His funeral marked the beginning of a prolonged struggle over his inheritance, pitching his eldest but illegitimate son, Zbigniew, against his sole legitimate son, Boleslaw. First, however, Wladyslaw's burial had to be delayed. His sons were away campaigning.[1] To this end, Archbishop Martin extended the opening obsequies to last five whole days. As soon as Boleslaw and Zbigniew arrived, they squabbled over their father's inheritance. In the end, Boleslaw received the two chief cities of the realm and its most populous regions, and Zbigniew the rest. 'Now', 'Gallus' concluded, 'that [Boleslaw] had this share of the patrimony and supported by his council and knights, the young Boleslaw set about developing his courage and his bodily strength, and in repute and years began to grow into a youth of fine character.'[2]

The young duke, either fifteen or sixteen years old, took to ruling with much gusto. He conquered the city of Bialograd,[3] and in 1103 married a daughter of the Grand Prince of Kiev. The presents distributed on that occasion, 'Gallus' noted, 'bear comparison with Boleslaw the Great.'[4] Meanwhile, Zbigniew had purportedly invited the Bohemians to invade Boleslaw's lands while the duke was distracted by his nuptials.[5] Boleslaw attacked Moravia in return,[6] but halted his campaign to welcome a papal legate to Poland. Together with the pope's emissary, Boleslaw convened a synod of the Polish higher clergy and assisted in the moral reform of the Polish Church.[7] Further campaigns followed in Pomerania, and efforts were made to forge closer ties with the king of Hungary.[8] Successive

---

[1] For background see above, Chapter 5.
[2] *Gesta Principum Polonorum*, ii.21, pp. 156–9. See also Dalewski, 'Begräbnis des Herrschers'.
[3] *Gesta Principum Polonorum*, ii.22, pp. 158–9.
[4] *Gesta Principum Polonorum*, ii.23, pp. 158–61. See also above, Chapter 6.
[5] *Gesta Principum Polonorum*, ii.24, pp. 160–1.
[6] *Gesta Principum Polonorum*, ii.25–6, pp. 162–7.
[7] *Gesta Principum Polonorum*, ii.27, pp. 166–7.
[8] *Gesta Principum Polonorum*, ii.28–33, pp. 166–81.

352   10. BEYOND ENTHRONEMENT

attempts to reach a concord with Zbigniew proved fruitless. In 1105/6, a planned conference collapsed when Zbigniew used it as a pretext to attack his brother.[9] When, in the summer of 1106, Boleslaw sent envoys once again, Zbigniew imprisoned them and sought to bring about an armed showdown.[10] Probably later that year or possibly in 1107, Zbigniew was defeated in battle. He had no choice but to submit to Boleslaw, who granted him Mazovia, 'but as a knight, not a lord. . . . Boleslaw could now move about Poland wherever he pleased'.[11]

Even from the highly partisan account of 'Gallus' it is possible to derive a sense of why Zbigniew may have felt aggrieved. He was the eldest son, yet he had to defend his claims against a younger half-sibling. He had to be satisfied with the less prosperous part of the realm and with its smaller towns. He was, from the outset, placed at a disadvantage. That was exacerbated by the humiliation of being ranked below his brother and the damage that did to his reputation and standing. His was the first case in Polish history when an eldest son did not succeed to the throne. Neither had anything similar happened in neighbouring Bohemia or Germany. Zbigniew had to act if he wanted to keep what was his already and if he wanted to see off his sibling. He searched for allies in Bohemia and among pagans, and tried to overcome his brother in battle. That he did so repeatedly, and to such little avail, probably helped accelerate his ultimate defeat. Still, he did what every claimant to the throne attempted: to garner support, to act like a good ruler and to outmanoeuvre his rivals.

He certainly presented a more formidable challenge than 'Gallus' let on. It took Boleslaw nearly five years before he could 'move about Poland wherever he pleased'. Zbigniew was able to pose so serious a threat because he did not act on his own. There were his Czech allies, but he would have been unable to muster troops without the backing of at least some Polish magnates, and certainly not without that of his own men. In fact, while only mentioned in passing by 'Gallus', princes and prelates played a prominent role throughout the conflict. Archbishop Martin may conceivably have sought to use the funeral to secure an amicable succession. The papal legate probably arrived thanks to the efforts of Bishop Baldwin of Kraków, who had been dispatched to secure papal dispensation for Boleslaw's consanguineous marriage. Baldwin was also named as one of the intercessors who facilitated the temporary reconciliation between the siblings in 1106/7.[12] No lay princes were granted such prominence. Still, when Boleslaw began his reign, he did so, as 'Gallus' noted, 'supported by his council and knights'. They guided him in 'developing

---

[9] Gesta Principum Polonorum, ii.32, pp. 174–5.
[10] Gesta Principum Polonorum, ii.36, pp. 184–7.
[11] Gesta Principum Polonorum, ii.38, pp. 190–1. The peace was not to last. The wars between the brothers continued until Boleslaw had Zbigniew blinded. See above, Chapter 5.
[12] Gesta Principum Polonorum, ii.38, pp. 188–9.

V. INAUGURATION 353

his courage and his bodily strength'.[13] That the magnates were not mere onlookers is further suggested by how 'Gallus' framed Zbigniew's surrender. Because he had allied himself with pagans, giving them generous gifts and ensuring that they attacked Boleslaw's lands, 'all the wise men of Poland were angry and their friendship with Zbigniew turned to hatred'. They complained of his untrustworthiness, lamented that he sowed division in Poland and that he 'listened to quite childish and harmful counsel'. They therefore decided to back Boleslaw.[14] This implies that Zbigniew's backing from among the Polish aristocracy was at least one factor that allowed him to continue competing not just for a share, but for the entirety of Wladyslaw's inheritance. The rivalry between the brothers had been made possible and had perhaps even been fuelled by some of the great men of the realm.[15]

When the 'wise men of Poland' chose to side with Boleslaw, they also fulfilled the obligation that had been laid upon them by Wladyslaw. In 1099 the duke had granted the right to choose his successor to the Polish princes. They should pick whichever of his sons would defend the honour of the realm and ward off foreign enemies.[16] In the rendering of 'Gallus' Boleslaw clearly was that person. Where Zbigniew was untrustworthy, Boleslaw was steadfast and patient even with his elder sibling. Where Zbigniew listened to childish and harmful advice, Boleslaw was guided by worthy knights and counsellors. They certainly enabled him to develop 'his courage and his bodily strength, [so that] in repute and years [he] began to grow into a youth of fine character'. Where Zbigniew was dependent on foreign invaders to pursue his claims, Boleslaw defeated the enemies of the realm. Where Zbigniew consorted with pagans, Boleslaw welcomed a papal legate.[17] And where Zbigniew desperately lavished gifts on pagan plunderers, Boleslaw III acted in the mould of Boleslaw I.[18] He was a worthy successor not just to his father, but to the first Polish king.

No inauguration was recorded for 1102, but the settlement of 1099 fulfilled many of the same functions. It set out what a ruler should do, what the basic principles were on which his authority would rest and in the service of which he should wield his power. Boleslaw and Zbigniew tried to demonstrate that they deserved their titles and that they were each more capable of ruling than the other sibling. They attempted to flesh out through concrete actions the

---

[13] *Gesta Principum Polonorum*, ii.21, pp. 156–9.
[14] *Gesta Principum Polonorum*, ii.35, pp. 182–5.
[15] The evidence is inconclusive at best, but it may be worth speculating whether the two unnamed bishops deposed by the papal legate could have been linked to Zbigniew: *Gesta Principum Polonorum*, ii.27, pp. 166–7.
[16] *Gesta Principum Polonorum*, ii.8, pp. 132–5. See above, Chapter 5.
[17] *Gesta Principum Polonorum*, ii.27, pp. 166–7.
[18] See above, Chapter 3. For the ritual contrast between the brothers, see the essential study by Zbigniew Dalewski, *Ritual and Politics. Writing the History of Dynastic Conflict in Medieval Poland* (Leiden and Boston, 2008).

354   10. BEYOND ENTHRONEMENT

abstract principles outlined by their father. In this regard, they were representative of broader European trends. The first few years of a ruler's reign
constituted an extended demonstration of his suitability for the throne, showing not only that he shared, but also that he was willing and able to enforce,
a common understanding of his duties. While the inauguration ceremony
highlighted norms, the king's subsequent performance spelt out what they
meant. It allowed his subjects to assess and, in a worst case scenario, to revisit
their earlier choice. This was the time when norms like justice or keeping the
peace were filled with concrete meaning. It was when the ability to balance the
conflicting expectations of subjects, of treading the fine line between equity
and largesse, between righteous anger and pious mercy had to be honed and
displayed. It was when new rulers had to deal with the unexpected and
unforeseen, with disruption and discontent. Elections and inaugurations
could be stage-managed to a considerable degree. Actual government less so.
How then could kings prove that they deserved to keep the crown?

10.1   Feasts, Processions and the Public

A ruler's enthronement celebrated the transition from candidate to king. It
represented the transfer of power not only from one monarch to the next, but
also from the people to their new ruler. Ideally, it would be a public event.
A sizable crowd implied if not complete unanimity, then at least strong
backing, especially if the succession was disputed. In 1152, Frederick
Barbarossa was elected at Bamberg on 4 March, and crowned at Aachen on
9 March, a distance of 450 km. His election had been as unexpected as the
death of his predecessor. There had been no time to gather the great men of the
realm.[19] Otto of Freising therefore marvelled at the many princes and prelates
who attended the coronation, including those from 'western Gaul', whom
nobody had expected to have received news of the event so quickly.[20]
Frederick's fame was such that even those not party to his election hurried to
attend his coronation.

Most of the time, just hoping for news to spread was not enough. In 1130,
Roger II of Sicily mandated that anyone of any dignity, honour or power be
present at Palermo to witness his coronation.[21] In 1170, Henry II of England
took similar steps for the crowning of his eldest son.[22] More commonly, the

---

[19]   See, however, Stefanie Dick's suggestion that Barbarossa utilised an event planned for the
installation of his eponymous cousin, the underage son of Conrad III: Dick, 'Die
Königserhebung'. For a critical response to Dick's thesis see Jan Paul Niederkorn, 'Zu
glatt und daher verdächtig? Zur Glaubwürdigkeit der Schilderung der Wahl Friedrich
Barbarossas (1152) durch Otto von Freising', *MIÖG* 115 (2007), 1–9.
[20]   Otto of Freising, *Gesta Frederici*, ii.3, pp. 286–7.
[21]   Alexander of Telese, *Ystoria Rogerii*, 25.
[22]   Roger of Howden, *Gesta*, vol. 1, 5.

V. INAUGURATION   355

ceremony was combined with religious festivities, at a venue that enabled the
assembly of a sufficient number of leading clerics and laymen. This was the
case in Castile in 1065 and in Denmark in 1170. Concerning the latter coronation, the *Annals of Lund* still marvelled a century later at the countless
populace, as well as the many prelates and magnates in attendance.[23] Bad
kings and tyrants, by contrast, had their inaugurations witnessed by only a few.
William of Malmesbury maintained that Stephen's in 1135 had been attended
'by only three bishops, no abbots, and only a handful of great men'.[24] Burchard
of Ursberg, writing about the Imperial Double Election of 1198, also stressed
that Otto IV was supported by just a few men, who were morally corrupt to
boot. An inability to demonstrate wide backing (and from the right kind of
people) denoted weakness, and carried with it the sheen of illegitimacy and
usurpation.

This posed challenges to rulers who came to the throne under circumstances
where a large public could not easily be assembled. Then, additional steps had
to be taken. In 1209, Otto IV repeated his coronation. Something comparable
occurred in England in 1220. On the death of King John in 1216, with London
supporting a rival claimant and Westminster therefore out of reach, the infant
Henry III had been crowned in a rather haphazard fashion at Winchester. In
1220, with Henry's claim secure, the coronation was repeated, this time at
Westminster and with the appropriate appurtenances of office.[25] In 1100,
Henry I of England had rushed to Winchester on hearing news of his brother's
death, seeking to pre-empt his older brother Robert's claiming the throne. In
fact, he did not even have an archbishop at hand to perform the coronation.
Anselm of Canterbury was still in exile, while Gerald of York was delayed.
Hence the bishop of Winchester had to officiate in their stead.[26] Another
option was to have a coronation recognised by either the pope or a papal
legate. This occurred in Germany in 1077, 1125, 1138 and 1212,[27] in England
during Stephen's reign,[28] in Sicily in 1193[29] and in Norway in 1160 and 1194.[30]
Whatever the means chosen, the lack of a public demanded that additional
measures be employed to ensure the legitimacy of a ruler's inauguration.

---

[23] *Annales Lundenses*, in *Danmarks Middelalderlige Annaler*, ed. Erik Korman
(Copenhagen, 1980), 59.
[24] William of Malmesbury, *Historia Novella*, 28–9.
[25] Roger of Wendover, *Rogeri de Wendover Chronica sive Flores Historiarum*, ed.
H. O. Coxe, 5 vols. (London, 1841–4), vol. 4, 2–3.
[26] William of Malmesbury, *Gesta Regum Anglorum*, v.393, vol. 1, 714–15; Green, *Henry I*,
42–4.
[27] Tilmann Schmidt, 'Eine unbekannte Urkunde Innocenz' III. mit dem Legatenbericht zur
Wahl und Krönung Friedrichs II. von 1212/1213', *Mitteilungen des Instituts für
Österreichische Geschichtsforschung* 115 (2007), 25–34, at 32–3.
[28] Richard of Hexham, *Historia de Gestis*, 147–8.
[29] Christian Reisinger, *Tankred von Lecce* (Cologne, Weimar and Vienna, 1992), 75–6.
[30] *Saga of King Sverri*, chapter 123, pp. 154–5.

356   10. BEYOND ENTHRONEMENT

Finally, a suitably large and prominent public constituted a warning to foes and rivals, and offered assurances to anyone wary of a new king. This dual role contextualises the importance attached to coronation feasts and processions. When, in the 1230s, Snorri Sturluson recounted the first coronation of a Norwegian king in 1160, he was far more concerned with the splendour of the feast than with the novel ceremony:

> Erling Skakki had a great banquet prepared in the great royal hall, which was hung with costly stuffs and tapestries and outfitted at very great expense. Both his following and all retainers were entertained there, with a great number of guests and many chieftains present. Magnus was then consecrated as king by Archbishop Eystein, and at the coronation there were present five other bishops, the papal legate, and many clerics. ... And on the day on which the coronation took place, the king and Erling had as their guests the archbishop, the papal legate, and all the bishops, and that banquet was a most splendid one. Both father and son gave [the guests] many magnificent presents.[31]

The feast was referred to twice, and both depictions were embedded in a record of Erling's wealth – the expensive hangings and costly cloths adorning the hall, as well as the splendid gifts given to those in attendance. It was deemed far more significant than the circumstance that, for the first time in Norwegian history, a formal coronation had taken place.

Why was this so? Feasts displayed the power of the new ruler, the extent of his backing and his suitability for office.[32] Particular care was taken in staging and planning them when a claim to the throne was in dispute. This had been the case in Norway in 1160. Not only was Magnus the first ruler not himself the son of a king, but he was also a mere eight years old.[33] In Scotland in 1214, Alexander II – who potentially faced several rival claimants – held a feast lasting three days. The inauguration, John de Fordun remarked, had been so

---

[31] Snorri Sturluson, *Heimskringla*, Saga of Magnus Erlingsson, chapter 22, p. 807.

[32] This has been explored primarily in an early medieval context: Gerd Althoff, 'Der frieden-, bündnis-, und gemeinschaftstiftende Charakter des Mahles im früheren Mittelalter', in *Essen und Trinken in Mittelalter und Neuzeit: Vorträge eines interdisziplinären Symposions vom 10. bis 13. Juni an der Justus-Liebig-Universität Gießen*, ed. Irmgard Bitsch, Trude Ehlert and Xenja von Ertzdorff (Sigmaringen, 1987), 13–26; Levi Roach, 'Hosting the king: hospitality and the royal *iter* in tenth-century England', *JMedH* 37 (2011), 34–46. For later periods: Hans Jacob Orning, 'Festive governance: feasts as rituals of power and integration in medieval Norway', in *Rituals, Performatives and Political Order in Northern Europe, c.650–1350*, ed. Wojtek Jezierski, Lars Hermanson, Hans Jacob Orning and Thomas Småberg (Turnhout, 2015), 175–208; Lars Kjaer, 'Feasting with traitors: royal banquets as rituals and texts in high medieval Scandinavia', in *Rituals, Performatives*, ed. Jezierski et al., 237–68.

[33] Snorri Sturluson, *Heimskringla*, Saga of Magnus Erlingsson, chapter 23–6, pp. 807–10. On the context see also: Kevin J. Wanner, '*At Smyrja Konung Til veldis*: royal legitimation in Snorri Sturluson's *Magnús Saga Erlingsonar*', *Saga-Book* 30 (2006), 5–38.

V. INAUGURATION   357

lavish that nobody had ever been enthroned 'with more grandeur and glory until then'.[34] Henry III's coronation as king of England in 1216 had been a similarly makeshift affair. Even so, Roger of Wendover noted about a decade later, the feast was most sumptuous, with the participants, seated according to their rank, full of hilarity and joy.[35] Even Geoffrey of Monmouth employed the trope: on his installation as king, Arthur had received so many knights that he ran out of gifts.[36]

A lavish feast displayed the extent of a king's backing and the resources at his disposal. The theme underpinned Alexander of Telese's account of Roger II's coronation feast in 1130:

> The royal palace was on its entire walls gloriously draped throughout. The pavement was bestrewed with multi-coloured carpets and showed off flowing softness to the feet of those who trod there. When the king went to church for the ceremony, he was surrounded by dignitaries, and the huge number of horses which accompanied them had saddles and bridles decorated with gold and silver. Large amounts of the choicest food and drink were served to the diners at the royal table, and nothing was served except in dishes or cups of gold or silver. There was no servant there who did not wear a silk tunic – the very waiters were clad in silk clothes! What more? The glory and wealth of the royal abode was so spectacular that it caused a great wonder and deep stupefaction – so great indeed that it instilled not a little fear in all those who had come from so far away. For many saw there more things than they had heard rumoured previously.[37]

The display was designed to awe Roger's people. Indeed, feasts could inspire fear and obedience. In 1171, Henry II of England received the submission of the rulers of Ireland. Gerald of Wales recounted that

> As the solemn festival of Our Lord's birth drew near, the princes of that land came to Dublin in great number to view the king's court. There they greatly admired the sumptuous and plentiful fare of the English table and the most elegant service by the king's domestics. Throughout the great hall, in obedience to the king's wishes they began to eat the flesh of the crane, which they had hitherto loathed.[38]

The events at Dublin were a demonstration of the wealth (the sumptuous fare), sophistication (the elegant service) and sheer might of the English ruler (Henry ordering his Irish subjects to eat crane – infamous for its bitter taste and tough

---

[34] John de Fordun, *Gesta Annalia*, vol. 1, 280, vol. 2, 276.
[35] Roger of Wendover, *Flores Historiarum*, vol. 2, 2.
[36] Geoffrey of Monmouth, *History of the Kings*, 192–3.
[37] Alexander of Telese, *Ystoria Rogerii*, 26; *Roger II.*, ed. Loud, 79.
[38] Gerald of Wales, *Expugnatio Hibernica. The Conquest of Ireland*, ed. and transl. A. B. Scott and F. X. Martin (Dublin, 1978), 96.

358   10. BEYOND ENTHRONEMENT

texture).[39] As at Palermo, feasting was not just about celebrating a king's succession. It also allowed him to instil fear into his people. To that end, harsh measures could sometimes be taken. On the day of his coronation, Sverrir of Norway reputedly had the last of his rivals put to death, with the severed head paraded before his guests.[40] The textual evidence for the festivities at Palermo and Dublin resembles how 'Gallus Anonymus' had framed the encounter between Duke Boleslaw I of Poland and Emperor Otto III in 999/ 1000. Boleslaw so shamed the emperor with the munificence of his gifts, the splendour of his court and the magnificence of his entourage, that Otto could only respond by placing his crown on Boleslaw's head.[41] Boleslaw and Roger became kings, and Henry the lord of Ireland, because they had the power, resources and men that raised them above their peers and subjects.

Behaving like a ruler in front of as many witnesses as possible was integral to the performance of kingship, and extended well beyond the inauguration and the feast. In 1092, Brestislav II was installed as duke of Bohemia:

> Approaching the burg of Prague with happy choirs of both girls and boys positioned at various crossroads, singing to pipes and drums, and with the bells ringing throughout the churches, the common folk joyfully received him. Together with the clergy and a magnificent procession, Bishop Cosmas himself took Duke Bretislav the Younger through the gate of the burg and led him to the throne before the Church of St Mary. There he was enthroned by all the *comites* and satraps according to the rite of the land.[42]

The procession displayed the ruler in regal (or quasi-regal) majesty. It signalled that he was ready to take charge of the affairs of the realm, and that he was supported by people, prelates and princes alike. When the underage Alfonso VII of Castile was enthroned as king in 1111, the festivities included a procession designed to display the king in his full regalia and thereby to establish his authority.[43] Conversely, when Duke Henry of Saxony sought to claim the throne in 984, he usurped the ritual language of kingship by having the *laudes regiae*, the liturgical acclamation of the ruler, sung to greet him.[44] Something similar occurred in twelfth-century Sicily. To Hugo Falcandus, writing almost contemporaneously with events, the constitutive element of the succession of William II in 1166 appears to have been a procession in which

---

[39] I owe this point to Hugh Thomas.
[40] Roger of Howden, *Chronica*, vol. 3, 270. Roger likely drew on what he heard from the exiled archbishop of Nidaros. Duggan, 'The English exile'; but see also Edward Carlsson Browne, 'Roger of Howden and the unknown royalty of twelfth-century Norway', *Quaestio Insularis* 11 (2010), 75–96.
[41] See above, Chapter 3.
[42] Cosmas of Prague, *Chronicon*, 157; Cosmas of Prague, *Chronicle*, 179–80.
[43] *Historia Compostellana*, 106.
[44] Thietmar, *Chronicon*, iv.2, pp. 116–17. See also above, Chapter 7.

V. INAUGURATION 359

the new ruler rode through the streets of Palermo.[45] No mention was made of anointing or crowning. When a few years earlier, a group of rebel barons imprisoned William I and sought to replace him, 'they took the king's elder son Duke Roger from the palace and made him ride round the whole city, showing him off to everyone and telling the common people not to call anyone else their king from now on'.[46] Hugo held the rebels in low regard. He established an implicit contrast between William II, who – despite being under age and in his mother's care – demonstrated agency by *choosing* to ride through Palermo, and Roger, who had been *forced* to do so. Still, in both instances kingship was established by the public display of the royal person to the populace at large. To paraphrase Timothy Reuter: in order to be king, one had to act like one, and that meant being seen to act like one.[47]

Feasts and processions continued a theme central to the enthronement ceremony as a whole: maintaining the right order of the world. In 1092 at Prague, the people greeted and welcomed the duke, who was escorted to the throne by the bishop, and acclaimed by the great men of the realm. Other sources emphasise that everyone was seated according to their rank. The king displayed his majesty and wealth with rich presents and lavish entertainment (seasoned, if need be, with a sprinkling of menace). All the great men of the realm were present, and demonstrated their place within the kingdom's hierarchy. Hence, at Westminster in 1189, the rivalry between the citizens of London and Winchester over who should serve as butler at the royal table. Hence, too, the importance attached to the ruler's demeanour. William of Malmesbury's account of Eadwig, who absconded from the coronation feast to cavort with his mistresses, derived its poignancy from the fact that the king violated the right order of the world. Worse still, he did so just after having solemnly sworn, before God and his people, to uphold it. Wipo's image of Conrad as ideal ruler also fixed on the king's conduct during the feast, but of course to very different effect. He vacated his seat in favour of a refugee who had sought succour, and commanded the princes to do justice. Feasts and processions marked the first stage in an extended performance during which kings proved that they intended to keep their solemn vows to be defenders of the realm, protectors of the church and guardians of their people.

These occasions helped tie together the component parts of the inauguration. In the days and weeks that followed, rulers did all they could to ensure

---

[45] *History of the Tyrants*, 138; Ugo Falcando, *Il regno di Sicilia*, 190. Romuald of Salerno, by contrast, stressed the royal anointing, followed by a procession: Romuald, *Chronicon*, 254. On William's coronation: Annkristin Schlichte, *'Der gute König'. Wilhelm II. von Sizilien (1166–1189)* (Tübingen, 2005), 7–8.

[46] *History of the Tyrants*, 110; Ugo Falcando, *Il regno di Sicilia*, 132.

[47] Timothy Reuter, *'Regemque, quem in Francia pene perdidit, in patria magnifice recepit*: Ottonian ruler representation in synchronic and diachronic comparison', in his *Medieval Polities*, 127–46, at 128–9.

360   10. BEYOND ENTHRONEMENT

that they were seen to hold the reins of power. In England in 973, or so Gaimar imagined c. 1140, during his coronation feast King Edgar 'established two bishoprics, three abbeys, and several religious houses and lordships. To those who had been disinherited he restored their land. To everyone he behaved so justly that ... each and everyone loved him.'[48] In Germany in 1024, the coronation and feast were followed in quick succession by the crowning of Conrad's queen and the appointment of officials. In Sicily, Roger designated a military leader for his armies right after his inauguration. In 1166, the queen, acting as regent for the underage William II of Sicily, decreed immediately after her son's coronation that all prisoners be set free, lifted unpopular taxes and appointed virtuous officials to oversee the king's administration.[49] The itineration of the realm, on which kings embarked soon after their inauguration, served similar ends. In 1024, the first stops of Conrad II were Lotharingia and Saxony, both regions whose nobles had been noticeably absent from his inauguration. At Aachen, he symbolically placed himself in succession to the first medieval western emperor by sitting on Charlemagne's throne, and won over those in attendance through his prudent application of the law. In Saxony, he received homage from the Saxons, confirmed their legal customs and extracted tributes from the regions bordering on his realm. He then travelled through east Francia before holding a festive diet at Konstanz.[50] Conrad traversed the kingdom and demonstrated his power in each of its constituent parts.

The *Gesta Stephani* place a similar emphasis in describing Stephen's early activities:

> The king therefore, attended by a large bodyguard, made a progress through England with the splendour that befits the royal majesty; those who submitted to his authority, he received with kindness and respect; in all the churches of both orders, also in the cities and castles, he was greeted with an enthusiastic welcome; to all who implored him for their own needs he gave his consent amiably and without pride; he made very great efforts to re-establish peace in the kingdom; he granted no small bounties to restore harmony among his subjects; he spent much sweat and likewise much money to pacify not only England, but also Wales.[51]

Stephen may have followed the precedent set by his grandfather, William the Conqueror. William of Poitiers, the Conqueror's biographer, portrayed him as

---

[48] Gaimar, *Estoire des Engleis*, ed. and transl. Ian Short (Oxford, 2009), ll. 3921–38, pp. 214–15.

[49] *History of the Tyrants*, 138; Ugo Falcando, *Il regno di Sicilia*, 190.

[50] Wipo, *Gesta Chuonradi*, 27–9; *Deeds of Conrad II*, 71–3; Roderich Schmidt, 'Königsumritt und Huldigung in ottonisch-salischer Zeit', in *Königtum, Burgen und Königsfreie / Königsumritt und Huldigung* (Sigmaringen, 1961), 97–233, at 106–14; Wolfram, *Konrad II.*, 74–84.

[51] *Gesta Stephani*, 14–15.

V. INAUGURATION   361

embarking on the moral reform of the realm immediately after his coronation. The king restored the liberties of the Church, shared the riches accumulated by Harold, did justice and collated the laws of the realm, before touring his kingdom.[52] He demonstrated and enacted kingship.

Touring the realm was what rulers did. They displayed and, in some ways, constituted the polity through their presence, and by bringing together leading men of the realm.[53] They did so in Germany and Norway as well as in Bohemia, Castile, Jerusalem and England.[54] For new rulers peripatetic kingship also offered an opportunity to solicit backing, and to seize the material sources of power. In England, Henry I and Stephen hastened to Winchester, where the royal treasury was located, as soon as they were able to. Alternatively, in the 1150s, Frederick Barbarossa in Germany and Valdemar I in Denmark used the opportunity to appoint new bishops at Magdeburg and Roskilde respectively to install trusted leaders, restore royal domains and crucially also to revive flows of revenue. In exemplary fashion, the itinerary of the realm combined pragmatic needs and moral norms. Abstract claims began to be filled with concrete meaning.

10.2   Justice

The reins of power should only be assumed in order that their holder work for the common good. That was *the* foundational principle on which secular power rested. It was enshrined in the Old Testament and in the writings of Cicero and of the Church Fathers. In Isidore of Seville's terms, he could not be

---

[52] William of Poitiers, *Gesta Guillelmi*, 158–67; Bates, *William the Conqueror*, 258–75. For England, see also, Gerald of Wales, *Instruction for a Ruler*, 494–5; Roger of Wendover, *Flores Historiarum*, vol. 3, 137–42; vol. 4, 1–3, 65–8; Church, 'Some aspects'; Julie Kanter, 'Peripatetic and sedentary kingship: the itineraries of John and Henry III', *Thirteenth Century England* 13 (2011), 13–26

[53] Reuter, 'Assembly politics', 192–8.

[54] Klewitz, 'Festkrönungen', 81; Schmidt, 'Königsumritt'; Brégaint, *Vox regis*, 35–7; Orning, *Unpredictability and Presence*; David Kalhous, 'Mittelpunkte der Herrschaft und Cosmas von Prag: Zum Charakter der Macht des frühmittelalterlichen Fürsten', in *Frühgeschichtliche Zentralorte in Mitteleuropa*, ed. Jiri Máchazek and Simon Ungermann (Bonn, 2011), 669–89; Charles Garcia, 'Itinérance de la cour et attaches sédentaires sous Alphonse VI et Urraque Ire', *e-spania* 8 (2013) (https://journals .openedition.org/e-spania/18692); and, though focussing on a later period, Fernando Arias Guillén, 'A kingdom without a capital? Itineration and spaces of royal power in Castile, *c*.1252–1350', *JMedH* 39 (2013), 456–76. In a like vein, it might be worth pondering whether the attention paid to Tripoli and Antioch by Baldwin II or Fulk I of Jerusalem might not reflect attempts to enact royal authority both symbolically and militarily. Albert of Aachen, *Historia*, 540–3; William of Tyre, *Chronicon*, 635–7; *History of Deeds*, vol. 2, 53–5. See also Alan V. Murray, 'Baldwin II and his nobles: Baronial factionalism and dissent in the kingdom of Jerusalem, 1118-1134', *Nottingham Medieval Studies* 38 (1994), 60–85; Murray, 'Dynastic continuity'.

362   10. BEYOND ENTHRONEMENT

a ruler (*rector*) who was not also a corrector. The principle underpinned the image and practice of kingship. Boleslaw I and Roger II merited a royal title because they did justice. First kings codified the law and enforced it with rigour. The willingness and the capacity to work for the common good, not private gain, guided the preparation of heirs for the succession, it underpinned deliberations during a king's election and it was rehearsed at length during his inauguration. But there could be no successful rulership without controlling its material foundations. They enabled a king to wield the sword of justice, but he also had to show that he would wield it with restraint and in a spirit of moral rectitude. How could this be done in practice? And how was that practice conceptualised?

The king's responsibility clearly extended to the moral and religious well-being of his people. An inauguration frequently coincided with the consecration of bishops, as it did during Frederick Barbarossa's and Philipp of Swabia's in Germany,[55] and Sverrir's in Norway.[56] To Otto of Freising, the confluence of events in 1152 was auspicious. With Bishop Frederick of Münster having been consecrated on the same day, in the same church and by the same prelates as the king (with whom he also shared a name), the two types of persons had simultaneously been installed who, according to the Bible, were alike in that they were both the anointed of the Lord.[57] Alternatively, the inauguration could coincide with the translation or the initiation of the liturgical commemoration of a new saint, as was the case in Iberia in 1065, in Denmark in 1170 and when in 1220 the archbishop of Canterbury interrupted Henry III's second coronation to announce that Hugh of Lincoln had been canonised by the pope. In other instances, newly enthroned kings held church councils soon after their inauguration, as Stephen did in 1136, Richard I in 1189 and Henry II in Ireland in 1172.[58] They went on pilgrimage, like Alexander III of Scotland in 1250. They resolved ecclesiastical disputes, as Frederick Barbarossa undertook in 1152.[59] Rulers also sought to ensure the moral reform of the realm. In 1066, William the Conqueror banned his men from consorting with prostitutes.[60] In 1100, William of Malmesbury informs us, Henry I put an end to the immoral practices of his late brother by restoring the use of lamps at night.[61] In 1180 Philipp Augustus of France decreed that any gambler caught swearing was to be drowned in a nearby river or lake.[62] Finally, kings sought papal recognition,

---

[55] Otto of Freising, *Gesta Frederici*, ii.3, pp. 288–9; *Heinrici Chronicon Livoniae*, ed. Leonid Arbusow and Albert Bauer, MGH SS sep. ed., 2nd edition (Hanover, 1955), 12.

[56] *Saga of King Sverri*, chapter 123, pp. 154–5.

[57] Otto of Freising, *Gesta Frederici*, ii.3, pp. 288–9.

[58] Gerald of Wales, *Expugnatio Hibernica*, 96–9.

[59] Otto of Freising, *Gesta Frederici*, ii.6, pp. 296–9.

[60] William of Poitiers, *Gesta Guillelmi*, 158–9.

[61] William of Malmesbury, *Gesta Regum*, v.393.1, vol. 1, pp. 714–15.

[62] Rigord, *Histoire*, 128–31.

V. INAUGURATION 363

as William the Conqueror had done by sending Harold's banner to Rome,[63] and both Stephen of Blois and Tancred of Lecce by having their right to rule confirmed by the *curia*. Similar motivations might have guided Boleslaw III in welcoming a papal legate and attending a synod of Polish bishops while locked in a struggle for the throne with Zbigniew. In short, kings liked to prove that they were ardent protectors of the Church, devout sons of the Lord and spirited defenders of the Faith and its servants.

Taking charge of ecclesiastical matters illustrates how closely entwined political necessity and religious symbolism were. Writers often constructed a direct link between kingship and a realm's ecclesiastical institutions. Kingship was established when a ruler organised the Church in his kingdom.[64] By exercising their royal duties, newly enthroned kings similarly demonstrated their oversight of the Church, normally framed as the restoration of moral rigour and religious vigour. That was certainly how 'Gallus' had represented the legate's activities in Poland in 1103. In England, William the Conqueror, once crowned, soon after set out to remove from his office Archbishop Stigand of Canterbury, the archetypal corrupt prelate in Anglo-Norman historical memory.[65] William's grandson Stephen, in his turn, convened a church council soon after he had been elected king.[66] At other times, the king's care for the Church manifested itself by combining peace-making with a reassertion of royal rights. Within weeks of his coronation, Frederick Barbarossa visited Saxony. There, he dealt with a disputed election at Magdeburg, where a divided chapter had elected two rival candidates. The king, Otto of Freising stressed, vainly tried to persuade, cajole and reconcile the clerics. In the end, he had no choice but to appoint a third candidate in Wichmann, formerly an imperial chaplain. Frederick did this, Otto claimed, because he asserted the prerogative that, in a split election, the decision on who occupied the see fell to the king.[67] That was a rather loose interpretation of established practice, and it was complicated further by the fact that Wichmann already held a bishopric, and therefore needed papal dispensation before he could

---

[63] William of Poitiers, *Gesta Guillelmi*, 152–3.

[64] See, for instance, Hucker, 'Liv- und estländische Königspläne'; Burian, 'Krönung'; *Register Innocenz' III.*, vol. 7, nos. 1–12, pp. 3–27; *Monumenta Bulgarica. A Bilingual Anthology of Bulgarian Texts from the Ninth to the Nineteenth Centuries*, ed. and transl. Thomas Butler (Ann Arbor, MI, 1996), 217–34; Erdmann, 'Das Papsttum'; Orrmann, 'Church and society', 428–31. Generally, above, Chapter 3.

[65] William of Poitiers, *Gesta Guillelmi*, 160–1. He did not, however, succeed until 1070. That after Harold's death the archbishop had organised resistance to William might also have been a factor: William of Poitiers, *Gesta Guillelmi*, 146–7. On Stigand: Mary Frances Smith, 'Archbishop Stigand and the eye of the needle', *ANS* 16 (1994), 199–219.

[66] *Gesta Stephani*, 24–9.

[67] Otto of Freising, *Gesta Frederici*, ii.6, pp. 291–3.

364   10. BEYOND ENTHRONEMENT

take up his new appointment.[68] Still, in Otto's version of events, the king
restored peace, ordered the Church and asserted royal rights.[69]

Comparable steps were taken by Valdemar I in 1157, not long after he had
become the sole king of Denmark. He travelled to Roskilde, where the death of
Bishop Asser had coincided with considerable turmoil. As in Magdeburg, there
had been a split election, with the populace and the cathedral canons backing
rival candidates. Violence soon erupted, pitching competing factions against
each other. Tensions culminated in an attack on and the plundering of the
estate of the overseer of the royal mint. To Valdemar, this posed a twofold
challenge. First, he had to ensure the unanimous election of a bishop. Like
Barbarossa, he claimed a right to choose a candidate in the case of a split vote,
and like Frederick, he ignored inconvenient provisions of canon law.
Valdemar furthermore asserted that, because Roskilde had been a royal foundation, he had a duty to intervene in its affairs. He therefore called together the
canons and asked them to repeat the election, this time in his presence. They
nominated the same candidates as before, but with the addition of Valdemar's
close confidant Absalon. To nobody's surprise, Absalon was elected, albeit,
Saxo stressed, in a secret ballot and unanimously.[70] The second challenge was
that the unrest threatened to undermine Valdemar's control of the whole
region. Armed men had attacked the royal minter and other officials.
Indeed, it took all of Absalon's considerable persuasive skills and moral
authority to assert his – and so also the king's – authority.[71]

At Magdeburg and Roskilde, Frederick and Valdemar encountered the type
of challenge that a king would face throughout his reign. Yet, because it
occurred so early, they were presented with an opportunity to demonstrate
the virtues they had sworn to uphold. Both rulers tried to bring about
a peaceful settlement, seeking to cajole and guide local factions to settle their
disputes amicably. They also adhered to – select – principles of canon law.
Neither usurped but rather merely upheld existing powers, and did so for the
greater benefit of aith and people. Both Frederick and Valdemar followed up
their respective engagements with further acts linking their kingship to the
divine. Frederick moved on to Bavaria, where he conducted a festive crown-
wearing at Regensburg, the central site of Bavarian ducal authority. The king
combined this with acts of generosity and patronage. That he did so in an area
hotly disputed between rival factions among his supporters, thereby

---

[68] Indeed, the appointment quickly soured relations with the papal court: Stefan Pätzold,
'Norbert, Wichmann und Albert: drei Magdeburger Erzbischöfe des 12. Jahrhunderts',
Concilium Mediii Aevi 3 (2000), 239–63, at 248; Görich, *Friedrich Barbarossa*, 118–20;
Freed, *Frederick Barbarossa*, 71–3.

[69] Görich, *Friedrich Barbarossa*, 119–20. Saxon chroniclers seem to have agreed: *Annales
Palidenses*, MGH SS 16, 88; *Annales Magdeburgenses*, MGH SS 16, 191.

[70] Saxo Grammaticus, *Gesta Danorum*, xiv.21.1–2, pp. 1113–17.

[71] Saxo Grammaticus, *Gesta Danorum*, xiv.21.3, pp. 1121–3.

V. INAUGURATION   365

establishing his authority over theirs, was probably part of the message that the act was meant to communicate. As soon as matters had been resolved at Roskilde, Valdemar led a campaign against the pagan Wends on the island of Rügen in the Baltic.[72] The combination of a forceful display of royal might and the demonstrative performance of royal duties was characteristic both of inauguration festivities and of a ruler's early deeds.

Indeed, kings, as soon as they had been enthroned, were expected to wage war almost at once. Alfonso I of Portugal led a campaign against Muslims neighbours within a few months of his succession,[73] as did Fernando I of Léon in the 1070s,[74] Alfonso VII of Galicia in 1111[75] and Baldwin II of Jerusalem in 1118.[76] According to 'Gallus Anonymus', Boleslaw I of Poland embarked on a campaign against Rus almost the moment he had received a crown from Emperor Otto III. 'Gallus' dated back to the beginning of Boleslaw's reign an expedition that did not in fact take place until almost twenty years later (1017/18). We do not know whether this was a conscious decision or the result of incomplete information. In either case, 'Gallus' established a causal link between the succession to royal status and the waging of war, either because this was what so exemplary a ruler as Boleslaw *would* have done or because it was what he *should* have done. Certainly, the reasoning attributed to Boleslaw suggests a link between kingship and war: the king sought to defend his honour. The ruler of Rus had refused to give him his sister in marriage. Boleslaw resorted to violence not for profit or material gain, but to defend his standing and implicitly that of his people. The Rus' campaign established a clear contrast between Boleslaw, who acted like a king even though he had only recently received the title, and his rival, whose royal status was well established. On receiving the news of an imminent attack, the ruler of Rus, who was sitting in a boat fishing, declared that, while he was good at catching fish, Boleslaw was good at fighting. It was thus clearly God's will that Boleslaw be victorious.[77] The ruler of Rus forfeited his realm because while he held the title, he lacked the character of a king.

Almost as soon as Stephen had been crowned, he followed a traditional course of action for English kings and waged war in Wales.[78] While the Normans had pacified the Welsh and brought order and justice, the *Gesta Stephani* explained, they had never been able to subdue its inhabitants, 'men of

---

[72] Saxo Grammaticus, *Gesta Danorum*, xiv.23.1, pp. 1122–3.
[73] Blöcker-Walter, *Alfons I.*, 151. The comparison between Portugal and Denmark is especially fruitful: Villards Jensen, 'Crusading at the fringe'.
[74] *Chronica Najerensis*, 156.
[75] *Historia Compostellana*, 106–7.
[76] Albert of Aachen, *Historia Ierosolimitana*, 874–5.
[77] *Gesta Principum Polonorum*, i.7, pp. 40–3.
[78] William of Malmesbury, *Gesta Regum*, iii.258, vol. 1, pp. 476–7; iv.306, vol. 1, pp. 544–5; iv.311.1, vol. 1, pp. 552–3; v.396, vol. 1, pp. 718–19; v.401, vol. 1, pp. 726–9.

366   10. BEYOND ENTHRONEMENT

an animal type, naturally swift-footed, accustomed to war, volatile always in breaking their word as in changing their abodes'.[79] The *Gesta*'s account culminated in extensive praise for Stephen's pacification of the realm.[80] By defeating his enemies abroad, he promised to bring about peace at home. But domestic foes also ought to be tackled. After his coronation, Roger II deliberated at length what a suitably king-like course of action would be before deciding upon a campaign to subjugate the rebellious townsmen of Amalfi.[81] Fulk of Anjou, on becoming king of Jerusalem in 1131, subdued the count of Tripoli and took control of Antioch.[82] Within a month of his enthronement in 1180, Philipp Augustus of France waged war on Ebbe VI de Charenton, a violent oppressor of the Church.[83] As a rule, such campaigns were portrayed as having been undertaken to restore justice or to maintain the peace. Fulk, William of Tyre tells us, had set out at the behest of the great men of Antioch, and Philipp Augustus, Rigord maintained, after emissaries from the clergy had alerted him to Ebbe's oppressions.

Kings set out to defend the honour of the realm and to restore the right order of the world. Military action was taken at the behest of loyal subjects oppressed by evil lords or against men who otherwise defied the king's authority. The principle underpinned the stark contrast painted by Peter of Eboli between Tancred of Lecce and Emperor Henry VI. On becoming king of Sicily, Tancred persecuted not evildoers but those who were just and generous.[84] He inverted the right order of the world. Henry, on the other hand, invaded Sicily only after envoys from its people had approached him, lamenting Tancred's tyranny.[85] A newly enthroned king was expected to protect those who could not protect themselves, to elevate the humble and to humble the proud. But war remained a last resort, to be used solely for the common good, and at the behest of the defenceless and the poor. It was a tool for restoring justice.

Justice was the root of all other virtues. Without it there could be no protection of the Church or defence of the fatherland. Because of that, it played a central role in Wipo's account of Conrad II's enthronement in 1024. En route to his coronation, Conrad was held up when a peasant, a widow and an orphan asked to have their cases heard. When members of Conrad's entourage

---

[79] *Gesta Stephani*, 14–15.

[80] *Gesta Stephani*, 22–3.

[81] Alexander of Telese, *Ystoria Rogerii*, 26. See also Kristjan Toomaspoeg, 'Frontiers and their crossing as representation of authority in the kingdom of Sicily (12th–14th centuries)', in *Representations of Power at the Mediterranean Borders of Europe (12th–14th centuries)*, ed. Ingrid Baumgärtner, Mirko Vagnoni and Megan Welton (Florence, 2014), 29–49.

[82] William of Tyre, *Chronicon*, 635–7; *History of the Deeds*, vol. 2, 53–5.

[83] Rigord, *Histoire*, 132–5.

[84] Peter of Eboli, *Liber ad honorem*, 118–19.

[85] Peter of Eboli, *Liber ad honorem*, 126–7.

V. INAUGURATION 367

protested that he should not delay his consecration, he responded with a short speech:

> I remember that you have said often that not the hearers of the law, but the doers are made just. If, however, one must haste to the consecration, as you say, it behooves met to set my footsteps firmly in the work of God so much the more carefully as I know that I draw near to that exacting dignity.[86]

Delivering justice was the chief purpose for which the royal office had been created. Acting like a king was therefore more important than the coronation:

> He [Conrad] feared to be thrown down, should he not show equity in the regal loftiness. It was quite laudable, amidst the new joys, amidst the pleasurable ministrations of the king, to hear the complaints of so many paupers and to decide their cases. He was unwilling to neglect what could swiftly be put in order. He declined to defer doing justice, since that was the essence of ruling. . . . Thus the king in such causes, for which the regal authority is wont to be solicited most of all – that is, for the defence of churches, widows, and orphans – prepared for himself that day the way to the remaining affairs of government.[87]

Justice was 'the essence of ruling'. Conrad would not allow so hallowed a duty to be postponed just so that he could savour the pomp and splendour of an inauguration. This desire marked him out as the very model that his son Henry (the recipient of Wipo's *Gesta*) was encouraged to emulate.[88]

Wipo's account is unusually detailed and conceptually sophisticated. He both defined the principles and described the practice of royal justice, where others focussed on the latter. In the *Gesta Principum Polonorum*, Boleslaw I's catalogue of virtues included the fact that he would not deny justice 'if some poor peasant or some ordinary woman' approached him for succour.[89] Neither would he pass judgement without having listened to both sides. Nor yet did he extract forced labour from peasants. He carefully planned his journeys through the realm, and, on his approach, 'no one on the road or at work would ever hide his sheep and cattle, but rich and poor alike would smile upon him as he passed and the whole country would come hurrying up to see him'.[90] 'His sense of justice and fairness', 'Gallus' concluded, 'raised Boleslaw to such glory and dignity – the virtues by which the Romans in the beginning rose to power and empire'.[91] Good kings showed that they cared *above all* about justice being done.

---

[86] Wipo, *Gesta Chuonradi*, 26; *Deeds of Conrad II*, 70.
[87] Wipo, *Gesta Chuonradi*, 26–7; *Deeds of Conrad II*, 71.
[88] An idea also expressed in Wipo's *Tetralogus*, an allegorical poem on the duties of kingship.
[89] *Gesta Principum Polonorum*, i.9, pp. 48–9. See also Chapter 3.
[90] *Gesta Principum Polonorum*, i.12; pp. 58–9.
[91] *Gesta Principum Polonorum*, i.9, pp. 50–1.

368   10. BEYOND ENTHRONEMENT

Widows and orphans featured as worthy recipients of a ruler's justice not only because biblical precept demanded as much. They also lacked the resources and networks that would allow them to defend their rights by force. They needed support from those mightier than themselves. Yet precisely because they could offer little in return, and because aiding them often meant confronting powerful men, anyone who came to their assistance demonstrated that they wielded power – and not for selfish ends, but in order to ensure the well-being of those given into their care. Only the most powerful in the realm could act unencumbered by obligations of friendship or the need to win allies and backers. Doing justice symbolised both moral rectitude and worldly might. Or as Saxo wrote about the Danish king Erik the Good (r. 1095–1103):

> To prevent the lords' greed weakening the ties of justice, he blocked their arrogance with firmness and, the farther away he was from these evildoers, the more he exerted his authority to inflict injury on them. When his absence diminished the fear that he used to strike into the oppressors of the populace, he had them seized abruptly by a band of his retainers, and made sure they were hanged. . . . For this reason he became a terror of the upper classes [*maiores*, the greater men], but was dearly beloved by the lower orders [*minores*, the lesser men], because he treated the latter with fatherly tenderness, the former with royal severity.[92]

Erik was pious and a generous patron of the Church. He secured the establishment of an archbishopric for his realm and died while on crusade. He also used his might for the common good. He was a good king. However, while Wipo was unusual because of his conceptual sophistication, Saxo was distinguished by his emphasis on unrelenting rigour. To him, there should be none of the hesitation, the concern for what one might term 'due process', central to 'Gallus' and evident in Wipo when Conrad did not do justice himself, but commanded the princes to do it in his stead.

Saxo reflected concerns peculiar to late twelfth-century Denmark. Kingship was rooted in the king's willingness both to act as moral exemplar and to force righteous actions upon his people. Showing leniency and mercy was viewed as a harbinger of corruption and unrest. Hence, for instance, the contrast that Saxo established between Knud and Harald in 1076. The latter, promising to introduce new and softer laws, gained the favour of his people, encouraging the laxity and decline halted only, and even then only temporarily, by Erik the Good.[93] Around 1180, Sven Aggesen's *Lex Castrensis* similarly sketched a history of decline. While the rigour of Knud the Great's laws had been maintained for generations, during the reign of King Niels (1104–34) it was decreed that retainers who committed a felony could atone for their deeds with a fine. 'After this, time passed and, with evil deeds growing more frequent,

---

[92] Saxo Grammaticus, *Gesta Danorum*, xii.3.4, pp. 874–5.
[93] Saxo Grammaticus, *Gesta Danorum*, i.10.4–5, pp. 824–5. See also, above, Chapter 8.

V. INAUGURATION   369

corruption gradually crept in'.[94] By failing to uphold the full rigour of the law, Niels encouraged depravity and enabled the already powerful to oppress the very people whom the king was supposed to protect. Unlike his brother Erik, who instilled fear and hence righteousness among the *maiores* so as to protect the *minores*, Niels absconded from his royal duties. As the *Chronicon Roskildense* put it, he was a benign and simple man, but no corrector.[95]

The emphasis on forceful implementation of the law, and on the evils of moderation therefore reflected a particular historical moment. Much of Valdemar's kingship rested on invoking an ideal *status quo ante*: the glory days of Erik the Good. Rigorous justice, equitable treatment of all and the determined prosecution of violators of the peace underpinned the concept of royal lordship celebrated during Knud VI's appointment as his father's heir in 1165, and at his coronation in 1170. Murderers and torturers of common men should not be allowed to extricate themselves from punishment because they were rich or of high status. Viewed in this context, the emphasis on rigour in the Danish materials reveals itself to be not a deviation from, but an affirmation of broader European norms. Kings had to be powerful enough to take on the mighty. Only then could the people at large live in prosperity and peace. In the generation or so before Valdemar's succession, however, rulers had softened the rigour of the law in expectation of an easy life, or because they were unable to restrain the violent ambitions of great men. At least that was how Saxo and Sven portrayed those years. Mercy and leniency, while laudable in themselves, had, through excessive use, paved the way for murder, oppression and tyranny. What may at first sight have seemed a case of Danish exceptionalism was rooted in a specific historical experience that determined the interpretation of a shared framework of norms. Indeed, to Sven Aggesen at least, Valdemar may even have gone too far. Without restraint, rigour all too easily veered into tyranny. In summarising the king's reign, the chronicler stated: 'For while he lived he was a man found acceptable in all things: courteous, discriminating, wise, most penetrating in counsel, vigorous, an outstanding warrior, an accomplished wit, victorious, popular, always successful; only more cruel towards his own people than was just.'[96]

Across the Latin west, new kings frequently sought to establish a clear contrast with their immediate predecessors. When Richard I of England and the regents for William II of Sicily set free prisoners and restored the goods of those unfairly dispossessed, their actions were intended also as an implicit criticism of the ruler whom they succeeded. The link between a new beginning

---

[94] Sven Aggesen, *Lex Castrensis*, in *Scriptores Minores*, ed. Gertz, vol. 1, 80–5; *Works of Sven Aggesen*, transl. Eric Christiansen, 39–41.
[95] 'virum mansuetum et simplicem, minime rectorem': *Chronicon Roskildense*, in *Scriptores Minores*, ed. Gertz, vol. 1, 25.
[96] Sven Aggesen, *Brevis historia*, in *Scriptores Minores*, ed. Gertz, vol. 1, 138–9; *A Short History*, 73.

370   10. BEYOND ENTHRONEMENT

and the overcoming of past abuses found its fullest expression in the *Gesta Stephani*. The 'false peace' of Henry I, its author claimed, had been based on fear, greed, and the oppression of the Church. It was now being replaced by a new and just concord. In Germany, Conrad III looked back not to his immediate predecessor, but to the ruler before him, while in Sicily, the reign of William II became the norm that successive rulers vowed to restore. Alternatively, an exemplary forebear was invoked – one whose accomplishments had been left in ruins by subsequent kings, and who now needed to be rescued from oblivion. Such thinking underpinned the Danish case, but also surfaces in Hungary, with St Stephen performing a similar role to Knud the Great and Erik the Good. A new reign heralded a fresh start, a highly visible attempt to abolish bad laws and customs and to enforce good ones.

The contrast between old king and new often related to issues of legal process and the ending of corruption. The sword of justice could be wielded only by someone mightier than the people against whom the law was supposed to be enforced. Yet this disparity in resources meant that royal justice, if not exercised with due restraint, would lapse into tyranny. With the partial exception of Denmark, particular emphasis was therefore placed on process. It was a safeguard against abuse. When Conrad II entrusted judgement to the princes of the realm, he acted as keeper, not maker of the law. Other steps were also taken to promise restraint in the exercise of royal power. Key among them was the dismissal of corrupt and the appointment of virtuous royal agents. Their counsel was most likely to reach the king's ear. They would sit in judgement on his behalf, or otherwise determine what cases reached the royal court. If need be, they were also meant to correct and chastise him.[97] Their character and reputation mattered. It was therefore a token of Conrad II's moral excellence that he appointed advisors of such standing that Wipo proclaimed that he could not remember any of Conrad's predecessors having surrounded themselves with such suitable and honourable officials.[98] Kings had to ensure that agents acting on their behalf were guided by a concern for the common good.

Equally, mercy and forgiveness ought to be shown to erstwhile foes. In 1024, the archbishop of Mainz exhorted Conrad II: having experienced first hand just how devastating the loss of royal grace could prove, he ought to restrain his anger, however righteous it might be.[99] Indeed, excessive rigour could be cause for criticism. In his *Gesta* of Frederick Barbarossa, Otto of Freising chastised Frederick when the new king refused to show forgiveness to a knight, who,

---

[97] Weiler, 'Clerical *admonitio*'; de Jong, 'Admonitio and criticism'; Monika Suchan, 'Monition and advice as elements of politics', in *Patterns of Episcopal Power*, ed. Körntgen and Waßenhoven, 39–50.

[98] Wipo, *Gesta Chuonradi*, 24; *Deeds of Conrad II*, 68–9. See also above, Chapter 9.

[99] Wipo, *Gesta Chuonradi*, 22; *Deeds of Conrad II*, 67.

V. INAUGURATION 371

having fallen out of favour, had approached him during the coronation feast, in the hope of regaining the new king's grace.[100] When Alfonso VII succeeded to the throne of León in 1126, he still had to quell rebellions against his mother's rule. He first declared that the leaders of the resistance to his rule would be forgiven if they surrendered peacefully. When they refused, he successfully laid siege to their fortifications, but then allowed them to depart unharmed. This, the *Chronicle of Alfonso the Emperor* commented, was done in a 'prudent spirit' (*prouida dispensatione*), and terrified the king's remaining enemies, who quickly submitted.[101] Alfonso had demonstrated the ability to wield power, and while, on this occasion he had exercised mercy, he also sent a warning that such leniency could not be relied upon in future. The portrayal by 'Gallus' of Boleslaw III's dealings with his brother follow a similar pattern. The younger sibling went out of his way to win Zbigniew over with kind words. He even took him back into his favour, notwithstanding Zbigniew's recurring betrayals. At the same time, he did not allow his brother's actions to remain unsanctioned. In the first instance, he reduced him to the rank of a knight instead of that of a lord. Mercy, if practised wisely, enhanced the power of the king. Yet it was a credible means for doing justice only if underpinned by a willingness and by the ability to use overwhelming might.

10.3   Force

Most new kings had been chosen not on a straightforward basis of heredity, but because they seemed the most capable of maintaining the peace or because they acted swiftly.[102] They still had to demonstrate that they deserved to wear the crown. Rivals needed to be won over – or at least isolated. Others princes and prelates would probably hedge their bets. The friends, dependants and followers of the previous king might eye the new regime warily, anxious about their own standing and safety. A new ruler's allies and companions would demand their share of royal patronage. The demonstrative promise of a new beginning, of a more just and equitable reign, would allow long-suppressed grievances to burst forth. The political cost of releasing prisoners, as Eleanor of Aquitaine had done on Richard I's behalf in 1189, was low. But the undertaking to restore lands unjustly seized by his father to their rightful owners meant that those to whom estates had been granted would be dispossessed and would have to be compensated. Every act with which a king's authority could be established, and with which legitimacy could be demonstrated, also created an opportunity to question, challenge or undermine the ruler.

---

[100] Krieg, 'Im Spannungsfeld'.
[101] *Chronicon Adefonsi Imperatoris*, 151.
[102] See above, Chapter 5.

372   10. BEYOND ENTHRONEMENT

Worse still, any misstep, setback or failure would raise questions about his suitability. This was probably one of the reasons why kings, when they embarked on their first military campaigns, sought out opponents who could easily be defeated, and whose actions had left them bereft of allies. The major tasks facing a new king were therefore to create consensus by acting in a manner demonstratively above the fray, to gain support by successfully tackling challenges as they arose and to win power by reclaiming wherever possible prerogatives and rights that had been misappropriated or neglected, but without alienating – or alienating too much – those who inevitably suffered as a result. The demonstrative exercise of the royal office, in carefully measured steps and over time, and in full view of the leading elites of the realm, was as much a practical necessity as it was a promise of good rule.

Because of all this, failure would prove all the more damaging, as the example of Stephen of Blois illustrates. Even what had in principle been a good beginning could turn into calamity. Stephen issued a charter of liberties, embarked upon an itinerary of the realm and led a campaign into Wales. Yet the backing he received was hesitant. Few bishops attended his coronation, and once he had won their support, they did so contingently, on condition of his future good behaviour.[103] He remained distrustful of many of his noble subjects. Increasingly, he relied on Flemish mercenaries instead.[104] And he failed to force into obedience Matilda's network of supporters and relatives. Matters came to the boil in 1137, when Stephen visited Normandy, accompanied, among others, by Matilda's illegitimate half-brother, Earl Robert of Gloucester. When the leader of Stephen's mercenaries accused Robert of disloyalty, the earl had to perform an oath to purge himself of the charges. It was dishonourable enough that the king evidently trusted a foreign man-for-hire more than someone of royal blood. But then, to aggravate matters further, whereas Stephen publicly embraced Robert as a friend, in private, William of Malmesbury claimed, 'he criticized him in spiteful terms, and fleeced him of what property he could'.[105] Consequently, Robert grew ever more distant, and ultimately renounced his allegiance.[106] Worse still, this occurred while the king was struggling to establish his authority in England. Lacking the backing of his barons, his attempts to reclaim royal estates resulted in ever more widespread acts of open defiance.[107] Then, in 1139, Stephen also lost the backing of most clergy when he arrested leading bishops.[108] That he did so at a church council only heightened the severity of his transgression. Many prelates decided to back Matilda, and almost fifteen years of civil war ensued. Stephen failed

[103] William of Malmesbury, *Historia Novella*, 32–7.
[104] William of Malmesbury, *Historia Novella*, 38–9; *Gesta Stephani*, 46–51.
[105] William of Malmesbury, *Historia Novella*, 38–9.
[106] William of Malmesbury, *Historia Novella*, 40–3.
[107] William of Malmesbury, *Historia Novella*, 40–1; *Gesta Stephani*, 28–31.
[108] William of Malmesbury, *Historia Novella*, 44–63; *Gesta Stephani*, 72–81.

V. INAUGURATION   373

because he lacked the resources to combine generosity with force, because his efforts proved to be either inconclusive or insufficient and because he alienated the very people he needed in order to rule.

It is worth setting his case alongside that of Frederick Barbarossa. Like Stephen, he succeeded with doubts about the legitimacy of his claim, and without the resources to act as if he were indeed more powerful than any of his subjects. While his family belonged to the upper echelons of the German aristocracy, it was by no means among the richest. Moreover, Frederick had been bequeathed a difficult legacy, with several overlapping rivalries threatening to engulf the realm as a whole. Yet he was more successful than Stephen in establishing his kingship. What did he do differently? The account offered in the *Gesta Frederici* by Otto of Freising and his erstwhile secretary, Rahewin, provides helpful clues. Immediately after his coronation, Frederick set out to subdue the rebellious citizens of Utrecht. However, rather than using force, he was content with issuing a fine.[109] In Saxony, he settled the Danish royal succession at Merseburg, and personally placed a crown on the head of King Sven. Once again, no force was used, with Sven's rivals receiving lands in Denmark.[110] The king proceeded to Magdeburg, where he secured the election of Wichmann, before heading to Regensburg, where he performed a festive crown-wearing.[111] All this occurred within roughly three months of Frederick's enthronement.

Like Stephen, Barbarossa embarked upon an itinerary of the realm, and settled disputes throughout the kingdom. Unlike Stephen, he was able to do so partly because he had the backing of most of his nobles. The king's itinerary communicated its extent. Merseburg and Magdeburg were located in eastern Saxony, a region increasingly beyond the purview of many of his predecessors. Indeed, when Frederick's uncle, Conrad III, had sought to establish rival centres of power to challenge ducal authority, unrest ensued. Matters had not been helped by Conrad's decision to deprive Henry, the duke of Saxony, of his Bavarian inheritance. By visiting Saxony so early in his reign, and doing so in Henry's company, Frederick signalled the restoration of royal authority and a renewed concord between king and duke. The kind of business conducted in Saxony reinforced the point. At Magdeburg, Frederick appointed a trusted ally to the duchy's foremost see and at Merseburg, he demonstrated power by making kings. Moreover, each meeting was attended by princes from across the realm. At Merseburg, when Frederick confirmed the privileges of the abbey of Corvey, the grant was witnessed by Sven and Knud of Denmark, the archbishop of Hamburg-Bremen, the bishops of Halberstadt, Strasbourg, Prague, Paderborn, Minden, Havelberg and Brandenburg, the abbots of

[109] Otto of Freising, *Gesta Frederici*, ii.4, pp. 288–91.
[110] Otto of Freising, *Gesta Frederici*, ii.5, pp. 290–1.
[111] Otto of Freising, *Gesta Frederici*, ii.6, pp. 292–3.

374   10. BEYOND ENTHRONEMENT

Fulda, Hersfeld and Niemburg, the duke of Saxony, Duke Welf, and the margrave of Meißen.[112] While men from Saxony and the eastern march predominated, the bishop of Strasbourg had to travel nearly 500 km to be there, the archbishop of Hamburg 330 km and the bishop of Prague 250 km. Their attendance testified to the reach of Frederick's authority. Similarly, a charter for the abbey of Gottesgnaden, issued at Regensburg, was witnessed not only by attendants from Bavaria, but also by the archbishop of Magdeburg, the bishops of Havelberg and Konstanz and the margraves of Brandenburg, Meißen and Istria, as well as the count palatine of the Rhine.[113] There was no need to use force because Frederick was able to show that he acted with the full backing of the princes of the realm.

All this set the scene for tackling the most difficult legacy bequeathed to Frederick: the Bavarian succession, which pitched his cousin, Henry the Lion, against his uncle, Henry Jasomirgott.[114] The display of royal majesty at Regensburg and Merseburg, the subjugation of the men of Utrecht and the investiture of Wichmann at Magdeburg communicated Frederick's power to act like a king. They allowed him to accrue political capital. They showed that he preferred the amicable resolution of conflicts to the use of force, but also that he could resort to the latter if circumstances called for it. That Frederick wore his crown at Regensburg – the symbolic centre of Bavarian ducal authority – constituted an assertion that any settlement was to be negotiated on his terms. Yet he still lacked the resources and standing to enforce one. In fact, the dispute was not resolved until 1156, when Henry the Lion was installed as duke of Bavaria, and Henry Jasomirgott became duke of Austria.[115] Both Otto and Barbarossa viewed ending the conflict as a major achievement. In 1157, Frederick wrote to Otto, commissioning him to write an account of his deeds. The emperor's letter contained an outline of what he considered to be his most noteworthy accomplishments. It included only two in Germany: Wichmann's election at Magdeburg and the settlement of the Bavarian question.[116] Otto agreed. So complete was the peace henceforth

---

[112] *Urkunden Friedrich Barbarossas*, no. 11.

[113] *Urkunden Friedrich Barbarossas*, no. 14. See also Theo Kölzer, 'Der Hof Kaiser Barbarossas und die Reichsfürsten', in *Deutscher Königshof, Hoftag und Reichstag im späteren Mittelalter*, ed. Peter Moraw (Stuttgart, 2002), 1–47.

[114] Otto of Freising, *Gesta Frederici*, ii.7, pp. 292–5. Thomas Zotz, 'Kaiserliche Vorlage und Chronistenwerk. Zur Entstehungsgeschichte der *Gesta Frederici* Ottos von Freising', in *Geschichtsvorstellungen: Bilder, Texte und Begriffe aus dem Mittelalter; Festschrift für Hans-Werner Goetz zum 65. Geburtstag*, ed. Steffen Patzold, Anja Rathmann-Lutz and Volker Scior (Cologne, Weimar and Vienna, 2012), 153–77.

[115] Otto of Freising, *Gesta Frederici*, ii.9, pp. 298–9; ii.11–12, pp. 300–3; ii.44–5, pp. 370–5; ii.49, pp. 378–81; ii.57–8, pp. 388–91. On the process: Freed, *Frederick Barbarossa*, 75–7, 158–9, 162–6; Görich, *Friedrich Barbarossa*, 127–34. Henry Jasomirgott was Otto's older brother.

[116] Otto of Freising, *Gesta Federici*, pp. 82–9, at 82–3 (Wichmann) and 88–9 (Bavaria).

V. INAUGURATION 375

enjoyed by the realm, he explained, that Frederick was called not only emperor and Augustus, but father of the fatherland.[117] To both king and chronicler, the Bavarian succession constituted a major challenge and its resolution an even greater achievement.

At least in Otto's and Rahewin's rendering, Barbarossa was also successful because he acted for the right reasons. Having ensured that the affairs of the realm prospered, and compelled by the fact that close relatives were in dispute,[118] Frederick anxiously contemplated how such strife could peacefully be resolved.[119] Each subsequent stage demonstrated his ability to act as keeper of law and peace. In 1152, proceedings opened after Frederick had punished the men of Utrecht, secured Wichmann's election at Magdeburg and settled the Danish succession. In June 1153, a first formal hearing coincided with Frederick, in cooperation with two Roman cardinals, deposing the archbishop of Mainz and the bishop of Eichstätt.[120] In September, another occurred after an embassy had been received, sent at the behest of Sicilian rebels, to petition for support against Roger II, while negotiations opened for a marriage between Frederick and a Byzantine princess.[121] In June 1154, a temporary resolution was reached, quickly followed by the assembly of an army at the borders between Swabia and Bavaria to prepare for Frederick's imperial coronation in Rome.[122] Barbarossa enacted royal lordship by proceeding in close cooperation with the papal see, by coming to the aid of those who could not defend themselves and by restoring the right order of the world. He acted like an emperor even before he was crowned one.

On returning from Italy in 1155, he visited Bavaria again. The previous year, Henry the Lion had been granted the duchy, but Henry Jasomirgott refused to concede. Barbarossa continued to search for a peaceful solution. He met with his uncle[123] and called yet another diet. In the interim, he settled scores. He met the duke of Bohemia and Margrave Albert of Saxony, who had been absent from his Italian campaign. In Otto's words, Frederick's 'great deeds had instilled fear [in those who remained behind], so that all went to him voluntarily, each striving to gain through obedience the grace of his friendship [*familiaritas*]'.[124] Frederick also meted out punishments. Bishop Hartwich of Regensburg was fined for having disposed of imperial fiefs without licence,[125] while the count palatine of the Rhine and the archbishop of Mainz were put on

---

[117] Otto of Freising, *Gesta Frederici*, ii.58, pp. 390–1. See also the discussion of the term in Seneca, *De Clementia*, i.14.1, pp. 120–1, above, Chapter 2.
[118] Otto of Freising, *Gesta Frederici*, ii.12, pp. 302–3.
[119] Otto of Freising, *Gesta Frederici*, ii.7, pp. 292–3.
[120] Otto of Freising, *Gesta Frederici*, ii.9, pp. 298–9.
[121] Otto of Freising, *Gesta Frederici*, ii.11, pp. 300–1.
[122] Otto of Freising, *Gesta Frederici*, ii.12, pp. 300–3.
[123] Otto of Freising, *Gesta Frederici*, ii.44, pp. 370–3.
[124] Otto of Freising, *Gesta Frederici*, ii.44, pp. 372–3.
[125] Otto of Freising, *Gesta Frederici*, ii.46, pp. 374–5.

376 10. BEYOND ENTHRONEMENT

trial for disturbing the peace during the emperor's absence. The metropolitan escaped sanctioning because of his clerical status, but the count was sentenced to the humiliating punishment of carrying a dog, which, Otto noted, was normally followed by the death penalty.[126] Frederick furthermore toured Germany to destroy illicit castles, sentencing robbers and other persistent violators of the peace to torture or the gallows.[127] This was followed by another meeting with Henry Jasomirgott, Frederick's second wedding[128] and, finally, the reconciliation of the two princes.

Otto's account shows a new ruler gradually accruing power, each step designed both to celebrate norms of good royal lordship and to heighten the king's authority. Incrementally, Frederick translated abstract principles into authority exercised in relation to increasingly powerful opponents, and with ever less reluctance to threaten the use of force. We can see him become king, one step at a time. But we can also observe how each stage reflected back upon and invoked the values and norms so demonstratively celebrated during his first few months on the throne. For example, harsh measures were taken against the count palatine and the archbishop of Mainz because their fighting during the king's absence had undermined the peace in Germany. Frederick fulfilled the functions of his office by forcefully subduing two of the foremost princes of the realm. His actions probably also sounded a warning to Henry Jasomirgott. Until a settlement was reached in Bavaria, Otto lamented, the duchy had been the only region in Germany not to enjoy the tranquillity that Frederick had brought to the remainder of his kingdom, and Henry was the culprit who prevented the emperor from doing his duty. Henry was a disturber of the peace and increasingly ran the risk of being treated like one. It is not implausible that Henry decided to surrender his claim in light of what had happened to other princes who defied Frederick.

Barbarossa did not act without the occasional misstep, duly recorded by Otto.[129] But in many respects he constituted the ideal type of the newly inaugurated ruler. There was, for instance, the avoidance of violence, yet with the threat of force always implicit and increasingly credible. The amassing of troops near Augsburg, en route to Rome but at the borders between Swabia and Bavaria, signalled Frederick's growing power. On his return, it was the fear of

---

[126] Otto of Freising, *Gesta Frederici*, ii.48, pp. 378–9. On the punishment: Bernd Schwenk, 'Das Hundetragen. Ein Rechtsbrauch im Mittelalter', *Historisches Jahrbuch* 110 (1990), 289–308.

[127] Otto of Freising, *Gesta Frederici*, ii.48, pp. 378–9.

[128] Otto of Freising, *Gesta Frederici*, ii.49–50, pp. 380–1.

[129] In 1155, for instance, he simply decreed that Henry the Lion should receive Bavaria. This, Otto stated, caused consternation among the princes. It was perhaps for this reason (the connection was never explicitly made) that the decision was confirmed by an imperial diet on Frederick's return from Italy: Otto of Freising, *Gesta Frederici*, ii.12, pp. 300–3. See also generally, Krieg, 'Im Spannungsfeld'.

V. INAUGURATION   377

imperial might that led the duke of Bohemia and the margrave of Saxony to seek
out his friendship. All of this was embedded in a narrative of keeping the peace,
of doing justice, and of ending past abuses.[130] Frederick rarely acted on his own.
He relied upon the counsel and consent of the princes. He did so when pushing
for Wichmann's appointment, when settling the Bavarian succession, humiliating the count palatine, sanctioning Bishop Hartwich and so on. This was not,
however, weakness. Rather, it was both a demonstration and the very source of
Frederick's power. Defying him meant defying the community of the realm.

That Barbarossa emerges as an exemplary ruler from Otto's and Rahewin's
account was to expected. But his incremental accumulation of power, his
building of broad coalitions and his piecemeal approach to tackling challenges
make him an ideal example of how abstract principles as rehearsed during
coronations, feasts and processions could be turned into concrete practice.
Indeed, his actions, like those of Stephen, Alfonso VI or Valdemar, mapped
neatly onto the duties outlined in coronation oaths and *ordines*: to offer peace to
the Church and all Christians, banish all iniquities and violence irrespective of
the standing of the perpetrators and judge with equity and mercy; to observe the
Catholic faith, defend the Church, protect the realm and rule it with justice. They
communicated a ruler's possession of the inner disposition and material means,
as well as the political and martial skills, to perform the functions of his office. By
no means did this indicate that henceforth all would be plain sailing. Events had
a habit of disrupting even the best-laid plans. And then there were pontiffs,
prelates, princes and predatory neighbours. But what his acts did ideally signal
was that a king was in a position strong enough to meet them. The performative
aspect of these first few years points back to the public nature of proceedings.
Audiences confirmed, legitimised and made possible the performance of royal
functions. While royal power was theoretically greater than that of any of
a ruler's leading subjects, in practice it depended on garnering their backing.
Rare indeed was the king, who, on his accession, possessed the means to proceed
without it. However, if kingship rested on the successful interplay of rulers and
ruled, how did that manifest itself? How could the people shape the exercise of
royal power? And how should rulers respond?

10.4   Disruption

Because the events of a ruler's inauguration depended on a sizable and
powerful public, disruption always lurked just beneath the surface. The larger

---

[130] The conflict, Otto explained, had begun when Conrad III exiled Henry the Lion's father
from Bavaria and granted the duchy to Henry Jasomirgott (Otto of Freising, *Gesta
Frederici*, ii.7, pp. 292–3). Indeed, in his *Chronica*, Otto had lamented the many evils
that befell Bavaria as a result of Conrad's decision (Otto of Freising, *Chronica*, vii.22,
p. 347).

378　　　　　　　　10. BEYOND ENTHRONEMENT

the audience, the easier it was for grievances to be voiced and for tensions to erupt, even if otherwise unrelated to the event at hand. When William the Conqueror was acclaimed as king of England in 1066, the approving shouts of those in congregated inside the church made the Normans outside fear that William had been assaulted. They started burning houses in the vicinity.[131] At other times, disturbances did carry a political message. In 1077, the coronation feast for Rudolf of Rheinfelden nearly ended in the king's death. The crowning had been performed at Mainz, whose populace, unlike its metropolitan, continued to support Henry IV. After the banquet, when some of the young men in Rudolf's entourage started engaging in games and disturbing the townspeople, the citizens seized the opportunity to attack the courtiers. The turmoil ended only when Rudolf's men grabbed their arms and started to slaughter the town's inhabitants.[132] What should have been a celebration of concord collapsed into violence and bloodshed.

Even if not primarily aimed at the king, disruption could pose a considerable challenge. How it was met revealed much about a ruler's ability to govern. The especially well-documented riots that erupted in London during the coronation of Richard I in 1189 are a case in point. The soon-to-be king had banned women and Jewish residents from attending the festivities, but large groups nonetheless congregated outside Westminster Abbey, amid a throng of other Londoners. A member either of the crowd or of the court (the sources are contradictory) assaulted one of the Jewish spectators. Violent altercations ensued.[133] Several churches were burned, and Jews were forcibly baptised.[134] The unrest posed a danger to Richard's authority even greater than that which had faced Valdemar I at Roskilde. It occurred in the economic and administrative heart of the realm. Worse still, it interrupted the festivities surrounding his enthronement: the king heard of the unrest during his coronation feast.[135] The context matters. The festivities had been designed in part as an enactment of the right order of the world, with the king presiding over the proceedings as the guarantor of law and peace. A riot led by townsmen, who played a subservient role, threatened to disturb and undermine that very order. Worse still, the Jewish community in England was, at least nominally, under the king's protection.[136] When even the justiciar had been unable to quell the violence – indeed, he had to withdraw when the angry mob threatened to turn

---

[131] William of Poitiers, *Gesta Guillelmi*, 150–1.
[132] Bruno of Merseburg, *De Bello Saxonixo Liber*, 86–7.
[133] William of Newburgh, *Historia*, vol. 1, 294–5.
[134] Roger of Howden, *Gesta*, vol. 2, 83–4 (who added the detail of women being banned, the burning of churches and that *curiales*, i.e. members of the court, started the violence).
[135] William of Newburgh, *Historia*, vol. 1, 297; Roger of Howden, *Chronica*, vol. 3, 12.
[136] R. C. Stacey, 'Crusaders, martyrdoms, and the Jews of Norman England, 1096–1190', in *Juden und Christen im Zeitalter der Kreuzzüge*, ed. Alfred Haverkamp (Munich, 1999), 233–53.

V. INAUGURATION 379

against him – this called into question Richard's ability to keep the peace.[137] This was perhaps also why, Roger of Howden recounted, most of the ringleaders were hanged[138] and privileges of protection were reissued to England's Jewish communities.[139] Still, these measures did not quell the disturbances. By the new year they had spread to Lincolnshire, and then York, which witnessed the worst pogroms since the First Crusade. Rioters directly challenged the authority of the king's representatives and the prelates who oversaw the affairs of the realm in his absence.[140]

What happened in London highlights the increasing political significance of urban communities. Yet, in most European monarchies, that had not translated into a legitimate political role. Consequently, violent disputes frequently erupted. It is likely that the conflict at Roskilde in 1157, for instance, was embedded in simmering rivalries between the town and the bishop. Frederick Barbarossa similarly had to settle violent disputes between urban communities and their episcopal lords at Magdeburg and Utrecht.[141] In 1160, he lost one of his most trusted allies when Archbishop Arnold of Mainz was killed by the townsmen in a quarrel over communal government.[142] This, it is worth stressing, does not imply that the London rioters had given vent to grievances over the town's exclusion from the political process. Ralph of Diss, the dean of St Paul's Cathedral, claimed that the unrest had been started by foreigners, not Londoners,[143] Roger of Howden blamed the London populace and William of Newburgh members of the court. Nonetheless, the exclusion of Londoners forms part of the context within which these events ought to be considered. That the resulting violence targeted groups under the king's protection or that it undermined the king's authority was, however, incidental. Jews were attacked not because but despite the fact that they were in the ruler's care.

---

[137] William of Newburgh, *Historia*, vol. 1, 297. See also Gillingham, *Richard I*, 108–9; Nicholas Vincent, 'William of Newburgh, Josephus and the New Titus', in *Christians and Jews in Angevin England: the York Massacres of 1190, Narratives and Contexts*, ed. Sarah Rees Jones and Sethina Watson (Woodbridge, 2013), 57–90.

[138] Roger of Howden, *Chronica*, vol. 3, 12; Roger of Howden, *Gesta*, vol. 2, 83–4.

[139] Roger of Howden, *Gesta*, vol. 2, 84.

[140] William of Newburgh, *Historia*, vol. 1, 309–22; Roger of Howden, *Gesta*, vol. 2, 107; Roger of Howden, *Chronica*, vol. 3, 33–5.

[141] Otto of Freising, *Gesta Frederici*, 304–5.

[142] *Vita Arnoldi archiepsicopi Moguntinensis. Die Lebensbeschreibung des Mainzer Erzbischofs Arnold von Selenhofen*, ed. and transl. Stefan Burkhardt (Regensburg, 2014), 186–9. See also *Lamberti Parvae Annales*, MGH SS 16 (Hanover, 1859), 647. See, generally, Natalie Fryde and Dirk Reitz, eds., *Murder of Bishops in the Middle Ages/ Bischofsmord im Mittelalter* (Darmstadt, 2003).

[143] Ralph de Diceto, *Ymagines Historiarum*, vol. 2, 69. This is about as close as we have to a contemporary London account. See, for later communal memory, *Cronica maiorum et vicecomitum Londoniarum et quedam, que contingebant temporibus allis ab anno 1188 ad annum 1274: De antiquis legibus liber*, ed. Thomas Stapleton (London, 1846), 1.

380   10. BEYOND ENTHRONEMENT

Disputes and rivalries could come to the fore simply because a ruler's inauguration created the opportunity for them to be pursued. This makes them no less significant. Richard I, after all, was forced to respond.[144] In 1077, Rudolf deemed it wiser to withdraw than to accept the forced loyalty of the citizens of Mainz.[145] Involving the king was part of a repertoire of stratagems with which rivalries and grievances that long pre-dated his presence could be pursued. When we talk about negotiating kingship, we are therefore concerned with how the ruled sought to utilise a well-established set of expectations and norms for their own ends, and how they exploited the king's need, especially prevalent during the early years of a reign, to demonstrate and enact good rulership in consultation and cooperation with his people. Of course, not all disruptions needed to be violent. Frequently, the mere presence of a sizable and politically powerful public provided an opportunity to seek redress, in the expectation that, given the occasion, the king had little option but to respond favourably. In the end, a ruler's availability to his subjects offered an indication of his willingness to do justice. Writing between 1059 and 1063, Cardinal Peter Damian recounted how Margrave Hugh of Tuscany went out of his way to hear the complaints of his subjects. He used to traverse the countryside incognito and without his entourage, enquiring of peasants tilling the land what they thought of the governance of Margrave Hugh. Peter even suggested that Hugh received spiritual rewards for his actions.[146] Walter Map applauded Henry I's willingness to interact with petitioners: 'He would have no man feel the want of justice or of peace.'[147] Henry II followed in his grandfather's steps: 'Whatever way he goes out', Map recounted, 'he is seized upon by crowds ... and, surprisingly to say, listens to each man with patience, and though assaulted by all with shouts and pullings and rough pushings, does not challenge anyone for it, nor show any appearance of anger.'[148]

Each example hinged on people of low rank being able to approach the ruler. Kings were supposed to provide succour to those most in need of it. The frequency with which subjects pleaded for help during coronation festivities and on comparable occasions is therefore noteworthy. Baldwin II of Jerusalem received the men of Antioch during his coronation feast. The Sicilians approached Frederick Barbarossa in the summer of 1152, and they petitioned Henry VI during his imperial coronation in 1194. There appears to have been an expectation that this was precisely when petitioners were supposed to seek succour. Indeed, in 1189, the monks of Christ Church Canterbury, locked in

---

[144] Even in York in 1190, the riots erupted in an environment that had pitched the archbishop against his chapter and the king. Roger of Howden, *Chronica*, vol. 3, 33.

[145] Bruno of Merseburg, *De Saxonico bello*, 87–8.

[146] *Briefe Peter Damian*, no. 68. He appeared in a vision and requested that his corpse be turned over so that it was no longer face down.

[147] Walter Map, *De Nugis*, v.6, pp. 470–3.

[148] Walter Map, *De Nugis*, v.6, pp. 484–7.

V. INAUGURATION 381

conflict with the archbishop, had been planning to do just that. They had heard that, following the coronation, the metropolitan intended to prostrate himself before the king to request a grant they opposed, and had prepared to respond with what Hugh Thomas called a 'counter prostration'. The moment the archbishop approached the ruler, they would throw themselves at Richard's feet. Their scheme was abandoned only when the archbishop failed to follow through with his rumoured plan.[149] That the citizens of London had been prevented from doing anything similar may, in turn, have been yet another factor contributing to the febrile atmosphere in the autumn of 1189. They had been prevented from seeking succour and redress.

Not all of these encounters were spontaneous. If nothing else, the act of disruption itself had to be planned, as in the case of the Canterbury monks. At other times, a degree of stage management is likely to have occurred. As with elections, public actions – including petitions – were often (though not always) the culmination of a prolonged process of advance negotiation.[150] Yet even if there had been preparing and planning, petitioning was still framed as a disruptive act. Embassies from distant lands arrived unexpectedly, just in time for a ruler's coronation or when he presided over an assembly of his princes and prelates. People unfairly driven from their homeland, widows and orphans emerged just in time for someone who was about to become king to see to their needs. Indeed, Boleslaw I, Henry I and Henry II were described as seeking to create an environment where unsolicited advances could easily be made. Boleslaw was eager to hear the complaints of even the lowliest of his people. Henry I let his subjects know well in advance where to meet him and Henry II patiently allowed himself to be thronged by men and women seeking succour. Providing an opportunity for disruption was part of the exemplary performance of kingship.

The king's suitability manifested itself in the way in which he responded to such episodes, and in his abiding by the unspoken rule that he was the one person not allowed to disrupt proceedings – unless he did so in response to petitions and pleas. Deviations from this pattern were few. When they did occur, they were used in paradigmatic fashion to chide and chastise the ruler. The case of the disgraced knight, who during Frederick Barbarossa's coronation in 1152 unsuccessfully pleaded for mercy, springs to mind. In Otto of Freising's account, criticism remained veiled. He simply noted that many in attendance were surprised at the king's severity.[151] Still, the point was made: supplicants were supposed to be heard, not dismissed out of hand. No less

---

[149] *Epistolae Cantuarienses. The Letters of the Prior and Convent of Christ Church Canterbury*, ed. William Stubbs, Rolls Series (London, 1865), no. 324. I am grateful to Hugh Thomas for this reference.
[150] Althoff, *Macht der Rituale, passim*; Claudia Garnier, *Die Kultur der Bitte: Herrschaft und Kommunikation im mittelalterlichen Reich* (Darmstadt, 2008).
[151] Otto of Freising, *Gesta Frederici*, ii.3, pp. 286–7. Krieg, 'Im Spannungsfeld'.

382   10. BEYOND ENTHRONEMENT

graphic a juxtaposition underpinned William of Malmesbury's depiction of Eadwig. He lacked the ability and willingness to perform the duties of kingship. Just as the ruler was supposed to listen to exhortations during the inauguration ceremony, so was he supposed to invite and welcome the supplications of his people. If he failed in this duty, if he acted harshly and unjustly, or sought to evade so solemn an obligation in order to consort with his concubines instead, the legitimacy of his rule was itself called into question.

For this reason, disruption lent itself to the construction of moral messages. When Bruno of Merseburg described the riots at Mainz, he commented on the legitimacy of Rudolf of Rheinfelden's kingship. Bruno lamented the courtiers having engaged in games after the feast, when they should have respected the solemnity of the occasion through sober and austere demeanour. Indeed, he stressed, in the coronation liturgy the assembled had been exhorted to rejoice in (that is, contemplate the glory of) Christ. That stood in stark contrast to the frivolous behaviour displayed by Rudolf's men. Bruno also referred to the vain luxury of the occasion. When the citizens of Mainz plotted to incite unrest, their actions involved cutting off pieces from the precious furs that adorned the courtiers' cloaks. Bruno specifically chided Rudolf's attendants for this display of superfluous wealth.[152] While Rudolf did not disrupt the proceedings himself, in their frivolous vanity his backers still failed to respect the occasion. Their demeanour presaged the future misfortunes of their king. Here, Bruno applied a widely used narrative technique. Richard of Devizes, who maintained an ambivalent attitude towards Richard I, reported that two inauspicious omens occurred during the coronation. First, a bat flew through Westminster Abbey at noon, repeatedly circling the royal throne, and then the church bells mysteriously rang without anyone having pulled them.[153] Only subsequent events would reveal the bat to stand for Richard's brother John. Similarly, writing in the 1140s, Orderic Vitalis gave the riots during William the Conqueror's coronation prognostic meaning: 'The English ... never again trusted the Normans who seemed to have betrayed them, but nursed their anger and bided their time to take revenge.'[154] Chronicling disruption provided an opportunity to pass judgement.

That was possible only because the literary trope was anchored in political reality. There was an expectation that petitioners would be heard, that their concerns would be addressed and that they would resolved in their favour: hence the monks of Christ Church preparing to counter their archbishop by throwing themselves at the king's mercy. The expectation reflected both the moral principles of the inauguration and the power of the audience in attendance. Disruption made it possible to assess the moral probity of a ruler – would

---

[152] Bruno of Merseburg, De Saxonico Bello, 87–8.
[153] Richard of Devizes, Chronicon, 3, 4.
[154] Orderic Vitalis, Ecclesiastical History, vol. 2, 184–5.

V. INAUGURATION   383

he offer justice, show largesse, offer forgiveness? – and with which to guide him
in the exercise of royal power. The examples of prelates interrupting a royal
inauguration, discussed in the previous chapter, provide a case in point. In
Hungary, the leader of the kingdom's Church refused to crown a ruler he
deemed to be a usurper. In France, the archbishop of Reims sought to halt the
coronation of Louis VI and in England, the archbishop of Canterbury interrupted the crowning of Henry I's queen. Each feared that the pre-eminence of
his see was under threat. Faced with so grave a disturbance of the right order of
the world, they engaged in disruption themselves. They demonstrated standing, but also, and more importantly, a willingness to discharge their responsibility for the spiritual and political well-being of the realm. Accepting, perhaps
even facilitating such moments of public intervention, especially if undertaken
on behalf of others or in order to highlight particular norms and ideals,
enabled bishops to show that they had been able to advise, counsel and guide
the monarch, and that they had used their access to the royal person for the
common good. Kings demonstrated suitability by enabling their electors to
demonstrate theirs.

Disruption in the service of the common good could overlap with more
mundane but, to the individuals involved, no less existential concerns. The
intervention by Archbishop Ralph of Reims in 1108 may serve as example. The
metropolitan, Suger claimed, had fallen out with Louis' father, King Philipp,
over the manner of his appointment.[155] After the death of Archbishop
Manasses, a split election had occurred. Eventually, a synod agreed that
Ralph should be archbishop, but he then proceeded to have himself invested
without royal assent. This context adds a distinctly personal note to his actions,
but without ruling out more principled concerns. Because the king had broken
with precedent, the status of Reims was at risk. Other motivations can be
surmised. Suger lamented the depravity of King Philipp who, preoccupied with
his adulterous union with the countess of Anjou, had let slip the reins of
governance. Peace and order were maintained solely through the efforts of
Prince Louis.[156] It is not inconceivable that Ralph's objections were an attempt
to encourage Louis to demonstrate suitability by redressing past wrongs. He
could do so by maintaining precedent and by recognising the demands of
ecclesiastical reform, which had underpinned the clash between king and
metropolitan. He should demonstrate preparedness to offer a new moral
beginning by casting aside his father's enmity. All these goals were closely
entwined with securing the metropolitan's position at court, with restoring

---

[155] Suger, *Vie*, 86–7. See also: Alain Erlande-Brandenburg, *Le Roi est mort. Étude sur les
    funérailles, les sepultures et les tombeaux des rois de France jusqu'à la fin du XIII siècle*
    (Geneva, 1975), 73–5.
[156] Suger, *Vie*, 80–3; Yves de Chartres, *Correspondance I*, ed. Jean Leclerq (Paris, 1949), nos.
    5, 9, 15, 22, 28, 47, 56. See, though, *Chronique de Morigny*, 11; Hugh de Fleury,
    Modernorum Regum Francorum Actus, MGH SS 9 (Hanover, 1851), 394.

384   10. BEYOND ENTHRONEMENT

him to his rightful place among the king's counsellors and with securing for him and his dependants the patronage and protection they needed. In fact, Ralph was in due course reconciled to Louis VI and became one of his most trusted allies.[157] Things were again as they should be.

Disruption was, however, legitimate only if it reflected or if it resulted in the restoration of the right order of the world. Interventions had to eschew violence and ought to occur in an appropriate setting. Hence the different treatment meted out on the one hand to the petitioners approaching Conrad II, the messengers from Antioch pleading with Baldwin II and from Sicily with Henry VI, and on the other to the townsmen of Roskilde and the London rioters. Indeed, where acts of disruption occurred during an inauguration, and when they were condoned or applauded, they appear to have been the prerogative both of individuals outside established power structures and of leaders of the Church. There are few examples of lower clergy engaging in them. When St Dunstan dragged Eadwig from his mistresses, he went searching for the king at the behest of the archbishop of Canterbury. Reminding the ruler of his duties was closely entwined with demonstrations and assertions of standing within the realm. The king's response, in turn, revealed his moral outlook. Rulers deserving of the throne provided succour to the powerless. They remained unperturbed in the face of upheaval, and punished men who violently disturbed the peace. They would know how to manage disruption, but would not cause it themselves.

Few secular leaders seem to have engaged in such acts during a king's enthronement. Most accounts simply noted their presence, often without even naming them. In others, they appear mostly in the context of their ceremonial functions. When Alfonso VII was crowned king of Galicia in 1111, leading nobles acted as butler and steward during the coronation feast,[158] and when Alexander III was crowned king of Scotland in 1249, earls greeted the king on his arrival, escorted him to the altar for his consecration and placed their cloaks at his feet.[159] If they caused disruption, then that was not primarily aimed at the king, but related to disputes over rank. In 1184, when Frederick Barbarossa knighted his eldest son Henry VI, the services of butler, steward and marshal, Arnold of Lübeck recounted, were performed by only by kings, dukes and margraves.[160] Gislebert of Mons reported that there were several princes, including Frederick's brother and nephew, who claimed that by right (*de jure*) they should carry the emperor's sword.[161] In the end, Frederick sidestepped the issue by having the count of Hainaut carry it

[157] Herman de Tournai, *Liber de Restauratione*, 282, 287.
[158] *Historia Compostellana*, 106.
[159] John de Fordun, *Gesta Annalia*, vol. 1, 294 (translation, vol. 2, 290).
[160] *Arnoldi Chronicon*, 88. Buchner, *Entstehung*, 137, overstates the case when he views this as a legal requirement.
[161] *Annales Cameracenses*, 523.

V. INAUGURATION   385

instead.[162] Gislebert stressed not only the military might of the princes in question, but also the great virtue of the duke of Austria, a 'generous and upright knight' (*miles probus et largus*), and of the landgrave of Thuringia, who was 'vigorous' (*strenuus*). All this highlighted the glory and character of the count of Hainaut. He was raised above even the emperor's relatives. Yet the association, however implicit, between might, virtue and standing reflects a set of expectations similar to that guiding the ruler.

Noble disruption of an inauguration was about the assertion of the standing of leading members of the aristocracy in relation to each other. Their status mirrored their position in relation to the ruler, but it rarely involved reminding the king, however obliquely, of his duties. The unknown knight who, during Barbarossa's coronation feast, had sought to regain the king's favour, was of low rank and a rare exception. And when individual nobles did break with precedent, their intervention was rarely perceived as legitimate. During the election of Rudolf of Rheinfelden in 1077, Otto of Northeim was reprimanded by the papal legate leading the proceedings when he demanded to have his grievances addressed.[163] In Denmark in 1165, Valdemar's kinsman Buris refused to do homage to Knud VI because enthroning a king during his father's lifetime was an unprecedent break with established custom. To Saxo, this foreshadowed Buris' treasonous alliance with the Norwegians the following year.[164] Unlike bishops, lay elites interrupting the inauguration were cast as rash or untrustworthy men who needed to be restrained and put in their place. Why this significantly different portrayal? Part of the answer resides in the fact that clergy, widows, peasants and orphans were people who, either *de facto* or in theory, lacked the means to protect themselves. Widowed women and fatherless children existed outside the networks of power with which claims could be pursued or enemies warded off. Members of the Church were not supposed to shed blood or engage in armed conflict.[165] Like the poor, they needed others to take up arms on their behalf. And the chief figure to offer such succour was the king. His office had been created, and his power had been granted by God, so as to protect, nurture and defend these very men and women. Allowing them to disrupt his inauguration gave him an opportunity to prove that he deserved to wear the crown.

Nobles, by contrast, had the means to defend themselves. If a king acted in a tyrannical fashion, magnates and princes could withdraw their services from him, or even take up arms against him. Indeed, from the largely clerical perspective of our sources, the king performed a different function in relation secular

---

[162] Gislebert of Mons, *Chronicon*, 156.
[163] See above, Chapter 8.
[164] Saxo Grammaticus, *Gesta Danorum*, xiv.33.2–4, pp. 1244–9; xiv.34.4, pp. 1250–1.
[165] In practice, they, of course, frequently did, but even then in carefully circumscribed ways, either so as to perform royal functions instead or in the absence of a ruler, or at his behest. See Kemp, 'Images of kingship'.

386   10. BEYOND ENTHRONEMENT

elites. He brought them to heel, restrained their violence and imposed order upon
them. Only then did he emerge as a true defender of the Church. Even dynastic
histories focussed on comparable qualities when they praised a noble family or its
leading members for performing king-like functions. The counts of Anjou or
Barcelona, Duke William of Normandy and the Welfs in Swabia and Bavaria
demonstrated their quasi-royal status by bringing to heel rebels and brigands.[166]
Moreover, there was no equivalent to an archbishop of Canterbury, Lund or
Nidaros who could claim to act as leader of a kingdom's aristocracy. Indeed, if
there was a single secular figure who, through wealth and standing, ranked above
all the other secular leaders, it should be the king.[167] If the aristocracy acted in
order to confront a ruler, then they could hope for success only when they did so
collectively, and often mediated through their clerical peers. That had been the
case in 1077, when rebel princes deposed Emperor Henry IV, and when, in 1153,
the English magnates forced Stephen of Blois and Henry of Anjou to settle their
dispute over the succession to Henry I.[168] In each instance, the withdrawal of
service was initiated by secular elites acting as a group, but it was communicated
through their clerical peers. At most, a section among the secular elites would be
singled out as having a particular responsibility towards the ruler. The companions of William Ironarm and Roger Guiscard, the descendants of the Seven
Leaders in Hungary and the group of princes who, Eike von Regpow claimed in
the 1220s, had the sole right to elect a king in Germany fall into this category. But
they still acted collectively, not individually. Most nobles lacked, if not the power,
then certainly the moral authority to act in a manner comparable to that of
a leader of the Church. Claiming to do so would in fact have meant questioning
the very foundations of a king's authority.

From a ruler's perspective, a further and final consideration also mattered.
Prelates and peasants would not normally claim the throne. Powerful nobles
who publicly disrupted a king's inauguration, by contrast, posed a direct
challenge. That had certainly been how Saxo Grammaticus presented events
in Denmark in 1165–7. Not only did Buris Hendriksen refuse to swear fealty to
Valdemar's son Knud, he did so publicly. The great men of the realm had been
summoned to Roskilde to promise their loyalty to the new co-king. Alone
among them, Buris denied Valdemar's request, 'and by doing so provoked
strong suspicion that he aspired to absolute power'. Worse still, he compared
the proposed arrangement to the customs of the much-despised Germans,
who, out of greed, would agree to serve two lords at once.[169] Buris not only

---

[166] *Historia Welforum*, 16–17, 18–21, 56–9; *Gesta Comitum*, 5, 7–8, 12–13; *Chronica de
Gestis*, 34–5, 37, 45; *Gesta Normannorum ducum*, vol. 2, 98–103, 120, 122, 126, 130;
Weiler, 'Kingship in dynastic chronicles'.
[167] See, especially, above, Chapter 3.
[168] See above, Chapters 5, 7 and 8.
[169] Saxo Grammaticus, *Gesta Danorum*, xiv.33.3, pp. 1246–7. For the Buris revolt:
Lars Hermanson, 'How to legitimate rebellion and condemn usurpation of the crown:

V. INAUGURATION   387

defied the king. He also jeopardised the carefully crafted narrative surrounding Knud's elevation, with its emphasis on the restoration of concord, and of the ideal *status quo ante* of the reign of Erik the Good.[170] His actions posed all the more of a challenge as Buris was a kinsman of Valdemar's, and hence a member of the royal *stirps*.[171] He was, moreover, well connected, counting Absalon, Saxo's patron and Valdemar's foster-brother, among his intercessors.[172] Hence, even after he defied Valdemar in public, the king still thought it prudent to conceal 'his wrath beneath mild replies and a calm expression'.[173] Buris was eminently throne-worthy, and a close eye had to be kept on him from the outset. When he suggested that the retainers of one of Valdemar's rivals be exiled, it was feared he would appoint himself to be their leader.[174] And when Valdemar visited Frederick Barbarossa in Germany, he insisted that Buris accompany him, 'in case he should try to promote national changes during their absence (*ne quid interim in patria novaret*)'.[175] Buris' act of defiance in full view of Valdemar's dependants and courtiers threatened to undermine the king's authority. Even if Buris' protestations that he did not seek the throne were true, his actions nonetheless intimated that Valdemar lacked a key qualification for being king: evidently, he was *not* more powerful than any of his people.

The Danish case constitutes a warning example of the risks of disruption, and hence a further explanation as to why nobles usually hesitated before disrupting a king's inauguration. Saxo remained silent about what happened to Buris after his confinement.[176] Thirteenth-century German accounts fill in the gap. At Valdemar's command, Albert of Stade and others report, Buris' eyes were gouged out.[177] It may well have been what Sven Aggesen referred to when he described the king as being unduly harsh towards his people. It also adds another layer to the proceedings of 1170. Knud VI's coronation and the translation of Knud Lavard asserted royal power. They also reinforced the message of stern and equitable justice that the two kings promised to mete out. Like Boleslaw's blinding of Zbigniew, the ferocity of the king's response was a mark of the severity of Buris' challenge. Like the bishop of Regensburg and the count palatine of the Rhine, who were shamed into submission on

---

discourses of fidelity and treason in the *Gesta Danorum* of Saxo Grammaticus', in *Disputing Strategies in Medieval Scandinavia*, ed. Kim Esmark, Hans Jacob Orning and Helle Vogt (Leiden and Bosten, 2013), 107–40, at 123–6.

[170] See above, Chapter 6.
[171] Saxo Grammaticus, *Gesta Danorum*, xiv.19.17, pp. 1110–13.
[172] Saxo Grammaticus, *Gesta Danorum*, xiv.30.7, pp. 1232–5; xiv.32.2, pp. 1240–3; xiv.33.4, pp. 1246–9.
[173] Saxo Grammaticus, *Gesta Danorum*, xiv.33.3, pp. 1246–7.
[174] Saxo Grammaticus, *Gesta Danorum*, xiv.28.5, pp. 1198–9.
[175] Saxo Grammaticus, *Gesta Danorum*, xiv.19.18, pp. 1112–13.
[176] Saxo Grammaticus, *Gesta Danorum*, xiv.34.9, pp. 1254–5.
[177] Hermanson, 'How to legitimate rebellion', 126 n. 47.

388   10. BEYOND ENTHRONEMENT

Frederick Barbarossa's return from Italy, he had assumed a degree of power that posed a direct challenge to the king's authority. Buris' actions resemble King Stephen's treatment of Earl Robert of Gloucester. The king had publicly humiliated Robert to such an extent, and so publicly, that the earl had no option but to back Stephen's rival Matilda.[178] Buris similarly crossed a line when he defied Valdemar before the assembled clergy and barons. The king had no option but to respond, and to do so with force.[179]

For this reason, aristocratic acts of disruption normally occurred at other points in the king-making process, notably the election. It was a means by which standing could be ascertained and grants solicited. That was certainly how the dukes of Saxony and Lotharingia utilised their absence from Conrad II's election in 1024. But once absentee princes recognised kingship, the act was framed so that both ruler and nobles gained from it. Recognition was usually offered in or a near a lord's domains, with dependants, allies and relatives in attendance.[180] Their presence enhanced the binding force of the submission, but also shielded lords from an overbearing or vengeful monarch. Buris may have attempted something similar. He had stood by Valdemar's side from the beginning, and had even been wounded in battle fighting on his behalf. When the king ended the practice of succession by election, Buris demanded, not unreasonably, that aristocratic lands should also pass automatically to a noble's heir. Like the princes who had been absent from Conrad II's election, he sought to translate hesitation into material gain. Unlike them, however, he failed. That had a good deal to do with the fact that he deprived the king of an opportunity to combine largesse with a display of royal might.

10.5   Consent and Consultation

None of this suggests that nobles lacked a voice in shaping the exercise of royal power. However, they did so collectively, as part of the community of the realm, normally outside the immediate context of the inauguration, and often in relation to royal patronage. Largesse was, after all, embedded in a series of conflicting demands and expectations. The mighty had to be won over, but

---

[178] Stephen D. White, 'Alternative constructions of treason in the Angevin political world: Traïson in the History of William Marshal', *e-spania* 4 (2007), https://journals .openedition.org/e-spania/2233 (accessed 28 January 2020).

[179] This offers a slightly different reading from Hermanson, 'How to legitimate rebellion', 125, who suggests that Buris reflected a 'feudal discourse of fidelity'.

[180] See above, Chapter 8. It is worth noting that Buris was imprisoned in Zealand and that Robert of Gloucester was humiliated in Normandy, both far from their respective strongholds. By contrast, Frederick Barbarossa demonstrated power by passing judgement on the archbishop of Mainz and the Count Palatine at Worms, which, while outside their respective domains, was nonetheless within easy travelling distance from Mainz, and close to the count's lands.

V. INAUGURATION 389

without letting them become too powerful. Followers should be rewarded, but not at the expense of seeming to value their particular interests above the common good. And so on. All this played out before a public that shifted from the community of the realm to that of a particular region and back again. For nobles, bishops and abbots, being able to assert standing in relation to the monarch had to translate into favours and benefits with which to maintain the loyalty of their own men. Equally, largesse must not veer into profligacy. Kings were supposed to reward where appropriate, but not to fritter away the wealth that was needed to defend the realm and maintain the peace. A satisfactory resolution of the resulting tensions required consent, which provided an opportunity to shape the king's exercise of his duties.

There is no shortage of examples. Most, however, are only very briefly documented. Conrad II's succession in 1024 is an important exception. After his election and coronation in September, the king visited Aachen and Saxony. The duke of Lotharingia, in whose lands the former was situated, had opposed Conrad's election. Likewise, few Saxons had backed him, and Conrad was the first non-Saxon king to rule east Francia in over a century. Both visits aimed to demonstrate the new ruler's status, and to reassure anyone still wary of his rule. At Aachen, the queen was crowned, and the king performed a festive crown-wearing.[181] Royal lordship was demonstrated, but without confronting the duke, who remained hostile. Matters were more complicated in Saxony.[182] On Christmas Day 1025, Conrad convened a diet at Minden, where, Wipo reports, he confirmed the 'barbaric' laws of the Saxons,[183] and where he was accepted as king by the nobles and prelates who had not been present at his election.[184] Extensive preparations had been required for this to happen. In November, Conrad had met the abbesses Sophie of Gandersheim and Adelheid of Quedlinburg, both daughters of Emperor Otto II.[185] The meeting constituted a quasi-designation, and smoothed the path towards Conrad's subsequent acceptance by the Saxon nobles. It also recognised the status of the surviving

---

[181] Wipo, *Gesta Chuonradi*, 28; *Deeds of Conrad II*, 69. See also Wolfram, *Konrad II.*, 76–7.

[182] See the detailed discussion in the revised online *Regesta imperii*: RI III,1 n. m, in Regesta Imperii Online, www.regesta-imperii.de/id/1024-09-04_1_0_3_1_0_12_m (accessed 14 August 2018).

[183] Wipo, *Gesta Chuonradi*, 29; *Deeds of Conrad II*, 69.

[184] *Annales Hildesheimenses*, 34.

[185] *Annales Quedlinburgenses*, 577. On Sophie: Otto Perst, 'Die Kaisertochter Sophie, Äbtissin von Gandersheim und Essen (975–1039)', *Braunschweiger Jahrbuch* 38 (1957), 5–46; Klaus Gereon Beuckers, 'Kaiserliche Äbtissinnen: Bemerkungen zur familiären Positionierung der ottonischen Äbtissinnen in Quedlinburg, Gandersheim und Essen', in *Frauen bauen Europa. Internationale Verflechtungen des Frauenstifts Essen*, ed. Thomas Schilp (Essen, 2011), 65–88. On Adelheid: Gerlinde Schlenker, 'Kaiserin und Reichsäbtissin: Macht und Einfluss von Adelheid und Mathilde von Quedlinburg', in *Auf den Spuren der Ottonen*, ed. Roswitha Jendryschik, Gerlinde Schlenker and Robert Werner (Halle a. D. Saale, 2002), 7–16.

390   10. BEYOND ENTHRONEMENT

women of the Ottonian imperial family, who, after the death of Henry II,
lacked a male relative on the throne to be their patron and protector. Soon
after, many of the Saxons met Otto at Dortmund (not far from Sophie's
community at Essen), and after pausing in Minden, Conrad continued his
journey through Saxony, visiting Halberstadt, Merseburg and Quedlinburg.

Conrad's actions followed established practice.[186] In 1002, Ekkehard of
Meißen had similarly sought to win Adelheid's backing for his pursuit of the
crown.[187] But it was Henry II who had probably set the immediate precedent
followed by Conrad. In 1002, the newly enthroned king had traversed the
realm, seeking to quell rebellions in Swabia and Lotharingia before heading to
Saxony. Along the way, he had been acclaimed as lord by the great men of
Thuringia.[188] At Merseburg, the Saxons deliberated whether to accept Henry
as king. Eventually, their duke addressed Henry in front of the assembled
prelates, princes and great men, and expounded on the expectations and
demands of his people. In particular, he rehearsed the legal customs of the
Saxons, and requested that Henry uphold them. Henry responded by praising
the Saxons for their past loyalty, and vowed to observe and protect their
laws.[189] The centrality granted to their customary laws clearly set the Saxons
apart from other component parts of the realm. The Thuringians, for instance,
merely received a royal grant that freed them from a tax on pork.[190] Moreover,
Saxony was the only region where the community as a whole deliberated
whether or not to accept the king. The Saxons clearly were different. That
raised the standing of their duke in relation both to his peers and to the king.
What had been true for Henry II applied also to Conrad a generation later.

This was not the end of affairs to be dealt with in Saxony. Even the resolution
of local disagreements required access to the king. The ability to involve him in
confirming grants, settling disputes and outlawing the actions of rivals communicated standing to local and regional as well as regnal audiences. Indeed,
proximity, especially early on in a ruler's reign, *should* translate into direct

---

[186] *Annales Quedlinburgenses*, 578; *Annalista Saxo. Die Reichschronik des Ananlista Saxo*,
ed. Klaus Naß, MGH SS (Hanover, 2006), 372.

[187] On which see, recently and persuasively, Sarah Greer, 'The disastrous feast at Werla:
political relationships and insult in the succession contest of 1002', *German History* 37
(2019), 1–16. See also, above, Chapter 7.

[188] Thietmar, *Chronicon*, v.14, pp. 206–9; *Ottonian Germany*, ed. Warner, 215.

[189] Thietmar, *Chronicon*, v.16, pp. 208–11; *Ottonian Germany*, ed. Warner, 216.

[190] Thietmar, *Chronicon*, v.14, pp. 206–9; *Ottonian Germany*, ed. Warner, 215. The grant,
however, was important enough that it was also recorded by the twelfth-century
Annalista Saxo, 286–7. Generally, on the role of Saxony: Hans-Werner Goetz, 'Das
Herzogtum der Billunger – ein sächsischer Sonderweg?', *Niedersächsisches Jahrbuch
für Landesgeschichte* 66 (1994), 167–97. This distinctiveness, while transformed, continued into the twelfth century: Bernd Schneidmüller, 'Landesherrschaft, welfische
Identität und sächsische Geschichte', in *Regionale Identität und soziale Gruppen im
deutschen Mittelalter*, ed. Peter Moraw (Berlin, 1992), 65–101.

V. INAUGURATION   391

backing. But it had to be solicited in an appropriate manner. In 1024, Archbishop Aribo of Mainz failed to heed that principle. He had been one of Conrad's most fervent supporters.[191] He had appeared as intercessor in several early charters[192] and acted as arch-chancellor (that is, the person nominally overseeing the king's administration).[193] In early 1025, while the king, accompanied by Aribo,[194] was still in Saxony, the metropolitan seized the opportunity to revive a simmering dispute with the bishop of Hildesheim.[195] The details need not concern us here. The *Gandersheimer Kirchenstreit*, a kind of high medieval *Jarndyce v Jarndyce*, centred on which of the two prelates should have oversight of the nunnery at Gandersheim. Initially, the archbishop was supported by none other than Abbess Sophie, who had been instrumental in gaining Conrad recognition in Saxony.[196] Aribo appears to have felt that his proximity to the new ruler, and his instrumental role in easing Conrad's path onto the throne, entitled him to the king's support. And yet he failed. He managed to offend the abbess,[197] who approached the bishop of Hildesheim for support instead. Meanwhile Conrad refused to involve himself in the dispute. The *Kirchenstreit* dragged on, inconclusively, for a few more years. In the end, the metropolitan, unpopular even at his own cathedral, lost the king's backing entirely and remained a marginal figure thereafter.[198] In pursuing his dispute with Hildesheim, a major Saxon cultural and political centre, at times purporting to act with authorisation from pope and emperor when he had in fact neither, Aribo, like Buris, overstepped the bounds of what was acceptable. The prelate's lack of support at Mainz made him a figure easily dispensed with. His efforts nonetheless do point to a more fundamental issue.

---

[191] Wolfram, *Konrad II.*, 64–66, 69–72. On Aribo: Peter Acht, 'Aribo (Mainz)', *Neue Deutsche Biographie* (Berlin, 1953), vol. 1, 351.

[192] *Die Urkunden Konrads II. mit Nachträgen zu den Urkunden Heinrichs II.*, ed. Harry Bresslau, MGH Diplomata (Hanover, 1909), nos. 9–10.

[193] *Urkunden Konrads II.*, nos. 11–14.

[194] *Urkunden Konrads II.*, nos. 9–10.

[195] *Vita Godehardi Prior*, MGH SS 11 (Hanover, 1854), 186–7.

[196] On the dispute's origins: Knut Görich, 'Der Gandersheimer Streit zur Zeit Ottos III. Ein Konflikt um die Metropolitanrechte des Erzbischofs Willigis von Mainz', *ZSRG: Kanonistische Abteilung 79* (1993), 56–94; on the dispute during Conrad's reign, Wolfram, *Konrad II.*, 108–13. For the otherwise unrecorded Mainz perspective, Steffen Patzold, 'Capitularies in the Ottonian realm', *EME 27* (2019), 112–32, at 127–31. I am grateful to Levi Roach for this last reference. Sophie and Aribo were certainly not the only ones to expect something in return for their backing. Also in spring 1025, Conrad's eponymous cousin, who had stepped aside to facilitate the king's election, approached Conrad to demand the duchy of Carinthia – a long-held grievance that, the younger Conrad seems to have argued, should now finally be settled. *Annales Sangallenses Maiores*, MGH SS 1 (Hanover, 1826), 83; Wolfram, *Konrad II.*, 91–102.

[197] Wolfram, *Konrad II.*, 108–9.

[198] *Die Konzilien Deutschlands und Reichsitaliens 1023–1059*, ed. Detlev Jaspert, MGH Concilia (Hanover, 2010), 69–73, 78–9, 111–16; Wolfram, *Konrad II.*, 275–6.

392   10. BEYOND ENTHRONEMENT

Backers expected to be rewarded. If kings hesitated, or if they refused to lend their full support, powerful men might well take matters into their own hands. Yet every gift meant that someone else would see his claims or ambitions thwarted, would lose out to rivals and see his standing diminished. Therefore, acts of patronage had to be carefully calibrated. In 1136, King Stephen sought to make Hugh le Poer earl of Bedford by marrying him to the heiress of Simon de Beauchamp. Her dowry included all of Simon's possessions, including the castle of Bedford. That, however, was held by Simon's nephew Miles, who consequently took up arms against the king and became one of Matilda's most fervent supporters.[199] More successful rulers therefore took care not to infringe the rights of nobles. In many cases, they initially limited themselves simply to confirming the grants of their predecessors. Conrad II's first grants consisted of re-issuing charters made out to the monasteries of Peterlingen[200] and Werden[201] or the Church of Freising,[202] and of donating some of his own possessions to the cathedral chapter at Speyer.[203] The pattern continued after the assembly at Minden. When visiting Franconia in the spring of 1025, Conrad issued several privileges for Bamberg Cathedral, his predecessor's foundation and burial place. But even these were mostly confirmations of grants originally issued by Henry II.[204] Royal largesse, especially while a king was still seeking to win over hesitant subjects, usually meant guaranteeing existing privileges, not issuing new ones.

And when rulers did issue new grants, they were supposed to draw on their own resources, especially when they provided for family members.[205] As long as a ruler was still without heirs, brothers and nephews remained putative successors. They had to be provided for. Yet they ought not to be privileged

[199] *Gesta Stephani*, 46–9; King, *King Stephen*, 83, 164, 224.
[200] *Urkunden Konrads II.*, no. 1.
[201] *Urkunden Konrads II.*, no. 2.
[202] *Urkunden Konrads II.*, no. 3.
[203] *Urkunden Konrads II.*, no. 4.
[204] *Urkunden Konrads II.*, nos. 11–14.
[205] See also, *Die Urkunden Heinrichs III.*, ed. Harry Bresslau and Paul Kehr, MGH Diplomata (Berlin,1931), nos. 1–9, 11–13; 15; *Die Urkunden Heinrichs IV.*, ed. Dietrich von Gladiss and Alfred Gawlik, MGH Diplomata (Berlin and Hanover, 1941–78), nos. 1–2, 4–6, 13–18, 20–3 (7–12 were grants to Speyer for the *memoria* of his father). We have as yet no edition of the charters of Henry V, and Lothar III and Conrad III were discussed above, Chapter 6. Similar patterns emerge in France, Sicily and the Latin kingdom of Jerusalem: *Actes Louis VI*, 26–8; *Guillelmi I. Regis Diplomata*, ed. Horst Enzensberger, Codex Diplomaticus Regni Siciliae (Cologne, Weimar and Vienna, 1996), nos. 1, 2, 5; *Tancredi et Wilelmi III Regum Diplomata*, ed. Herbert Zielinski, Codex Diplomaticus Regni Siciliae (Cologne and Vienna, 1982), nos. 1–5; *Constantiae Imperatricis et Reginae Siciliae Diplomata (1195-1198)*, ed. Theo Kölzer, Codex Diplomaticus Regni Siciliae (Cologne and Vienna, 1983), nos. 1, 2, 5, 7; *Urkunden Könige Jerusalem*, nos. 19, 21, 82–3, 128, 211–12, 308–10, 451, 453, 474, 568–70.

V. INAUGURATION   393

over magnates and prelates. Kings generally sought to avoid issuing grants that might challenge or alienate leading members of the realm. In the lead-up to his inauguration in 1189, Richard I of England gave lands to his younger brother John, for whom he also secured a marriage to the heiress to the earldom of Gloucester.[206] On becoming king of France in 1031, Henry I granted his brother possession of the duchy of Burgundy,[207] while in 1152 Frederick Barbarossa made his eponymous cousin duke of Swabia.[208] Yet John received the earldom of Gloucester only because the earl had died, Burgundy used to be Henry I's possession and Swabia Barbarossa's. There were no rival claimants to feel aggrieved or disappointed.

At the same time, the approach could only be taken so far. Indeed, one of the criticisms levelled at Richard I over his gifts to John was that many evils arose from his 'immoderate and unwise largesse'.[209] Normally, therefore, rulers assured themselves of broad backing before making strikingly generous grants. This was manifestly the case in the sequence of charters surviving from King Stephen's early reign. One of his earliest privileges, issued on Christmas Day 1135 to the abbey and bishopric of Bath, merely confirmed an earlier donation. It had three witnesses.[210] When Beverley Minster received generous gifts in February 1136, the charter was witnessed by ten prelates and magnates.[211] When, that same year, Stephen restored to Winchester estates and rights alienated as far back as the reign of William the Conqueror, the number of witnesses had swollen to between fourteen and twenty-seven.[212] This act of lavish patronage necessitated a considerable redistribution of resources. It also demonstrated Stephen's intention to be a good king by ending past abuses. And it greatly enriched a see held by his brother. Hence a sizable audience was required. We have seen similar strategies at play in the case of Frederick Barbarossa and his handling of the Bavarian succession. The one time he decided to proceed on his own, his rashness delayed a peaceable solution. Otherwise, he demonstratively purported to act in unison with the princes, at their behest and on their advice. This was a matter of performing royal lordship, but also of respecting the practicalities of what was feasible and necessary. Princes and prelates would need to enforce a decision alongside the king. Securing their consent might not altogether avoid rivalries, but it

---

[206] Roger of Howden, *Gesta*, vol. 2, 78.
[207] Rodulfus Glaber, *Historiarum libri quinqui*, 156–9.
[208] Görich, *Friedrich Barbarossa*, 137–41. See also Freed, *Frederick Barbarossa*, 82–5, 179–82.
[209] William of Newburgh, *Historia*, vol. 1, 302. Similar concerns were voiced by Richard of Devizes, *Chronicle*, 6.
[210] *Regesta Regum Anglo-Normannorum*, vol. 3, no. 45.
[211] *Regesta Regum Anglo-Normannorum*, vol. 3, no. 99.
[212] *Regesta Regum Anglo-Normannorum*, vol. 3, nos. 945–9.

394   10. BEYOND ENTHRONEMENT

ensured that anyone disappointed would find it harder to challenge the monarch or the recipients of his largesse.

This need for consultation provided prelates and princes with an opportunity to influence the governance of the realm. They did so collectively, not individually, and by both restraining royal power and working towards their own advancement. In 1136 Stephen was forced to abandon the siege of Exeter. The townsmen had asked for terms of surrender and begged for royal clemency, which the king, egged on by the bishop of Winchester, denied. At this, many of the barons, who had friends and relatives among the besieged, baulked. They then interceded with the king:

> he [Stephen] had won a complete victory over his enemies in at last obtaining, by superior strength what was his by right, and therefore it was more consonant with his lofty position and more befitting royal clemency to grant life to supplicant prisoners than by inflicting the death penalty ruthlessly to deprive them of the little they had left. They added that the besieged had not sworn allegiance to the king's majesty, and had taken up arms only in fealty to their lord ... Wherefore they judged it wiser and more to the advantage of his kingdom to have done with that wearisome siege by which they were so much distressed, that he might both take over the castle to the increase of his glory and gird himself more readily and eagerly to perform other tasks.[213]

By refusing to continue to lend him their backing, the barons forced the king to practise generosity and clemency, and not to exercise revenge. Of course, that some of the barons should have sympathised with the besieged also mattered, as did the fact that the inhabitants and defenders of Exeter were tied to Stephen's men by networks of friendship and family. But it was above all the language attributed to the barons that is of interest here – all the more notably, as it was recorded in the Gesta Stephani, an account that, while by no means uncritical, was nonetheless favourably inclined towards the king. The barons invoked the duties of kingship, and reminded Stephen of just why it was that they had chosen him to be their ruler. They had helped the king secure victory and in the recovery of one of his chief cities. They had met their own set of obligations. But their assistance was conditional on Stephen upholding his by heeding their advice.

Comparable incidents occurred across Europe. Three will suffice by way of illustration. In each, a ruler faced opposition early on in his reign. In each, criticism was sometimes openly voiced, sometimes implicitly, but always by lay elites acting collectively, and centring on the duties of kingship. In 1152, Otto of Freising recounted, the German princes denied Frederick's request to man an expedition against the king of Hungary.[214] No reason for their refusal has

---

[213] Gesta Stephani, 42–3.
[214] Otto of Freising, Gesta Frederici, ii.6, pp. 292–3.

V. INAUGURATION   395

been recorded, but that Frederick turned his attention to the Bavarian question instead may be an indication of what they thought his priorities should be. There were good reasons why he might. If Otto is to be believed, Barbarossa had been elected king because he was related to both families behind the dispute. The princes had hoped that he would thus be best placed to end it.[215] In that sense, Frederick was reminded of why he wore the crown. Of course, that he planned to embark on a campaign against the rulers of Hungary fits an established pattern: waging wars against neighbouring foes – or, in Otto's version of events, forcing rebels back into the fold – was exactly what newly enthroned kings ought to do. Yet Barbarossa's efforts were thwarted because his leading subjects appear to have felt that upholding other norms, such as keeping the peace at home, was a more pressing concern. However dimly, a process of negotiation comes into view, with ruler and ruled determining what abstract norms signified in practice.

Something quite similar happened a few years later in Denmark. In 1154, Valdemar had become one of three kings reigning simultaneously. Three years later, one of them, Sven had invited his rival Knud to a feast. There, Knud was murdered at Sven's instigation. Sven was subsequently slain in battle, which left Valdemar I as the sole surviving ruler of Denmark. Knud's erstwhile retainers 'approached the king in a body', and demanded that Sven's men be outlawed for their participation in so heinous a crime. Valdemar faced a dilemma. On the one hand, sending so many men into exile would potentially turn them into recruits for ambitious relatives and future rivals. Indeed, these were the men, who it was feared, Buris might seek to lead. On the other hand, not satisfying the desire for revenge and justice would risk driving away Knud's followers, and would undermine Valdemar's role as keeper of the law. 'Finally, subdued by the persistence of this pressure group',[216] Valdemar developed an elaborate stratagem. Or so Saxo claimed. It ensured both that justice was done, and that he could embrace Sven's allies as his own, granting them his friendship the more easily, 'the further he recognized they were from being party to that seditious assassination'. Valdemar had to weigh up the respective merits and risks of rigour and mercy, the need to be a strict defender of the law, with his duty to maintain peace within the realm, even if as a result he let guilty men go free. He was forced to make that choice because he had been confronted by the community of Knud's retainers. Unlike Barbarossa, however, he was not forced to choose one norm over the other, but managed to find a way to satisfy both at once. He decreed that all the men named by Knud's followers would be exiled, but that it would be the responsibility of Knud's men

---

[215] Otto of Freising, *Gesta Frederici*, ii.2, pp. 284–7.
[216] The Latin sounds rather less as if it might have inspired the writers of *The West Wing*: 'Ad ultimum instantium perseverantia victus': 'In the final instance defeated by perseverance'.

396 10. BEYOND ENTHRONEMENT

to welcome them back. For, Saxo argued, the king knew that 'the human mind easily switches from dislike to partiality'.[217] What he left unsaid was that Knud's followers would be held accountable for any undue harshness by the remaining friends and relatives of the men they had exiled, while those who escaped unscathed would be all the more grateful for the king's display of mercy and largesse. He also left unsaid that Valdemar had no choice but to concede. All he could do was lay responsibility for any troubles that might ensue on the magnates who had forced his hand.

Successful kings used moments of crisis to strengthen their authority. For this to work, royal authority had to be asserted. It had, after all, been challenged: the English nobles refused to lay Exeter waste, the German princes declined to campaign in Hungary and the Danes forced Valdemar to choose between expediency and justice. To prevent disruption from veering into disorder, a course of action had to be agreed that demonstrated the king's authority, and that had the backing of his people. That was more easily accomplished if disputes were conducted within a shared view of what royal authority entailed. Hence Otto's and Saxo's portrayal of Frederick and Valdemar respectively as seizing the initiative. In fact, during a diet at Würzburg later in 1152, called by Barbarossa to tackle the Bavarian question, he demonstratively received envoys from Sicily who asked for support against their king. This time, the princes willingly agreed to embark on a campaign against the enemies of the realm.[218] In the English context, even the *Gesta Stephani* painted Stephen as casting aside the false counsel of his brother and winning over the men of Exeter with his generosity and kindness.

Yet such common ground could also be used to reject criticism, as happened in Bohemia in 1158. That year, Duke Vladislav had received a royal crown and the title of king from Frederick Barbarossa. In return, he promised to provide troops for Frederick's imminent campaign against Milan. The new king and his entourage returned in great splendour to Prague. Vladislav convened an assembly of the great men of the realm, where he announced his decision. Several of the Bohemian nobles objected. The king had entered into an agreement without their consent. Vladislav managed to sway most of them by promising that he would cover the expenses of all who joined him. The ones who refused, he mockingly declared, should rest assured that they would remain in the king's peace while being lazy and playing womanly games.[219] Vincent of Prague, to whom we owe this account, clearly sided with the king. The context is important: the newly appointed king presented himself to his people in royal majesty. While there was much rejoicing at so great a dignity,

---

[217] Saxo Grammaticus, *Gesta Danorum*, xiv.19.18, pp. 1112–13. For the context see also Kjaer, 'Feasting with traitors'.

[218] Otto of Freising, *Gesta Frederici*, ii.7, pp. 292–5.

[219] *Vincentii Pragensis Annales*, 667–8.

one that cast ruler and ruled alike in glory, the Prague assembly still created a forum in which subjects dissatisfied with the king's decision could voice their dissent and insist on their participation in the governance of the realm. The king's mocking response should not deceive us. He had been forced to make concessions. He had to pay the expenses of the nobles joining him (rather than being able to demand their participation) and he had to keep under his protection and in his favour anyone who decided to remain behind.

Reminding the king of his duties was by no means something that happened only during a ruler's enthronement. Neither, for that matter, was it something confined to leading members of the clergy. It was central to the performance of kingship and to the negotiation of relations both between ruler and ruled and among the ruled. It formed an integral part of the exercise the royal office during a ruler's early reign, and was something frequently employed by the ruled to help shape the governance of the realm. In many ways, it constituted an attempt to enact the right order of the realm, and to do so in the presence of the leading secular and spiritual princes of the realm, as well as before their dependants and followers. This also poses problems of interpretation. The need to uphold norms, to fashion acts and petitions in a manner that made them conform to the expectations of how kings and their subjects ought to behave, can too readily obscure the more material needs served in the process. But then this merely reinforces the importance of the phenomenon itself. Invoking values was a means with which the manifold and diverse tensions at the heart of the king-making process could be negotiated, with which these tensions could be reconciled, and with which the violence and unrest, the disturbances and civil war that constantly lurked beneath the surface, might yet be averted.

The practices discussed in this and previous chapters were remarkably consistent across Latin Europe. It did not greatly matter whether kings were inaugurated by unction and crowning, by taking a sword from the altar of a church, by being placed on a giant stone or handed a pair of hazel twigs. The norms and how adherence to them was demonstrated unfolded along similar (though not identical) lines. Moments of remonstration and challenge helped to reinforce a normative framework of power, and of expectations of good kingship, and to ensure that they were passed on from one generation to the next. They provided precedent with which to fashion and with which to evaluate the exercise of power in the present. This is particularly striking in the emergence of transpersonal concepts of the realm, which underpinned the ideal of royal succession, and which were so central both to the liturgy and to the performance of kingship. These were among the lasting legacies that the high Middle Ages bequeathed to subsequent generations. They provided the foundations on which kingship was created, passed on, conferred and enacted. They were the means by which the tensions between reality and practice, between suitability and right and between consensus and authority could if

398   10. BEYOND ENTHRONEMENT

not necessarily be reconciled, then at least be navigated. Perhaps they could even be harnessed for the common good.

This is not to suggest that violence was always avoided. The centrality of warfare to the king-making process, as well as of rigorous and sometimes brutal enforcement of justice, has been amply demonstrated. And sometimes kings simply did prove unable to convince enough of their subjects that they had both the character and the means to impose order. Rival claimants emerged, and rulers were either dispatched on a path towards martyrdom and future sainthood, or towards becoming exemplars of the useless, inept and evil king, warning precedents to their successors, among the half-remembered bogeymen of yore. But most of the time, in most parts of Europe, if a ruler made it through those first few years without alienating too many princes and prelates, if he won over most of his erstwhile rivals and defeated the others, if he rewarded his allies and retainers without exhausting the resources at his disposal or starting new disputes, if he could demonstrate that he knew how to balance mercy with rigour, the threat of force with a preference for peaceful settlements, then he was unlikely to die at the hands of his successor or at those of his people. He had found a path to kingship.

Conclusion

Choosing the right path to the throne entailed not just having power, but knowing – and showing that one knew – how to wield it. In order to be a good king, a ruler ought to be more powerful than any of his subjects. He would not be able to protect those who could not protect themselves, to humble the mighty and to elevate the humble, if he lacked the means to take on the former on behalf of the latter. He also ought to be of a virtuous disposition. A weak and ineffectual ruler would not be able to perform his duties, but one holding power without moral restraint would become an oppressor of his people, not their protector, a tyrant, not a guardian. Power should therefore be both the result of virtue and its reward. Moral outlook and material means were the twin foundations on which the edifice of high medieval kingship rested.

Yet virtue lay in the eye of the beholder. One man's rigorous enforcement of the law was another's act of tyranny, one man's just reward another's wasteful profligacy. Still, values and norms could not be interpreted at will. There remained a relatively consistent set of expectations about what qualified someone for the royal office. Good kings embarked upon upholding the law, protecting the weak, being generous to the Church and keeping the enemies of the realm at bay. They took up the royal office not because they wished to rule others, but because it was a most solemn duty, an onerous obligation thrust upon them by both their people and their Creator. Doing justice was both the root and the apex of good governance. It was concerned with enforcing both the law of the land, and, more importantly, that of God. It aimed to maintain the right order of the world.[1] Upholding divine law furthermore laid upon rulers responsibility for the spiritual well-being of their people. Kings owed their position to God, and they demonstrated both their devotion and their willingness to act like kings by overseeing matters of faith. The numinous was woven into the very fabric of kingship. It just meant something different to high medieval observers than to many of their modern readers.

Good kingship also demanded that rulers surround themselves with men of good repute. They needed trustworthy men to assist them in wielding the

---

[1] *Isidori Hispalensis Etymologiarum*, ii.24.6; Fredric L. Cheyette, 'Suum cuique tribuere', *French Historical Studies* 6 (1976), 287–99.

400   CONCLUSION

sword of justice. But, as Peter of Blois had explained to Henry II, a ruler could
not enforce the law of God if he did not know what it was. Virtuous kings
therefore sought out wise men with whom to discuss 'the nature of things'.
They assembled libraries like the one at Hagenau. They commissioned and
received treatises on how to lead a moral life. As William of Malmesbury had
put it: an illiterate king – one without an interest in learning – was but
a crowned ass.[2] Furthermore, learned advisors helped reinforce the foundational principles on which they and their peers drew in thinking and writing
about power. They knew their Cicero from their Seneca, had at least a passing
acquaintance with Isidore and had probably been reared on a diet of selections
from Augustine and Gregory the Great. They provided guidance on how to
relate abstract concepts to concrete action.

They also provided a link with their peers advising princes and prelates.
Collectively, they helped shape and enforce a normative framework in which to
engage with the business of power. That framework was anchored in biblical
precedent, as well as in classical and patristic writings. However, it was
a framework, not a rigid template. It could be amended and revised so as to
reflect the realities of power. Advice and counsel, for example, played a far
more significant role in the eyes of high medieval writers than they did in the
Old Testament. There were no barons and princes in the books of Samuel and
Kings whose agreement had to be sought. The role of the Israelites ceased once
they had agreed to God's choice of king for them. Not so in high medieval Latin
Europe. The burden of reprimanding the king, shouldered by figures like
Samuel and Nathan, was shared among the ruled. In that sense, the principle
of oversight, of the participation of the ruled in the governance of the realm,
was an innovation. Yet it also had been present in the conceptualisation of
kingship from the outset. It was not born out of a crisis, whether of accountability or otherwise.

Depictions of king-making were also shaped by the material conditions and
political needs of a particular realm. Being able to keep foreign foes at bay
mattered everywhere. But it was of particular concern in kingdoms facing
powerful neighbours who might be – or might feel – called upon to intervene.
Hence warding off such rulers assumed far greater prominence in Scotland,
Hungary, Poland, Denmark and Jerusalem than it did in England and Norway.
Yet such differences were variations on a common theme, not altogether
different tunes. Writers operated within a shared framework that made it
possible to accommodate change with relative ease. William of Normandy
conquering England or Roger II becoming king of Sicily had a profound
impact on their respective polities, but their actions nonetheless conformed
to a common set of expectations about what constituted a legitimate path to
kingship.

[2] William of Malmesbury, *Gesta Regum Anglorum*, v.390, pp. 710–11.

CONCLUSION 401

Inevitably, histories and chronicles did not necessarily set out coherent conceptual models. The same text could contain contradictory readings of the same principle. One would expect nothing else, given that authors and the actors whose deeds they recorded frequently faced situations where equally valid principles had to be weighed up, and where the expedient might have to be chosen over the desirable. Often, a decision would have to be made whether to elect a candidate who was present, an adult, with a proven track record in warfare and peace-keeping, or one who may have been more closely related to the late king, but who was under age or had a reputation for profligacy and wanton cruelty. At other times, the question was whether to enforce the full rigour of the law, even if that would result in rebellion and unrest. The interpretation of norms was tailored to the concrete challenge and problems at hand. Determining the right course of action was therefore a matter of forging consensus.

While mechanisms existed to facilitate agreement, they also created tensions of their own. Elections provide a good example. On one level, they were concerned with finding the candidate most capable of leading a people and of being pleasing to God. The emphasis on unanimity and probity flowed from this premise. On another level, elections reflected practical needs. Patrilineal succession was normative, but not the norm. Succession disputes were frequent. They also provided an incentive to define the royal office and to rehearse the principles on which its exercise should be based. Across Latin Europe, they were essential stages in the king-making process. If civil strife was to be avoided, as many of the great men of the realm as possible had to agree on one candidate. Yet, in order for that to happen, promises had to be made. Grants had to be offered. Scheming and plotting and secret negotiations could not be avoided. That is, steps had to be taken that violated the very principles without which the act could not legitimately be performed. The ensuing tensions could not always be resolved, but they could be lessened. Ensuring that key stages of the process demonstratively enacted adherence to what should be was one way of accomplishing that. Another was to show through concrete actions that fundamental principles would be upheld. The legitimacy of an election was rooted in choosing a ruler who would prove that he had been raised to his dignity by the right people and for the right reasons. But that, too, required consent.

Paths to kingship were therefore not the ruler's alone to tread. His relatives, teachers and followers guided him along the way. They might even force him into action, as the Birkibeinar had done with Sverrir. The king's subjects decided whether and how far they would follow. However powerful a ruler might be as an individual, without the backing of princes and magnates, of bishops and abbots, he would never have gained the crown, and was unlikely to have it for long. Just as he was a keeper of the realm, so his leading subjects were the keepers of the common good. They acted collectively, as

402   CONCLUSION

representatives of the community of the realm. If the great men chose a bad
king, if they preferred vain promises to virtue, lavish gifts to moral rigour, easy-
going sociability to truthfulness, they would in the eyes of God be just as
culpable for the evils that subsequently befell the realm as the *rex inutilis* they
had placed upon the throne. Their actions would invite rebellions and foreign
invasions. They would provide rivals with an opportunity to attack their men
and properties. Choosing the right person mattered.

The authority to make or legitimise kings was therefore as much an opportunity as it was a duty. It also involved responsibility towards the *populus*, the
populace at large. On the one hand, it was very much excluded from the
process. The people were meant to provide a festive backdrop, a mass of
cheering crowds, respectful and jubilant, or be humble petitioners seeking
redress. But they were not supposed to have a say in determining who occupied
the throne. When they did, as in London in 1136 and 1141, or in Palermo in
1166, then it was under exceptional circumstances. Even the citizens of Mainz,
who, in 1077, attacked the followers of Rudolf of Rheinfelden, were viewed as
being in the wrong by Bruno, despite his hostility towards Rudolf. On the other
hand, considerable importance attached to 'the people'. There could be no
kingdom without a people. In their own myths of origin, Poles pre-dated
Piasts, Hungarians Árpads and Bohemians Přemyslids. The *populus* made
kingship possible. It had chosen someone to be its leader, but he, his descendants and successors could wield legitimate authority only as long as they
protected and shielded the community of the realm. Seeing to its needs,
remedying injustices, liberating it from evil and oppressive lords was precisely
why kings had been granted their power. 'The people' provided an opportunity
to pass comment on the behaviour of the mighty and to reinforce the moral
imperative of protecting those who could not protect themselves. Failing to
come to their assistance, refusing to act or proving incapable of protecting
them, inevitably called into question the right to rule over them.

'The people' was a rhetorical figure so broad that it could encompass widows
and orphans as well as claimants to the Danish throne. It was shorthand for
those requesting succour from the king. By portraying themselves as the poor
in need of assistance, petitioners could force a ruler's hand. Refusing to heed
their pleas would equal forfeiting the moral foundations of his power. A ruler
who refused to treat them with equity and justice would prove unlikely to ward
off the enemies of the realm, to control his officials and to restrain his
supporters. Indeed, stepping in to give assistance to the poor and powerless
was a legitimising strategy. It was to ease their suffering that Stephen had set
out to claim the English throne. It was to provide succour to the men of
Antioch that Fulk I had intervened in the affairs of the principality. It was to
free the Sicilians from the yoke of Tancred's tyranny that Henry VI fought to
secure his wife's inheritance. How a ruler engaged with the people at large
provided a way of judging his performance. Would he shoulder what Peter

CONCLUSION

Damian had described as the burden of justice? Would he act for the common good? Did he take the throne out of ambition and greed or to lead an easy life? Conversely, the suffering of the populace at large also offered grounds to take up arms against the ruler, or at least to demand that he reform his governance. That, at least, was how the Golden Bull of Hungary had been framed. Similar thinking underpinned Rudolf of Rheinfelden's election in 1077, and it was why the Birkibeinar demanded that Sverrir become their leader. The *populus* may have lacked a formal role, but it nonetheless framed how kings should be chosen, and how they should rule.

What about change over time? At first sight, the emphasis on an unbroken succession of rulers and the frequent invocation of antiquity militates against tracing such change. This impression of timelessness is, of course, misleading. Change was inherent in the king-making process, but it occurred at different rates, in different forms and not necessarily where modern historians would expect it to have happened. It also unfolded in different categories of time: during the process of king-making, during the life cycle of an individual and across historical time. Change and timelessness were not polar opposites, but mutually reinforcing.

King-making could take several years. It began with the death of one ruler and ended only once a successor had been able to overcome rival claimants and firmly take control of the material and symbolic sources of power. It marked the transition from a moment of uncertainty to one of relative stability. If successful, it would ensure the continuity of the realm, and maintain the right order of the world. Unrest would be averted and hostile neighbours kept at bay. The process was also about overcoming ruptures, about *returning* to a time when things had been as they should be. What seemed a chronologically rational sequence of steps forward in time culminated in a backwards leap. It was a fragile process. It could fall apart at any point. Missteps, unexpected challenges or the sheer inability to navigate the pitfalls of rulership could turn a moment of putative hope into one of deep anxiety and profound despair.

As far as individual experiences are concerned, the transition from candidate to king, and from someone who was king by dint of coronation and election to one who sat securely on the throne, would have been experienced by any ruler throughout this period. However, to get to that stage, a putative king already needed to have reached a degree of maturity. He had to be able to distinguish right from wrong, mount a horse, lead his men into battle, be an avid hunter, marry and know how to 'discuss the nature of things' with learned clerics. The process of change continued once a king had seized the reins of power. He gradually grew into his new role – a theme central to Otto of Freising's portrayal of Frederick Barbarossa. The king learned to rule, as William of Malmesbury had claimed of Henry I, with a lighter hand. Or, as 'Gallus' had put it concerning Boleslaw III: 'he set about developing his courage and his bodily strength'. Notwithstanding any training and instruction, it was quite a step from acting as the heir to the throne to actually occupying it. No longer were there fathers at hand who could be called upon to intervene. No longer was one's authority limited to only part of the realm or to certain types of business. Old friends might have to be abandoned and new enemies would arise. Successful rulers learned how to handle this kind of ultimately predictable change.

They also had to act with an eye to developments beyond their own lifetimes. Ideally, kings would live long enough, and have children who lived long enough, to secure the succession of their progeny, or at least to nominate someone to rule after them. Their responsibility encompassed not only relatives and dependants, but the realm at large. In most kingdoms, whoever was king was but the most recent in a long line of rulers. It was his duty to ensure that the line was continued, but also to see to it that the gains made by his forebears were preserved and even enlarged and losses recovered. Rights had to be defended or restored so that the fame of illustrious ancestors would not be dimmed. Once again, looking forward and looking back appear as a single package. Ideal rulership manifested itself not as venturing into a new age, but as reviving and re-enacting if not a glorious past, then at least one that was respectable and worth emulating. Simultaneously, kings were supposed to take charge of the continuing liturgical commemoration of those who had ruled before. And, as churchmen frequently pointed out, they would themselves be held accountable by God. *Memoria*, in this regard, was certainly about liturgical commemoration, but it was also concerned with ensuring that, after the king's death, peace and tranquillity prevailed, and that the right order of the world be maintained. That way, a king's own place as part of a sequence of exemplary rulers would be assured.

Thus far, the changes discussed were structurally determined – they reflected the process of king-making and the life cycle of the individuals involved. What, however, about changes *to* established structures? As far as high medieval writers were concerned, by far the most decisive such change to occur was the adoption of Christianity into hitherto largely 'pagan' polities. In Hungary, Poland and Norway, Christianisation coincided with the creation of kingship. But the acquisition of a crown, while certainly important, was not what mattered most. That was the conversion. It established a polity as part of a community of Christian nations. It also initiated an indigenous ecclesiastical organisation. As always, there were exceptions. In Jerusalem, the conquest of 1099 constituted the key point of change, while in Sicily it was the arrival of the Normans around the year 1000. In other realms, moments of crisis provided a focal point, like the murder of St Stanislas in Poland or the conquest of 1066 in England. But even these were embedded in a narrative of divine retribution and salvation. To 'Gallus', the killing of St Stanislas threatened to undo the accomplishments of Boleslaw I, but the visions about Boleslaw III and the divine backing they implied for him promised a return to how things should

CONCLUSION   405

be. In England, William of Malmesbury linked the Norman Conquest explicitly to the sinfulness of the Anglo-Saxon aristocracy.[3] The affairs of the realm were rooted in Christian time, and it was not only being subject to it, but being able to participate in it that mattered.

Medieval authors were not wrong to have stressed the importance of conversion. Christianisation facilitated the spread and reception of shared cultural foundations and reinforced a common structural framework.[4] It is because of this that we can compare Poland, Hungary, England, France, Germany, Sicily, Iberia, Bohemia, Denmark and the crusader states. The Bible, traditions of biblical exegesis and the importance of classical antiquity as a route into the acquisition of Latin and a tool with which to flesh out biblical precedent ensured that references to Isidore of Seville, St Augustine, Pseudo-Cyprian and Cicero surface in Thietmar, Fulcher of Chartres, Cosmas of Prague, Alexander of Telese, Walter Map and Sven Aggesen. They also ensured that Wipo's concept of kingship would have been accessible to Saxo, William of Malmesbury's to Vincent Kadlubek and Otto of Freising's to the Anonymous Notary. Shared reference points and structural features facilitated a considerable consistency across regions and across the central Middle Ages in how authors wrote about king-making.

Because it created a framework, not a template, high medieval thinking about power could easily accommodate change. Conquests and new dynasties did not alter the fundamental pattern of how kings ought to be chosen or of the norms by which rulers ought to abide. For instance, the Investiture Controversy, as beloved of contemporary medievalists as it was largely ignored by medieval contemporaries, had little discernible impact on the king-making process. There was no crisis of sacrality. Hildebrandine tantrums did not undermine the basic principle that kingship was rooted in the divine will, and that its moral obligations were as binding to rulers as to those who chose them. In fact, as far as the Church was concerned, Frederick Barbarossa, Valdemar I and Sverrir got away with a lot more than their eleventh-century predecessors could ever have imagined. Rulers ran into difficulties only when they pursued their goals so ruthlessly that they provided an opening for disgruntled subjects to accuse them of violating what they purported to protect. Reformist zeal provided an additional way of framing these accusations.[5] But the principles on which resistance was based long predated the particular concerns of the Lombard monk and his followers.

---

[3] William of Malmesbury, *Saints' Lives, Vita Wulfstani*, 58–9.

[4] See above, Chapters 1 and 2.

[5] See, generally, Steven Vanderputten's sceptical remarks about 'reform': 'Individual experience, collective remembrance and the politics of monastic reform in high medieval Flanders', *EME* 20 (2011), 70–89.

406   CONCLUSION

Moreover, rebellion and resistance did not question the framework sketched here, but a ruler's adherence to it. Partly because the precise meaning of norms was a matter of interpretation, they enabled protest, and provided a means by which resistance could be legitimised. At the same time, because challenges to royal authority still operated within a shared set of expectations, they could be appropriated. The ease with which the cult of Thomas Becket was turned into a means of strengthening royal rule provides a case in point. Within a few years of his canonisation, the archbishop had been transformed from a victim of royal tyranny into a protector of the right order of the realm, with the king among his most devout followers.[6] Just as easily, the principles invoked in mounting challenges could be turned against the people mounting them. Adolf of Cologne, Eskil of Lund and Eystein of Nidaros left themselves open to attack when they could convincingly be portrayed as working no longer for the common good, but for personal or partisan gain. Debate and contest were woven into the very fabric of power.

The massive expansion of literacy in the course of the twelfth century had a far greater impact than the Investiture Controversy. It is a major reason for the chronological imbalance in this book. There is more to be said about twelfth-century images of kingship because more was being written, not just in terms of chronicles. Seneca's *De Clementia* and Cicero's *De Amicitia* were copied and transcribed with renewed vigour. As Michael Clanchy has pointed out, written records provided new ways of gathering and collecting revenue, of enshrining, asserting and enforcing royal power and royal prerogatives. However, exploiting these tools required wealth. Training and recruiting clerics adept in these skills necessitated considerable outlay. In consequence, the already mighty became even mightier. In Aragon, England, France, Sicily and Hungary royal power grew exponentially compared to that of magnates and prelates.[7] The renewed interest in Cicero and Seneca, with their emphasis on power being wielded for the common good, probably reflected this changing landscape. So did the engagement in works of biblical exegesis with questions of oversight, of ensuring that rulers abide by the norms of their office. By the thirteenth century the assertion of communal rights was framed as a defence not against the tyranny of the king (with Magna Carta the exception that proves the rule), but against that of his agents, if left unchecked by baronial or episcopal oversight. The moral character of the king's chief advisors always reflected on the ruler. Hence Wipo's praise for Conrad II's choice of counsellors. But it acquired far greater significance towards the end of our period. Where Conrad picked an inner circle of close advisors, Richard I appointed judges and justiciars, replaced sheriffs and seneschals.

---

[6] Paul Webster and Marie-Pierre Gelin, eds., *The Cult of Thomas Becket in the Plantagenet World, c.1170–1220* (Woodbridge, 2016).

[7] Clanchy, *From Memory to Written Record*, 102; Bisson, *Crisis*.

CONCLUSION 407

Written records also created precedent. Through them, custom acquired the patina of history. Hence the emergence of Aachen, Reims, Scone and Westminster as 'traditional' sites of a king's inauguration. In England, the decades around 1120 witnessed the refashioning of the pre-Conquest past on a monumental scale. The first indigenous histories of Poland, Norway, Hungary, Denmark and Bohemia were written. They enshrined precedent for future usage. It was a lot easier to assert as customary a particular office during royal crownings or crown-wearings if there was written evidence with which to back up the claim, or on the basis of which it had been communicated as well known and hence normative. In consequence, the public demonstration of status became progressively more important, especially as the audience now extended to future generations. In accounts of princely lineages, the distinctive virtues of a noble *stirps* were often visualised in their relationship with kings who were either morally surpassed by a dynast's forebears or who owed their thrones to them. Royal lordship depended upon and was rooted in the consent and backing of the ruled. But memories of that relationship had to be preserved, recorded and defended.

The relationship also had to be codified. The act of recording history preserved – or even created – a memory of rights and claims, but for these to be translated into political reality, it had to be recorded in a manner that conferred upon them enforceable authority. Hence the proliferation of forgeries, so characteristic of the eleventh and twelfth centuries,[8] as well as the creation of aristocratic cartularies and *Traditionsbücher* (though most were kept by religious houses on the behalf of lay patrons).[9] From the end of the twelfth century, the practice extended to formal charters of liberties. Magnus Erlingsson's coronation charter was an early outlier. It was, however, representative of contemporary thinking about royal power in that it granted the archbishop of Nidaros a role of oversight on behalf of the community at large. That was what prelates were supposed to do. In this regard, the Norwegian example provides a useful reminder not to mistake form for content. Thinking about royal accountability – how to get the ruler to abide by shared norms of the royal office and how to ensure that he act for the common good not private

---

[8] Bernd Schneidmüller, 'Zwischen frommer Lüge und schnödem Betrug: Fälschungen im Mittelalter', *AKG* 73 (1991), 217–32.

[9] Adam J. Kosto, 'The *Liber feudorum maior* of the Counts of Barcelona: the cartulary as an expression of power', *JMedH* 27 (2001), 1–22; John B. Freed, 'The creation of the Codex Falkensteinensis (1166): self-representation and reality', in *Representations of Power in Medieval Germany*, ed. Simon MacLean and Björn Weiler (Turnhout, 2006), 189–210; Peter Johanek, 'Zur rechtlichen Funktion von Traditionsnotiz, Traditionsbuch und früher Siegelurkunde', in *Recht und Schrift im Mittelalter*, ed. Peter Classen (Sigmaringen, 1977), 131–62; Alice Taylor, 'Formalising aristocratic power in royal "acta" in late twelfth- and early thirteenth-century France and Scotland', *TRHS*, 6th series, 28 (2018), 33–64; Adam J. Kosto and Anders Winroth, eds., *Charters, Cartularies, and Archives: the Preservation and Transmission of Documents in the Medieval West* (Toronto, 2002).

408   CONCLUSION

gain – was integral to high medieval engagements with power. It was not
necessary that contemporaries be exposed to new techniques of estate management for them to grasp the significance of that accountability.

Increasing bureaucratisation of royal government brought with it the need
to defend established liberties and practices, and new means with which to do
so. In England, France and Hungary, the target of oversight shifted from the
king to his officials. The re-issue of the Golden Bull, Louis IX's investigation of
royal officials in the 1240s and the Provisions of Oxford in England in 1258
aimed to restrain and oversee the king's agents in the localities and in relation
to the realm's established elites. These developments occurred within
a conceptual framework still recognisable to Thietmar of Merseburg and
William of Malmesbury. Wielding power over others was a duty, not an
opportunity. Kings ought to restrain the haughty and protect those who
could not protect themselves, even if this meant taking on judges of the forest
rather than castellans and knights. Bishops had a particular responsibility for
ensuring that the governance of the realm promoted the common good.
Anyone holding power would be held accountable for his actions before
God.[10] However, just as patristic writers had to mould biblical precept and
classical precedent to fit the conditions of late antique Roman and post-Roman
societies, and just as high medieval authors had to translate that inheritance to
apply to post-Carolingian Europe, so late medieval observers had to accommodate the social, cultural, economic and religious transformation of the
thirteenth century. They also had new tools to work with. But they still drew
as much on Cicero and Seneca, Gregory the Great and St Augustine, as their
high medieval forebears had done.

Indeed, if many of the norms invoked seem familiar even today, then it is
probably not so much because of any continuing reception of Thietmar, Saxo
and Otto of Freising, as a consequence of the centrality of the sources on which
they drew. Well into the 1970s, Cicero formed part of the staple diet of elite
education. Gregory and St Augustine were integral to reformist Catholic social
theology. High medieval sources therefore do not provide the foundations of
modern political norms. They constitute a point along a continuum of the
reception and application of texts considered to be authoritative. Even so, high
medieval authors struggled with challenges that recur in any polity where
a single figurehead is charged with exercising authority on behalf of and over
the community at large. How could government be held accountable? How
could the ruled restrain and direct the power of the ruler? How could they
ensure that public office was held by trustworthy and truthful men and
women? How could one ensure that those wielding power did not succumb
to its lures? The answers given to these questions are rooted in each historical

[10] Frédérique Lachaud, *L'éthique du pouvoir au Moyen Âge: l'office dans la culture politique
(Angleterre, vers 1150–vers 1330)* (Paris, 2010).

CONCLUSION 409

moment. They reveal how contemporaries thought about the right order of the world, what they imagined it to look like, and what they deemed feasible tools for securing it. They make it possible to situate our own experience in a broader historical context. They may even make us rethink how we engage with that experience.

The model sketched here reflects a particular space and a particular moment in time: Europe between the late tenth and the early thirteenth centuries. It cannot easily be applied to other periods or to cultures outside Latin Europe. Still, three aspects are significant beyond this book's immediate chronological and thematic focus and lend themselves to further comparison. First, given the dominance in a modern context of the vernacular and of the concept of the nation state, it is all the more important to look beyond both. There is nothing natural or inevitable about the emergence of the latter, while the undoubted significance of the former should not blind us to the extent to which cultural exchange and transfer permeate linguistic boundaries. What is true of high medieval kingship also applies to other aspects of life. Merchants, townspeople, clerics and monks, religious minorities and perhaps even peasants had as much in common with their peers across the medieval world as with their immediate neighbours, and certainly more than with their ecclesiastical and secular superiors. In order to get at the distinctiveness of their experience, in order to be able to recognise the impact of environmental factors or that of law, demographics, culture and politics, we need to look beyond the artificial constructs of nineteenth-century political geography.

Kingship demands a transeuropean approach not only because of over-whelming structural similarities between the component polities of the Latin west, but also because contemporary engagements were largely the pursuit of a well-connected, highly mobile, international elite that drew on a shared corpus of foundational texts. Indeed, this is one area where the proliferation of vernacular texts, and the increasing codification of legal customs from the thirteenth century onwards could turn out to have created a degree of distinct-iveness that had not existed before. In terms of education, Hedwig Röckelein has pointed out that the cosmopolitan world of the high Middle Ages did not survive the proliferation of local universities and *studia*.[11] Paradoxically, the expansion of educational opportunities curtailed the common intellectual foundations of Latin Europe. How far did that hold true of engagements with royal power and other aspects of elite life? And what was the impact of the widening social foundation of late medieval elites on concepts like the *populus*? Even if 'the people' remained excluded from the larger political process, did the fact that non-aristocratic and non-religious communities both claimed and wielded power change the position allocated to them within

[11] Hedwig Röckelein, *Schriftlandschaften, Bildungslandschaften und religiöse Landschaften des Mittelalters in Norddeutschland* (Wiesbaden, 2015).

410   CONCLUSION

the hierarchy and within the conceptual underpinnings of late medieval political thought and practice?

Second, the high medieval case alerts us to the importance of norms, and of the complicated relationship between what should be, what could be and what was. Ideals and expectations mattered. King-makers and kings went to considerable lengths to ensure that they were seen to adhere to, uphold and enforce shared expectations about what kings should do, and how they should be chosen. These norms were foundational to and were deeply ingrained in the practice of royal governance. Nobody wanted to be viewed – and neither would anybody want to view themselves – as abetting grifters and tyrants. That ideals were not absolutes, but open to interpretation, does not militate against this. If anything, it ensured their longevity. Their normative force was, however, dependent upon a public that would confirm adherence to them, and that would use any deviation from them to justify resistance, or at least the withdrawal of their services. Expectations and ideals were no mere ornaments. Indeed, attention to this normative framework is essential to our understanding of royal government, political organisation and political practice in the medieval Latin west.

Finally, what of the world beyond Latin Europe? Ultimately, the values discussed in this book were not specifically western or European. That those in power owed their position to one or more higher beings, that they were supposed to wield it for the common good and to maintain the right order of the world and that they ought to listen to wise counsel are principles just as familiar to writers in China, Byzantium and the Islamic world. This is not the place to attempt a transcultural or global comparison.[12] It would, in any case,

---

[12] Catherine Holmes, Jonathan Shepard, Jo Van Steenbergen and Björn Weiler, eds., *Political Culture in the Latin West, Byzantium and the Islamic World, c. 700–c. 1500: A Framework for Comparing Three Spheres* (Cambridge, forthcoming); Alexander Beihammer, 'A transcultural formula of rule: the Byzantine-Frankish discourse on the formation of the kingdom of Cyprus', in *Union in Separation: Diasporic Groups and Identitites in the Eastern Mediterranean (1100–1800)*, ed. Karl Christ and Franz-Julius Morche (Rome, 2015), 435–52; Jenny Rahel Oesterle, *Kalifat und Königtum. Herrschaftsrepräsentation der Fatimiden, Ottonen und frühen Salier an religiösen Hochfeste* (Darmstadt, 2009); Almut Höfert, *Kaisertum und Kalifat: der imperiale Monotheismus im Früh- und Hochmittelalter* (Frankfurt a.M., 2015); Hugh N. Kennedy, *Caliphate: the History of an Idea* (New York, 2016); Aziz al-Azmeh, *Muslim Kingship: Power and the Sacred in Muslim, Christian and Pagan Polities* (Edinburgh, 2001); Eric J. Hanne, *Putting the Caliph in His Place: Power, Authority, and the Late Abbasid Caliphate* (Teanick, NJ, 2007); Roy P. Mottahedeh, *Loyalty and Leadership in an Early Islamic Society* (Princeton, NJ, 1980); Paul Magdalino, 'Aspects of Twelfth-Century Byzantine "Kaiserkritik"', *Speculum* 58 (1983), 326–46; Catherine J. Holmes, *Basil II and the Governance of Empire (976–1025)* (Oxford, 2005); Jonathan Shepard, 'Aspects of moral leadership: the imperial city and lucre from legality', in *Authority in Byzantium*, ed. Pamela Armstrong (Farnham, 2013), 9–30; Andrew Eisenberg, *Kingship in Early*

have to move beyond the values themselves to consider how they were communicated and how they were incorporated into wider political structures, thought worlds and practices. Nonetheless, several aspects merit further exploration. What was the role of foundational texts in shaping contemporary political practices, how were they understood and how was compliance with them ascertained? The world of eleventh- and twelfth-century Constantinople was, after all, as far removed from that of ancient Rome or Old Testament Israel as contemporary Norway, Scotland or Hungary. Abbasids and Fatimids, Seljuks and Almohads, inhabited a very different world from that of Muhammad and his followers. All the invocations of an idealised past notwithstanding, Song China had little in common with the state of Lu. What were the parameters within which debates over the meaning of norms and the extent of their adaptation could be conducted? Who was involved in conducting them? And what do the answers to these questions reveal about broader structural patterns? What was the impact of the considerably more advanced bureaucratic machineries at the disposal of Byzantine emperors, of Abbasid and Fatimid caliphs and of the sons of heaven? How far did the absence of a distinctive caste of interpreters of scripture in the Islamic world shape debates about the meaning of precedent? What was the role of external factors: climate, geography, seasons? How were conquerors and invaders familiarised with concepts and practices that pre-dated them? Now that we have a better sense of the extent to which kingship was a transeuropean phenomenon, we can begin to place it in a broader global context.

Medieval China (Leiden, 2008); Julia Ching, *Mysticism and Kingship in China: the Heart of Chinese Wisdom* (Cambridge, 1997).

SELECT READING

I Primary Sources

Acerbus of Morena in *Ottonis Morenae et continuatorum Historia Frederici I*, ed. Ferdinand Güterbock, MGH SS sep. ed. (Hanover and Leipzig, 1930).

Ágrip a Nóregskonungasgum. A Twelfth-Century Synoptic History of the Kings of Norway, ed. and transl. M. J. Driscoll, 2nd edition (London, 2005).

Albert of Aachen, *Historia Ierosolomitana. History of the Journey to Jerusalem*, ed. and transl. Susan B. Edgington (Oxford, 2007).

Alexander of Telese, *Alexandri Telesini Abbatis Ystoria Rogerii Regis Sicilie Calabriae atque Apulie*, ed. Ludovica de Nava, with a historical commentary by Dione Clementi (Rome, 1991); English translation in *Roger II*, 63–128.

Alexandri III epistolae et privilegia, PL 200 (Paris, 1855).

Amatus of Montecassino, *Storia de' Normanni volgarizzata in antico francese*, ed. Vincenzo de Bartholomaeis (Rome, 1935).

Amatus of Montecassino, *The History of the Normans*, transl. Prescott N. Dunbar, rev. and introduction by Graham A. Loud (Woodbridge, 2004).

Ambrose of Milan, *De Officiis Ministrorum*, PL 16 (Paris, 1845).

Ambrose of Milan, *Expositio Evangelii secundum Lucam*, in *Sancti Ambrosii Mediolanensis Opera IV*, ed. M. Adriaen, CCSL 14 (Turnhout, 1957).

Ambrosiastri qui dicitur commentarius in epistolas Paulinas, ed. Heinrich Joseph Vogel, CSEL, 3 vols. (Vienna, 1966–9).

Anglo-Scottish Relations 1174–1328. Some Selected Documents, ed. and transl. E. L. G. Stones (London, 1965).

Annalen van Egmond. Het Chronicon Egmundanum, ed. J. W. J. Burgers, transl. Marijke Gumbert-Hepp and J. P. Gumbert (Hilversum, 2007).

Annales Altahenses Maiores, ed. Wilhelm Giesebrecht and Emund Oefele, MGH SS sep. ed., 2nd edition (Hanover and Leipzig, 1890).

Annales Aquenses, MGH SS 24 (Hanover, 1879), 33–9.

Annales Augustani, MGH SS 3 (Hanover, 1839), 123–36.

Annales Cameracenses, MGH SS 16 (Hanover, 1859), 509–54.

Annales Colbazienses, MGH SS 19 (Hanover, 1866), 710–20.

Annales Cremonenses, MGH SS 31 (Hanover, 1903), 1–21.

Annales Engelbergenses, MGH SS 17 (Hanover, 1861), 278–82.

Annales Hildesheimenses, ed. Georg Waitz, MGH SSrG sep. ed. (Hanover, 1878).

SELECT READING

Annales Londonienses, in *Chronicles of the Reigns of Edward I and Edward II*, vol. 1, ed. W. Stubbs (London, 1882), 1–252.

Annales Lundenses, in *Danmarks Middelalderlige Annaler*, 21–70.

Annales Magdeburgenses, MGH SS 16 (Hanover, 1859), 105–96.

Annales Marbacenses Qui Dicuntur (Cronica Hohenburgensis cum Continuatione et Additamentis Neoburgensibus), ed. Hermann Bloch, MGH SS sep. ed. (Hanover and Leipzig, 1907).

Annales Monastici, ed. H. R. Luard, 5 vols. (London, 1864–9).

Annales Palidenses, MGH SS 16 (Hanover, 1859), 48–98.

Annales Parmenses maiores, MGH SS 18 (Hanover, 1863), 664–790.

Annales Patherbrunnenses. Eine verlorene Quellenschrift des zwölften Jahrhunderts, aus Bruchstücken wiederhergestellt, ed. Paul Scheffer-Boichorst (Innsbruck, 1870).

Annales Pegavienses, MGH SS 16 (Hanover, 1859), 232–70.

Annales Placentini Ghibellini, MGH SS 18 (Hanover, 1863), 457–581.

Annales Quedlinburgenses, ed. Martina Giese, MGH SSrG sep. ed. (Hanover, 2004).

Annales Ratisponenses, MGH SS 17 (Hanover, 1861), 579–88.

Annales Romani, MGH SS 5 (Hanover, 1849), 468–80.

Annales S. Disibodi, MGH SS 17 (Hanover, 1861), 4–30.

Annales S. Pauli Virdunensis, MGH SS 16 (Hanover, 1859), 500–2.

Annales Sangallenses Maiores, MGH SS 1 (Hanover, 1826), 72–85.

Annales Stadenses, MGH SS 16 (Hanover, 1859), 271–379.

Annales Zwetlenses, MGH SS 9 (Hanover, 1851), 541–4.

Annalista Saxo. Die Reichschronik des Ananlista Saxo, ed. Klaus Naß, MGH SS (Hanover, 2006).

Annalium Corbeiensium Continutio Saeculi xii et Historia Corbeiensis Monasterii Annorum MCXLV–MCXLVII (Chronographus Corbeiensis). Fortsetzung der Corveyer Annalen des 12. Jahrhunderts und die Geschichte des Klosters Corvey der Jahre 1145–1147 mit Zusätzen (Der Corveyer Chronograph), ed. and transl. Irene Schmale-Ott (Münster, 1989).

Anonimi Bele regis notarii Gesta Hungarorum et Magistri Rogerii Epistolae in miserabile Carmen super destruction Regni Hungariae per tartaros facta, ed. and transl. Martin Rady, János M. Bak and László Veszprémy (Budapest and New York, 2010).

Arnold of Lübeck, *Chronica Slavorum*, ed. Johann M. Lappenberg, MGH SS 21 (Hanover, 1869).

Arnold of Lübeck, *The Chronicle of Arnold of Lübeck*, transl. Graham A. Loud (Abingdon, 2019).

Augustine of Hippo, *De Civitate Dei*, ed. Bernard Dombart and Alphons Kalb, CCSL 47–8, 2 vols. (Turnhout, 1955).

Aurea Gemma Oxonienses, in *Die Jüngere Hildesheimer Briefsammlung*, ed. Rolf de Kegel, MGH Epistolae: Briefe der Deutschen Kaiserzeit (Munich, 1995), nos. 134–144.

414 SELECT READING

Baldric of Bourgeuil, *Historia Ierosolimitana*, ed. Steven Biddlecombe (Woodbridge, 2014).

Baldric of Trier, *Gesta Alberonis Auctore Balderico*, in *Lebensbeschreibungen einiger Bischöfe des 10.–12. Jahrhunderts*, transl. Hatto Kallfelz (reprinting the Latin from MGH SSrG 8, 243–60) (Darmstadt, 1973).

Baldric of Trier, *A Warrior Bishop of the Twelfth Century. The Deeds of Albero of Trier, by Balderich*, transl. Brian A. Pavlac (Toronto, 2008).

Die Chroniken Bertholds von Reichenau und Bernolds von Konstanz 1054–1100, ed. I. S. Robinson, MGH SS NS (Hanover, 2003).

Bertholds and Bernolds Chroniken, ed. and transl. Ian Stuart Robinson (Darmstadt, 2002).

Bracton, De Legibus et consuetudinibus Angliae, ed. George E. Woodbine, 4 vols. (New Haven, CT, 1915–42).

'The *Brevis relatio de Guilelmo nobilissimo comite Normannorum*, written by a monk of Battle Abbey', ed. Elizabeth M. C. van Houts, *Camden Miscellany* 34 (1997), 1–48.

Das Briefbuch des Abts Wibald von Stablo und Corvey, ed. Martina Hartmann based on preparatory work by Heinz Zatschek and Timothy Reuter, MGH Epistolae, 3 vols. (Hanover, 2012).

Die Briefe des Abtes Bern von Reichenau, ed. Franz-Josef Schmale, Veröffentlichungen der Kommission für geschichtliche Landeskunde in Baden-Württemberg Reihe A: Quellen 6 (Stuttgart, 1961).

Die Briefe des Abtes Walo von St. Arnulf vor Metz, MGH Epistolae, ed. Bernd Schütte (Hanover, 1995).

Briefsammlungen der Zeit Heinrichs IV., MGH Epistolae, ed. Carl Erdmann and Norbert Fickermann (Hanover, 1977).

Briefsteller und Formelbücher des elften bis vierzehnten Jahrhunderts, ed. Ludwig Rockinger, 2 vols. (Munich, 1863–4).

Bruno of Merseburg, *De Bello Saxonixo Liber*, ed. Hans-Eberhard Lohmann, MGH Deutsches Mittelalter (Leipzig, 1937).

Brun[o] of Querfurt, *Brunonis Querfurtensis epistola ad Henricum regem*, in *Monumenta Poloniae Historica. Nova Series*, ed. Jadwiga Karwasińska (Warsaw, 1973), vol. 4, 97–106. English translation by William North, https://apps.carleton.edu/curricular/mars/assets/Bruno_of_Querfurt_Letter_to_Henry_II_for_MARS_website.pdf (accessed 12 November 2016).

Brunos Buch vom Sachsenkrieg, ed. Hans-Eberhard Lohmann, MGH SSrG (Leipzig, 1937).

Brut y Tywysogyon or The Chronicle of the Princes. Peniarth Ms. 20 Version, transl. Thomas Jones (Cardiff, 1952).

Burchard of Ursberg, *Burchardi Praepositi Urspergensis Chronicon*, ed. Oswald Holder-Egger and Bernhard von Simson, MGH SS sep. ed., 2nd edition (Hanover and Leipzig, 1916).

Carmen Campodoctoris, in *Chronica Hispana Saeculi XII*, ed. Emma Falque, Juan Gil and Amtonio Maya, CCCM (Turnhout, 1990), 99–108.

SELECT READING

Carpentier, Elisabeth and Georges Pon, 'Chronique de Saint-Nicolas de la Chaize-le-Vicomte', *Revue Historique de Centre Ouest* 6 (2007), 339–91.

Chesnutt, Michael, 'The medieval Danish liturgy of St Knud Lavard', in *Bibliotheca Arnamagnaeana xlii: Opuscula XI*, ed. Britta Olrik Fredericksen (Copenhagen, 2003), 1–160.

Chronica de Gestis Consulum Andegavorum, in *Chroniques des Comtes d'Anjou et des Seigneurs d'Amboise*, ed. Louis Halphen and René Poupardin (Paris, 1913), 25-73.

Chronica Naierensis, ed. Juan A. Estévez Sola (Turnhout, 1995).

Chronica Regia Coloniensis (Annales Maximi Colonienses), ed. Georg Waitz, MGH sep. ed. (Hanover, 1880).

Chronica Reinhardsbrunnensis, MGH SS 30 (Hanover and Leipzig, 1896), 514–656.

Chronica S. Petri Erfordensis Moderna, in *Monumenta Erphesfurtensia saec. xii, xiii, xiv*, ed. Oswald Holder-Egger, MGH SS sep. ed. (Hanover and Leipzig, 1899), 354–472.

Chronicle of Alfonso X, transl. Shelby Thacker and Jose Escobar (Lexington, KY, 2002).

The Chronicle of Jocelin de Brakelond, Concerning the Acts of Samson, Abbot of the Monastery of St Edmunds, ed. and transl. H. E. Butler (London, 1949).

Chronicles of the Reigns of Stephen, Henry II, and Richard I, ed. Richard Howlett, Rolls Series, 4 vols. (London, 1884–9).

Chronicon Adefonsi Imperatoris, in *Chronica Hispana Saeculi XII*, ed. Emma Falque, Juan Gil and Amtonio Maya, CCCM (Turnhout, 1990), 109–248.

Chronicon Monasterii Casinensis, ed. Hartmut Hoffmann, MGH SS 34 (Hanover, 1980).

Chronicon Roskildense, in *Scriptores Minores*, ed. Gertz, vol. 1, 1–33.

Chronicon rhythmicum Austriacum, MGH SS 25 (Hanover, 1880), 350–68.

La Chronique attribuée au connétable Smbat, transl. Gérard Dédéyan (Paris, 1980).

Chronique d'Ernoul et de Bernard le Trésorier, ed. Louis de Mas Latrie (Paris, 1871).

La Chronique de Morigny, ed. Léon Mirot (Paris, 1909).

Chronique de Saint-Pierre-le-Vif de Sens, dite Clarius: Chronicon Sancti Petri Vivi Senonensis, ed. and transl. Robert-Henri Bautier, Monique Gilles and Anne-Amrie Bautier (Paris, 1979).

Chroniques des Comtes d'Anjou et des Seigneurs d'Amboise, ed. Louis Halphen and René Poupardin (Paris, 1913).

Cicero, *De Amicitia*, transl. William Armistead Falconer (Cambridge, MA, 1946).

Cicero, *De Officiis*, transl. William Miller (Cambridge, MA, 1913).

Codex Diplomaticus et Epistolaris Regni Bohemiae, ed. Gustav Friedrich et al., 9 vols. (Prague, 1904–93).

Codex Udalrici, ed. Klaus Nass, MGH Briefe, 2 vols. (Wiesbaden, 2017).

Colker, Marvin, 'The "Karolinus" of Aegidius Parisiensis', *Traditio* 29 (1973), 199–326.

Conrad of Scheyern, *Annales*, MGH SS 17 (Hanover, 1861), 615–23.

416   SELECT READING

Constantiae Imperatricis et Reginae Siciliae Diplomata (1195–1198), ed. Theo Kölzer, Codex Diplomaticus Regni Siciliae (Cologne and Vienna, 1983).

Continuatio Admuntensis, MGH SS 9 (Hanover, 1851), 580–93.

Continuatio Chronici Willelmi de Novoburgo, in *Chronicles of the Reigns of Stephen, Henry II and Richard I*, vol. 2 (London, 1885).

Cosmas of Prague, *Cosmae Pragensis Chronica Boemorum*, ed. Bertold Bretholz, MGH SSrG NS (Berlin, 1923).

Cosmas of Prague, *The Chronicle of the Czechs*, transl. Lisa Wolverton (Washington, DC, 2009).

Cronica maiorum et vicecomitum Londoniarum et quedam, que contingebant temporibus allis ab anno 1188 ad annum 1274: De antiquis legibus liber, ed. Thomas Stapleton (London, 1846).

Danmarks Middelalderlige Annaler, ed. Erik Korman (Copenhagen, 1980).

Davis, H. W. C., 'Henry of Blois and Brian fitz Count', *EHR* 25 (1910), 297–303.

Decrees of the Ecumenical Councils, ed. and transl. Norman P. Tanner, 2 vols. (London and Washington, DC, 1990).

Decretum Magistri Gratiani, in *Corpus Iuris Canonici*, ed. Emil Ludwig Richter and Emil Friedberg, 2 vols., 2nd edition (Leipzig, 1879; repr. Graz, 1955).

Die deutsche Königserhebung im 10.–12. Jahrhundert, ed. Walter Böhme, 2 vols. (Göttingen, 1970).

Dialogus de Scaccario. The Dialogue of the Exchequer; Constitutio Domus Regis. The Disposition of the King's Household, ed. Emilie Amt and S. D. Church (Oxford, 2007).

Diplomatari i Escrits Literaris de l'Abbat i Bisbe Oliba, ed. Eduard Junyent i Subirà and Anscari M. Mundó (Barcelona, 1992).

Diplomatarium Norvegicum, 23 vols. (Oslo, 1847–). (Online: www.dokpro.uio.no /dipl_norv/diplom_felt.html; accessed 11 January 2021).

Diplomatic Documents Preserved in the Public Record Office 1101–1272, ed. Pierre Chaplais (London, 1964).

Eadmer, *Eadmeri Historia Novorum in Anglia*, ed. M. Rule, Rolls Series (London, 1884).

Eadmer, *Vita St Anselmi*, ed. and transl. Richard W. Southern (Oxford, 1962).

Ebonis Vita S. Ottonis Epsicopi Babenbergensis, ed. Jan Wikarjak and Kasimierz Liman, Monumenta Poloniae Historica Series Nova (Warsaw, 1969).

Eike von Repgow, *Sachsenspiegel*, ed. K. A. Eckhardt, MGH Fontes iuris Germanici antiqui Nova Series 1–2, 2 vols. (Hanover, 1964–73).

Ekkehard of Aura, *Ekkehardi Uraugiensis Chronica*, MGH SS 6 (Hanover, 1844), 1–267.

Eleventh-Century Germany. The Swabian Chronicles, transl. I. S. Robinson (Manchester, 2008).

English Coronation Records, ed. and transl. L. G. Wickham Legg (Westminster, 1901).

SELECT READING 417

Epistola de morte Friderici imperatoris, in *Quellen zur Geschichte des Kreuzzuges Kaiser Friedrichs I.*, ed. A. Chroust, MGH SS sep. ed. (Hanover and Berlin, 1928), 173-178.

Epistolae Cantuarienses. The Letters of the Prior and Convent of Christ Church Canterbury, ed. William Stubbs, Rolls Series (London, 1865).

Epistolae Pontificum Romanorum Ineditae, ed. Samuel Loewenfeld (Leipzig, 1885).

Fagrskinna. A Catalogue of the Kings of Norway, transl. Alison Finlay (Leiden and Boston, 2004).

Falcone de Benevento, *Chronicon Beneventanum*, ed. Edoardo D'Angelo (Florence, 1998).

Flores Historiarum, ed. H. R. Luard, Rolls Series, 3 vols. (London, 1890).

Die Formeln der deutschen Königs- und der römischen Kaiserkrönung vom zehnten bis zum zwölften Jahrhundert, ed. Georg Waitz (Göttingen, 1872).

Fürstenspiegel des frühen und hohen Mittelalters, ed. and transl. Hans Hubert Anton (Darmstadt, 2006).

Frutolfs und Ekkehards Chroniken und die anonyme Kaiserchronik, ed. and transl. Franz-Josef Schmale and Irene Schmale-Ott (Darmstadt, 1972).

Fulcher of Chartres, *Fulcheri Carnotensis Historia Hierosolymitana, 1095–1127*, ed. Heinrich Hagenmeyer (Heidelberg, 1913).

Gaimar, *Estoire des Engleis*, ed. and transl. Ian Short (Oxford, 2009).

Galbert of Bruges, *De multro, traditione, et occisione gloriosi Karoli comitis Flandriarum*, ed. Jeff Rider, CCCM (Turnhout, 1994).

Geoffroi Malaterra, *Histoire du Grand Comte Roger et de son frère Robert Guiscard; vol. I (books 1 & 2)*, ed. Marie-Agnès Lucas-Avenel (Caen, 2016); online: www .unicaen.fr/puc/sources/malaterra/accueil (accessed 28 July 2018).

Geoffrey of Monmouth, *The History of the Kings of Britain. An Edition and Translation of De gestis Britonum [Historia Regum Britanniae]*, ed. Michael D. Reeve, transl. Neil Wright (Woodbridge, 2007).

Gerald of Wales, *Expugnatio Hibernica. The Conquest of Ireland*, ed. and transl. A. B. Scott and F. X. Martin (Dublin, 1978).

Gerald of Wales, *Giraldi Cambrensis opera*, 8 vols., vol. 5, *Topographia Hibernica et Expugnatio Hibernica*, ed. J. F. Dimock, Rolls Series (London, 1867).

Gerald of Wales, *Instruction for a Ruler: De Principis Instructione*, ed. and transl. Robert Bartlett (Oxford, 2018).

Gerald of Wales, *The Life of St Hugh of Avalon, Bishop of Lincoln 1186–1200*, ed. and transl. Richard M. Loomis (New York and London, 1985).

Gerbert d'Aurillac, *Correspondance*, ed. P. Riché and J. P. Callu, 2 vols. (Paris, 1993).

Gervase of Canterbury, *The Historical Works of Gervase of Canterbury*, ed. William Stubbs, Rolls Series, 2 vols. (London, 1879).

Die Gesetze der Angelsachsen, ed. F. Liebermann, 3 vols. (Halle, 1903–16).

Gesta Comitum Barcinonensium. Textos Llatí i Català, ed. L. Barrau Dihigo and J. Massó Torrents (Barcelona, 1925).

418 SELECT READING

Gesta episcoporum Halberstadensium [781–1209], MGH SS 23 (Hanover, 1874), 78-123.

Gesta Episcoporum Leodiensium, MGH SS 25 (Hanover, 1880), 1-129.

The Gesta Normannorum Ducum of William of Jumieges, Orderic Vitalis and Robert of Torigni, ed. and transl. Elisabeth M. C. van Houts, 2 vols. (Oxford, 1995).

Gesta Principum Polonorum. The Deeds of the Princes of the Poles, ed. and transl. Paul W. Knoll and Frank Schaer, with a preface by Thomas N. Bisson (Budapest, 2003).

Gesta Stephani, ed. K. R. Potter and R. H. C. Davis (Oxford, 1976).

Gilbert of Mons, *Chronicle of Hainaut*, transl. and intro. Laura Napran (Woodbridge, 2005).

Gislebert of Mons, *La Chronique de Gislebert de Mons*, ed. Léon Vanderkindere (Brussels, 1904).

Godfrey of Viterbo, *Denumeratio regnorum imperio subiectorum*, in *Littérature latine et histoire du Moyen Âge*, ed. Léopold Delisle (Paris, 1890), 41–50.

Godfrey of Viterbo, *Speculum Regum*, MGH SS 22 (Hanover, 1872), 21–93.

Gregory the Great, *Moralia in Job*, ed. Marc Adriaen, CCSL, 3 vols. (Turnhout, 1979–85).

Gregory the Great, *Regula Pastoralis*, ed. Floribert Rommel, transl. Charles Morel, intro., notes and index Bruno Judic, Sources chrétiennes 381-2, 2 vols. (Paris, 1992).

Guibert of Gembloux, *Guiberti Gemblacenses Epistolae*, ed. Albert Derolez, CCCM, 2 vols. (Turnhout, 1988–9).

Guibert of Nogent, *Dei Gesta Per Francos et cinq autres textes*, ed. R. B. C. Huygens (Turnhout, 1996).

Guillaume le Breton, *Philippide*, in *Oeuvres de Rigord et de Guillaume le Breton*, ed. H.-François Delaborde, 2 vols., vol. 2 (Paris, 1885).

Guillelmi I. Regis Diplomata, ed. Horst Enzensberger, Codex Diplomaticus Regni Siciliae (Cologne, Weimar and Vienna, 1996).

Gumpoldi Vita Vencezlai Ducis Bohemiae, MGH SS 4 (Hanover, 1841), 211–23.

Hafner, P. Wolfram, 'Der "Planctus Philippi" im Engelberger Codex 1003', in *Festschrift für Bernhard Bischoff*, ed. Johanna Autenrieth and Franz Brunhölzl (Stuttgart, 1971), 398–405.

Heinrici Chronicon Livoniae, ed. Leonid Arbusow and Albert Bauer, MGH SS sep. ed., 2nd edition (Hanover, 1955).

Helgaud of Fleury, *Vie de Robert le Pieux*, ed. Robert-Henri Bautier and Gilette Labory (Paris, 1965).

Henry, Archdeacon of Huntingdon, *Historia Anglorum. The History of the English People*, ed. and transl. Diana Greenway (Oxford, 1996).

Hermann of Reichenau (Hermann the Lame), *Herimanni Augiensis Chronicon*, MGH SS 5 (Hanover, 1844), 74–133.

Herman de Tournai, *Liber de Restauratione S. Martini Tornacensis*, MGH SS 14 (Hanover, 1883).

Hincmar of Rheims, *Collectio de ecclesiis et capellis*, ed. Martina Stratmann, MGH Fontes Iuris sep. ed. (Hanover, 1990).

Hincmar of Rheims, *De cavendis vitiis et virtutibus exercendis*, ed. Doris Nachtmann, MGH Quellen zur Geistesgeschichte (Munich, 1998).

Hincmar of Rheims, *De Fide Carolo Regi Servanda*, PL 125 (Paris, 1852).

Hincmar of Rheims, *De Ordine Palatii*, ed. and transl. Thomas Gross and Rudolf Schieffer, MGH Fontes Iuris sep. ed. (Hanover, 1980).

Hincmar of Rheims, *De Regis Persona et Regio Ministerio*, PL 125 (Paris, 1852).

'Histoire anonyme des rois de Jérusalem (1099–1187)', ed. Charles Kohler, *Revue d'Orient latin* 5 (1897), 211–53.

Historia Compostellana, ed. Emma Falque Rey, CCCM 70 (Turnhout, 1988).

Historia de expeditione Friderici imperatoris, in *Quellen zur Geschichte des Kreuzzuges Kaiser Friedrichs I.* ed. A. Chroust, MGH SS sep. ed. (Hanover and Berlin, 1928).

Historia Francorum Senonensis, MGH SSrG 9 (Hanover, 1851), 364–9.

Historia Norwegie, ed. Inger Ekrem and Lars Boje Mortensen, transl. Peter Fisher (Copenhagen, 2003).

Historia Ricardi, Priore Ecclesiae Haugustaldensis, De Gestis Regis Stephani, in *Chronicles of the Reigns of Stephen, Henry II and Richard I*, vol. iii (London, 1886).

Historia Silense, ed. Justo Perez de Urbel and Atilano Gonzalez Ruiz-Zorilla (Madrid, 1959).

Historia translationis Sancti Isidori, in *Chronica Hispana saeculi xiii*, ed. Luis Charlo Brea, Juan A. Estévez Sola and Rocío Carande Herrero, CCM (Turnhout, 1997), 119–79.

Historia Welforum, ed. and transl. Erich König, Schwäbische Chroniken der Stauferzeit (Stuttgart, 1938; repr. Sigmaringen, 1978).

History of William Marshal, ed. A. J. Holden, transl. S. Gregory, notes by D. Crouch, 3 vols. (London, 2002).

Hugh de Fleury, *Modernorum Regum Francorum Actus*, MGH SS 9 (Hanover, 1851), 373–94.

Hugh de Fleury, *Hugonis monachi Floriacensis tractatus de regia potestate et sacerdotali dignitate*, ed. Ernst Sackur, MGH Libelli de Lite 2 (Hanover, 1892).

Hugo Falcandus, *Il regno di Sicilia*, transl. Vito Lo Curto (Cassino, 2007) (reprinting the Latin edition of *La Historia o Liber de Regno Sicilie e la Epistola ad Petrum Panormitane Ecclesie Thesaurium di Ugo Falcando*, ed. G. B. Siragusa (Rome, 1897)).

Hugo Falcandus, *The History of the Tyrants of Sicily by 'Hugo Falcandus'*, transl. Graham A. Loud and Thomas Wiedemann (Manchester, 1998).

In passione sancti Kanuti, in *Vitae Sanctorum Danorum*, 189–200.

In translatione sancti Kanuti, in *Vitae Sanctorum Danorum*, 200–4.

Innocentii II Pontificis Romani Epistolae et Privilegia, PL 179 (Paris, 1855).

420   SELECT READING

Isidore of Seville, *Isidori Hispalensis Episcopi Etymologiarum Sive Originum Libri XX*, ed. W. M. Lindsay, Scriptorum Classicorum Bibliotheca Oxoniensis, 2 vols. (Oxford, 1911).

Ivo of Chartres, *Correspondance I*, ed. Jean Leclercq (Paris, 1949).

Jacques de Vitry, *The Historia Occidentalis of Jacques de Vitry*, ed. J. F. Hinnebusch (Fribourg, 1972).

Johannes Codagnelli, *Annales Placentini*, ed. Oswald Holder-Egger, MGH sep. ed. (Hanover and Leipzig, 1901).

Johannis de Fordun, *Chronica Gentis Scotorum et Gesta Annalia*, ed. William F. Skene, 2 vols. (Edinburgh, 1872).

John of Ibelin, *Le Livre des Assises*, ed. Peter W. Edbury (Leiden, 2003).

John of Salisbury, *Historia Pontificalis. Memoirs of the Papal Court*, ed. and transl. Marjorie Chibnall (London, 1956).

John of Salisbury, *Policraticus sive de nugis curialium et vestigiis philosophorum libri viii*, ed. Clemens C. I. Webb, 2 vols. (Oxford, 1909).

John of Worcester, *The Chronicle of John of Worcester*, ed. and transl. R. R. Darlington, P. McGurk and Jennifer Bray, 3 vols., vols. 2 and 3 (Oxford, 1995–8).

Jonas d'Orléans, *De Institutione Regia*, ed. and transl. Alain Dubreucq, SC 407 (Paris, 1995).

Die jüngere Translatio S. Dionysii Aeropagitae, ed. and transl. Veronika Lukas, MGH SSrG sep. ed. (Wiesbaden, 2013).

Kaiserchronik eines Regensburger Geistlichen, ed. Eduard Schöder, MGH Deutsche Chroniken 1 (Hanover, 1895).

[Kaiserchronik.] The Book of Emperors, transl. Henry A. Myers (n.p., 2013).

Die Konzilien Deutschlands und Reichsitaliens 1023–1059, ed. Detlev Jaspert, MGH Concilia (Hanover, 2010).

Lamberti Parvae Annales, MGH SS 16 (Hanover, 1859), 645-650.

Lampert of Hersfeld, *Annales*, ed. Oswald Holder-Egger, transl. Adolf Schmidt (Darmstadt, 1973).

Lantbert of Deutz, *Vita Heriberti; Miracula Heriberti; Gedichte; liturgische Texte*, ed. Bernhard Vogel, MGH SSrG sep. ed. (Hanover, 2001).

Die Lateinische Fortsetzung Wilhelms von Tyrus, ed. Marianne Salloch (Greifswald, 1934).

Latinske Dokument til Norsk Historie fram til År 1204, ed. and transl. Eirik Vandvik (Oslo, 1959).

The Laws of the Medieval Kingdom of Hungary, transl. and ed. J. Bak, G. Bónis and J. R. Sweeney, 2 vols. (Bakersfield, CA, 1989).

Legenda S. Gerhardi episcopi, ed. Imre Madszar, in *Scriptores Rerum Hungaricarum*, vol. 2, 461–506.

Legenda S. Ladislai regis, ed. Emma Bartoniek, in *Scriptores Rerum Hungaricarum*, vol. 2, 507–28.

Legenda S. Stephani regis maior et minor, atque legenda ab Hartwico episcopo conscripta, ed. Emma Bartoniek, in *Scriptores Rerum Hungaricarum*, vol. 2, 363–440.

SELECT READING   421

Leo of Vercelli, *Versus de Ottone et Henrico*, ed. Karl Strecker, MGH Poetae Latini Medii Aevii (Berlin, 1939), 480–3.

The Letters and Charters of Gilbert Foliot, ed. Adrian Morey and C. N. L. Brooke (Cambridge, 1967).

The Letters and Poems of Fulbert of Chartres, ed. and transl. Frederick Behrends (Oxford, 1976).

The Letters of Arnulf of Lisieux, ed. Frank Barlow, Camden Series Third Series 61 (London, 1939).

The Letters of Lanfranc Archbishop of Canterbury, ed. and transl. Helen Clover and Margaret Gibson (Oxford, 1979).

The Letters of Osbert of Clare, Prior of Westminster, ed. E. W. Williamson (Oxford, 1929).

The Letters of Peter the Venerable, ed. Giles Constable, 2 vols. (Cambridge, MA, 1967).

Libellus de institutione morum, ed. Joseph Balogh, in *Scriptores Rerum Hungaricarum*, vol. 2, 619–27.

Liber Eliensis, ed. E. O. Blake, Camden Third Series 92 (London, 1962).

Liudprand of Cremona, *Antapodosis*, ed. P. Chiesa, in *Liudprandi Cremonensis Opera Omnia*, CCCM 156 (Turnhout, 1998).

Magna Carta, ed. and transl. David Carpenter (London, 2015).

Magna Vita Sancti Hugonis. The Life of St Hugh of Lincoln, eds. and transl. Decima L. Douie and David Hugh Farmer, 2 vols. (Oxford, 1961–85).

Marianus Scotus, *Chronicon*, MGH SS 17 (Hanover, 1861), 495–562.

Matthew of Edessa, *Armenia and the Crusades, Tenth to Twelfth Centuries: the Chronicle of Matthew of Edessa*, transl. Ara Edmond Dostourian (Lanham, MI, 1993).

Matthew Paris, *Chronica Majora*, ed. Henry R. Luard, Rolls Series, 7 vols. (London, 1872–4).

Matthew Paris, *Historia Anglorum*, ed. Frederick Madden, Rolls Series, 3 vols. (London, 1866–9).

Memorials of St Dunstan, Archbishop of Canterbury, ed. William Stubbs, Rolls Series (London, 1874).

The Metrical Life of St Hugh of Lincoln, transl. Charles Garton (Lincoln, 1986).

Monumenta Bulgarica. A Bilingual Anthology of Bulgarian Texts from the Ninth to the Nineteenth Centuries, ed. and transl. Thomas Butler (Ann Arbor, MI, 1996).

Monumenta Historica Norwegiae. Latinske Kildeskrifter til Norges Historie i Middlealderen, ed. Gustav Storm (Kristiana, 1880).

Morkinskinna. The Earliest Icelandic Chronicle of the Norwegian Kings (1030–1157), transl., intro. and notes Theodore M. Andersson and Kari Ellen Gade (Ithaca, NY, 2000).

Narratio de electione Lotharii Saxoniae ducis in regem Romanorum, MGH SS 12 (Hanover, 1856), 510-512.

Niederquell, Theodor, 'Die Gesta Marcuardi', *Fuldaer Geschichtsblätter* 38 (1962), 173–99.

SELECT READING

Orderic Vitalis, *The Ecclesiastical History of Orderic Vitalis*, ed. and transl. Marjorie Chibnall, 6 vols. (Oxford, 1969–80).

Ordines Coronationis Franciae. Texts and Ordines for the Coronation of Frankish and French Kings and Queens in the Middle Ages, ed. Richard A. Jackson, 2 vols. (Philadelphia, PA, 1995–2000).

Otto of Freising, *Chronica sive historia de duabus civitatibus*, ed. Walther Lammers, transl. Adolf Schmidt (Darmstadt, 1960).

Otto of Freising and Rahewin, *Gesta Frederici, seu rectius Cronica*, ed. Franz-Josef Schmale, transl. Adolf Schmidt (Darmstadt, 1965).

Otto of St Blasien. *Ottonis de Sancto Blasio Chronica*, ed. Adolf Hofmeister, MGH SS sep. ed. (Hanover and Leipzig, 1912).

The Papal Reform of the Eleventh Century: Lives of Pope Leo IX and Pope Gregory VII, transl. I. S. Robinson (Manchester, 2004).

Paschalis II Pontificis Romani Epistolae et Privilegia, PL 163 (Paris, 1854).

Peregrinationes tres: Saewulf, John of Würzburg, Theodericus, ed. R. B. C. Huygens with a study on the voyages of Saewulf by John H. Pryor, CCCM 149 (Turnhout, 1994).

Peter Damian, *Die Briefe des Peter Damian*, ed. Kurt Reindel, MGH Epistolae, 4 vols. (Hanover, 1983–93).

Peter Damian, *Petri Damiani Vita Beati Romualdi*, ed. Giovanni Tabacco, Fonti per la storia d'Italia (Rome, 1957).

Peter of Blois, *The Later Letters of Peter of Blois*, ed. Elizabeth Revell (Oxford, 1993).

Peter of Blois, *Opera Omnia*, ed. J. A. Giles, 4 vols. (Oxford, 1846–7).

The Peterborough Chronicle 1070–1154, ed. Cecily Clark (Oxford, 1958).

Peter of Eboli, *Book in Honour of Augustus (Liber ad Honorem Augusti) by Piedro da Eboli*, transl. Gwenyth Hood (Tempe, AZ, 2012), reprinting the Latin text from *Liber in Honorem Augusti di Pietro da Eboli. Secondo il Cod. 120 della Biblioteca Civica de Berna*, ed. G. B. Siragusa (Rome, 1906).

Petrus Tudebodus, *Historia de Hierosolymitano Itinere*, ed. John and Laurita L. Hill (Paris, 1977).

Le Pontifical romano-germanique du dixième siècle, ed. Cyrille Vogel and Reinhard Elze, 2 vols. (Vatican, 1963).

Pontificum Romanorum qui fuerunt inde ab exeunte saeculo 9 usque ad finem saeculi 13 Vitae ab aequalibus conscriptae, ed. I. M. Watterich, 2 vols. (Leipzig, 1862).

Prologues to Ancient and Medieval History: A Reader, ed. Justin Lake (Toronto, 2013).

Pseudo-Cyprianus, *De xii Abusivis Saeculi*, ed. Siegmund Hellmann, *Texte und Untersuchungen zur Geschichte der altchristlichen Literatur*, 3rd ser. 4 (1910), 1–62.

Radulfus Niger – Chronica: eine englische Weltchronik des 12. Jahrhunderts, ed. Hanna Krause (Frankfurt/Main et al., 1985).

Radulfus Niger, *De Re Militari et Triplici Via Peregrinationis Ierosolimitane (1187/ 88)*, ed. Ludwig Schmugge, Beiträge zur Geschichte und Quellenkunde des Mittelalters 6 (Berlin and New York, 1977).

SELECT READING   423

Ralph of Coggeshall, *Chronicon Anglicanum*, ed. J. Stevenson, Roll Series (London, 1875).

Ralph de Diceto, *Ymagines Historiarum*, in *Radulfi de Diceto Opera Historica*, ed. William Stubbs, Rolls Series, 2 vols., vol. 2 (London, 1876).

Raymond d'Aguilers, *Le 'Liber' de Raymond d'Aguilers*, ed. John Hugh Hill and Laurita L. Hill (Paris, 1969).

Raymond d'Aguilers, *Historia Francorum qui ceperunt Iherusalem*, transl. John Hugh Hill and Laurita L. Hill (Philadelphia, PA, 1968).

Recueil des actes de Louis VI, roi de France (1108–1137), ed. Robert-Henri Bautier and Jean Dufour, 4 vols. (Paris, 1992–4).

Recueil des actes de Philippe Ier, roi de France (1059–1108), ed. M. Prou and M. H. d'Arbois de Jubainville (Paris, 1908).

Regesta Imperii. Die Regesten des Kaiserreichs, ed. Johann Friedrich Böhmer et al. 13 vols. in 89 (Vienna et al., 1844–). Online edition: www.regesta-imperii.de (accessed 11 January 2021).

Regesta Regum Anglo-Normannorum 1066–1154, ed. H. W. C. Davis, H. A. Cronne and Charles Johnson, 4 vols. (Oxford, 1913–69).

Regesta Regum Scottorum, ed. G. W. S. Barrow et al., 6 vols. (Edinburgh, 1971–2011).

Regestum Innocentii III Papae super negotio Romani Imperii, ed. Friedrich Kempf, Miscellanea Historiae Pontificiae xii (Rome, 1947).

Regino of Prüm, *Chronicon cum continuatione Treverensi*, ed. Friedrich Kurze, MGH SS sep. ed. (Hanover, 1890).

Das Register Gregors VII., ed. Erich Caspar, MGH Epistolae Selectae, 2 vols. (Berlin, 1920–3).

The Register of Pope Gregory VII, transl. H. E. J. Cowdrey (Oxford, 2002).

Die Register Innocenz' III. Band VII: 7. Pontifikatsjahr, 1204/1205, ed. Christoph Egger et al. (Vienna, 1997).

Reineri Annales, MGH SS 16 (Hanover, 1859), 651–80.

Richard of Devizes, *The Chronicle of Richard of Devizes of the Reign of Richard I*, ed. and transl. John T. Appleby (Oxford, 1963).

Richard of Hexham, *De gestis regis Stephani*, in *Chronicles of the Reigns of Stephen, Henry II and Richard I*, vol. 2, 139–78.

Richer of St Remi, *Historiarum Libri Quarti*, ed. Hartmut Hofmann, MGH SS (Hanover, 2000).

Richer of St Remi, *Histories*, transl. Justin Lake, 2 vols. (Cambridge, MA, 2011) (reprint of Hoffmann's Latin text).

Rigord, *Histoire de Philippe Auguste*, ed. and transl. Elisabeth Carpentier, Georges Pon and Yves Chauvin (Paris, 2006).

Robert de Clari, *La Conquête de Constantinople*, ed. and transl. Peter Noble (Edinburgh, 2005).

Robert of Torigny, *The Chronicle of Robert of Torigny*, in *Chronicles of the Reigns of Stephen, Henry II and Richard I*, vol. 4 (London, 1889).

424 SELECT READING

Roberts, Phyllis B., *Thomas Becket in the Medieval Latin Preaching Tradition. An Inventory of Sermons about Thomas Becket, c. 1170 – c. 1400* (Steenbruggen, 1992).

Roderici Ximenii de Rada, Historia de Rebus Hispaniae sive Historia Gothorum, ed. Juan Fernández Valorde, in *Ximenii de Rada Opera Omnia I*, CCCM (Turnhout, 1987).

Rodulfus Glaber, *Historiarum libri quinqui*, in *Rodulfus Glaber: Opera*, ed. and transl. John France, Neithard Bulst and Paul Reynolds (Oxford, 1989).

Roger II and the Creation of the Kingdom of Sicily, transl. and annotated Graham A. Loud (Manchester, 2012).

Roger of Howden, *Chronica: Chronica Magistri Rogeri de Houdene*, ed. W. Stubbs, Rolls Series, 4 vols. (London, 1868–71).

Roger of Howden, *Gesta Henrici II: the Chronicle of the Reigns of Henry II and Richard I AD 1169–1192, known commonly under the name of Benedict of Peterborough*, ed. William Stubbs, Roll Series, 2 vols. (London, 1867).

Roger of Wendover, *Rogeri de Wendover Chronica sive Flores Historiarum*, ed. H. O. Coxe, 5 vols. (London, 1841–4).

Romuald of Salerno, *Chronica*, ed. Giousue Carducci and Vittorio Fiorini (Città di Castello, 1909–35).

Ruotgers Lebensbeschreibung des Erzbischofs Bruno von Köln: Ruotgeri Vita Brunonis archiepiscopi Coloniensis, ed. Ingrid Ott, MGH SS sep. ed. NS (Hanover, 1951).

Rupert of Deutz, *De Gloria et Honore Filii Hominis Super Mattheum*, ed. Hrabanus Haacke, CCCM (Turnhout, 1979).

Rupert of Deutz, *De Sancta Trinitate*, ed. Hrabanus Haacke, CCCM, 4 vols. (Turnhout, 1971–2).

The Saga of Hacon and a fragment of the Saga of Magnus, transl. G. W. Dasent, in *Icelandic Sagas and Other Historical Documents Relating to the Settlements and Descents of the Northmen on the British Isles*, ed. Gudbrand Vigfusson, 4 vols., Rolls Series, vol. IV (London, 1887–94).

The Saga of King Sverri of Norway (Sverrisaga), transl. J. Sephton (London, 1899).

Saxo Grammaticus, *Gesta Danorum: the History of the Danes*, ed. Karsten Frijs-Jensen, transl. Peter Fisher, 2 vols. (Oxford, 2015).

Schmidt, Tilmann, 'Eine unbekannte Urkunde Innocenz' III. mit dem Legatenbericht zur Wahl und Krönung Friedrichs II. von 1212/1213', *Mitteilungen des Instituts für Österreichische Geschichtsforschung* 115 (2007), 25–34.

Scriptores Minores Historiae Danicae Medii Aevii, ed. M. C. Gertz, 2 vols. (Copenhagen, 1917–18, repr. 1970).

Scriptores Rerum Hungaricarum, ed. Emré Szentpétery, 2 vols. (Budapest, 1937–8).

Selected Letters of Pope Innocent III Concerning England (1198–1216), ed. and transl. C. R. Cheney and W. H. Semple (London, 1953).

Seneca, *De Clementia*, ed. and transl. Susanna Braund (Oxford, 2009).

Sigebert of Gembloux, *Chronica*, MGH SS 6 (Hanover, 1844), 300–74.

SELECT READING 425

Simon de Kéza, *Gesta Hungarorum*, ed. and transl. László Veszprémy and Frank Schaer (Budapest and New York, 1999).

Slocum, Kay Brainerd, *Liturgies in Honour of Thomas Becket* (Toronto, 2004).

Snorri Sturluson, *Heimskringla. History of the Kings of Norway*, transl. Lee M. Hollander (Austin, TX, 1964, repr. 1999).

Die St Gallener Annalistik, ed. and transl. Roland Zingg (Ostfildern, 2019).

Suger, *Oeuvres*, ed. and transl. Françoise Gasparri, 2 vols. (Paris, 1996–2001).

Suger, *Vie de Louis VI le Gros*, ed. and transl. Henri Waquet (Paris, 1929).

Suger, *Deeds of Louis the Fat*, transl. Richard C. Cusimano and John Moorhead (Washington, DC, 1992).

Sven Aggesen, *Svenonis Aggonis F. opuscula*, in *Scriptores Minores*, vol. 1, 55–144.

Sven Aggesen, *The Works of Sven Aggesen, Twelfth-Century Historian*, transl. Eric Christiansen (London, 1992).

Tancredi et Wilelmi III Regum Diplomata, ed. Herbert Zielinski, Codex Diplomaticus Regni Siciliae (Cologne and Vienna, 1982).

Die Tegernseer Briefsammlung des 12. Jahrhunderts, ed. Helmut Plechl and Werner Bergmann, MGH Epistolae (Hanover, 2002).

Theodoricus Monachus, *Historia de Antiquitate Norvegiensum*, in *Monumenta Historica Norwegiae*, 1–68.

Theodoricus Monachus, *An Account of the Ancient History of the Norwegian Kings*, transl. David McDougall and Ian McDougall, introduction by Peter Foote (London, 1998).

Thietmar of Merseburg, *Chronicon*, transl. Werner Trillmich (Darmstadt, 1974) (reprinting the Latin text of *Thietmari Merseburgensis episcopi Chronicon*, ed. Friedrich Kurze, MGH SSrG (Hanover, 1889)).

Thietmar of Merseburg, *Ottonian Germany. The Chronicon of Thietmar of Merseburg*, transl. David A. Warner (Manchester, 2001).

Die Urkunden der lateinischen Könige von Jersualem, ed. Hans Eberhard Mayer with Jean Richard, MGH Diplomata, 4 vols. (Hanover, 2010).

Die Urkunden Friedrichs I., ed. Heinrich Appelt et al, MGH Diplomata, 5 vols. (Hanover, 1975–90).

Die Urkunden Heinrichs III., ed. Harry Bresslau and Paul Kehr. MGH Diplomata (Berlin, 1931).

Die Urkunden Heinrichs IV., ed. Dietrich von Gladiss and Alfred Gawlik, MGH Diplomata (Berlin and Hanover, 1941–78).

Die Urkunden Konrads II. mit Nachträgen zu den Urkunden Heinrichs II., ed. Harry Bresslau, MGH Diplomata (Hanover, 1909).

Die Urkunden Konrads III. und seines Sohns Heinrich, ed. Friedrich Hausmann, MGH Diplomata (Vienna, Cologne and Graz, 1969).

Die Urkunden Lothars III. und der Kaiserin Richenza, ed. Emil von Ottenthal and Hans Hirsch, MGH Diplomata (Berlin, 1927).

Vincent Kadlubek, *Die Chronik der Polen des Magster Vincentius*, transl. Eduard Mühle (Darmstadt, 2014) (reprinting the Latin text of *Magistri Vincentii dicti*

426 SELECT READING

Kadubek Chronica Polonorum, ed. Marian Plezia, Monumenta Poloniae Historica Nova Series (Kraków, 1994)).

Vincent of Beauvais, *Bibliotheca mundi seu speculi maioris Vincentii Burgundi praesulis Bellovacensis, ordinis praedicatorum, theologi ac doctori eximii, tomus quartus qui Speculum Historiale inscribitur* (Douai, 1624).

Vincent of Beauvais, *De Morali Principis Institutione,* ed. Robert J. Schneider, CCCM (Turnhout, 1995).

Vincentii Pragensis Annales, MGH SS 17 (Hanover, 1861), 658–83.

Vita Annonis Minor. Die jüngere Annovita, ed. and transl. Mauritius Mittler (Siegburg, 1975).

Vita Arnoldi archiepsicopi Moguntinensis. Die Lebensbeschreibung des Mainzer Erzbischofs Arnold von Selenhofen, ed. and transl. Stefan Burkhardt (Regensburg, 2014).

Vita Burchardi episcopi Wormatiensis, MGH SS 4 (Hanover, 1841), 829–46.

Vita Caroli comitis auctore Waltero archidiacono Tervannensi, MGH SS 12 (Hanover, 1856), 537–61.

Vita Godehardi Prior, MGH SS 11 (Hanover, 1854), 167–218.

Vita Heinrici IV Imperatoris, ed. Wilhelm Eberhard, MGH SSrG sep. ed., 3rd edition (Hanover and Leipzig, 1899).

Vita Lanfranci, ed. Margaret Gibson, in *Lanfranco di Pavia e l'Europa de secolo xi,* ed. Giulio Donofrio (Rome, 1995), 639–715.

Vita Meinwerci epsicopi Patherbrunnensis. Das Leben Bischof Meinwerks von Paderborn, ed. and transl. Guido M. Berndt (Paderborn, 2009).

Die Vita Sancti Heinrici regis et confessoris und ihre Bearbeitung durch den Bamberger Diakon Adelbert, ed. Marcus Stumpf, MGH SSrG (Hanover, 1999).

Vita Sancti Stanislai Cracoviensis Episcopi (Vita Maior), ed. Wojciech Kętrzyński, *Monumenta Poloniae Historica,* vol. 4 (Lwów, 1864; repr. Warsaw, 1964).

Vitae Sanctorum Danorum, ed. M. C. Gertz (Copenhagen, 1908–12).

Walter Bower, *Scotichronicon,* ed. and transl. D. E. R. Watt et al., 9 vols. (Aberdeen, 1987–96).

Walter Map, *De Nugis Curialium: Courtiers Trifles,* ed. and transl. M. R. James, rev. C. N. L. Brooke and R. A. B. Mynors (Oxford, 1983).

Wenrich of Trier, *Epistolae sub Theodoerici episcopi Virdunensis nomine composita,* ed. K. Francke, MGH Libelli 1 (Hanover, 1891), 280–99.

Widukind of Corvey, *Die Sachsengeschichte,* in *Quellen zur Geschichte der sächsischen Kaiserzeit,* ed. and transl. Albert Bauer and Reinhold Rau (Darmstadt, 1977).

Widukind of Corvey, *Deeds of the Saxons,* transl. Bernard S. Bachrach and David S. Bachrach (Washington, DC, 2014).

William FitzStephen, *Vita Sancti Thomae Cantuariensis Archiepiscopi et Martyri,* in *Materials for the History of Thomas Becket,* ed. J. C. Robertson, Rolls Series, 7 vols. (London, 1875–85), vol. 3.

William of Apulia, *La Geste de Robert Guiscard,* ed. and transl. Marguerite Mathieu (Palermo, 1965).

SELECT READING

William of Malmesbury, *Gesta Pontificum Anglorum: the Deeds of the English Bishops*, ed. and transl. Rodney N. Thomson and Michael Winterbottom, 2 vols. (Oxford, 2007).

William of Malmesbury, *Gesta Regum Anglorum: the History of the English Kings*, ed. and transl. R. A. B. Mynors, continued by R. N. Thomson and M. Winterbottom, 2 vols. (Oxford, 1998–9).

William of Malmesbury, *Historia Novella*, ed. Edmund King, transl. K. R. Potter (Oxford, 1998).

William of Malmesbury, *Saints' Lives. Lives of SS. Wulfstan, Dunstan, Patrick, Benignus and Indract*, ed. and transl. M. Winterbottom and R. M. Thomson (Oxford, 2002).

William of Newburgh, *Historia Rerum Anglicarum*, ed. Richard Howlett, in *Chronicles of the Reigns of Stephen, Henry II and Richard I*, vols. 1 and 2 (London, 1884–5).

William of Newburgh, *History of English Affairs*, ed. and transl. P. G. Walsh and M. J. Kennedy, 2 vols. (Oxford, 1988–2007) [covers the period up to 1174].

William of Poitiers, *The Gesta Guillelmi of William of Poitiers*, ed. and transl. R. H. C. Davis and Marjorie Chibnall (Oxford, 1998).

William of Rishanger, *The Chronicle of William of Rishanger of the Barons' War*, ed. J. O. Halliwell (London, 1840).

William of St Thierry, *Expositio super epistolam ad Romanos*, ed. Paul Verdeyen, CCCM (Turnhout, 1989).

William of Tyre, *Chronicon*, ed. R. B. C. Huygens, CCCM, 2 vols. (Turnhout, 1986).

William of Tyre, *A History of Deeds Done Beyond the Sea*, transl. Emily Atwater Babcock and A. C. Krey, 2 vols. (New York, 1943).

Wipo, *Gesta Chuonradi*, in *Wiponis Opera*, ed. Harry Bresslau, MGH SSrG sep. ed., 3rd edition (Hanover and Leipzig, 1915), 1–62.

Wipo, *Deeds of Conrad II*, in *Imperial Lives and Letters of the Eleventh Century*, transl. Theodor E. Mommsen and Karl F. Morrison (New York, 2000), 52–100.

Wulfstan of York, *Die 'Institutes of Polity, Civil and Ecclesiastical'. Ein Werk Erzbischofs Wulfstans von York*, ed. and transl. Karl Jost (Bern, 1959).

Yves de Chartres, *Correspondance I*, ed. Jean Leclercq (Paris, 1949).

II   Secondary Literature

Acht, Peter, 'Aribo (Mainz)', *Neue Deutsche Biographie* (Berlin, 1953), vol. 1, 351.

Affeldt, Werner, *Die weltliche Gewalt in der Paulus-Exegese. Röm.13, 1–7 in den Römerbriefkommentaren der lateinischen Kirche bis zum Ende des 13. Jahrhunderts*, Forschungen zur Kirchen- und Dogmengeschichte 22 (Göttingen, 1969).

Ailes, Marianne, 'Charlemagne "Father of Europe": a European icon in the making', *Reading Medieval Studies* 38 (2012), 59–76.

Album Elemèr Mályusz, no editor (Brussels, 1976).

428   SELECT READING

Althoff, Gerd, 'Christian values and noble ideas of rank and their consequences on symbolic acts', *e-Spania* 4 (2007), 2–13.

Althoff, Gerd, 'Der frieden-, bündnis-, und gemeinschaftstiftende Charakter des Mahles im früheren Mittelalter', in *Essen und Trinken in Mittelalter und Neuzeit: Vorträge eines interdisziplinären Symposions vom 10. bis 13. Juni an der Justus-Liebig-Universität Gießen*, ed. Irmgard Bitsch, Trude Ehlert and Xenja von Ertzdorff (Sigmaringen, 1987), 13–26.

Althoff, Gerd, 'Friedrich von Rothenburg. Überlegungen zu einem übergegangenen Königssohn', in *Festschrift für Eduard Hlawitschka zum 65. Geburtstag*, ed. Karl Schnith and Roland Pauler (Kallmünz, 1993), 307–16.

Althoff, Gerd, *Kontrolle der Macht. Formen und Regeln politischer Beratung im Mittelalter* (Darmstadt, 2016).

Althoff, Gerd, *Die Macht der Rituale. Symbolik und Herrschaft im Mittelalter* (Darmstadt, 2003).

Althoff, Gerd, *Spielregeln der Politik im Mittelalter. Kommunikation in Frieden und Fehde* (Darmstadt, 1997).

Althoff, Gerd, *Verwandte, Freunde und Getreue. Zum politischen Stellenwert der Gruppenbildungen im frühen Mittelalter* (Darmstadt, 1990); English translation: *Family, Friends and Followers. Political and Social Bonds in Early Medieval Europe* (Cambridge, 2004).

Althoff, Gerd, ed., *Heinrich IV.* (Ostfildern, 2009).

Amaral, Luis Carlos Correia Ferreira do, 'As sedes de Braga e Compostela e a restauraçâo da métropole galaica', in *O século de Xelmírez*, ed. Fernando López Alsina, Henrique Monteagudo, Ramón Villares and Ramón José Yzquierdo Perrín (Santiago, 2013), 17–44.

Andenna, Cristina and Gert Melville, eds., *Idoneität – Genealogie – Legitimation. Begründung und Akzeptanz von dynastischer Herrschaft im Mittelalter* (Cologne, 2015).

Andersson, Theodore M., 'The king of Iceland', *Speculum* 74 (1999), 923–34.

Andersson, Theodore M., *The Sagas of Norwegian Kings (1130–1265). An Introduction* (Ithaca, NY, 2016).

Anton, Hans Hubert, 'Anfänge säkularer Begründung von Herrschaft und Staat im Mittelalter. Historiographie, Herkunftssagen, politische Metaphorik (Institutio Traiani)', *AKG* 86 (2004), 75–122.

Anton, Hans Hubert, *Fürstenspiegel und Herrscherethos in der Karolingerzeit* (Bonn, 1968).

Anton, Hans Hubert, 'Pseudo-Cyprian. *De duodecim abusivis saeculi* und sein Einfluß auf dem Kontinent, insbesondere auf die karolingischen Fürstenspiegel', in *Die Iren und Europa im frühen Mittelalter*, ed. Heinz Löwe, 2 vols. (Stuttgart, 1982), vol. 2, 568–617.

Anton, Hans Hubert, 'Zu neueren Wertung Pseudo-Cyprians ("De duodecim abusivis saeculi") und zu seinem Vorkommen in Bibliothekskatalogen des Mittelalters', *Würzburger Diözesangeschichtsblätter* 51 (1989), 463–74.

SELECT READING

Antonsson, Haki, *Damnation and Salvation in Old Norse Literature* (Woodbridge, 2018).

Antonsson, Haki, *St. Mágnus of Orkney. A Scandinavian Martyr-Cult in Context* (Leiden, 2007).

Appelt, Heinrich, 'Der Anteil der Empfänger an der Ausfertigung der Diplome Friedrichs I.', in *Geschichte und ihre Quellen. Festschrift für Friedrich Hausmann zum 70. Geburtstag*, ed. Günter Cerwinka, Walter Höflechner, Othmar Pickl, Hermann Wiesflecker and Reinhard Härtel (Graz, 1987), 381–6.

Arnold, Benjamin, *Power and Property in Medieval Germany: Economic and Social Change c.900–1300* (Oxford, 2004).

Aurell, Jaume, *Medieval Self-Coronations: the History and Symbolism of a Ritual* (Cambridge, 2020).

Aurell, Martin, 'Le refus de la royauté d'Aragon par Raimond Bérenger IV selon Guillaume de Newburg', in *Figures de l'autorité médiévale: mélanges offerts à Michel Zimmermann*, ed. Pierre Chastang, Patrick Henriet and Claire Soussen Max (Paris, 2016), 33–44.

Aurell, Martin, 'Political culture and medieval historiography: the revolt against King Henry II, 1173–1174', *History* 102 (2017), 752–71.

Aurell, Martin, *The Lettered Knight. Knowledge and Behaviour of the Aristocracy in the Twelfth and Thirteenth Centuries* (Budapest, 2016).

Baaken, Gerhard, 'Die Altersfolge der Söhne Friedrich Barbarossas und die Königserhebung Heinrichs VI.', in Gerhard Baaken, *Imperium und Papsttum. Zur Geschichte des 12. und 13. Jahrhunderts. Festschrift zum 70. Geburtstag*, ed. Karl-Augustin Frech und Ulrich Schmidt (Cologne, Weimar and Vienna, 1997), 1–30.

Baaken, Gerhard, 'Recht und Macht in der Politik der Staufer', in Gerhard Baaken, *Imperium und Papsttum. Zur Geschichte des 12. und 13. Jahrhunderts. Festschrift zum 70. Geburtstag*, ed. Karl-Augustin Frech und Ulrich Schmidt (Cologne, Weimar and Vienna, 1997), 143–58.

Bachrach, Bernard S., 'Feeding the host: the Ottonian royal fisc in military perspective', *Studies in Medieval and Renaissance History*, 3rd series 9 (2012), 1–43.

Bachrach, David S., 'Bruno of Merseburg and his historical method, c.1085', *JMedH* 40 (2014), 381–98.

Bachrach, David S., 'Toward an appraisal of the wealth of the Ottonian kings of Germany, 919–1024', *Viator* 44/2 (2013), 1–27.

Bagge, Sverre, 'Christianization and state formation in early medieval Norway', *Scandinavian Journal of History* 30 (2005), 107–34.

Bagge, Sverre, *Cross and Scepter: the Rise of the Scandinavian Kingdoms from the Vikings to the Reformation* (Princeton, NJ, 2014).

Bagge, Sverre, 'Die Herausbildung einer Dynastie. Thronfolge in Norwegen bis 1260', in *Idoneität – Genealogie – Legitimation*, ed. Andenna and Melville, 257–72.

Bagge, Sverre, 'Early state formation in Scandinavia', in *Der frühmittelalterliche Staat – europäische Perspektiven*, ed. Walter Pohl and Veronika Wieser (Vienna, 2009), 145–54.

430   SELECT READING

Bagge, Sverre, *From Viking Stronghold to Christian Kingdom: State Formation in Norway, c. 900–1350* (Copenhagen, 2010).

Bagge, Sverre, *Kings, Politics, and the Right Order of the World in German Historiography c. 950–1150* (Leiden, 2002).

Bagge, Sverre, 'Theodoricus Monachus: the kingdom of Norway and the history of salvation', in *Historical Narratives and Christian Identity on a European Periphery: Early History Writing in Northern, East-Central, and Eastern Europe (c. 1070–1200)*, ed. Ildar H. Garipzanov (Turnhout, 2011), 71–90.

Bagge, Sverre, *The Political Thought of the King's Mirror* (Odense, 1987).

Baier, Thomas, 'Cicero und Augustinus. Die Begründung ihres Staatsdenkens im jeweiligen Gottesbild', *Gymnasium* 109 (2002), 123–40.

Bainton, Henry, 'Literate sociability and historical writing in later twelfth-century England', *ANS* 34 (2011), 23–40.

Bak, János M., ed., *Coronations. Medieval and Early Modern Monarchic Ritual* (Berkeley, Los Angeles and Oxford, 1990).

Banaszkiewicz, Jacek, 'Königliche Karrieren von Hirten, Gärtner und Pflügern', *Saeculum* 33 (1982), 265–86.

Banaszkiewicz, Jacek, 'Slavonic *origines regni*: hero the law-giver and founder of monarchy (introductory survey of problems)', *Acta Poloniae Historica* 69 (1989), 97–131.

Banaszkiewicz, Jacek, 'Slawische Sagen "De origine Gentis" (al-Masudi, Nestor, Kadlubek, Kosmas). Dioskurische Matrizen der Überlieferung', *Mediaevalia Historia Bohemica* 3 (1993), 29–58.

Bande, Alexandre, *Le cœur du roi. Les Capétiens et les sépultures multiples XIIIe–XVe siècles* (Paris, 2009).

Bannermann, John, 'The King's Poet and the inauguration of Alexander III', *Scottish Historical Review* 68 (1989), 120–49.

Barker, Rodney, *Legitimating Identities: the Self-Presentation of Rulers and Subjects* (Cambridge, 2001).

Barnwell, P. S., ed., *Political Assemblies in the Earlier Middle Ages* (Turnhout, 2003).

Barrau, Julie, *Bible, lettres et politique: l'écriture au service des hommes à l'époque de Thomas Becket* (Paris, 2013).

Barrau, Julie, 'Did medieval monks actually speak Latin?', in *Understanding Monastic Practices of Oral Communication (Western Europe, Tenth–Thirteenth Centuries)*, ed. Steven Vanderputten (Turnhout, 2011), 293–317.

Bartlett, Robert, *Gerald of Wales and the Ethnographic Imagination* (Cambridge, 2013).

Bartlett, Robert, *The Making Of Europe: Conquest, Colonisation and Cultural Change* (London, 1993).

Bates, David, *William the Conqueror* (New Haven, CT, 2016).

Baumann, Daniel, *Stephen Langton. Erzbischof von Canterbury im England der Magna Carta* (Leiden and Boston, 2009).

SELECT READING 431

Becher, Matthias, 'Dynastie, Thronfolge und Staatsverständnis im Frankenreich', in *Der frühmittelalterliche Staat – europäische Perspektiven*, ed. Walter Pohl and Veronika Wieser (Vienna, 2009), 183–99.

Becher, Matthias, 'Karl der Gute als Thronkandidat im Jahr 1125. Gedanken zur norddeutschen Opposition gegen Heinrich V.', in *Heinrich V. in seiner Zeit. Herrschen in einem europäischen Reich des Hochmittelalters*, ed. Gerhard Lubich (Cologne, Weimar and Vienna, 2013), 137–50.

Becher, Matthias, 'Die mittelalterliche Thronfolge im europäischen Vergleich. Einführende Überlegungen', in *Die mittelalterliche Thronfolge*, ed. Becher, 9–19.

Becher, Matthias, ed., *Die mittelalterliche Thronfolge im europäischen Vergleich* (Ostfildern, 2017).

Becquette, John, 'Aelred of Rievaulx's *Life of Saint Edward, king and confessor*: A saintly king and the salvation of the English people', *Cistercian Studies Quarterly* 43 (2008), 17–40.

Beihammer, Alexander, 'A transcultural formula of rule: the Byzantine-Frankish discourse on the formation of the kingdom of Cyprus', in *Union in Separation: Diasporic Groups and Identitites in the Eastern Mediterranean (1100–1800)*, ed. Karl Christ and Franz-Julius Morche (Rome, 2015), 435–52.

Beihammer, Alexander, Stavroula Constantinou and Maria Papani, eds., *Court Ceremonies and Rituals of Power in Byzantium and the Medieval Mediterranean. Comparative Perspectives* (Leiden, 2015).

Berend, Nora, 'Introduction', in *Christianization*, ed. Berend, 1–46.

Berend, Nora, 'The mirage of East Central Europe: historical regions in a comparative perspective', in *Medieval East Central Europe in a Comparative Perspective: From Frontier Zones to Lands in Focus*, ed. Gerhard Jaritz and Katalin G. Szende (London, 2016), 9–23.

Berend, Nora, 'Writing Chistianization in medieval Hungary', in *Historical and Intellectual Culture*, ed. Heebøll-Holm, Münster-Swendsen and Sønnesyn, 31–50.

Berend, Nora, Przemysław Urbańczyk and Przemysław Wiszewski, *Central Europe in the High Middle Ages: Bohemia, Hungary and Poland, c. 900 – c. 1300* (Cambridge, 2013).

Berend, Nora, ed., *Christianization and the Rise of Christian Monarchy. Scandinavia, Central Europe and Rus', c.900–1200* (Cambridge, 2007).

Bergsagel, John, 'Between politics and devotion: the canonizations of Knud Lavard and Edward Confessor', in *Political Plainchant? Music, Text and Historical Context of Medieval Saints' Offices*, ed. Roman Hankeln (Ottawa, 2009), 49–58.

Berkhofer, Robert, Alan Cooper and Adam J. Kosto, eds., *The Experience of Power in Medieval Europe 950–1350: Essays in Honor of Thomas N. Bisson* (Aldershot, 2005).

Beuckers, Klaus Gereon, 'Kaiserliche Äbtissinnen: Bemerkungen zur familiären Positionierung der ottonischen Äbtissinnen in Quedlinburg, Gandersheim und

432   SELECT READING

Essen', in *Frauen bauen Europa. Internationale Verflechtungen des Frauenstifts Essen*, ed. Thomas Schilp (Essen, 2011), 65–88.

Beumann, Helmut, 'Die Historiographie des Mittelalters als Quelle für die Ideengeschichte des Königtums', *HZ* 180 (1955), 449–88.

Beumann, Helmut, 'Historische Konzeption und politische Ziele Widkunds von Corvey', in *Settimane di studio del centro Italiano di studi sull'alto medioevo* 17 (Spoleto, 1970), 857–94.

Beumann, Helmut, *Widukind von Korvey. Untersuchungen zur Geschichtsschreibung und Ideengeschichte des 10. Jahrhunderts* (Weimar, 1950).

Beumann, Helmut, 'Zur Entwicklung transpersonaler Staatsvorstellungen', in *Das Königtum. Seine geistigen und rechtlichen Grundlagen*, ed. Theodor Mayer (Sigmaringen, 1956), 185–224.

Beyer, Katrin, *Witz und Ironie in der politischen Kultur Englands im Hochmittelalter* (Würzburg, 2012).

Bhreathnach, Edel, ed., *The Kingship and Landscape of Tara* (Dublin, 2005).

Biddle, Martin, 'Seasonal festivals and residence: Winchester, Westminster and Gloucester in the tenth to the twelfth centuries', *ANS* 8 (1986), 51–72.

Bishko, C. J., 'The liturgical context of Fernando I's last days according to the so-called *Historia Silense*', in C. J. Bishko, *Spanish and Portuguese Monastic History 600–1300* (Aldershot, 1984), vol. 7, 47–58.

Bisson, Thomas N., 'Hallucinations of power: climates of fright in the early twelfth century', *HSJ* 16 (2005), 1–11.

Bisson, Thomas N., 'On not eating Polish bread in vain: resonance and conjuncture in the *Deeds of the Princes of the Poles* (1109–1113)', *Viator* 29 (1998), 275–89.

Bisson, Thomas N., *The Crisis of the Twelfth Century. Power, Lordship and the Origins of European Government* (Princeton, NJ, 2009).

Bisson, Thomas N., *Tormented Voices. Power, Crisis and Humanity in Medieval Catalonia, 1140–1200* (Cambridge, MA, 1998).

Bláhová, Marie, 'Die Anfänge des böhmischen Staates in der mittelalterlichen Geschichtsschreibung', in *Von sacerdotium und regnum. Geistliche und weltliche Gewalt im frühen und hohen Mittelalter. Festschrift für Egon Boshof zum 65. Geburtstag*, ed. Franz-Reiner Erkens and Hartmut Wolff (Cologne, Weimar and Vienna, 2002), 67–76.

Bláhová, Marie, 'Herrschergenealogie als Modell der Dauer des "politischen Körpers" des Herrschers im mittelalterlichen Böhmen', *Genealogie* 57 (2008), 380–97.

Blattmann, Marita, '"Ein Unglück für sein Volk". Der Zusammenhang zwischen Fehlverhalten des Königs und Volkswohl in Quellen des 7. – 12. Jahrhunderts', *FmSt* 30 (1996), 80–102.

Blöcker-Walter, Monica, *Alfons I. von Portugal* (Zürich, 1966).

Boardman, Stephen, 'Chronicle propaganda in fourteenth-century Scotland: Robert the Steward, John of Fordun and the "Anonymous Chronicle"', *Scottish Historical Review* 76 (1997), 23–43.

SELECT READING 433

Bobrycki, Shane, 'The royal consecration *ordines* of the Pontifical of Sens from a new perspective', *Bulletin du centre d'études médiévales d'Auxerre* 13 (2009), 131–42.

Bojcov, Michail A., 'Die Plünderung des toten Herrschers als allgemeiner Wahn', in *Bilder der Macht in Mittelalter und Neuzeit. Byzanz, Okzident, Russland*, ed. Michail A. Bojcov and Otto Gerhard Oexle (Göttingen, 2007), 53–118.

Borgolte, Michael, *Europa entdeckt seine Vielfalt* (Stuttgart, 2002).

Borgolte, Michael and Ralf Lusiardi, eds., *Das europäische Mittelalter im Spannungsbogen des Vergleichs: Zwanzig internationale Beiträge zu Praxis, Problemen und Perspektiven der historischen Komparatistik* (Berlin, 2004).

Bornscheuer, Lothar, *Miseriae Regum. Untersuchungen zum Krisen- und Todesgedanken in den herrschaftstheologischen Vorstellungen der ottonisch-salischen Zeit* (Berlin, 1968).

Bougard, François, Hans-Werner Goetz and Régine Le Jan, eds., *Théorie et pratiques des élites au Haut Moyen Âge: conception, perception et réalisation sociale* (Turnhout, 2001).

Bouman, C. A., *Sacring and Crowning: the Development of the Latin Ritual for the Anointing of Kings and the Coronation of an Emperor before the Eleventh Century* (Utrecht, 1957).

Boureau, Alain and Claudio Sergio, eds., *La royauté sacrée dans le monde chrétien. Colloque de Royaumont, mars 1989* (Paris, 1992).

Bozóky, Edina, 'The sanctity and canonisation of Edward the Confessor', in *Edward the Confessor*, ed. Mortimer, 173–86.

Breen, Aidan, 'De XII Abusivis: text and transmission', in *Ireland and Europe in the Early Middle Ages: Texts and Transmission. Irland und Europa im früheren Mittelalter: Texte und Überlieferung*, ed. Próinséas Ní Chatháin and Michael Richter (Dublin, 2002), 78–94.

Breen, Aidan, 'Pseudo-Cyprian *De Duodecim Abusivis Saeculi* and the Bible', in *Irland und die Christenheit: Ireland and Christendom. Bibelstudien und Mission: the Bible and the Missions*, ed. Próinséas Ní Chatháin and Michael Richter (Stuttgart, 1987), 230–45.

Breen, Aidan, 'Towards a critical edition of De XII Abusivis. Introductory essays with a provisional edition of the text and an English translation' (unpublished PhD thesis, Trinity College Dublin, 1988), available online at www.tara.tcd.ie/handle/2262/77107 (accessed 9 October 2018).

Brégaint, David, 'Staging deaths: King Sverre or a usurper's path to the throne', *Medievalista Online* 23 (2018), https://journals.openedition.org/medievalista/1591 (accessed 30 January 2020).

Brégaint, David, *Vox regis. Royal Communication in High Medieval Norway* (Leiden, 2016).

Brennecke, Hanns Christof, 'Heiligkeit als Herrschaftslegitimation', in *Sakralität zwischen Antike und Neuzeit*, ed. Berndt Hamm, Klaus Herbers and Heidrun Stein-Kecks (Stuttgart, 2007), 115–22.

434 SELECT READING

Brink, Stefan, 'Legal assembly sites in early Scandinavia', in *Assembly Places and Practices in Medieval Europe*, ed. Aliki Pantos and Sarah Semple (Dublin, 2004), 205–16.

Brittain, Charles, 'St Augustine as a reader of Cicero', in *Tolle lege: Essays on Augustine and on Medieval Philosophy in Honor of Roland J. Teske, SJ*, ed. Richard C. Taylor (Milwaukee, WI, 2011), 81–114.

Broekmann, Theo, *Rigor Iustitiae. Herrschaft, Recht und Terror im normannisch-staufischen Süden (1050–1250)* (Darmstadt, 2005).

Broun, Dauvit, 'Contemporary perspectives on the inauguration of Alexander II', in *The Reign of Alexander II, 1214–1249*, ed. Richard Oram (Leiden, 2005), 79–98.

Brühl, Carlrichard, *Fodrum, Gistum, Servitium regis. Studien zu den wirtschaftlichen Grundlagen des Königtums im Frankenreich und in den fränkischen Nachfolgestaaten Deutschland, Frankreich und Italien vom 6. bis zur Mitte des 14. Jahrhunderts*, 2 vols. (Cologne, 1968).

Brühl, Carlrichard, 'Fränkischer Krönungsgebrauch und das Problem der "Festkrönungen"', *Historische Zeitschrift* 194 (1962), 265–326.

Brühl, Carlrichard, 'Kronen- und Krönungsgebrauch im frühen und hohen Mittelalter', *Historische Zeitschrift* 234 (1982), 1–31.

Buc, Philippe, 'Exègése et pensée politique: Radulphus Niger (vers 1190) et Nicolas de Lyre (vers 1330), in *Représentation, pouvoir et royauté á la fin du Moyen Âge*, ed. Joël Blanchard (Paris, 1995), 145–64.

Buc, Philippe, *Holy War, Martyrdom, and Terror: Christianity, Violence, and the West* (Philadelphia, PA, 2015).

Buc, Philippe, *L'Ambiguïté du livre. Prince, pouvoir, et peuple dans les commentaires de la Bible au Moyen Âge* (Paris, 1994).

Buc, Philippe, '*Principes gentium dominantur eorum*: princely power between legitimacy and illegitimacy in twelfth-century exegesis', in *Cultures of Power. Lordship, Status, and Process in Twelfth-Century Europe*, ed. T. N. Bisson (Philadelphia, PA, 1995), 310–28.

Buchner, Max, *Die Entstehung der Erzämter und ihre Beziehung zum Werden des Kurkollegs: mit Beiträgen zur Entstehungsgeschichte des Pairskollegs in Frankreich* (Paderborn, 1911).

Buck, Andrew D., 'Settlement, identity, and memory in the Latin East: an examination of the term "Crusader States"', *EHR* 135 (2020), 271–302.

Bühler-Thierry, Geneviève, Régine Le Jan and Loré Vito, eds., *Acquérir, prélever, contrôler: les ressources en compétition (400–1100)* (Turnhout, 2017).

Bühler-Thierry, Geneviève, Steffen Patzold and Jens Schneider, eds., *Genèse des espaces politiques IXe – XIIe siècle: autour de la question spatiale dans les royaumes francs et post-carolingiens* (Turnhout, 2018).

Burian, Marie Luise, 'Die Krönung des Stephan Prvovencani und die Beziehungen Serbiens zum Heiligen Stuhl', *AKG* 23 (1933), 141–51.

Buringh, Eltjo, *Medieval Manuscript Production in the Latin West: Explorations with a Global Database* (Leiden, 2011).

SELECT READING

Burkhardt, Stefan, *Mit Stab und Schwert: Bilder, Träger und Funktionen erzbischöflicher Herrschaft zur Zeit Friedrich Barbarossas. Die Erzbistümer Köln und Mainz im Vergleich* (Stuttgart, 2010).

Buschmann, Erna, 'Ministerium dei – idoneitas. Um ihre Deutung aus den mittelalterlichen Fürstenspiegeln', *Historisches Jahrbuch* 82 (1962), 70–102.

Campbell, James, 'The late Anglo-Saxon state: a maximum view', *Proceedings of the British Academy* 87 (1994), 39–65.

Carozzi, Claude, 'Die drei Stände gegen den König: Mythos, Traum, Bild', in *Träume im Mittelalter. Ikonologische Studien*, ed. Agostino Paravacini Bagliani and Giorgio Stabile (Stuttgart and Zürich, 1989), 149–60.

Carpenter, David, 'Archbishop Langton and Magna Carta: his contribution, his doubts and his hypocrisy', *EHR* 126 (2011), 1041–65.

Cerda, Jose M., 'Cum consilio et deliberatione episcoporum, comitum, et baronum nostrorum: consultation, deliberation and the crafting of parliamentary assemblies in England and the Spanish kingdoms', in *Podział władzy i parlamentaryzm w przeszłości i współcześnie – prawo, doktryna, praktyka*, ed. Wacław Uruszczak (Warsaw, 2007), 264–76.

Cerda, José Manuel, 'The parliamentary calendar of Spanish and English assemblies in the twelfth century', *Parliaments, Estates and Representation* 26 (2006), 1–18.

Church, Stephen D., 'Some aspects of the royal itinerary in the twelfth century', *Thirteenth Century England* 11 (2007), 31–45.

Clanchy, M. T., *From Memory to Written Record: England, 1066–1307*, 3rd edition (Oxford, 2012).

Clancy, Thomas Owen, 'King making and images of kingship in Gaelic literature', in *The Stone of Destiny*, ed. Welander, Breeze and Clancy, 107–22.

Clayton, Mary, 'De Duodecim Abusiuis, lordship and kingship in Anglo-Saxon England', in *Saints and Scholars: New Perspectives on Anglo-Saxon Literature and Culture in Honour of Hugh Magennis*, ed. Stuart McWilliams (Cambridge, 2012), 141–63.

Clayton, Mary, 'The Old English *Promissio regis*', *Anglo-Saxon England* 37 (2008), 91–150.

Clement, Richard W., 'A handlist of manuscripts containing Gregory's Regula Pastoralis', *Manuscripta* 28 (1984), 33–44.

Clement, Richard W., 'The production of the Pastoral Care: King Alfred and his helpers', in *Studies in Earlier Old English Prose*, ed. Paul E. Szarmach (Albany, NY, 1996), 129–52.

Clementi, D. R., 'A twelfth-century account of the parliaments of the Norman kingdom of Sicily in the *Liber de regno Sicilie*, 1154–1169', *Parliaments, Estates and Representation* 19 (1999), 23–56.

Collard, Judith, 'Henry I's dream in John of Worcester's Chronicle (Oxford Corpus Christi College, MS 157) and the illustration of twelfth-century English chronicles', *JMedH* 36 (2010), 105–25.

436 SELECT READING

Constable, Giles, 'Letter collections in the Middle Ages', in *Kuriale Briefkultur im späteren Mittelalter: Gestaltung – Überlieferung – Rezeption*, ed. Tanja Broser, Andreas Fischer and Matthias Thumser (Cologne, 2015), 35–54.

Cooper, Alan, '"The feet of those that bark shall be cut off": timorous historians and the personality of Henry I', *ANS* 23 (2001), 47–67.

Cooper, Alan, 'Walter Map on Henry I: the creation of eminently useful history', *The Medieval Chronicle* 7 (2011), 103–14.

Csendes, Peter, 'Die Doppelwahl von 1198 und ihre europäischen Dimensionen', in *Staufer und Welfen: zwei rivalisierende Dynastien im Hochmittelalter*, ed. Werner Hechberger and Florian Schuller (Regensburg, 2009), 156–71.

Csendes, Peter, *Heinrich VI*. (Darmstadt, 1993).

Dale, Johanna, 'Conceptions of kingship in high medieval Germany in historiographical perpective', *History Compass* 16 (2018), 1–11.

Dale, Johanna, 'Imperial self-representation and the manipulation of history in twelfth-century Germany: Cambridge, Corpus Christi College MS 373', *German History* 29 (2011), 557–83.

Dale, Johanna, *Inauguration and Liturgical Kingship in the Long Twelfth Century. Male and Female Accession Rituals in England, France and the Empire* (Woodbridge, 2019).

Dalewski, Zbigniew, 'Begräbnis des Herrschers. Ritual und Streit um die Thronfolge im Polen des früheren Mittelalters', *FmSt* 43 (2009), 327–47.

Dalewski, Zbigniew, 'Boleslaw Wrymouth's penance and Gallus Anonymus' chronicle', in *Gallus Anonymus in the Context of Twelfth-Century Historiography from the Perspective of the Latest Research*, ed. Krzysztof Stopka (Kraków, 2010), 125–40.

Dalewski, Zbigniew, *Ritual and Politics. Writing the History of Dynastic Conflict in Medieval Poland* (Leiden and Boston, 2008).

Dalewski, Zbigniew, 'The knighting of Polish dukes in the early Middle Ages: ideological and political significance', *Archivum Poloniae Historiae* 80 (1999), 15–43.

Dall'Aglio, Francesco, 'L'immagine della Bulgaria in occidente al tempo della quarta crociata', *Annuario Istituto Romeno di Cultura e ricerca Umanistica* 5 (2003), 79–103.

Dalton, Paul, 'The accession of Henry I, August 1100', *Viator* 43 (2012), 79–109.

Dalton, Paul, 'William the Peacemaker: the submission of the English to the duke of Normandy, October 1066–January 1067', in *Rulership and Rebellion in the Anglo-Norman World, c. 1066–c.1216. Essays in Honour of Professor Edmund King*, ed. Paul Dalton and D. E. Luscombe (Aldershot, 2015), 21–44.

Dartmann, Christoph, 'Adventus ohne Stadtherr. "Herrschereinzüge" in den italienischen Stadtkommunen', *Quellen und Forschungen aus italienischen Archiven und Bibliotheken* 86 (2006), 64–94.

Davidson, Ivor J., 'A tale of two approaches: Ambrose, "De officiis" 1.1–22 and Cicero "De officiis" 1.1–6', *Journal of Theological Studies* NS 52 (2001), 61–84.

SELECT READING

Davies, R. R., *The Age of Conquest. Wales, 1063–1415* (originally published as Conquest, Coexistence and Change. Wales 1063–1415) (Oxford, 1987; repr. Oxford, 1991).

de Jong, Mayke, 'Admonitio and criticism of the ruler at the court of Louis the Pious', in *La culture du haut moyen âge, une question d'élites?*, ed. François Bougard, Régine Le Jan and Rosamond McKitterick (Turnhout, 2009), 315–38.

Delivré, Fabrice, 'The foundations of primatial claims in the western Church (eighth–thirteenth centuries)', *Journal of Ecclesiastical History* 59 (2008), 383–406.

Deliyannis, Deborah Mauskopf, 'A biblical model for serial biography: the Book of Kings and the Roman *Liber Pontificalis*', *Revue Bénédictine* 107 (1997), 15–23.

Desi, Rosa Maria, 'La double conversion d'Arduin d'Ivrée: Pénitence et conversion autour de l'An Mil', in *Guerriers et moines. Conversion et sainteté aristocratiques dans l'Occident médiéval (IXe – XIIe siècle)*, ed. Michel Lauwers (Antibes, 2002), 317–48.

Deswarte, Thomas, 'Liturgie et royauté dans les monarchies asturienne et léonaise (711–1109)', *Cahiers de civilisation médiévale* 58 (2015), 279–90.

Dick, Stefanie, 'Die Königserhebung Friedrich Barbarossas im Spiegel der Quellen – Kritische Anmerkungen zu den "Gesta Friderici" Ottos von Freising', *Zeitschrift der Savigny-Stiftung für Rechtsgeschichte (Germanistische Abteilung)* 121 (2004), 200–37.

Dittelbach, Thomas, 'The image of the private and the public king in Norman Sicily', *Römisches Jahrbuch der Bibliotheca Hertziana* 35 (2005), 149–72.

Dormeier, Heinrich, 'Un vescovo in Italia alle soglie del mille. Leone di Vercelli "Episcopus imperii, servus sancti Eusebi"', *Bolletino storico vercellese* 28:53 (1999), 37–74.

Driscoll, Stephen T., 'Govan: an early medieval center on the Clyde', in *The Stone of Destiny*, ed. Welander, Breeze and Clancy, 77–84.

Duggan, Anne, 'The English exile of Archbishop Øystein of Nidaros (1180–3)', in *Exile in the Middle Ages*, ed. Laura Napran and Elisabeth van Houts (Turnhout, 2004), 109–30.

Duggan, Anne, ed., *Kings and Kingship in Medieval Europe* (London, 1993).

Duncan, A. A. M., 'Before coronation: making a king at Scone in the 13th century', in *The Stone of Destiny*, ed. Welander, Breeze and Clancy, 139–68.

Edbury, Peter W., *John of Ibelin and the Kingdom of Jerusalem* (Woodbridge, 1997).

Eggert, Wolfgang, 'Wie "pragmatisch" ist Brunos Buch vom Sachsenkrieg?', *DA* 51 (1995), 543–53.

Ehlers, Joachim, *Heinrich der Löwe. Eine Biographie* (Munich, 2008).

Ehlers, Joachim, 'Le pouvoir des morts: lieux de sépulture, rites funéraires et mémoire des rois allemands (Xe–XIIe siècles)', in *Lieux de pouvoir au Moyen Âge et à l'époque moderne*, ed. Michal Tymowski (Warsaw, 1995), 29–59.

438   SELECT READING

Elze, Rainer, 'Eine Kaiserkrönung um 1200', in *Adel und Kirche. Festschrift Gerd Tellenbach*, ed. Josef Fleckenstein and Karl Schmid (Freiburg/Br. and Basel, 1968), 365–73.

Elze, Reinhard, 'The ordo for the coronation of Roger II of Sicily: an example of dating by internal evidence', in *Coronations*, ed. Bak, 165–78.

Elze, Reinhard, 'Zum Königtum Rogers II. von Sizilien', in *Festschrift für Percy Ernst Schramm zu seinem 70. Geburtstag*, 2 vols. (Wiesbaden, 1964), ii, 102–16.

Engels, Jens Ivo, 'Das "Wesen" der Monarchie? Kritische Anmerkungen zum "Sakralkönigtum" in der Geschichtswissenschaft', *Majestas* 7 (1999), 3–39.

Engels, Odilo, 'Friedrich Barbarossa und Dänemark', in *Friedrich Barbarossa*, ed. Haverkamp, 353–85.

Erdmann, Carl, 'Das Papsttum und Portugal im ersten Jahrhundert der portugiesischen Geschichte', *Abhandlungen der Preußischen Akademie der Wissenschaften: Philosophisch-Historische Klasse* 5 (1928), 1–63.

Erdmann, Carl, *Das Papsttum und Portugal im ersten Jahrhundert der portugiesischen Geschichte* (Berlin, 1928).

Erkens, Franz-Reiner, *Die Erzbischöfe von Köln und die deutsche Königswahl, Studien zur Kölner Kirchengeschichte, zum Krönungsrecht und zur Verfassung des Reiches (12. Jahrhundert bis 1806)* (Siegburg, 1987).

Erkens, Franz-Reiner, *Herrschersakralität im Mittelalter. Von den Anfängen bis zum Investiturstreit* (Stuttgart, 2006).

Erkens, Franz-Reiner, ed., *Das frühmittelalterliche Königtum. Ideelle und religiöse Grundlagen* (Berlin and New York, 2005).

Erkens, Franz-Reiner, ed., *Die Sakralität von Herrschaft: Herrschaftslegitimierung im Wechsel der Zeiten und Räume; fünfzehn interdisziplinäre Beiträge zu einem weltweiten und epochenübergreifenden Phänomen* (Berlin, 2002).

Erlande-Brandenburg, Alain, *Le Roi est mort. Étude sur les funérailles, les sepultures et les tombeaux des rois de France jusqu'à la fin du XIII siècle* (Geneva, 1975).

Ertl, Thomas, 'Der Regierungsantritt Heinrichs VI. im Königreich Sizilien (1194): Gedanken zur zeremoniellen Bewältigung der *unio regni ad imperium*', *FmSt* 37 (2003), 259–89.

Ewig, Eugen, 'Zum christlichen Königsgedanken im Frühmittelalter', in Eugen Ewig, *Spätantikes und fränkisches Gallien. Gesammelte Schriften (1952–73)*, ed. Hartmut Atsma, Beihefte der Francia 3, 2 vols. (Munich, 1976–9), i, 3–71, originally in *Das Königtum. Seine geistigen und rechtlichen Grundlagen*, Vorträge und Forschungen 3 (Sigmaringen, 1956), 7–73.

Fairbairn, Henry, 'Was there a money economy in Late Anglo-Saxon and Norman England?', *EHR* 134 (2019), 1081–135.

Fawcett, Richard, 'The buildings of Scone Abbey', in *The Stone of Destiny*, ed. Welander, Breeze and Clancy, 169–81.

Fichtenau, Heinrich, *Arenga. Spätantike und Mittelalter im Spiegel von Urkundenformeln* (Graz, 1957).

SELECT READING

Fitzpatrick, Elizabeth, 'Royal inauguration assembly and the Church in medieval Ireland', in *Political Assemblies in the Early Middle Ages*, ed. Paul S. Barnwell and Marco Mostert (Turnhout, 2003), 73–93.

Fleckenstein, Josef, 'Friedrich Barbarossa und das Rittertum. Zur Bedeutung der Mainzer Hoftage von 1184 und 1188', in *Festschrift Hermann Heimpel zum 70. Geburtstag*, 2 vols. (Göttingen, 1971–3), ii, 1023–41.

Fletcher, Richard, 'A twelfth-century view of the Spanish past', in *The Medieval State. Essays Presented to James Campbell*, ed. J. R. Maddicott and D. M. Palliser (London, 2000), 147–61.

Fletcher, Richard A., 'Reconquest and crusade in Spain c. 1050–1150', *TRHS* 5th series 37 (1987), 31–47.

Fletcher, R. A., *Saint James's Catapult. The Life and Times of Diego Gelmírez of Santiago de Compostela* (Oxford, 1984).

Flori, Jean, *Chevaliers et chevalerie au Moyen Âge* (Paris, 2004).

Foerster, Thomas, 'Neue Herrschaft in neuen Reichen. Genealogie, Idoneität und die Ursprünge weiblicher Nachfolge im 12. Jahrhundert', in *Idoneität – Genealogie – Legitimation*, ed. Andenna and Melville, 139–66.

Foerster, Thomas, 'Political myths and political culture in twelfth-century Europe', in *Erfahren, erzählen, erinnern: narrative Konstruktionen von Gedächtnis und Generation in Antike und Mittelalter*, ed. Herwig Brandt, Benjamin Pohl, William Maurice Sprague and Lina Hörl (Bamberg, 2012), 83–116.

Foerster, Thomas, '"Romanorum et regni Sicilie imperator": Zum Anspruch Kaiser Heinrichs VI. auf das normannische Königreich Sizilien', *AfD* 54 (2008), 37–46.

Foerster, Thomas, *Vergleich und Identität. Selbst- und Fremddeutung im Norden des hochmittelalterlichen Europas* (Berlin, 2009).

Fößel, Amalie, *Die Königin im mittelalterlichen Reich* (Stuttgart, 2000).

Fößel, Amalie, 'Ottonische Äbtissinnen im Spiegel der Urkunden. Einflussmöglichkeiten der Sophia von Gandersheim und Essen auf die Politik Ottos III.', in *Frauen bauen Europa. Internationale Verflechtungen des Frauenstifts Essen*, ed. Thomas Schilp (Essen, 2011), 89–106.

Frankfort, Henri, *Kingship and the Gods. A Study of Ancient Near Eastern Religion as the Integration of Nature and Society* (Chicago, 1978).

Freed, John B., 'The creation of the Codex Falkensteinensis (1166): self-representation and reality', in *Representations of Power in Medieval Germany*, ed. MacLean and Weiler, 189–210.

Freed, John B., *Frederick Barbarossa. The Prince and the Myth* (New Haven, CT, 2017).

Fried, Johannes, 'Die Königserhebung Heinrichs I. Erinnerung, Mündlichkeit und Traditionsbildung im 10. Jahrhundert', in *Mittelalterforschung nach der Wende 1989*, ed. Michael Borgolte, Historische Zeischrift Beiheft 20 (Munich, 1995), 267–318.

Fried, Johannes, *Der päpstliche Schutz für Laienfürsten. Die politische Geschichte des päpstlichen Schutzprivilegs für Laien (11.-13. Jhdt.)*, Abhandlungen der

440 SELECT READING

Heidelberger Akademie der Wissenschaften: Philosophisch-historische Klasse (Heidelberg, 1980).

Fügedi, Eric, 'Coronation in medieval Hungary', *Studies in Medieval and Renaissance History* 3 (1980), 157–89.

Führer, Julian, 'Gegenwart der Vorgänger und genealogisches Bewusstsein bei den Kapetingern (987–1223)', in *Genealogisches Bewusstsein als Legitimation: Inter- und intragenerationelle Auseinandersetzungen sowie die Bedeutung von Verwandtschaft bei Amtswechseln*, ed. Herwig Brandt, Katrin Köhler and Ulrike Sievert (Bamberg, 2010), 145–66.

Führer, Julian, 'Royauté et réforme en France au début du XIIe siècle', *Bulletin d'Information de la Mission Historique Française en Allemagne* 40 (2004), 214–21.

Fuhrmann, Horst, 'Studien zur Geschichte mittelalterlicher Patriarchate, 1–3', *ZSRG (Kanonistische Abteilung)* 39 (1953), 112–76; 40 (1954), 1–84; 41 (1955), 95–183.

Gabriele, Matthew, and Jayce Stuckey, eds., *The Legend of Charlemagne in the Middle Ages: power, faith, and crusade* (New York, 2008).

Ganz, Peter, 'Friedrich Barbarossa: Hof und Kultur', in *Friedrich Barbarossa*, ed. Haverkamp, 623–50.

Garcia, Charles, 'Itinérance de la cour et attaches sédentaires sous Alphonse VI et Urraque Ire', *e-spania* 8 (2013), https://journals.openedition.org/e-spania/18692 (accessed 11 January 2021).

Garipzanov, Ildar H., *Graphic Signs of Authority in Late Antiquity and the Early Middle Ages, 300–900* (Oxford, 2018).

Garipzanov, Ildar H., *The Symbolic Language of Authority in the Carolingian World* (Leiden, 2008).

Garipzanov, Ildar, ed., *Historical Narratives and Christian Identity on a European Periphery. Early Historical Writing in Northern, East-Central, and Eastern Europe* (Turnhout, 2011).

Garnett, George. *Conquered England: Kingship, Succession and Tenure, 1066–1166* (Oxford,2007).

Garnier, Claudia, *Die Kultur der Bitte: Herrschaft und Kommunikation im mittelalterlichen Reich* (Darmstadt, 2008).

Geary, Patrick J., *Myths of Nations: the Medieval Origins of Europe* (Princeton, NJ, 2003).

Geary, Patrick J., *Women at the Beginning. Origin Myths from the Amazons to the Virgin Mary* (Princeton, NJ, 2006).

Gelting, Michael H., 'Two early twelfth-century views of Denmark's Christian past', in *Historical Narratives and Christian Identity on a European Periphery. Early Historical Writing in Northern, East-Central, and Eastern Europe*, ed. Ildar Garipzanov (Turnhout, 2011), 33–55.

Giese, Wolfgang, 'Das Gegenkönigtum des Staufers Konrad 1127–1135', *Zeitschrift der Savigny-Stiftung für Rechtsgeschichte: Germanistische Abteilung* 95 (1978), 202–20.

SELECT READING 441

Gillingham, John, 'At the deathbeds of the kings of England, 1066–1216', in *Herrscher- und Fürstentestamente im westeuropäischen Mittelalter*, ed. Brigitte Kasten (Cologne, Weimar and Vienna, 2008), 509–30.

Gillingham, John, *Richard I* (New Haven, CT, 1999).

Gillingham, John, 'The cultivation of history, legend and courtesy at the court of Henry II', in *Writers of the Reign of Henry II*, ed. Ruth Kennedy and Simon Meecham-Jones (New York, 2006), 25–52.

Gillingham, John, 'Two Yorkshire historians compared: Roger of Howden and William of Newburgh', *HSJ* 12 (2003), 15–37.

Gillingham, John, 'Writing the biography of Roger of Howden, king's clerk and chronicler', in *Writing Medieval Biography, c. 750–1250. Essays in Honour of Frank Barlow*, ed. David Bates, Julia Crick and Sarah Hamilton (Woodbridge, 2006), 207–20.

Gödel, Caroline, *Servitium regis und Tafelgüterverzeichnis. Untersuchung zur Wirtschafts- und Verfassungsgeschichte des deutschen Königtums im 12. Jahrhundert* (Sigmaringen, 1997).

Goez, Werner, 'Von Bamberg nach Frankfurt und Aachen: Barbarossa's Weg zur Königskrone', *Jahrbuch für fränkische Landesforschung* 52 (1992), 61–72.

Goetz, Hans-Werner, 'Der "rechte" Sitz: Die Symbolik von Rang und Herrschaft im hohen Mittelalter im Spiegel der Sitzordnung', in *Symbole des Alltags, Alltag der Symbole. Festschrift für Harry Kühnel zum 65. Geburtstag*, ed. Gertrud Blaschitz, Helmut Hundsbichler, Gerhard Jaritz and Elisabeth Vavra (Graz, 1992), 11–47.

Goetz, Hans-Werner, 'Fortuna in der hochmittelalterlichen Geschichtsschreibung', in *Das Mittelalter* 1 (1996), 75–89.

Görich, Knut, 'Der Gandersheimer Streit zur Zeit Ottos III. Ein Konflikt um die Metropolitanrechte des Erzbischofs Willigis von Mainz', *Zeitschrift der Savigny-Stiftung für Rechtsgeschichte: Kanonistische Abteilung* 79 (1993), 56–94.

Görich, Knut, 'Eine Wende im Osten: Heinrich II. und Boleslaw Chobry', in *Otto III. – Heinrich II. Eine Wende?*, ed. Bernd Schneidmüller and Stefan Weinfurter (Sigmaringen, 1997), 95–167.

Görich, Knut, *Friedrich Barbarossa. Eine Biographie* (Munich, 2010).

Görich, Knut, 'Karl der Große – ein politischer Heiliger?', in *Religion und Politik im Mittelalter*, ed. Körntgen and Waßenhoven, 117–55.

Görich, Knut, 'Verletzte Ehre? König Richard Löwenherz also Gefangener Kaiser Heinrichs VI.', *Historisches Jahrbuch* 123 (2003), 65–91.

Gourgues, Pascal, 'Royauté et élection au Xe siècle', in *Dieu, le prince et le peuple au Moyen Âge (VIe – XVe siècles)*, no editors (Paris, 2011), 65–88.

Gouttebroze, Jean-Guy, 'Robert de Gloucester et l'écriture de l'histoire', in *Histoire et littérature au Moyen Âge*, ed. Danielle Buschinger (Göppingen, 1991), 143–60.

Graeber, David and Marshall Sahlins, *On Kingship* (Chicago, 2017).

Graus, František, 'Die Herrschersagen des Mittelalters als Geschichtsquelle', in *Ausgewählte Aufsätze von František Graus (1959–1989)*, ed. Hans-Jörg Gilomen, Peter Moraw and Rainer C. Schwinges (Stuttgart, 2002), 3–28.

442   SELECT READING

Graus, František, *Volk, Herrscher und Heiliger im Reich der Merowinger: Studien zur Hagiographie der Merowingerzeit* (Prague, 1965).

Green, Judith A., 'Forest laws in England and Normandy in the twelfth century', *Historical Research* 86 (2013), 416–31.

Green, Judith A., *Forging the Kingdom. Power in English Society, 973–1189* (Cambridge, 2017).

Greer, Sarah, 'The disastrous feast at Werla: political relationships and insult in the succession contest of 1002', *German History* 37 (2019), 1–16.

Groh, Martin, 'Das Deutschlandbild in den historischen Büchern der Gesta Danorum', in *Saxo and the Baltic Region. A Symposium*, ed. Tore Nyberg (Odense, 2004), 143–60.

Grosse, Rolf, 'La royauté des premiers Capétiens: "Un mélange de misère et de grandeur"?', *Le Moyen Age* 114 (2008), 255–71.

Guillén, Fernando Arias, 'A kingdom without a capital? Itineration and spaces of royal power in Castile, *c*.1252–1350', *JMedH* 39 (2013), 456–76.

Güntzel, Anette, 'Godfrey of Bouillon: the stylization of an ideal ruler in universal chronicles of the 12th and 13th centuries', *Amsterdamer Beiträge zur älteren Germanistik* 70 (2013), 209–22.

Hägermann, Dieter, 'Die wirtschaftlichen Grundlagen der ersten Kapetinger (987–1108)', in *Pouvoirs et libertés au temps des premiers Capétiens*, ed. Elisabeth Magnou-Nortier (Maulevrier, 1992), 111–23.

Haider, Siegfried, *Die Wahlversprechungen der römisch-deutschen Könige bis zum Ende des 12. Jahrhunderts* (Vienna, 1968).

Halfter, Peter, *Das Papsttum und die Armenier im frühen und hohen Mittelalter. Von den ersten Kontakten bis zur Fixierung der Kirchenunion im Jahre 1198* (Cologne, Weimar and Vienna, 1996).

Hamilton, Bernard, 'Women in the crusader states: the queens of Jerusalem, 1100–1190', in *Medieval Women. Dedicated and Presented to Professor Rosalind M.T. Hill on the Occasion of her Seventieth Birthday*, ed. Derek Baker (Oxford, 1978), 143–74.

Hamilton, Sarah, 'A new model for royal penance? Helgaud of Fleury's Life of Robert the Pious', *EME* 6 (1997), 189–200.

Hamm, Stefanie, 'Regentinnen und minderjährige Herrscher in normannischen Sizilien', in *Roma, magistra mundi. Itineraria culturae medievalis. Mélanges offerts au Père L. E. Boyle à l'occasion de son 75e anniversaire*, ed. Jacqueline Hamese, 3 vols. (Louvain-la-Neuve, 1998), vol. 3, 123–39.

Hanspeter, Heinz, 'Der Bischofsspiegel des Mittelalters. Zur Regula Pastoralis Gregors des Großen', in *Sendung und Dienst im bischöflichen Amt: Festschrift der Katholisch-Theologischen Fakultät der Universität Augsburg für Bischof Josef Stimpfle zum 75. Geburtstag*, ed. Anton Ziegenaus (St Ottilien, 1991), 113–36.

Hartmann, Florian, 'Das Gerücht vom Tod des Herrschers im frühen und hohen Mittelalter', *Historische Zeitschrift* 302 (2016), 340–62.

SELECT READING

Hartmann, Florian, 'Thronfolgen im Mittelalter zwischen Erbe und Wahl, zwischen Legitimität und Usurpation, zwischen Kontingenz und (konstruierter) Kontinuität', in *Die mittelalterliche Thronfolge*, ed. Becher, 449–67.

Hartmann, Florian, 'Wie sag ich's dem Kaiser? Friedrich Barbarossa als fiktiver Kommunikationspartner in der italienischen Rhetoriklehre', in *Friedrich Barbarossa*, no editor (Göppingen, 2017), 32–47.

Hauck, Karl, 'Geblütsheiligkeit', in *Liber floridus. Mittellateinische Studien. Paul Lehmann zum 65. Geburtstag*, ed. Bernhard Bischoff (St Ottilien, 1950), 187–240.

Haverkamp, Albrecht, ed., *Friedrich Barbarossa: Handlungsspielräume und Wirkungsweisen des staufischen Kaisers* (Sigmaringen, 1992).

Hayward, Paul, 'The importance of being ambiguous: innuendo and legerdemain in William of Malmesbury's Gesta Regum and Gesta Pontificum Anglorum', *ANS* 33 (2011), 75–102.

Hechberger, Werner, *Adel im fränkisch-deutschen Mittelalter. Zur Anatomie eines Forschungsproblems* (Ostfildern, 2005).

Heebøll-Holm, Thomas, Mia Münster-Swendsen and Sigbjørn Olsen Sønnesyn, eds., *Historical and Intellectual Culture in the Long Twelfth Century: the Scandinavian Connection* (Toronto, 2015).

Henriet, Patrick, 'Mahomet expulsé d'Espagne par Isidore de Séville. Sur la postérité moderne d'un épisode hagiographique rejeté par les bollandistes', in *Vitae Mahometi. Reescritura e invención en la literatura cristiana de controversia*, ed. Cándida Ferrero Hérnandez and Oscar de la Cruz Palma (Madrid, 2014), 255–76.

Herbers, Klaus, 'Herrschernachfolge auf der Iberischen Halbinsel. Recht – Pragmatik – Symbolik', in *Die mittelalterliche Thronfolge*, ed. Becher, 231–52.

Hering, Kai, '"Fridericus primus [. . .] natus ex clarissima progenie Carolorum". Genealogie und Idoneität bei den frühen Staufern', in *Idoneität – Genealogie – Legitimation*, ed. Andenna and Melville, 305–28.

Hermanson, Lars, 'How to legitimate rebellion and condemn usurpation of the crown: discourses of fidelity and treason in the *Gesta Danorum* of Saxo Grammaticus', in *Disputing Strategies in Medieval Scandinavia*, ed. Kim Esmark, Hans Jacob Orning and Helle Vogt (Leiden and Bosten, 2013), 107–40.

Heslin [Duggan], Anne, 'The coronation of the Young King in 1170', *Studies in Church History* 2 (1965), 165–78.

Hlawitschka, Eduard, 'Merkst Du nicht, daß Dir das vierte Rad am Wagen fehlt? Zur Thronkandidatur Ekkehards von Meißen (1002) nach Thietmar, *Chronicon*, iv.c.52', in *Geschichtsschreibung und geistiges Leben im Mittelalter. Festschrift für Heinz Lôwe zum 65. Geburtstag*, ed. Karl Hauck and Hubert Mordek (Cologne and Vienna, 1978), 287–311.

Höfert, Almut, *Kaisertum und Kalifat: der imperiale Monotheismus im Früh- und Hochmittelalter* (Frankfurt a.M., 2015).

444   SELECT READING

Hoffmann, Erich, *Königserhebung und Thronfolgeordnung in Dänemark bis zum Ausgang des Mittelalters* (Berlin and New York, 1976).

Hoffmann, Hartmut, 'Eigendiktat in den Urkunden Ottos III. und Heinrichs II.', *DA* 33 (1988), 390–423.

Hollister, C. Warren, 'The Anglo-Norman succession debate of 1126: Prelude to Stephen's Anarchy', *JMedH* 1 (1975), 19–41.

Holmes, Catherine, Jonathan Shepard, Jo Van Steenbergen and Björn Weiler, eds., *Political Culture in the Latin West, Byzantium and the Islamic World, c. 700–c. 1500: A Framework for Comparing Three Spheres* (Cambridge, forthcoming).

Houben, Hubert, 'Melfie Venosa. Due città sotto il dominio normanno-svevo', in *Itinerari e centri urbani nel Mezzogiorno normanno-svevo*, ed. Giosuè Musca (Bari, 1993), 311–32.

Houben, Hubert. *Roger II. von Sizilien. Herrscher zwischen Orient und Okzident* (Darmstadt, 1997).

Howard, Ian, 'Harold II, a throneworthy king', in *King Harold II and the Bayeux Tapestry*, ed. Gayle Owen-Crocker (Woodbridge, 2005), 34–52.

Hucker, Bernd Ulrich, 'Liv- und estländische Königspläne', in *Studien über die Anfänge der Mission in Livland*, ed. Manfred Hellmann (Sigmaringen, 1989), 65–106.

Hundahl, Kerstin, Lars Kjaer and Niels Lund, eds., *Denmark and Europe in the Middle Ages, c. 1000–1525. Essays in Honour of Professor Michael H. Gelting* (Farnham, 2014).

Huth, Volker, 'Wipo, neugelesen. Quellenkritische Notizen zur "Hofkultur" in spätottonisch-frühsalischer Zeit', in *Adel und Königtum im mittelalterlichen Schwaben. Festschrift für Thomas Zotz zum 65. Geburtstag*, ed. Andreas Bihrer, Matthias Kälble and Heinz Krieg (Stuttgart, 2009), 155–68.

Hyams, Paul, *Rancor and Reconciliation in Medieval England* (Ithaca, NY, 2003).

Jacobsen, Peter Christian, 'Das Totengericht Kaiser Heinrichs II. Eine neue Variante aus dem Echternacher "Liber aureus"', *Mittellateinisches Jahrbuch* 33 (1998), 53–8.

Jaeger, C. Stephen, *The Origins of Courtliness: Civilizing Trends and the Formation of Courtly Ideals, 939–1210* (Philadelphia, PA, 1985).

Jakobsson, Ármann, 'Image is everything: the Morkinskinna account of King Sigurðr of Norway's journey to the Holy Land', *Parergon* 30 (2013), 121–40.

Jakobsson, Ármann, 'Inventing a saga form: the development of the kings' sagas', *Filologia Germanica* 4 (2012), 1–22.

Jakobsson, Ármann, 'King Sverrir of Norway and the foundations of his power: kingship ideology and narrative in Sverrissaga', *Medium Aevum* 84 (2015), 109–35.

Jakobsson, Ármann, 'Our Norwegian friend: the role of kings in the family sagas', *Arkiv för nordisk filologi* 117 (2002), 145–60.

Jakobsson, Sverrir, 'The early kings of Norway, the issue of agnatic succession and the settlement of Iceland', *Viator* 47 (2016), 171–88.

SELECT READING

Jäschke, Kurt-Ulrich, 'Frühmittelalterliche Festkrönungen? Überlegungen zu Terminologie und Methode', *HZ* 211 (1970), 556–88.

Jäski, Bart, *Early Irish Kingship and Succession* (Dublin, 2000).

Jensen, Kurt Villads, *Crusading at the Edges of Europe. Denmark and Portugal c.1000 – c. 1250* (Abingdon, 2017).

Jezierski, Wojtek, Lars Hermanson, Hans Jacob Orning and Thmoas Småberg, eds., *Rituals, Performatives and Political Order in Northern Europe, c.650–1350* (Turnhout, 2015).

Johanek, Peter, 'Zur rechtlichen Funktion von Traditionsnotiz, Traditionsbuch und früher Siegelurkunde', in *Recht und Schrift im Mittelalter*, ed. Peter Classen (Sigmaringen, 1977), 131–62.

Johansson, Karl G., and Elise Kleivane, eds., *Speculum septentrionale. Konungs skuggsjá and the European Encyclopedia of the Middle Ages* (Oslo, 2018).

John, Simon, *Godfrey of Bouillon: Duke of Lotharingia, Ruler of Latin Jerusalem, c. 1060–1100* (London and New York, 2018).

John, Simon, 'Royal inauguration and liturgical culture in the Latin kingdom of Jerusalem, 1099–1187', *JMedH* 43 (2017), 485–504.

John, Simon, 'The papacy and the establishment of the kingdoms of Jerusalem, Sicily and Portugal: twelfth-century papal political thought on incipient kingship', *Journal of Ecclesiastical History* 68 (2017), 223–59.

Jordan, William C., *A Tale of Two Monasteries: Westminster and Saint-Denis in the Thirteenth Century* (Princeton, NJ, 2009).

Kaeuper, Richard W., *Holy Warriors: the Religious Ideology of Chivalry* (Philadelphia, PA, 2009).

Kalhous, David, 'Mittelpunkte der Herrschaft und Cosmas von Prag: Zum Charakter der Macht des frühmittelalterlichen Fürsten', in *Frühgeschichtliche Zentralorte in Mitteleuropa*, ed. Jiri Máchazek and Simon Ungermann (Bonn, 2011), 669–89.

Kamp, Hermann, *Friedensstifter und Vermittler im Mittelalter* (Darmstadt, 2001).

Kamp, Hermann, 'Tugend, Macht und Ritual: Politisches Verhalten beim Saxo Grammaticus', in *Zeichen, Rituale, Werte. Internationales Kolloquium*, ed. Gerd Althoff (Münster, 2004), 179–200.

Kannowski, Bernd, 'The impact of lineage and family connections on succession in medieval Germany's elective kingdom', in *Making and Breaking the Rules*, ed. Lachaud and Penman, 13–22.

Kanter, Julie, 'Peripatetic and sedentary kingship: the itineraries of John and Henry II', *Thirteenth Century England* 13 (2011), 13–26.

Keller, Hagen, 'Die Herrschaftsurkunden: Botschaften des Privilegierungsaktes – Botschaften des Privilegientextes', *Settimane di Studio del centro Italiano di Studi sull'Alto Medioevo* 52 (2005), 231–83.

Keller, Hagen, 'Die Investitur. Ein Beitrag zum Problem der "Staatssymbolik" im Hochmittelalter', *FmSt* 27 (1993), 51–86.

Keller, Hagen, 'Meinwerk von Paderborn und Heimrad von Hasungen: Spätottonische Kirchenmänner und Frömmigkeitsformen in Darstellungen

446 SELECT READING

aus der Zeit Heinrichs IV. und Friedrich Barbarossas', *FmSt* 39 (2005), 129–50.

Kemp, Ryan, 'Images of kingship in bishops' *vitae* and *gesta*: England and Germany in the long twelfth century' (PhD thesis, Aberystwyth University, 2019).

Kempshall, Matthew, *Rhetoric and the Writing of History, 400–1500* (Manchester, 2011).

Kerner, Max and Hans Kloeft, *Die Institutio Traiani. Ein pseudo-plutarchischer Text im Mittelalter. Text – Kommentar – zeitgenössischer Hintergrund* (Stuttgart, 1992).

Kershaw, Paul, *Peaceful Kings: Peace, Power and the Early Medieval Political Imagination* (Oxford, 2011).

Kersken, Norbert, *Geschichtsschreibung im Europa der 'nationes'. Nationalgeschichtliche Gesamtdarstellungen im Mittelalter* (Cologne, Weimar and Vienna, 1995).

Kienast, Walter, 'Germanische Treue und "Königsheil"', *HZ* 227 (1978), 265–324.

Kirchweger, Franz, ed., *Die Heilige Lanze in Wien: Insignie, Reliquie, 'Schickalsspeer'* (Vienna, 2005).

Kjaer, Lars, 'Feasting with traitors: royal banquets as rituals and texts in high medieval Scandinavia', in *Rituals, Performatives*, ed. Jezierski et al., 269–94.

Kjaer, Lars, 'Political conflict and political ideas in twelfth-century Denmark', *Viking and Medieval Scandinavia* 13 (2017), 61–100.

Kjaer, Lars, 'Runes, knives and Vikings: the Valdemarian kings and the Danish past in comparative perspective', in *Denmark and Europe*, ed. Hundahl, Kjaer and Lund, 255–67.

Klaniczay, Gábor, *Holy Rulers and Blessed Princesses. Dynastic Cults in Medieval Central Europe*, transl. Éva Pálmai (Cambridge, 2002).

Klaniczay, Gábor, 'La royauté sacrée des Arpadiens dans l'historiographie hongroise médiévale et moderne', *Comptes rendus. Académie des Inscriptions et Belles-Lettres* 157 (2013), 595–619.

Klaniczay, Gábor, 'Representations of the evil ruler in the Middle Ages', in *European Monarchy. Its Evolution and Practice from Roman Antiquity to Modern Times*, ed. Heinz Duchhardt, Richard A. Jackson and David J. Sturdy (Stuttgart, 1992), 69–79.

Klaniczay, Gábor, 'Rex iustus: Le saint fondateur de la royauté chrétienne', *Cahiers d'études hongroises* 8 (1996), 34–58.

Klauser, Renate, 'Der Heinrichs- und Kunigundenkult im mittelalterlichen Bistum Bamberg. Idee und Wirklichkeit', *Bericht des Historischen Vereins für die Pflege der Geschichte des ehemaligen Fürstbistums Bamberg* 95 (1956), 1–211.

Klewitz, Hans-Walter, 'Die Festkrönungen der deutschen Könige', *Zeitschrift der Savigny-Stiftung für Rechtsgeschichte* 59 (*Kanonistische Abteilung* 28) (1939), 45–96; separate reprint (Darmstadt, 1966).

Kłoczowski, Jerzy, 'Saint Stanislas, patron de la Pologne au XIIIe siècle', in *Pascua Mediaevalia. Studies voor Prof. Dr. J.M. De Smet*, ed. R. Lievens, Erik van Mingroot and W. Verbeke (Leuven, 1983), 62–5.

SELECT READING

Kölzer, Theo, 'Der Hof Kaiser Barbarossas und die Reichsfürsten', in *Deutscher Königshof, Hoftag und Reichstag im späteren Mittelalter*, ed. Peter Moraw (Stuttgart, 2002), 1–47.

Körntgen, Ludger, 'Der Investiturstreit und das Verhältnis von Religion und Politik im Frühmittelalter', in *Religion und Politik im Mittelalter*, ed. Körntgen and Waßenhoven, 89–115.

Körntgen, Ludger, *Königsherrschaft und Gottes Gnade: zu Kontext und Funktion sakraler Vorstellungen in Historiographie und Bildzeugnissen der ottonisch-frühsalischen Zeit* (Berlin, 2001).

Körntgen, Ludger, '"Sakrales Königtum" und "Entsakralisierung" in der Polemik um Heinrich IV.', in *Heinrich IV.*, ed. Althoff, 127–60.

Körntgen, Ludger, and Dominik Waßenhoven, eds., *Patterns of Episcopal Power. Bishops in Tenth- and Eleventh-Century Europe* (Berlin, 2011).

Körntgen, Ludger, and Dominik Waßenhoven, eds., *Religion und Politik im Mittelalter: England und Deutschland im Vergleich* (Berlin, 2013).

Kosto, Adam J., 'The elements of practical rulership: Ramon Berenguer I of Barcelona and the revolt of Mir Geribert', *Viator* 47 (2016), 67–94.

Kosto, Adam J., 'The *Liber feudorum maior* of the Counts of Barcelona: the cartulary as an expression of power', *JMedH* 27 (2001), 1–22.

Koziol, Geoffrey, 'England, France, and the problem of sacrality in twelfth-century ritual', in *Cultures of Power. Lordship, Status, and Process in Twelfth-Century Europe*, ed. T. N. Bisson (Philadelphia, PA, 1995), 124–48.

Krieg, Heinz, 'Im Spannungsfeld zwischen christlichen und adligen Normvorstellungen. Zur Beurteilung Friedrich Barbarossas in stauferzeitlicher Historiographie', *FmSt* 41 (2007), 447–66.

Krieg, Heinz, 'Zur Spiegelung Friedrich Barbarossas in der stauferzeitlichen Historiographie', in *Macht und Spiegel der Macht*, ed. Kersken and Vercamer, 255–72.

Krieg, Heinz, *Herrscherdarstellung in der Stauferzeit. Friedrich Barbarossa im Spiegel seiner Urkunden und der staufischen Geschichtsschreibung* (Stuttgart, 2003).

Krier, Silvia-Irene, 'Studien zum Herrscherbild in lateinischen Viten vornormannischer Könige in England' (PhD thesis, Bonn, 1965).

Kuehn, Evan F., 'Melchizedek as exemplar for kingship in twelfth-century political thought', *History of Political Thought* 31 (2010), 557–75.

Kypta, Ulla, *Die Autonomie der Routine. Wie im 12. Jahrhundert das englische Schatzamt entstand* (Göttingen, 2014).

Lachaud, Frédérique, *L'éthique du pouvoir au Moyen Âge: l'office dans la culture politique (Angleterre, vers 1150–vers 1330)* (Paris, 2010).

Lachaud, Frédérique, and Michael Penman, eds., *Making and Breaking the Rules: Succession in Medieval Europe, c. 1000–c.1600/Etablir et abolir les normes: la succession dans l'Europe médiévale, vers 1000–vers 1600* (Turnhout, 2008).

Lambert, Sarah, 'Queen or consort: rulership and politics in the Latin East, 1118–1228', in *Queens and Queenship in Medieval Europe*, ed. Ann Duggan (Woodbridge, 1997), 153–69.

448   SELECT READING

Laudage, Johannes, 'Der Hof Friedrich Barbarossas: eine Skizze', in *Rittertum und höfische Kultur der Stauferzeit*, ed. Johannes Laudage and Yvonne Leiverkus (Cologne, Weimar and Vienna, 2006), 75–92.

Lay, Stephen, 'A leper in purple: the coronation of Baldwin IV of Jerusalem', *JMedH* 23 (1997), 317–34.

Lay, Stephen, *The Reconquest Kings of Portugal: Political and Cultural Reorientation on the Medieval Frontier* (Basingstoke, 2009).

Le Goff, Jacques, 'Aspects religieux et sacrés de la monarchie française du Xe au XIIIe siècle', in *La royauté sacrée*, ed. Boureau and Sergio, 19–28.

Le Goff, Jacques, 'The symbolic ritual of vassalage', in Jacques Le Goff, *Time, Work and Culture* (Chicago, 1980), 237–87.

Le Goff, Jacques, Éric Palazzo, Jean-Claude Bonne and Marie-Noël Colette, eds., *Le sacre royal à l'époque de Saint Louis d'après le manuscrit Latin 1246 de la BNF* (Paris, 2001).

Lejbovicz, Max, ed., *Les relations culturelles entre chrétiens et musulmans au Moyen Âge: quelles leçons en tirer de nos jours?* (Turnhout, 2005).

Lewis, Andrew W., 'Anticipatory association of the heir in early Capetian France', *American Historical Review* 83 (1978), 906–27.

Lewis, Andrew W., *Royal Succession in Capetian France: Studies on Familial Order and the State* (Cambridge, MA, 1981).

Leyser, Karl, 'The Anglo-Norman Succession 1120–1125', *ANS* 13 (1990–1), 225–42.

Leyser, Karl J., *Rule and Conflict in an Early Medieval Society: Ottonian Saxony* (Oxford, 1979).

Leyser, Conrad, David Rollason and Hannah Williams, eds., *England and the Continent in the Tenth Century: Studies in Honour of Wilhelm Levison (1876–1947)* (Turnhout, 2010).

Licence, Tom, 'Edward the Confessor and the succession question: a fresh look at the sources', *ANS* 39 (2017), 113–28.

Lieberman, Max, 'A new approach to the knighting ritual', *Speculum* 90 (2015), 391–423.

Lilie, Ralph-Johannes, 'Erbkaisertum oder Wahlmonarchie? Zur Sicherung der Herrschaftsnachfolge in Byzanz', in *Die mittelalterliche Thronfolge*, ed. Becher, 21–39.

Lilie, Ralph-Johannes, 'Der Kaiser in der Statistik. Subversive Gedanken zur angeblichen Allmacht der byzantinischen Kaiser', in *Hypermachos: Studien zur Byzantinistik, Armenologie und Georgistik. Festschrift für Werner Seibt zum 65. Geburtstag*, ed. Chrestos Staurakos (Wiesbaden, 2008), 211–34.

Lincoln, Bruce, *Between History and Myth: Stories of Harald Fairhair and the Founding of the State* (Chicago, 2014).

Linehan, Peter, *History and Historians of Medieval Spain* (Oxford, 1993).

Linehan, Peter, 'The king's touch and the dean's ministrations: aspects of sacral monarchy', in *The Work of Jacques Le Goff and the Challenges of Medieval History*, ed. Miri Rubin (Woodbridge, 1997), 189–206.

SELECT READING 449

Lohrmann, Dietrich, 'Der Tod König Heinrichs I. von England in der mittellateinischen Literatur Englands und der Normandie', *Mittellateinisches Jahrbuch* 8 (1972), 90–107.

Lönnroth, Lars, 'Sverrir's dreams', *Scripta Islandica* 57 (2007), 97–110.

Loud, G. A., *The Age of Robert Guiscard. Southern Italy and the Norman Conquest* (Harlow, 2000).

Loud, G. A., *The Latin Church in Norman Sicily* (Cambridge, 2007).

Loud, G. A., 'William the Bad or William the Unlucky? Kingship in Sicily 1154–1166', *HSJ* 8 (1996), 99–114.

Lubich, Gerd, 'Beobachtungen zur Wahl Konrads III. und ihrem Umfeld', *Historisches Jahrbuch* 117 (1997), 311–39.

Lubich, Gerd, 'Das Kaiserliche, das Höfische und der Konsens auf dem Mainzer Hoffest (1184). Konstruktion, Inszenierung und Darstellung gesellschaftlichen Zusammenhalts am Ende des 12. Jahrhunderts', in *Staufisches Kaisertum im 12. Jahrhundert. Konzepte – Netzwerke – Politische Praxis*, ed. Stefan Burkhardt, Thomas Metz, Bernd Schneidmüller and Stefan Weinfurter (Regensburg, 2010), 277–93.

Lyon, Jonathan R., 'Fathers and sons: preparing noble youths to be lords in twelfth-century Germany', *JMedH* 34 (2008), 291–310.

Lyon, Jonathan R., *Princely Brothers and Sisters: the Sibling Bond in German Politics, 1100–1250* (Ithaca, NY, 2013).

MacLean, Simon, *Kingship and Politics in the Late Ninth Century. Charles the Fat and the End of the Carolingian Empire* (Cambridge, 2003).

MacLean, Simon, 'Recycling the Franks in twelfth-century England: Regino of Prüm, the monks of Durham, and the Alexandrine Schism', *Speculum* 87 (2012), 649–81.

MacLean, Simon, 'Shadow kingdom: Lotharingia and the Frankish world, c.850–c.1050', *History Compass* 11 (2013), 443–57.

MacLean, Simon, 'The Carolingian past in post-Carolingian Europe', in *'The Making of Europe': Essays in Honour of Robert Bartlett*, ed. Sally Crumplin and John G. H. Hudson (Leiden, 2016), 11–31.

MacLean, Simon, and Björn Weiler, eds., *Representations of Power in Medieval Germany, c. 800–1500* (Turnhout, 2006).

Madeline, Fanny, *Les Plantagenêts et leur empire: construire un territoire politique* (Rennes, 2014).

Maisel, Witold, *Rechtsarchäologie Europas* (Cologne, Vienna and Weimar, 1992).

Maleczek, Walter, 'Abstimmungsarten. Wie kommt man zu einem vernünftigen Wahlergebnis?', in *Wahlen und Wählen im Mittelalter*, ed. Reinhard Schneider (Sigmaringen, 1990), 79–134.

Malegam, Jehangir, *The Sleep of Behemoth. Disputing Peace and Violence in Medieval Europe, 1000–1200* (Itahca, NY, 2013).

Markus, R. A., 'Gregory the Great's rector and his genesis', in *Gregoire le Grand*, ed. Jacques Fontaine, Robert Gillet and Stan Pollistrandi (Paris, 1986), 137–46.

450 SELECT READING

Marritt, Stephen, 'Prayers for the king and royal titles in Anglo-Norman charters', *ANS* 32 (2009), 184–202.

Martin, Jean-Marie, 'Quelques remarques sur les sceaux des princes lombards et normands de Capoue', in *Ut sementem feceris, ita metes. Studi in onore di Biagio Saitta*, ed. Carmelina Urso (Acireale, 2016), 437–46.

Mattoso, José, 'À propos du couronnement des rois portugais', in *L'espace rural au Moyen Âge, Portugal, Espagne, France (XIIe–XIVe siècle), Mélanges en l'honneur de Robert Durand*, ed. Monique Bouron and Stéphanie Boissellier (Rennes, 1999), 133–46.

May, Georg, 'Der Erzbischof von Mainz als primas', in *Der Mainzer Kurfürst als Reichserzkanzler. Funktionen, Aktivitäten, Ansprüche und Bedeutung des zweiten Mannes im alten Reich*, ed. Peter Claus Hartmann (Stuttgart, 1997), 35–76.

Mayer, Hans Eberhard, 'Das Pontifikale von Tyrus und die Krönung der Lateinischen Könige von Jerusalem: Zugleich ein Beitrag zur Forschung über Herrschaftszeichen und Staatssymbolik', *Dumbarton Oaks Papers* 21 (1967), 141–232.

Mayer, Hans Eberhard, 'The succession to Baldwin II of Jerusalem: English impact on the East', *Dumbarton Oaks Papers* 39 (1985), 139–47.

Mayer, Roland, 'Seneca *Redivivus*: Seneca in the medieval and Renaissance world', in *The Cambridge Companion to Seneca*, ed. Shadi Bartsch and Alessandro Schiesaro (Cambridge, 2015), 277–88.

McDougall, Sara, *Royal Bastards. The Birth of Illegitimacy, 800–1230* (Oxford, 2017).

McEvitt, Christopher, 'The Chronicle of Matthew of Edessa: Apocalypse, the First Crusade and the Armenian diaspora', *Dumbarton Oaks Papers* 61 (2007), 157–81.

McTurk, Rory, 'Sacral kingship in ancient Scandinavia: A review of some recent writings', *Saga-Book* 19:2–3 (1975–6), 139–69.

McTurk, Rory, 'Scandinavian sacral kingship revisited', *Saga-Book* 24:1 (1994), 18–32.

Meens, Rob, 'Politics, mirrors of princes and the Bible: sins, kings and the well-being of the realm', *EME* 7 (1998), 345–57.

Melve, Leidulf, 'Assembly politics and the "rules of the game" (ca. 650–1150)', *Viator* 41 (2010), 69–90.

Melve, Leidulf, '"Even the very laymen are chattering about it": the politicization of public opinion, 800–1200', *Viator* 44:1 (2013), 25–48.

Melve, Leidulf, 'Performance, argument, and assembly politics (ca. 1080 – ca. 1160)', *Super alta perennis* 10 (2010), 85–108.

Metcalfe, Alex, 'The Muslims of Sicily under Christian rule', in *The Society of Norman Italy*, ed. Graham A. Loud and Alex Metcalfe (Leiden, 2002), 289–318.

Michałowski, Roman, 'Polen und Europa um das Jahr 1000. Mit einem Anhang: zur Glaubwürdigkeit des Berichts von Gallus Anonymus über das Treffen in

SELECT READING 451

Gnesen', in *Der Hoftag von Quedlinburg 973. Von den historischen Wurzeln zum neuen Europa*, ed. Andreas Ranft (Berlin, 2006), 51–72.

Mitteis, Heinrich, *Die deutsche Königswahl. Ihre Rechtsgrundlagen bis zur Goldenen Bulle* (Brünn, Munich and Vienna, 1944).

Moeglin, Jean-Marie, '"Rex crudelis": über die Natur und die Formen der Gewalt der Könige vom 11. zum 14. Jahrhundert (Frankreich, Reich, England)', in *Gewalt und Widerstand in der politischen Kultur des späten Mittelalters*, ed. Martin Kintzinger, Frank Rexroth and Jörg Rogge (Ostfildern, 2015), 19–52.

Moers, Stephanie L., 'Networks of power in Anglo-Norman England', *Medieval Prosopography* 7 (1986), 25–54.

Mortensen, Lars Boje, 'Sanctified beginnings and mythopoetic moments. The first wave of writing on the past in Norway, Denmark, and Hungary, c. 1000–1230', in *The Making of Christian Myths in the Periphery of Latin Christendom (c. 1000–1300)*, ed. Lars Boje Mortensen (Copenhagen, 2006), 247–73.

Mortensen, Lars Boje, 'Saxo Grammaticus' View of the Origin of the Danes and his Historiographical Models', *Cahiers de l'Institut du moyen-âge grec et latin (Université de Copenhague)* 55 (1987), 169–83.

Mortensen, Lars Boje, 'The glorious past: entertainment, example or history? Levels of twelfth-century historical culture', *Culture and History* 13 (1994), 57–71.

Mortensen, Lars Boje, 'The Nordic archbishoprics as literary centres around 1200', in *Archbishop Absalom of Lund and His World*, ed. Karsten Frijs Jensen and Inge Skovgaard-Petersen (Roskilde 2000), 133–57.

Mortimer, Richard, ed., *Edward the Confessor: the Man and the Legend* (Woodbridge, 2009).

Mottahedeh, Roy P., *Loyalty and Leadership in an Early Islamic Society* (Princeton, NJ, 1980).

Müller, Jan-Dirk, *König Philipp und seine Krone. Über Fremdheit und Nähe mittelalterlichen Denkens* (Berlin, 2014).

Münster-Swendsen, Mia, 'Lost chronicle or elusive informers? Some thoughts on the source of Ralph Niger's reports from twelfth-century Denmark', in *Historical and Intellectual Culture*, ed. Heebøll-Holm, Münster-Swendsen and Sønnesyn, 189–210.

Murray, Alan V., 'Dynastic continuity or dynastic change? The accession of Baldwin II and the nobility of the kingdom of Jerusalem', *Medieval Prosopography* 13 (1992), 1–28.

Murray, Alan V., 'Women in the royal succession of the Latin Kingdom of Jerusalem (1099–1291)', in *Mächtige Frauen?*, ed. Claudia Zey, 131–62.

Muylkens, Michaela, *Reges geminati. Die Gegenkönige in der Zeit Heinrichs IV.* (Husum, 2011).

Naß, Klaus, 'Hofgeschichtsschreibung bei den Welfen im 12. und 13. Jahrhundert', in *Die Hofgeschichtsschreibung im mittelalterlichen Europa*, ed. Rudolf Schieffer and Jarosław Wenta (Toruń, 2006), 107–17.

SELECT READING

Naus, James, 'Negotiating kingship in France at the time of the early crusades: Suger and the *Gesta Ludovici Grossi*', *French Historical Studies* 36 (2013), 525–41.

Naus, James, 'The "Historia Iherosolimitana" of Robert the Monk and the coronation of Louis VI', in *Writing the Early Crusades: Text, Transmission and Memory*, ed. Marcus Bull and Damien Kempf (Woodbridge, 2014), 105–15.

Nechutová, Jana, *Die lateinische Literatur des Mittelalters in Böhmen*, transl. Hildegard Boková and Václav Bok (Cologne, Weimar and Vienna, 2007).

Nef, Anneliese, 'Muslims and Islam in Sicily from the mid-eleventh to the end of the twelfth century: contemporary perceptions and today's interpretations', in *Routledge Handbook of Islam in Europe*, ed. Roberto Tottoli (London, 2015), 55–69.

Nelson, Janet L., 'Kingship, law and liturgy in the political thought of Hincmar of Rheims', *EHR* 92 (1977), 241–79.

Nelson, Janet L., 'Tenth-century kingship comparatively', in *England and the Continent*, ed. Leyser, Rollason and Williams, 293–308.

Nelson, Janet L., 'The rites of the Conqueror', *ANS* 4 (1982), 117–32, 210–21.

Nelson, Janet L., *Rituals and Politics in Early Medieval Europe* (London, 1986).

Nemerkényi, Előd, *Latin Classics in Medieval Hungary: Eleventh Century* (Budapest and New York, 2005).

Nemerkényi, Előd, 'The religious ruler in the *Institutions* of St Stephen of Hungary', in *Monotheistic Kingship. The Medieval Variants*, ed. Aziz al-Azmeh and János Bak (Budapest 2004), 231–48.

Niederkorn, Jan Paul, 'Friedrich von Rothenburg und die Königswahl von 1152', in *Von Schwaben bis Jerusalem. Facetten staufischer Geschichte*, ed. Sönke Lorenz and Ulrich Schmidt (Sigmaringen, 1995), 51–60.

Niederkorn, Jan Paul, 'Zu glatt und daher verdächtig? Zur Glaubwürdigkeit der Schilderung der Wahl Friedrich Barbarossas (1152) durch Otto von Freising', *Mitteilungen des Instituts für Österreichische Geschichtsforschung* 115 (2007), 1–9.

Noble, Thomas F. X. and John Van Engen, eds., *European Transformations. The Long Twelfth Century* (Notre Dame, IN, 2012).

Nonn, Ulrich, 'Geblütsrecht, Wahlrecht, Königswahl: die Wahl Lothars von Supplinburg 1125', *Geschichte in Wissenschaft und Unterricht* 44 (1993), 146–57.

O'Callaghan, Joseph F. , *The Cortes of Castile-León 1188–1350* (Philadelphia, PA, 1989).

Oesterle, Jenny Rahel, *Kalifat und Königtum. Herrschaftsrepräsentation der Fatimiden, Ottonen und frühen Salier an religiösen Hochfeste* (Darmstadt, 2009).

Oexle, Otto Gerhard, 'Die Gegenwart der Lebenden und der Toten. Gedanken über Memoria', in *Gedächtnis, das Gemeinschaft stiftet*, ed. Karl Schmid and Joachim Wollasch (Munich and Zurich, 1985), 74–107.

Oliński, Piotr, 'Am Hofe Bolesław Schiefmunds. Die Chronik des Gallus Anonymus', in *Die Hofgeschichtsschreibung im mittelalterlichen Europa*, ed. Rudolf Schieffer and Jarosław Wenta (Toruń, 2006), 93–106.

Olsen, Birger Munk, 'Comment peut-on déterminer la popularité d'un texte au Moyen Âge? L'exemple des oeuvres classiques latines', *Interfaces* 3 (2016), 13–27.

Orning, Hans Jacob, *Unpredictability and Presence. Norwegian Kingship in the High Middle Ages*, transl. Alan Crozier (Leiden and Boston, 2008).

Parisse, Michel, and Xavier Barral Altet, eds., *Le roi de France et son royaume autour de l'an mil. Actes du colloque Hugues Capet 987–1987. La France de l'an Mil, Paris – Senlis, 22–25 juin 1987* (Paris, 1992).

Parkes, Henry, 'Henry II, liturgical kingship, and the birth of the "Romano-German Pontifical"', *EME* 28 (2020), 104–41.

Partner, Nancy F., *Serious Entertainments: the Writing of History in Twelfth-Century England* (Chicago, 1977).

Pätzold, Stefan, 'Norbert, Wichmann und Albrecht II.: drei Magdeburger Erzbischöfe des 12. Jahrhunderts', *Concilium Medii Aevi* 3 (2000), 239–63.

Patzold, Steffen, 'Königserhebungen zwischen Erbrecht und Wahlrecht? Thronfolge und Rechtsmentalität um das Jahr 1000', *DA* 58 (2002), 467–507.

Patzold, Steffen, 'Konsens und Konkurrenz. Überlegungen zu einem aktuellen Forschungskonzept der Mediävistik', *FmSt* 41 (2007), 75–103.

Patzold, Steffen, 'Wie bereitet man sich auf einen Thronwechsel vor? Überlegungen zu einem wenig beachteten Text des 11. Jahrhunderts', in *Die mittelalterliche Thronfolge*, ed. Becher, 127–57.

Paul, Nicholas L., *To Follow in Their Footsteps. The Crusades and Family Memory in the High Middle Ages* (Ithaca, NY, 2012).

Perst, Otto, 'Die Kaisertochter Sophie, Äbtissin von Gandersheim und Essen (975–1039)', *Braunschweiger Jahrbuch* 38 (1957), 5–46.

Péter, László, 'The Holy Crown of Hungary, visible and invisible', *Slavonic and Eastern European Review* 81 (2003), 421–510.

Peters, Edward M., *The Shadow King: Rex Inutilis in Medieval Law and Literature, 751–1327* (New Haven, CT, 1970).

Petersohn, Jürgen, *Echte und falsche Insignien im deutschen Krönungsbrauch des Mittelalters? Kritik eines Forschungsstereotyps* (Frankfurt, 1993).

Petersohn, Jürgen, 'Kaisertum und Kultakt in der Stauferzeit', in *Politik und Heiligenverehrung im Hochmittelalter*, ed. Jürgen Petersohn (Sigmaringen, 1994), 101–46.

Plassmann, Alheydis, '[...] et clauses thesaurorum nactus est, quibus fretus totam Angliam animo subiecit suo [...]. Herrschernachfolge in England zwischen Erbschaft, Wahl und Aneignung (1066–1216)', in *Die mittelalterliche Thronfolge*, ed. Becher, 193–227.

Plassmann, Alheydis, *Origo gentis. Identitäts- und Legitimitätsstiftung in früh- und hochmittelalterlichen Herkunftserzählungen* (Berlin, 2006).

454 SELECT READING

Pletl, Renate, *Irdisches Regnum in der mittelalterlichen Exegese. Ein Beitrag zur exegetischen Lexikographie und ihren Herrschaftsvorstellungen, 7.-13. Jahrhundert* (Frankfurt/Main, 2000).

Portera Silva, Ermelindo, 'Diego Gelmírez y el trono de Hispania. La coronación real del año 1111', in *O século de Xelmírez*, ed. Fernando López Alsina, Henrique Monteagudo, Ramón Villares, and Ramón José Yzquierdo Perrín (Santiago, 2013), 45–74.

Prado-Vilar, Francisco, 'Lacrimae rerum: San Isidoro de León y la memoria del padre', *Goya: Revista de Arte* 329 (2009), 195–221.

Pryce, Huw, 'Negotiating Anglo-Welsh relations: Llewellyn the Great and Henry III', in *England and Europe in the Reign of Henry III (1216–1272)*, ed. Björn Weiler with Ifor Rowlands (Aldershot, 2002), 13–30.

Purkis, William J. and Matthew Gabriele, eds., *The Charlemagne Legend in Medieval Latin Texts* (Woodbridge, 2016).

Rader, Olaf B., 'Prismen der Macht. Herrschaftsbrechungen und ihre Neutralisierung am Beispiel von Totensorge und Grabkulten', *HZ* 271 (2000), 311–46.

Rady, Martyn J., 'Election and descent in medieval Hungarian kingship', in *Élections et pouvoirs politiques du VIIe au XVIIe siècle: actes du colloque réuni à Paris 12 du 30 novembre au 2 décembre 2006*, ed. Corinne Péneau (Pompignac, 2008), 383–90.

Rady, Martin J., 'Hungary and the Golden Bull of 1222', *Banata* 24 (2014), 87–108.

Raffensperger, Christian, *Reimagining Europe: Kievan Rus' in the Medieval World* (Cambridge, MA, 2012).

Ray, R. D., 'Medieval historiography through the twelfth century: problems and progress of research', *Viator* 5 (1974), 33–60.

Reinke, Martina, 'Die Reisegeschwindigkeit des deutschen Königshofes im 11. und 12. Jahrhundert nördlich der Alpen', *Blätter für deutsche Landesgeschichte* 123 (1987), 225–51.

Reisinger, Christian, *Tankred von Lecce* (Cologne, Weimar and Vienna, 1992).

Reuling, Ulrich, 'Zur Entwicklung der Wahlformen bei den hochmittelalterlichen Königserhebungen im Reich', in *Wahlen und Wählen im Mittelalter*, ed. Reinhard Schneider (Sigmaringen, 1990), 227–70.

Reuter, Timothy, 'A Europe of bishops. The age of Wulfstan of York and Burchard of Worms', in *Patterns of Episcopal Power*, ed. Körntgen and Waßenhoven, 17–38.

Reuter, Timothy, *Medieval Polities and Modern Mentalities*, ed. Janet L. Nelson (Cambridge, 2006).

Reuter, Timothy, 'Vom Parvenü zum Bündnisparter: das Königreich Sizilien in der abendländischen Politik des 12. Jahrhunderts', in *Die Staufer im Süden. Sizilien und das Reich*, ed. Theo Kölzer (Sigmaringen, 1996), 43–56.

Rexroth, Frank, 'Tyrannen und Taugenichtse. Beobachtungen zur Ritualität europäischer Königsabsetzungen im späten Mittelalter', *HZ* 278 (2004), 27–54.

SELECT READING

Rey, Emma Falque, 'De Sevilla a León: el último viaje de San Isidor', *Annuario de Historia de la Iglesia andaluza* 9 (2016), 11–31.

Reydellet, Marc, *La royauté dans la littérature latine de Sidoine Apollinaire à Isidore de Séville* (Paris, 1981).

Reynolds, Leighton D., *The Medieval Tradition of Seneca's Letters* (Oxford, 1965).

Reynolds, Susan, *Kingdoms and Communities in Western Europe, 900–1300*, 2nd edition (Oxford, 1997).

Richardson, H. G., 'The coronation in medieval England: the evolution of the office and the oath', *Traditio* 16 (1960), 111–202.

Riches, Theo, review of *The Crisis of the Twelfth Century: Power, Lordship, and the Origins of European Government* (review no. 754), www.history.ac.uk/reviews/review/754 (accessed 26 August 2018).

Riis, Thomas, 'Saxo und die offizielle Königsideologie', in *Saxo and the Baltic Region. A Symposium*, ed. Tore Nyberg (Odense, 2004), 93–104.

Riis, Thomas, 'The significance of 25 June 1170', in *Of Chronicles and Kings: National Saints and the Emergence of Nation States in the High Middle Ages*, ed. John D. Bergsagel, David Hiley and Thomas Riis (Copenhagen, 2015), 91–102.

Roach, Levi, 'Hosting the king: hospitality and the royal *iter* in tenth-century England', *JMedH* 37 (2011), 34–46.

Robinson, I. S., *Henry IV of Germany, 1056–1106* (Cambridge, 1999).

Robinson, I. S., *The Papacy, 1073–1198. Continuity and Innovation* (Cambridge, 1990).

Röckelein, Hedwig, *Schriftlandschaften, Bildungslandschaften und religiöse Landschaften des Mittelalters in Norddeutschland* (Wiesbaden, 2015).

Rollason, David, *The Power of Place. Rulers and Their Palaces, Landscapes, Cities, and Holy Places* (Princeton, NJ, 2016).

Rosenthal, Joel T., 'Letters and letter collections', in *Understanding Medieval Primary Sources: Using Sources to Discover Medieval Europe*, ed. Joel T. Rosenthal (London, 2012), 72–85.

Rotondo-McCord, Jonathan, '*Locum sepulturae meae ... elegi*: property, graves, and sacral power in eleventh-century Germany', *Viator* 26 (1995), 77–106.

Rubenstein, Jay, 'Holy Fire and sacral kingship in post-conquest Jerusalem', *JMedH* 43 (2017), 470–84.

Rucquoi, Adeline, 'La royauté sous Alphonse VIII de Castille', *Cahiers de linguistique hispanique médiévale* 23 (2000), 215–41.

Ruiz, Teofilo F., 'Unsacred monarchy: the kings of Castile in the late Middle Ages', in *Rites of Power. Symbols, Ritual and Politics since the Middle Ages*, ed. Sean Wilentz (Philadelphia, PA, 1985), 109–45.

Sandaaker, Odd, 'Magnus Erlingssons Kroning: ein "politiserande" Sagatradisjon?', *Historik Tijdskrift* 77 (1998), 181–96.

Sanmark, Alex, 'At the assembly: a study of ritual space', in *Ritual, Performatives*, ed. Jezierski et al., 79–112.

Sassier, Yves, 'La Corona regni: émergence d'une persona ficta dans la France du XIIe siècle', in *La puissance royale: image et pouvoir de l'Antiquité au Moyen Âge*, ed. Emmanuelle Santinelli and Christian-Georges Schwentzel (Rennes, 2012), 99–110.

Sassier, Yves, '"La royauté ne s'acquiert pas par droit héréditaire". Réflexion sur la structure du discours attribué à Adalbéron de Reims en faveur de l'élection de Hugues Capet', in *Élections et pouvoirs politiques du VIIe au XVIIe siècle: actes du colloque réuni à Paris 12 du 30 novembre au 2 décembre 2006*, ed. Corinne Péneau (Pompignac, 2008), 341–50.

Scheel, Roland, *Skandinavien und Byzanz: Bedingungen und Konsequenzen mittelalterlicher Kulturbeziehungen*, 2 vols. (Göttingen, 2015).

Schieffer, Rudolf, 'Die Ausbreitung der Königssalbung im hochmittelalterlichen Europa', in *Die mittelalterliche Thronfolge*, ed. Becher, 43–80.

Schieffer, Rudolf, 'Gregor VII. und die Könige Europas', *Studi gregoriani per la storia della Libertas Ecclesiae* 13 (1989), 189–211.

Schieffer, Rudolf, 'Mediator cleri et plebis. Zum geistlichen Einfluß auf Verständnis und Darstellung des ottonischen Königtums', in *Herrschaftsrepräsentation im ottonischen Sachsen*, ed. Gerd Althoff and Ernst Schubert (Sigmaringen, 1998), 345–61.

Schlenker, Gerlinde, 'Kaiserin und Reichsäbtissin: Macht und Einfluss von Adelheid und Mathilde von Quedlinburg', in *Auf den Spuren der Ottonen III*, ed. Roswitha Jendryschik, Gerlinde Schlenker and Robert Werner (Halle a. D. Saale, 2002), 7–16.

Schlesinger, Walter 'Die sogennante Nachwahl Heinrichs II. in Merseburg', in *Geschichte in der Gesellschaft. Festschrift für Karl Bosl zum 65. Geburtstag*, ed. Friedrich Prinz, Franz-Josef Schmale and Ferdinand Seibt (Stuttgart, 1974), 350–69.

Schlichte, Annkristin, *'Der gute König'. Wilhelm II. von Sizilien (1166–1189)* (Tübingen, 2005).

Schmidt, Roderich, 'Königsumritt und Huldigung in ottonisch-salischer Zeit', in *Königtum, Burgen und Königsfreie / Königsumritt und Huldigung*(Sigmaringen, 1961), 97–233.

Schmidt, Ulrich, '"Ein neues und unerhörtes Dekret": der Erbreichsplan Heinrichs VI.', in *Kaiser Heinrich VI. Ein mittelalterlicher Herrscher und seine Zeit* (Göppingen, 1998), 61–81.

Schmidt, Ulrich, *Königswahl und Thronfolge im 12. Jahrhundert* (Cologne and Vienna, 1987).

Schmitz-Esser, Romedio, *Der Leichnam im Mittelalter. Einbalsamierung, Verbrennung und die kulturelle Konstruktion des toten Körpers* (Ostfildern, 2014), 213–20.

Schneider, Reinhard, 'Wechselwirkungen von kanonischer und weltlicher Wahl', in *Wahlen und Wählen im Mittelalter*, ed. Reinhard Schneider (Sigmaringen, 1990), 135–71.

SELECT READING

Schneidmüller, Bernd, 'Die einzigartig geliebte Stadt: Heinrich II. und Bamberg', in *Kaiser Heinrich II. 1002-1024*, ed. Josef Kirmeier, Bernd Schneidmüller and Stefan Weinfurter (Stuttgart, 2002), 30-51.

Schneidmüller, Bernd, 'Konsensuale Herrschaft. Ein Essay über Formen und Konzepte politischer Ordnung im Mittelalter', in *Reich, Regionen un Europa in Mittelalter und Neuzeit. Festschrift für Peter Moraw*, ed. Paul Joachim Heinig, Sigrid Jahns, Hans-Joachim Schmidt, Rainer Christoph Schwinges and Sabine Wefers (Berlin, 2000), 53-97 (shortened English version: 'Rule by consensus. Forms and concepts of political order in the European Middle Ages', *The Medieval History Journal* 16 (2013), 449-71).

Schneidmüller, Bernd, 'Mittelalterliche Geschichtsschreibung als Überzeugungsstrategie: eine Königswahl des 12. Jahrhunderts im Wettstreit der Erinnerungen', *Heidelberger Jahrbücher* 52 (2008), 167-88.

Schneidmüller, Bernd, 'Reich und Thronfolgeregelung im hochmittelalterlichen Frankreich', *HZ* 238 (1984), 95-104.

Schneidmüller, Bernd, 'Zwischen frommer Lüge und schnödem Betrug: Fälschungen im Mittelalter', *AKG* 73 (1991), 217-32.

Schneidmüller, Bernd, 'Zwischen Gott und den Getreuen. Vier Skizzen zu den Fundamenten mittelalterlicher Monarchie', *FmSt* 36 (2002), 193-224.

Scholz, Sebastian, 'Die "Wiener Reichskrone": Eine Krone aus der Zeit Konrads II.?', in *Grafen, Herzöge, Könige: der Aufstieg der frühen Staufer und das Reich (1079 - 1152)*, ed. Hubertus Seibert and Jörg Dendorfer (Ostfildern, 2005), 341-62.

Schramm, Percy Ernst, 'Herrschaftszeichen: gestiftet, verschenkt, verpfändet. Belege aus dem Mittelalter', *Nachrichten der Akademie der Wissenschaften in Göttingen: Philosophisch-Historische Klasse* 1957, 159-226.

Schramm, Percy Ernst, *Herrschaftszeichen und Staatssymbolik. Beiträge zu ihrer Geschichte vom dritten bis zum sechzehnten Jahrhundert*, 3 vols. (Stuttgart, 1954-6).

Schramm, Percy Ernst, *Kaiser, Könige und Päpste. Gesammelte Aufsätze zur Geschichte des Mittelalters*, 4 vols. in 5 (Stuttgart, 1969).

Schramm, Percy Ernst, 'Nachträge zu den Ordines-Studien 2-3', *Archiv für Urkundenforschung* 16 (1939), 279-86.

Schramm, Percy Ernst, 'Ordines-Studien 2: Die Krönung bei den Westfranken und den Franzosen', *Archiv für Urkundenforschung* 15 (1938), 3-55.

Schramm, Percy Ernst, 'Ordines-Studien 3: Die Krönung in England', *Archiv für Urkundenforschung* 15 (1938), 305-91.

Schröder, Sybille, *Macht und Gabe: materielle Kultur am Hof Heinrichs II. von England* (Husum, 2004).

Schulze-Dörrlamm, Mechtild, *Die Kaiserkrone Konrads II. (1024-1039). Eine archäologische Untersuchung zu Alter und Herkunft der Reichskrone* (Sigmaringen, 1991).

Schütte, Bernd, 'Das Königtum Philipps von Schwaben im Spiegel zeitgenössischer Quellen', in *Philipp von Schwaben: Beiträge der internationalen Tagung*

458 SELECT READING

anlässlich seines 800. Todestages, ed. Andrea Rzihacek and Renate Spreitzer (Vienna, 2010), 113–28.

Schwarzmaier, Hansmartin, '*Pater imperatoris*. Herzog Friedrich II. von Schwaben, der gescheiterte König', in *Mediaevalia Augiensia. Forschungen zur mittelalterlichen Geschichte*, ed. Jürgen Petersohn (Stuttgart, 2001), 247–84.

Schwedler, Gerhard, 'Kaisertradition und Innovation. Die Bezugsnahme Barbarossas auf andere Kaiser', in *Staufisches Kaisertum im 12. Jahrhundert. Konzepte – Netzwerke – Politische Praxis*, ed. Stefan Burkhardt, Thomas Metz, Bernd Schneidmüller and Stefan Weinfurter (Regensburg, 2010), 231–52.

Shepard, Jonathan, 'Adventus, arrivistes and rites of rulership in Byzantium and France in the tenth and eleventh century', in *Court Ceremonies*, ed. Beihammer, Constantinou and Papani, 337–72.

Shepard, Jonathan, 'Aspects of moral leadership: the Imperial city and lucre from legality', in *Authority in Byzantium*, ed. Pamela Armstrong (Farnham, 2013), 9–30.

Shepard, Jonathan, 'Byzantium's overlapping circles', *Proceedings of the 21st International Congress of Byzantine Studies* (Aldershot, 2006), 15–55.

Shepard, Jonathan, 'Conversion and regimes compared: the Rus' and the Poles, c. 1000', in *East Central & Eastern Europe in the Early Middle Ages*, ed. Florin Curta (Ann Arbor, MI, 2005), 254–82.

Shepard, Jonathan, 'Crowns from the Basileus, crowns from heaven', in *Byzantium, New Peoples, New Powers: the Byzantino-Slav Contact Zone, from the Ninth to the Fifteenth Century*, ed. Miliana Kaimakamova, Maciej Salamon and Malgorzata Smorag Rózycka (Krakow, 2007), 140–55.

Sierck, Michael, *Festtag und Politik. Studien zur Tagewahl karolingischer Herrscher* (Cologne, 1995).

Simon, Gertrud, 'Untersuchungen zur Topik der Widmungsbriefe mittelalter-licher Geschichtsschreiber bis zum Ende des 12. Jahrhunderts', *Archiv für Diplomatik und Urkundenforschung* 4 (1958), 52–119; 5–6 (1959), 73–153.

Smalley, Beryl, 'Sallust in the Middle Ages', in *Classical Influences on European Culture AD 500–1500*, ed. Robert R. Bolgar (Cambridge, 1971), 165–75.

Smith, Mary Frances, 'Archbishop Stigand and the eye of the needle', *ANS* 16 (1994), 199–219.

Smith, R. J., 'Henry II's heir: the *Acta* and seal of Henry the Young King, 1170–83', *EHR* 116 (2001), 297–326.

Sønnesyn, Sigbjørn Olsen, *William of Malmesbury and the Ethics of History* (Woodbridge, 2012).

Southern, R. W., 'Aspects of the European tradition of historical writing', parts 1–4, *TRHS*, 5th series, 20 (1970), 173–96; 21 (1971), 159–79; 22 (1972), 159–80, 23 (1973).

Spiegel, Gabrielle M., 'The cult of Saint Denis and Capetian kingship', *JMedH* 1 (1975), 43–70.

Spiegel, Gabrielle M., 'The *Reditus Regni ad Stirpem Karoli Magni*: a new look', *French Historical Studies* 7 (1971), 145–74.

Stafford, Pauline, 'The laws of Cnut and the history of Anglo-Saxon royal promises', *Anglo-Saxon England* 10 (1982), 173–90.

Staunton, Michael, *The Historians of Angevin England* (Oxford, 2017).

Steger, Hugo, *David rex et propheta. König David als vorbindliche Verkörperung des Herrschers und Dichters im Mittelalter* (Nuremberg, 1961).

Stehkämper, Hugo, 'Geld bei deutschen Königswahlen im 13. Jahrhundert', in *Wirtschaftskräfte und Wirtschaftswege. Festschrift Hermann Kellenbenz*, ed. Jürgen Schneider, 5 vols. (Stuttgart, 1978–81), vol. 1, 83–136.

Stehkämper, Hugo, 'Über das Motiv der Thronstreit-Entscheidungen des Kölner Erzbischofs Adolf von Altena 1198–1205: Freiheit der fürstlichen Königswahl oder Aneignung des Mainzer Erstkurrechts?', *Rheinische Vierteljahrsblätter* 67 (2003), 1–20.

Stock, Brian, *The Implications of Literacy: Written Language and Models of Interpretation in the Eleventh and Twelfth Centuries* (Princeton, NJ, 1983).

Stoob, Heinz, 'Zur Königswahl Lothars von Sachsen im Jahre 1125', in *Historische Forschungen für Walter Schlesinger*, ed. Helmut Beumann (Cologne and Vienna, 1974), 438–61.

Stopka, Krzysztof, ed., *Gallus Anonymus in the Context of Twelfth-Century Historiography from the Perspective of the Latest Research* (Kraków, 2010).

Strickland, Matthew, *Henry the Young King, 1155–1183* (New Haven, CT, 2016).

Strickland, Matthew, 'On the instruction of a prince: the upbringing of Henry, the Young King', in *Henry II. New Perspectives*, ed. Christopher Harper-Bill and Nicholas Vincent (Woodbridge, 2008), 184–214.

Strömberg, J. B. L. D., 'The Swedish kings in progress – and the centre of power', *Scandia: Tidskrift for Historisk Forskning* 70 (2004), 167–217.

Suchan, Monika, 'Fürstliche Opposition gegen das Königtum im 11. und 12. Jahrhundert als Gestalterin mittelalterlicher Staatlichkeit', *FmSt* 37 (2003), 141–65.

Suchan, Monika, 'Monition and advice as elements of politics', in *Patterns of Episcopal Power*, ed. Körntgen and Waßenhoven, 39–50.

Sulovsky, Vedran, 'Sacrum imperium: Lombard influence and the "sacralization of the state" in the mid-twelfth-century Holy Roman Empire', *German History* (https://doi.org/10.1093/gerhis/ghaa085) (2020).

Taylor, Alice, *Shape of the State in Medieval Scotland, 1124–1290* (Oxford, 2016).

Teunis, Henry B., 'The coronation charter of 1100: a postponement of decision. What did not happen in Henry I's reign', *JMedH* 4 (1978), 135–44.

Thomas, Hugh M., 'Violent disorder in King Stephen's England: a maximum argument', in *King Stephen's Reign: 1135–1154*, ed. Graeme J. White and Paul Dalton (Woodbridge, 2008), 139–70.

Thompson, Kathleen H., 'Affairs of the state: the illegitimate children of Henry I', *JMedH* 29 (2003), 129–51.

460 SELECT READING

Thomson, Rodney M., Emily Dolmar and Emily Winkler, eds., *Discovering William of Malmesbury* (Woodbridge, 2017).

Torre, Chiara, 'Seneca and the Christian tradition', in *The Cambridge Companion to Seneca*, ed. Shadi Bartsch and Alessandro Schiesaro (Cambridge, 2015), 266–76.

Trilling, Renée, 'Sovereignty and social order: Archbishop Wulfstan and the Institutes of Polity', in *The Bishop Reformed: Studies in Episcopal Power and Culture in the Central Middle Ages*, ed. Anna T. Jones and John S. Ott (Aldershot, 2007), 58–85.

Truax, Jean A., 'Winning over the Londoners: King Stephen, the Empress Matilda and the politics of personality', *HSJ* 8 (1996), 42–62.

Turner, Ralph V., 'King John's concept of royal authority', *History of Political Thought* 17 (1996), 158–78.

Ubl, Karl, 'Der kinderlose König. Ein Testfall für die Ausdifferenzierung des Politischen im 11. Jahrhundert', *HZ* 292 (2011), 323–63.

Ukena-Best, Elke, 'Die Lyrik Kaiser Heinrichs VI. und König Konrads (Konradin)', in *Dichtung und Musik der Stauferzeit*, ed. Volker Gallé (Worms, 2011), 147–73.

Ulewicz, Tadeusz, 'St Stanislaus of Szczepanów in old Polish literature and culture', *Aevum: Rassegna di scienze storiche linguistiche e filologiche* 54 (1980), 287–314.

Ullmann, Walter, 'The bible and principles of government in the Middle Ages', *Settimane di studio del centro Italiano di studi sull'alto medioevo* 10 (Spoleto, 1963), 181–227.

Ullmann, Walter, *Medieval Political Thought* (Harmondsworth, 1975).

Utz, Hans, 'Erste Spuren von Nationalismus im spätmittelalterlichen Schottland. Forduns "Chronica Gentis Scottorum"', *Schweizerische Zeitschrift für Geschichte* 29 (1979), 305–29.

Vagnoni, Mirko, 'The sacrality of Queen in the Norman Sicily. The pattern of Ordo coronationis', *Mirabilia. Revista Eletrônica de História Antiga e Medieval* 17 (2013), 174–86.

Van Engen, John, 'Letters, schools and written culture in the eleventh and twelfth centuries', in *Dialektik und Rhestorik im früheren und hohen Mittelalter. Rezeption, Überlieferung und gesellschaftliche Wirkung antiker Gelehrsamkeit vornehmlich im 9. und 12. Jahrhundert*, ed. Johannes Fried (Munich, 1997), 97–132.

van Houts, Elisabeth, *Married Life in the Middle Ages, 900–1300* (Oxford, 2019).

van Houts, Elisabeth, 'The writing of history and family traditions through the eyes of men and women: the Gesta Principum Polonorum', in *Gallus Anonymus and His Chronicle in the Context of Twelfth-Century Historiography from the Perspective of the Latest Research*, ed. Krzysztof Stopka (Krakow, 2010), 189–203.

Vercamer, Grischa, 'Vorstellung von Herrschaft bei Magister Vincentius von Krakau (um 1150–1223)', in *Macht und Spiegel der Macht*, ed. Kersken and Vercamer, 309–40.

SELECT READING

Vercamer, Grischa, and Norbert Kersken, eds., *Macht und Spiegel der Macht: Herrschaft in Europa im 12. und 13. Jahrhundert vor der Hintergrund der Chronistik* (Wiesbaden, 2013).

Veszprémy, Lászlo, 'Chronicles in charters. Historical narratives (*narrationes*) in charters as substitutes for chronicles in Hungary', *The Medieval Chronicle* 3 (2004), 184–99.

Veszprémy, Lászlo, 'The invented eleventh century of Hungary', in *The Neighbours of Poland in the 11th Century*, ed. Przemysław Urbańczyk (Warsaw, 2002), 137–54.

Veszprémy, László, '"More paganismo": reflections on the pagan and Christian past in the Gesta Hungarorum of the Hungarian Anonymous Notary', in *Historical Narrative*, ed. Garipzanov, 183–201.

Veszprémy, László, 'Umwälzungen im Ungarn des 13. Jahrhunderts: vom "Blutvertrag" zu den ersten Ständeversammlungen', in *Macht und Spiegel der Macht*, ed. Kersken and Vercamer, 383–402.

Villards Jensen, Kurt, 'Crusading at the fringe of the Ocean: Denmark and Portugal in the twelfth century', in *Medieval History Writing and Crusading Ideology*, ed. Tumoas M. S. Lehtonen and Kurt Villards Jensen with Janne Malkki and Katja Ritari (Helsinki, 2005), 195–206.

Vincent, Nicholas, 'Conclusion', in *Noblesses de l'espace Plantagenet (1154–1224). Table ronde tenue à Poitiers le 13 mai 2000*, ed. Martin Aurell (Poitiers, 2001), 207–14.

Vincent, Nicholas, 'King Henry III and the blessed Virgin Mary', *Studies in Church History* 39 (2006), 126–46.

Vincent, Nicholas, 'The court of Henry II', in *Henry II: New Interpretations*, ed. Christopher Harper-Bill and Nicholas Vincent (Woodbridge, 2007), 278–334.

Vincent, Nicholas, 'The great lost library of England's medieval kings? Royal use and ownership of books, 1066–1272', in *1000 Years of Royal Books and Manuscripts*, ed. Kathleen Doyle and Scot McKendrick (London, 2013), 73–112.

Vincent, Nicholas, 'The pilgrimages of the Angevin kings of England, 1154–1272', in *Pilgrimage. The English Experience from Becket to Bunyan*, ed. Colin Morris and Peter Roberts (Cambridge, 2002), 12–45.

Vincent, Nicholas, 'Rank insubordination: disobedience and disinheritance amongst the Anglo-French nobility, 1050–1250', in *Rank and Order: the Formation of Aristocratic Elites in Western and Central Europe, 500–1500*, ed. Jörg Peltzer (Ostfildern, 2015), 131–70.

Vogtherr, *Thomas*, '"Weh dir, land, dessen König ein Kind ist." Minderjährige Könige um 1200 im europäischen Vergleich', *FmSt* 37 (2003), 291–314.

Ward, Emily Joan, 'Child kingship and notions of (im)maturity in north-western Europe, 1050–1262', *ANS* 40 (2018), 197–211.

Ward, John O., 'What the Middle Ages missed of Cicero, and why', in *Brill's Companion to the Reception of Cicero*, ed. William H. F. Altman (Leiden, 2015), 307–26.

462   SELECT READING

Warner, David A., 'Thietmar of Merseburg: the image of the Ottonian bishop', in *The Year 1000: Religious and Social Response to the Turning of the First Millennium*, ed. Michael Frassetto (New York, 2000), 85–110.

Warntjes, Immo, 'Regnal succession in early medieval Ireland', *JMedH* 30 (2004), 377–410.

Wasselynck, René, 'Les compilations des "Moralia in Job" du VIIe au XIIe siècle', *Recherches de théologie ancienne et médiévale* 29 (1962), 5–32.

Waßenhoven, Dominik, 'Bischöfe als Königsmacher?: Selbstverständnis und Anspruch des Episkopats bei Herrscherwechseln im 10. und frühen 11. Jahrhundert', in *Religion und Politik im Mittelalter*, ed. Körntgen and Waßenhoven, 31–50.

Weiler, Björn, 'Clerical admonitio, letters of advice to kings and episcopal self-fashioning, c.1000–1200', *History* 102 (2017), 557–75.

Weiler, Björn, 'Historical writing in Europe, c. 1100–1300', in *Medieval Welsh Chronicles*, ed. Ben Guy and Owain Bryn Jones (forthcoming).

Weiler, Björn. 'Kingship, usurpation and propaganda in twelfth-century Europe', *Anglo-Norman Studies* 23 (2001), 299–326.

Weiler, Björn, 'Knighting, homage, and the meaning of ritual: the kings of England and their neighbours in the thirteenth century', *Viator* 37 (2006), 275–300.

Weiler, Björn, 'Politics', in *The Central Middle Ages*, ed. Daniel J. Power (Cambridge, 2006), 91–120.

Weiler, Björn, 'Rebellious sons: revolt, succession, and the culture of kingship in Western Europe, c.1170 – c.1280', *Historical Research* 82 (2009), 17–40.

Weiler, Björn, 'Royal virtue and royal justice in Walter Map's *De Nugis Curialium* and William of Malmesbury's *Historia Novella*', in *Virtue and Ethics in the Twelfth Century*, ed. Istvan Bejczy and Richard Newhauser (Leiden, 2005), 317–39.

Weiler, Björn, 'Suitability and right: imperial succession and the norms of politics in early Staufen Germany', in *Making and Breaking the Rules*, ed. Lachaud and Penman, 71–86.

Weiler, Björn, 'Tales of trickery and deceit: the election of Frederick Barbarossa (1152), historical memory, and the culture of kingship in later Staufen Germany', *JMedH* 38 (2012), 295–317.

Weiler, Björn, 'The rex renitens and medieval ideals of kingship, c. 950–1250', *Viator* 31 (2000), 1–42.

Weiler, Björn, 'Thinking about power before Magna Carta: the role of history', in *Des chartes aux constitutions. Autour de l'idée constitutionnelle en Europe (XIIᵉ–XVIIᵉ siècles)*, ed. François Foronda and Jean-Philippe Genet (Paris, 2019), 3–26.

Weiler, Björn, 'William of Malmesbury, Henry I, and the Gesta Regum Anglorum', in *ANS* 31 (2009), 157–76.

Weiler, Björn, 'William of Malmesbury on Kingship', *History* 90 (2005), 3–22.

Weinfurter, Stefan, 'Bamberg und das Reich in der Herrscheridee Heinrichs II', *Bericht des Historischen Vereins für die Pflege der Geschichte des ehemaligen Fürstbistums Bamberg* 137 (2001), 53–82.

Weinfurter, Stefan, *Heinich II. Herrscher am Ende der Zeiten* (Regensburg, 1999).

Welander, Richard, David J. Breeze and Thomas Owen Clancy, eds., *The Stone of Destiny. Artefact and Icon* (Edinburgh, 2003).

Weller, Tobias, *Die Heiratspolitik des deutschen Hochadels im 12. Jahrhundert* (Cologne, Weimar and Vienna, 2004).

Werner, Karl Ferdinand, 'Gott, Herrscher und Historiograph: der Geschichtsschreiber als Interpret des Wirkens Gottes in der Welt und Ratgeber der Könige (4. bis 12. Jahrhundert)', in Karl Ferdinand Werner, *Einheit der Geschichte. Studien zur Historiographie*, ed. Werner Paravicini (Sigmaringen, 1998), 89–119.

White, Stephen D., 'Alternative constructions of treason in the Angevin political world: *Traïson* in the *History of William Marshal*', *e-spania* 4 (2007), https://journals.openedition.org/e-spania/2233 (accessed 28 January 2020).

Wickham, Chris, 'Problems in doing comparative history', in *Challenging the Boundaries of Medieval History: the Legacy of Timothy Reuter*, ed. P. J. Skinner (Turnhout, 2009), 5–28.

Wickham, Chris, *Sleepwalking into a New World: the Emergence of Italian City Communes in the Twelfth Century* (Princeton, NJ, 2015).

Wiedemann, Benedict G. E., 'The kingdom of Portugal, homage and papal "fiefdom" in the second half of the twelfth century', *JMedH* 41 (2015), 432–45.

Wieruszowski, Helene, 'Roger II of Sicily. *Rex tyrannicus* in twelfth-century political thought', *Speculum* 38 (1963), 46–78.

Williams, J. J, 'León: the iconography of the capital', in *Cultures of Power: Lordship, Status, and Process in Twelfth-Century Europe*, ed. T. N. Bisson (Philadelphia, PA, 1995), 231–58.

Winterbottom, Michael, 'The transmission of Cicero's De Officiis', *Classical Quarterly* 43 (1993), 215–42.

Wolfram, Herwig 'Political theory and narrative in charters', *Viator* 26 (1995), 39–52.

Wolverton, Lisa, *Cosmas of Prague: Narrative, Classicism, Politics* (Washington, DC, 2014).

Wormald, Patrick, 'Archbishop Wulfstan: eleventh-century state-builder', in *Wulfstan, Archbishop of York. The Proceedings of the Second Alcuin Conference*, ed. Matthew Townend (Turnhout, 2004), 9–27.

Zey, Claudia, ed., *Mächtige Frauen. Königinnen und Fürstinnen im europäischen Mittelalter* (Stuttgart, 2015).

Zotz, Thomas, 'Kaiserliche Vorlage und Chronistenwerk. Zur Entstehungsgeschichte der *Gesta Frederici* Ottos von Freising', in *Geschichtsvorstellungen: Bilder, Texte und Begriffe aus dem Mittelalter; Festschrift für Hans-Werner Goetz zum 65. Geburtstag*, ed. Steffen Patzold, Anja Rathmann-Lutz and Volker Scior (Cologne, Weimar and Vienna, 2012), 153–77.

INDEX

Aachen, 173, 221, 265, 272, 323, 324, 327, 354, 389
Absalon, archbishop of Lund, 103, 167, 184, 189, 193, 364, 387
Acerbus of Morena, 348
Adalbero, archbishop of Reims, 294
Adalbert, archbishop of Mainz, 254, 295, 299
Adelheid, abbess of Quedlinburg, 389
Adolf, archbishop of Cologne, 112, 301, 406
Aethelred II, king of England, 182
Ailred of Rievaulx, 190
Alan Durward, Scottish magnate, 318
Albero, archbishop of Trier, 269, 281, 296
Albert of Aachen, 74, 140, 248, 288
Albert of Stade, 254, 387
Alexander II, king of Scotland, 221, 320, 323, 329, 356
Alexander II, pope, 60
Alexander III, king of Scotland, 202, 312, 318, 329, 362, 384
　　inauguration of, 320
Alexander III, pope, 171, 189, 254
Alexander of Telese, 14, 74, 84, 91, 92, 140, 179, 194, 197, 357
　　on kingship of Roger II, 84–93
Alfonso I, king of Portugal, 198, 310, 330, 365
Alfonso VI, king of Castile, 311
Alfonso VII, king of Castile, 178, 311, 332, 358, 365, 371, 384
　　coronation as king of Galicia (1111), 329, 330, 332–3
Alfonso X, king of Castile, 349
Álmos, Magyar leader, 71, 73, 75, 105, 110

Amalfi, 366
Amatus of Montecassino, 71, 86
Ambrose of Milan, 27, 39, 47, 48, 50
Ambrosiaster, 50, 51
Anaclete II, pope, 91
Andrew II, king of Hungary, 13
Andrew, archbishop of Lund, 322
Angus, earls of, 329
Annales Marbacenses, 162, 209, 413
Annals of Quedlinburg, 123, 139
Anno, archbishop of Cologne, 184, 193
Anonymous (Hungarian) Notary, 69, 103, 105, 106, 110, 260
Anselm of Bec, archbishop of Canterbury, 143, 185, 355
Anselm of Laon, 54
Antioch, 25, 366, 380, 384
Aquileia, patriarch of, 208
Aragon, kings of: *see* James, Peter II
Arduin of Ivrea, 238, 241, 242, 245, 250
Aribo, archbishop of Mainz, 312, 335, 370, 391
Aristotle, 26, 185, 187
Arnold of Lübeck, 384
Arnold, archbishop of Mainz, 379
Arnulf of Lisieux, 254
Árpad, leader of the Magyars, 324, 325
Árpads, Hungarian royal dynasty, 79, 105
Arthur of Brittany, 134, 135, 198
Arthur, legendary ruler of Britain, 357
Ascelin fitzArthur, 129
assembly sites, 278, 286
　　Frohse, 272, 273, 274, 275
　　Isøre, 237, 277, 286
　　Kamba, 267
　　Werla, 272, 273, 274, 275, 276

INDEX 465

Asser, bishop of Roskilde, 364
Atholl, earls of, 329
Augsburg, 201
Augustine of Hippo, 27, 39, 48, 50, 51, 53, 75, 77, 122, 228

Baldwin I, king of Jerusalem, 53, 54, 73, 140, 211, 222, 246, 256, 288
Baldwin II, king of Jerusalem, 140, 141, 222, 248, 264, 322, 365, 380
  election of (1118), 140, 246, 288–9, 299
Baldwin III, king of Jerusalem, 187, 188, 193, 195
Baldwin IV, king of Jerusalem, 136
Baldwin, bishop of Kraków, 352
Baldwin, II king of Jerusalem, 227
Bamberg, 275, 354
Battle Abbey, 189
bears, mating, untimely end of, 179
Berengar, count of Sulzbach, 263
Bergamo, 209
Bergen, 223, 266, 273
Bern of Reichenau, 109, 187, 192
Bernard of Clairvaux, 182
Berthold of Reichenau, 243
Bethlehem, 323
Bialograd, 351
Bible
  exegesis of, 10, 40, 54–5, 110, 345
  images of kingship, 40–3, 129, 139, 160, 186, 251
Bigfoot, 8
Birgi, Swedish magnate, 251
Birkibeinar, 234, 250, 251, 254, 266, 297, 298, 301, 305
Blood Oath (Hungary), 105, 260, 300
Bohemia, rulers of, 250; see also Borivojc I, Bretislav I, Bretislav II, Jaromir, Vladislav
Boleslaw I, ruler of Poland, 71, 73, 74, 75, 77, 78, 79, 80, 83, 85, 88, 95, 99, 101, 102, 111, 112, 114, 147, 148, 149, 190, 227, 325, 353, 358, 362, 365, 367, 381
Boleslaw II, king of Poland, 77, 78, 83, 143, 147
Boleslaw III, ruler of Poland, 80, 83, 144, 149, 150, 179, 180, 181, 196,

197, 202, 208, 212, 225, 329, 351, 353, 363, 371
  conflict with Zbigniew, 351–4
  designation of, 143–9
Bologna, 209
Borivojc I, duke of Bohemia, 305
Braga, archbishops of, 31, 76
Bremen, archbishops of, 76
Bretislav I, duke of Bohemia, 298
Bretislav II, duke of Bohemia, 358
Brittany, 95, 134, 144
Brixen, bishops of, 241, 274
Bruno of Merseburg, 382
Bruno, bishop of Augsburg, 313
Buchan, earls of, 329
Burchard of Ursberg, 270, 355
Burchard, bishop of Worms, 274, 280, 300, 301
Burgundino of Pisa, 188, 189, 193
Buris Hendriksen, Danish magnate, 301, 385, 386, 395
  and Valdemar I, king of Denmark, 386–8
Byzantium, 12, 25, 26, 28, 29, 89, 93, 97, 99, 101, 102, 208, 304, 327, 328, 375; see also Manuel Komnenos, Constantine X Monomachos

Canterbury, archbishops of, 111, 280; see also Anselm of Bec, Hubert Walter, Lanfranc of Bec, Ralph, Stephen Langton, Stigand, Thomas Becket, William
Capetians, French royal dynasty, 139; see also Hugh Capet, Robert II, Henry I, Philipp I, Louis VI, Louis VII, Philipp Augustus
Carolingians, 7, 9, 28, 37, 55, 325
Casimir, ruler of Poland, 124
Castile, 144; see also Fernando I, Alfonso VI, Sancho II, Alfonso VII, Alfonso X, Sancho IV
Celestine III, pope, 159
Charlemagne, 6, 28, 37, 109, 173, 187, 203, 208, 220, 324, 325, 326, 327, 349, 360
  translation of relics (1215), 173–4
Charles the Good, count of Flanders, 124, 235, 270, 274, 301

466 INDEX

Charles, duke of Lotharingia, 279, 283
Chester, 126
Chichester, bishops of, 189
Chlodwig, Frankish king, 220
Chronicon Rhythmicum Austriacum, 295
Chronicon Roskildense, 67, 73, 169, 369
Cicero, 21, 27, 39, 45, 46, 47, 48, 50, 51, 52, 56, 57, 63, 75, 190, 191, 203, 228, 361
  De Officiis, 43–6
Cologne, 30, 100, 121, 142, 235, 429, 441, 443, 444, 446
  archbishops of, 111, 162, 199, 221, 263, 280; *see also* Heribert, Anno, Adolf
Coloman, king of Hungary, 106
Compiègne, 222, 278, 279
Conrad I, ruler of east Francia, 121, 125, 139, 149, 159, 214, 219, 224, 256
  death of and succession to, 121–4
Conrad II, western emperor, 190, 202, 203, 220, 249, 271, 272, 286, 312, 322, 325, 327, 349, 360, 366, 370
  coronation of, 312–14
  election of (1024), 286–8, 294
  Gandersheimer Kirchenstreit, 392
Conrad III, ruler of Germany, 61, 93, 138, 141, 211, 213, 216, 217, 218, 219, 220, 228, 265, 276, 278, 281, 296, 322, 323, 349, 370, 373
Constance, queen of Sicily, 201, 208, 291
Constans, legendary king of the Britons, 96
Constantine X Monomachos, Byzantine emperor, 97
Constantine, Roman emperor, 109, 185
Corvey, 125
Cosmas of Prague, 14, 69, 70, 77, 149, 259
crane
  tough meat of, 357
Crema, 209
Cremona, 209

Dagobert, Frankish king, 220
Dál Riata, 319
David I, king of Scotland, 190, 320

David, biblical king, 40, 41, 45, 63, 88, 111, 123, 139, 185, 223, 224, 291, 335
David, earl of Huntingdon, 315
Denmark: *see* Erik the Good, Erik the Memorable, Frothi III, Harald, Knud the Great, Knud VI, Magnus the Good, Niels, Olaf Hunger, Sven Estrithson, Valdemar I, Valdemar II
Diego Gelmírez (arch)bishop of Santiago de Compostela, 330
dogs, 78, 268, 376
Dortmund, 390
Dover, 266
dreams, visions and portents, 73–4, 79, 87, 137, 146, 148, 172, 223, 236, 239, 404
Dublin, 357
Dunkeld, bishops of, 318
Dunstan, archbishop of Canterbury, 333
Durham, bishops of, 314

Eadwig, king of England, 384
Edgar, king of England, 326, 360
Edith, queen of England, 194
Edward I, king of England, 202, 320
Edward the Confessor, king of England, 137, 152, 172, 213, 218, 324
Eichstätt, bishop of, 375
Eike von Regpow, 386
Ekkehard, margrave of Meißen, 233, 238, 257, 268, 272, 273, 275, 276, 390
Eleanor of Aquitaine, queen of England, 317, 371
Eleanor of Castile, queen of England, 202
Elvira, queen of Sicily, 202
Ely, bishops of, 317
Emma, queen of England, 194
Encomium Emmae Reginae, 139
England: *see* Aethelred II, Eadwig, Edgar, Edward the Confessor, Harold II, William I, William II, Henry I, Stephen, Henry II, Henry the Young King, Richard I, John, Henry III, Edward I

INDEX

467

Erfurt, 136, 201
Erik the Good, king of Denmark, 137, 163, 168, 169, 175, 184, 218, 368, 369, 370, 387
Erik the Memorable, king of Denmark, 233, 253, 284
Eskil, archbishop of Lund, 175, 284, 406
Eustace, son of Stephen, king of England, 157, 158, 159, 161, 205, 207
Exeter, 126
Eystein, archbishop of Nidaros (Trondheim), 103, 112, 330, 406

Faenza, 209
feasts, 82, 101, 136, 203, 233, 249, 303, 309, 320, 325, 329, 332, 348, 360, 371, 378, 380, 382, 395
  as demonstration of power, 356–8
Fernando I, king of Castile, 172, 311, 330, 365
  settlement of succession, 144, 172
Fife, earls of, 318, 329
Flanders, counts of, 329
Fontrevault, 220
Forchheim, 244, 293
France: *see* Capetians, Hugh Capet, Robert II, Henry I, Philipp I, Louis VI, Louis VII, Philipp Augustus, Louis VIII
Frederick Barbarossa, western emperor, 14, 93, 102, 112, 136, 141, 163, 169, 171, 173, 179, 181, 182, 187, 188, 189, 190, 193, 198, 208, 211, 213, 216, 217, 218, 219, 225, 253, 254, 255, 256, 257, 267, 269, 274, 276, 278, 281, 295, 302, 322, 330, 347, 348, 354, 361, 362, 363, 370, 373, 379, 380, 381, 384, 387, 388, 393, 396
  and the Bavarian succession, 373–7
  election of, 138, 140, 141–2
  knighting of Henry VI, 198–201
Frederick II, western emperor, king of Sicily, 154, 173, 210
  translation of relics of Charlemagne (1215), 173–4
Frederick, bishop of Münster, 362

Frederick, duke of Swabia, 254, 256, 262, 282, 296
Frothi III, legendary king of Denmark, 103, 260, 325
Fulbert of Chartres, 271
Fulcher of Chartres, 53, 54, 107, 108
Fulda, abbot of, 199, 200, 374
Fulk, count of Anjou, 60, 227, 264, 270, 366
  kingship of Jerusalem, 16, 227
Fulk, king of Jerusalem, 136

Gaimar, 360
Gaithel Glas, son of Neoilus and Scota, 319
Galbert of Bruges, 274
Galicia, 144
Gallus Anonymus, 14, 68, 71, 80, 81, 82, 83, 84, 89, 93, 94, 101, 103, 111, 112, 124, 145, 146, 147, 148, 149, 150, 179, 180, 197, 212, 259, 260, 326, 351, 352, 353, 358, 363, 365, 368, 371
Gandersheim, 194
Gelnhausen, 201
Geoffrey of Monmouth, 69, 95, 96, 186, 357
Geoffrey, archbishop of York, 317
Gerald of Wales, 58, 138, 141, 309, 357
  De Principis Instructione, 57–9
Gerald, archbishop of York, 355
Gerbert of Aurillac, 183
Gerhard, bishop of Csanád, 330
Germany: *see* Conrad I, Henry I, Otto I, Otto II, Otto III, Henry II, Conrad II, Henry III, Henry IV, Henry V, Lothar III, Conrad III, Frederick Barbarossa, Henry VI, Frederick II, Richard of Cornwall
  Double Election of 1198, 100, 112, 138, 355
Gerstungen, 242
Gesta Stephani, 155, 203, 249, 273, 276, 279, 297, 360, 365, 370, 394, 396
Giles of Paris, 187
Gisela, western empress, 202
Gislebert of Mons, 141, 384
Glasgow, bishops of, 329
Gloucester, 134, 198

468 INDEX

Gniezno, 74, 77, 80, 82, 84, 85, 94, 144, 148
Godehard, bishop of Hildesheim, 391
Godfrey of Calw, count palatine of the Rhine, 263
Godfrey of Viterbo, 187, 192
Godfrey, ruler of the Latin kingdom of Jerusalem, 53, 73, 107, 211, 288
   later reputation, 107–8
Golden Bull of Hungary (1222), 13, 19, 38, 105, 106, 107, 113, 300
   and Stephen, king of Hungary, 107
Gregory I, pope, 27, 39, 49–50, 51, 53, 63, 191, 228, 252
   Regula Pastoralis, 49
Gunnhild, 73

Hagenau, 270
   library at, 187, 193, 281, 400
Hainaut, 196, 199
Håkon IV, king of Norway, 208
Halberstadt, 390
Hamburg-Bremen, archbishops of, 278
Harald Fairhair, king of Norway, 68, 132, 261
Harald Hardrada, king of Norway, 233, 324
Harold II, king of England, 152, 213, 218, 227, 233, 305, 323, 343
Hartwich, bishop of Regensburg, 375
Hastings, 227
Hengist and Horsa, 70
Henry I, king of England, 128, 143, 150, 160, 188, 190, 194, 210, 213, 214, 255, 265, 331, 355, 370
   death of, 158
   settlement of succession, 150–9
   succession to, 245–6
Henry I, king of France, 285, 393
Henry I, ruler of east Francia, 121, 125, 139, 159, 214, 248, 256
Henry II, king of England, 134, 144, 150, 164, 171, 172, 184, 185, 192, 218, 220, 314, 320, 354, 357, 380, 400
Henry II, western emperor, 79, 182, 221, 236, 237, 249, 256, 270, 286, 295, 301, 312, 328
   body snatching, 221, 257

   election of, 237–42, 274–5
Henry III, king of England, 97, 134, 198, 349, 355, 362
Henry III, western emperor, 97, 109, 161, 187, 249, 323
Henry IV, western emperor, 63, 106, 128, 142, 143, 161, 165, 181, 184, 194, 196, 197, 220, 242, 305, 378, 386
Henry V, western emperor, 143, 218, 220, 261, 281, 301, 305
Henry VI, western emperor, 28, 102, 135, 136, 137, 142, 153, 162, 163, 168, 187, 188, 192, 196, 198, 201, 208, 210, 211, 216, 228, 270, 272, 278, 281, 291, 305, 344, 346, 366, 380, 384
   and the latrine, 136
   knighting of, 198–201
   settlement of succession, 162–3
   wedding (1186), 208–10
Henry Jasomirgott, duke of Austria, 374
Henry of Blois, bishop Winchester, 204
Henry of Huntingdon, 68, 152, 158, 163, 245, 252, 255
Henry the Lion, duke of Bavaria and Saxony, 374
Henry the Troublesome, duke of Bavaria, 239
Henry the Young King, king of England, 176, 180, 184, 201
   revolt of, 201
Heribert, archbishop of Cologne, 238, 295
Herman, duke of Swabia, 238, 272
Hermann of Reichenau, 161
Hildebrand, false monk, 73, 98, 99, 112, 244
Hildesheim, 183, 192, 272
Historia Norwegie, 68, 70, 73, 132, 134, 419
Historia Welforum, 16, 419
Honorius II, pope, 60, 92
Honorius III, pope, 319
Hubert Walter, archbishop of Canterbury, 291
Hugh Capet, king of France, 279, 322
   election of, 283

INDEX

Hugh of Honau, 188
Hugh. margrave of Tuscany, 380
Hugo Falcandus, 214, 358
Hungary: *see* Stephen I, Solomon,
    Ladislaus, Coloman, Peter II,
    Andrew II

Iceland, 3, 32, 68, 261, 428
inauguration
    forms of, 309–11
    sites, 323–5
Ingeborg of Denmark, queen of France,
    202
Innocent II, pope, 60, 92
Innocent III, pope, 60, 76, 98, 138, 141,
    154
insignia, 79, 80, 95, 97, 217, 218, 254,
    287, 315, 321, 329
    crown, 54, 76, 79, 83, 94, 96, 99, 100,
        315, 328, 331–2
    crown-wearing, 200, 208, 323, 329,
        331, 345, 347, 364, 373
    mantle, 315, 335
    meaning of, 336, 337
    ring, 61, 335
    rod (staff), 54, 316
    sceptre, 315, 324, 335
Ioannitsa, ruler of Bulgaria, 76, 99, 102
Ireland, 26, 51, 144, 309, 330, 357, 358,
    362
Isidore of Seville, 39, 50, 51, 172, 361,
    420
    translation of relics (1063), 172

James II, king of Aragon, 311
Jaromir, duke of Bohemia, 259
Jeroboam, Biblical king, 94, 186, 192
Jerusalem, Latin kingdom of: *see*
    Godfrey, Baldwin I, Baldwin II,
    Fulk, Baldwin III
John de Fordun, 312, 318, 320, 323, 327,
    356
John of Salisbury, 57, 157, 176, 420
John of Worcester, 155, 420
John, earl of Gloucester, 315
John, king of England, 134, 135, 291,
    355
Josiah, biblical king, 185
Julius Caesar, 185, 327

justice, 156
Justinian, Roman emperor, 185, 192
Jütland, 301

Kaiserchronik, 69, 186, 259, 261, 325,
    327, 349, 420
kings and kingship
    and ecclesiastical elites, 3, 4, 6, 12,
        76–7, 110–14, 185, 282–3, 330–5
    and justice, 13, 34, 41, 42, 44–5, 50–1,
        54, 57, 58, 60, 77, 78, 85, 89, 112,
        122, 127, 155, 172, 175, 176, 181,
        182, 185, 186, 190, 191, 193, 197,
        201, 205, 207, 209, 223, 249, 264,
        290, 297, 300, 313, 315, 317, 325,
        335, 359, 361, 366–9, 377, 380–1,
        387, 396, 399
    and secular elites, 3, 4, 6, 12, 110, 235,
        284–5, 329–30, 384–8, 389–94
    and the populace at large, 30, 191,
        299, 382, 403
    and the sacred, 13, 43, 73–4, 87,
        171–4, 236, 336–8, 342–6
    and warfare, 75, 88, 178–80, 287,
        292
    and wordly power, 368
    character of, 5, 83, 95, 96, 121–2, 125,
        181, 182, 191, 212, 248–50, 252–4,
        337, 363
    concepts of, 10, 12, 21, 31, 36–7,
        39–62, 67–77, 114–15, 125,
        166–77
    death and burial of, 128–30, 225, 238,
        244, 245, 257, 262, 270, 278, 289,
        316, 320, 351
    literacy of, 193
    marriage, 71, 194, 195, 201–3, 208,
        351, 376
    moral obligations of subjects, 53,
        62–3, 96, 115, 131–2, 245–7,
        256–8, 282–3, 328
    origins of, 67–77
    oversight of, by subjects, 93–4, 109,
        110, 111–14, 115, 291–2, 345,
        394–7, 400, 406
    practice of, 10, 20, 398
    proliferation of, 2, 32
    recognition of, 94, 96–102
    succession, instability of, 134–7

INDEX

kings and kingship (cont.)
  suitability for, 74–6, 77–80, 83, 137–42
  transpersonal concept of, 325–8
  wealth and power, 36, 72–3, 84, 88, 110, 123, 124, 370, 387
  widows, orphans and exiles, protection of, 43, 60, 72, 77, 78, 112, 190, 205, 313, 314, 335, 337, 350, 366–8, 381, 385, 402
Knud Lavard, 169, 170, 171, 174, 175, 176, 177, 180, 184, 218, 269, 285
  translation of relics (1170), 174–6, 387
Knud the Great, king of Denmark, England and Norway, 103–5, 110, 189, 325, 368
Knud VI, king of Denmark, 164, 165, 167, 169, 176, 177, 184, 187, 189, 193, 195, 202, 203, 210, 216, 218, 301, 322, 369, 385, 387
  coronation (1170), 169–71, 174–6
  designation of (1165), 168–9
Koblenz, 265
Körntgen, Ludger, 12, 13

Ladislaus, king of Hungary, 53, 98, 143, 178, 182, 248, 343, 344, 348
Lampert of Hersfeld, 242, 248, 420
Lanfranc of Bec, archbishop of Canterbury, 54
Latin
  and literacy, 2, 25, 36, 260, 406–8
  importance of, 17–18, 27
Latin Europe
  concept of, 25–7
  development of, 28–9
latrines, 163
Leo, bishop of Vercelli, 270
  and the kingship of Italy, 272
León, 172
Leopold, duke of Austria, 282
letters, images of kingship in, 59–62
Lewon II, king of Armenia, 98, 99, 102, 347
Liber Eliensis, 153
Libuše, 70, 111
Lincoln, 203
Liudprand of Cremona, 122, 123, 281

Loch Ness Monster, 8
London, 191, 205, 280, 324, 329, 355, 378, 381
  bishops of, 317
Lothar III, western emperor, 92, 93, 109, 218, 220, 224, 233, 248, 250, 254, 259, 263, 265, 278, 282, 301, 305
  election of (1125), 255, 264
Lotharingia, dukes of, 222, 238, 240, 270, 275
Lothian, earls of, 329
Louis VI, king of France, 143, 179, 180, 181, 182, 184, 192, 193, 196, 201, 219, 322, 383, 384
  coronation of (1108), 331, 383–4
Louis VII, king of France, 179, 189
Louis VIII, king of France, 187
Lund, archbishops of, 31, 103, 169, 280; see also Absalon, Anders, Eskil

Magdeburg, 239, 363
  archbishops of, 278, 361; see also Wichmann
Magna Carta, 19, 38, 292, 300
Magnus Erlingsson, king of Norway, 112, 221, 250, 273, 343
  coronation charter of, 112
  coronation feast, 356
Magnus the Good, king of Denmark, 136
Mainz, 67, 198, 199, 200, 201, 210, 240, 262, 265, 267, 278, 279, 287, 312, 313, 324, 329, 378, 380, 382
  archbishops of, 136, 218, 239, 243, 263, 280, 294; see also Adalbert, Aribo
Malcolm IV, king of Scotland, 320
Malta, 88
Mantes, 126, 130
Manuel Komnenos, Byzantine emperor, 93
Martin, archbishop of Gniezno, 103
Matilda, empress, claimant to the English throne, 140, 150, 160, 191, 203, 210, 249, 265, 294
  and Stephen, king of England, 150–9
  designation of, 245–6
Matthew Paris, 291
  succession of King John (1199), 291–2

INDEX

Meinwerk, bishop of Paderborn, 273, 274, 280, 300
Melfi, 86, 88, 90, 329, 444
Melisende, queen of Jerusalem, 210
Menteith, earls of, 318, 329
Merseburg, 125, 241, 297, 373, 390
Metz, bishops of, 243
Mieszko II, ruler of Poland, 80, 147
Mieszko III, ruler of Poland, 143
Milan, 209, 249
Minden, 297, 389
Moravia, 351
Morkinskinna, 100, 101

Namur, 196, 199, 200
Narratio de Electione Lotharii, 267, 268, 269, 279, 282, 298
Nathan, biblical prophet, 41, 63, 94, 115, 400
Neoilus, king of Athens, 319
Nero, Roman emperor, 327
networks, importance of, 34, 125, 233–5
Nicholas, bishop of Stavanger, 330
Nidaros (Trondheim), 295, 297
   archbishops of, 31, 133, 266, 277, 280; *see also* Eystein
Niederaltaich, 276, 280
Niels, king of Denmark, 104, 368
Norway
   royal succession in, 132–4, 135; *see also* Håkon IV, Harald Fairhair, Harald Hardrada, Magnus Erlingsson, Olaf Haraldso, Olaf Tryggvason, Sigurd, Sverrir, Magnus Erlingsson

Odo, bishop of Bayeux, 128
Odo, count of Blois, 249, 257, 276
Olaf Haraldson, king of Norway, 132
Olaf Hunger, king of Denmark, 63
Olaf Tryggvason, king of Norway, 73, 74, 76, 133, 137, 142, 261
Oliba of Vic, 187, 189, 192
Orderic Vitalis, 214, 296, 382
   death of William the Conqueror, 126–30
Orléans, 331
Osbert de Clare, 156

Otto I, western emperor, 123
Otto II, western emperor, 140
Otto III, western emperor, 13, 72, 73, 79, 80, 110, 111, 114, 183, 215, 221, 238, 239, 241, 265, 272, 275, 296, 328, 358, 365
Otto IV, western emperor, 153, 323, 355
Otto of Freising, 14, 193, 211, 216, 218, 228, 248, 257, 325, 354, 362, 363, 370, 373, 381, 394
Otto, bishop of Bamberg, 261, 300, 301
Otto, count of Northeim, 257, 276, 301, 385
Ovid, 27, 70

Paderborn, 272
Palermo, 84, 90, 91, 94, 184, 266, 278, 280, 354, 358, 359
   archbishops of, 187, 283
Paschal II, pope, 60
Paul of Bernried, 243
Paul, bishop of Poznan, 103
Pavia, 209, 327
Piast
   legendary ancestor of the Piasts, 74, 111, 147, 148
Peter Damian, cardinal, 72, 77, 79, 182, 380, 422
Peter I, king of Hungary, 330
Peter II, king of Aragon, 311
Peter of Blois, 184, 185, 186, 188, 189, 190, 192, 193, 225, 400
   on the education of Henry the Young King, 185–7
Peter of Eboli, 280, 283, 290, 366
   on the succession to William II, king of Sicily, 290–1
Peter, count of Trava, 178
Philipp Augustus, king of France, 179, 198, 202, 314, 323, 362, 366
Philipp I, king of France, 160, 219, 333
Philipp of Swabia, ruler of Germany, 163, 270, 278, 362
Piacenza, 209
Piasts, Polish ducal and royal dynasty, 79, 80, 84, 114, 148, 192, 207, 259
pig, devilish, 136
Pipewell, 316

472 INDEX

Pippin, Merovingian palace official, 139
Poland: see Boleslaw I, Boleslaw II,
    Boleslaw III, Casimir, Mieszko I,
    Mieszko III, Wladyslaw, Zbigniew
Pomerania, 144, 207
Pontius Pilate, 244
pork, lifting taxes on, 390
Pseudo-Cyprianus
    De xii Saeculi Abusivis, 51–2

Quedlinburg, 239, 390

Rahewin, 14, 373, 375, 377
Ralph (Radulfus) Niger, 57, 252, 345
Ralph of Coggeshall, 317
Ralph of Diss, 379
Ralph, archbishop of Canterbury, 331
Ralph, archbishop of Reims, 383
Ramiro I, king of Aragon, 311
Regensburg, 272, 364, 373
Reggio, 86, 209
Reims, 222
    archbishops of, 111, 189, 323,
        331
Reuter, Timothy, 23, 48, 359
Richard I, king of England, 60, 99, 100,
    134, 135, 198, 210, 220, 291, 312,
    314, 320, 326, 335, 362, 369, 371,
    378, 380, 382, 393, 419
    coronation of (1189), 314–18
Richard of Cornwall, ruler of Germany,
    349
Richard of Devizes, 382
Richer of Saint-Rémi, 68, 278, 279
Rigord, 179, 366
Rike, bishop of Schleswig, 284
Ripoll, 282
Robert Curthose, duke of Normandy,
    127, 150, 252, 255, 265, 355
    kingship of Jerusalem, 252–3
Robert de Clari, 102
Robert Guiscard, Norman leader in
    Sicily, 86, 89, 92
Robert II, king of France, 183,
    270
Robert Pullen, 54
Robert, earl of Gloucester, 152, 154,
    191, 372, 388
Robert, earl of Leicester, 315

Rodrigo Jiménez de Rada, 69
Rodulfus Glaber, 95, 249, 276
    succession to Rudolf III, king of
        Burgundy, 249
Roger Guiscard, Norman leader in Sicily,
    386
Roger II, king of Sicily, 14, 28, 32, 72,
    74, 75, 84, 85, 87, 88, 95, 96, 101,
    102, 114, 135, 140, 144, 171, 176,
    179, 180, 182, 189, 194, 196, 202,
    227, 278, 328, 333, 354, 357, 362,
    366, 375, 412
    coronation of, 333, 335–6
    creation of kingship, 84–93
Roger of Howden, 221, 312, 320
    coronation of Richard I (1189),
        314–18
Roger of Wendover, 357
Roncaglia, 189
Roskilde, 378, 386
    bishops of, 361
Rotrou, archbishop of Rouen, 185
Rouen, 316
Rudolf III, king of Burgundy, 249
    succession to, 249
Rudolf of Rheinfelden, duke of Swabia,
    claimant to the German throne,
    242, 243, 247, 248, 256, 257, 276,
    278, 284, 285, 293, 301, 305, 343,
    378, 382, 402
    election of (1077), 244
Rügen, 170, 178, 365
Rupert of Deutz, 54
Rus, Kiev, 25

Salerno, 79, 85, 166
Salians, German imperial dynasty, 220;
    see also Conrad II, Henry III,
    Henry IV, Henry V
Salisbury, 317
    bishops of, 317
Samuel, biblical prophet, 41, 42, 63, 77,
    91, 94, 111, 223, 224, 251, 336, 337,
    400
Sancho II, king of Castile, 311
Sancho IV, king of Castile, 311
Santiago de Compostela, archbishops
    of, 111
Sardinia, 199

INDEX

473

Saul, biblical king, 40, 41, 42, 49, 52, 63, 111, 115, 122, 123, 139, 186, 214, 223, 291, 337, 343

Saxo Grammaticus, 9, 17, 69, 103, 129, 167, 178, 184, 212, 233, 235, 254, 255, 260, 284, 289, 290, 300, 325, 385, 386, 395
    and Sven Aggesen, on royal justice, 368–9
    on Danish royal elections, 260, 289–90

Saxony, 28, 159, 195, 238, 239, 240, 265, 272, 305

Scone, 323, 324, 329, 330

Scone Abbey, 310, 318

Scota, daughter of Pharaoh Chentres, 319

Scotland, 310; *see also* David I, Malcolm IV, William the Lion, Alexander II, Alexander III

Seneca, 39, 46, 47, 48, 53, 57, 63, 77, 190, 203, 228, 375
    De Clementia, 43, 46–7

Senlis, 222, 278, 455

Sens, archbishops of, 331

Serbia, 25, 31

Shetlands, 261

Shropshire, 151

Sigebert of Gembloux, 27, 128

Sigebert, Frankish king, 220

Sigurd, king of Norway, 74, 100, 101, 114
    and Roger II, king of Sicily, 100–2

Simon de Kéza, 324

Skjalm, Danish noble, 177, 178, 184

Skjold, 75

Snorri Sturluson, 273, 356

Solomon, biblical king, 40, 42, 45, 88, 123, 161, 185, 224

Solomon, king of Hungary, 98, 143

Sophie, abbess of Gandersheim, 389, 391

St Adalbert of Prague, 81, 348

St Andrews, bishops of, 318

St Andrews, earls of, 329

St Denis, 181, 182, 184, 192, 323

St Evroul, 296

St Wenzel, 348

Stanislas, bishop of Kraków, 77, 79, 80, 83, 84, 89, 94, 111, 143, 147

Star Trek, 19

Staufen, German imperial dynasty, 188, 218, 233, 257; *see also* Conrad III, Frederick Barbarossa, Henry VI, Philipp of Swabia, Frederick II

Stephen I, king of Hungary, 13, 55, 62, 71, 74, 75, 78, 79, 91, 94, 102, 106, 107, 110, 165, 181, 189, 328, 370
    Libellus de institutione morum, 56–7

Stephen Langton, archbishop of Canterbury, 345

Stephen, bishop of Uppsala, 175

Stephen, king of England, 60, 150, 191, 203, 207, 213, 218, 245, 247, 250, 265, 282, 294, 295, 305, 355, 360, 363, 365, 372
    and Matilda, 150–9
    election of, 245–6
    siege of Exeter (1136), 394

Stigand, archbishop of Canterbury, 363

Strasbourg, bishop of, 278

Strathearn, earls of, 318, 329

Sturla Thordarsson, 207

Suger of St Denis, 137, 179, 181, 184, 193, 331, 383

Sven Aggesen, 110, 138, 184, 237, 325, 369, 387
    and saxo Grammaticus, on royal justice, 368–9
    Brevis Historia Regum Dacie, 75
    Lex Castrensis, 103–5, 107, 110, 124, 368

Sven Estrithson, king of Denmark, 168

Sverrir, king of Norway, 14, 28, 73, 74, 112, 133, 134, 137, 142, 178, 182, 183, 196, 219, 221, 222, 223, 224, 225, 234, 235, 250, 251, 256, 266, 289, 295, 297, 298, 301, 305, 330, 358, 362
    and Magnus Erlingsson, burial of, 224
    death of, 225
    election of, 234, 250–1, 297–8

Sverrisaga, 14, 225, 251, 266, 295

Székesfehérvár, 324, 325

474 INDEX

Tancred of Lecce, king of Sicily, 135, 291, 363, 366
Tarquin, king of Rome, 327
Tegernsee, 190
Theobald the Deceiver, count of Blois, 249
Theodoric the Monk, 103
  Historia de Antiquitate Regum Norwagiensium, 68
Theodoric, Roman emperor, 327
Theodosius, Roman emperor, 185
Thietmar of Merseburg, 68, 121, 125, 130, 214, 236, 237, 248, 272, 274, 282, 298, 408
  and the election of Henry II, western emperor (1002), 237–42
Thomas Becket, archbishop of Canterbury, 176, 332
Treviso, 209
Tripoli, 366
Trøndelag, 266

Ulrich of Kemenaten, abbot of Fulda, 263
Utrecht, 373
Urraca, queen of Castile, 210, 332

Valdemar I, king of Denmark, 28, 129, 142, 165, 166, 167, 178, 181, 187, 189, 207, 208, 216, 225, 233, 254, 256, 305, 361, 364, 378, 385, 395
  and Buris Hendriksen, 386–8
  coronation of Knud VI (1170), 169–71, 174–6
  designation of Knud VI (1165), 168–9
  translation of relics of Knud Lavard (1170), 174–6
  treatment of defeated nobles, 396
Valdemar II, king of Denmark, 169, 207, 322
Värmland, 266
Verona, 209
Vexin, 201
Victor III, pope, 254, 256
Vienne, archbishops of, 208
Vincent Kadlubek, 69, 83, 94, 192
Vincent of Prague, 396
Vladislav, duke of Bohemia, 149

Vortigern, legendary king of the Britons, 95, 96, 204

Walter Bower, 251, 318
  Macduff, 251–2
Walter Map, 380
Walter of Céfalu, 178
Walter of Trier, 124
Welfs, German princely dynasty, 16, 77, 257, 281
Wenrich of Trier, 244
Werinhar, 313
Werinhar, bishop of Strasbourg, 313
Werla, 275
Westminster, 134, 266, 323, 359
Westminster Abbey, 315, 328, 378, 382
Wichmann, archbishop of Magdeburg, 363, 373
Widukind of Corvey, 122, 123, 130, 139, 214
William, archbishop of Canterbury, 154, 245, 273, 282, 294
William Clito, 150
William, duke of Apulia, 140
William I, king of England (the Conqueror), 60, 125, 126, 135, 142, 143, 147, 149, 150, 159, 185, 189, 210, 214, 215, 216, 218, 227, 246, 252, 256, 299, 301, 322, 324, 332, 344, 360, 362, 363, 378, 382, 393
  death and burial, 126–30, 158
William I, king of Sicily, 135, 178, 214, 359
William II, king of England, 127, 149, 265
William II, king of Sicily, 184, 193, 280, 283, 290, 358, 369
William Ironarm, Norman leader in Sicily, 86, 89, 329, 386
William Marshal, 184, 193
William of Malmesbury, 14, 67, 70, 151, 154, 157, 186, 187, 188, 191, 192, 205, 214, 245, 246, 252, 255, 279, 294, 348, 355, 359, 362, 372, 382, 400, 408
  Gesta Regum Anglorum, 14, 67, 152, 186, 187
  Historia Novella, 151
William of Newburgh, 156, 317, 379

INDEX

William of Poitiers, 360
William of Tyre, 67, 73, 140, 187, 222, 246, 272, 284, 288, 366
William the Lion, king of Scotland, 221, 320, 323
Winchester, 316, 329, 355
  royal treasure at, 266
Winchester, bishops of, 317, 331, 332
Wipo, 187, 202, 203, 267, 272, 279, 280, 284, 286, 287, 289, 294, 295, 298, 299, 312, 313, 314, 318, 319, 320, 321, 324, 325, 327, 335, 359, 366, 367, 368, 370, 389
  coronation of Conrad II, western emperor (1024), 312–14
  election of Conrad II, western emperor (1024), 286–8, 294
Wladyslaw, ruler of Poland, 143, 144, 145, 146, 147, 148, 149, 171, 177, 179, 181, 194, 196, 207, 222, 351, 353
  settlement of succession (c. 1099), 143–9
women, royal
  and concepts of kingship, 202–7
  and education, 193–5

and succession, 287, 312, 317, 389–90, 391
  as regents, 195, 215
  as rulers, 210–11
  See also Adelheid of Quedlinburg, Constance, Edith, Emma, Eleanor of Aquitaine, Eleanor of Castile, Elvira, Gisela, Ingeborg of Denmark, Matilda, Melisende, Sophie of Gandersheim, Urraca
Worms, 287
Wulfstan of York, 55
  Institutes of Polity, 55–6
Würzburg, bishops of, 243

York, 266
  archbishop of, 332

Zamora, 198, 311, 330
Zbigniew, claimant to the Polish throne, 144, 145, 146, 148, 149, 150, 194, 233, 351, 352, 353, 363, 371, 387
  conflict with Boleslaw III, 351–4
zombies
  desacralisation of kingship, 342
  Königsheil and Geblütsheiligkeit, 340